THE HOLY SACRIFICE OF THE MASS

Dogmatically, Liturgically, and Ascetically Explained

By
REV. DR. NICHOLAS GIHR

TRANSLATED FROM THE GERMAN

B. HERDER BOOK CO.
15 & 17 SOUTH BROADWAY, ST. LOUIS 2, MO.
AND
33 QUEEN SQUARE, LONDON, W. C.

Printing Statement:

Due to the very old age and scarcity of this book, many of the pages may be hard to read due to the blurring of the original text, possible missing pages, missing text and other issues beyond our control.

Because this is such an important and rare work, we believe it is best to reproduce this book regardless of its original condition.

Thank you for your understanding.

Part 2

CHAPTER XX

THE KYRIE AND THE GLORIA

1. After the Introit the priest returns to the middle of the altar and recites the Kyrie eleison [1] (= *Domine miserere:* "Lord, have mercy"); alternately with the acolyte he nine times addresses to the triune God fervent petitions for mercy. The Kyrie is a cry for help of touching humility and simplicity, one proceeding naturally and directly from the heart that is in distress and want; hence we come across it in many parts of the Old and the New Testament, and formerly it resounded thousands of times from the lips of the people supplicating God in penitential procession. In Rome the Kyrie was originally sung by the clergy and people; later by two choirs that repeated it alternately until the celebrant gave the sign to cease.[2] The custom of invoking the divine mercy nine consecu-

---

[1] This cry is derived from the Greek Κύριε ἐλέησον. The latter word is the aorist imperative of ἐλεέω = *misereor,* and in the Latin Church language it is read *eleison;* for the Church favors Itacism, that is, she pronounces η as *i*. Besides, as it is read according to the Greek accent, the *i* is short and the word *e-lé-ï-son* has four, not three syllables. (Cf. Stadler, *Ordo divini officii,* II, i, 2, § 105.) The Kyrie must be recited by the priest at all Masses without exception; hence also on Holy Saturday. Very appropriately this prayer of supplication is said before the image of the Crucified, whereas in former times it was recited on the Epistle side (as it is still done in the Solemn Mass).

[2] The Kyrie chant is, of course, differently arranged in all the liturgies of the East and West. As the Second Council of Vaison (529) says, it was at that time the universal custom to recite the Kyrie at Mass *frequentius cum grandi affectu et compunctione.* St. Gregory the Great writes to Bishop John of Syracuse concerning the divergence existing in his time in regard to the Kyrie chant in the Roman and Greek Churches: "The Greeks recite *Kyrie eleison* all together, but with us the clerics say it, while the people answer; we also recite *Christe eleison* as often, which the Greeks do not." (Cf. Bona, *Rer. liturg.,* II, iv, 1.) In the Ambrosian liturgy the priest alone recites *Kyrie eleison* three times, and that at three different times: after the Gloria, after the Gospel, and after the Communion. Formerly the Kyrie was omitted at Rome in the Mass itself if it had immediately before been said in the Litany. Thus it was still practised in the twelfth century. Kyrie non dicitur propter Litaniam processionis, ubi dictum est Kyrie (*Ordo Rom.* XI, n. 63).

tive times in the Roman liturgy has been prescribed and practiced since the eleventh century.

2. The frequent repetition of the Kyrie denotes in general the ardor, perseverance, and importunity with which we, conscious of our sinfulness and unworthiness, implore mercy and assistance. There is also a still higher, mystical meaning in the threefold repetition of the three invocations. The three divine persons are separately and consecutively invoked: first the Father by the *Kyrie eleison;* then the Son by the *Christe eleison;* and finally the Holy Ghost by the *Kyrie eleison.* The invocation of each of the divine persons is repeated exactly three times to signify that with each of the divine persons the two others are at least virtually invoked,[3] since by the fact of their mystical indwelling in one another (*circuminsessio*) all three of the divine persons are eternally in one another.[4] Other meanings founded for the most part in devotion have also been given to this ninefold cry for mercy; thus, for instance, the ninefold signification of the Kyrie is devoutly thought to refer to the nine kinds of sins and wants, or it has been said that thereby we express our desire of union with the nine choirs of angels.[5]

3. The Kyrie is the only prayer in Greek still retained in the Mass rite. The principal reason for this may be that the common supplication of the people for help passed already in the earliest times from the Eastern into the Western Church, and on account of its frequent use the Kyrie became universally known and loved; hence this venerable form of supplication was not translated into

[3] Quoniam unus est Patris et Filii Spiritus, necesse est ut dum invocatur Pater aut Filius, in Patre et Filio etiam ille qui unus est utriusque Spiritus invocetur (S. Fulgent., *Contra Fabian.*, fragm. 31).

[4] Secunda pars praeparationis continet commemorationem praesentis miseriae, dum misericordia petitur, dicendo: *Kyrie eleison,* ter quidem pro persona Patris; ter autem pro persona Filii, cum dicitur: *Christe eleison,* et ter pro persona Spiritus sancti, cum subditur: *Kyrie eleison,* contra triplicem miseriam ignorantiae, culpae et poenae, vel ad significandum, quod omnes personae sunt in se invicem (S. Thom., IIIa, q. 83, a. 4).

[5] Singulis in Trinitate personis ternam miseriam, nimirum culpae, poenae et defectus bonorum spiritualium exponimus, ut oculis misericordiae suae nos respicientes auferre dignentur a nobis miseriam culpae indulgendo, miseriam poenae auferendo afflictiones, miseriam defectus donando spiritualia, quibus maxime indigemus; atque ita ss. Trinitatis misericordia novem choris Angelorum aliquando consociemur. Ut autem attentius et devotius haec verba proferamus, expedit speciatim meminisse culparum nostrarum in prima harum vocum recitatione, poenarum et afflictionum in secunda, ac defectum in tertia (Van der Burg, *Brevis elucidatio totius Missae,* chap. 2, §4).

THE KYRIE

Latin. In addition to the Greek *Kyrie*, the Hebrew expressions, *amen*, *alleluja*, *sabaoth*, and *hosanna*, appear in the Latin Mass prayers, and thus in the celebration of the unbloody sacrifice those three languages are still united which proclaimed to the world, in the glorious title on the cross, Christ's sovereignty (John 19:19).[6]

The Kyrie, as an expression of our wants, is never omitted in the celebration of Mass, and has a very appropriate place in its rite; while it follows the Introit quite naturally, at the same time it forms a suitable preparation for the Collect or for the Gloria. The Introit expresses, sometimes in a vein of joy and praise, again in a strain of tender pity or humble supplication, such thoughts and sentiments as should principally occupy the soul at the daily celebration of Mass, and thus serves as an introduction to the special feast. At the remembrance of this celebration we are so overpowered by the conviction of our own unworthiness, weakness, and indigence, that our heart is involuntarily compelled to break out into the oft-repeated supplications of the Kyrie since God's mercy alone can make us worthy of celebrating the holy mysteries in a proper manner.

The special celebration of the day, begun with the Introit, gives us, then, an opportunity at once to present our particular intentions and petitions to the Lord: here the Kyrie is best adapted to place the soul in suitable dispositions for prayer and to prepare it for the reception of gifts.[7] Humility, confidence, and desire constitute the key to the riches of divine mercy. Now, precisely in the repeated cry of the Kyrie is expressed the humble acknowledgment of one's own misery, as well as one's firm confidence in divine mercy and ardent desire for divine help. It therefore disposes us for the recitation of the Collects that follow it. "By considering our own wretchedness, we are taught to pray for what we need; by meditating on the divine mercy we are admonished with what fervent desires we

---

[6] Ecclesia latina merito et satis convenienter retinet voces aliquas, tum graecas, tum hebraicas, eisque utitur in Missa, in Officio, in Litaniis etc., praesertim *Kyrie eleison*, i.e. Domine miserere. Primo quia habent peculiarem quandam emphasim, et ob frequentem usum aeque intelliguntur ac voces latinae. Secundo retinentur ob venerationem antiquitatis. Tertio ad indicandam Ecclesiae catholicae unitatem, praesertim ex populis hebraeis, latinis et graecis, quorum omnium litteris conscriptus fuit titulus crucis Christi (Quarti, *De Litaniis Sanctorum*, sect. I, punct. 6).

[7] Ideo et *Kyrie eleison* cantatur, ut subsequens oratio sacerdotis exaudiatur (Honor. Augustod., *Gemma animae*, I, chap. 92). Cf. Amalar., *De eccles. offic.*, III, chap. 6.

should present our petitions. On these two wings, the misery of man and the mercy of our divine Redeemer, prayer ascends heavenwards." With humility and confidence, therefore, we should repeat the Kyrie, and in this disposition "go with confidence to the throne of grace, that we may obtain mercy and find grace in seasonable aid" (Heb. 4:16).[8]

The Kyrie is, moreover, a fitting preface to the Gloria; filled with joy and gratitude at the very thought of the graces and favors of our merciful God, we are impelled to bless His holy name. "The *Kyrie eleison*,—that cry for mercy which is to be found in every liturgy of East and West,—seems introduced as if to give grander effect to the outburst of joy and praise which succeeds it in the *Gloria in excelsis;* it is a deepening of our humiliation, that our triumph may be the better felt."[9]

4. As long as we children of Eve are constrained to remain in this vale of tears weeping and mourning, in exile and misery, no prayer is so necessary, none so befitting our condition, as the Kyrie, this heartfelt appeal, this humble cry for mercy to the triune God,[10]

---

[8] In omni Dei obsequio, praesertim in oratione et laude divina, duo nobis consideranda incumbunt, videlicet Dei misericordia et nostra miseria. Intelligo autem pro misericordia Dei omnia, quae ad bonitatem ejus respiciunt, scilicet caritatem ejus et liberalitatem et patientiam super nos. Per nostram vero miseriam universa intelligo, quae nostram imperfectionem, culpam et fragilitatem concernunt. Haec igitur intente nobis pensanda sunt, quatenus ex contemplatione divinae bonitatis atque clementiae respiremus et cum fiducia ad thronum gratiae accedamus, in plenitudine fidei, certissime agnoscentes, quia quidquid oraverimus Patrem in nomine Filii, dabitur nobis, si tamen perseveranter infatigabiliterque pulsemus. Dici non valet, quantum omnipotenti Deo perseverans ac fiducialis oratio placeat. Ex consideratione vero nostrae miseriae humiliemur et displiceamus nobis vilesque simus in oculis nostris. . . . Sic ergo sacrosancta Ecclesia convenienter instituit, ut post Introitum, in quo laus Dei cantata est, ad nos ipsos redeamus et Dei misericordiam imploremus dicentes: *Kyrie eleison*, i.e. Domine miserere. Et dicitur novies, quatenus nostram imperfectionem novies profitentes ad perfectionem ac societatem novem ordinum Angelorum perducamur (Dion. Carthus., *Expos. Miss.*, a. 9).

[9] Wiseman, *loc. cit.*

[10] Inter omnia verba deprecativa verbum hoc *Miserere* videtur efficacissimum et insuperabile esse et Omnipotenti quodammodo praevalere. Nam quidquid dicenti *Miserere* dixerit Deus, ipse orans opponere potest et dicere: *Miserere.* Si dixerit Deus: "Impius es et omni misericordia mea indignus," respondeat miser: *Miserere.* Nam quia indignus sum, imo indignissimus et quasi infinite indignior, quam ego ipse comprehendere valeo, ideo dico et oro: *Miserere mei.* Et quidquid huic orationi objiciatur, scil. quod non oro ex zelo justitiae, ex caritatis affectu, idem verbum resumam dicamque: *Mise-*

who is compassionate and merciful, long-suffering and plenteous in mercy (Ps. 102:8). "Man born of woman, living for a short time, is filled with many miseries" (Job 14:1), "all his days are full of sorrows and miseries" (Eccles. 2:23); who can enumerate them: the sins, temptations, dangers, defects, weaknesses, sufferings, wants, diseases, cares, adversities, hardships, and tribulations that here below surround man and oppress his heart? Freedom and redemption, protection and assistance, consolation and refreshment, poor man finds only with God, who is good and whose mercy endureth forever (Ps. 117:1). "As a father hath compassion on his children, so hath the Lord compassion on them that fear Him; for He knoweth our frame. He remembereth that we are dust" (Ps. 102:13 f.). The mercy of God will follow us all the days of our life (Ps. 22:6); and like a never-setting star in the heavens, it sheds its gentle and consoling rays upon us, in the morning as well as in the evening of life. But in order that the plenitude of divine mercy may descend upon us, the cry of the Kyrie must proceed from a heart penetrated with a lively sense of its poverty and misery.[11]

The Gloria

1. After the Kyrie the Gloria frequently follows. It is called the greater doxology because, in comparison with the *Gloria Patri*, it contains more extensive praise of the triune God; it is called the Angelic Hymn [12] because its opening words were sung by a host of heavenly spirits on the plains of Bethlehem on the night of Christ's birth.

---

rere. Etenim quia ex zelo justitiae et caritate non oro, peto ut mihi miserrimo miserearis et des mihi ex zelo justitiae atque ex caritate et ut tibi placeat orare. A tua justitia ad misericordiam tuam confugio, quae in infinitum major est omni malitia et miseria mea: ideo *miserere mei*, a cujus verbi prolatione numquam cessabo (Dion. Carthus., *De orat.*, a. 27).

[11] Constat ex his, cum quanta humilitate et affectione contritioneque cordis haec sacratissima verba Kyrie eleison dicenda sint, non cursorie, sed morose, quatenus presbyter omne genus peccati sibi indulgeri desideret, et tanto haec verba ferventius dicat quanto ea saepius iterat. Nam et ideo saepius iterantur, ut semper devotius explicentur (*idem.*, *Exposit. Miss.*, 9).

[12] If the Gloria is called *hymnus angelicus*, the Te Deum *hymnus ss. Ambrosii et Augustini*, the Preface *hymnus gloriae*, then the word *hymnus* is not used as a technical term, but mainly in the general sense of a chant or song of praise; for, in a stricter sense, by a church hymn is understood a spiritual canticle expressing religious sentiments in a concise form and composed, or at least adapted, for public liturgical use.

The compiler of this ancient hymn cannot be historically ascertained; only this much is undoubtedly certain: the Gloria is not of Latin, but of Greek origin, and it came from the East.[13] The Latin text, therefore, is not the original one, but a somewhat free translation or rearrangement of the original Greek text, which for good reasons is ascribed to St. Hilary of Poitiers, Doctor of the Church (d. 366).

In the Orient it was customary in the third century to make use of the greater doxology in the liturgy, but only as a morning hymn in the little hours of the Divine Office, not at the Eucharistic celebration. Even now it is not recited at Mass by the Greeks; but only the words of the angels, without further additions, are to be found in some Oriental liturgies, for instance, in that of St. James, where they are repeated three times.

With regard to the insertion of the Gloria into the Roman Mass, we have only obscure and uncertain accounts.[14] The use of the Gloria was originally and for a long period rather restricted: it served for the expression of Christmas joy and Easter exultation.[15] Until nearly the close of the eleventh century the rubrics of the Gregorian

[13] In a somewhat altered composition, but which in all probability is the original, we find the greater doxology already in the *Apostolic Constitutions* (VIII, chap. 47) as an ecclesiastical morning prayer.

[14] According to the *Liber Pontificalis*, Pope Telesphorus (d. 136 or 138) prescribed the Angelic Hymn for Christmas night; and Pope Symmachus (d. 514) for Sundays and the feasts of martyrs. Telesphorus constituit, ut . . . Natali Domini noctu Missae celebrarentur . . . et ante sacrificium hymnus diceretur angelicus, h. e. *Gloria in excelsis Deo*. Symmachus constituit, ut omne die dominica vel natalicia martyrum *Gloria in excelsis* hymnus diceretur (Duch., I, 129, 263). About the middle of the eleventh century, the ordinance of *Sacrament. Gregor.* was still in force: Dicitur *Gloria in excelsis Deo*, si episcopus fuerit, tantummodo die dominico sive diebus festis; a presbyteris autem minime dicitur nisi solo in Pascha. (Cf. Bern. Augiens. [d. 1048], *Libell. de quibusdam rebus ad Missae officium pertinentibus*, chap. 2.)

[15] Until the ninth century the Gloria, as the Te Deum at present, was sung in solemn thanksgiving. Since the eleventh century at the Introit, Kyrie, Gloria, Sanctus, and Agnus Dei there occur many so-called tropes, that is, explanatory and amplified additions with an abundance of melody. These insertions or adornments of the liturgical text, as a rule, took place only on feast days and were often collected in separate books (*libri troparii vel troponari*). An amplified Gloria, *Gloria Marianum*, was still recited here and there at the time of the revision of the missal, in spite of the issued prohibition; therefore, in the *Ordo Missae* of the Roman Missal, after the Gloria the express ordinance was inserted: Sic (*thus, as it is given in the missal and without addition*) dicitur Gloria in excelsis Deo, etiam in Missis beatae Mariae, quando dicendum est.

THE GLORIA

Sacramentary prevailed, which granted or prescribed the recitation of the Gloria by the bishop on all Sundays and feast days; by the priest, on the contrary, only at Easter. But from that time this privilege of the bishops has been extended also to priests. Now the Gloria is said in almost all Masses except those celebrated with purple vestments and ferial Masses celebrated with green vestments. The Gloria and the Te Deum are enthusiastic, sublime chants of joy and exultation, expressive of festal rejoicing; hence both are omitted on days and in seasons which are devoted mainly to mourning and penance, or which at least are without a festive character.[16]

2. The greater Doxology is as follows:

Gloria in excelsis Deo, et in terra pax hominibus bonae voluntatis.

Laudamus te: benedicimus te: adoramus te: glorificamus te: gratias agimus tibi propter magnam gloriam tuam: Domine Deus, Rex coelestis, Deus Pater omnipotens.

Domine, Fili unigenite, Jesu Christe: Domine Deus, Agnus Dei, Filius Patris. Qui tollis peccata mundi, miserere nobis. Qui tollis peccata mundi, suscipe deprecationem nostram. Qui sedes ad dexteram Patris, miserere nobis.

Quoniam tu solus Sanctus, tu solus Dominus, tu solus Altissimus, Jesu Christe, cum sancto Spiritu, in gloria Dei Patris. Amen.

Glory to God in the highest, and on earth peace to men of good will.

We praise Thee, we bless Thee, we adore Thee, we glorify Thee. We give thanks to Thee for Thy great glory, O Lord God, heavenly King, God the Father Almighty.

O Lord Jesus Christ, the only-begotten Son, O Lord God, Lamb of God, Son of the Father, who takest away the sins of the world, have mercy on us. Who takest away the sins of the world, receive our prayer. Who sitteth at the right hand of the Father, have mercy on us.

For Thou only art holy, Thou only art the Lord, Thou only, O Jesus Christ, together with the Holy Ghost, art most high in the glory of God the Father. Amen.

[16] Micrologus (chap. 2) wrote at the close of the eleventh century: In omni festo, quod plenum habet officium, excepto intra Adventum Domini et Septuagesimam et natali Innocentium tam presbyter quam episcopus *Gloria in excelsis* dicunt. Quod etiam numquam post meridiem legitur dicendum nisi in Coena Domini, ubi chrisma conficitur et in sabbatis Paschae et Pentecostes. According to Amalarius (IV, chap. 30), the Gloria was omitted dur-

The Gloria is the sublime triumphal chant of redemption, part of which first resounded from the choir of heavenly hosts; the rest is an outpouring from the heart of the Church. Choirs of angels intoned it at the birth of the Saviour; the Church, initiated in the mysteries of God, has continued and completed it.[17] On the plains of Bethlehem the heavenly notes of the *"Gloria in excelsis"* resounded;[18] they pealed forth with the sublimity and power of tones of thunder, full and melodious as "the roaring of many waters." The angels glorify the Child in the crib. With His birth honor is restored to God and peace to men. And this makes the angels rejoice greatly. When at Bethlehem, amid the silence of the midnight hour, the flower from the root of Jesse came forth and bloomed, visible to mortal eye, filling the world with its fragrance, then could the heavens open, then did the angels sing melodies, such as the listening earth had never heard before, melodies as might be sung only to

---

ing Advent about the ninth century *in aliquibus locis*. The same statement is made by Honorius of Autun (d. 1145) in the twelfth century (cf. *Gemma animae*, III, chap. 1). In the Roman Church, on the contrary, the Sundays of Advent were celebrated in a festive manner until toward the close of the twelfth century, with white vestments and the Angelic Hymn (cf. *Ordo Rom. XI*, n. 4). From this date Rome also took up the practice that had for a long time existed in other churches, *ut hymnus angelicus laetius solemniusque Dominici natalis die repeteretur*.

[17] Hymnum angelicum, in quo verbis quaedam ab angelis circa nativitatem dominicam in laudem Dei sunt prolata, sequentes ss. Patres ad communem sanctae et individuae Trinitatis laudationem dulcissimas et congruentissimas dictiones addiderunt, ut sicut ejus principium a coelestibus est ordinatum ministris, ita etiam tota ejus series divinis esset plena mysteriis (Walafrid. Strabo, chap. 22).

[18] "Glory to God in the highest, and on earth peace to men of good will" (Luke 2:14). The angelic hymn of praise is to be considered not as a wish but as an assertion, and, therefore, not ἔστω, *sit*, but ἐστίν, *est*, is to be understood. By the birth and the whole work of the Saviour, infinite glory is given to God reigning in heaven, and on earth peace (the fullness of all the supernatural goods of salvation) to men, on whom, instead of anger, the divine good will or pleasure (bona voluntas Dei; cf. Ps. 5:13; 50:20) now again rests. In their liturgical use the angels' words form a chant of praise, intoned by the Church or by us, and may then properly be considered as a wish (*sit*). Here, indeed, there is question of the subjective realization and individual application of that which in the Angelic Hymn is represented as already realized and accomplished. In like manner, we may refer the words *bonae voluntatis* also to the good will of men redeemed, effected by the divine favor and grace; this good disposition, this desire of salvation, is indispensable if we wish to draw down on ourselves the divine pleasure and the plenitude of peace.

grace a triumph wherein the eternal God celebrated the victories of His own boundless love.

Gloria in excelsis Deo, et in terra pax hominibus bonae voluntatis. ("Glory to God in the highest, and on earth peace to men of good will.") Thus do we joyfully sing at the celebration of Mass in unison with the choir of heavenly hosts; for it is at the altar that this joyful message of the angel has its perfect fulfillment. There all due honor and the highest glory are rendered to God; for an infinite person, the God-man Jesus Christ, humbles and sacrifices Himself to the praise and adoration of the divine Majesty. There true peace is imparted to man; for Christ, by His sacrifice, purchased for us pardon, reconciliation, and happiness. The words, *Gloria Deo et pax hominibus*, constitute the theme of the entire hymn. The Gloria is a chant of praise, thanksgiving, and petition; for the praise of God is interrupted by thanksgiving and petition, which are likewise acts of adoration and contribute to proclaim the divine glory.

Gloria in excelsis Deo ("Glory to God in the highest"). The heavenly hosts never weary of praising and magnifying God. St. John in a vision heard the heavenly chant: "Let us be glad and rejoice and give glory to Him," the Lord our God, the Almighty (Apoc. 19:7). In this grand hymn, this eternal canticle of praise once heard on the plains of Bethlehem, all creation, and especially man, should unite. In praise of the Most High do the stars twinkle, the flowers bloom, the birds sing; but far more precious and exalted is the praise which man consciously and freely presents to God by prayer. Hence out of the fullness of our heart we cry to the Lord: *Laudamus te* [19] ("We praise Thee"). Yes, let us praise the Lord, for

---

[19] At the words *laudare, benedicere, adorare, glorificare,* the varied meaning and the proper succession is worthy of consideration. The most general idea, contained in all four expressions, is that of honoring; for they denote religious veneration, but each in a different manner. *Laus* and *benedictio* are marks of honor which consist in acknowledging, extolling, and announcing the perfections, privileges, virtues, and merits of others with heart and mouth. *Laus Dei est sapida quaedam cognitio majestatis et perfectionis divinae, ejusque per verba interiora et exteriora magnificatio et exaltatio* (Alvarez de Paz, *De studio orationis*, Bk. IV, Part III, chap. 14). *Laudare* and *benedicere* are indeed often used without distinction, but here their signification may be somewhat distinct; for *benedicere* (= to praise) expresses an intensive, corroborated, and increased praise, as is evident from the liturgical doxological formula *Benedictus Deus* ("May God be highly praised"). Through the liturgical use of this formula, the word *benedictus* has obtained a certain solemnity, and in the Old Testament, as well as in the New,

He is great and exceedingly worthy of praise, and of His greatness there is no end (Ps. 144:3). Let us proclaim aloud, let us with heart and lips exalt His infinite power and majesty, His never-failing goodness and mercy, His boundless holiness and justice, His impenetrable ways and decrees. It is the blessed duty and vocation of the priest always to praise God, seven times a day to withdraw from the world and in the hours of prayer to chant the praises of the Lord.[20]

Benedicimus te ("We bless Thee").[21] The blessing, that is, the praising of God, is a spirited and sublime praise, proceeding from the overflowing sentiments of the heart, which we offer to the Lord chiefly to acknowledge Him as the source of all blessings, graces, and mercies imparted to us. The consideration of the divine mercies inflames the heart to bless the name of the Lord, who above all is deserving of praise.[22] To the praise of the Most High, St. Paul, the Apostle of the Gentiles, exhorts us: "Let the word of Christ dwell in you abundantly, in all wisdom, teaching and admonishing one another in psalms, hymns and spiritual canticles, singing in grace in

---

where it occurs in eight passages, it is almost always employed only with reference to God (Rom. 8:5). Not merely in degree, but essentially different from *laus* and *benedictio*, is *adoratio* (adoration). In this restricted meaning *adorare* is to be taken, as it otherwise often designates religious veneration in general. If to the knowledge and confession of the infinite majesty of God a corresponding subjection is added, then *laus* and *benedictio* become *adoratio* (adoration). The word *glorificare* (to exalt, to ennoble) includes a further quality: it designates a special *laudare, benedicere, et adorare*, such as brings about among other persons glory for the one that is praised, extolled, and adored. Gloria idem fere est quod honorifica laus; addit enim effectum quemdam, quem laus efficit in aliis, scil. bonam existimationem de re laudata. Est enim gloria clara cum laude notitia; unde glorificare aliquem nihil aliud est quam eum ita laudare, ut apud alios bona ejus existimatio inde oriatur (cf. Suarez, disp. LI, sect. 1, n. 1–4).

[20] Non est laboriosa, sed amabilis et optanda servitus, in Dei laudibus perpetuo assistere (Beda Venerab., I, homil. IX).

[21] Cf. S. August., *Enarrat. in Ps.*, 66:1. Benedicimus Deum, in quantum ejus bonitatem corde recognoscimus et ore confitemur (S. Thom., *In ep. ad Rom.*, chap. 1, lect. 7).

[22] *Benedicimus te* = bonum de te vel tibi dicimus. Nos benedicimus Deo, et Deus benedicit nobis, sed differenter valde. Nam benedictio Dei est collatio munerum divinorum et multiplicatio eorundem; benedictio igitur Dei est causa bonitatis et gratiae et sanctitatis in nobis. Benedictio vero, qua nos Deum benedicimus, est quaedam professio, qua omnia bona Deo adscribimus tanquam fonti bonitatis et sanctitatis ac gratiae (Dion. Carthus., *Expos. Miss.*, a. 10).

your hearts to God" (Col. 3:16). "Singing and making melody in your hearts to the Lord" (Eph. 5:19) for all gifts and favors conferred.

Adoramus te ("We adore Thee"). Adoration in itself is far more sublime than the praise and extolling of God; for it is that supreme honor which may not be given to a mere creature, but which is due and may be rendered only to the divine Majesty. It is by adoration that man worships his God as the infinitely perfect Being, before whom all that is created vanishes as mere nothingness. Adoration is peculiarly the prayer of the angels and saints in heaven. And we also in this vale of tears, being animated with holy joy and fear, should "adore and fall down and weep before the Lord that made us" (Ps. 94:6), so that heaven and earth may form together a choir of humble, joyous adoration.

Glorificamus te ("We glorify Thee"). The Lord for His own honor and glory hath created all things (Prov. 16:4); the faithful hath He called, redeemed, and sanctified, that they may be "unto the praise of the glory of His grace" (Eph. 1:6). Every creature is in its way destined to glorify God. All that we do should be done for the greater glory of God, should tend to promote God's honor: *Omnia ad majorem Dei gloriam*. We principally proclaim God's glory by praising Him, exalting Him, and adoring Him. When we praise, exalt, and adore God, we bear a public testimony to His power, wisdom, and goodness, we acknowledge His absolute perfection and supreme dominion, spread His fame and His honor, make known His name.[23] The Psalmist admonishes us: "Bring to the Lord glory and honor, bring to the Lord glory to His name, adore ye the Lord in His holy court!" (Ps. 28:2.)

Now the hymn of praise, exaltation, and adoration changes to a canticle of thanksgiving of almost ecstatic joy: *Gratias agimus tibi propter magnam gloriam tuam* ("We give Thee thanks for Thy great glory").[24] These words have a wonderful and profound mean-

---

[23] *Glorificamus te.* Dicimur Deum sanctificare vel magnificare, dum ei in sanctitate et aequitate servimus sicque eum magnum et sanctum esse ostendimus. Sic quoque Deum glorificamus, dum nomen ipsius aliis manifestamus, ac per hoc ipsum famosum et in animo aliorum gloriosum efficimus (*ibid.*).

[24] The words *propter magnam gloriam tuam* may likewise be referred to the four foregoing expressions, and thus the "great glory" of the heavenly Father may be indicated as the reason and object of our praise as well as of our adoration and glorification, but even then it needs to be explained how we may also thank God "on account of His great glory." In the Celtic Stowe

ing, springing as they do from an ardent and pure love of God. We thank God for gifts and benefits received; but how can we thank Him because of His great glory? Many writers, in seeking to solve the difficulty here presented, would have, for example, the Incarnation or the mercy of God understood to be the glory and magnificence that inspire our grateful thanks. This meaning is evidently too restricted, for the expression "glory" is here to be taken in its most comprehensive sense: it refers to the internal as well as to the external glory of God. We therefore thank God because of His great glory, which from all eternity He has in Himself and of Himself; we also thank Him by reason of that great glory which He has procured and continues to procure for Himself in time by the works of His hands.

God in Himself, that is, according to His nature, is infinitely glorious, infinitely worthy of glory, the uncreated glory itself. This interior, eternally unchangeable, and impenetrable glory of God we must admire, praise, adore; it may also be a subject of gratitude for us, inasmuch as by the perfect love of God, the divine glory becomes in a manner our property and the source of joy to us.[25] For this love of benevolence unites us most intimately with God. "He that abideth in charity, abideth in God, and God in him" (I John 4:16). Nothing pleases the loving soul more than the consideration of the infinite majesty, beauty, goodness, holiness, wisdom, power, and mercy of God; therefore, it is not surprising that the soul breaks out into a joyous chant of thanksgiving because of the eternal and infinite glory of God.

Still our thanks have reference principally to the exterior glory of God, wherewith heaven and earth are filled. The rays of the glory of the Creator and Redeemer strike us everywhere. In the works of His power, the magnanimous deeds of His love and mercy,

---

Missal of the seventh or eighth century we read: *Gratias agimus tibi propter magnam misericordiam tuam.*

[25] Gaudium est quies animi in bono suo jam adepto. Bonum autem proprium non solum est quod quisque in se habet, sed etiam quod habet in aliis sibi conjunctis. Aspicies ergo Dominum ut benignissimum et dilectissimum Patrem tuum, a quo genitus es, et (ut speras) ad aeternam haereditatem efficaciter vocatus, et omnia ejus bona propria reputabis. Gaudebis de omnibus perfectionibus Dei tui, ut de ejus sapientia, bonitate et potentia et reliquis, ut de bonis benignissimi Patris tui. Et sufficiat tibi, quod ipse sit infinite beatus et dives adeoque exsultes de gloria ejus (Alvarez de Paz, *De studio orationis*, Bk. VI, Part III, chap. 12, exercit. 11).

the Lord has exteriorly revealed His interior glory. If God acts outwardly, He glorifies Himself; but this self-glorification of God redounds to man's profit and constitutes our happiness and bliss.[26] God's glory is our salvation; that which gives God glory, gives us an abundance of graces and blessings. The creation of heaven and earth, the Incarnation, the life, passion, death, resurrection, and ascension of Jesus Christ, the institution of the Eucharistic sacrifice and of the sacraments, the guidance of the Church throughout all ages, the sanctification and happiness of man, the future transformation of the world—all these works have for their object, first of all, the glory and honor of the Most High, and, at the same time, the welfare and salvation of man. Our supreme good, our eternal happiness, is the highest glory of God: nowhere is God more glorified than in heaven, where the blessed contemplate, enjoy, love, praise, and glorify forever face to face His infinite goodness and beauty.[27] The thanksgiving offered to the Lord on account of His great glory thus has reference principally to the marvelous works and ways of God in the kingdom of nature and of grace, from which flows our happiness and beatitude.[28] The Church does not say: We thank Thee, O Lord, for Thy many benefits or mercies; but she expresses herself in terms exceedingly beautiful and ingenious: "We thank Thee for Thy great glory."

[26] Deus "omnia operatus est propter se," h. e. operatus est omnia ad hoc, ut suam bonitatem, sapientiam, potentiam, magnificentiam, gloriam etc. creaturis ostenderet et communicaret, quod est bonum creaturarum, non Dei. Deus enim ex hac sui communicatione nihil acquisivit, cum nihil ei addi possit (unde et gloria, qua eum glorificant homines, Angeli et creaturae omnes, nihil ei addit, cum ipse in se habeat gloriam increatam et infinitam); sed creaturae suam essentiam, proprietates, dotes, omneque bonum suum hauserunt a Deo (Corn. a Lap., *In Proverb. Salom.*, 16:4).

[27] Dei glorificatio completur ipsa exaltatione et beatitudine Sanctorum, seu potius ipsa exaltatio et beatitudo Sanctorum est suprema Dei gloria objectiva et formalis, quod Deus ut summum bonum a creatura per visionem, amorem et inde consequentem beatitudinem in perpetuas aeternitates possidetur (Franzelin, *De Deo uno*, thes. 29).

[28] Dum Deus spectat suam summam gloriam, eo ipso necessario spectat et intendit summum bonum nostrum, quia summa ejus gloria est summum bonum nostrum et summum bonum nostrum non potest esse nisi summa ejus gloria. Unde non minus Deo gratias agere debemus, quod quaerat gloriam suam, quam quod quaerat salutem nostram, quia gloria ejus est nostra salus. Hoc in Hymno angelico Ecclesia innuit, cum ait: "Gratias agimus tibi propter magnam gloriam tuam;" beneficia enim ipsius in nos sunt gloria ejus (Lessius, *De perfect. divin.*, XIV, chap. 3).

From the heights of the holy and enthusiastic praise of God the Gloria descends to the depths of a humble prayer of supplication; now follows a more detailed amplification of these words of the angels: *"In terra pax hominibus bonae voluntatis"* ("On earth peace to men of good will"). Peace and reconciliation with God proceed from the Child in the manger, who by His death on the cross established peace and reconciliation between heaven and earth (Col. 1:20). Thus amid the loud jubilant strains of the Gloria, the Church reminds us of our sinfulness and poverty, and humbly petitions our Lord, who brought peace into the word, to relieve our miseries, to reconcile us with the Father and grant us peace. The petition is addressed to Jesus Christ,[29] and the most moving reasons are set forth for Him to hear our prayer and to listen to the voice of our supplication (Ps. 129:2).

Domine, Fili unigenite, Jesu Christe: Domine Deus, Agnus Dei, Filius Patris ("O Lord Jesus Christ, the only-begotten Son, O Lord God, Lamb of God, Son of the Father"). With this invocation the Church exhausts herself in extolling her heavenly chief and spouse: she exalts His divinity and sovereignty over all creatures; she praises Him as the only-begotten Son, whom the Father begot before the morning star, before all time (Ps. 109:3), and in whom He is eternally well pleased (Matt. 17:5); she celebrates Him as the divine victim for the honor of God and the salvation of the world; she combines all His divinely human perfections and privileges in the name of Jesus (= Saviour, Redeemer), and Christ (= the anointed, that is, the highest prophet, priest, and king).[30]

Qui tollis peccata mundi, miserere nobis ("Who takest away the sins of the world, have mercy on us"). In torrents and to the

---

[29] Dominus Christus, qui nos exaudit cum Patre, orare pro nobis dignatus est ad Patrem. Quid felicitate nostra certius, quando ille pro nobis orat, qui dat quod orat? Est enim Christus homo et Deus: orat ut homo; dat, quod orat, ut Deus (S. August., *Serm.*, CCXVII, n. 1). Petere et orare competit Christo secundum naturam assumptam, sed posse implere debetur ei secundum naturam assumentem (S. Bonav., III, dist. 17, a. 2, q. 1).

[30] Clarificatio nominis Christi est manifestatio cognitionis habitae de Christo, qua cognoscitur esse Dei Filius et Christus et Jesus, et quodlibet istorum est nomen super omne nomen. Nam Filius Dei nominat personam in una natura; Christus autem et Jesus nominant personam in duabus naturis; sed Christus nominat personam in humana natura relata ad divinam, quia dicitur unctus. Jesus autem nominat personam in divina natura relata ad humanam, quia Jesus dicitur Salvator esse et ideo in nomine Jesu Christi debet omne genu curvari (Phil. 2:10), sicut in nomine Filii Dei (*ibid.*, dist. 18, dub. 2).

THE GLORIA

last drop did Christ shed His precious blood for the atonement and the cleansing of all sins, which unceasingly deluged the world and provoked God's justice to punish. The Son of God assumed a truly human heart, making it the throne of mercy, even allowing it to be opened and pierced with a lance, in order to show mercy and compassion on our weaknesses and errors.

Qui tollis peccata mundi, suscipe deprecationem[31] *nostram* ("Who takest away the sins of the world, receive our prayer"). Almost the same words are repeated; for the Church is greatly moved by the mercy and condescension of our divine Saviour, who has loved us and washed our sins in His blood (Apoc. 1:5). Since He has given Himself for all as a propitiatory sacrifice, He will also attend to the petitions of them that fear Him, and He will save them (Ps. 144:19).

Qui sedes ad dexteram Patris, miserere nobis ("Who sitteth at the right hand of the Father, have mercy on us"). In the holy of holies in heaven Christ reigns at the right of the Father, that is, He excels, even according to His human nature, all creatures in dignity, power, and plenitude of grace; in the fullest measure He shares in the power, sovereignty, and glory of God. In His heavenly exaltation and glorification He is not only our all-powerful mediator and advocate with the Father, but also our most merciful God and Master, who is ever ready with divine power and clemency to forgive us, to succor us in every want, and to assist us in every danger.

In the beginning of the Gloria, we present the Lord our God our homage and our thanks; mindful of our constant necessities, we then address the most ardent supplication to Jesus Christ, who died and rose from the dead, who sitteth at the right hand of God and intercedes for us (Rom. 8:34). This cry for mercy and for a favorable hearing is changed, at the end, into spirited tones of joy; the Gloria now peals forth in sublime praise of the triune God.

---

[31] *Deprecatio* = the solicitous, urgent, earnest petition, and also, the petition to avert, the petition for grace and pardon. Precationem et deprecationem, multi nostri hoc idem putant, et hoc quotidiano usu jam omnino praevaluit. Qui autem distinctius latine locuti sunt, precationibus utebantur in optandis bonis, deprecationibus vero in devitandis malis. Precari enim dicebant esse precando bona optare; imprecari mala, quod vulgo jam dicitur maledicere; deprecari autem, mala precando depellere (S. August., *Epist.* 149 [al. 59], *ad Paulin*, n. 13).

Quoniam tu solus [32] *Sanctus, tu solus Dominus, tu solus Altissimus, Jesu Christe, cum sancto Spiritu in gloria Dei Patris. Amen.* ("For Thou only art holy, Thou only art the Lord, Thou only, O Jesus Christ, together with the Holy Ghost, art most high in the glory of God the Father. Amen.") The more profoundly Jesus Christ has debased and humbled Himself for us and for our salvation, so much the more joyfully and gratefully do we chant these words, so replete with an enthusiastic confession of His absolute holiness, sovereignty, and majesty: of His divinity. "The All Holy, the Lord God, the Most High"—these titles are frequently used in Holy Scripture to designate the true God. The Father, the Son, and the Holy Ghost are by their essence "the only Holy," [33] "the only (boundless) Lord," and "the only Most High." [34]

Jesus Christ is "the (infinitely) Holy One" and, therefore, the source and prototype of all created holiness; even in His humanity

---

[32] The word *solus* may relate either to the preceding subject *tu* or to the following predicate *Sanctus, Dominus, Altissimus:* "Thou alone art (with the Holy Ghost and the Father) the Holy One, the Lord, the Most High," or "Thou art (with the Holy Ghost and the Father) the only (essentially) Holy One, the only Lord, the only highest." If *tu* is combined with *solus,* then naturally only the creatures, but not the two other divine persons, are excluded from the possession of the predicate. Non dicimus absolute, quod solus Filius sit Altissimus, sed quod sit Altissimus cum sancto Spiritu in gloria Dei Patris (S. Thom., IIa, q.31, a.4 ad 4). A passage parallel to *solus* and *Sanctus* combined together, is found in the prayer of our Saviour to His Father: *Haec est vita aeterna, ut cognoscant te, solum Deum verum* ("This is eternal life, that they may know Thee, the only true God"; John 17:3). Divinae naturae propria attribuuntur Filio Dei, cum ipse *solus Sanctus, solus Dominus* et *solus Altissimus* esse enuntiatur. In quibus quidem tribus Filii Dei celebrationibus particula "solus" non excludit reliquas duas divinas personas, Patrem, inquam, et Spiritum Sanctum, quin potius eas includit, cum illa tria praedicata Sanctus, Dominus et Altissimus sint essentialia et divinitatis concernant substantiam. . . . Ex quo protinus evadit dilucidum, particulam illam "solus" naturas alias a divina, ut angelicam et humanam, hic excludere. Non enim angelus aut homo secundum eam rationem sanctus est, qua dicitur Deus sanctus, quandoquidem Deus est absolute Sanctus, Dominus et Altissimus, natura sanctitatem habens, dominatum et altitudinem, et ex se Angelus autem et homo non suapte natura neque ex se sanctimoniam habet, dominium et celsitudinem, sed participatione et sola gratia quadamque a Deo dependentia, perinde atque aër et aqua claritatem mutuantur a sole per se lucido (Clichtov., *Elucidat.,* III).

[33] Like *Dominus* et *Altissimus,* the word *Sanctus* also is not to be taken here as an adjective, but as a substantive: it designates Him whose whole essence is holiness and from whom proceeds all created holiness.

[34] "Let them know that the Lord is Thy name; Thou alone art the Most High (*tu solus altissimus*) over all the earth" (Ps. 82:19).

are to be found all the treasures of grace and virtue. He is still "the Lord," [35] the absolute proprietor, sovereign, and judge of the universe; He is the King of kings and the Lord of lords (I Tim. 6:15), whom all creatures serve and to whom man in particular owes the most profound reverence and submission. He is "the Most High," since by reason of His divine greatness, grandeur, and majesty He infinitely excels all created things. His holy humanity also is exalted and glorified above all things; for God raised Him from the dead and placed Him at His right hand in heaven, above all kingdoms, above all power and might and every name that is mentioned, not only in this world, but also in the world to come.

Thus ends the glorious hymn of praise with a joyous look to heaven and to the glorious majesty of the triune God. We exult because the Son of God possesses with the Holy Ghost the same glory which the Father has from eternity. "Every tongue should confess that the Lord Jesus Christ is in the glory of God the Father" (Phil. 2:11).

3. While the priest recites the Gloria, he stands erect at the middle of the altar with hands joined; only a few simple ceremonies are prescribed to emphasize certain words of the text. At the words *Gloria in excelsis*, the priest, without raising his eyes at the time, extends and elevates his hands to the shoulders, thus giving vent to his eagerness and longing to praise and magnify God. At *Deo* he again joins his hands and bows his head profoundly toward the crucifix on the altar (or toward the Blessed Sacrament when it is exposed). This profound inclination of the head is several times repeated: to express the interior acts of adoration (*adoramus te*), of gratitude (*gratias agimus tibi*), of petition (*suscipe deprecationem nostram*), of reverence (*Jesu Christe*), and to give expression to these acts of homage not merely in words, but also by movements of the body. At the last words of the Gloria the celebrant signs himself with the sign of the cross, principally to close the sublime hymn in a suitable and worthy manner. But as the sign of the cross is of itself a symbolical representation of the Trinity, it may also be referred to the glory of the Holy Trinity expressed in the concluding words of the hymn; for the acknowledgment of the three

---

[35] Nomen et ratio Domini soli omnipotenti Deo plene, summe, pure ac proprie competit, quippe qui solus universale, primordiale, independens ac nulli subjectum habet dominium (Dion. Carthus., *In Luc.*, 1:68).

divine persons is often, although not always, accompanied by the sign of the cross.[36]

4. This Angelic Hymn should be recited and sung with angelic devotion.[37] During its recitation we should unite in heart and lips with the choirs of the heavenly hosts, who daily assemble around the altar and never grow weary of chanting God's praise and our happiness, as they once sang at the crib of the newborn Saviour.[38]

In this hymn we are reminded of the marvelous joy which came to the whole world when God sent to condemned man a Saviour from heaven. This hymn the Church of God likewise sings with great joy, like unto that joy which any man might in all reason experience on favorably and bounteously receiving what he stood in great need of, for which he had entertained an ardent desire, and for which he had earnestly and suppliantly prayed. As though our cries to God had just now been heard and we had just obtained from God the fulfillment of our desires, the priest begins with great joy to praise God: "Honor and glory be to God in the highest," and the choir, in the place of all the congregation, who can no longer restrain their hearts overflowing with exultation, unite with the priest and with lips and heart jointly sing the praises of

---

[36] Litania Kyrie eleison finita, dirigens se Ponifex contra populum incipit Gloria in excelsis Deo et statim regyrat se (*he turns around*) ad Orientem (*to the altar*) usquedum finiatur (*Ordo Rom. I*, n. 9). This turning of the celebrant to the people while intoning, which probably was meant to invite and summon them to praise God, was no longer customary in the ninth century. According to Amalarius (d. 857) the Gloria was intoned while facing the east (that is, toward the altar, where our Lord is), but on the Epistle side (cf. *De ecclesiast. offic.*, III, chap. 8). Later on it was judged more suitable to recite the Angelic Hymn before the image of the Crucified in the middle of the altar (cf. Durand., *Ration.*, IV, xiii, 1).

[37] Hoc angelicum canticum cum magna cordis laetitia ac devotione dulcissima est cantandum sive legendum, quod fieri nequit, nisi intellectus in contemplatione Dei stabiliter atque sincere firmetur. Quanto enim verba fuerint diviniora, tanto ampliorem advertentiam et elevationem mentis puriorem requirunt; quo etiam sensus divinorum verborum affectuosior est atque profundior, eo modica cordis distractio vehementius nocet ac impedit. Postremo quum Deus attente orandus sit, attentius tamen laudandus est, et tanto attentius quanto majus ac dignius est Deum laudare quam orare (Dion. Carthus., *Expos. Miss.*, a. 10).

[38] Quaedam dicuntur a choro, quae pertinent ad populum, quorum quaedam chorus totaliter prosequitur, quae scil. toti populo inspirantur; quaedam vero populus prosequitur sacerdote inchoante, qui personam Dei gerit, in signum quod talia pervenerunt ad populum ex revelatione divina, sicut fides et gloria coelestis, et ideo sacerdos inchoat Symbolum fidei et Gloria in excelsis Deo (S. Thom., IIIa, q.83, a.4 ad6).

THE GLORIA

God, who has acted so mercifully toward us, praising and extolling His graces in many joyful words.[39]

Cardinal Wiseman says of the Gloria: "No composition ever lent itself more perfectly to the musician's skill; none ever afforded better play to the rich and rapid succession of every mode, gay and grave; none better supplied the slow and entreating cadence, or the full and powerful chorus. In the simple Gregorian chant, or in the pure religious harmonies of Palestrina, it is truly 'the Hymn of Angels.' "[40]

The glorious apostle and protector of Rome, St. Philip Neri, on the day of his death (the feast of Corpus Christ, May 26, 1595) celebrated a low Mass at a very early hour. At the *Gloria in excelsis* he was suddenly rapt in ecstasy and he began to sing; full of devotion and jubilation of heart, in a clear, loud voice, he sang the "Angelic Hymn" from the beginning to the end, as though he had already departed from earth and was rejoicing among the choirs of the blessed spirits.

[39] *Ein Vergissmeinnicht*, p. 65.
[40] "On Prayer and Prayer-Books," *Essays on Various Subjects*, II, 199.

CHAPTER XXI

THE COLLECT

AFTER the Gloria, or the Kyrie, follows the principal prayer, that is, the special prayer for the day or the feast, which is usually called the Collect.[1] It has here an appropriate place in the arrangement of the Mass rite; for by the humble and confident cry for mercy in the Kyrie, as well as by the praising of the divine power and goodness in the Gloria, we have placed ourselves in the proper attitude for prayer, disposing ourselves to receive from God a favorable answer to our petitions. "He hath had regard to the prayer of the humble, and He hath not despised their petition" (Ps. 101:18); "the prayer of the humble and the meek hath always pleased Thee" (Judith 9:16). The Collects are prayers of petition,[2] in which the Church by the mouth of the priest presents to God her maternal desires and interests, in order to obtain for her children the special gifts and graces corresponding to the different feasts and seasons of the year. The Collect, although but a small part of the liturgy

---

[1] In the Roman Missal the heading of this prayer is *Oratio*, whereby it is in an eminent sense characterized as a prayer. The name *Collecta* is ascribed to it in the summarized exposition of the Mass rite (*Ritus celebr. Miss.*, tit. 11, n. 1). To the proper prayer of the day there are generally added some others; they too are called *Collectae*, whether prescribed by the rubrics and decrees (*Orationes praescriptae*) or ordered (*Orationes imperatae*, sc. *a Superiore*) by ecclesiastical superiors (pope or bishop), or on certain days of lower rite, when they are added by the celebrant (*ex privata devotione*) to the others (*Orationes votivae*).

[2] In officio Missae est ordinatissima mixtio commemorationis divinae excellentiae, quam laudamus, et recognitionis nostrae miseriae, pro qua oramus; nam post Confessionem ante altare, in qua nostram profitemur miseriam, inchoatur Introitus, qui est cantus laudis divinae, et statim subjunguntur *Kyrie eleison*, in quo rursus humiliamus nos ipsos, nostram miseriam declarantes. Hoc finito ad Dei laudem convertimur, dicentes *Gloria in excelsis Deo*, quo completo *Oratio* sequitur, in qua denuo consideramus nos ipsos et misericordiam imploramus miseriae nostrae (Dion. Carthus., *Expos. Miss.*, a. 11).

THE COLLECT

of the Mass, presents some very important and interesting features.

1. **The name *Collecta*.**[3] The formulas for Mass are uniformly arranged; they all have the same arrangement of prayers and readings. The first prayer comes before the Epistle and is called *Oratio*, or the Collect (collected prayer); the second forms the conclusion of the Offertory and is called the Secreta (silent prayer); the third and last follows the Communion and is called the Postcommunion (Communion prayer). The origin and meaning of the name Collect is interesting.

The word *collecta*[4] frequently designated in former times the congregation of the faithful assembled for religious services, and principally for the Sacrifice of the Mass; then it was made to designate the celebration of divine worship itself: the ordinary morning and night prayer, the prayer in choir, the Holy Sacrifice. *Collecta* was the name especially given to the preparatory divine service held on the station days in a particular church (*ecclesia collecta*), which preceded the procession to the station church. At this preliminary celebration the blessing and concluding prayer of the celebrant, the *Oratio ad Collectam* (the prayer at the assembly), formed the principal part. The longer term *Oratio ad Collectam* was then abbreviated and merely the word *Collecta* was used to designate the prayer, thus transferring the name of the whole service to the principal part. Now, if the name Collect was originally given to that prayer which was addressed to the assembled people at the preparatory service of the station celebration (*super populum collectum*), then it was evident that the first Mass prayer to be said soon after in the station church should likewise be called Collect, since it also was a prayer at the *collecta*, that is, at the assembly held for divine worship.[5]

---

[3] Sequitur oratio prima, quam Collectam dicunt (*Ordo Rom. II*, n. 6). Prima oratio dicitur aliquando Oratio, aliquando Collecta (Amalar. [d. 857], *Eclog.*, n. 23). Oratio sive Collecta statim subsequitur, quamtumvis Collecta proprie vocetur oratio illa, quae fit in processione, cum populus et universus clerus ab una ecclesia procedit ad alteram (Beleth., chap. 37).

[4] *Collecta* (from *colligere* = to collect or to gather) is a substantive form instead of *collectio*. In the Vulgate and the Fathers *Collecta* is also the name of the (public) gathering of alms for charity. (Cf. I Cor. 16:2.) The corresponding Greek word *synaxis* (σύναξις from συνάγω) is also frequently used to denote the assemblies of the faithful for divine worship, the celebration of the Eucharistic sacrifice, and especially Holy Communion.

[5] Collectam proprie dici volunt eam orationem, quae olim super populum

Like the Mass prayers in general, this prayer before the Epistle is not merely a private prayer of the priest, but a liturgical one, a public prayer which the celebrant recites in the name and by the commission of the Church, and with a special intention for the welfare of the whole Christian people.[6] At the altar the priest stands as mediator between God and man, he there presents the desires and interests of all before the throne of God. To him applies what is said of the prophet Jeremias: "This is a lover of his brethren and of the people Israel, this is he that prayeth much for the people and for all the city" (II Mac. 15:14). The faithful assisting at the sacrifice are of one heart and one soul, they pray interiorly and unite with the priest, who, as their representative, collects their supplications and desires to present them before God.[7]

As a collective prayer, the Collect is still to be considered under another aspect. It is considered as a prayer which in comprehensive brevity embodies the most important petitions: a summary of all that we, in consideration of the day's celebration, especially seek to obtain from God.[8] In a similar manner the Collect returns in almost every hour of the Divine Office as a concluding prayer summarizing all that precedes.[9] It is thus the peculiar prayer of the day, the prayer in which the Church repeatedly expresses what is nearest to her heart and what she principally desires for her children.

Finally, some writers, in a manner more edifying than solid, see in the name *Collecta* an admonition for priest and people to keep all

---

fieri solebat, quando collectus in unum erat cum universo Clero in una Ecclesia, ut ad aliam procederet, in qua Statio celebranda erat. Ex quo fieri potuit, ut ad reliquas hujusmodi orationes Collectae nomen dimanarit (Bona, *Rer. liturg.*, II, v, 3).

[6] Oratio publica est, quae a ministris Ecclesiae pro populo manifeste ac solemniter funditur, quam oportet non solum esse mentalem, sed etiam vocalem (Dion. Carthus., IV, dist. 15, q.6).

[7] Orationes, quae circa principium Missae dicuntur, Collectae vocantur eo quod sacerdos, qui fungitur ad Deum legatione pro populo petitiones omnium in eis colligat et concludat (Innocent. III, *De sacr. altar. myster.*, II, chap. 27).

[8] "This name of Collects, in fine, has its origin in the fact that the words, of which they are composed, are taken from all that is most touching and beautiful in Holy Scripture, in the treasures of tradition, or even in the lives of the saints whose feasts are celebrated; it is a wonderful epitome, a substantial abridgment which sums up everything" (Pichenot, *Les Collectes*, p. 8).

[9] Prime and Compline have, as liturgical morning and evening prayers, always the same Oration, and in the Vespers of Lent the *Oratio super populum* is recited.

THE COLLECT   455

their senses and thoughts collected in order to offer to God in profound recollection of spirit (*collectis animis*) the supplications comprised in the prayer.[10] Collect is, therefore, an ingenious, deeply significant term for the first prayer of the Mass; the name itself recalls the beautiful station solemnities of early Christian ages, at the same time it characterizes the Oration as a liturgical prayer of the priest, draws attention to the rich contents embodied in its few words, and reminds us of the pious disposition of soul required for its recitation.[11]

2. **The kissing of the altar.**[12] The Collect is introduced by the kissing of the altar, the mutual salutation, and the invitation to prayer. After the celebrant at the conclusion of the Gloria has made the sign of the cross on himself, he immediately, without joining his hands,[13] kisses the altar in the middle, because the altar stone there represents Jesus Christ, the living head and cornerstone of the Church, and there rest the relics of the martyrs. In the kissing of the altar we may distinguish a twofold meaning: first, it is an expres-

[10] Sequitur oratio, quae Collecta dicitur eo quod omnes adstantes Missae se debeant devote colligere et cum sacerdote fideliter orare (S. Bonav., *Exp. Miss.*, chap. 2).

[11] Brevis haec oratio ideo Collecta dicitur, quia populo in unum congregato et collecto recitatur, vel quia sacerdos legatione apud Deum pro omnibus fungens omnium vota in unum colligit, vel quia ex selectis s. Scripturae et Ecclesiae verbis compendiosa brevitate colligitur, vel quia omnes collectis animis affectus suos et mentem ad Deum attollunt (Bona, *loc. cit.*).

[12] Already the ancient Roman *Ordines* and all the missals of the Middle Ages prescribe the kissing of the altar several times during the celebration of the Eucharistic sacrifice. The unauthorized assertion that the kissing of the altar in this manner at the celebration of Mass is, "without doubt, repeated too frequently" (Lüft, *Liturgik*, II, 542), is absolutely to be rejected; for the present ordinance and practice of the Church, according to which the celebrant kisses the altar quite often, is based on the signification of this liturgical *osculum*. As the specially dedicated place of sacrifice, as the resting place of the body and blood of Christ, as the tomb of the relics of the martyrs, and as the symbol of Christ, our divine victim, the altar is incontestably the most excellent and the holiest part of the Church and therefore deserving of all the veneration rendered by the kissing. This liturgical kiss does not merely apply to the sanctified place of sacrifice, but principally to the invisible victim and sacrificing priest, whom the altar symbolically indicates. If the priest thinks of this, he will be touched by this ceremony and incited to devotion, and will joyfully repeat the kissing of the altar in order, in his own name and in the name of the faithful, to present anew to our Saviour sacrificing Himself for us, due love, veneration, and gratitude.

[13] In like manner the hands must not be joined after the sign of the cross at the end of the Credo and Sanctus (S. R. C., November 12, 1831).

sion of benevolent love; secondly, a sign of reverence and devotedness. The special meaning of kissing the altar at this part of the Mass is now evident. In a full sense, the altar is a symbol of Christ and the saints united with Him in glory; it represents the triumphant Church in heaven, of which Christ is the head and the elect are His members. Now, since the priest stands at the altar as a mediator between heaven and earth, he therefore first salutes with a kiss the triumphant Church,[14] then by the *Dominus vobiscum* he salutes the Church militant in words that call down upon the latter salvation and blessing.

3. **The priest's salutation.** With hands joined before his breast and with downcast eyes, the priest reverently turns toward the people; then, while slowly extending and joining the hands (without raising them), he salutes the entire Church with the benediction: *Dominus vobiscum* ("The Lord be with you").[15] This motion of the hands, which is repeated in precisely the same manner at the *Oremus*, harmonizes perfectly with the meaning of the words spoken. The extending of the hands expresses the earnest desire of the priest that the blessing he invokes may be bestowed; the joining of the hands signifies that the priest humbly mistrusts his own strength and confidently abandons himself to the Lord.

This salutation [16] is repeated eight times during the celebration of Mass to continually excite and increase the spiritual union of the priest and people during the Holy Sacrifice. As the meaning of this general formula of salutation varies, its special signification must be

---

[14] The priest kisses the altar each time before turning to the people, and, with the words *Dominus vobiscum*, wishes the people to their very face, as it were, the divine blessing in a more impressive manner. He would not turn to the people without having previously evinced toward the sanctuary this reverence, and he would at the same time indicate that all the help and all the blessings of grace that he wishes to the people present, must come from the altar and from our union with the Saviour sacrificing Himself upon it.

[15] This formula of well-wishing dates back to the Old Testament. In the book of Ruth it is related that Booz greeted his reapers in the field with the words: "The Lord be with you," and that they answered him: "The Lord bless thee" (Ruth 2:4). To the Blessed Virgin the archangel Gabriel said: *Dominus tecum*, "The Lord be with thee" (Luke 1:28).

[16] At the recitation of the Divine Office only the priest and deacon (but not the subdeacon) may say the *Dominus vobiscum* before and after the prayer; by this is signified that there is here a question of a canonical salutation, which presupposes the sacrament of orders on the part of him who pronounces the blessing.

explained in connection with what occurs. Where the Lord is, there He imparts manifold graces and blessings. By the formula *Dominus vobiscum* are wished all the goods which are connected with the presence of the Lord.

While expressing his wish that the Lord come into the hearts of the people, the priest at the same time intends to implore for the faithful the grace, light, and strength necessary for a good and perfect prayer.[17] The words *Dominus vobiscum* in this place are, consequently, a request for the assistance of divine grace to enable the faithful to pray efficaciously and to ask for what is proper, since all our sufficiency is from God, and without Christ we can do nothing profitable for salvation (II Cor. 3:5; John 15:5). Prayer presupposes the assistance of divine grace, without which its practice is not possible. "We know not what we should pray for as we ought"; therefore the Spirit must help our infirmity. Yes, the Holy Ghost Himself "asketh for us with unspeakable groanings" (Rom. 8:26), that is, He awakens in us the desire to pray, He urges us to pray, He grants us devotion and perseverance in prayer, He renders our prayer pleasing and meritorious in the sight of God.[18] "The spirit of grace and of prayers" (Zach. 12:10), which the Lord pours out over His Church, is indeed a great and precious gift, since prayer itself is the source of so many blessings.

In addition to the grace of prayer, which is here first of all desired, the salutatory blessing of the priest comprises numberless other graces; for when the Lord enters into a pure and penitent heart, at the same time all good things come along with Him: riches, glory, peace, joy, and happiness. When our Lord is with us, He imparts the desire for all that is good, strength in all combats and persecutions, consolation in all sufferings, and encouragement in all temptations. Therefore, the priest could not wish anything better to the faithful than what is included in the greeting, *Dominus vobiscum*.

[17] *Dominus vobiscum*, i.e. gratiam vobis infundat devote mecum orandi et sacra verba digne atque salubriter audiendi, et haec verba ex libro Ruth sumpta videntur, suntque affectuose a sacerdote dicenda, velut a mediatore inter Deum et populum, secundum exigentiam caritatis fraternae, quae in sacerdotibus exuberantior esse debet (Dion. Carthus., *Expos. Miss.*, a. 11).

[18] Illo modo recte accipitur, quo solet significari per efficientem id quod efficitur, i.e. gemere, desiderare et postulare nos faciat Spiritus sanctus, dum scilicet gemendi atque postulari cordibus nostris inspirat affectum (S. Fulgent., *Contra Fabian.*, fragm. 5).

And how do the people respond to this greeting of the priest? By the lips of the acolyte or the choir they answer with the corresponding greeting: *Et cum spiritu tuo* ("And with thy spirit").[19] The same or a similar wish for a blessing St. Paul frequently employed in his Epistles.[20] Out of gratitude for the imparted salutation and blessing, the people express the wish that the Lord would with His enlightening and strengthening grace replenish and penetrate the spirit [21] of the celebrant, that he may, as a man of God, a truly spiritual man, be enabled to present in a worthy manner the petitions and supplications of the whole Church. The priest does indeed greatly stand in need of the assistance of this grace when he is standing at the altar; for "holy is this place, where the priest prays for the transgressions and sins of the people." In that he prays and offers as a minister of the Church, he discharges the most exalted duty that the Church has to fulfill toward God. The priest appears at the altar by commission of the Church, the immaculate spouse of Christ, there to recite for the welfare of the living and the dead those venerable prayers which she herself, inspired by the Holy Ghost, has composed and prescribed. Now, if we are already obliged to prepare our soul carefully for every private prayer, how much more is this preparation necessary for the prayers of the Mass.[22] How fitting, then, is this response

---

[19] "If the Holy Ghost were not in this your common father and teacher, you would not recently, when he ascended this holy chair and wished you all peace, have cried out with one accord: 'And with thy spirit.' Thus you cry out to him, not only when he ascends his throne and when he speaks to you and prays for you, but also when he stands at this holy altar to offer the sacrifice. He does not touch that which lies on the altar before wishing you the grace of our Lord and before you have replied to him: 'And with thy spirit.' By this cry you are reminded that he who stands at the altar does nothing, and that the gifts that repose thereon are not the merits of a man, but that the grace of the Holy Ghost is present and, descending on all, accomplishes this mysterious sacrifice. We see indeed a man, but God it is who acts through him. Nothing human takes place at this holy altar" (Chrysostom, *First Homily for the Feast of Pentecost,* n. 4).

[20] Dominus Jesus Christus cum spiritu tuo (II Tim. 4:22). Gratia Domini nostri Jesu Christi cum spiritu vestro (Gal. 6:22).

[21] Nec vacat mysterio, quod sacerdoti dicenti: *Dominus vobiscum* non respondeatur: *Et tecum,* sed: *Et cum spiritu tuo,* quod verbum est majoris momenti magisque spirituale, quasi respondentes optent, Dominum implere spiritum ejus devotione, ut magno fervore pro omnibus oret, ita ut ejus oratio non solum lingua proferatur, sed multo magis corde et spiritu (De Ponte, *De christ. hom. perfect.,* IV, tr. II, chap. 11, §2).

[22] Quamvis oratio boni sacerdotis efficacior sit ad impetrandum quam mali, tamen oratio, imo et totum officium mali sacerdotis virtutem sortitur et im-

of the people, begging God to be with the spirit of the praying priest.

The bishop also salutes the faithful during Mass with the *Dominus vobiscum*, except in this place, before the Collect, on those days on which the Gloria is said, when his salutation is: *Pax vobis* ("Peace be to you").[23] The connection between this salutation and the Angelic Hymn should be noted: the bishop invokes that peace which is announced in the Gloria.[24] Therefore, as it was the privilege of the bishop to recite the Angelic Hymn on all Sundays and feast days, whereas priests were permitted to recite it only at Easter, so the bishops alone were allowed to salute the faithful immediately after the Gloria with the *Pax vobis*. From the end of the eleventh century the recitation of the Gloria ceased to be the exclusive privilege of bishops, but the greeting, *Pax vobis*, was still reserved to them. This formula has a certain preference over *Dominus vobiscum;* this preference does not lie in its contents, but in the fact that our Lord Himself frequently used the salutation, *Pax vobis*, and thus sanctified it. Therefore, if the bishop salutes the faithful with *Pax vobis*, in a special manner he manifests himself to be the representative of the Lord, who after His resurrection said to His disciples: "Peace be to you." [25] As successors of the apostles, bishops also pos-

---

petrandum fit efficax, in quantum sacerdos talis orat et agit in persona totius Ecclesiae. Praeterea quamvis ubique et semper Deus ab omni christiano reverenter et pure atque sollicite exorandus consistat, a sacerdote tamen in Missa tanto ardentius sinceriusque orandus est, quanto causa orandi est major et ipsum officium dignius, persona quoque Christo vicinior, ut puta mediator Dei et plebis (Dion. Carthus., *loc. cit.*).

[23] Postea salutans populum Pontifex dicit *Pax vobiscum* sive *Pax vobis*. Respond. *Et cum spiritu tuo* (*Ordo Rom. II*, n. 6). Before the Offertory it says (n. 9): Salutat episcopus populum dicens: *Dominus vobiscum*. The words *Pax vobis* were regarded, even in the tenth century, as a festive, joyful formula of salutation and were, therefore, not used on penitential days. The *Ordo Rom. XIV* (written before the middle of the fourteenth century) contains the rubric: Ante orationem non dicit: *Pax vobis*, sed tantum: *Dominus vobiscum*, et sic in omnibus feriis et dominicis tam Quadragesimae quam et Adventus, exceptis Dominica Gaudete et Laetare (chap. 79).

[24] Episcopus celebrans in festis in prima salutatione dicit: *Pax vobis*, quod post resurrectionem discipulis dixit Dominus, cujus personam repraesentat praecipue Episcopus (S. Thom., IIIa, q.83, a.5 ad6).

[25] Pontifex salutationem praemittit ad populum dicens: *Pax vobis;* illius utens eulogio, cujus fungitur pontificio. Minor autem sacerdos ait: *Dominus vobiscum*. Ut episcopus se ostendat Christi vicarium, prima vice dicit: *Pax vobis*. Quoniam haec fuit prima vox Christi ad discipulos, cum eis post resur-

sess (in addition to other privileges) a greater power of dispensing graces and blessings than priests enjoy; for they possess the plenitude of the power of orders for the administration and dispensation of the heavenly treasures of grace. This sublime and more complete power of blessing, connected with the bishop's consecration and dignity, is very appropriately exhibited by this salutation of the bishop at the beginning of Mass, as well as by the concluding benediction at the end of Mass, wherein the threefold sign of the cross is given. The salutation of peace, *Pax vobis*, which the bishop, after the example of Christ and the apostles, utters on certain days in the Mass, contains in itself the plenitude of every good. However, salvation and blessing for time and eternity are also essentially comprised in the *Dominus vobiscum*; for where our Lord is, there also is His peace.[26]

Both the sacerdotal and the episcopal salutation come from the lips of the representative of Christ, not as a mere empty wish, but as a blessing spoken with the efficacy of higher power, containing within itself supernatural strength; so that in reality it imparts the good it expresses to all whose hearts are capable of receiving it.[27] The Lord stands at the door and knocks; to any one who hears His voice and opens the door to Him, He will come and enter with His peace (Apoc. 3:20).[28]

4. **The *Oremus*.** Standing at the Epistle side of the altar, the priest humbly and reverently bows his head to the crucifix upon the altar, extends his hands and presently joins them again, while saying the word: *Oremus* ("Let us pray"). This is an invitation to pray in common, which the priest directs both to himself and to those present; he invites all to honor God, to raise the heart and mind to Him. We will pour out our heart to the Lord, acknowledge our poverty and misery, and expect and implore from God, the all-

---

rectionem apparuit. Ad instar vero sacerdotum ceterorum dicit postea: *Dominus vobiscum*; ut se unum ex ipsis ostendat (Innoc. III, *De sacr. alt. myst.*, II, chap. 24).

[26] The Greeks always use the formula: "Peace be to all," to which the congregation answer: "And with thy spirit."

[27] Sola est oratio, quae Deum vincit (Tertull., *De Oratione*, chap. 29).

[28] Post introitum sacerdotis ad altare litaniae aguntur a clero, ut generalis oratio praeveniat specialem sacerdotis; subsequitur autem oratio sacerdotis et pacifica primum salutatione populum salutans, pacis responsum ab illo accipit, ut vera concordia et caritatis pura devotio facilius postulata impetret ab eo, qui corda aspicit et interna dijudicat (Raban. Maur., *De clericor. institut.*, I, chap. 33).

THE COLLECT

merciful and the all-powerful, salvation and help in all our necessities. That this prayer of the Mass should be made in common is indicated, not only by the name, *Collect*, and the invitation to prayer, *Oremus*,[29] but, moreover, by the priest's speaking aloud. For the priest prays aloud to call the attention of the faithful to join at least mentally with him in his prayer and to pray along with him. Prayer is the liturgical accompaniment of the sacrifice. The best and the most profitable participation in the Holy Sacrifice consists in this, that those present follow the priest step by step, praying and offering with him.[30]

The priest's greeting to the people has for its purpose to encourage them, attracting and directing their hearts to prayer. And it is meant for us all. For prayer in church is not a simple act of one alone, nor is it for one alone, but it is *Collecta*, that is, a joint prayer said by the entire congregation of the faithful and in behalf of the whole congregation. Although but one pronounces the words, yet all the others should with heart and mind pray with him. Therefore we are reminded of the Lord, that we may seriously recollect ourselves and put aside all levity and frivolous thoughts, for we are in the presence of the greatest and the most powerful of Lords, treating with Him and beseeching Him who is our Master, who has power over our life and death, over fortune and misfortune, who has the power to cast both our soul and body into eternal fire, as He says Himself, but who is also bountiful and merciful, and who will gladly bestow upon us all the good which we earnestly and with firm confidence ask of Him. Consequently, every Christian should be attentive to the greeting: "The Lord be with you," and to the admonition: "Let us pray." Then we should, as members of God's Church, unite in prayer. Whoever does not understand the words of the prayer, can indeed in general be mindful of God and beseech Him graciously to receive the prayer of His Church and grant to us who are on earth what is needful and profitable for soul and body, through Christ our Lord.[31]

Some of the liturgical prayers are recited standing, and some kneeling. In ancient times it was customary on the Sundays of the

[29] Non *Oro*, sed *Oremus* dicit, quia vocem totius Ecclesiae exprimit (Honor. Augustod., *op. cit.*, I, chap. 93).

[30] Sacerdos salutatione praemissa dicit *Oremus*, ubi oraturus alios hortatur ut secum orent. Tunc ejus pro nobis maxime suscipitur oratio, si nostra ei jungatur devotio. . . . Oportet ergo ut et in Missa et in ceteris officiis cor nostrum jungamus cum voce sacerdotis (Robert. Paulul., *De offic. eccles.*, chap. 15).

[31] *Ein Vergissmeinnicht*, pp. 67 f.

year and during the whole Eastertide to pray standing.[32] The standing up should remind us of the Lord's glorious resurrection and of life eternal. On these days the invitation to common prayer has always been made by the simple formula, *Oremus*. And although we stand up at the prayers, we ought at the same time to abase ourselves in humility of heart before the face of the Lord. During the seasons when the spirit of penance should be more prominent, it is befitting to manifest even exteriorly, by genuflecting, the interior humility and reverence of the heart.[33] Hence, for example, on the Ember days as well as on other days that have several lessons and prayers (Wednesday after *Laetare* Sunday, Wednesday of Holy Week, Good Friday, Holy Saturday, and the vigil of Pentecost), some of the prayers are introduced by the words, *Flectamus genua* (let us bend the knees) and the answer *Levate* (arise).[34] Before we address our petitions to God, we will profoundly humble ourselves in the consciousness of our sinfulness, and also express our repentance and contrition.

[32] "On Sundays we consider it improper to pray kneeling (*de geniculis*). The same privilege we enjoy from Easter until Pentecost" (Tertull., *De corona militis*, chap. 3). The various methods of prayer in use among Christians already in the most ancient times, Prudentius (*Cathermerin.*, II, verses 48 ff.) has collected very beautifully in the following lines:

> Te, Christe, solum novimus:
> Te mente pura et simplici,
> Te voce, te cantu pio,
> Rogare curvato genu,
> Flendo et canendo discimus.

In them is expressed the inmost prayer of the heart, which is the requisite foundation of every other mode of prayer, *mente pura et simplici;* vocal prayer without singing, *voce,* and with singing, *canto pio;* prayer with genuflection, *curvato genu,* and prayer with singing and tears, *flendo et canendo.* Cf. Arevalo, *loc. cit.* (Migne, LIX, p. 789).

[33] Cf. Honor. Augustod., *Gemma animae*, chap. 117. In Quadragesima ideo ad Missam *Flectamus genua* dicimus, quia corpus et animam in poenitentia nos humiliare innuimus.

[34] Formerly the deacon said the *Flectamus genua* (upon which all present prayed kneeling for some time in silence) as well as the *Levate.* According to the present rite the priest recites the *Oremus,* the deacon *Flectamus genua* (and all except the celebrant bend the knee), and the subdeacon the *Levate.* But if the priest says the *Flectamus genua,* he must also genuflect; the acolyte in that case answers *Levate.* The reason for this difference is that in the latter case the celebrant considers himself among those whom he summons to genuflect, while in the former case it suffices for the deacon to unite in genuflecting, to which he invites those present (with the exception of the celebrant). Cf. Quarti, *Comment. in Rubr. Missal.*, I, xvii, 3.

Frequently a double *Oremus* occurred in the Mass: the first was followed by an announcement for whom and for what intention the prayer should be made; the second preceded the prayer proper. This original form is still retained in the liturgy of Good Friday at the great or solemn intercessory prayers, which date from the first Christian centuries; in them the Church shows herself as the loving mother of the entire human race, inasmuch as she prays at the foot of the cross for the redemption of the whole world.

5. **Contents of the Collects.** The Collect itself is distinguished as much for the beauty and perfection of its form as for the depth of its contents. The Collects are prayers of petition: the innumerable needs and necessities of soul and body form the substance of the supplications therein expressed. In them we seek to obtain all kinds of favors and blessings, and implore the averting of every evil. The Collects indeed ask of God no more than what is petitioned for in the Lord's Prayer; but the object of these petitions is presented in various expressions. Thus we pray for the grace to serve God, to let the light of divine faith shine in our works, to become rich in good works, to know well our duty and to be strengthened in its fulfillment, to become interiorly changed and renewed according to the image of our Saviour, to be supported by His continual help and to be confirmed in all righteousness, to grow strong spiritually and corporally so as to be able to overcome every evil, to be rescued from all sufferings and tribulations, to be safeguarded against all perverting error, to draw down upon ourselves by purity of body and mind the good pleasure of heaven, to abhor all that is unchristian, to faithfully observe the divine commandments, to love the commandments of God and to long for His promises, to understand and put in practice what is right and perfect, to be enabled to serve God in undisturbed and pure cheerfulness, to grow in every virtue, to walk in accordance with God's pleasure; thereby to arrive at the enjoyment of the beatific vision, the happy enjoyment of eternal life.

Each Collect contains a special petition. The reason for imploring precisely this or that favor lies in the special character of the Mass on the various days and feasts, or the special motive for the celebration of the Mass. In the liturgical cycle of feasts the sacred history and the entire work of redemption are repeated and renewed. The Church celebrates the mysteries of Christ and of His blessed Mother, as well as the anniversaries of His saints, so that they may become for priest and people a school and a source of supernatural life. The ecclesiastical year, by reason of its instruction and the stream of grace flowing throughout its channel, should induce and enable us so to employ the shortness of time that we may happily arrive at the blissful life of eternity. At the same time the weekdays and Sundays and feast days during the course of the year should constantly bring before our mind other truths and mysteries, and continually secure for us new graces. In this way the Collects and other variable parts of the Mass enable us to celebrate the Church year to our profit and advantage, to lead an interior life in harmony with it, and to manifest its spiritual fruit in our conduct.

6. **Form of the Collects.** The Collect is, therefore, a prayer of petition for the particular grace of the day; but in what form is this petition clothed? Amid all the variety and diversity of the Collects there still prevails a certain uniformity in their construction, which shows that they have been composed according to a specified rule. The petition is not simply presented to God by itself, but is supported by other kinds of prayer, in order that it may be made so much the more fervent and efficacious. Praise, adoration, thanksgiving—in short, all kinds of prayer are finally resolved in petitions, for petitions are for us in our present state the most important and necessary kind of prayer. Petition also forms the peculiar essence of the Collects. But by what other acts is this petition usually accompanied? St. Paul mentions—and probably here there is question of public worship—supplications (urgent entreaty, to which a powerful motive is added that the prayer may be heard the sooner), prayers, petitions, and thanksgivings.[35] These four kinds of prayer

[35] Obsecro primum omnium fieri obsecrationes, orationes, postulationes, gratiarum actiones pro omnibus hominibus (I Tim. 2:1). These expressions of the Apostle are differently interpreted. (Cf. S. Thom., IIa IIae, q. 83, a. 17. Suarez, *De Relig.*, Tr. IV, Bk. II, chap. 3, n. 3–8.) St. Augustine finds indicated in them the whole course of the Mass. Aliqua singulorum istorum proprietas inquirenda est, sed ad eam liquido pervenire difficile est: multa quippe hinc dici possunt, quae improbanda non sint. Sed eligo in his verbis hoc intelligere, quod omnis vel paene omnis frequentat Ecclesia, ut precationes (sc. obsecrationes) accipiamus dictas, quas facimus in celebratione Sacramentorum, antequam illud quod est in Domini mensa incipiat benedici; orationes, cum benedicitur et sanctificatur et ad distribuendum comminuitur, quam totam petitionem fere omnis Ecclesia dominica oratione concludit. . . . Interpellationes (sc. postulationes) fiunt, cum populus benedicitur: tunc enim antistites velut advocati susceptos suos (*their clients*) per manus impositionem

THE COLLECT

are not only found alternately in the course of the celebration of the Holy Sacrifice, but they are, for the most part, combined in each Collect,[36] and thus form a most effectual prayer of petition. The person praying must approach God, elevate himself to God (*oratio*), and then present his petitions (*postulatio*); and to obtain more speedily what is asked for, he joins to it his motives, one of which is gratitude or thanksgiving (*gratiarum actio*); for in so far as we are grateful for benefits received, do we obtain graces yet more plentifully.[37] But the most efficient means for having our petitions granted, is to beg them of God by the merits and intercession of Jesus Christ; hence the concluding words, "through Christ our Lord," words which express the entreaty (*obsecratio*).

The Collect for Pentecost, for example, is as follows:

Deus (*oratio*), qui hodierna die corda fidelium sancti Spiritus illustratione docuisti (*gratiarum actio*), da nobis in eodem Spiritu recta sapere et de ejus semper consolatione gaudere (*postulatio*). Per Dominum nostrum . . . (*obsecratio*).	O God (*elevation of the soul*), who today by the light of the Holy Ghost didst instruct the hearts of the faithful (*thanksgiving*), give us by the same Holy Spirit a love for what is right and just and a constant enjoyment of His comforts (*petition*). Through our Lord Jesus Christ . . . (*supplication*).

Thus the Church complies with the admonition of the Apostle: "In everything, by prayer and supplication with thanksgiving, let your petitions be made known to God" (Phil. 4:6).

---

misericordissimae offerunt potestati. Omnibus peractis et participato tanto sacramento, gratiarum actio cuncta concludit, quam in his etiam verbis ultimam commendavit Apostolus (S. August., *Epist.*, 149 [al. 59], *ad Paulin.*, n. 15 f.).

[36] Cf. Guyet, *Heortologia*, III, chap. 2, q. 4. The *oratio* (elevation of the mind to God) is usually contained in the words *Domine* or *Deus* or *Domine Deus* or *Omnipotens et misericors Deus;* the *gratiarum actio* in the mention of some benefit of God; the *postulatio* in the expressions: *concede, da, largire, praesta, tribue;* the *obsecratio* in the concluding formula: *per Dominum nostrum.*

[37] De acceptis beneficiis gratias agentes, meremur accipere potiora ut in Collecta dicitur (S. Thom., *loc. cit.*). Gratiarum actio est orationis completio et integralis pars ejus, per quam tam ipsa oratio Deo fusa exaudibilis redditur, quam sequentibus orationibus via ac praeparatio exauditionis aperitur. Qui enim gratus est de acceptis et de minoribus regratiatur, majoribus donis efficitur dignus (Dion. Carthus., *De oratione*, a. 3).

The prayers may be addressed to the holy and indivisible Trinity or to any one of the divine persons. When it is addressed to only one of the divine persons, it is self-evident that the other two persons are not excluded, but rather virtually included; and to make this obvious they are, as a rule, expressly mentioned. It is the same with respect to the Collects. Whether they are directed to the Father or to the Son, there follows at any rate at the conclusion an explicit confession and solemn acknowledgment of the Holy Trinity.[38]

The Collects were originally and without exception addressed to the Father; for the Father is the First Person of the Blessed Trinity and as such He is, in a manner, the original source, not only of the divine nature which from all eternity He imparts to the Son and with the Son to the Holy Ghost,[39] but of all created things. To the Father are principally attributed (appropriated) power and majesty, which are revealed in the creation of the world; the Father has sent us His only-begotten Son, and together with Him He has given us all things. Jesus Christ Himself offered His whole life, actions, sufferings, and especially His prayers to God the Father. The Saviour in His prayer to God was not only our advocate, but also our model in prayer, our leader in prayer. He always prayed to His Father, "to show that the Father is His origin, from whom He from eternity receives His divine nature and by whom His human nature also was created, and from whom it received all the good that it possessed."

When the Church while praying usually has recourse to the Father, she follows in this respect not merely the example of Christ, but also His teaching: "Amen, amen I say to you, if you ask the Father anything in My name, He will give it you" (John 16:23). In this a further reason is indicated why the Collects, for the most part, are addressed to the Father. Our petitions should be presented "in

---

[38] Neque enim praejudicium Filio vel sancto Spiritui comparatur, dum ad Patris personam precatio ab offerente dirigitur; cujus consummatio, dum Filii et Spiritus sancti complectitur nomen, ostendit nullum esse in Trinitate discrimen. Quia dum ad solius Patris personam honoris sermo dirigitur, bene credentis fide tota Trinitas honoratur, et cum ad Patrem litantis destinatur intentio, sacrificii munus omni Trinitati uno eodemque offertur litantis officio (S. Fulgent. [d. 533], *Ad Monim.*, II, chap. 5).

[39] Patrem sancta Ecclesia in precibus poscit, quem esse originem Filii et Spiritus sancti recta credulitate cognovit. Ideo autem nomine Filii et Spiritus sancti orationes precesque consummat, ut sanctam Trinitatem unius esse naturae ac majestatis ostendat (S. Fulgent., *Contra Fabian.*, fragm. 29).

THE COLLECT 467

the name of Jesus." Jesus is the mediator through whom all our prayers and supplications ascend to heaven, and through whom all graces and merits descend upon earth; hence we conclude the Collects with these words, "through our Lord Jesus Christ." This rule is especially observed at Mass, in which the Son offers Himself to the heavenly Father.

Some of the Collects are now addressed to the Second Person of the Blessed Trinity, because they have a particular and closer relation to the mystery of the Incarnation or to the incarnate Word.[40] On the other hand, we do not find in our missal a single Collect addressed to the Holy Ghost, although in the liturgy there are other prayers to the Holy Ghost and hymns in His honor, wherein He is invoked and glorified as God.[41]

The form of the conclusion of the Collect may vary somewhat according to the context of the prayer.[42] The usual form of conclusion

---

[40] For example, the prayer to the Most Blessed Sacrament, on the feast of the Finding of the Cross, on several feasts of the Passion and of St. Joseph.

[41] Tota Trinitas una et eadem adoratione colenda est, puta unus Deus, cum in ipsis personis sit una numero majestas et deitas; nihilominus cum unaquaeque increata persona sit in se vere subsistens persona, potest unusquisque fidelis preces suas specialiter dirigere ad quamlibet divinam personam et eam secundum se specialiter exorare, non tamen cum actuali aliarum personarum exclusione, quasi ipsa sola sit adoranda. Hinc in Missae Officio orationes Ecclesiae ad Patrem specialiter effunduntur, interdum ad Filium, ut cum dicimus: "Fidelium Deus omnium Conditor et Redemptor," communiter vero ad Patrem, tanquam ad totius Trinitatis principium, i.e. primam fontalem personam a nullo manantem; sic et aliquae laudes, orationes, hymni, sequentiae ad Spiritum sanctum specialiter depromuntur (Dion. Carthus., *Elementat. theolog.*, prop. 128).

[42] The prayers to the Father usually conclude: *Per Dominum nostrum J. Chr. . . .* ; those to the Son always: *Qui vivis et regnas cum Deo Pater. . . .* Sometimes the Collects addressed to the Father conclude: *Per eundem Dominum . . .* (when, for instance, the Son was mentioned at the beginning or in the middle), or: *Qui tecum vivit et regnat . . .* (if this mention is made at the conclusion). This naming of the Son may be done by the words *Christus, Verbum, Unigenitus, Salvator*, and so forth, or also merely according to the sense (S. R. C., March 11, 1820). When the person of the Holy Ghost is mentioned directly and actually, as is not the case in such expressions as *spiritus dilectionis, fortitudinis, fervoris, adoptionis, gratiae salutaris*, the concluding formula is: *. . . in unitate ejusdem Spiritus sancti . . .* (S. R. C., November 12, 1831). But in order to obtain these modifications of the conclusions, the naming of the Son or of the Holy Ghost must not merely be in one of the preceding Orations, but it must be found in the last, to which the conclusion is attached (S. R. C., May 23, 1835; April 8, 1865). Outside of the Divine Office and the Mass, all Orations have the shorter concluding formula: *Per (eundem) Christum Dominum nostrum* or *Qui vivis et regnas in* (or *per*

is as follows: *Per Dominum nostrum Jesum Christum Filium tuum, qui tecum vivit et regnat in unitate Spiritus sancti Deus: per omnia saecula saeculorum.* ("Through our Lord Jesus Christ Thy Son, who with Thee in the unity of the Holy Ghost liveth and reigneth forever and ever.") Thus the Collects end with a magnificent praise of the Holy Trinity. How solemn, how overpowering, how grand are these concluding words! With what courage and confidence, with what consolation and consciousness of victory should they fill us! "Were it not for the intercession of our mediator, without doubt, the cry of our supplication would go up unheard in the presence of God." [43] The Church prays with a lively faith in the mediatorship of Jesus and an unshaken confidence in His merits; since Christ has merited for us all grace, He has, therefore, secured a favorable answer also to our prayers. For Christ's sake we are favored and blessed by God. Whenever God looks upon the face of His Anointed, in whom He is eternally well pleased, He will

---

omnia) saecula saeculorum, if in the liturgical books the longer one is not expressly ordered, as, for example, in the Litany of the Saints (S. R. C., December 20, 1864). When several prayers occur, only the first (to which, however, at times another *sub una conclusione* is joined) and the last have a special concluding formula. The *Oremus* precedes only the first and second Orations at Mass, while in the Divine Office all the prayers are introduced with this cry, as here the antiphon together with the versicle is inserted between the separate orations.

As the prayers are addressed to the omniscient God, in them only the simple or the double proper names may be employed (for example, *Joanna Francisca, Petrus Coelestinus*) and similar designations which express their dignity (for example, *Apostolus, Martyr, Confessor, Virgo*, but never *Vidua*, because this is not a title of honor). To them may also be added the names *Joannes Chrysostomus* and *Petrus Chrysologus;* for *nomina Chrysostomi et Chrysologi adjectiva potius sunt et vel facundiam vel vim et efficaciam divini sermonis recensitis Sanctis quasi supernaturali inditam virtute designant.* (S. R. C., March 8, 1825; December 7, 1844 ad 9.) All other surnames, of any nature whatsoever (*cognomina*, for example, *de Matha, a Cruce, Benitius, Nonnatus, Quintus;* and *patria*, for instance, *de Cortona, de Paula, Nepomucenus*, with the exception of *Maria Magdalena*), must be omitted, as they are necessary only for us to distinguish the saints one from another. The name *rex* and *regina* may be added, but not of the kingdom over which the saints have reigned (for example, *Danorum, Scotiae*). (S. R. C., December 22, 1629; June 23, 1736.) Cf. Guyet., *Heortolog.,* III, chap. 2, q. 5; Cavalieri, *Oper. liturg.,* II, chap. 38; Beleth, *Ration.,* chap. 54.

[43] Adjutor quaeritur, ut desiderium exaudiatur, quia nisi pro nobis interpellatio mediatoris intercederet, ab aure Dei procul dubio postrarum precum voces silerent (S. Greg., *Moral.,* XXII, chap. 17).

through Christ [44] and for the sake of Christ graciously receive our petitions and graciously hear them by pouring out upon us His abundant mercies and blessings.[45]

The *Amen* that the acolyte says at the end of the Collect in the name of the people,[46] is a solemn expression of the wish that the petitions offered be graciously heard and fulfilled: "So be it done." This word occurs even in the Old Testament, especially in the divine worship; and on account of its antiquity and solemnity, and its frequent use also by our Lord, the term is highly venerable and has, therefore, been adopted, without being translated, into the Church's liturgy.[47] "This word was so frequently on the lips of our Saviour, that it pleased the Holy Ghost to preserve it in the Church of God." [48] In the New Testament our Lord frequently uses it in His exhortations at the beginning of sentences to arouse the attention of His hearers and forcibly to emphasize and impress some thought.[49]

---

[44] Patri dicimus orantes "Per Dominum nostrum J. Chr. Filium tuum" poscentes, ut per ipsum faciat quod oramus, per quem nos facere dignatus est ut essemus. Omnia enim Pater per Filium fecit et facit, quia unus Dominus J. Chr. per quem omnia (I Cor. 8:6). (S. Fulgent., *Contra Fabian.*, fragm. 31.)

[45] *Per Dominum nostrum Jesum Christum:* hoc est, per ipsius dignitatem et per virtutem ejus et efficaciam et per ejus meritum et per intercessionem orationemque ejus. Quae omnia significat hoc verbum omniaque sub eo Ecclesia comprehendit, allegans omnes titulos, quos Christus habet, ut omnes ejus orationes ab aeterno Patre exaudiantur et impleantur (Arias, *Thesaur. inexhaust.*, I, tr. III, cap. 16).

[46] In the first centuries the entire congregation responded. Already St. Justin Martyr writes in his first Apology (chap. 67) that all the congregation join in the liturgical prayers and thanksgivings, by saying "Amen." St. Jerome says of the Roman Basilicas: *ad similitudinem coelestis tonitrui Amen reboat* (*Commentar. in epist. ad Galat.*, II). *Amen* hebraeum est, quod ad omnem sacerdotis orationem seu benedictionem respondet populus fidelium (Raban. Maur., *De clericor. institut.*, I, chap. 33). Amen confirmatio est orationis a populo (Pseudo-Alcuin., *De divin. offic.*, chap. 40).

[47] Duo verba *Amen* et *Alleluja* nec Graecis nec Latinis nec barbaris licet in suam linguam omnino transferre vel alia lingua enuntiare. Nam quamvis interpretari possint, propter sanctiorum tamen auctoritatem servata est ab Apostolis in iis propriae linguae antiquitas. Tanto enim sacra sunt nomina, ut etiam Joannes in Apocalypsi referat se Spiritu revelante vidisse et audivisse vocem coelestis exercitus tamquam vocem aquarum multarum et tonitruum validorum dicentium *Amen* et *Alleluja:* ac per hoc sic oportet in terris utraque dici sicut in coelo resonat (S. Isid., *Etymolog.*, VI, xix, 20 f.).

[48] *Catech. Rom.*, IV, chap. 17, q. 3, n. 1.

[49] Christus geminavit dixitque "Amen, Amen" ad ostendendam rei gravitatem, sublimitatem et certitudinem (Corn. a Lap., *In Joann.* 3:3).

At the conclusion of prayers, blessings, creeds, doxologies, and hymns it is sometimes the expression of the ardent desire of the heart (= *fiat*, be it so); sometimes the formula of solemn confirmation and consent (= *verum est*, it is so).⁵⁰ Such is its meaning in the liturgy, and to this meaning entirely corresponds the grave and solemn manner in which it is sung by the choir at the conclusion of the Gloria and the Credo. The concluding *Amen* is, therefore, a repetition and confirmation of the petitions which have been presented in the Collects; it is an expression of the ardent desire and confident hope of being favorably heard by God.⁵¹ The people, as it were, put their seal upon the petitions made by the priest by answering: *Amen:* "Be it done, be it as you have asked." We should, then, always pronounce this short but significant word with recollection of mind and fervor of heart, as do the angels in heaven (Apoc. 7:12).⁵²

7. **How the Collects are to be said.** According to the prescription of the Church, during the recitation of the Collects the hands of the priest are to be extended and elevated before the breast, but in such a way that the ends of the fingers do not reach beyond the breadth and height of the shoulders.⁵³ This rubric leaves room for no extravagant and unbecoming gestures. "If we pray with modesty and humility, we recommend our petitions to God far better, inasmuch as we do not raise our hands too high, but only moderately and becomingly." ⁵⁴ This position of the body in praying (the extending and raising of the hands) is proper and well calculated to increase

---

⁵⁰ In Hebrew the Amen as an adjective signifies reliable, faithful, true, firm; as a substantive: fidelity, truth; as an adverb: truly, assuredly.

⁵¹ Omnes respondent *Amen*, h. e. utinam fiat, sicut petis, et ita verum est, sicut dixisti. In quo solo verbo continetur, quidquid sacerdos pluribus dixit, et tanto affectu verbum illud dici potest, ut non minus promereatur unico illo verbo prolato, quam si protulisset omnia. Deus enim Dominus noster non tam verborum multitudinem respicit, quam fervorem affectuum (De Ponte, *loc. cit.*).

⁵² Amen est orationis signaculum fructuosum et animi recollectivum. Dicendo enim *Amen*, anima summatim fertur ad omnia praeinducta et renovatur affectio impetrandi, sicque oratio cum fervore finita pleniorem sortitur effectum (Dion. Carthus., *In Matt.*, chap. 6).

⁵³ Digitorum summitas humerorum altitudinem distantiamque non excedat. On this Lohner remarks: Unde colligitur, in altum elevatos digitos esse debere et non in aequali cum palma altitudine constitutos et quasi jacentes, ut multi faciunt. Sed et distantia manuum cum decore servanda est (*De sacrif. Miss.*, VI, tit. 5).

⁵⁴ Tertull., *De Orat.*, chap. 17.

THE COLLECT

devotion in him who prays and to edify those present; it is, at the same time, so natural and expressive that it has always been the customary position at prayer among all nations. Israel was victorious in its battle against Amalek when Moses raised his hands in prayer; but when he allowed them to fall ever so little, Amalek triumphed (Exod. 17:8-11). Solomon placed himself before the altar of the Lord in the presence of the people of Israel and extended his hands towards heaven (III Kings 8:22). David cries out: "Hear, O Lord, the voice of my supplication when I pray to Thee, when I lift up my hands to Thy holy temple" (Ps. 27:2). The adorable hands of Jesus were also extended and elevated on the cross, when along with His bloody sacrifice He offered prayers and intercession for the whole world. This divine model the primitive Christians had before their eyes and imitated when they prayed with arms outstretched in the form of a cross.[55]

Hundreds of paintings, tombstones, enamels and sculpturings of the catacombs represent the blessed in heaven and the faithful on earth praying with arms extended in the form of the cross. "We have the command," writes St. Maximus, "to pray with uplifted hands, so that even by our corporal bearing we may confess the passion of the Lord." And St. Peter Chrysologus remarks: "Does not he who extends his hands, pray even by the position of his body?" . . . When, therefore, in the first ages the clergy and faithful in general were accustomed to pray with outstretched arms, and when the martyrs often even suffered and died in this posture, they thereby confessed the Saviour extended on the cross, and presented His merits to the heavenly Father.[56]

The manner in which the priest, according to the rubrics, must now hold his hands at the altar, presents no longer the form of the cross, as was the case in the ancient Christian manner of prayer; but the position of his uplifted hands should still remind us of our Saviour praying and sacrificing Himself upon the cross.[57] The extending of the hands is, so to speak, an embracing, a collecting to-

---

[55] Non ausa est cohibere poena palmas
In morem crucis ad Patrem levandas
—Prudent., *Peristephanon*, hymn VI, verses 106 f.

[56] P. Wolter, O. S. B., *Die römischen Katakomben*, II, 43.

[57] Passis quondam sublatisque brachiis orabant, ut statum, quo Christus oravit in cruce, imitarentur. Consultius vero existimavit Ecclesia, si ad eum modum, quo nunc utimur, Collectae recitarentur, ne veteri retenta consuetudine orandi passis extensisque brachiis, inconcinnis et ridiculis figuris aperiretur locus (Benedict XIV, *De Miss. sacrif.*, II, vi, 5).

gether of all the wants and desires and necessities of the faithful. The elevating of the hands denotes and promotes the uplifting of the heart to God,[58] the soaring of the soul above earthly things to that which is above, where Christ ascended with arms extended. This position of the hands extended and raised is a sign of the ardent desire for help, an expression of the fervor and urgency with which the petitions are presented, a symbol of confidence, and an assurance of being favorably heard. Thus the priest stands at the altar and cries to the Lord and stretches out his hands for rescue and redemption, which must come from above. If he at the concluding formula of the Collect again joins his hands, he thereby manifests the sentiments of ardent devotion, the humble disavowal of his own strength, the devout desire to give himself entirely to the Lord and to rest in the Lord; he also acknowledges God as the Supreme Good, whence, as from the fountain and source of all graces, every gift comes to us through Jesus Christ.[59]

As is evident from many testimonies of the Fathers,[60] it was an ancient custom to turn toward the east when praying; accordingly the churches were generally built in this direction, so that the priest and the faithful, when at prayer, might look toward the rising of the sun. The principal symbolical reasons for this are, according to St. Thomas,[61] the three following. First, the position of the person who prays is considered with reference to the divine Majesty, revealed to us in the movement of the heavens; this movement of the heavens takes place from the east. Secondly, we seek to express by this position that we desire to return to Paradise, which was situated in the east. Thirdly, we turn in that direction because we thereby think of Jesus Christ, who is the true light of the world and is, therefore, called the *Oriens*, that is, the rising Sun of justice, and who at His second coming, as judge of the living and the dead, will appear as lightning coming out of the east and passing even into the west (Matt. 24:27).

[58] Levat sacerdos manus orando ad designandum, quod oratio ejus dirigitur pro populo ad Deum (S. Thom., IIIa, q.83, a.5 ad 5).

[59] Manuum junctio significat omnium bonorum a Deo fluentium in ipso unitatem et conjunctionem (Durand., *Ration.*, IV, vii, 5).

[60] "Who will not admit at once that the direction of the rising sun is evidently the one toward which we should turn when at prayer, to show that the soul looks to the rising of the true light [Jesus Christ]?" (Origen, *On Prayer*, chap. 32.)

[61] IIa IIae, q.84, a.3 ad 3.

THE COLLECT 473

8. **The number and value of the Collects.** From apostolic times a number of prayers and supplications were offered at the celebration of the Holy Sacrifice. In our missals may be found Collects which date from the first Christian centuries. The saintly popes, Leo I (440–61), Gelasius (492–96), and Gregory I (590–604) deserve great credit, not only for having faithfully preserved the treasure of traditional prayers, but also for having added new ones. Most of our Collects are venerable for their antiquity and their use throughout many centuries.

Until about the twelfth century, the Roman Church was accustomed to recite but one Collect before the Epistle. However, in the eleventh century other churches departed from this original practice by reciting several Collects; only the consecrated number of seven was not to be exceeded.[62] With the development of the liturgical calendar, a fixed law was gradually formed regulating the number of prayers to be said at Mass. Since the thirteenth century the prescribed number of prayers has been determined according to the respective rank (*ritus*), dignity (*dignitas*), and solemnity (*solemnitas*) of the feasts of the ecclesiastical year. The greater the feast, the more deeply recollected we should enter into its spirit, the more we should concentrate all our thoughts and sentiments upon the mystery celebrated; hence for the feasts of the highest rank (*duplex*) only one Collect is properly appointed.[63] The cele-

[62] Amalarius (d. about 847) attests in the *praefatio altera* to his principal work, that even in his time some *juxta affectum* recited two or three Collects, although in Rome only one was said, even on Sundays upon which the feast of a saint fell. Micrologus (in the eleventh century) defends this *antiqua vel romana traditio*, but adds these remarks: Sed hoc jam pauci observant, imo plures in tantum orationes multiplicant, ut auditores suos sibi ingratos efficiant et populum Dei potius avertant quam ad sacrificandum alliciant. Hoc autem sapientioribus multum displicet, qui etsi aliquando antiquam traditionem aliis morigerando excedunt, in ipsa tamen sua excessione modum tenere et aliquam rationem attendere solent. Unde et in Missa, etsi non semper una tantum oratione sint contenti, septenarium tamen numerum in orationibus raro excedunt. . . . Hoc autem summopere solent observare, ut in Missa aut unam, tres aut quinque aut septem orationes dicant (*De eccles. observat.*, chap. 4). Debet dici una oratio, sicut una epistola et unum evangelium, propter fidei unitatem . . . sed ex Patrum institutionibus quandoque dicuntur tres vel quinque vel septem. Praetor hos numeros alius est, non dico reprehensibilis, sed extraordinarius. . . . Pares non sunt dicendae, quia "numero Deus impare gaudet." . . . Quotcunque dicantur, sola prima conclusione debita terminentur (Sicard. [d. 1215], *Mitral.* III, chap. 2).

[63] Oratio est explicativa desiderii. Sed desiderium tanto est sanctius, quanto

bration of a feast of a lesser rite (*semiduplex*) is of less importance, hence other commemorations and petitions may find expression in our prayer; on feasts of such rite three Collects are generally said. The lowest rite (*simplex*) allows the priest to go beyond the consecrated number of three and to present to the Lord various needs. As often as the rubrics leave the priest free to add one or more prayers to those prescribed, he must take care that the number be an uneven one,[64] for this symbolizes the indivisibility of the Supreme Being and the unity of the Church. Never should more than seven Collects be said.

As to the value of the prayers of the Mass, but one opinion can be expressed in their regard: as to form and contents they are incomparable models of prayer. The language of the Collects is calm, simple, and plain, yet not without ornament; their contents exceedingly rich and profoundly dogmatic. One need but reflect in devout meditation on the text of a Collect, and he will discover what a wealth of sublime thoughts and holy emotions is embodied in those brief, substantial words. It is, therefore, very difficult, often even impossible, to translate these prayers without impairing their full meaning and weakening their force. That profound connoisseur of the Roman liturgy, Cardinal Wiseman, says of the Church's prayers:

> There is a fragrance, a true incense in those ancient prayers which seems to rise from the lips, and to wind upwards in soft, balmy clouds, upon which angels may recline, and thence look down upon us, as we utter them. They seem worthy to be caught up in a higher sphere, and to be heaped upon the altar above, at which an angel ministers. . . . They partake of all the solemnity and all the stateliness of the places in which they were first recited: they retain the echoes of the gloomy catacomb, they still resound with the jubilee of gilded basilicas, they keep the harmonious reverberations of lofty groined vaults. . . .
>
> Nothing can be more perfect in structure, more solid in substance,

---

magis ad unum restringitur, secundum illud Ps. 26:4: "Unum petii a Domino, hanc requiram" (S. Thom., IIa IIae, q.83, a.14).

[64] The priest, however, is not bound, *in simplicibus, feriis* et *votivis*, to add another prayer, so that the *numerus impar* may be observed (S. R. C., December 2, 1684). Regarding the *Missa quotidiana* for the departed *curandum est, ut orationes sint numero impares* (S. R. C., September 2, 1741). Quod si in quotidianis Missis pro defunctis plures addere orationes celebranti placuerit, uti rubricae potestatem faciunt, id fieri potest tantum in Missis lectis, impari cum aliis praescriptis servato numero et orationi pro omnibus defunctis postremo loco assignato (S. R. C., June 30, 1896).

more elegant in conception, or more terse in diction, than the Collects, especially those of the Sundays and of Lent. They belong essentially to the traditional deposits of the Church. . . . There is, in fact, hardly a Collect in which some singular beauty of thought, some happy turn of phrase, is not to be found. . . . Each is almost invariably composed of two parts, which may be called the recital and the petition. The first contains either a declaration of our wants, . . . or a plea for mercy, or for a favorable hearing. . . . Nothing strikes one so much as the noble and appropriate terms in which the Deity is addressed, and the sublime greatness in which His attributes are described. . . . The petition itself is ever most solemn, devout and fervent; often containing a depth of thought which would supply materials for a long meditation. . . . If any one thinks that these prayers, so easy in appearance, require no great power to imitate them, let him try to compose a few, and he will soon find their inferiority to the old ones; he will see that it is far from easy to put so much meaning into such a small compass, and still more difficult to come up to the beauty and greatness of thought generally condensed in the ancient form.[65]

The Collects are to be reckoned among the most precious liturgical treasures of the Church; they are masterly, unsurpassable prayers, distinguished alike for their solid force and pithy brevity, as for their fragrant charm and imperishable freshness.

9. **Examples.** The petition contained in the Collect is, as a rule, based on the Mass of each day. This is evident in the various feasts of the ecclesiastical year. The birth of the Saviour of the world is the mystery, the great joy of the holy feast of Christmas. On this holy night the Holy Sacrifice is offered three times to the glorious Trinity (*in nocte, in aurora, in die*). Now what are the desires and petitions of the Church on this great feast? In the first Collect she implores of God, who "enlighteneth this most holy night with the brightness of Him who is the true light, to grant that we who have known the mysteries of this light of earth, may likewise come to the enjoyment of it in heaven." In the prayer of the second Mass the Church addresses to almighty God the petition that He would "grant to us, who are flooded (*perfundimur*) by the new light of the Word made flesh, the grace that this light may be so reflected by our actions, as it shines through faith in our mind." The Collect of the third Mass contains the petition that "the new birth in the flesh of Thy only-begotten Son may free us, whom the ancient

[65] "On Prayer and Prayer-Books," *Essays*, II, 148 f., 170 ff.

slavery holds under the yoke of sin." On the feast of the Ascension we beg of God the grace which elevates us above all that is earthly that "we also may with our mind dwell among heavenly things."

In the Masses in honor of the saints, the subject of the petition is, in general, that by their example and merit, by their doctrine and intercession, we may advance in the spiritual life and attain eternal joys; that we may enjoy their mediation, protection, and intercession; that, animated by their example, we may be converted to God, produce worthy fruits of penance, walk in the simplicity and innocence of heart, endure all adversity with constant patience, despise all that is earthly, temporal, and perishable, and, on the contrary, long for and strive after all that is heavenly, eternal, and imperishable; that we may love what they loved, do what they taught, imitate what they have done, and obtain what they possess. Frequently the Church prays for their imitation in a particular virtue, for example, love of our neighbor, constancy in faith, confidence in God, the spirit of prayer, mortification; or for special protection against a particular evil. Such petitions for special graces and virtues are usually based upon some fact, miracle, or prominent characteristic in the life of the saint whose feast is celebrated. Thus the Church prays to almighty God on the Nativity of St. John Baptist that He would grant "His people the grace of spiritual joys, and direct the minds of all the faithful into the way of eternal salvation." On the feast of St. Thomas Aquinas the Collect is as follows: "O God, who by the wonderful learning of blessed Thomas, Thy confessor, dost enlighten Thy Church, and by his holy works dost render her fertile; grant, we beseech Thee, that we may perceive with our mind what he taught, and in our lives fulfill by our imitation what he practised."

On the Sundays of Advent we implore the Lord to "stir up Thy power and come; that by Thy protection we may deserve to be freed from the imminent dangers of our sins, and be saved by Thy deliverance"; and we beg God to "stir up our hearts to prepare the ways of Thy only-begotten Son, that through His coming we may be enabled to serve Thee with purified minds." The Collects of the Lenten liturgy have reference almost always to the same subject, for they generally implore the grace to worthily and profitably employ this solemn time of penance. With an astonishing variety this petition is expressed in an ever new and changeable form. Thus, for example, the Church begs God to "grant that our mind, chastened by the mortification of the body, may shine brightly in Thy sight with the desire for Thee"; she prays "that the faithful who by abstinence mortify their body, may by the fruit of good works become quickened in spirit"; "that we, who are commanded to abstain from carnal food, may also refrain from pernicious vices"; "that, fervently persevering in fasting and prayer, we may be delivered from the enemies of both soul and body"; "that the chastisement which we have inflicted on the body may serve to the strengthening and fortifying of the soul"; that "our fast may be pleasing to the Lord, make us worthy of divine grace, and lead us to the fountains of eternal salvation."

The second half of the ecclesiastical year, the time from Pentecost to Advent, represents the pilgrimage of the children of God to their eternal home, their heavenly country. This pilgrimage is indeed accompanied with hardship and labor, but is also full of hope and consolation.[66] We feel that we are pilgrims and strangers coming from afar, who seek a better heavenly country, the city which God hath prepared for us (Heb. 11:13–16). Therefore, in the Collects of this season, the Church prays that God, the strength of all that hope in Him, may send us the help of His grace, that, in the fulfillment of His commandments, we may please Him by thought and by deed; she prays that God would multiply His mercies toward us, that guided by Him we may make use of temporal goods in such a manner as not to lose those which are eternal; that under the guidance of God, the world may be ruled peacefully and the Church may enjoy undisturbed devotion; that God, who has prepared invisible goods for all who love Him, may pour into our hearts the fire of His charity, that, by loving Him in all things and above all things, we may obtain His promises which surpass all understanding; that God's infallible providence may avert from us all that is hurtful and grant us all that is profitable for us; that God may give us the spirit of always knowing and accomplishing what is right and just; that He would give us an increase of faith, hope, and charity, and in order that we may attain the happiness that He has promised, He

---

[66] Deliciae spiritus nostri divina cantica, ubi et fletus sine gaudio non est. Fideli homini et peregrino in saeculo nulla est jucundior recordatio quam civitatis illius unde peregrinatur; sed recordatio civitatis in peregrinatione non est sine dolore atque suspirio. Spes tamen certa reditus nostri etiam peregrinando tristes consolatur et exhortatur (S. August., *Enarrat. in Ps.*, 145:1).

may fill us with love for His holy commandments. As faithful children, who are pilgrims as yet at a distance from their true home, suffering and struggling,[67] we can ask or desire nothing better than what is expressed in these Sunday prayers.

[67] Ab octavis Pentecostes usque Adventum Domini (Ecclesia) recolit tempus peregrinationis. In hoc est nobis perpetua pugna et lucta adversus tres infestissimos hostes, mundum videlicet, carnem et diabolum. Mundus est hostis sophisticus, caro hostis domesticus, diabolus hostis antiquus. Nullus tamen istorum hostis est efficacior ad nocendum quam inimicus noster familiaris, scil. caro, quam fovemus indumentis et reficimus alimentis, cui tanquam jumento tria debentur: cibus ne deficiat, onus ut mansuescat, virga ut non indirecte, sed directe incedat (Beleth., *Ration.*, chap. 56).

CHAPTER XXII

THE EPISTLE

1. With the *Amen* of the Collect the service of prayer comes to an end. Now follow the readings from the Bible, which are connected with each other by various forms of chant and are often crowned by the Creed. What signification have the readings from Holy Scripture in the liturgy of the Mass? In the Mass the Saviour's entire work of redemption is shown forth and renewed; the celebration of the Mass embraces in its several parts the whole operation of the Redeemer. As the Lord exercised during His mortal life the office of mediator, thus He continues to exercise it in His Church, and that in a sacramental manner. Christ came as mediator between God and man, to reconcile and unite Heaven and earth with each other. God sent His Son to save the world and to bring godliness and the promise of the life which is to come (John 3:17; I Tim. 4:8). Christ has come from God unto "wisdom and justice and sanctification and redemption" (I Cor. 1:30), that is, as Redeemer He is the source not only of grace and sanctification, but also of enlightenment in all truth for mankind.

The first office of the Redeemer was to teach the truth and the law of God, exteriorly by the words which fell from His lips, and interiorly by the light which He infused into hearts. Already the Prophet remarks that in the days of the Messias "the earth is filled with the knowledge of the Lord, as the covering waters of the sea" (Isa. 11:9). The Spirit of God hovered over the Saviour, anointed Him and sent Him "to preach the gospel to the poor" (Luke 4:18). Christ came into the world to give testimony to the truth, and He taught the way of God in truth (John 18:37; Matt. 22:16). In Him were "hid all the treasures of wisdom and knowledge" and the fullness of His grace we have all received (Col. 2:3; John 1:14-16).

Only after the Lord, as the teacher of truth, had shown the way to heaven, did He die on the cross to unite man again with God in grace and love. Now all this is repeated in the Holy Sacrifice of the Mass. Before the Saviour becomes present on the altar at the Consecration as a mystical victim, He speaks to us words of eternal life, first by His prophets and apostles, then by Himself. The Epistle and Gospel come before the sacrificial action. In this arrangement is revealed the connection between the teaching of truth and the mystery of the altar, between the word of God and the divine eternal Word, who was made flesh and who under the Eucharistic veil is again present and dwells among us.

The sacramental God-man is not merely the life, but also the way and the truth for us men (John 14:6); only where the fountain of grace of the Eucharistic sacrifice flows, does the truth of Christ shine forth in full and undimmed splendor. The altar of grace and the pulpit of truth are sanctuaries intimately connected: they are in the same house of God, and the priest who offers the sacrifice also proclaims the heavenly doctrine. The Church, therefore, most appropriately combines the reading of the prophetical and evangelical word with the celebration of the Eucharistic sacrifice, which is eminently termed "the mystery of faith."[1] The announcement of the truth precedes the accomplishment of the sacrifice; for knowledge is the beginning of salvation. The living word of God is the seed whence proceeds the imperishable life of faith, which here below is perfected by grace and in the next life is transformed into glory.

The Church prefers to employ in her liturgy the words of Scripture, because they are especially holy and venerable, efficacious and full of grace; they are, indeed, the words of God, words that have the Holy Ghost for their author. Therefore are they so well adapted to manifest to the Lord our sentiments, desires, and petitions. To commune with God in prayer, to praise Him, to thank Him, to supplicate Him, to pour out to Him in chant our heart's joys and plaints, we can find no words more fitting than those which God Himself has put into our mouth and inspired through His "Holy

---

[1] Instructio fidei est duplex: una quae fit noviter imbuendis, scil. catechumenis et talis instructio fit circa baptismum. Alia autem est instructio, qua instruitur fidelis populus, qui communicat huic mysterio et talis instructio fit in hoc sacramento et tamen ab hac instructione non repelluntur etiam catechumeni et infideles (S. Thom., IIIa, q.83, a.4 ad4).

Spirit, who within us beseeches Heaven in our behalf with unutterable groanings." In the readings which now follow the service of prayer, we have the word of God, by which He speaks to us and instructs us in all doctrine and truth. These readings teach us the science of the saints and show us the kingdom of God. They afford us abundant material for growth "in grace and in the knowledge of our Lord and Saviour Jesus Christ" (II Pet. 3:18).

2. From apostolic times the canonical books have been read aloud at the assemblies of divine worship, and principally at the celebration of the Eucharistic sacrifice.[2] For a long time it belonged to the bishop to select the parts of Scripture which were to be read. St. Justin Martyr (d. 166 or 167), who describes the order of divine worship among the Christians, says that at the Sunday assemblies the writings of the apostles (the books of the New Testament) or the writings of the prophets were read as long as time permitted.[3] With the gradual development of the liturgical year, the distribution of the passages to be read changed more and more according to the new feasts, until finally, in the sixteenth century, the present arrangement of the Epistles and Gospels for the missal was determined. In this matter St. Jerome, who, by order of Pope Damasus I (366–384), completed and corrected the traditional arrangement of the biblical passages for the Mass, deserves great credit.

What rule was followed in the choice and arrangement of the biblical readings? The Epistles and the Gospels bear the closest connection with the course and spirit of the ecclesiastical year; the Church's selection, therefore, was made in conformity with the celebration of the feast or day. Indeed, among the variable parts of the Mass formula, the lessons selected from Holy Scripture occupy the principal place. In them, as a rule, the idea of the ecclesiastical season or feast finds its most perfect expression.

3. According to a general rule that has few exceptions, every

---

[2] In the first four centuries the liturgical celebration of Mass began with the reading of Scripture, at which the different books of the Bible were read (as they are still in the breviary) in a continuous order (*in continua serie*). (Cf. the 124 sermons of St. Augustine on the Gospel of St. John and St. John Chrysostom's homilies on the epistles of St. Paul.) For the highest feasts there were chosen already from the beginning appropriate passages, that is, such passages as had reference to the mysteries celebrated. With the progressive evolution of the ecclesiastical year, the *lectio continua* was replaced by a series of biblical extracts arranged for the various feasts and festal seasons.

[3] *First Apology*, chap. 67.

Mass formula has two biblical readings,[4] the first of which is called the Epistle and the other the Gospel. The first reading may be taken from any part of the Old and New Testaments except the four Gospels and the Book of Psalms; but generally—for example, on all the Sundays of the year—the Epistle is taken from the writings of the apostles. Hence it is that the name *Epistola* (letter) was used to designate the first pericope, even when it was not taken from the Epistles of the apostles but from some other part of Holy Scripture.[5] And from the fact that this pericope was not sung in former times, but only read,[6] it is still called in the superscription or heading of the missal, *Lectio*, that is, lesson or reading.[7]

[4] In the Mozarabic and Ambrosian liturgies, the Gospel is usually preceded by two lessons (generally one from the Old, the other from the New Testament). On Ember Saturdays there were formerly, according to the Roman rite, twelve lessons read by twelve lectors (that is, six lessons read first in Latin and then in Greek); hence in the ancient liturgical books these Saturdays are called *Sabbata duodecim lectionum s. in duodecim lectionibus*. At present they still retain the six lessons (five from the Old Testament and one from the New) before the Gospel, while Ember Wednesdays have but two. In the pope's High Mass the Epistle and Gospel are still sung both in Latin and Greek.

[5] Because this first reading was more frequently taken from St. Paul's epistles, it was called also ἀπόστολος to distinguish it from εὐαγγέλιον. Under the former term were included not only the epistles of the apostles, but also the Acts of the Apostles and the Apocalypse. *Postmodum dicitur Oratio; deinde sequitur Apostolus* (*Sacrament. Gregor.*).

[6] *Lectio dicitur quia non cantatur ut psalmus vel hymnus, sed legitur tantum. Illic enim modulatio, hic sola pronuntiatio quaeritur* (Isid., *Etymolog.*, VI, xix, 9). The present mode of delivering the Epistle is a tone between singing and simple reading: it is a manner of singing in which the whole text is delivered in a monotone (*tono recto*) without modulation (except at an interrogation, when the voice descends half a tone, but in the last syllable returns to the dominant tone). The rubrics designate this as chanting. *Subdiaconus cantat Epistolam alta voce* (*Cerem. Episc.*, II, viii, 40). The ancient liturgists called it *choraliter legere* (reading in a choral manner). The reading or singing tone of the Gospel is somewhat more melodious and, therefore, more festive.

[7] In regard to the superscription *Lectio libri Sapientiae*, it is to be observed that it is given not only to extracts from the Book of Wisdom itself, but also to selections from the Book of Jesus the son of Sirach (Ecclesiasticus), from Ecclesiastes, the Canticle of Canticles, and the Book of Proverbs—all these taken together are called by the Fathers and in the liturgy, Books of Wisdom (*libri Sapientiales*). *Notandum est, non omnia verba ex s. Scriptura esse desumpta, sed initium fere semper et interdum etiam finem ab Ecclesia dumtaxat additum esse, ut convenientius inchoetur aut claudatur Epistola. Hinc Epistolae desumptae ex s. Paulo initium vox "fratres" et finis frequenter*

THE EPISTLE

In former times, perhaps up to the fifth century, it was the duty of the lector to read the Epistle; but from that time forward the solemn reading of the Epistle was assigned to the subdeacon, who only since the fourteenth century was especially empowered for that office by a special rite at his ordination.[8] In ancient churches the ambo [9] stood in the space between the sanctuary and the nave. If a church had two ambos, one served for the reading of the Gospel and the other for that of the Epistle. If there was but one ambo, then the Gospel was read from the highest step and the Epistle from

---

"in Christo Jesu Domino nostro." Si vero ex aliorum Apostolorum Epistolis sumatur, vox "carissimi"; si ex Prophetis, verba "in illo tempore" ab initio praeponuntur, et in fine non raro verba "dicit Dominus omnipotens" subjunguntur (Lohner, *De ss. Miss. sacrif.*, VI, tit. 6).

[8] In the thirteenth century Durandus answers the question: Quare subdiaconus legit lectiones ad Missam, cum non reperiatur hoc sibi competere vel ex nomine vel ex ministerio sibi concesso? (*Ration.*, II, viii, 4.) In former times even the lectors were allowed to read the Gospel. St. Cyprian mentions this when speaking of the confessors Aurelius and Celerinus, whom he had ordained lectors about the year 250 (cf. *Epist.*, 38, 39). Antiquioribus temporibus Lectorum ordo legendo Evangelio fuit destinatus. Verum saeculo IV visum est Patribus nostris, reverentiam et venerationem Evangelio debitam omnino exigere, ut tantum munus non amplius Lectoribus, qui jam ut plurimum ex puerili aetate eligebantur, sed ministris sacris, saltem Diaconis committeretur, qui ad sacerdotalem dignitatem proxime accedebant (Krazer, IV, a.1, §235). However, the handing of the Book of the Gospels at the ordination of the deacon came into use only gradually after the tenth century. (Cf. Amalar., *De ecclesiast. offic.*, II, chaps. 11 f.; Morin., *De sacris ordinat.*, III, ix, 1; *ibid.*, xii, 2.)

In a High Mass without the assistance of the *ministri sacri*, a lector in surplice sings the Epistle (*Rubr. Miss.*, II, vi, 8). On April 23, 1875, the S. R. C. gave this answer: Quum Missa cantatur sine ministris et nullus est clericus inserviens qui superpelliceo indutus Epistolam decantet juxta Rubricas, satius erit quod ipsa Epistola legatur sine cantu ab ipso Celebrante; nunquam vero in Ecclesiis monialium decantetur ab una ex eis. Accordingly it is indeed more proper (*satius*) that the celebrant in a High Mass without sacred ministers should merely read the Epistle, but he is not forbidden to sing it. The priest in this matter should conform to the ordinance or general practice of the diocese. Only in a case of actual necessity may a superior permit a cleric who is not in a higher order to vest as subdeacon (however, without maniple) and sing the Epistle in a *Missa solemnis* and perform the remaining functions of a subdeacon (S. R. C., July 15, 1698).

[9] The ambo is an immovable tribune or oblong pulpit up to which a few steps lead. It serves for the solemn reading of the Holy Scriptures, the announcement of divine worship, and so forth. In the Basilica of St. Clement at Rome are to be found three ambos; beside the ambo for the Epistle, is another marble stand arranged for the Old Testament lessons.

a lower one. Thus the prominence due the Gospel over the Epistle was expressed both by the manner of delivery and by the person of the reader and the place of reading.[10]

All the books of the Old and New Testaments possess the same divine character, the same divine dignity and authority, inasmuch as they have God for their author and are inspired by the Holy Ghost, and are, therefore, in a true and full sense the word of God; but in other respects a certain distinction of rank can and must be given to them. That which the Holy Ghost imparts through the medium of the inspired writers can be more or less important, the manner of communication can be more or less perfect. In this respect the superiority of the New Testament over the Old is surely manifest, and again in the New Testament itself the four Gospels take precedence of the Acts of the Apostles, the Epistles, and the Apocalypse. For in the work of divine revelation there is a continual and gradual progression. The foundations laid in the Old Dispensation, were brought to perfection in Christ and His apostles. The Old Testament is included, developed, and completed in the New.

The crown of the supernatural revelation consists in this, that God spoke to us, not only by the prophets and apostles, but also through His only-begotten Son (Heb. chap. 1). The prophets and apostles were, indeed, organs of the Holy Ghost, who announced through them heavenly truths; still they were only human messengers of salvation. Jesus Christ, on the contrary, is a divine person; He is truth itself; He is the true light of the world; all His words, works, and miracles are eminently divine works and actions, full of divine spirit and life, of infinite truth and depth. The Gospels place before our eyes the life of Jesus Christ, the word and

---

[10] From the most ancient times (cf. *Ordo Rom. I*, n. 10), it was customary to sit in choir with head covered at the solemn reading of the Epistle, whereas from the beginning it was customary to stand with head uncovered while the Gospel was sung. Although the subdeacon no longer reads the Epistle to the people from the ambo (as he formerly did until towards the end of the Middle Ages), but at the left side turned towards the altar, he must, nevertheless, both before and after reading it make a genuflection (*in gradu*) in the middle of the altar. The subdeacon receives the blessing from the celebrant, who represents Christ, only after he has finished reading, because the Old Law, symbolized by the Epistle, was fulfilled, or annulled, by Christ (Math. 5:17-20); the deacon, on the contrary, is blessed by the celebrant before he reads the Gospel, because the Gospel is derived from Christ (cf. Durand., *op. cit.*, IV, chap. 17).

example of the eternal Wisdom made flesh; in them appears the God-man Himself, teaching and acting, suffering and triumphing, whereas in the Epistles the Holy Ghost speaks to us, instructs and admonishes us, only by His human messengers and servants. Hence it is usually said that the instruction of the people takes place first in the Epistle, in a preparatory and imperfect manner through the doctrine of the prophets and apostles; then the faithful are more perfectly instructed through the teachings of Christ as contained in the Gospel.[11] The Epistle, therefore, is read before the Gospel because it is subordinate to it, prepares for it, leads to the understanding of it.[12] Both readings harmonize with one another and mutually complete each other; they would express a common thought, or at least kindred ideas. But as the subject or the mystery of the ecclesiastical celebration appears more closely and more fully exposed at one time in the Epistle, at another time in the Gospel, it may in general be said that both readings mutually explain and throw light on each other, so as to constitute together a whole. On the feast of the Most Holy Trinity, for example, the Apostle in his grand Epistle (Rom. 11:33-36) glorifies the impenetrable secrets of the Divinity, while in the Gospel (Matt. 28:18-20) the adorable mystery of three persons in God, which forms the foundation of faith and is its crown, is clearly and distinctly set forth. The Epistle of Pentecost (Acts 2:1-11) announces and describes in detail the coming of the Holy Ghost, while the Gospel (John 14:23-31) contains the promise of the Comforter and His blessed gifts.

Many of the Epistles are taken from the Old Testament, for the following reasons. The Old Testament is a divine testimony to Christ and to His kingdom. Whenever the Church found in it some

---

[11] Instructio fidelis populi dispositive quidem fit per doctrinam prophetarum et apostolorum, quae in Ecclesia legitur per lectores et subdiaconos;—perfecte autem populus instruitur per doctrinam Christi in Evangelio contentam, quae a summis ministris legitur, scilicet a diaconibus (S. Thom., IIIa, q.83, a.4). Epistolarum doctrina respectu evangelicae doctrinae, quae immediate a Christo profluxit, est imperfecta et ordinatur ad eam sicut ad finem. Intellectus namque Epistolarum disponit ad intellectum Evangeliorum; propterea Epistola ante Evangelium legitur (Dion. Carthus., *Expos. Miss.*, a. 12).

[12] Anteponitur in ordine quod inferius est dignitate, ut ex minoribus animus audientium ad majora proficiat et gradatim ab imis ad summa conscendat (Walaf. Strabo, chap. 23). According to the liturgists of the Middle Ages, the Epistle precedes the Gospel because it represents the Law and the Prophets, or the efficacy of the Precursor of Christ, or the preaching of the seventy-two disciples, who prepared the way for the Saviour.

striking prophecy or figure of a New Testament mystery or event, she incorporated it, if possible, as an Epistle in the Mass, as a supplement to the Gospel or an explanation of it. Most of the Masses in honor of the Mother of God have Epistles taken from the Old Testament, and these have preferably been selected from the Books of Wisdom.

Another reason why the Church inserted in the liturgy of the Mass lessons from the Old Testament is found in the following reflection. In the Old Law salvation had not yet appeared and the light had not as yet risen, but darkness and the shadow of death enveloped all nations; it was a time of anxious and painful expectancy, a time of sighing and longing for redemption. Lessons taken from this dark period are well fitted to impress the character of penance on those days on which they are used. This explains why the Church on all ferial days from Ash Wednesday until Tuesday in Holy Week exclusively uses lessons from the Old Testament. They are intended to awaken, nourish, and strengthen within us a true penitential spirit; for, like so many voices from the ages before Christ, they impressively admonish us that by sin we have become estranged from God and have strayed back into the night of death. On those days which have several Old Testament lessons, such as the Wednesdays and Saturdays of Ember weeks,[13] the earnest spirit of penance is still more deeply stamped. Coming down to us from apostolic times, the Ember days are, according to their original intent and purpose, days of penance, on which we are expected, by prayer, fasting and alms-giving, to purify and to sanctify our souls; they are also days of thanksgiving and petition for the blessings of the seasons. Later on they became also ordination days, because they were specially suitable for the conferring of holy orders.

4. At the conclusion of the Epistle the acolyte, in the name of the people, answers: *Deo gratias* ("Thanks be to God"). What is more befitting than that we should thank the Lord from the bottom of our heart for the divine instruction which He has impared to us by the mouth of His messenger? In the Epistle almighty God, so to speak, sends a letter, a writing from heaven, to us miserable crea-

---

[13] Only on the Wednesday of the Pentecost Ember week are there two New Testament lessons; the reason is that the penitential character of this Ember Week is in many respects superseded by the festal spirit of the octave.

tures.[14] Should we not with faith and reverence receive His words which are of infinite dignity, power, and depth of meaning, and obey them with cheerfulness and alacrity? Every word emanating from the mouth of God is supernatural and heavenly food for the life of the soul. Holy Scripture, more than any other writing, is fit to instruct us for salvation, to teach, reprove, correct, indoctrinate in justice, that the man of God may be perfect, furnished for every good work (II Tim. 3:15–17). By means of the biblical readings the minister of God plants and waters the field of our heart; let us be grateful for this, and the Lord will then give the increase, so that the heavenly seed of the living word may germinate and thrive, blossom and produce fruit, thirty, sixty, and a hundredfold (I Cor. 3:6–9; Matt. 13:3–23). But in order that this fruit of salvation may ripen, in order that we may advance in the holy love of God and in every Christian virtue to perfection, we must not only receive and preserve the divine word with a perfect heart, but we must persevere in patience amid all sufferings and contradictions, amid all temptations and combats.

It is peculiar to the Christian always to return thanks to God through Christ our Lord, who has revealed Himself to us full of truth and grace, who in the character of a penitent has taken our place and submitted to the death of the cross, who is our mediator and advocate with the Father. Hence the words *Deo gratias* were, at the time of the persecution of the Christians, the watchword or the mark by which, as a short profession of faith, the *ostiarius* (the doorkeeper) recognized as Christians those who sought admission into the place of public worship. At the same time there was comprised in this expression of gratitude a confession of the sentiments with which the Christians were urged to assist at divine worship, which they regarded as a grace from God. No wonder that the words *Deo gratias* found their way into the liturgy and occur so frequently. They are found already in St. Paul's Epistles (I Cor. 15:57; II Cor. 2:14).

---

[14] Sunt et Angeli cives nostri: sed quia nos peregrinamur, laboramus, illi autem in civitate exspectant adventum nostrum. Et de illa civitate, unde peregrinamur, literae nobis venerunt: ipsae sunt Scripturae, quae nos hortantur, ut bene vivamus (S. August., *In Ps. 90 serm.*, II, n. 1).

CHAPTER XXIII

THE INTERPOSED CHANTS

THE Church has assigned to the choir the task of executing, in the name of the congregation, the various parts that are to be sung. These are very appropriately and skilfully inserted in the liturgy of the Mass, for sacred chant produces many wholesome results: [1] it makes divine worship more solemn and more majestic, elevates the mind, exhilarates the heart, renders the disposition more peaceable, inclines to devotion, excites to piety, softens to mildness and compunction of spirit, produces a flow of tears and raises a desire of amendment, enables the soul to soar above the earth and all that is earthly and to lose itself in heavenly meditation. St. Augustine depicts the powerful impression made by the chant of the Ambrosian hymns upon his soul: "How I wept, O Lord, amid Thy hymns and chants, greatly moved by the voices of Thy sweetly singing Church! They poured themselves into my ears, these voices, and like drops Thy truth penetrated my heart: the fervor of devotion was awakened, tears flowed, and ah, how happy I was then!" [2] Thus the chants at the celebration of Mass, by a pleasing variety, drive away weariness and keep the participation of the faithful in the divine service ever on the alert. Formerly they had a larger scope and were in the form of responsories, or alternate singing, conducted, according to a certain rule of repetition, by precentors and the choir.

The chant which follows the Epistle and precedes the Gospel is a connecting link between these two biblical readings. It varies at

---

[1] Psallendi utilitas tristia corda consolatur, gratiores mentes facit, fastidiosos oblectat, inertes exsuscitat, peccatores ad lamenta invitat. Nam quamvis dura sint carnalium corda, statim ut psalmi dulcedo insonuerit, ad affectum pietatis animum eorum inflectit (S. Isid., *Sentent.*, III, vii, 31).

[2] *Confess.*, IX, chap. 6.

the different periods of the ecclesiastical year, and accordingly bears different names. Sometimes the Gradual alone occurs; but for the most part it is followed by an Alleluja or the Tract. Sometimes the Gradual, or the Alleluja, or the Tract, is followed by the Sequence. During the Easter season the Gradual is entirely replaced by the greater Alleluja, and once (on Good Friday) by the Tract.

THE GRADUAL

The word *Graduale*[3] comes from *gradus* = step. To distinguish the responsory that occurs between the Epistle and the Gospel from the responsories of the Divine Office, it was, in time, called *Graduale*, from the place in which it was sung; for the leading singer who intoned the longer chant after the Epistle and sang it alternately with the choir, stood (in the Roman Church) on an elevated step, that is, on the same step of the ambo from which the Epistle had previously been read.[4]

The Apostolic Constitutions (II, chap. 57) already prescribe a chant of psalms after the reading from the Old Testament. St. Augustine several times mentions that between the apostolic reading

---

[3] The original designation was: *Responsum, Responsorium, Responsorium graduale, Responsorius (sc. cantus vel psalmus)*. The name *Responsorium* (from *respondere*), that is, alternate singing, expresses the way and manner of the singing, namely, *quod uno canente chorus consonando respondet* (Isidor., *De offic. eccles.*, I, chap. 8). Accordingly, the responsory-hymn consists of two parts, of the *Responsorium* proper (R.) and the *Versus* (V.). Often (but not always) the other explanation holds good, by which *Responsorium* would designate a chant of the choir answering the contents of the preceding reading, *quia lectioni convenire et quodammodo respondere debet* (Benedict. XIV, *De ss. Miss. sacrif.*, II, v, 15). Responsoria dicuntur a respondendo. Tristria namque tristibus, et laeta laetis debemus succinere lectionibus (Rupert. Tuitiens., *De divin. offic.*, I, chap. 15).

[4] Subdiaconus ascendit in ambonem (—non tamen in superiorem gradum, quem solus solet ascendere qui Evangelium lecturus est—*Ordo Rom. II*, n. 7) et legit (sc. Epistolam). Postquam legerit, cantor cum cantatorio (*Antiphon or Gradual*) ascendit et dicit Responsum (*Ordo Rom. I*, n. 10). Non tamen ascendit superius, sed stat in eodem loco, ubi et lector, et solus inchoat Responsorium et cuncti in choro respondent et idem solus Versum Responsorii cantat (*Ordo Rom. II*, n. 7). Lectionem quae legitur post sessionem, sequitur cantus, qui vocatur responsorius (Amalar., *De ecclesiast. offic.*, III, chap. 11; cf. Amalar., *Eclog. in Ord. Rom.*, n. 14). According to others this chant was called *Graduale*, because it was sung while the deacon with his attendants went from the altar to the steps (*gradus*) of the choir-stand and ascended them, in order to sing the Gospel. (Cf. Bellarm., *De Missa*, II, chap. 16.)

(Epistle) and the Gospel an entire psalm should be sung responsorily.[5] Thus in this place whole psalms were sung until the fifth century; but in the *Antiphonarium* of St. Gregory the Great, this psalm-chant is reduced to a few verses, as it now stands in our missal. Even in its present abridgment the Gradual chant has preserved its previous responsory form; for all the Graduals consist of two parts: the first retains the name, *responsorium*, the other bears the title, *versus* (V).[6] In most cases both parts are taken from the Psalms; not unfrequently, however, passages from other books of the Old and New Testaments are used; only a few times do we meet with texts which are not from the Bible.[7] Thus do we find everywhere in the liturgy "words of Holy Scripture which the Church, with a delicacy of thought, has appropriately selected and causes, like so many brilliant gems, to glisten in her divine service."

The object and meaning of the Gradual can generally be easily seen and determined if we take into consideration that this choir chant, with the three other variable chants (Introit, Offertory, Communion), forms a whole which bears the impress or idea of the feast or of the ecclesiastical year, that is, gives in various ways expression to the fundamental thought of the liturgical celebration of the day. Sentiments and resolutions similar to those of the Introit are again expressed or amplified in the chant that comes between the readings, that we may be ever more penetrated with the spirit of the day's celebration. Hence the intimate connection between the Gradual chant and the two scriptural lessons which it binds together is made evident. The Epistle and Gospel, as well as the Gradual chant which comes between them, are selected with regard to the central idea of the liturgical celebration; accordingly, the

[5] Primam lectionem audivimus Apostoli. Deinde cantavimus Psalmum. Post haec evangelica lectio decem leprosos mundatos nobis ostendit et unum ex eis alienigenam gratias agentem mundatori suo (S. August., *Serm.*, CLXXVI, n. 1).

[6] Formam habet Responsorii Graduale, imo et Responsorium semper appellatur in Antiphonario S. Gregorii, et frequentius a Radulpho et aliis rituum interpretibus. Unde sicut Responsorii duae sunt partes, ita et Gradualis: prior una, quae ipsa *Responsorii* nomen retinet, posterior altera huic cohaerens et annexa, quae *Versus* dicitur (Guyet., Heortolog., III, chap. 25, q. 3).

[7] This is the case, for example, in the Gradual of the feast of the Seven Dolors of the Blessed Virgin Mary: *Dolorosa et lacrymabilis* . . . ; and in the Gradual, *Benedicta et venerabilis* . . . , which occurs in many Masses of the Blessed Virgin Mary. Here also belongs the first part of the Gradual in Requiem Masses: *Requiem aeternam.* . . .

THE GRADUAL

readings and the chant harmonize with one another: in both the peculiarity of each ecclesiastical celebration is reflected, but in a different way, as the character of an instructive reading or an inspiring chant demands.[8] In the reading God descends to us, speaks to us, makes known His mysteries and His will to us, addresses exhortations and admonitions to us, terrifies us by threats, and consoles us with His promises; in the chant, on the contrary, we soar upwards to God, make known our devotion and fervor, we praise, thank, love, admire, implore, lament, and rejoice. This harmonious blending of instructive readings with affective singing brings along a beneficial variation in the divine service.

In the Gradual chant we give appropriate expression to our lofty dispositions, we utter sentiments of joy or sorrow, various impressions and resolutions which have been awakened in us by the day's celebration and by the Mass in general, as well as by the reading of the Epistle in particular.[9] In a certain sense, then, we may say that the interposed chant is an echo of the Epistle and a suitable transition to the Gospel. In order, then, to expound thoroughly the meaning of the Gradual chant, it must always be conceived and explained in its twofold relation: to the preceding Epistle and the following Gospel.

Usually the Gradual is not sung or recited alone, but it has an appendix, which, according to the tenor of the ecclesiastical celebration, bears the impress of joy or of sorrow. Expressive of joy is the Alleluja, which is generally added to the Gradual throughout the year. It consists of two allelujas, a verse, and another alleluja; hence it is often called the Alleluja verse.[10] In this addition the

---

[8] In lectione auditores pascuntur, sed in cantu quasi aratro compunctionis corda conscinduntur; habet enim musica quamdam vim ad flectendum animum (Sicard., *Mitral.*, III, chap. 3).

[9] Utraque Gradualis pars, perinde atque Introitus, modo invitationem et exhortationem continet, modo collaudationem et congratulationem, nonnumquam prosopopoeiam vel apostrophen, saepissime vero omnium narrationem aut invocationem (Guyet., *loc. cit.*).

[10] Alleluja canimus, quoniam ad laudes angelicas in hoc itinere festinamus; Versus, quoniam sic euntes, laborantes, festinantes ad Dominum revertimur, unde et Versus cantantes ad Orientem nos convertimur; et attende, quod Alleluja, prius summotenus dictum, praesentis contemplationis gaudium repraesentat, sed postea repetitum cum jubilo gaudium designat aeternum et tam angelorum quam beatarum animarum convivium. Unde et hoc hebraicum nomen in officio remanet peregrinum, quoniam gaudium illud peregrinatur ab hac vita et nos a Domino peregrinamur. Congrue igitur post Graduale

Gradual expands and rises into a joyful chant, which thrills through the soul.[11] The verse between the three allelujas is frequently not a mere continuation, but rather a clearer development and a more perfect expression of the thoughts contained in the Gradual. The reason for this is the fact that in selecting the verse the Church gave herself freer scope. While she compiled the Gradual almost always entirely from the Psalms, she did not adhere so strictly to this rule in the composition of the Alleluja verse, but she often employed therein other biblical texts and, especially in Masses celebrated in honor of the saints, verses of ecclesiastical origin. In this way it was easier to designate more distinctly the subject of the day's celebration. One of the verses thus composed by the Church is sung on the feast of the Assumption of the Blessed Virgin: *Assumpta est Maria in coelum, gaudet exercitus angelorum.*

The Gradual lies midway between the mournful Tract and the exultant Alleluja: it denotes the laborious and difficult pilgrimage of the children of God through life to their heavenly country.[12] Therefore, at one time the Gradual is connected with the Tract, at another with the Alleluja, according as the sufferings and pains of penance or the consolations and hopes of future eternal rest predominate in our earthly pilgrimage.[13] At certain times the Gradual is entirely omitted or gives place to the Tract, for the reason that grief of soul has reached is profoundest depths, as on Good Friday;

---

cantatur, quia post actionem sequitur contemplatio, post luctum poenitentiae canticum laetitiae, post irriguum dilationis magnitudo consolationis, quoniam ... qui seminant in lacrymis, in exsultatione metent. Congrue quoque in Alleluja jubilamus (= we continue to sing the last syllable with varied melodious turns), ut mens illuc rapiatur, ubi Sancti exsultabunt in gloria et laetabuntur in cubilibus suis (Ps. 149), quod gaudium nec potest verbis exprimi nec omnino taceri: non exprimitur propter magnitudinem, non tacetur propter amorem (Sicard., *loc. cit.*).

[11] Versus nihil sinistrum aut triste, sed totum jucundum et dulce debent sonare (Innoc. III, *op. cit.*, II, chap. 33).

[12] Graduale significat non jam requiem remuneratorum, sed laborem operantium (Rupert. Tuit., I, chap. 24). In hoc quidem tempore peregrinationis nostrae ad solatium viatici dicimus Alleluja: modo nobis Alleluja canticum est viatoris, tendimus autem per viam laboriosam ad quietam patriam, ubi retractis omnibus actionibus non remanebit nisi Alleluja (S. August., *Serm.*, CCLV, n. 1).

[13] Post lectionem cantatur a choro Graduale, quod significat profectum vitae, et Alleluja, quod significat spiritualem exsultationem, vel Tractus in officiis luctuosis, quod significat spiritualem gemitum: haec enim consequi debent in populo ex praedicta doctrina (S. Thom., IIIa, q. 83, a. 4).

or it is displaced by the Alleluja, because the soul, as it were, forgets the troubles of this life and can but rejoice with the blessed of heaven, as during Eastertide.

The Tract

At certain times the joyful Alleluja chant after the Gradual is replaced by the Tract, which is of an entirely different tenor. Whereas the Gradual with the Alleluja is a spirited hymn of joy, the Tract adds a grave, mournful, and penitential character to the interposed chant.

Tractus[14] is a musical term; it relates primarily, not to the contents, but to the manner of singing. The peculiar, characteristic manner of singing called *tractus* consisted in this, that all the verses were continuously sung by one singer in a slow, protracted measure, without interruption from the choir. This uniform and measured way of chanting, in contrast to the animated, alternate singing of the Gradual and Alleluja verse, is evidently suited for the expression of sorrow and penitential sentiments. For this reason the Tract replaced the jubilant alleluja, and became the peculiar characteristic of the Lenten rite: it occurs only on days especially devoted to exercises of prayer and mortification, to works of penance, and fervent prayers for divine grace and mercy. What the somber purple is to the eye on these days of penance, the touching chant of the Tract is to the ear, a sigh of penitential grief.

The Tract is a continuation or amplification of the Gradual, and according to its contents harmonizes with it: at times it expresses quiet sentiments of joy, hope, and confidence; more frequently, however, it utters the supplication of a contrite heart oppressed with distress and suffering. The Tract is nearly always taken from Holy

[14] *Tractus* = the drawing, the extension, the slow movement of the words; *tractim* = in one strain, drawn, extended, slowly. We find the Tract already in the most ancient Roman *Ordines*. Cantor dicit Reponsum. Si fuerit tempus ut dicat Allelujam, bene; sin autem, Tractum; sin minus, tantummodo Responsum (*Ordo Rom. I*, n. 10). Saeculo decimo complures sibi persuaserunt, quod tractim canere nihil aliud significaret, quam cunctanter lento et tristi tono canere; hinc jusserunt, ut non amplius unus, sed plures et quidem bini Tractum alternis canerent vicibus, ea tantum servata lege, ne chorus eos interrumperet (Krazer, sect. 4, art. 1, cap. 4, § 234). Tractus dicitur a trahendo, vel quia lente et lugubriter cantatur, vel quia olim tractim et sine interruptione a cantore canebatur (De Carpo, *Biblioth. liturg.*, I, a. 2).

Scripture, especially from the Psalms; often various biblical texts are freely joined together; only seldom is it partly or wholly of ecclesiastical origin. Sometimes it is long, sometimes short; it always comprises, with but few exceptions, more than two verses. On three occasions (on the first Sunday of Lent, Palm Sunday, and Good Friday) almost an entire psalm is chanted. Not all those days have a Tract on which the joyful Alleluja chant is omitted; it rather serves to distinguish certain more strictly penitential days from others, or to bring the festive expression of some Masses more into harmony with the spirit of Lent. The most sorrowful day of the year, Good Friday, has two Tracts; at other times only one is prescribed.[15]

The Mondays, Wednesdays, and Fridays in Lent were, from the earliest period, the most prominent days of penance;[16] hence they have a tract specially arranged for penitents. With the exception of Wednesday in Holy Week, this Tract is always the same. It is as follows:

Ps. 102:10. Domine, non secundum peccata nostra, quae fecimus nos: neque secundum iniquitates nostras retribuas nobis.	Ps. 102:10. O Lord, deal not with us according to our sins: nor reward us according to our iniquities.
V. Ps. 78:8 f. Domine, ne memineris iniquitatum nostrarum antiquarum: cito anticipent nos misericordiae tuae, quia pauperes facti sumus nimis.	V. Ps. 78:8 f. Remember not, O Lord, our former iniquities: let Thy mercies speedily prevent us, for we are become exceedingly poor.
V. (*Ad hunc versum genuflectitur.*) Adjuva nos, Deus salutaris noster: et propter gloriam nominis tui, Domine, libera nos; et propitius esto peccatis nostris, propter nomen tuum.	V. (*Genuflect.*) Help us, O God, our Saviour: and for the glory of Thy name, O Lord, deliver us; and forgive us our sins for Thy name's sake.

[15] On Ember Saturdays the Tract follows the Epistle only, and thus closes the five chants (Graduals) that are annexed to the five preceding lessons and are, thus to speak, regarded as one single Gradual. Rupert of Deutz remarks on this circumstance, that on Ember Saturdays and on Wednesday in Holy Week, after the Epistle, as well as on Good Friday after the (two) lessons, not the Gradual with the Tract, but merely the Tract without the Gradual follows, whereby the expression of penitential sorrow is augmented in the highest degree (*De divin. off.*, V, chap. 13).

[16] They are called *feriae legitimae*, that is, official penitential days, the

THE TRACT

This Tract is a fervent supplication for mercy, for the pardon of sin, and for obtaining the assistance of grace to persevere in a life of virtue.[17] For all this we pray, not indeed relying on our merits, but wishing to honor the name of God, that He may thereby be glorified and praised. But to make our cry of supplication and our petition still more pressing, we bend the knee at the last verse in token of our profound humility and compunction.

The ecclesiastical year has no influence whatever on the Requiem Mass, which is always the same. It has throughout the entire year a Gradual with a Tract,[18] which, with the exception of an inserted verse from the Psalms, was composed by the Church herself. The Gradual and Tract for the Requiem Mass is always as follows:

Graduale. Requiem aeternam dona eis, Domine: et lux perpetua luceat eis.	*Gradual.* Eternal rest grant unto them, O Lord: and let perpetual light shine upon them.
V. Ps. 11:7. In memoria aeterna erit justus: ab auditione mala non timebit.	V. Ps. 7. The just shall be in everlasting remembrance: he shall not fear the evil hearing.
Tractus. Absolve, Domine, animas omnium fidelium defunctorum ab omni vinculo delictorum.	*Tract.* Release, O Lord, the souls of all the faithful departed from the bonds of their sins.
V. Et gratia tua illis succurrente, mereantur evadere judicium ultionis.	V. And by the assistance of Thy grace may they escape the sentence of condemnation.
V. Et lucis aeternae beatitudine perfrui.	V. And enjoy the bliss of eternal light.

---

observance of which was transplanted from the East to the West. The mystical reasons for selecting the *feriae legitimae* (fer. II, IV, VI) are given by Quadt, *Die Liturgie der Quatembertage*, pp. 111 f.

[17] Admiranda est virtus orationis versuum horum et omnino saluberrimum est mentali affectu cum attentione ingenti, cum praecordiali sapore hos sacros versus depromere, quoniam possibilius foret coelum et terram perire quam talem orationem inefficacem existere (Dion. Carthus., *In Ps.*, 78:8).

[18] Tam Graduale quam Tractus in Missis defunctorum nullam unquam mutationem subeunt; adeo luctuosa officia sunt Missae de Requiem, quae nobis objiciunt Purgatorii animas a facie Dei projectas, in immanissimis tormentorum generibus excruciatas, ut aptae haud sint suscipere vel intermixta admittere laetitiae signa, unde et respuunt vocem Alleluja (Cavalieri, *Oper. liturg.*, III, x, 3).

As a tenderly solicitous mother, the Church begs God the Father to take His and her suffering children out of purgatory into the peace of heaven and light of glory. The Church is encouraged thus to pray and intercede, because the souls that are expiating in purgatory led God-fearing and devout lives here on earth. She then implores the Lord to remove the last obstacle to glory; and while she suddenly represents to herself these souls at the moment of their departure from the body and out of this world, she entreats for them a favorable judgment, that they may soon be admitted to the possession of eternal joys.

The Alleluja and Tract are, therefore, at different times added to the ordinary Gradual to express the various interior sentiments of the Church. Although the times of Advent and Lent are in many respects liturgically alike, there is a distinction made with regard to the Alleluja. Advent has a character partly grave and partly joyful; it is indeed still night, but the first rays of the dawn and of the rising Sun already chase away the dark shadows. On the four Sundays of Advent, the somber hue of the purple vestments of the Church announces the penitential spirit of the holy season, while the Alleluja after the Gradual gives expression to the joyful expectation.[19] The Church stamps this season with the seal of her joy and of her anxious solicitude; she intermingles the Alleluja amid her sighs, knowing well that "joy will drown all sorrow on that night which is brighter than the clearest day."

The case is entirely different during the period from Septuagesima until Easter. This is the greatest and strictest penitential season of the Church; hence the Alleluja is totally withheld from her lips.[20] She is overwhelmed with sorrow; she weeps over the malice of sin, which covers the earth. As faithful children of the Church we should heed her admonition and exercise ourselves in works of penance. Our hearts, sullied by sin and the love of the world, we should bathe in the tears of sorrow and compunction before we presume to per-

---

[19] Quamvis cum gaudio boni servi spectent, adventum Domini sui, tamen maximum gaudium recolunt in praesentia ejus (Amalar., *De eccles. offic.*, IV, chap. 30). Adventus partim est laetitiae, quia Alleluja dicitur et cantus in jucunditate cantatur; partim tristitiae, quia *Te Deum, Gloria in excelsis* et *Ite Missa est* reticentur (Radulph. Tungren., *De canon. observantia*, prop. 16).

[20] Alleluja certis quidem diebus cantamus, sed omni die cogitamus. Si enim hoc verbo significatur laus Dei, etsi non in ore carnis, certe in ore cordis—"semper laus ejus in ore meo" Ps. 33:2 (S. August., *Enarrat. in Ps.*, 106:1).

mit that hymn of pure souls, the alleluja, to again cross our lips.[21]

The alleluja, that chant of the heavenly Jerusalem, ceases to resound during the season of Lent, which so deeply impresses our hearts with the consciousness of our earthly banishment and pilgrimage; the modest and tranquil melody of the Tract alone expresses our silent grief, our longing, our petition to be heard, our lament and hope.[22] Yet we lovingly cling to the jubilant Alleluja chant, and only reluctantly separate ourselves from it; and this we express at the Vespers on the Saturday preceding Septuagesima,[23] by repeating twice the alleluja after the *Benedicamus Domino* and *Deo gratias*.[24] And after that it resounds no more within the hallowed precincts of the sanctuary until it is again introduced with solemnity in the High Mass on the vigil of the feast of Easter. Then after the Epistle the alleluja forms the beginning of the Gradual chant, and is sung three times alternately by the priest and the choir, each time on a higher tone. As Easter dawns, not only the Tract but also the Gradual must now be laid aside; the joyful peal of the alleluja rings out again and again during Eastertide.

[21] Cf. S. Benedicti, *Regula*, chap. 15. Speciale caput s. Benedictus instituit de Alleluja, tanquam de voce divina vereque angelica nec nisi ad Angelis aut certe ab hominibus vitae puritate angelicos spiritus imitantibus decantanda (Martene, *Regul. commentata*, chap. 15).

[22] Cuncti tractus fletum et tristitiam in humilitate sonorum denuntiant. Tristitiae tempus exigit, ut Alleluja, quod laetantium carmen est, intermitteretur. Bene ergo tractus, qui interim pro Alleluja cantatur, altitudinem atque excellentiam gaudii, gravi succentu et modestis declinat incessibus (Rupert. Tuit., *De div. off.*, IV, chap. 6).

[23] According to the prescription of St. Benedict, the Alleluja was sung *usque ad caput Quadragesimae*, that is, until the first Sunday of Lent; this was customary in many order of monks (Benedictines and Cistercians) for a long period, and it is still in use in the Ambrosian rite. Thus writes Radulph of Rivo, Dean of Tungern (d. 1403): Benedictini et Ambrosiani servant Alleluja usque ad Dominicam Quadragesimae (*De canon, observantia*, prop. 16). The breviary ascribes the present practice to St. Gregory the Great: constituit, ut extra id tempus, quod continetur Septuagesima et Pascha, Alleluja diceretur.

[24] In the Middle Ages, antiphons, hymns, and sequences, filled with childlike naïveté and simplicity, were sung on the eve of Septuagesima as a farewell to the Alleluja. (Cf. Guéranger, *Le temps de la Septuagésime*, p. 121; Sicard., *Mitral.*, VI, chap. 1.)

The Greater Alleluja

The Hebrew word *alleluia* signifies literally: "Praise the Lord!" [25] And because it has a peculiar meaning and dignity, a force of expression and emphasis peculiarly its own, it has not been translated into other languages.[26] Thus in the cry of the alleluja are the tongues of all nations lifted up in unison to praise and adore God even here on earth with one voice and one sound, as will most perfectly be done in the world to come.[27] The blessed inhabitants of the heavenly Jerusalem, the angels and saints, sing without ceasing their endless alleluja, as already Tobias (13:21 f.) announced in prophetic vision: "The gates of Jerusalem shall be built of sapphire and of emerald, and all the walls thereof round about of precious stones. All its streets shall be paved with white and clean stones, and alleluja shall be sung in its streets." The beloved disciple describes a vision which he beheld in heaven: "After these things I heard, as it were,

---

[25] In view of the joy and consolation found in the pious death (*mors pia vel sacra*) of the Christian (*Beati mortui, qui in Domino moruntur*; Apoc. 14:13), the Alleluja formerly was sung even in the liturgy of the dead; this is still the case among the Greeks, who even during Lent do not omit the Alleluja. From Rome, St. Jerome writes (*Ad Oceanum, Epis.*, 77) that at the funeral obsequies of Fabiola "Psalms were sung and the allelujas resounding aloft re-echoed (*quatiebat*) throughout the gilded ceilings of the temples." Even outside of divine worship in the primitive times of Christianity, the chanting of alleluja was very common. Thus St. Jerome remarks that young children even had been trained to sing the alleluja *balbutiente lingua*, and that in the fields of Bethlehem this chant might everywhere be heard (*Quocunque te verteris, arator stivam tenens Alleluja decantat*). Seamen sang the alleluja, and the shores re-echoed the cry (*responsantibus ripis*; Sidon. Apollin., II, ep. 10). In many places it was customary by this word to call the inmates of the convent to the hours of common prayer.

[26] Illud advertendum, multo majorem vim apud Hebraeos habere hanc vocem "Alleluja" quam apud Latinos "Laudate Deum"; hoc est enim exhortantis vel excitantis ad Deo laudes reddendas: at Alleluja vim potius habet interjectionis quam verbi, et vehementem sonat affectum acclamantis prae gaudio et ex laude Dei exsultantis atque in jubilum vocemque laetitiae erumpentis (Bona, *De divin. Ps.*, chap. 16, §7, n.7). Alleluja vox hebraica est et sonat "laudate Dominum" vel "laus Deo," cum gaudii tamen laetitiaeque plenitudine (Carli, *Biblioth. liturg.*).

[27] Rectissime et pulcherrime generalis sanctae Ecclesiae mos inolevit, ut hoc divinae laudationis carmen propter reverentiam primae auctoritatis a cunctis per orbem fidelibus hebraea voce cantetur. Quod ideo fit, ut per talis consonantiam devotionis admoneatur Ecclesia, quia et nunc in una fidei confessione ac dilectione Christi consistere debeat, et ad illam in futuro patriam festinare, in qua nulla diversitas mentium, nulla est dissonantia linguarum (Beda Venerabilis, II, hom. 10).

THE ALLELUJA

the voice of much people in heaven, saying: Alleluja. Salvation and glory and power is to our God. . . . And I heard . . . the voice of many waters, and as the voice of great thunders, saying: Alleluja, for the Lord our God the Almighty hath reigned. Let us be glad and rejoice, and give glory to Him; for the marriage of the Lamb is come, and His wife hath prepared herself" (Apoc. 19:1, 6 f.). The souls of the blessed in heaven overflow with joy and happiness; hence their language becomes a canticle of praise. Thus they continue for all eternity in heaven what upon earth was their delight and felicity; for the Church sings in an antiphon: "When clothed with mortality, Thy saints, O Lord, cried out: Alleluja, alleluja, alleluja."

The literal meaning of the word alleluja (hallĕlū = praise, iah = God) is no longer clearly felt; in the mouth of the Church the word alleluja becomes transformed as a powerful cry of joy and exultation, and especially of happy Easter jubilation.[28] The Church on earth is midway between the Synagogue and the heavenly Jerusalem; accordingly the cry of the alleluja resounds more frequently in the divine worship than it did in the service of the Old Law, but yet not without interruption, as it peals forth in the Church triumphant. This cry of triumphant praise and salvation (Ps. 117:15), which descended from heaven to our poor earth, resounds in the

[28] Quinquagesima (*the fifty days of Eastertide*) ab ipso dominicae resurrectionis die inchoare et gaudiis potius laudibusque divinis quam jejuniis (Patres nostri) voluerunt esse celebrem, quatenus annuis ejus festis dulcius admoneremur, desiderium nostrum ad obtinenda festa, semper accendere fixumque tenere, quia non in tempore mortalitatis hujus, sed in aeternitate futurae incorruptionis vera nobis quaerenda felicitas, vera est invenienda solemnitas, ubi cessantibus cunctis languoribus tota in Dei visione ac laude vita geritur—juxta hoc quod propheta corde pariter et carne in Deum vivum exsultans ajebat: "Beati qui habitant in domo tua, Domine; in saecula saeculorum laudabunt te" (Ps. 83). Unde merito Quinquagesimae diebus in memoriam hujus nostrae quietissimae ac felicissimae actionis crebrius ac festivius Alleluja canere solemus (*ibid.*). Dum s. Gertrudis cum devotione et intentione omnes vires et sensus tam interiores quam exteriores extenderet, et se ad cantandum Matutinas in gloriam Dominicae resurrectionis praepararet, dum imponeretur Invitatorium Alleluja, dixit ad Dominum: "Doce me, instructor benignissime, quali devotione te laudare possim per Alleluja, quod toties in festo isto repetitur." Respondit Dominus: "Convenientissime poteris me per Alleluja collaudare in unione laudis supercoelestium qui per idem jugiter collaudant in coelis." Et adjecit Dominus: "Nota igitur quod in illa dictione Alleluja omnes vocales inveniuntur praeter solam vocalem *o*, quae dolorem signat, et pro illa duplicatur prima, scil. vocalis *a*." (S. Gertrud., *Legat. divinae pietatis*, IV, chap. 27).

liturgy principally from Holy Saturday until the Saturday after Pentecost; for this great octave of weeks is a joyful time. The celebration of holy Eastertide is nothing else than the triumph of the Redeemer and the redemption wrought by Him: the celebration of the victory over sin, death, and hell. All the liturgy refers to the eternal, blessed life of glory, upon which Christ has entered and which He has acquired for us. The resurrection and ascension of Christ, as well as the descent of the Holy Ghost, are sources of true and lasting joy, so that for a time we seem to forget the combats and labors of our earthly pilgrimage, and, full of joy and gratitude, we join in the alleluja of the citizens of heaven without ever becoming weary of repeating it again and again. The alleluja is the outpouring of that grand Easter joy with which our hearts are filled to overflowing; it is the festive song, the exultant cry over the happiness of our redemption.

What is the form of the Alleluja chant during Eastertide? Whereas the Gradual is still retained during Easter week, it is omitted on the Saturday before Low Sunday, and thenceforth until the feast of the Holy Trinity two allelujas are sung (as antiphons) followed by two verses, each with an alleluja. "The Gradual, as a canticle of mourning, is omitted during Eastertide, and the alleluja is repeated almost without measure, to note that salvation has been purchased for us, by the death and resurrection of Christ, and the way to eternal joys has been opened, where with all the blessed we shall sing to our Lord an eternal alleluja." [29]

On the feast of Christ's ascension, the Epistle and Gospel narrate the glorious entrance of the Redeemer into His eternal glory and beatitude. The intermediate chant likewise announces this triumphant and solemn entrance of Christ.

Alleluja, alleluja.	Alleluja, alleluja.
V. Ps. 46:6. Ascendit Deus in jubilatione, et Dominus in voce tubae. Alleluja.	V. Ps. 46:6. God hath ascended with jubilee, and the Lord with the sound of trumpet. Alleluja.
V. Ps. 67:18 f. Dominus in Sina in sancto; ascendens in altum, captivam duxit captivitatem. Alleluja.	V. Ps. 67:18 f. The Lord is among them in Sinai, in the holy place; He hath ascended on high, and hath led captivity captive. Alleluja.

[29] *Ein Vergissmeinnicht*, p. 78.

When our Lord entered victoriously and gloriously into the holy of holies of heaven, which is the true Sinai, the angelic choirs rejoiced that the King of Glory ascended on high leading captivity captive: bringing with Him the just of ancient times, whom He delivered as the prize of victory from limbo and introduced into the kingdom of eternal light as captives of His redeeming love.

That the Gradual is still continued during Easter week appears strange. The liturgy of the Easter vigil is already radiant with the splendor of light and fire, it resounds throughout with the joyous exultation of the Resurrection. During the entire week following Easter, the Church cries out: *Haec dies, quam fecit Dominus: exsultemus et laetemur in ea* ("This is the day, which the Lord hath made; let us rejoice and be glad therein"). (Ps. 117:24.) [30] During the first thousand years of Christianity the Church had a special reason for inserting the Gradual during the octave of Easter; this reason lay in the peculiar form of divine worship, which had reference especially to the newly baptized, who on Holy Saturday, by means of the laver of regeneration, had risen to a new life. During the entire week they were instructed in the truths and mysteries of the Christian religion, and went about wearing white robes all the while in token of the innocence and holiness acquired in baptism.[31] On Saturday the baptismal solemnities were ended and the white garment was laid aside.[32] Like the rest of the liturgical celebration, the Gradual of Easter week was also arranged with special regard to the neophytes,[33] but it is difficult to determine more minutely what was the purpose and meaning of the Gradual for the newly baptized.

[30] Merito cantatur hic versiculus in die Paschae tam frequenter, quoniam Christus, sol justitiae, candor lucis aeternae, lux lucis et fons luminis, qui erat in die Parasceves passionis caligine obscuratus atque in monumento lapideo tanquam densissima nube absconditus, in die Paschae de sepulcro glorificatus, candidus et rubicundus processit, illuminans mundum, noctem infidelitatis et tenebras ignorantiae de cordibus discipulorum ejiciens (Dion. Carthus., *In Ps.*, 117:23).

[31] In the *Gregorian Sacramentary* all the days of Easter week are designated as *feriae in Albis*.

[32] As the practice varied in the different churches, this did not take place in many localities until Sunday; hence we still have the name *Sabbatum in Albis* and *Dominica in Albis scil. depositis*. In ancient liturgical books the octave day of the feast of Easter is also called *Dominica post Albas (depositas)*.

[33] Graduale, quod est cantus laborantium in hac peregrinatione, jam dictum est ad hos dies resurrectionis usque in Pentecosten non pertinere, sed propter baptizatos per hanc hebdomadam in officiis additum esse (Rupert. Tuit., *De divin. offic.*, VIII, chap. 1).

The Sequence

On certain days the Alleluja's joyful praise [34] or the mournful melody of the Tract continues to resound in a prolonged canticle, which is universally called Sequence (*Sequentia*): the sentiment of joy or sorrow already awakened finds its greatest intensity and its fullest expression in the Sequence. How did the Sequences originate, and at what time were they inserted in the liturgy? Already before the ninth century it was customary to continue singing melodiously the last syllable of the alleluja without any further text. To this harmonious series of many notes to one syllable (a textless melody) different names were given: *Neuma, Jubilus, Jubilatio, Sequentia*.[35] Such *Neumae* (songs without words) are an exultation of the soul carried away with holy enthusiasm; they indicate the transcendent joy of the blessed, which is endless and unspeakable; for so surpassingly great and above all measure is the happiness of heaven, that the feeble language of poor mortals has not words to adequately express it.[36] In the ninth century various hymn verses began to be set to these joyful airs, and to them the name Sequence was then transferred.[37] The first composition of such chants, as well as their introduction into the celebration of Mass, is ascribed to a monk of St. Gall, St. Notker (*Balbulus*, the Stammerer; d. 912). Of him it is said: "at the time his equal was not to be found, he was a vessel of the Holy Ghost" and "favored by God with the gift of divine praise for the edification of the faithful." Such religious poems soon won great public praise and were extensively circulated; they increased to the extent that every Sunday, except during the season of Septuagesima,

---

[34] Post Alleluja Sequentia jubilatur (*Consuetud. Cluniac.*, I, chap. 43).

[35] This extension of the Alleluja according to Cardinal Bona (*Rer. liturg.*, II, vi, 5) is called Sequence, quia est quaedam veluti sequela et appendix cantici Alleluja, quae sine verbis post ipsum sequitur. Probably *sequentia* = regulated succession or series (cf. Boëth., *De Arithmetica*, I, chaps. 10 and 23).

[36] Pneumata, quae in Alleluja fiunt, jubilum significant, qui fit, cum mens aliquando sic in Deum afficitur et dulcedine quadam ineffabili liquescit, ut quod sentit, plene effari non possit. *Beatus populus, qui scit jubilationem* (Ps. 88), id est, qui saepe experitur et praegustat hanc dulcedinem, et sic interius movetur, ut quod praesentit nec dicere sufficiat nec possit tacere (Robert. Paulul., *De offic. eccl.*, II, chap. 19). Cf. S. August., *Enarrat. in Ps.*, 99:4.

[37] The other name for these hymns is *Prosa*. It is meant to indicate that in the Sequences neither metrical rules nor a homogeneous arrangement of stanzas are strictly observed, as is the case with actual hymns (cf. Clichtoveus, *Elucidator. eccles.*, IV).

and almost every feast had a Sequence. Among many inappropriate compositions, many excellent chants full of lyrical animation are to be found.

The revised Roman Missal has retained but five Sequences, which serve to distinguish particular feasts (Easter, Pentecost, Corpus Christi, and the two feasts of the Seven Dolors of the Blessed Virgin) and the Requiem Masses. Even though the authors of the Sequences cannot always be assigned with certainty,[38] these hymns "proved how completely in those golden ages of devotion men might be the tongues, so to speak, of the Church, and express her holiest feelings."[39] The five Sequences of our missal belong incontestably to the most glorious and most sublime creations of the hymnology of the Church; they are variegated but equally fragrant blossoms "of Christian poetry, of that poetry, forsooth, which sings on earth the mysteries of heaven and prepares us for the canticles of eternity" (Guéranger); each of them has its peculiar beauties and excellencies.

a) The Easter Sequence, *Victimae paschali*, which in the Middle Ages found numerous imitations, is a *dulce canticum dramatis*, a sweet dramatical chant, in the form of a dialogue, that sings the praises of the glorious resurrection of the Saviour. In it the Christians are exhorted to offer, out of gratitude, sacrifices of praise to our true Easter Lamb, Jesus Christ; for Christ, the Lamb of God, was immolated to purchase and redeem the sheep: Christ, the Good Shepherd, innocence itself, laid down His life for His flock, that He might reconcile the guilty to His Father. Death and life struggled together, engaged in a marvelous combat; but now the Prince of life, who had died, reigns in the imperishable life of glory. Then Mary Magdalen is appealed to as an eyewitness of the Resurrection: "Tell us, O Mary, what hast thou seen in the way?" She testifies to the Lord's resurrection: "I saw the tomb of the living one and the glory of the

---

[38] In all probability the Easter Sequence, *Victimae paschali*, is erroneously ascribed to St. Peter Damian (d. 1072); in an Einsiedeln manuscript (Schubiger, *Sängerschule von St. Gallen*, p. 91 ff.) of the eleventh century, the court chaplain of Conrad II, Wipo of Burgundy, is mentioned as its author. The Pentecost Sequence, *Veni Sancte Spiritus*, is said to have been composed by King Robert of France (d. 1031), or by Innocent III (d. 1216). St. Thomas (d. 1274) composed the Sequence for the feast of Corpus Christi. It is said that the *Stabat Mater* was composed by Jacopone da Todi (d. about 1306), and the *Dies irae* by Thomas of Celano (d. about 1255).

[39] Wiseman, "On Prayer and Prayer-Books," *Essays*, II, 150.

resuscitated; as witnesses of this, I beheld the angels, the napkin and the linen cloths." And triumphantly she adds: "Christ, my hope, is risen," and she announces to the apostles that the risen one will go before them into Galilee. Upon this assertion follows the joyful acknowledgment of the faithful: "We know that Christ is truly risen from the dead." This Easter hymn concludes with the fervent petition, that the King of Glory, who has overcome the sting of death, may have mercy on us.

b) The Sequence for Pentecost, *Veni sancte Spiritus*, can have come but from a heart wholly inflamed with the fire of the Holy Ghost. It is an incomparable hymn, breathing of the sweetness of paradise. This Pentecostal hymn contains a wealth of deep thought and affections, in a form remarkable as much for beauty as for brevity.[40] The entire hymn is an ardent and devout supplication to the Holy Ghost, in which, on the one hand, His mysterious imparting of grace is depicted in a manner uncommonly tender and charming, and, on the other hand, the wants of our earthly pilgrimage is represented in a manner exceedingly simple and touching. The Holy Ghost is called by the Church: "The finger of God's right hand," that is, the treasurer and dispenser of all the gifts and graces which Christ has merited for us. But He not only gives us His gifts, but He comes Himself and dwells in a sanctified soul as in His living temple. How beautifully expressed is the strong and ardent desire for the joyful coming of the Holy-Ghost into the soul, in the four consecutive invocations: *Veni:* "Come," O Holy Ghost. "O most blessed Light," continues the Church in her prayer to the Holy Ghost, "fill the inmost hearts of Thy faithful! Without Thy will there is nothing in man, nothing harmless." And because our wretchedness is unspeakably great and manifold, the Church goes on imploring for her children: "Wash what is soiled, water what is parched, heal what is wounded. Bend what is stiff, warm what is cold, guide what is astray." As at the beginning, she repeats at the close with equal ardor and earnestness four consecutive times the

---

[40] Omni commendatione superior est, tum ob miram ejus suavitatem cum facilitate apertissima, tum ob gratam ejus brevitatem cum ubertate et copia sententiarum, tum denique ob concinnam ejus in contextu venustatem, qua opposita inter se aptissimo nexu compacta cernuntur. Crediderimque facile, auctorem ipsum (quisquis is fuerit) cum hanc contexuit orationem, coelesti quadam dulcedine fuisse perfusum interius, qua Spiritu sancto auctore tantam eructavit verbis adeo succinctis suavitatem (Clichtov., *loc. cit.*).

petition: *Da:* "Give," O Holy Ghost. "Give to Thy faithful confiding in Thee, Thy sevenfold gifts. Give them the merit of virtue; give a happy end; give them never-ending joy." [41]

c) The *Lauda Sion*, the Sequence for the feast of Corpus Christi, belongs to those "supernatural hymns uniting the strictness of dogma with a sweetness and a melody more like echoes of heaven than mere poetry of earth." [42] St. Thomas, the angel of the schools, is the author of this hymn of praise to the adorable sacrifice and sacrament of the altar; he reveals therein the profound learning of a cherub as well as the inflamed love of a seraph; with a clearness and a penetration of thought equaled only by ardor of feeling he unveils the hidden, unfathomable riches, beauties, and sweetnesses of the Holy Eucharist, which is our heaven in this vale of tears and sin.

One of the most useful literary productions of St. Thomas, in which the Church even now takes great delight, is the office of the Blessed Sacrament, which on the occasion of the institution of the feast of Corpus Christi, Pope Urban IV engaged St. Thomas to compose. Not only are the psalms and antiphons, lessons and responsories chosen by him replete with the most beautiful and fruitful references to the mystery of the altar, but also the hymns composed by him, as the *Pange lingua, Sacris Solemniis, Verbum supernum* and *Lauda Sion*, are full of fervor and devotion and pearls beyond price in the hymnal treasury of the Church. The same grand mind that, like the whale, dived down into the lowest depths of the sea of Christian speculation and, like the lion, destroyed with fiery strength the errors against faith, soared like the eagle into the greatest heights of Christian poetry. No element pertaining to the Deity was foreign to him.[43]

---

[41] To this Sequence also apply the beautiful words, written by Denis the Carthusian in reference to the hymn *Veni Creator Spiritus:* Hunc hymnum cum omni puritate et elevatione mentis ad superdulcissimum Spiritum sanctum cantemus. Cumque nihil impedit nos a desiderata plenitudine susceptionis Spiritus sancti et exuberantia charismatum ejus, nisi negligentiae nostrae, distractiones corporeae et vitia, praesertim sensuales affectus, satagamus haec omnia evitare ac erubescamus. Dominum illum majestatis immensae, hospitem sanctitatis atque munditiae penitus infinitae, invitare ad visitandum, ingrediendum et inhabitandum corda nostra adhuc imparata ac sordida. Menta ergo contrita, recollecta, affectuosa invocemus, laudemus, adoremus Spiritum sanctum. Toto corde afficiamur ad eum, cujus omnia attributa, proprietates et nomina dulcedinem redolent, amabilissima exstant consolationemque largiuntur (*Hymn. aliq. veter. eccles. Enarratio*).

[42] Faber, *The Blessed Sacrament*, p. 14.

[43] Laurent, *Hagiolog.*, II, 388.

Incomparably beautiful and heartfelt are the concluding words, wherein the Church prays to the Saviour as the Good Shepherd concealed in the Sacrament, that He would here below guide the sheep purchased with His precious blood, protect them, and finally lead them to the ever-green pastures of paradise.

> O Good Shepherd, our true bread,
> Jesus, mercy on Thy flock;
> Deign to feed us, to protect us,
> Deign to make us see Thy blessings
>   In the land of living men.
>
> Thou who knowest and canst all things,
> Who here feedest us mortal men,
> Grant that we may be Thy guests;
> Make us coheirs and companions
>   Of Thy saintly citizens.

d) How touching is the *Stabat Mater*, this dolorous lamentation on the Sorrowful Mother of God! At first the Sequence depicts the overwhelming anguish of the Virgin Mother. She stood at the foot of the cross wholly plunged in grief (*dolorosa*) and bathed in tears (*lacrymosa*) while her Son was shedding all His blood on the cross. "Who, unmoved, can behold her bewailing her Son?" Therefore the loving soul implores the Sorrowful Mother that she would permit us to realize and share her grief. "Holy Mother, grant that the wounds of the Crucified may be deeply impressed in my heart. . . . Grant that I may be wounded by His wounds, that I may be inebriated with His Cross and with the blood of thy Son." Finally there follows a supplication to Christ for the full fruit of His redeeming sufferings: "When my body shall die, then grant that the glory of paradise be given to my soul." [44]

[44] The *Stabat mater dolorosa* is outwardly simple in form and versification: and this, indeed, is precisely the mark of true poetry, which with little outward show, almost unadorned, attains the highest object, and understands how to place in the most simple form the richest contents. If we abstract from its form in order to briefly grasp the contents of the beautiful Sequence, we observe that they also are very simply arranged. The first, second, and fourth stanzas in a few words unfold the historical event which took place beneath the Cross, according to St. John (19:25) and St. Luke (23:35). The remaining stanzas, on the contrary, contain reflections, affections, petitions and resolutions, that the passion and death of Christ may, in view of the sorrows of His holy Mother, not be devoid of fruit for us, but may impart

e) The grandest, most magnificent hymn of the Church is the chant for the funeral rites, the world-renowned and ever-admired *Dies irae*, which is remarkable for its majesty, sublimity, and affective power, and its language of the most childlike simplicity and expressiveness; through its realistic illustration and poetical description, its words fall upon the soul as claps of thunder. Very appropriate to its contents is also the choice of the three-versed stanza, which has a touching pause in its movement. As to contents and form, this hymn is a perfect work of art; the judgment of all connoisseurs designates it as the most sublime composition that human genius ever produced in this style of poetry. The terrors of the general judgment, before which all the vain pride of this world shall sink into dust and ashes, are depicted in this chant for the dead in lines of such dread sublimity and grand simplicity that the soul spontaneously imagines herself removed to the gates of eternity and already beforehand feels penetrated with the woes and dread of that day of tribulation and anguish, of lamentation and misery.

> Then what terror shall befall us
> When the Judge shall come to call us,
> To judge all things most rigorously.
>
> Wondrous sound the trumpet flingeth,
> Through earth's sepulchers it ringeth,
> All before the throne it bringeth.
>
> Death and nature are amazed
> When the creatures are upraised
> To make answer to their Judge.
>
> When the Judge shall then be seated,
> All that's hid shall be revealed;
> Nothing unavenged remaineth.

The contemplation of so terrifying a spectacle draws from sinful man the exclamation:

---

to us vigor in life, comfort in suffering, and in the end be to us the source of bliss. . . . Happily and beautifully does the form bear out the context in this poem. The solemn, sonorous beginning places us at once in the mournfulness of the occasion. How resigned is the language in the resolutions, how gentle in the petitions, how melodious when announcing in advance the happiness of paradise, in the last stanza in which the soul longs for heaven! (Kröll, *Kanzelreden*, II, 870 f.)

> What shall I, poor wretch, be pleading?
> Who for me be interceding,
> When the just are mercy needing?

There is nothing left for him to do but to have recourse to the mercy of the "King of dreadful majesty." This is done in the following humble, childlike, and trustful appeal for grace and favor:

> Think, kind Jesus! My salvation
> Caused Thy wondrous Incarnation;
> Leave me not to reprobation.
>
> Faint and weary Thou has sought me,
> On the Cross of suffering bought me;
> Shall such grace in vain be brought me?
>
> Righteous Judge of vindication,
> Grant Thy gift of absolution
> Ere that day of retribution.

The concluding petition is for all the faithful departed: "Kind Jesus, Lord, grant them rest."

The insertion of the last two Sequences (*Stabat Mater* and *Dies irae*) in their respective Masses belongs to a later period and is to be regarded as a departure from the general rule; for, from earliest times, sequences were always festive and joyful chants which followed the Alleluja and replaced the sounds of jubilant praise without text. The *Dies irae* always follows the Tract, while the *Stabat Mater* follows either the Tract or the Alleluja verse. To both sequences the words of Wiseman are applicable: "Even when the Church mourns, she must have her song—attuned in a deeper key, but still enlivening sorrow itself with hope." [45] Singing always introduces a cheerful, refreshing element into the divine service, even though the service bears the grave character of a holy grief.[46]

---

[45] *Op. cit.*, p. 157.

[46] Defunctorum Missae et neumate et ipso Alleluja carent, et nihilominus Sequentia quadam, quae simul maeroris et aliqualis gaudii argumentum est, easdem condecorat Ecclesia in symbolum consolationis, quam defunctorum animae inter purgatorii gemitus habent super securitate de sua aeterna beatitudine, praxis instar, quam servat Ecclesia in Sabbato sancto, in quo tractum unit cum Alleluja, ut semiplenam laetitiam ostendat ac paschale gaudium in spe proxima. Quae Sequentia etiam alia habet commoda, majus scilicet defunctorum suffragium et commiserationem ac nostram admonitionem super novissimis (Cavalieri, III, x, 6).

THE SEQUENCE

If we compare the varied form and composition of the chant intervening between the Epistle and Gospel, we cannot but admire with what refined delicacy the Church understands how to set forth the manifold dispositions and shades of the soul's interior life, from the most profound sorrow to the height of joy. Thus the soul becomes ever more worthily prepared and disposed to receive the word of God, now about to be announced in the Gospel.[47]

[47] Ideo non ab apostolica vel evangelica lectione, quod majus esse constat, Missa inchoatur, sed potius canendo et psallendo, quatenus dulcedo suavitatis corda audientium prius demulceat, et sic post modulationem suavis cantilenae in spiritualibus rebus populus per compunctionem mentis intentus, salutifera Evangelii verba ardenti affectu suscipiat (Pseudo-Alcuin., *De divin offic.*, chap. 40). The Alleluja chant denotes the joy of the heart in view of the glad tidings of the Gospel. Alleluja ante lectionem evangelicam a cantore interponitur, ut laudetur ab omnibus, cujus gratia salvantur omnes, quasi dicat. Quia verba Evangelii salutem conferentia mox audituri estis, laudate Dominum, cujus beneficio hanc gratiam percipere meruistis (*ibid.*).

CHAPTER XXIV

THE GOSPEL

THE reading of the Gospel constitutes the highest point of the first part of the Mass. The word Gospel is here employed in the strictest sense, and according to this interpretation it designates a pericope (περικοπή), that is, a part or fragment selected for liturgical purposes from the four Gospels. In the New Testament, as a rule, "gospel" has a more comprehensive meaning. *Evangelium* (εὐαγγέλιον) means good or joyful tidings. Joyful tidings in its sublimest sense is the entire revelation of God through Christ; it is the fullness of all truth and grace, which Christ brought into the world. These joyful tidings of salvation and peace resounded first from the mouth of angels to the devout shepherds of Bethlehem: "Behold, I bring you good tidings (*evangelizo*) of great joy, that shall be to all the people; for this day is born to you a Saviour, who is Christ the Lord, in the city of David" (Luke 2:10 f.). Our Saviour Himself testifies that the Holy Ghost anointed and sent Him to announce good tidings to the poor (*evangelizare pauperibus*), to heal the contrite of heart, to preach deliverance to the captives, and give sight to the blind (Luke 4:18). Justly, therefore, is the work of redemption called the gospel, that is, good and joyful tidings.[1] For is it not a joy to be delivered from the bondage of sin and Satan, to have been rescued from the depth of misery, the abyss of endless torment and insupportable darkness? Is it not an ecstatic joy to be blessed with the fullness of peace, to have God in human form redeem us and from on high visit us and live among us? The redemption which Christ accomplished shed immeasurable blessings upon the earth; for the poor human race it became an endless source of unutterable joy and divine consolation.

---

[1] Lex nova est perfecte et simpliciter evangelium, i.e. bona annuntiatio, quia annuntiat maxima bona, scil. coelestia, spiritualia et aeterna (S. Thom., *In ep. ad Galat.*, chap. 1, lect. 2).

THE GOSPEL

How precious, therefore, must the holy Gospels be to us, in which are recorded by God's own hand the wonderful deeds and mysteries of redemption! The words of the Gospel are words of eternal wisdom, of the uncreated Word Himself, who in the simplicity of human language and human actions, in parables intelligible to children, but also publicly and without figures, has taught the plenitude of divine truth and science. As in the beginning He called into existence the whole natural world, so He likewise gave being to the whole supernatural world of Christianity by short and simple words, but words full of infinite meaning and creative power. The value of the Gospels consists principally in the fact that they give us a perfect, living picture of the person, of the conversation and actions, of the life and passion of our divine Saviour, by the description of chosen eyewitnesses and, what is infinitely more significant, through the inspiration of the Holy Ghost. Grace flowed from the lips of Jesus, and a divine beauty transfigured His countenance; now in the Gospel we continue to hear "the sweetness of His words" and to look at His face full of heavenly benignity and majesty.

The readings from the Gospels at Mass serve not merely for instruction and edification, but are at the same time a liturgical action by which religious veneration and homage are paid to the word and truth of God, hence to God Himself, who is present in His word as our teacher. This explains the customs, full of meaning, which surround the reading of the Gospel, especially at the solemn celebration of Mass. Next to the body and blood of the Lord in the Blessed Sacrament and the grace of the Holy Ghost, the Church esteems nothing so highly as the word of God in the Gospel. To the Gospel are paid the honors of a divine service: when it is solemnly chanted, it is surrounded with the splendor of lights and the fragrance of incense.

1. Liturgical preparation for announcing the Gospel. To announce the words of eternal life at the Holy Sacrifice, is an exalted and sublime office. Since the fourth century the solemn reading of the Gospel at divine service belongs to the deacon or to the priest, but both must specially prepare themselves that they may be worthy to now lend, as it were, their heart and mouth to the Lord for the announcement of His heavenly truth. Suitable preparation for announcing the divine word consists in a perfect purification and sanctification of heart and mouth. Indeed, the soul should not only be free from all sin, from all base, earthly, and selfish motives, but should moreover, be sanctified by a blessing from above. For this purpose two prayers are now recited: the one for purification, the other for the bestowal of the blessing. The priest stands in the middle of the altar; raising his eyes aloft, as if "to the mountain whence assistance comes," he soon lowers them again; with body profoundly inclined and with hands joined, but without resting them on the altar, he prays:

Munda cor meum ac labia mea, omnipotens Deus, qui labia Isaiae Prophetae calculo mundasti ignito: ita me tua grata miseratione dignare mundare, ut sanctum Evangelium tuum digne valeam nuntiare. Per Christum Dominum nostrum. Amen.	Cleanse my heart and my lips, O almighty God, who didst cleanse the lips of the prophet Isaias with a burning coal: vouchsafe so to cleanse me by Thy gracious mercy, that I may be able worthily to proclaim Thy holy Gospel. Through Christ our Lord. Amen.
Jube, Domine, benedicere.	Give me Thy blessing, O Lord.
Dominus sit in corde meo, et in labiis meis, ut digne et competenter annuntiem Evangelium suum. Amen.	The Lord be in my heart and on my lips, that I may worthily and in a becoming manner announce His holy Gospel. Amen.

First comes the petition for interior purification (*Munda cor meum*). The Fathers frequently mention that the soul should receive the word and truth of God with a purity similar to that required for receiving the Eucharist. Wisdom enters not into an unclean soul nor does it dwell in a body subject to sin (Wisd. 1:4). How difficult it is to walk undefiled on the dusty path of this earthly life! The heart is not only sullied by sin, but its purity is likewise dimmed by passion, distraction, earthly inclinations, and worldly attachments. Hence the humble petition of the priest, that the Lord would purify his heart; for only a stainless heart is a vessel worthy of divine truth and wisdom. This purity of the inner man is the first and principal requisite; but that is not all: the lips also which pronounce words so holy must be pure. "For the lips of the priest shall keep knowledge, and they shall seek the law at his mouth; because he is the angel of the Lord of hosts" (Mal. 2:7). The mouth of the priest is consecrated for heavenly mysteries, hence no profane sound should proceed therefrom. But with what ease and levity does not the talkative tongue sin, if we endeavor not with all our might to master it. Incalculable is the multitude of the sins of the tongue. Hence the priest is fully aware how necessary it is that his lips be purified anew from all stains of idle, worldly, and sinful talk. Thus for interior and exterior cleansing the priest prays before he begins to announce God's word.

This petition has its foundation in a symbolical reference to a mysterious event in the life of the prophet Isaias (6:5-10). He relates his call, consecration, and mission to exercise the office of a prophet. In a marvelous vision he beheld the glory of the God of hosts and heard the canticle of the angels praising Him; filled with holy awe, he acknowledged and confessed his sinfulness and unworthiness. Then a seraph took from the heavenly altar of incense a live coal, touched with it the lips of the Prophet, saying these words: "Behold! this hath touched thy lips, and thy iniquities shall be taken away, and thy sin shall be cleansed." Then only did Isaias say: "Lo, here am I, send me!" The live coal in the Prophet's vision is a symbol of grace and of its efficacy. Grace is like a spiritual fire which so consumes and destroys all earthly dross in the soul that it becomes more brilliant and radiant than the finest gold and silver. The fire of the grace of the Holy Ghost not only purifies the heart, but also enlightens the mind with exalted wisdom and inflames the soul with heavenly love.

"Give me Thy blessing, O Lord." [2] The blessing asked for is two-

---

[2] *Jubere* in this formula, much used in the liturgy, in order to express the petition with more humble modesty and reverence, has the signification of *velle* or *dignari* = deign. The deacon says: *Jube Domne benedicere*, because he does not ask the blessing immediately from God, the absolute Master (*Dominus*), but from the priest (*Domnus*). The name *Dominus* was given to God the Lord alone, while the abbreviated word *Domnus* was a distinguished title bestowed upon personages high in authority. In the Litany of the Saints the pope is called *Domnus Apostolicus*. From *Domnus* originated the form Dom and Don. Also among the Greeks there is a difference between Κύριος (= *Dominus, Deus*) and Κύρις (= *domnus*). (Cf. Bona, *De Psalm. divin.*, chap. 16, § 14, n. 5.) Sacerdos ad altare ratione excellentissimi ministerii, quod exercet, aptus non videtur alium quam Deum in superiorem agnoscere, et ideo sicut ratione pontificiae dignitatis Papae et episcopalis Episcopo, dum ad Matutinum in choro lectionem legunt, datum est dicere Jube Domine et non Domne, ita idipsum datum est sacerdoti celebranti (Cavalieri, II, chap. 34).

fold: that the Lord would be in the purified heart as well as on the purified lips of the priest. If the Lord be in the heart of the priest, then will he worthily (*digne*) announce the tidings of salvation, that is, with recollection and attention, with a holy joy and zeal, with profound humility and reverence. If the Lord be on his lips, then will the priest announce the Gospel competently (*competenter*), that is, in a proper manner, clearly and distinctly, with power and energy, so that all may be edified.[3] Prepared in this manner, the priest is a pure channel which receives within itself the salutary waters of the Gospel and then conveys them into the hearts of the faithful.

2. **Delivery of the Gospel.** After the above preparatory prayers the priest goes from the middle of the altar to the Gospel side, where the missal must be placed so that the back of the book is not parallel with the back of the altar, but is turned diagonally toward the corner of the altar, so that the priest, when reading the Gospel, is half turned toward the people (*semiversus*) and looks northward. In this position the priest reads or sings the Gospel; of which the beginning, middle, and conclusion are now to be considered.

a) The opening formula comprises the mutual salutation and the announcement of the Gospel to be read. What graces do priest and people mutually wish each other in this place by the well known salutation, *Dominus vobiscum: Et cum spiritu tuo?* Here there is question that the word of God be correctly understood, that it be embraced with faith and faithfully followed. For the Lord says by the prophet: "As the rain and snow come down from heaven and return no more thither, but soak the earth and water it and make it to spring and give seed to the sower and bread to the eater: so shall My word be which shall go forth from My mouth; it shall not return to Me void, but it shall do whatsoever I please, and shall prosper in the things for which I sent it" (Isa. 55:10 f.). It does not suffice that the sound of the word penetrates our ears; but it is more necessary that the Spirit of truth, together with His unction and heavenly light of grace, should teach us interiorly, in order that we may be

---

[3] Monendi sunt sacerdotes, ut internae devotioni etiam externam conjungant, ita ut majori pausa et distinctione, quam alia, quae clara voce dicuntur, Evangelium pronuntient, quia est verbum Verbi et sapientia incarnatae Sapientiae. Et quidem praemissis tot diligentiis et petita attentione populi valde indecens esset, sanctissima verba praecipitare (Quarti, *Comm. in Rubr. Miss.*, II, vi, 2).

able to understand and love the wonderful sublimity and unfathomable riches of the Gospel. The Spirit of God, with His mysterious power, also moves and attracts us that we may unreservedly abandon ourselves to the divine word in thought, will, and deed. A lively, clear, and ardent faith is a precious gift which God bestows on us, and, at the same time, a virtue which we must acquire and increase. By the mutual salutation, therefore, priest and people implore for each other the grace of the Lord to love, embrace, and obey the divine truths with a cheerful faith.[4]

The Gospel passage to be read is announced in simple words. If the pericope begins with the first words of one of the four Gospels, which is rarely the case, the heading is, for instance: *Initium sancti Evangelii secundum Matthaeum* ("The beginning of the holy Gospel according to St. Matthew").[5] If the extract to be read is taken from the context that follows the beginning of the Gospel, which as a rule is the case, then the announcement runs thus: *Sequentia*[6] *sancti Evangelii secundum Matthaeum* ("Continuation of the Holy Gospel, according to St. Matthew"). The acolyte thereupon answers in the name of the people: *Gloria tibi, Domine* ("Glory be to Thee, O Lord"). When the good tidings are announced, how can we do otherwise than break forth in words of praise to our Lord? He has revealed Himself to us in an altogether incomparable manner, preferring us to millions who still remain in darkness.[7]

---

[4] Doctrina sine adjuvante gratia, quamvis infundatur auribus, ad cor nunquam descendit: foris quidem perstrepit, sed interius nil proficit. Tunc autem Dei sermo infusus auribus ad cordis intima pervenit, quando Dei gratia mentem interius ut intelligat tangit. Sicut enim quosdam flamma caritatis suae Deus illuminat, ut vitaliter sapiant, ita quosdam frigidos torpentesque deserit, ut sine sensu persistant (S. Isid., *Sentent.*, III, x, 1 f.).

[5] The headings of the Gospels are very ancient, but they are of ecclesiastical origin. They appropriately express that one and the same Gospel of Jesus Christ was written under the inspiration of the Holy Ghost by the Evangelists in a fourfold manner. This is comprised in the little word *secundum* = according. Evangelistae, quum sint quatuor, non tam quatuor Evangelia, quam unum quatuor (Quartetto) varietate pulcherrima consonum ediderunt (Beda Vener., *Prooem. in Luc.*).

[6] Vox *Sequentia* non singularis est numeri, sed pluralis, significatque ea, quae sequuntur in textu Evangelistae (Guyet., *Heortolog.*, III, chap. 27, q. 2).

[7] Respondet populus: *Gloria tibi, Domine.* In Evangelio agitur de gloria Dei et nostra, scil. quod diabolum vicit et victor ad gloriam Dei Patris ascendit; quod nos redemit et nobis majora promisit. Audientes igitur Evangelii mentionem, nos ad Orientem vertimus et exclamamus in laudem Creatoris:

At the words *Sequentia* (or *Initium*) *sancti Evangelii*, the priest with his thumb imprints a cross on the first words of the Gospel passage, then on his forehead, mouth, and breast. The sign of the cross is made on the book [8] to express that the whole Gospel, the whole doctrine and work of salvation, is comprised and contained in the one mystery of the Cross, the bloody sacrificial death of the God-man, undergone for the redemption of the world. Hence St. Paul calls the Gospel simply "the word of the Cross," and although he had been taken up to the third heaven, where he saw and heard things not given to man to utter, yet he wished to know and to preach nothing else than Jesus Christ and Him crucified: his only glory he sought in the Cross of Christ, in which is our salvation, life, and resurrection. The mystery of the Cross, which is to the world a scandal and a folly but to us the power and wisdom of God, includes in itself all other mysteries of Christianity. The Cross shows forth the love, wisdom, and providence of God; it teaches all Christian virtues: renunciation of the world and of self, humility, obedience, faith, patience, hope, love of God and of our neighbor. The cross with which the Gospel in the missal is signed, is intended to remind us of all this.

On their forehead, mouth, and breast [9] the priest and the faithful make the sign of the cross, in order to express, by this beautiful symbolism, that they wish to bear and preserve the doctrine of the Cross in their mind, on their lips, and in their heart, and that they are not ashamed to proclaim openly and joyfully to the world, both

---

Gloria tibi, Domine, quasi dicamus: Quod in Evangelio praedicatur, et nos credimus et speramus, nobis proficiat, nobis eveniat, sine fine permaneat. Et exinde: Non nobis, Domine, non nobis, sed nomini tuo inest et inerit gloria, et ita populus glorificat Deum qui misit nobis verbum salutis et fecit redemptionem plebis suae, juxta quod in Act. Apost. (11:18) dicitur: Et glorificaverunt Deum (Sicard., *Mitral.*, III, chap. 4).

[8] This is not a *benedictio libri*, but merely a symbolical *signatio* of it. Libro crucem imprimit sacerdos, tanquam si dixerit: hic est liber Crucifixi (Beleth., *Ration.*, chap. 39).

[9] The *Ecloga Amalarii Abb. in Ord. Rom.* mentions here only the *signatio frontis*, and the *Ordo Rom. II*, n. 8, has in addition the *signatio pectoris*. But already Honorius of Autun wrote in the first half of the twelfth century: Per cordis signationem fides verbi accipitur; per oris signationem confessio Christi intelligitur; per frontis signationem operatio Evangelii exprimitur (*Gemma animae*, I, 23). In pectoris signo fides et in oris signo confessio, in frontis signo intelligitur operatio, quasi dicat: Signo me in fronte, ore et pectore, quia crucem Christi non erubesco, sed praedico et credo (Sicard. [d. 1215], *loc. cit.*).

by word and deed, the glory of the cross of Christ. For the priest, who is to preach Christ crucified, this sign of the cross is at the same time a serious admonition to lead a life hidden with Christ in God, to be attached with Christ to the cross, and to be crucified to the world. Our Lord Himself once revealed to Blessed Angela of Foligno that the word of the Gospel penetrates powerfully to the soul only when it proceeds from lips reddened with His precious blood. But since the cross is not only a significant sign but also an efficacious one, it can here be considered principally as a protection against the Evil One, to prevent his coming and snatching the seed of the divine word out of our hearts.[10]

b) As has been said above, each Gospel is selected with regard to the ecclesiastical year with its cycle of feasts and holy seasons. Indeed, the Gospel excels in meaning and importance all the other variable parts of the Mass formula;[11] it gives most perfect expression to the fundamental thought of the day's celebration. The Gospel is to be explained in harmony with the other portions of the Mass which are to be read and sung; but in order that the true and entire sense may be obtained, the Gospel must often be explained allegorically or in a liturgically mystical manner.[12]

The prominent position and sublime signification of the Gospel is clearly evident in the ecclesiastical rite. First, the Gospel is read

---

[10] In order to obtain this grace, they formerly signed themselves again with the holy cross after the reading of the Gospel. Perlecto Evangelio, iterum se signo sanctae crucis populus munire festinat (*Ordo Rom. II*, n. 8). Debet quilibet post Evangelium se signo crucis munire contra diabolum, qui Evangelio lecto confestim insidiatur, ne capiat in nobis sermo (*lest the word of God may take root in our hearts*). (Sicard., *loc. cit.*)

[11] Sanctum Evangelium principale est omnium, quae dicuntur ad Missae officium. Sicut enim caput praeeminet corpori, et illi cetera membra subserviunt, sic Evangelium toti officio praeeminet et omnia, quae ibi leguntur vel canuntur, intellectuali ratione illi consentiunt (Rupert. Tuitiens., *De divin. offic.*, chap. 37).

[12] Exaggerated is the assertion, that "the Evangelical pericope appears as a pure, bright precious stone, in which the idea of each day is depicted in wonderful clearness" (Kindhäusser); for frequently the *sensus accommodatius* or the mystical reference of the Gospel to the mysterious life of the Church is not so clear to the eye, but deeply hidden, and, therefore, it is not always easily discerned. If we would at all times adhere merely to the literal explanation, then the pericope would often be too superficially conceived, and its signification in the ecclesiastical year would not be grasped according to the sense of the Church. This, for example, applies to many of the Sunday Gospels after Pentecost.

on the right side of the altar, as the right side is generally regarded as the more honorable. As the churches and altars, in consequence of a very ancient custom, were usually built to face the east, the book on the Gospel side is so placed as to be turned toward the north,[13] and in this there is a mystical meaning.[14] For as the beautiful life of nature in the warm sunny south is a symbol of the higher life of grace, so the dark and frigid north is considered to have an evil significance and to symbolize the kingdom of the Evil One.[15] The dormant, snowbound regions of the North, enchained in the death grip of winter's frosts, represent in a suitable manner the dreary and lifeless condition of heathenism. But now the Gospel is read toward the north as a sign that the good tidings of heaven have changed the icy night and coldness of mankind into the mild warmth of summer, and awakened them to an imperishable spiritual spring of grace and mind.[16] The Gospel's bright rays have changed rugged winter into gentle spring.

In like manner, the fact that all present stand when listening to the Gospel, has a deep significance.[17] This rite probably dates from

---

[13] Formerly the deacon read the Gospel looking toward the South (*ad quam partem viri solent confluere*). Thus it is prescribed in the very ancient *Ordo Rom. II*, n. 8. Still Honorius of Autun (*Gemma animae*, I, chap. 22) already in the beginning of the twelfth century remarks that the deacon, when reading the Gospel, should turn no longer *secundum Ordinem* to the South, but *secundum solitum morem* to the North.

[14] The assertion is erroneous, that the ordinance of reading the Gospel at the right side of the altar has its origin exclusively in a reason of necessity; in the circumstance, namely, that the left side of the altar must be left free for the sacrificial gifts, that is, for the presentation of the sacrificial elements. For this, it would suffice merely to remove the missal after the reading of the Gospel. The present rubric has its origin, therefore, in a higher or mystical reason.

[15] Isa. 14:13; Jer. 1:14; 4:6.

[16] Verba Evangelii levita pronuntiaturus contra septentrionem faciem vertit, ut ostendat verbum Dei et annuntiationem Spiritus Sancti contra eum dirigi, qui semper Spiritui Sancto contrarius existit et in nullo ei communicat. . . . Sicut enim per austrum, qui ventus est calidus et leniter flat, Spiritus Sanctus designatur, qui corda quae tangit ad amorem dilectionis inflammat, ita et per aquilonem, qui durus et frigidus est, diabolus intelligitur, qui eos quos possidet ab amore caritatis atque dilectionis torpentes et frigidos reddit. Quod enim per aquilonem diabolus designetur, ostendit propheta dicens: O Lucifer, qui dicebas in corde tuo: "Sedebo in lateribus aquilonis" (Isa. 14:13). (Pseudo-Alcuin., *De divin. Offic.*, chap. 40.)

[17] In the *Liber Pontificalis* we read that the holy Pope Anastasius I (399–401) prescribed or rather inculcated anew to the priests the very ancient

apostolic times and has a manifold mystical meaning. By standing at the Gospel we would first testify that God's gospel of peace and glory fills us with great joy, and that the truth of Christ has made us truly free and brought us spiritual resurrection; for by "the sword of the Spirit, which is the word of God" (Eph. 6:17), the fetters of slavery, the bonds of sin and passion, are cut asunder. Furthermore, standing is a mark of the profound reverence, esteem, and attention due to the word of Jesus Christ. Finally, to stand is the posture of the servant in the presence of his master. In the Gospel, Christ our Lord appears as our teacher; and by the fact that we receive His word standing, we express our obedience and our readiness to serve Him; we avow our alacrity and willingness to do all that He requires of us and recommends to us, in order that we may be not merely hearers, but also doers of His commandments and counsels (James 1:22).[18]

At Solemn Mass the reading of the Gospel is honored by the splendor of lighted tapers and the fragrance of incense. During the singing of the Gospel, the two acolytes hold lighted torches and stand one on each side of the book. St. Jerome already defended the higher meaning of this ancient custom of lighting candles at the Gospel, inasmuch as he insists that thereby we should give expression to the joy and jubilation of our hearts at the good tidings of salvation. Above all, the light by its brightness and its glow symbolizes Jesus Christ, the Sun that knows no setting and the Light of the City of God on earth as well as in heaven. By means of the Gospel, God has called us to the wonderful light of Christian truth and grace. In this dark vale of the earth "Thy word is a lamp to my feet, and a light to my paths" (Ps. 118:105).

---

custom of standing at the reading of the Gospel (*Constit. Apost.*, II, chap. 57). Hic constituit, ut quotiescunque Evangelia sancta recitantur, sacerdotes non sederent, sed curvi starent. According to a pseudo-Isidorian letter (in opposition to an abuse which had crept in), he ordained "that while the holy Gospels were read in the church, the priest and all present should not remain seated, but reverently bow . . . and stand, while attentively listening to and devoutly honoring the words of the Lord."

[18] Martene gives (*Regula commentat.*, chap. 11) the following reasons for standing during the reading of the Gospel: a) Honor et reverentia s. Evangelii; b) quod non deceat alios sedere stante s. Evangelii lectore, qui "Domini nostri Jesu Christi personam gerit" (Rupert., II, *in regul. s. Ben.*); c) ut hac nostri corporis dispositione demonstremus, nos tanquam veros Dei servos ad ejus, quae proferuntur, exsequenda mandata semper esse paratos.

Wherever in the world the word of God does not shine and enlighten, profound darkness hovers over the ways of man and over man himself. For then not only the surety as to how to act rightly, but even the origin and end of our pilgrimage . . . is enveloped in darkness. This darkness is enlightened and becomes marvelously bright through the word of God; by this word the ground on which we stand becomes clear, and the way we have to follow to reach our destiny is made manifest. From the word of God beams a secure light to guide us amid the various directions and helps, as well as amid the various wants, obstacles, and dangers we meet on this path so stern and so difficult to be determined (Reischl).

By the gospel we should become as light in the Lord and shine always as children of light, by producing fruits of light in all goodness, justice, and truth. If, enlightened and filled with fervor by the light of the gospel, we lead a life resplendent with the brightness of virtue and purity, we shall then be fulfilling that admonition of the Lord: "So let your light shine before men, that they may see your good works and glorify your Father who is in heaven" (Matt. 5:16).

The incensing at the Gospel is also rich in symbolism.[19] In the first place, the incensing of the book of the Gospels is to be regarded as an act of reverence and honor paid to "the words of eternal life," which the Lord here speaks to us. The fragrant clouds that envelop the book call to mind how the good odor of the knowledge of Jesus Christ is spread abroad by the announcement of the Gospel. "Thanks be to God, who always maketh us to triumph in Christ Jesus, and manifesteth the odor of His knowledge [20] by us in every place. For we are the good odor of Christ unto God, in them that are saved . . . the odor of life unto life" (II Cor. 2:

---

[19] Sicard of Cremona (d. 1215) mentions the incensing of the book of the Gospels. After signing himself with the cross, "the deacon incenses the book" (*Mitral.*, III, chap. 4). The incensing of the celebrant, after the reading of the Gospel, is first mentioned in the *Ordo Rom. V*, n. 7. Subdiaconus accipiat a diacono Evangelia, et exhibeat ea ad deosculandum episcopo, quibus exosculatis exhibeatur ei et incensorium. In the Middle Ages the celebrant, while putting incense into the censer, at this place frequently said these words: Odore coelestis inspirationis suae accendat et impleat Dominus corda nostra ad audienda et implenda Evangelii sui praecepta.

[20] *Odor notitiae* is, according to St. Thomas, *notitia de Deo, quae habetur per fidem, et illuminat intellectum et delectat affectum;* therefore, a loving, fervent, blissful knowledge of the divine mysteries. (Cf. *In Epist. II ad Cor.*, chap. 2, lect. 3.)

14–16). The incense furthermore admonishes us with what heavenly ardor of devotion the words of the Gospel should be announced by the deacon or the priest and be listened to by the faithful and laid up in their hearts. As the bright flame of the lighted taper is an image of a pure life, so the sweet fragrance of incense also symbolizes a virtuous, God-fearing life. Christ's doctrine and grace should make of us a good odor unto God and men. This will be the case if, by innocence and purity, by mildness and mercy, by humility and meekness, by constancy and patience, by mortification and austerity, we propitiate and please God, and also edify and console our neighbor. Virtue, indeed, exhales a sweet and a refreshing perfume; in testimony of this, the Lord has often wonderfully provided that the bodies of the saints during their lifetime or after death exhale a sweet scent, altogether supernatural and heavenly.[21]

c) When the reading of the Gospel has ended, the acolyte answers in the name of the people: *Laus tibi, Christe* ("Praise be to Thee, O Christ").[22] The priest kisses the initial words of the passage just read, saying at the same time: *Per evangelica dicta deleantur nostra delicta* ("By virtue of the words of the Gospel may our sins be blotted out"). Thus the reading of the holy Gospel is closed, not only with a chant of thanksgiving, but also with a kiss and a prayer.[23]

[21] The body of St. Peter of Alcantara remained, after the soul had departed, still supported by his brethren in a kneeling posture, with hands raised heavenward; the cell was filled with a marvelously sweet odor, a celestial light surrounded the venerable remains, and the ravishing melodies of the angelic choirs filled the air with their glorious strains. His body, which had previously been emaciated and worn out, withered and wasted from continual mortification, bronzed by the air and the heat of the sun, suddenly became dazzling white and slightly rosy, like the flesh of a delicate child, and emitted a bright light; but his eyes especially, which during life had been so carefully guarded, sparkled like two precious stones of rare beauty.

[22] Formerly the answer was *Amen* or *Deo gratias* or *Benedictus, qui venit in nomine Domini*. Lecto Evangelio quisque dicere debet *Amen*. Vel ut alii volunt, recitato Evangelio, statim dicamus oportet *Deo gratias*, quemadmodum post quamlibet lectionem sive capitulum. Sed melius est ut dicatur *Amen* ac nos cruce contra diabolum muniamus, ne ipse sermones Domini ex pectore nostro rapiat (Beleth. [d. about 1165], *Ration.*, chap. 39; cf. Sicard., *loc. cit.*). Already St. Benedict prescribes in his *Rule* (chap. 11): Legat abbas lectionem de Evangelio, cum honore et tremore, stantibus omnibus. Qua perlecta respondeant omnes *Amen*. Here *Amen* mainly denotes devout assent.

[23] The book of the Gospels, or rather, the sacred text of the Gospels in general, represents our divine Savior Himself and was, therefore, ever a

Jesus Christ teaches the science of salvation and points out the way of life by word and example, announced to us by the Gospel. Joyfully moved by a feeling of heartfelt gratitude for the blessed truth and grace of the Gospel, the faithful break forth into words of praise and glorification, saying: "Praise be to Thee, O Christ!" This concluding formula corresponds in sentiment to the introductory formula: "Glory be to Thee, O Lord," just as the kiss of the book and the signing of it with the cross also harmonize with each other.

What is the meaning of kissing the Gospel? After having tasted and experienced in the Gospel how sweet the Lord is, how faultless His doctrine, how good and refreshing His consolations and promises, the heart of the priest overflows with happiness and joy, and he kisses the words of eternal life in order to testify his profound reverence, his great and ardent love for them. This liturgical kiss, therefore, expresses the thought of the Psalmist: "More to be desired than gold and many precious stones [are the words of the Lord], and sweeter than honey and the honeycomb" (Ps. 18:11; cf. Ps. 118 *passim*). "What the world values most is threefold: riches, whose principal symbol is gold; beauty, represented by precious stones; and pleasure, symbolized by the honeycomb. Yet nothing of all that the earth can bestow is comparable to the joy and refreshment imparted by the word of God" (Reischl). The Gospel be-

---

subject of religious veneration, as were the images of Christ. The manifold ceremonies at the reading of the Evangelical pericope are likewise so many symbols and signs of veneration for the holy Gospels and of grateful joy at the glad tidings of salvation. The kissing of the Gospel after it has been read, is also the expression and, so to speak, the seal of these sentiments. Formerly it was customary to present to all present the book of the Gospels (in some places closed, in others open) to be kissed. (Cf.*Ordo Rom. II,* n. 8.) Under Pope Honorius III (1216-27) this was forbidden. According to the present practice one person only kisses the Gospel, and that, as a rule, is the celebrant. But if a prelate (that is, the pope, a cardinal, a nuncio, the patriarch, the archbishop or the bishop of the diocese) assist at the Mass, the book is kissed only by him (and if there are more than one, by the highest in dignity). (Cf. *Cerem. Episc.*, I, chap. 30.) In Requiem Masses the introductory benediction formula (*Jube . . . Dominus sit . . .*) and at the close of the Gospel the kiss with the accompanying words (*Per evangelica . . .*) are omitted. The Church evidently wishes to respond to the just exigencies of human nature, when in Requiem Masses for the departed she avoids exterior signs of joy and, therefore, omits such rites and prayers (as those just mentioned) which denote joyful sentiments and impart to the holy action a more festive disposition, or which tend to impart a blessing to the living. (Cf. Quarti, *Comment. in Rubr. Miss.*, II, xiii, 1.)

stows that heavenly wisdom of which Solomon says: "I preferred her before kingdoms and thrones, and esteemed riches nothing in comparison of her. Neither did I compare unto her any precious stone: for all gold, in comparison of her, is as a little sand, and silver in respect to her shall be counted as clay. I loved her above health and beauty, and chose to have her instead of light; for her light cannot be put out" (Wisd. 7:8–10).

If the Gospel is taken into the heart and preserved therein with all that esteem and submission, love and joy, which the kissing of the book denotes, then is the Gospel also able "to blot out our sins." However, the words of the Gospel do not blot out sins as do baptism and penance: they are only a kind of sacramental in a more general sense and have, therefore, the power of awakening and promoting that disposition of soul by which venial sins are effaced, or which renders one worthy of receiving the sacraments. The word of God, which is accompanied by the interior working of grace, exercises a redeeming, healing, and sanctifying influence on man when he is properly disposed, by exciting faith, hope, and charity, fear and contrition, conversion and amendment of life. It is not only a powerful means of ridding the soul of sin and imperfections, but it possesses other beneficial effects besides. "Are not My words as a fire, saith the Lord, and as a hammer that breaketh the rock in pieces?" (Jer. 23:29.) Indeed, the words of the Lord are spirit and life; they are powerful, two-edged, penetrating. When Christ on the road to Emmaus "opened" to the two disciples the meaning of the Scriptures, their hearts burned within them (Luke 24:32). The word of God has a marvelous power for enlightening the eyes, for imparting wisdom to the lowly and the humble, for rejoicing the heart and refreshing the soul. In like manner, may the living and life-giving word of God, which abides forever, impart to us "salvation and protection," [24] may it purify, consecrate, and sanctify our souls ever more and more. For the Gospel "is the power of God unto salvation to every one that believeth" (Rom. 1:16).[25]

---

[24] Cf. the benediction in the third nocturn: Evangelica lectio sit nobis salus et protectio. (Cf. S. Ambr., *Enarrat. in Ps.*, 39:16.)
[25] Verbum Dei animam vivificat, infundens ei spirituale gaudium, sicut etiam apparet in hominibus laicis et idiotis, qui licet non intelligant quae leguntur, sentiunt tamen gaudium Spiritus et inde ad poenitentiam animantur. Verbum etiam Dei efficacem reddit animam ad virtutes et quaecunque bona et penetrat eam omnia ejus interiora illustrando (S. Mechtild., *Lib. spec. grat.*, III, chap. 19).

CHAPTER XXV

THE CREED

1. On certain days and feasts, the announcement of the good tidings of salvation is followed by the solemn profession of faith. The heart, full of joy and gratitude, exclaims: *Credo* ("I believe"). When the Credo occurs, it forms the answer to the voice of God, who has spoken to us by His prophets and apostles, even by His own Son. The liturgical symbol recited at Mass is as follows:

Credo in unum Deum, Patrem omnipotentem, factorem coeli et terrae, visibilium omnium et invisibilium. Et in unum Dominum Jesum Christum, Filium Dei unigenitum. Et ex Patre natum ante omnia saecula. Deum de Deo, lumen de lumine, Deum verum de Deo vero. Genitum, non factum, consubstantialem Patri: per quem omnia facta sunt. Qui propter nos homines, et propter nostram salutem descendit de coelis. (*Hic genuflectitur.*) Et incarnatus est de Spiritu sancto ex Maria Virgine: et homo factus est. Crucifixus etiam pro nobis: sub Pontio Pilato passus et sepultus est. Et resurrexit tertia die, secundum Scripturas. Et ascendit in coelum: sedet ad dexteram Patris.	I believe in one God, the Father Almighty, Maker of heaven and earth, and of all things visible and invisible. And in one Lord Jesus Christ, the only-begotten Son of God; born of the Father before all ages: God of God, light of light, true God of true God; begotten not made, consubstantial to the Father; by whom all things were made. Who for us men and for our salvation came down from heaven; (*here genuflect*) and became incarnate by the Holy Ghost, of the Virgin Mary; and was made man. He was crucified also for us, suffered under Pontius Pilate, and was buried. And the third day he rose again according to the Scriptures; and ascended into heaven, sitteth at

THE CREED

Et iterum venturus est cum gloria judicare vivos et mortuos: cujus regni non erit finis. Et in Spiritum sanctum, Dominum et vivificantem: qui ex Patre Filioque procedit. Qui cum Patre et Filio simul adoratur et conglorificatur: qui locutus est per Prophetas. Et unam sanctam catholicam et apostolicam Ecclesiam. Confiteor unum baptisma in remissionem peccatorum. Et expecto resurrectionem mortuorum. Et vitam venturi saeculi. Amen.

the right hand of the Father; and he is to come again with glory to judge the living and the dead, of whose kingdom there shall be no end. And in the Holy Ghost, the Lord and giver of life, who proceedeth from the Father and the Son, who together with the Father and the Son is adored and glorified; who spoke by the prophets. And one holy, catholic, and apostolic Church. I confess one baptism for the remission of sins. And I expect the resurrection of the dead, and the life of the world to come.

There are a number of ecclesiastical symbols of faith, which contain the principal points of dogma in pregnant brevity,[1] and hence such symbols of belief serve for the profession of faith in communion with the Church.[2] The first in origin and the simplest is the Apostles' Creed, which most probably is of strictly apostolical origin and forms the basis of the others, as all later symbols are only a development and extension of it.[3] Next to the Apostles' Creed (*symbolum Apostolorum*), the so-called *Nicene-Constantinopolitan Creed* (*symbolum Patrum*) holds the most prominent place. This Creed is called Nicene because the definition of the first General Council of Nice (325) regarding the divinity of the Son is therein

---

[1] Symbolum est regula fidei brevis et grandis: brevis numero verborum, grandis pondere sententiarum (S. August., *Serm*, LIX, n. 1).

[2] *Symbolum* (σύμβολον) = mark, characteristic, true sign, by which a person may be recognized or be identified. By the profession of faith the faithful are distinguished from heretics and unbelievers. Beati Apostoli Ecclesiae Dei, quam adversus militiam diabolici furoris armabant, mysterium symboli tradiderunt, ut quia sub uno Christi nomine credentium erat futura diversitas, signaculum symboli inter fideles perfidosque secerneret et alienus a fide atque hostis appareret Ecclesiae (S. Maxim. Taurin., *Homil.*, LXXXIII, *de traditione symboli*). Symbolum per linguam graecam signum vel collatio interpretatur. Discessuri enim Apostoli ad evangelizandum in gentibus hoc sibi praedicationis signum vel indicium posuerunt (S. Isid., *Etymolog.*, VI, xix, 57).

[3] Cf. MacDonald, *The Apostles Creed*.

almost literally recorded; it is called Constantinopolitan because, although not first arranged in this order by the Second Ecumenical Council of Constantinople (381), it was, however, there received and confirmed as Catholic. The fact that not only the divinity of the Father, but also the divinity of the Son and of the Holy Ghost are so expressly and emphatically emphasized in this symbol of faith, rendered this Creed particularly suited for the solemn profession of the true faith at divine worship. This Creed was introduced into the sacrificial liturgy of the East in the beginning of the sixth century, mainly in opposition to the Arian and Macedonian heresies. Later the great National Council of Toledo (589), in Spain, resolved and decreed that in the Mozarabic rite, immediately before the Pater Noster, the profession of faith of Constantinople should be recited aloud by all the people.[4] Toward the end of the eighth century the same Creed was incorporated into the Mass rite in France and Germany.[5]

It is far more difficult to determine at what period the Roman Church began to recite or sing the Credo during Mass. Since apparently contradictory testimonies on this point exist in the ancient documents, liturgists differ greatly in their opinions. According to the lucid and reliable information of the Abbot Berno of Reichenau [6] (d. 1048), the general adoption of the Credo into the Roman

---

[4] In the Mozarabic celebration of Mass the priest says: *Fidem, quam corde credimus, ore autem dicamus.* He then elevates the sacred host so that it may be seen by the people, and holding it over the chalice, he recites the Symbol alternately with the choir or assistants. Its recitation, therefore, is here an act of immediate preparation for Holy Communion.

[5] Symbolum quoque fidei catholicae recte in Missarum solemniis post Evangelium recensetur, ut per sanctum Evangelium "corde credatur ad justitiam," per Symbolum autem "ore confessio fiat in salutem." Et notandum, Graecos illud Symbolum, quod nos ad imitationem eorum intra Missas assumimus, potius quam alia in cantilenae dulcedinem ideo transtulisse, quia Constantinopolitani concilii proprium est, et fortasse aptius videbatur modulis sonorum quam Nicaenum, quod tempore prius est, et ut contra haereticorum venena in ipsis etiam sacramentorum celebrationibus medicamenta apud regiae suae urbis sedem confecta fidelium devotio replicaret. Ab ipsis ergo ad Romanos ille usus creditur pervenisse; sed apud Gallos et Germanos post dejectionem Felicis (*Bishop of Urgel*) haeretici (*Adoptianists*), sub gloriosissimo Carolo Francorum rectore damnati, idem Symbolum latius et crebrius in Missarum coepit officiis iterari (Walafrid. Strabo [d. 849], *De exord. et increm.,* chap. 23).

[6] In his document, *De quibusdam rebus ad Missae officium pertinentibus,* chap. 2, he mentions what he witnessed during his sojourn in Rome. Baronius,

Mass rite took place only at the beginning of the eleventh century, during the pontificate of Pope Benedict VIII and at the request of the emperor, Henry II. On February 14, 1014, which fell that year on Sunday, Henry II was anointed and crowned Emperor in the Basilica of St. Peter's. The devout Emperor noticed that during the coronation Mass the Credo had not been sung, as was customary throughout Christendom. Inquiring into the cause for this omission, he was informed that the Roman Church, which had never departed from the Catholic faith and had never been corrupted by heresy, had no need for such a profession of faith. But the Emperor requested as a coronation gift for himself and for the edification of the faithful, who from all parts of the world flocked to Rome, that the Pope would prescribe the insertion of this profession of faith into the Solemn Mass; the Pope deemed it advisable to introduce into Rome a custom which henceforth for all times would be a testimony of the lively faith of the holy Emperor and which, in consequence, would enkindle this ardor of faith in thousands of hearts.

The rite for the recitation of the Creed is simple. Its recitation in a loud voice invites all present to unite in heart and mind with the priest and joyfully to repeat the Creed with him. At the first words, the hands of the priest are raised and extended, to evince the joyful, believing, adoring sentiments of the heart. During its recitation, the hands remain joined before the breast; this devout attitude corresponds with the humble homage and the confiding abandonment of oneself to the absolute truth and veracity of God, and with the perfect submission of the will and of the understanding to the infinite majesty and sovereignty of God. The three devout inclinations of the head, at the words *Deum, Jesum Christum,* and *simul adoratur* (at the confession of faith in the Father, the Son, and the Holy Ghost), express due reverence to the three divine persons. The words, *Et incarnatus est,* are accompanied by a genuflection, slowly made in order appropriately to revere and glorify the Incarnation, this mystery of God's inconceivable condescension.[7] At the last

---

Bona, Menardus, Lupus, Gavantus, Renaudot, Bellotte, Mari, Lesley, and Zaccaria have adopted this explanation.

[7] If the celebrant, the deacon, and subdeacon are seated while these words are sung by the choir, as a rule they make only a profound bow with head uncovered. But at Christmas and at the Annunciation (when the latter feast is transferred, *in ipsa die translationis;* S. R. C., September 25, 1706) they must rise from their seats and kneel down on the lowest step of the altar, on the

words, *et vitam venturi saeculi*, the priest makes the sign of the cross. This sign of the cross has been variously interpreted: it can be understood as referring to the entire symbol, or merely to the words immediately preceding. In the former case it is evident how appropriate it is to conclude and seal the Credo with the sign of the cross, because the latter is not only a brief profession of our faith, but also our shield and buckler against all the adversaries of our faith.[8] With this signification we can easily harmonize the other, which places the sign of the cross in special relation to the concluding words: "and the life of the world to come." According to this explanation, it would here signify the fundamental truth that only the royal road of the Cross, the way of sorrow and suffering, leads to the home of imperishable joys. Besides this allusion, that the way of the Cross is the path to eternal glory, it contains the admonition that the sign of the resplendent cross will appear in the heavens with Christ at His second coming to judge the world.

While in the Greek liturgy the symbol of faith is placed after the kiss of peace which follows the Offertory, the Roman liturgy orders its recitation after the Gospel; and whereas in the former the Creed is a constituent part of every Mass celebrated, it occurs in the latter only on certain days as a mark of special distinction. The Credo has the more suitable position in the Roman liturgy. It makes no difference whether it is regarded as the end of the first part of the Mass or as the beginning of the second part, it is in any case the most proper connecting link between the two parts. As the blossom and fruit of the preceding Scriptural readings,[9] it forms a fitting conclusion of the general divine service; but at the same time it is also the basis for the special sacrificial celebration about to begin, which is called the "mystery of faith."

2. Since, therefore, only certain Masses are distinguished and

---

Epistle side (*utroque genu cum capitis inclinatione*), because on these days the mystery of the Incarnation is celebrated in a special manner. (S. R. C., June 11, 1701; May 23, 1846.)

[8] Signaculum crucis virtutem passionis Christi ostendit. Hoc ergo quando fronte imprimitur, christianus munitur. Quando contra imminens periculum opponitur, adversaria virtus fugatur. Primum ad arma, secundum ad tela; primum ad defensionem, secundum ad impugnationem (Hugo de s. Vict., *De Sacrament.*, Bk. II, Part IX, chap. 8).

[9] Quia Christo credimus tanquam divinae veritati (Joan. 8:46), lecto Evangelio, symbolum fidei cantatur, in quo populus ostendit se per fidem Christi doctrinae assentire (S. Thom., q.83, a.4).

THE CREED

privileged above others by the solemn profession of faith, we must consider what were the reasons for admitting the symbol into the sacrificial rite.[10] As a rule, liturgists classify under three heads the principal reasons for the recitation of the symbol, and these they designate by the words, *mysterium, doctrina, solemnitas.*

a. Accordingly, the first principal reason for the adoption of the Credo lies in the mystery celebrated. The Credo is recited on certain days and feasts whose historical foundation or dogmatic subject is contained in the symbol, that is, one of the mysteries expressly mentioned therein or at least acknowledged as included therein.[11] Since the celebration of divine worship on such days is consecrated to the commemoration and to the honor of a special mystery of faith, it is proper to confess this mystery by the solemn singing or recitation of the Credo. Among such days are reckoned:

a. All Sundays. Sunday is devoted to the commemoration of many mysteries recited in the symbol. Its celebration is especially ordained to honor the triune God, who wrought so many great works of salvation on the first day of the week, which corresponds to our Sunday. For on this day was commenced the creation of the world in the beginning of time; and in the fullness of time the new creation of the fallen world was accomplished by Christ's resurrection[12] and the sending of the Holy Ghost. Some writers hold that on this day Jesus Christ was born, and at the Circumcision shed His first blood. Not only the resurrection of the Lord, but the other mysteries also commemorated on Sunday occasioned the recitation of the Credo on this day.

b) The feasts of the Holy Trinity and Pentecost, as well as all the feasts of Jesus Christ and of His Blessed Mother. In the Credo

---

[10] From the statement of Innocent III (*De sacr. alt. myst.*, II, chap. 51) it follows that already in the twelfth century certain rubrics had obtained regarding the recitation or omission of the Credo on certain days. The practice was, and continued to be, widely different until the liturgical development was concluded in the revision and the new edition of the missal under Pius V.

[11] According to John Beleth, the Credo was recited in the twelfth century in *eorum tantummodo festis, quorum in Symbolo fit mentio* (*Ration.*, chap. 40).

[12]
      Primo dierum omnium
      Quo mundus exstat conditus
      Vel quo resurgens Conditor
      Nos morte victa liberat.
           —St. Gregory the Great

we proclaim the name and glory of the three divine persons. Hence it is entirely fitting that we recite the Credo on the feasts of the Holy Trinity and of each of the three divine persons. The principal mysteries of Christ's life are, moreover, specifically mentioned in the Credo. These we celebrate with special feasts during the course of the ecclesiastical year. In these mysteries the Blessed Virgin, Mother of God, is inseparably connected with her Son; therefore these special feasts of Mary are distinguished by the Credo.

c) *The feasts of the angels.* The reason for reciting the Credo on the feast of the angels is found in the mention made of them in the word *invisibilium*, by which the angels are understood. The recitation of the Credo in the Masses of the angels can be further based on their mission and calling; for they are "all ministering spirits, sent to minister for them who shall receive the inheritance of salvation" (Heb. 1:14). As messengers of God, the angels are active in the work of redemption; they announce to man the decrees and revelations of God. An angel brings to Mary the joyful tidings that she is to become the mother of the Saviour. They appear at His birth, resurrection, and ascension, and they will accompany Him on His return to judge the world. They labor untiringly for the extension and progress of the kingdom of God upon earth; to the Church they are a heavenly, protecting guard in all her sufferings and combats with the powers of hell and the hatred of the world.

d) *The feast of All Saints.* The Credo is recited on the feast of All Saints because they are the triumphant, glorious members of the "one, holy, catholic and apostolic Church."

e) *The celebration of the Dedication of the Church and its anniversary* are also distinguished by the recitation of the Credo, for the material house of God is a figure of the Church militant and triumphant, of the kingdom of Christ on earth and in heaven.

b) The second principal reason for the recitation of the Symbol is designated by the word doctrine. For this reason the honor of the Creed is bestowed upon the principal and secondary feasts of the apostles, evangelists, and doctors of the Church when they are celebrated *sub ritu duplici*.

a) The Symbol contains the doctrine taught by the apostles, and it mentions expressly as one of the four marks of the true Church that she is apostolic. The apostles introduced into the world the Church instituted by Christ and they spread it over the whole earth.

THE CREED

They were the organs of the Holy Ghost and the infallible bearers of revelation; they announced all that Christ did and suffered for our salvation.[13]

b) By the hands of evangelists the Holy Ghost Himself wrote down the history of redemption, the tidings of salvation of the kingdom of Christ, the doctrines and mysteries of our faith, and the means of grace handed over and entrusted to the Church as a precious treasure.

c) The doctors of the Church are chosen and glorious men,[14] of whom "nations shall declare his wisdom, and the Church shall show forth his praise" (Ecclus. 39:14). With the depth of their knowledge corresponded the height of their sanctity. Enlightened with light from above and inflamed with ardor for the truth, they have in their conversation and writings gradually developed, confirmed, and defended the doctrine of Christ against the attacks of error and calumny. Because they have illumined the whole world with the light of faith, their feasts are distinguished by the recitation in the Mass of the joyful and solemn profession of faith.

All the other saints—martyrs and confessors, holy women and sacred virgins—possessed indeed the virtue of faith in a heroic degree, and some of them even merited for themselves the immortal honor to extend the faith, yet in this respect they are outranked by the apostles, evangelists, and doctors of the Church, and in the Mass of their feast the Credo is properly left out.[15]

d) Only on the feast of St. Mary Magdalen does the Church make an exception; besides the Mother of God, to St. Mary Magdalen alone among all the female saints is given the distinction of the rec-

---

[13] Isti [scil. Apostoli] sunt viri sancti, quos elegit Dominus in caritate non ficta, et dedit illis gloriam sempiternam: quorum doctrina fulget Ecclesia, ut sole luna (*Breviar. Roman.*).

[14] At present the following saints are venerated as Doctors of the Church: 1. Athanasius; 2. Basil the Great; 3. Gregory of Nazianzum; 4. John Chrysostom; 5. Ambrose; 6. Jerome; 7. Augustine; 8. Gregory the Great; 9. Thomas Aquinas; 10. Bonaventure; 11. Anselm; 12. Isidore of Seville; 13. Peter Chrysologus; 14. Leo the Great; 15. Peter Damian; 16. Bernard; 17. Hilary; 18. Alphonsus Maria de Liguori; 19. Francis de Sales; 20. Cyril of Jerusalem; 21. Cyril of Alexandria; 22. John Damascene; 23. Venerable Bede; 24. John of the Cross; 25. Albert the Great; 26. Robert Bellarmine; 27. Anthony.

[15] Hence the mnemonic:
D A credit; M V C, per se, non credit.
D = Doctores, A = Apostoli, M = Martyres, V = Virgines et Viduae, C = Confessores.

itation of the Creed on her feast. Why is this? Probably because Magdalen, after the Mother of God, first beheld the risen Saviour and, as an eyewitness of His resurrection, she was sent by Him to the apostles as the first promulgator of the mystery of His resurrection. Mary Magdalen went to the disciples and announced to them: "I have seen the Lord, and these things He said to me" (John 20:18). St. Jerome in the life of St. Marcella writes: "Mary Magdalen, on account of her fervor and the ardor of her faith, received the name of one 'standing on a high tower,' [16] and she was found worthy, the first of all even before the apostles, of beholding the risen Lord."

c) The third reason for inserting the Credo in the ritual of the Mass is some special solemnity: the profession of faith is often sung or recited publicly to enhance the exterior splendor of the feast or Mass. According to this rule, the following feasts or Masses are entitled to the Creed:

a) The so-called patronal feasts, that is, the feast of the principal patron of the church and of the place.[17] The patron of a church is that saint under whose invocation and in whose honor the church has been erected and dedicated. Since the church has received its name (its title) from this saint, he is usually called in liturgical language, the titular of the church, even if he be not at the same time the patron of the place. Moreover, the title of a church is not always that of a saint or an angel, but is taken from some mystery, for example, that of the Holy Trinity. By the patron of the place, on the other hand, we understand that saint who is chosen as the special intercessor or protector of a parish, diocese, province, or nation, and who is invoked and honored as such.[18]

---

[16] Magdalena from *Migdol* = the observatory or the tower.

[17] Titularis sive patronus ecclesiae is dicitur, sub cujus nomine seu titulo ecclesia fundata est et a quo appellatur. Patronus autem loci proprie is est, quem certa civitas, dioecesis, provincia, regnum etc. delegit velut singularem ad Deum patronum (S. R. C., May 9, 1857).

[18] Churches, therefore, have either titular feasts in a stricter sense, or patronal feasts; places, on the contrary, have only patronal feasts. There is a distinction between *patronus vel titulus principalis* and *patronus vel titulus minus principalis s. secundarius*. The Symbol properly is only for the chief (*festum primarium*), but not for the secondary feast (*festum secundarium*) of the principal patron or principal patrons, as only the principal feast *sub ritu dupl. I. cl. cum oct.* is celebrated. The feast of the *patronus vel titulus minus principalis* is usually celebrated only *sub ritu dupl. maj. vel min.*, and that without octave, and has, therefore, no Credo. (Cf. S. R. C., December 2, 1684; September 15, 1691; August 22, 1744.) The regular priests recite the

b) The Credo is recited in the Mass of the feast of a saint in that church in which the body or at least a notable relic (*reliquia insignis*) is preserved.[19] The Credo is also recited in the Solemn Mass which, "on account of an extraordinary concourse of people" is celebrated in honor of the saint who has a special altar in the church.

c) The solemn votive Masses which, on important occasions, are celebrated by order or with permission of the bishop, also have the Credo; those however have no Credo which are sung on ordinary weekdays in purple vestments.

The octave is nothing else than the continuation and completion of the celebration of the feast; therefore, if a feast has a Credo, the whole octave of the feast receives also this distinction. If feasts that have no Credo fall during such an octave or on a Sunday, they then receive it on account of the day on which they are celebrated.

Thus the Church has, according to well established principles, prescribed the Credo as a special distinction of the feasts and days which have a close relation to the profession of faith. This profession of faith, proclaimed so loudly and solemnly at the Holy Sacrifice, should always emanate from hearts filled with joy and gratitude to God; for great indeed is the grace of the Catholic faith.

Sprouting from heaven and descending to earth, faith unites earth with heaven; coming forth from out of the boundless ocean of eternal light, its rays penetrate the dark night which envelops man, enlightening his pathway through this dark vale of life. What was man before this heavenly light penetrated darkness, when the nations were still sitting in the shadow of death (Luke 1:79; Ps. 106:10; Matt. 4:16), and what would the child of earth be, even now, were he not enlightened from a higher world? What a sad, dark picture humanity presents without faith! The light of faith dawns, and where previously there ruled but folly and passion, and strife and fear, and darkness and ruin, there are now found truth and virtue and peace and light and life eternal. Faith

---

Credo also on the principal feast of their founder, but not of the other saints of their order (S. R. C., March 12, 1836; July 22, 1848).

[19] As notable relics of a saint are considered, for example, the head, an arm, or leg, if they are entire, that is, consisting of both bones, and every other portion, in which the martyr specially suffered, provided it is still entire and not too small, and is regularly approved by the bishop. The integrity of a relic may also be restored by the artificial joining of the separate fragments of a member. A hand, a foot, a thigh bone or shin bone alone does not answer as *reliquia insignis s. major* (S. R. C., January 13, 1631; S. C. Indulg., June 12, 1822).

brings to man consolation, instruction, warning, confidence, fortitude, and self-denial on his journey through life; faith inspires him with courage and hope in death; and faith accompanies him beyond the tomb to a blissful immortality, and in the more beautiful land of light and glory it removes the dark veil from his eyes and enables him to behold his God face to face. Thus the holy, Christian faith is to man a true heavenly messenger that religion sends before him to prepare his way. Again, faith is a brilliant star which serves him as an unfailing guide on his dangerous passage to his heavenly country. Faith is to him an angel, who supports him in his arms, a strong defence and refuge in every danger. Thus faith renders us truly happy here and hereafter.[20]

[20] Geissel, III, 123.

SECTION II

The Offertory

THE first part of the Mass rite is prescribed to purify the heart and to enlighten the mind, as well as to enliven faith and to excite devotion. Now, after the proper dispositions have been formed in priest and people by means of these preliminary prayers and readings, the celebration of the Eucharistic sacrifice proper begins. Since this holy mystery is not only offered and consecrated as a sacrifice, but also received as a sacrament, the representation of the real sacrificial service is naturally divided into three distinct parts:

1. The Oblation, that is, the offering of the sacrificial elements.
2. The Consecration, that is, the accomplishment of the sacrificial action.
3. The Communion, that is, the participation in the accomplished sacrifice.

The Offertory, Consecration, and Communion are the principal parts of the Mass: they are intimately connected with one another, but are not of equal significance, importance, or necessity in the accomplishment of the sacrifice. The sacrificial act proper (*sacrificatio vel immolatio corporis et sanguinis Christi*) is accomplished in the Consecration, which, therefore, forms the center and essence of the Mass. In the second place, according to rank, comes the Communion of the officiating priest, which belongs, although not to the essence, yet to the completeness of the Eucharistic sacrifice. Less important and significant than these two parts is the Offertory, in which the elements of bread and wine, requisite for the accomplishment of the Eucharistic sacrifice, are dedicated and offered to God.

In the Oblation, therefore, the sacrifice is prepared, at the Consecration it is really accomplished, and during the Communion it is entirely concluded and finished.

CHAPTER XXVI

PREPARATION FOR THE OBLATION

THE prayers and ceremonies of the Offertory constitute a most appropriate, although not an essentially necessary, preparation for the sacrificial action accomplished at the moment of Consecration. To comprehend the true sense and the abundant contents of the rite and prayers of the Offertory, the following points should be considered.

The words and the rite of the oblation before the Consecration relate to a twofold object: to the elements of bread and wine, and also to Christ's body and blood. In the first place, the oblation (*oblatio*) relates to the Eucharistic elements: the bread and wine are withdrawn from common use, consecrated to God, and previously sanctified, that they may be in a manner prepared and made fit for their unspeakably exalted destiny. We give up all claim to these earthly gifts and offer them to the Most High, with the intention and desire that He would change them in the course of the sacrifice into the most holy body and blood of Christ. Accordingly, this portion of the Mass rite includes manifold petitions to the Most High, that He graciously accept and bless or consecrate the bread and wine offered.[1]

Yet the Offertory has not exclusively for its object the mere elements of bread and wine, but also the real object of the sacrifice of the New Law: the body and blood of Christ, which by Consecration take the place of the former substances of bread and wine, and thus become present on the altar.[2] The Church, therefore, does not

---

[1] During the Middle Ages, many prayers were said during the Offertory for the consecration of the elements. Sanctifica ✠, quaesumus Domine Deus, hanc oblationem, ut nos Unigeniti corpus (*or* sanguis) fiat.—Oblatum tibi, Domine, munus sanctifica, ut nobis unigeniti Filii tui D. N. J. C. corpus et sanguis fiat. (Cf. Ebner, *Quellen und Forschungen*, p. 296 ff.)

[2] Respondeo, illam oblationem panis et vini, quae fit in Missa, non esse obla-

wait until the change of substance has taken place to offer the victim; already in the Offertory she offers the divine victim to the divine Majesty, regarding, as it were, the approaching Consecration of the sacrificial elements as having already taken place.³ The offering (*oblatio*) of the sacrificial gifts may precede and follow the accomplishment of the actual sacrificial act (*immolatio, sacrificatio*), as in our Mass rite, in which a similar oblation repeatedly takes place for the glorification of the divine name and for the salvation of the living and of the dead. From this point of view it can be explained why the Church already designates her oblation by such names as: *immaculata hostia, calix salutaris, sancta sacrificia illibata, sacrificium laudis*, which in their full sense are applicable only to Christ's sacrificial body and blood.

From the liturgical prayers of the Offertory, therefore, we may by no means conclude that the offering of the elements of bread and wine is a real sacrifice or constitutes a part of the Eucharistic sacrifice.⁴ Only Jesus Christ, present on our altars under both species as

---

tionem sacrificativam, sed simplicem oblationem, qua offertur materia, ex qua facienda est hostia sacrificanda. . . . Dicitur autem panis hostia, quia in ipso tanquam in materia, ex qua facienda est, praeexistit hostia et quia ipsam repraesentat: unde cum nondum sit praesens hostia, offertur Deo simplici oblatione tanquam praeparatoria in pane tanquam in typo. Quia cum sit futura panis spiritualis et vestita accidentibus panis, assumitur panis ut materia praevia tanquam typus illius (Pasqualigo, *De sacrific. N. L.*, I, q. 30, n. 8).

[3] This view is not opposed to the meaning of the Offertory prayers, which are here considered; for even according to the ordinary mode of speaking, the demonstrative pronoun *hic* (this) generally refers to things near the person speaking. Now such things can either really and perceptibly be near (*demonstratio ad sensum*), or be merely represented as present and thought to be present (*demonstratio ad intellectum*). All scholastics of the Middle Ages acknowledge this distinction in explaining the words of consecration. Pronomen hoc facit demonstrationem ad intellectum et ad sensum simul, sic intelligendo, quod demonstrat aliquid quod est objectum intellectus et aliquid quod est objectum sensus (Richard. a Med., IV, viii, a. 3, q. 1). The expressions: *hanc hostiam, hanc oblationem, hoc sacrificium*, and so forth, that often occur in the Offertory prayers before the Consecration, may, therefore, grammatically be referred equally as well to Christ's body and blood, which in the light of faith are seen as already present, as to the bread and wine which the celebrant beholds with his corporeal eyes immediately before him.

[4] Dico, hanc oblationem nullo modo pertinere ad substantiam hujus sacrificii, neque ut essentialem partem neque ut integralem, sed tantum esse ceremonialem quamdam praeparationem ab Ecclesia institutam ad conciliandam devotionem et reverentiam animosque fidelium excitandos ad mysterium ipsum peragendum (Suarez, disp. 75, sect. 3, n. 1). Vera sacrificalis oblatio

symbols of His death, is the perpetual sacrifice of the Catholic Church, our real and true sacrifice.

As soon as Christ, by virtue of the Consecration, has descended from heaven, as soon as He has taken up His abode with us under the humble appearances of bread and wine, He offers Himself to His Father a clean oblation amid a sin-stained human race, shows His wounds to His Father and holds up His death before Him, and in His wounds and death exhibits all His obedience, all His humiliations and His love. And we, fully conscious of our unworthiness, take up this clean oblation with a thrill of joy and offer it to the Father. The offering of the bread and wine, which previously takes place in the Mass, removes the bread and the wine from ordinary use and dedicates them to God, that He may change this inefficacious offering into the true oblation that worketh salvation. This offering of bread and wine should serve to prepare us and to raise our hearts to the Lord, who is to appear and to whom the prayers of the Church already beforehand refer, and whom the Church meets with rejoicings as she, in the spirit of meditation, beholds Him approaching: "Blessed is He, that cometh in the name of the Lord. Hosanna in the highest!" But when He does come, it is not in the splendor of His glory that He appears, but under the images of His passion and death.[5]

Until far into the thirteenth century, the Roman Church had in this portion of the Mass rite only the Offertory chant (*Offertorium*) of the choir and the secret oblation prayer of the priest (*Oratio super oblata* = Secreta);[6] all the other intervening prayers of the Offertory were only later admitted into the Roman rite,[7] after they had already been adopted by other churches. All these prayers collectively were in former times not improperly styled the *canon minor*, as their contents indicate they were in many ways connected with the *canon major*, the real Canon.

---

non intellegitur esse, donec materia illa, quae ad divinum cultum dicata jam est, benedicitur et sanctificatur; nulla ergo petitio fit per hanc oblationem, sistendo in pane et vino, sed in ordine ad eorum consecrationem, per quam Christus vere sacrificatur et offertur; quod est petere per incruentam Christi sacrificationem ex pane et vino sub eorumque speciebus faciendam (*ibid.*, disp. 83, sect. 2, n. 8).

[5] Eberhard, I, 337.

[6] Circa oblationem duo aguntur: scil. laus populi in cantu offertorii, per quod significatur laetitia offerentium, et oratio sacerdotis, qui petit ut oblatio populi sit Deo accepta (I Par 29:17). (S. Thom., IIIa, q.83, a.4.)

[7] Romanus Ordo nullam orationem instituit post Offerendam ante Secretam (Microlog., chap. 11). The prayers now prescribed we meet for the first time in *Ordo Rom. XIV*, chap. 53. Perfect unity in regard to the rite and prayers at the offering of the sacrificial elements was restored only in the sixteenth century by the publication of the newly revised missal.

PREPARATION FOR THE OBLATION 539

The Offertory Chant

1. The Offertory is introduced by the kissing of the altar and the mutual salutation: *Dominus vobiscum. Et cum Spiritu tuo.*[8] By these words priest and people reciprocally express the desire that the Lord would assist them by His grace and power, in order that with lively faith and with proper dispositions they may celebrate the Eucharistic sacrifice and in union with it offer themselves to the Most High as an acceptable gift. The nearer the moment of the sacrifice approaches, the more urgently do we require assistance from above.

The *Oremus*, which the priest then says, relates not merely to the Offertory chant, but also to the whole series of prayers that are said during the Offertory. All present are thereby exhorted to unite with the celebrant in sentiments of devotion, in a spirit of recollection, with attention, with heartfelt fervor, and, in union with him, to pray and make the offering in silence; for the interior sentiments of prayer and sacrifice alone impart to our offering true value in the sight of God.

After the *Oremus*, the priest recites an antiphon, which in the missal is called *Offertorium*.[9] From apostolic times until about the eleventh century, there was always a procession at the Offertory. All the faithful who were to be admitted at the table of the Lord, and only these, were authorized and at the same time bound to offer

---

[8] Quartum officium (= distinctio, *part*) Offertorium vel Offerenda vocatur, quod incipit a *Dominus vobiscum*. Consuetudo est quod cum nuper ad operarios ingredimur, eos salutemus. Sic, secundum quosdam, cum de uno officio ad aliud transitum facimus (*that is, at the beginning of a new part of the Mass*), salutationem praemittimus (Sicard., *op. cit.*, III, chap. 5). Lecto Evangelio populus offert, chorus cantat, sacerdos suscipit, Deoque corde et ore et manibus repraesentat et incurvatur et orat. Officium igitur, quod nos dicimus Offerendam, ab eo loco inchoatur, ubi post Evangelium sacerdos dicit *Dominus vobiscum* et finitur in eo loco, ubi excelsa voce dicit: *Per omnia saecula saeculorum* (Hildeb. Turon., *De exposit. Missae*).

[9] The word *Offertorium* designates in a more comprehensive sense also the so-called Little Canon, that is, all the prayers and rites of the Offertory until the conclusion of the Secreta. Already in the *Ord. Rom.* the antiphon in question is called *Offertorium*, and it is distinguished from the added verses: Canitur offertorium cum versibus (*Ord. Rom. II*, n. 9). The word *offertorium*, which is found only in Church Latin, had previously several other meanings. Thus in old documents it designated, for example, the book in which the Offertory chants were contained, then the sacrificial gifts themselves. Pontifex, Offertorio lecto, . . . accipit offertorium (*the lighted candles*) ab omnibus ordinatis (*Pontif. Roman., De ordinat. Presbyt.*).

their gifts at the Offertory. The rite of this offering differed at various places and times. For the most part, only bread and wine could be brought to the altar as an offering; from these gifts the materials for the sacrifice were selected.[10] The Offertory procession of the clergy and the people was accompanied by singing, to excite a joyful disposition in the givers, since God "loveth a cheerful giver." We cannot determine when the chant accompanying the procession was introduced.[11] Its particular development is ascribed to St. Gregory the Great. In his Antiphonary the Offertory chant consists of an antiphon and several verses. The whole antiphon was first entirely sung, and then partly repeated after several verses. It was a responsorial chant sung by two choirs. When, after the twelfth century, the ancient custom at the Offertory gradually disappeared,[12] the psalm chant was abridged. In our missal there remains

---

[10] According to an ancient custom and an ecclesiastical ordinance, the faithful formerly offered, in more or less close reference to the Eucharistic sacrifice, all manner of material gifts (*oblationes*, προσφοραί), to provide the material for the divine service, as well as for the maintenance of the clergy and the poor. Thus they offered, for example, corn, fruit, grapes, milk, honey, wax, oil, later on money also. The offering of such objects, however, could not be made at the same time as that of the bread and wine, which served for consecration, but it was done generally before or after Mass in a particular place in the Church, or also in the house of the bishop. These religious offerings were already in themselves a meritorious and satisfactory act of virtue; in addition to this, they who offered them would thereby participate in the Eucharistic sacrifice and gain the Eucharistic sacrificial fruits in more abundant measure. In this twofold connection the oblations of the faithful served *pro remedio vel pro redemptione animae*, that is, to efface sin, as is often expressed in the old documents. From this ancient custom there was gradually developed the present practice, in existence for many centuries, of giving Mass stipends for the special application of the so-called ministerial sacrificial fruits. Of the loaves presented, only a portion was ordinarily blessed and at the close of the celebration distributed to the non-communicants, later on to all present, or sent to the absent as a mark of union with the Church, the so-called Eulogies, εὐλογία, *benedictio, panis benedictus*, ἀντίδωρον (substitute for Holy Communion). Among the Greeks Eulogies are still in use.

[11] Offertorium, quod inter offerendum cantatur, quamvis, a priori populi consuetudine in usum christianorum venisse dicatur, tamen quis specialiter addiderit officiis nostris, aperte non legimus, sicut et de Antiphona, quae ad communionem dicitur, possumus fateri: cum vere credamus priscis temporibus Patres sanctos *silentio* obtulisse vel communicasse, quod etiam hactenus in Sabbato sancti Paschae observamus (Walafrid. Strabo, chap. 23).

[12] Remains of these are the offerings still in use at Requiem Masses and the festal offerings practised in many congregations; likewise the offering of a lighted candle when receiving holy orders, as well as the presentation of

PREPARATION FOR THE OBLATION

only the antiphon designated by the name *Offertorium*, which the priest recites immediately before offering the sacrificial gifts; but it is still sung by the choir, as in former times, during the Offertory.

2. The *Offertorium* is now a shorter or longer verse, generally taken from the Psalms, sometimes from the other books of Holy Scripture; only a few have been composed by the Church herself. As to its contents, it does not relate to the oblation, as the name would seem to imply.[13] Rather it changes during the course of the ecclesiastical year, and gives expression to the dominant thought of the feast or season; therefore it has precisely the same significance and purpose as have the foregoing Introit and Gradual chants. The same spirit that pervades these two choral chants, resounds again in the Offertory, strengthens the festal dispositions, reawakens the thoughts and feelings with which we should offer or assist at the sacrifice.

The following Offertory read in Requiem Masses deserves special notice:

Domine, Jesu Christe, Rex gloriae, libera animas omnium fidelium defunctorum de poenis inferni et de profundo lacu: libera eas de ore leonis, ne absorbeat eas tartarus, ne cadant in obscurum: sed signifer sanctus Michael repraesentet eas in lucem sanctam: Quam olim Abrahae promisisti et semini ejus.	Lord Jesus Christ, King of Glory, deliver the souls of the faithful departed from the flames of hell, and from the deep pit. Deliver them from the lion's mouth, lest hell swallow them, lest they fall into darkness: and let the standard-bearer, St. Michael, bring them into the holy light: Which thou hast promised of old to Abraham and his posterity.
V. Hostias et preces tibi, Do-	V. We offer Thee, O Lord,

---

two large lighted candles, of two loaves and two small casks of wine at the consecration of a bishop and at the benediction of an abbot. Cf. *Pontif. Roman.*

[13] Oblationes offeruntur a populo et Offertorium cantatur a clero, quod ex ipsa causa vocabulum sumpsit quasi offerentium canticum (Raban. Maur., *De clericor. institut.*, I, chap. 33). Dicto Symbolo cantatur Offertorium sive Offerenda, ut aliqui dicunt. Appellatur autem Offertorium ab offerendo, quia tunc offerimus. Sed necessario hic considerandum est, tria omnino esse quae offerre debemus: primo nosmetipsos, ac deinde ea quae sacrificio sunt necessaria, scil. panem, vinum et aquam, et si qua sunt alia sacrificio apta (Beleth, *Ration.*, chap. 41).

mine, laudis offerimus: tu suscipe pro animabus illis, quarum hodie memoriam facimus: fac eas, Domine, de morte transire ad vitam: Quam olim Abrahae promisisti et semini ejus.	a sacrifice of praise and prayers: accept them in behalf of the souls we commemorate this day: and let them pass from death to life. Which Thou didst promise of old to Abraham and his posterity.

This is the only Offertory which has retained its original form: it consists of an antiphon, a verse, and the concluding antiphonal words repeated. The text is difficult to understand; hence so many different interpretations have been given to it.[14]

THE SACRIFICIAL ELEMENTS

Wheaten bread (*panis triticeus*) and wine of the grapes (*vinum de vite*) are the two elements which are necessary for the accomplishment of the Eucharistic sacrifice; hence they are frequently called the matter of the Holy Sacrifice. This mode of speech, however, must not be misunderstood. It does not say that bread and wine belong to the Eucharistic offerings in the same way that the body and blood of Christ are offered. As on the cross, so on the altar Jesus Christ alone is our victim. The substances of bread and wine appertain to the Eucharistic sacrifice, inasmuch as they are changed into Christ's body and blood; the species of bread and wine serve to

[14] St. Peter designates the place of punishment of the damned by the words *infernus* and *tartarus*, writing, that "God spared not the angels that sinned: but delivered them, drawn down by infernal ropes to the lower hell, unto the torments, to be reserved unto judgment" (*rudentibus inferni detractos in tartarum tradidit cruciandos*). By the words: *Ad infernum detraheris in profundum laci* (Isa. 14:15), which apply to the chief of the fallen angels, hell is likewise designated. St. Michael is the "standard-bearer" (*signifer*), that is, the prince and leader of the angelic choirs that protect the faithful in the agony of death against the attacks of the infernal spirits and conduct the souls that have faithfully struggled into the heavenly paradise. Hence the Church sings in an Antiphon: *Archangele Michael, constitui te principem super omnes animas suscipiendas* ("Archangel Michael, thee have I constituted as prince, to receive all souls"). The promise of salvation (of eternal light and life) was repeatedly made to Abraham as the "Father of believers" and to his spiritual children. The earthly Chanaan promised him (Gen. 12:7; 17:8), "the land of promise," was a type (figure) of the true Chanaan, that is, of the kingdom of God here below and in heaven (Heb. 11:8–12). Terra promissionis erat figura regni coelestis seu patriae et quies illius figura fuit quietis beatorum in coelis (Dion. Carthus., *In Ps.*, 94:11). Cf. also God's word to Abraham: Ego merces tua magna nimis (Gen. 15:1).

make the offering of the body and blood of Christ a visible sacrifice. Considering the close relation of the elements of bread and wine to the Eucharistic sacrifice, we should handle them with great care and reverence even before their consecration.

1. Our Lord and Saviour, at the first celebration of the Eucharistic sacrifice, consecrated bread and wine and prescribed the use of these elements for the accomplishment of the unbloody sacrifice in His Church for all future time. Christ indeed freely and out of His good pleasure chose bread and wine for this sacred purpose; but since His divine wisdom orders all things sweetly, there are certainly some reasons which show the suitableness of these sacrificial elements. The Eucharist is not only a sacrifice, but it is also a sacrament; under both of these points of view the bread and wine are clearly proper for their high destiny.[15] In this place only the fitness of these gifts for the purpose of the Eucharistic sacrifice is chiefly to be considered.

When God united the human soul with the body, thereby imparting life to the body, He, for the support of this life within us, directed us to the natural life without, and in the beginning ordered us to draw the nourishment of our life from the vegetable kingdom. In the state of man's innocence, the trees of Paradise yielded spontaneously for man their fruits, substantial and succulent, delightful to the taste; but after his fall, banished from Paradise to the earth, which of itself yields but thorns and thistles, man has been obliged to wrest support from the earth by hard labor in the sweat of his brow. The grain of wheat, which is the fat of the land, and the grape, which ripens in the sun, in a manner contain the marrow and blood of the earth, and are intended mainly to renew man's substance and to refresh his blood; therefore they are the chief means for the nourishment of his life. Nowhere do these grow

---

[15] Si quaeratur, cur panis et vinum sint hujus sacramenti materia, dicendum, quod principalis causa institutio est divina, cujus institutionis multiplex est ratio. Primo ex parte usus sacramenti, quoniam panis et vinum communius in cibum et potum proveniunt, sicque per ea in spiritualem refectionem manuducimur magis apte. Secundo ex sacramenti effectu, quia panis prae ceteris cibis sustentat corpus et vinum laetificat cor. Ita et hoc sacramentum magis laetificat et sustentat caritate inebriatos, quam alia sacramenta. Tertio ex ritu celebrationis, quoniam duo ista tractantur mundius ac frequentius, quam cetera alimenta. Quarto ex significatione duplicis rei sacramenti istius. Panis namque ex multis granis conficitur et vinum ex multis acinis confluit, quod competit ad significandum corpus Christi verum ac mysterium. Quinto ex repraesentatione ejus, quod praecessit. Grana namque in area conculcantur, panis in fornace decoquitur et vinum in torculari exprimitur, et ita per ea Christi passio designatur (Dion. Carthus., IV, dist. 11, q. 3).

wild, but in all places they thrive only by man's careful and laborious cultivation; and when he has harvested the ears and gathered in the grapes, it is still by renewed labor that he must prepare them for food and drink.

If, therefore, on one hand, bread and wine are gifts of God, they are, on the other, products of man; the sweat of his brow cleaves to them before they are changed into his flesh and blood. Hence they are eminently suited as gifts of man to God; in presenting them we offer to God our fatigue and labor, and in the offering of these gifts we bring to God, so to speak, our flesh and blood, our body and life. Therefore, before our Lord can give and leave us His flesh and blood as a sacrifice, we must offer to Him bread and wine, by separating and withdrawing these articles from the ordinary wants of life, and reserving and sanctifying them for Him for His sacrifice. Consequently, in ancient times the Church permitted the faithful to bring bread and wine to the house of God and to place them on the altar, and the priest accepted them both for the sacrifice and for his daily support.[16]

Ears of wheat and bunches of grapes are the most noble and most valuable products of the vegetable world; they compose, so to speak, the flesh and blood of the earth. These "firstlings of God's creatures and gifts" [17] represent, therefore, nature in her entirety, which is in a manner offered to God in the oblations of bread and wine obtained from the wheat and from the grapes. The offering of bread and wine symbolizes also the donation of man himself and of his life; for bread and wine are the most excellent means of nourishment.[18] In the bread and wine, then, man offers himself and all that he is and has.[19]

[16] Laurent, *Christol. Predigten*, II, 67.
[17] S. Iren., *Adv. haeres.*, IV, xvii, 5).
[18] Prima causa (*for the offering of bread, wine and water*) est, quia inter omnia humanae vitae sustentandae necessaria, haec tria sunt mundiora et utiliora et magis necessaria, propterea potius debuerunt apponi quam alia, et in id quod mundius est et utilius omnibus et super omnia ad vitam aeternam capessendam magis necessarium, transferri et transformari, i.e. in corpus Christi et sanguinem (*Lib. de canone mystici libam.*, chap. 2). This little work is no longer ascribed to John of Cornwallis, but to Richard, a Premonstratentian of the monastery of Wedinghausen (diocese of Cologne).
[19] On the words of the Canon, *qui tibi offerunt pro se suisque omnibus*, Robert Paululus remarks, the small word "*pro*" hoc sensu non inconvenienter accipitur, ut haec, scil. panem et vinum quae in victu vitae animalis principalia sunt, offerendo seipsos et sua omnia, i.e. totum victum suum offerre dicantur. Praecipua quippe illius portio sunt et totum figurant (*De offic. eccles.*, II, chap. 29).

PREPARATION FOR THE OBLATION

2. The Church requires that the matter used for the consecration be not only valid and genuine, but also licit and as perfect as possible. The bread destined for the sacrificial action must have been made of pure wheaten flour that has been mixed with natural water and baked in the fire; the bread should be pure and fresh. The sacrificial wine must have been pressed from ripe grapes and fully fermented, not soured nor settled nor artificially composed; as to the color or taste, it may be red or white, strong or light, naturally sweet or tart. With regard to the color, it is to be remarked that, although red wine symbolizes more perfectly than the white the blood of Christ, still white wine is to be preferred because in its use at the altar cleanliness can more easily be observed. Another prescription respecting the sacrificial elements is that the bread is required to be unleavened and the wine to be mixed with a little water. The use of unleavened bread and the mixing of wine with water have a higher meaning and are, therefore, strictly prescribed by the Church; although they are not required for the validity of the sacrifice, yet they are absolutely required for the lawfulness of the consecration.

a) The bread should be unleavened.[20] This is a strict ordinance of the Church for the priests of the Latin rite, while the uniate Greeks [21] are strictly enjoined, according to an old custom, to consecrate only leavened bread.[22] Unleavened and leavened bread are

[20] *Azymus panis* = *panis sine fermento* (instead of *fervimentum* = fermentation, fermenting mixture, leaven, ζύμη) *vel non fermentatus*, from ἄζυμος. Substantive *azymon* = unleavened bread. The second syllable is made short by Prudentius and others. Bread raised with leaven, leavened bread, is called by Isid. (*Etymolog.*, XX, ii, 15) *panis fermentacius, i.e. fermentis confectus*, also *panis fermentalis vel fermentatus*. In omnibus Scripturis invenimus panem indifferenter dici, sive fuerit azymus sive fuerit fermentatus (Humbert., *Adversus Graecor. calumnias*, n. 12).

[21] In the East the Armenians and Syro-Maronites (like the Latins) use unleavened bread.

[22] Among the Greeks it appears that leavened sacrificial bread, from the most ancient times, was exclusively or at least generally used. The historic question has not as yet been solved, what kind of bread the Western Church used for the sacrifice during the first ten centuries. Three different views regarding it prevail among Catholic theologians since the seventeenth century when the controversy was most animated. P. Sirmond, S. J. (d. 1651), in his *Disquisitio de azymo, semperne in usu altaris fuerit apud Latinos*, defended the assertion (in its universality, at any rate, exaggerated and incorrect), that the Western Church in the middle of the ninth century consecrated exclusively leavened bread. Christopher Lupus, O. S. Aug. (d. 1681), first opposed this opinion. But as its chief opponent, Mabillon, O. S. B. (d. 1707), came forth, who principally in his *Dissertatio de pane eucharistico azymo ac*

equally valid matter of the sacrifice; the one as well as the other has its peculiar mystical signification. Yet there are more numerous and better reasons for the usage prevalent in the Latin Church; hence the rite of the latter is to be preferred. These reasons are principally the following:

a) At the institution of the Eucharist, Christ used unleavened bread. "On the first day of unleavened bread" the Saviour kept the Pasch with His disciples; therefore, at the time in which the Jews, according to the ordinance of the law, were obliged to have nothing leavened in the house or to partake of it. Consequently it is generally admitted that Christ consecrated unleavened bread.[23] Although the words of the Lord to His apostles and their successors commanding them to do the same as He had done at the Last Supper, may not have been a formal command to consecrate unleavened bread, still it is evident that in so grave and sacred a matter the example of Christ should not easily be departed from. The Church has not the slightest reason to depart from it; on the contrary, she has every reason to retain the use of unleavened bread after the example of Christ, since in many respects the unleavened bread is preferable to the leavened bread.

b) The unleavened bread symbolizes very appropriately the Eucharistic victim and the Eucharistic food of the soul. The leaven penetrates and soon leavens the entire mass of flour in which it is mixed, changing it into savory bread. The Saviour Himself (Matt. 13:33) calls the divine truth and grace a heavenly leaven that trans-

---

fermentato, defended the diametrically opposite opinion, namely, that in the West the constant and general use of unleavened sacrificial bread had prevailed; he admits the partial use of leavened bread only among the apostles. Cardinal Bona, O. Cist. (d. 1674), takes a middle view, employing the inconclusive arguments used by both opponents to make it probable that the Roman Church, until late in the ninth century, permitted the use of leavened as well as of unleavened sacrificial bread. The views of Mabillon and Bona since that time have had the greater number of adherents. On the side of Mabillon are, for example, Martene, Macedo, Ciampini, Cabassutius, Boucat, Berti, Simmonet, Sandini; on Bona's side, for example, Tournely, Witasse, Bocquillot, Grancolas, Graveson, Natalis Alexander.

[23] Credimus panem illum, quem primum Dominus in coena mystica in mysterium corporis sui consecravit, infermentatum fuisse, maxime cum in tempore paschae nullum fermentum cuiquam vesci, sed nec in domo habere illi licebat (Raban. Maur., *De cleric. instit.*, I, chap. 31). Even though our Saviour had anticipated the Paschal meal, which can by no means be proved, the use of leavened bread would not in consequence follow.

forms mankind. Otherwise leaven is usually employed in an evil sense;[24] in its fermentation it works decomposition or decay; therefore it serves as a figure of the unclean, perverse, and corrupted. Unleavened bread, on the contrary, which has undergone no such process of fermentation, is a symbol of purity and cleanliness. Accordingly only unleavened bread can appropriately indicate the superhuman holiness and purity of the Eucharistic victim, as well as the incomparable purity and incorruption of the Eucharistic food of the soul.

c) Inasmuch as unleavened bread calls to our mind how unspeakably pure and bright the transfigured body of Christ is, at the same time it also reminds us of the purity of heart and body with which we should approach the table of the Lord and receive the food of angels. According to the counsel of the Apostle (I Cor. 5:7 f.), we must purge out the old leaven of sin and passion, of wickedness and wantonness, that we may be a new paste, and be enabled, when thus sanctified, to partake of the immaculate flesh of the Eucharistic victim. These thoughts are beautifully expressed in the paschal hymn which says: "Christ is our paschal sacrifice, while for unleavened bread we need but heart sincere and purpose true" (*pura puris mentibus sinceritatis azyma*).[25]

b) To the sacrificial wine a small quantity of natural water must

---

[24] Fermentum significat caritatem propter aliquem effectum, quia scil. panem facit sapidiorem et majorem; sed corruptionem significat ex ipsa ratione suae speciei (S. Thom., IIIa, q.74, a.4 ad 3). In another passage he says: In fermento duo possunt considerari. Primo sapor, quem tribuit pani, et secundum hoc per fermentum significatur sapientia Dei, per quam omnia quae sunt hominis sapida redduntur; secundo in fermento potest considerari corruptio, et secundum hoc per fermentum potest intelligi uno modo peccatum, alio modo homo peccator (*In 1 Cor.*, chap. 5, lect. 2).

[25] Unleavened bread is also different in appearance and taste from the daily bread that we eat; hence it is suitable, by its appearance, to indicate that under the Eucharistic veil no ordinary bread, but the true and living bread of heaven, is concealed, that preserves the spiritual life of grace and ensures the blessed life of immortality. The unleavened bread, which was eaten with the paschal lamb and bitter herbs, is called "bread of tribulation" (*panis afflictionis;* Deut. 16:3), because it was a reminder of the labors and oppression endured in Egypt; in this it also symbolizes the Eucharistic banquet celebrated in memory of the bitter passion and death of Christ. Cf. Algerus, *De sacramentis corp. et sang. dominici,* II, chap. 10. The ferment that penetrates and invigorates the mass of meal, is indeed a figure of the divinity, clothing itself with human nature, but *panis est proprie sacramentum corporis Christi, quod sine corruptione conceptum est, magis quam divinitatis ipsius* (S. Thom., IIIa, q.74, a.4).

be added, according to apostolic ordinance and the strict discipline of the Church. As this commingling is a holy ceremony, it must take place at the altar before the oblation and be made in the chalice itself. Even a drop answers the purpose. It is advisable and always safer to pour but a little water into the chalice,[26] so that the wine is not too much weakened and thus perhaps be spoiled. This mixture is so important and, therefore, so strictly prescribed that a priest would never be allowed to begin the Holy Sacrifice if he foresaw that no water could be procured. Profoundly significant are the reasons that favor the fitness of this strict ecclesiastical ordinance and practice.

a) It is certain that the Lord at the institution of the Eucharist consecrated wine mixed with water, since the addition of water to the wine at the paschal meal was a permanent and universally practiced custom from which the Lord surely did not depart.[27] The ancient liturgies and holy Fathers are unanimous in asserting that the Saviour mixed water with the wine at the Last Supper.[28] Thus from the time of the apostles the Church has everywhere and at all times faithfully followed the example of her divine Master and has ever consecrated only wine mixed with water. She regarded it, as St. Cyprian writes in his letter to Caecilius, as proper that at the mixing and offering of the chalice of the Lord, she should observe the true tradition, so that at His glorious and triumphant return He

---

[26] The *Florentinum* gives: *aqua modicissima* and *paululum aquae;* the rubric: *parum aquae*. Hence the well known adage: *quanto paucior, tanto potior.* "Although the reasons for the mingling of the water are so manifest that without mortal sin it may not be omitted, yet the Sacrament exists when it is not done. But priests should be attentive that, as in Mass water must be taken with the wine, yet only a little must be added. For according to the opinion and judgment of ecclesiastical commentators, this water is changed into wine" (*Catech. Rom.*, II, chap. 4, q. 16). Vino consecrando miscenda est aqua naturalis tantum et modica, et per modum sacrae ceremoniae, ad altare et in calice (Sporer, *Theol. sacrament.*, II, chap. 3, sect. 2, §3).

[27] As a rule, red wine mingled with water was used for the paschal celebration.

[28] The mingling of the wine with water is not *de necessitate sacramenti neque praecepti divini*, but only *de necessitate praecepti ecclesiastici*, that is, *apostolici*. In the Fathers and in councils and liturgies, the Eucharistic chalice, that is, its contents (before the Consecration), has, for example, the following denominations: κρᾶσις, κρᾶμα, ποτήριον κεκραμένον, *calix mixtus, temperamentum calicis, poculum aquae et vini, calix dominicus vino mixtus, calix vini et aquae plenus, vinum aqua mixtum, calix dominicus vino et aqua permixtus, mixtum, temperatum*.

may find us adhering strictly to that which He had exhorted us, observing what He had taught and doing what He had done.

Besides this historical reason there are also mystical and symbolical reasons.[29]

b) The wine destined to be changed into the blood of Christ is mixed with water at the altar, that by these two elements the blood and water which flowed from the wound in the side of Christ may be represented.[30] The piercing and opening of the heart of Jesus, from which the stream of blood and water flowed forth, is a wonderful event [31] and, at the same time, one full of mystical meaning, which should in a very special manner engage the attention of men. For this occurrence not only proves the truth and reality of the sacrificial death of Christ, but it moreover involves a profound symbolism; for the stream of blood and water which proceeded from the pierced heart of Jesus symbolizes all the graces and blessings that flow to us from His passion and death. The water symbolizes baptism, which is the laver of purification and regeneration; the blood signifies the Eucharist, the fountain of reconciliation and strength for life eternal. But since baptism is the beginning, the Eucharist, the end and complement of the remaining sacraments, they are all included in these two principal ones. The outpouring of blood and water from the pierced side of the Redeemer, therefore, symbolically expresses that all the sacraments have their origin in His sacrificial death, that is, that they derive from it their power and plenitude of grace. But the Church is the only lawful possessor and administrator of the sacraments, by virtue of which she in her members is ever undergoing purification and sanctification; hence

---

[29] Sicut propter imitationem magis exactam, et propter mysterium Ecclesia latina praecipit consecrationem in azymo, sic propter eamdem imitationem, et propter mysterium Ecclesia universalis praecipit consecrationem in vino non puro, sed lymphato (Lugo, *loc. cit.*).

[30] It is the better established and the more general opinion that the right side of the Saviour (together with His Sacred Heart) was opened by the lance. Dominus meus Jesus post cetera inaestimabilis suae erga me beneficia pietatis, etiam dextrum sibi propter me passus est latus fodi: quod videlicet nonnisi de dextera mihi propinare vellet, nonnisi in dextera locum parare refugii. Utinam ego talis merear esse columba, quae in foramine petrae habitet et in foramine lateris dextri (S. Bernard., *In Ps. 90 serm.*, VII, n. 15).

[31] In this outpouring of blood and water from a heart that beat no longer, the holy Fathers behold a great miracle. Contumelia a Judaeis illata in signum prodiit, quia de corpore exstincto sanguis verus et aqua pura miraculose manavit (Ludolph. de Saxon., II, lxiv, 13).

the holy Fathers behold in the pierced heart of Jesus also the divine origin of the Church. They say that from the opened side of the second Adam, while slumbering in death, the new Eve, that is, the Church, was formed and came forth.[32] Thus from the pierced heart of Jesus, the pure, immaculate Church was born, and thence the inexhaustable fountain of her graces originated. The rite of the mixing of wine and water in the chalice should remind us of these mysteries.

c) The commingling of wine and water in the chalice refers also to that intimate, mystical relationship existing between Christ and His Church.[33] The wine is a symbol of Christ; the water is a symbol of man. "The waters which thou sawest," said the angel to John, "are peoples and nations" (Apoc. 17:15). The drops of water which have been poured into the chalice no longer exist as water, but they are diffused in and incorporated into the wine, partaking of its qualities. Similar is the union of the faithful with Christ,[34] by virtue of which they are made partakers of the divine nature, that is, by sanctifying grace they are made children of God and His heirs. For from the head, Jesus Christ, who is filled with all the treasures of the divinity, the unction of grace flows down to His members, descending even to the hem and extremity of the garment of the Church (Ps. 132:2), so that she becomes wholly penetrated with the precious flow of heavenly gifts. By the commingling of wine and water before the oblation, we are to understand, first of all, the sacrificial communion between Christ and the Church, that is, this ceremony is intended to place before our eyes Christ, as the head, in union with the Church, as His mystical body, offering sacrifice and being offered in sacrifice at the celebration of Mass. At the same time, is indicated that unspeakably intimate and exalted

---

[32] Sopor ille viri (*Adam*; Gen. 2:21) mors erat Christi, cujus examinis in cruce pendentis latus lancea perforatum est atque inde sanguis et aqua profluxit (John 19:34): quae sacramenta esse novimus, quibus aedificatur Ecclesia (S. August., *De civit. Dei*, XXII, chap. 17). Cf. Pius XII, Encyclical *Mystici corporis*.

[33] Consulte a prioribus statutum est, ne vinum in sacrificio sine aquae admixtione offeratur, ut videlicet per hoc significetur, populos qui secundum Joannem (Apoc. 17:15) aquae sunt, a Christo, cujus sanguis in calice est, dividi non debere (Walafr. Strabo, *De exord. et increm.*, chap. 16).

[34] Cum aqua in vinum convertitur, significatur, quod populus Christo incorporatur (S. Thom., IIIa, q.74, a.8 ad 2). Aqua significat populum, qui est insipidus, et sapidus fit per conjunctionem cum Sapientia, Christo, sicut aqua, cum adjungitur vino (S. Bonav., IV, dist. 11, p.2, a.1, q.3 ad 6).

relation which is realized between the children of the Church and our Redeemer by the sacrifice and sacrament of the Eucharist. This is that supernatural espousal of which the Apostle wrote to the Christians of Corinth: "I have espoused you to one husband, that I may present you as a chaste virgin to Christ" (II Cor. 11:2). It commences here below in sanctifying grace and is consummated above in eternal glory.

d) Finally, our rite is calculated to symbolize that mystery by which the divine and human natures are united together in one person, the incarnate Son of God. This mystery is the root and source of every supernatural relation of man with God in time and eternity.

3. To the elements of the sacrifice are due the most scrupulous care and the greatest reverence, even before the oblation.[35] Every

---

[35] The bread selected for the consecration was generally called *oblata* or *hostia*. The figure and size were not prescribed in the first centuries, but left to the judgment of the celebrant and people, *prout erat cuique studium atque devotio in religione divina* (Bernold., *Constant.*). Si de primis Ecclesiae saeculis agitur, quando ipsae populi oblationes immolabantur, perspicuum est, alia tum forma non fuisse, quam quae panum erat oblatorum. Integri enim ac solidi, ut oblati fuerant, consecrabantur consecratique in partes ad distribuendum comminuebantur (Sirmondus, *Disquis. de azymo*, chap. 4). In reference to the example of our Saviour, who consecrated a loaf (a cake, a slice, a round) of the unleavened paschal bread, the round form had even at a very early period the preference, the more so as it is regarded as a symbol of perfection. Already St. Epiphanius (d. 403) mentions that the Eucharistic sacrificial bread is round in shape (*The Anchor*, chap. 57). In the Middle Ages it received names that allude to its circular form, for example, *corona oblationum, circulus, rotula panis, panis rotularis*. According to an ordinance of the Sixteenth Synod of Toledo (693), the sacrificial bread should be specially and carefully prepared, be white and of moderate size; finally, not a piece, but whole loaves were to be consecrated (*panis integer et nitidus, qui ex studio fuerit praeparatus, neque grande aliquid, seu modica tantum oblata*). It was already then baked in iron moulds, provided with symbolical pictures and Scriptural signs (host-irons, *ferrum oblatorium, ferrum oblatarum, ferramentum characteratum*). Moreover, in the eleventh century the consecrated breads were still so large that they had to be broken and divided for the Communion of the faithful (*particulae*). Tenues oblatas ex simila (*of the finest wheaten flour*) praeparatas integras et sanas sacris altaribus superponimus et ex ipsis post consecrationem fractis cum populo communicamur (Humbert. Card. [d. about 1064], *Advers. Graec. calumn.*, n. 33). From this time on they gradually became smaller and thinner, until they received the present (coin) form. As a rule, now only hosts that are whole may be distributed; but the name *particulae*, that has clung to them, still reminds us of the ancient practice of the breaking of bread. Decet revera panem candidissimum esse et mundissimum, si facultas non defuerit, qui transferri debet

precaution must be taken to procure freshly and properly made hosts and pure grape wine for the sacrifice of the altar. During the Middle Ages devout princes and princesses esteemed it a high honor to be allowed to prepare and to provide the bread and wine for the Holy Sacrifice.[36] In convents the preparation of the sacrificial bread was even accompanied with religious solemnity and a kind of divine service. Thus was it prepared in the world-renowned Benedictine abbey of Cluny.[37] At prescribed hours the monks performed manual labor; but that they might also be sanctified in the midst of their occupations, they worked amid the singing of psalms. But special care was bestowed upon the preparation of the bread for the sacrifice; amid the singing of psalms the seed destined for it was confided to the earth and the ripe grain was gathered; amid divine praises grain after grain was selected, carefully washed, and carried in a special sack to the mill by one of the most exemplary monks. There he first washed the two millstones, covered them with cloths, robed himself in white, and then, with veiled face so that his eyes alone were uncovered, he began to grind the wheat. With similar care the sieve was then washed and the flour sifted. To prepare the bread from the flour was the duty of the highest official of the monastic church; two monks and a recently admitted brother shared the holy labor with him. Being well washed and clothed in white garments, they baked the hosts in a blessed vessel. It is proper that even today persons consecrated to God prepare with reverence the bread for the Holy Sacrifice, regarding this preparation as a work of love.

---

in splendidissimum corpus Agni immaculati (Algerus, *De sacram. corp. et sang. dom.*, II, chap. 9). Cf. Mabillon, *Acta SS. O. S. B.*, III, praef. n. 57–60; Gerbert, *Vetus Liturgia Alemannica*, I, disp. IV, chap. 3.

[36] S. Wenceslaus summa religione sacerdotes veneratus suis manibus triticum serebat et vinum exprimebat, quibus in Missae sacrificio uterentur (*Brev. Rom.*).

[37] Cf. *Consuetud. Cluniac.*, III, chap. 13 (*De hostiis qualiter fiant*); Krazer, sect. III, art. 2, chap. 3.

CHAPTER XXVII

THE OBLATION

The Offering of the Host

THE next preparation of the elements of the sacrifice takes place during the Mass itself,[1] and it includes the separation, dedication, and blessing of the bread and wine for the exalted end to which they are destined. This preliminary sanctification of the Eucharistic elements, if not essentially necessary, is yet in the highest degree just and proper.[2] The earthly elements are to be taken from the sphere of nature into the higher order of grace: they are to become holy things before the Holy Ghost changes them into the body and blood of Christ. At the Last Supper, Jesus Himself, in His character of high priest, took the bread and the chalice with wine "in His holy and venerable hands, and raising His eyes to heaven to God, His almighty Father, giving thanks, He blessed" the earthly gifts of bread and wine.[3] The Church, therefore, imitates

---

[1] The preparation of the offering, that is, the pouring of the wine into the chalice and the mixing of water in it, took place, in the Middle Ages, usually before the prayers at the foot of the altar, that is, immediately after the priest had ascended the altar, and also the bread and the wine were then often offered to God not one after the other, but both together by a single prayer. Cf. the present rite of the Dominicans.

[2] Per prolationem sacrorum verborum et signa crucis panis et vinum aptantur et quasi meliorantur, ut sint condigna materia, quae in corpus et sanguinem Christi convertatur. Si enim vestes et templum ac vasa ecclesiae benedicuntur et sanctificantur, ut sint apta instrumenta divini obsequii, quanto rationabilius est, panem et vinum ante consecrationem benedici, ut sint apta materia transsubstantiationis supermirabilis atque divinae. Nam et aliorum sacramentorum materiae propter reverentiam sacramenti ante usum suum sanctificantur, ut aqua baptismi vel chrisma seu oleum (Dion. Carthus., *Expos. Miss.*, a. 18).

[3] The Lord celebrated the Pasch of the New Testament by blessing (εὐλογήσας, *benedicens*) the bread and the chalice, as also by giving thanks (εὐχαριστήσας, *gratias agens*) to God the Father. Both words εὐλογεῖν and εὐχαριστεῖν are not simply synonymous, but are often used to designate one

our Lord when, in the course of the sacrificial celebration up to the time of the consecration, she repeatedly blesses the Eucharistic elements and implores of God their acceptance, sanctification, and transformation.

The offering of the elements begins with the offering of the host, wherein we may distinguish the act and the prayer of oblation.

1. The act of oblation. The priest takes the paten with the host and elevates it; he offers it as a sacrificial gift to the Lord God "who dwells in the highest," and he does this by holding it before His eyes and praying that the Lord would graciously accept it.[4] The raising of the host is intended to express the act of presentation. At the same time the priest, in conformity with the first words of the accompanying prayer, raises his eyes to the crucifix on the altar and lowers them again almost immediately, mindful of his unworthiness. After the conclusion of the prayer, the celebrant makes with the paten and host the sign of the cross over the place on which the host is to be placed.[5] This ceremony is intended to bring before the mind in a

---

and the same prayer, in so far as the blessing therein contained is connected with thanksgiving. At all events by this εὐλογεῖν or εὐχαριστεῖν we must not understand merely the uttering of the words of consecration; for there is thereby designated another act entirely different from the consecration, that is, a preparatory prayer of blessing and thanksgiving preceding the consecration, the conclusion of which are the words of the consecration. This presanctification of the elements was wholly appropriate, since their species remained after the consecration, and, in like manner, the thanksgiving also was appropriate before and during the performance of a mystery equally glorious for God as beneficial for men. (Cf. Knabenbauer, *Ad Matt.*, 26:26; Cornely, *Ad I Cor.*, 10:16 and 11:24.)

[4] In oblatione panis et vini dicuntur aliquae orationes valde tenerae, devotae ac sanctae a sacerdote, quasi spiritualiter *habente in manibus thus lucidissimum et panes propositionis* (Lev. 24:7), qui in mensa Domini offeruntur. Et quamvis sacerdos satisfaciat, orationes illas eo affectu dicens, quem ipsa verba insinuant, bene ad ea attentus, tamen magis adhuc specialiter quum accipit Patenam cum hostia in manibus, debet spiritualiter in ea cor proprium ponere et corda omnium circumstantium, imo et omnium fidelium, ut ea etiam Deo offerat cum ea celsissima intentione, quod quemadmodum hostiam illam offert, quae est purus panis, ut ejus substantia destructa convertatur in corpus ipsius Christi, ita cor suum et omnium fidelium offerat, ut in eis destruat quidquid terrenum est, et convertat ac per amorem et imitationem transformet in ipsum Christum, ita ut desinant esse quod erant et vivere more antiquo, incipiant autem esse et vivere sicut ipse omnium Redemptor (De Ponte, *De christ. hom. perf.*, IV, tr. II, chap. 12, § 1).

[5] There is, moreover, already a cross cut in the altar stone and anointed with chrism, when the altar was consecrated, in the very place (the middle

striking manner that the cross and altar are holy places, where, though in a different manner, one and the same sacrifice was once or is now offered. The very same body that hung upon the cross, is laid on the altar; as the cross was once deemed worthy to bear the atoning sacrifice for the world, so is now the altar.

2. **The oblation prayer.**

Suscipe, sancte Pater, omnipotens aeterne Deus, hanc immaculatam hostiam, quam ego indignus famulus tuus offero tibi Deo meo vivo et vero, pro innumerabilibus peccatis et offensionibus et negligentiis meis, et pro omnibus circumstantibus, sed et pro omnibus fidelibus Christianis, vivis atque defunctis: ut mihi et illis proficiat ad salutem in vitam aeternam. Amen.	Accept, O holy Father, almighty and eternal God, this unspotted host, which I Thy unworthy servant offer unto Thee, my living and true God, for my innumerable sins, offences, and negligences, and for all here present; as also for all faithful Christians, both living and dead, that it may avail both me and them for salvation unto life everlasting. Amen.

This prayer, which is as terse in composition as it is rich in thought, affords an answer to various questions that may be asked with regard to the Eucharistic sacrifice. Who is to receive and accept the host? "The holy Father, the almighty and eternal God." [6] The Church in the Mass generally addresses herself to God the Father, uniting herself to the Saviour, who on the altar offers Himself to His heavenly Father. In the full and complete sense God alone deserves the name of Father, as Christ says: "Call none your father upon earth; for one is your Father, who is in heaven" (Matt. 23:9). Yes, God is our Father; we are His children. Through His only-begotten Son, Jesus Christ, He has conferred upon us the dignity as well as the goods and privileges of children of God. What love has He not thereby shown us! God is not merely the

---

of the altar) where the host is placed. Quod sacerdos oblata in altari deponit super crucem in consecratione altaris cum chrismate factam, hic est Christus, qui carnem suam cruci affixit (Sicardus, *Mitrale*, III, chap. 6).

[6] Pensa, cui offeras, utpote Deo Patri omnipotenti et aeterno, ex cujus bonitatis, dilectionis, pietatis, munificentiae ac beneficiorum contemplatione debes vehementi dilectione accendi, atque ex consideratione suae majestatis et aequitatis debes reverentiali timore et omni humiliatione tui ipsius repleri. Hinc ante celebrationem et in ea debes bonitatem, caritatem, liberaliter et misericordiam Dei Patris ad homines intueri, mirari et honorare (Dion. Carthus., *De sacr. altar.*, a. 16).

best and the most liberal of fathers, but He is also the infinitely "holy Father." Thus does the Saviour call Him in His sacrificial prayer as high priest (John 17:11). Therefore as His children, it is incumbent on us to be, after the Saviour's example, holy in all our conduct; for we should be perfect as is our Father in heaven (Matt. 5:48). God, whom we may with confidence call our Father, is, moreover, the "almighty, eternal God," to whom, on account of His majesty and glory, the sacrifice of the most profound reverence and humble subjection is due. Finally, He is the "living and true God," to whom alone sacrifice may and should be offered. In the liturgy the Lord is often designated as the living and true God (I Thess. 1:9), in contradistinction to the inanimate and false gods, which are vain, powerless, without life, and full of deception. The priest offers to the "living and true God," who created heaven and earth. The "living" God is life itself, the eternal, uncreated life, the source of all life: from Him proceeds both natural and supernatural life, the life of grace and glory in the world of angels and of men. In God all things live and move; without Him there is no life. The "true" God is truth itself, the primordial and purest truth, the fountainhead of all truth.

What is offered to God the Father? An "unspotted host." [7] By this expression the Eucharistic sacrificial body of Christ, as well as the Eucharistic sacrificial bread, is to be understood. That the term, "unspotted host," is not exclusively applied to the bread there present, but is to be referred also to the body of the Lord soon to be present under the appearance of bread, is clearly evident from the context, as also from the comparison of this prayer with other oblation prayers recited before the consecration. Only the body of Christ is that unspotted host which secures for us atonement of sin and salvation, for which supplication is made.[8] The Church,

---

[7] This spotlessness is frequently commented upon in the liturgy, because it it the first and essential requisite, in order that the sacrificial gift may be acceptable to God.

[8] Panis non est immaculata illa hostia pro expiatione peccatorum oblata, sed solus Christus. Itaque sensus horum verborum hic est: Suscipe, sancte Pater, immaculatam hostiam, quam ego indignus servus tuus ex hoc pane per mirabilem conversionem confecturus sum et tibi oblaturus. . . . Unde sacerdos in Offertorio orat Deum, ut acceptet hostiam a se ex hoc pane conficiendam et offerendam, et ut victima ex pane conficienda prosit sibi et aliis. Atque simul per caerimoniam illam sacrat Deo materiam remotam sacrificii ad sacrificium eucharistiae decentius peragendum (Antoine, *De sacrif. Missae*, q. 2).

therefore, looks on the bread resting on the paten and chosen for the consecration as already consecrated, and in offering it has already Christ's body in view. Hence the priest already before the consecration calls the gift that he offers immaculate, unspotted; for Christ is the absolutely pure, holy, and spotless victim. The unspotted host on the altar is, therefore, that "clean oblation" announced by the prophet Malachias. This offering of the body of Christ is, in a measure, to be distinguished from the offering which takes place after the consecration; and the difference consists in this, that here at the same time the bread is still presented and dedicated to the Lord God with the desire that He would accept it for the purpose of consecration, bringing the oblation of the bread to its final termination by the consecration. Consequently the expression, "unspotted host," can and ought to be understood of the sacrificial bread lying on the paten.[9] To two things therefore, namely, to the sacrificial body of the Lord, in spirit regarded as already present, and to the sacrificial bread soon to be changed, which is present in reality, the eye and heart of the priest are directed while he raises on the paten the "unspotted host," imploring its favorable acceptance by the heavenly Father.

Who performs the offering? The priest, who acknowledges himself an unworthy servant of God. The priest is God's servant; the Lord has called him into His sanctuary, that he may serve Him there all the days of his life. But it is especially at the altar that the priest is penetrated with a sense of his unworthiness to discharge this honorable and sublime service. The humblest office in the house of God is more exalted than the greatest worldly position. Now, when the priest considers his misery and frailty, his ingratitude and sinfulness, how painfully should he not realize that he is quite unworthy to serve the Most High, above all, in the most holy mystery of the altar!

For whom does the priest offer the sacrifice? In the first place, for

[9] After the Consecration not only the body and blood of Christ, but also the figurative bread and wine offerings of Melchisedech are designated as *immaculata hostia*. Bishop Odo of Cambrai (d. 1113) remarks in respect to this designation (*Expos. in Canon. Miss.*, dist. 3): Ab immaculata [Virgine] sumpta est haec hostia, ideo et ipsa immaculata. Et hoc loco admonemur quod panis appositus altari debet esse candidissimus et in quo nulla possit inspici macula, ut hoc appareat in figura, quod praedicatur de substantia, ut pura et immaculata videatur exterius figura, cujus substantia dicitur interius pura et immaculata.

himself, then for all present, and finally, for all Christians. The celebrant, therefore, first offers the unspotted host as a sacrifice of propitiation for his own sins, to obtain remission of all guilt and punishment. The priest knows full well that he is not (as he should be) holy, innocent, undefiled, separated from sinners, but that he is encompassed with infirmity; therefore in the first place he offers sacrifice for his own sins, and afterward for those of his people (Heb. 7:26).[10] He confesses his sins and faults and negligences to be "innumerable." [11] *Delicta quis intelligit?* (Ps. 18:13.) Who can understand and take a note of all his sins? [12] The possibilities of failing and stumbling are numerous. Even the just man falls seven times a day, and we all fail in many things. Though our sins be but trivial, they are still many, and in their number lurks the danger. All the sins incident to the very living of this wretched life of ours, the priest

[10] Christus Dominus noster, qui aeternitate sacerdotii sui omnes tibi [Deo] servientes sanctificat sacerdotes, quoniam mortali carne circumdati, ita quotidianis peccatorum remissionibus indigemus, ut non solum pro populo, sed etiam pro nobis [sacerdotibus] ejusdem te Pontificis sanguis exoret (*Sacrament. Gregor.*).

[11] Tu Christi sacerdos considera temetipsum, *quis sis*, h. e. quam defectuosus et fragilis in natura . . . quam culpabilis in vita, quam *innumerabilibus* vicibus quotidie peccans, saltem in venialibus, per omissionem et commissionem, per interiorum et exteriorum incustodiam sensuum, per irrefrenationem linguae, per inexemplaritatem et scandalum, per cogitationes inutiles, per distractiones, levitates, negligentias etiam in divinis, per immoderantias cibi ac potus, per inordinatas circa quaecunque creata affectiones. In his et consimilibus multis adverte te quotidie toties esse culpabilem ac peccantem, ut *nequeas numerare*, nec singula possis attendere, imo exorare indigeas et exclamare ad Dominum: *Delicta quis intelligit? Ab occultis meis munda me* (Dion. Carthus, *De sacramento altaris serm.*, 3).

[12] P. Roothaan, S. J., distinguishes in his *Annotations* to the *Exercitia spiritualia* of St. Ignatius the *peccata et offensiones et negligentiae* of our oblation prayer in the following manner: a) Peccata quaevis, seu gravia seu levia, sive cogitationis sint, sive verborum sive operum sive etiam omissionis. Peccata, intelligo culpas proprie sic dictas. b) Offensiones, culpae minus proprie dictae, seu involuntariae, in quas scilicet offendere fragilitatem nostram in tot tamque variis vitae hujus casibus pronum est, ferme ut per viam salebrosam incedenti frequenter offendere seu impingere vel nolenti accidit. Et tamen, cautius incedendo, offensiones hujusmodi minuere Dei famulus potest et debet. c) Negligentiae eae, quae ad rationem quidem peccati omissionis non pertingunt, sed in actiones nostras irrepere, easque si minus vitiare omnino, tamen imperfectas minusque acceptas Deo reddere solent, suntque profecto innumerae, sive intentionis puritatem et intensionem spectes sive modos omnes, quibus actiones nostras ornari ac perfici in Dei conspectu decet, pro mensura luminis et gratiae nobis a Domino communicatae.

THE OBLATION

would daily atone for and efface by the sacrifice of the altar.[13] The priest, in the second place, offers and prays expressly for all present: for all those who are devoutly assisting at the divine service and who are uniting in the sacrifice; such persons, consequently, receive a more special and abundant share in the fruits of the sacrifice. But like a loving, solicitous mother, the Church forgets none of her children; she therefore permits the priest to offer and pray for all the faithful who belong to the communion of saints and who still stand in need of assistance, consequently, for all her children, "whether this present world yet retains them in the flesh or the world to come has already received them stripped of their mortal bodies," whether they still are combating on earth or suffering in purgatory.

For what purpose is the sacrifice offered? That to all it may avail for eternal life, that it may apply to them the benefits and blessings of redemption, not merely for time, but for all eternity. Salvation (*salus*) is the ideal and the sum of all the good things that Christ brought into the world, for we acquire possession of these goods when we obtain salvation. This salvation begins for us already here below but is completed only in the blessedness of the world to come. Now, on the altar there flows the universal and inexhaustible fountain of salvation, whence all spiritual gifts come to us. Hence the priest prays that the Eucharistic sacrifice may be so efficacious a means of salvation that all may attain to glory of soul and body in eternity.[14]

---

[13] Non solum lavit Christus nos a peccatis nostris in sanguine suo, quando sanguinem suum dedit in cruce pro nobis, vel quando unusquisque nostrum mysterio sacrosanctae passionis illius baptismo aquae ablutus est, verum etiam quotidie tollit peccata mundi. Lavat itaque nos a peccatis nostris quotidie in sanguine suo, cum ejusdem beatae passionis ad altare memoria replicatur, cum panis et vini creatura in sacramentum carnis et sanguinis ejus ineffabili Spiritus sanctificatione transfertur, sicque corpus et sanguis illius non infidelium manibus ad perniciem ipsorum funditur et occiditur, sed fidelium ore suam sumitur in salutem (Beda Venerab., I, homil. XIV).

[14] After the offering of the host, the paten, when the Mass is not a solemn one, is concealed under the corporal until after the Pater noster (cf. Microl., *op. cit.*, chap. 10). In Solemn Masses, however, the subdeacon holds the paten enveloped in the veil that hangs from his shoulders. The original and peculiar reason for keeping it thus covered is, that the paten (as also the chalice), being a blessed and sacred object, should, as far as possible, be withdrawn from profane gaze (cf. Lebrun, *op. cit.*, III, a. 6).

The Offering of the Chalice

In a similar manner the chalice also is dedicated and offered to the heavenly Father;[15] but the offering is preceded by the preparation.

1. The preparation of the chalice comprises the pouring of the wine into the chalice and the mixing with it of a little water which was previously blessed by the sign of the cross. It is asked why the sign of the cross is made over the water only and not over the wine and why in Requiem Masses the blessing of the water also is omitted. The most reliable explanation rests on the symbolical meaning to be found in the mingling of the wine and water. The wine symbolizes Christ, who has no need of a blessing and gains no advantage from His union with the people; hence the wine is not blessed. The water symbolizes the faithful, who greatly need divine grace and receive the greatest gain from their union with Christ; hence the sign of the cross is made over the water before it is mingled with the wine.[16] The sign of the cross, therefore, does not apply so much to the water itself, as to the people signified by the water.[17] This also explains why the sign of the cross is omitted in Requiem Masses. The whole rite of the Requiem Mass aims at giving to the departed souls the greatest possible assistance, hence some parts which refer exclusively to those present (the living) are omitted. Thus, for example, the celebrant at the Introit makes the sign of the cross, not over himself, but over the book, which here in a certain way represents the suffering souls; and at the conclusion of the Mass he does not bestow the blessing on those present. For the same reason, at the

---

[15] That the Oblation prayer of the chalice is always addressed to the Father, is manifest from the Mozarabic Missal, in which the prayer is as follows: Offerimus tibi, Domine, Jesu Christi Filii tui calicem humiliter implorantes clementiam tuam, ut ante conspectum divinae majestatis tuae cum odore suavitatis ascendat. Per eundem Chr. (Migne, *P.L.*, LXXXV, 528).

[16] Vinum in hoc loco Christum significat, qui nulla eget benedictione; aqua populum qui in hac vita nequit esse sine peccato, propter quod indiget benedictione Dei, ut reddatur dignus ad unionem cum Christo. Ad hoc igitur significandum aqua benedicitur, quando vino admiscetur (Durand., IV, xxx, 21).

[17] The former rite had not this signification; it was differently constituted, as the cross was not made over the water, but the water was poured into the chalice in the form of a cross: *Archdiaconus infundit (aquam) faciens crucem (= in modum crusis) in calice (Ordo Rom. I*, n. 14). The *Ordo Rom. XIV*, chap. 72, had the rubric: *demum* (after pouring the water into the wine) *signat super calicem semel.*

Offertory he omits to bless the water, that is, the people symbolized by the water.

The prayer recited at the mixing of the water with the wine is as follows:

Deus, qui humanae substantiae dignitatem mirabiliter condidisti, et mirabilius reformasti: da nobis per hujus aquae et vini mysterium, ejus divinitatis esse consortes, qui humanitatis nostrae fieri dignatus est particeps, Jesus Christus, Filius tuus, Dominus noster; Qui tecum vivit et regnat in unitate Spiritus Sancti, Deus: per omnia saecula saeculorum. Amen.	O God, who in creating human nature hast wonderfully dignified it, and still more wonderfully reformed it: grant that by the mystery of this water and wine, we may be made partakers of the divine nature of Him who vouchsafed to become partaker of our human nature, namely, Jesus Christ, our Lord, Thy Son, who liveth and reigneth with Thee in the unity of the Holy Ghost, one God, world without end. Amen.

The foregoing prayer, which occurs in the ancient sacramentaries as a Christmas Collect,[18] contains in part the mystical meaning of the mingling of the water and wine. In it we beg for that participation in the divine nature (II Pet. 1:4) which consists in this, that poor, frail human nature, by the communication of heavenly gifts and graces, is elevated to a supernatural state, endowed with inestimable riches, and clothed with incomparable beauty. Hence the holy Fathers speak of a deification of man, by which they understand a supernatural, mystical, blissful union with God. "They in whom the Holy Ghost dwells become deified." [19] The virgin martyr Agnes referred to these gifts of grace when, full of enthusiasm, she spoke of her heavenly spouse: "With sparkling and glittering gems hath He covered my breast, with golden garments hath He clothed me, with artistic and precious jewels hath He adorned me, and, moreover, He hath shown me incomparable treasures, which are to be mine if I remain true to Him." To particpate in the divine life, in the divine glory of Jesus Christ, we therefore pray: *per hujus aquae et vini mysterium*, that is, by the mystery which is represented by the present mingling of water and wine. This mystery is manifold:

[18] There the words *per hujus aquae et vini mysterium* are wanting.
[19] S. Athanas., *Epist. l ad Serap.*, n. 24.

at one time it represents the Incarnation (the union of the human and divine natures) and also the passion and death of the Saviour (the issue of water and blood from Christ's pierced heart), hence the whole work of redemption; for these two mysteries are the original source of all grace for us. Another mystery signified by the mixing of wine and water is the mystical union of the faithful with Christ, principally as accomplished in the reception of the Eucharist.[20] By this union with the head, divine life diffuses itself throughout the members, as from the stock of the vine the vivifying and fructifying sap flows on to the branches. The more intimately we become incorporated with Christ by means of the Eucharist, the nearer we draw to the fountain of all graces, and the more plentifully are they diffused in our soul.

That we may be the more readily heard, we gratefully acknowledge the exceedingly great mercy the Lord has shown us in creating and redeeming us.[21] Therefore we implore that the work which God has wonderfully begun, He may mercifully complete in us by imparting to us the divine life of grace here below and of glory hereafter.[22] In a wonderful manner did God create man: He made man the king of the visible world, setting him but a little below the angels, with honor and glory He crowned him; but He enriched and adorned human nature with supernatural gifts. From the blissful heights of Paradise man precipitated himself into the depth of sin and misery; then God in a still more wonderful manner restored him and raised him up from his fall. God's love, wisdom, and power are incomparably more gloriously displayed in the redemption

---

[20] "Under the form of bread the body is given to thee, and under the form of wine the blood is given to thee, that, by partaking of the body and blood of Christ, thou mayst become one body and blood with Him. In this manner we also become Christ-bearers, in that His body and blood are distributed throughout our members. Therefore, according to the blessed Peter, we become partakers of the divine nature" (S. Cyrill. Hierosol., *Cat. mystag.*, IV, n. 3).

[21] Ipse erit reformator tuus, qui fuit formator tuus (S. August., *Enarrat. in Ps.*, 103:4). Duo sunt, quae principaliter attendere debet humana circumspectio: dignitatem suae conditionis et excellentiam suae reformationis. Dignitatem suae conditionis, ut peccare timeat; excellentiam redemptionis, ut gratiae redimentis ingratus non existat (Ivon. Carnot., *Serm.*, XXII).

[22] Grace is the beginning, the principle and the root of glory, and glory is the completion, the blossom and the fruit of grace. Gratia et gloria ad idem genus referuntur; quia gratia nihil aliud est quam quaedam inchoatio gloriae in nobis (S. Thom., IIa IIae, q. 24, a. 3 ad 2).

THE OBLATION

than in the creation of the world. *Nihil nobis nasci profuit, nisi redimi profuisset*, sings the Church. "It would have availed us nothing to have been born, unless the regeneration had been added."

2. The oblation of the chalice also comprises the act and the prayer of oblation.

a) **The act of oblation.** The priest raises the chalice as though he would present it to God; but here the celebrant does not cast his eyes down, as at the offering of the host, but he keeps them fixed on the crucifix while he is offering the chalice. The reason lies in the accompanying prayer of offering, with which this raising of the eyes harmonizes, since the prayer contains the petition that this sacrificial offering "may ascend as an agreeable odor" to the throne of the Most High. Moreover, this offering prayer does not expressly remind the celebrant of his unworthiness. Before the priest puts down the chalice,[23] he makes the sign of the cross with it over the altar, to signify that in the chalice and upon the altar that same precious blood is offered which was shed on the wood of the holy cross.

b) **The oblation prayer.**

Offerimus tibi, Domine, calicem salutaris, tuam deprecantes clementiam, ut in conspectu divinae majestatis tuae, pro nostra et totius mundi salute cum odore suavitatis ascendat. Amen.	We offer unto Thee, O Lord, the chalice of salvation, beseeching Thy clemency that it may ascend before Thy divine Majesty as a sweet odor for our salvation and for that of the whole world. Amen.

As the above prayer shows, "the chalice of salvation" (Ps. 115: 13) is here offered. Although the chalice now contains merely the wine mixed with water, it is yet called the chalice of salvation (a chalice bringing salvation) because the sacrificial wine will soon be

---

[23] During the Middle Ages the chalice was not put behind the host as now, but was placed to the right, that is, towards the Epistle side, near the host, by which was symbolically indicated, that blood and water flowed from the right side of our Lord. *Ita juxta Romanum Ordinem in altari (panis et vinum aqua mixtum) componenda sunt, ut oblata (i.e. hostia) in corporali posita, calix ad dextrum latus oblatae ponatur, quasi sanguinem Domini suscepturus, quem de latere dominico profluxisse credimus* (Microl., *De eccles. observat.*, cap. 10). This practice continued in the Roman Church until the fifteenth century, while in other places the present rite was introduced still earlier, *ut Christi stantis ante crucem memoria haberetur*, or rather, *ob majorem securitatem, ne calix tam facile effundi posset*.

changed into the sacrificial blood of Christ. In the offering of the chalice there is contained, at the same time, the petition that the Lord would change the wine into Christ's blood and graciously accept this blood from our hands: [24] "may it ascend before Thy divine Majesty as a sweet odor." Only the consecrated chalice is truly a "chalice of salvation," as it alone contains that divine blood which was shed on the cross as a sacrifice and ransom.[25] In the chalice we daily offer that sacred blood which once flowed through the members of the Saviour's body and gave Him strength to love, to labor, and to suffer for us, that divine blood, the source of salvation and life, which throughout eternity flows through the heart of Jesus. In the chalice is offered that blood which has brought eternal salvation to all the elect; for in heaven the blessed stand around the throne of the Lamb of God, singing unto Him: "Thou wast slain, and hast redeemed us to God in Thy blood, out of every tribe and tongue and people and nation, and hast made us to our God a kingdom and priests, and we shall reign on the earth" (Apoc. 5:9 f.).

Who offers the chalice of salvation? "We offer," the priest says here, whereas at the offering of the host he said, "I offer." It makes no great difference whether the singular or plural number is used. The priest stands at the altar as the representative and authorized agent of the Church; therefore he offers the host, as well as the chalice, in the name of all the faithful, and they, especially those who are present, offer in conjunction with the priest.[26] This participation of the

---

[24] According to an *Ordo Missae* of the beginning of the twelfth century, the priest says here, hence before the consecration, at the offering of the chalice: Offerimus tibi, Domine, Jesu Christi Filii tui sanguinem. Humiliter imploramus clementiam tuam, ut ante conspectu divinae majestatis tuae cum odore suavitatis accedat. *Odor suavitatis* (= *odor suavissimus*) is a figurative expression, often occurring in the Old Testament. "To ascend as a pleasing odor" is to say, that God takes pleasure in the offering and graciously receives it.

[25] Orat sacerdos, ut calix oblatus "in conspectu divinae majestatis cum odore suavitatis ascendat," cum illo scil. mystico odore, qui ex ipso calice, cum consecratus fuerit, suavissime exspirat (Bona, *Rer. liturg.*, II, ix, 5). It is only the chalice changed into Christ's blood that is truly an *odor suavitatis*.

[26] St. Cyprian says that the Christians assemble in common with the brethren and celebrate with the priest of God the divine sacrifice (*in unum cum fratribus convenimus et sacrificia divina cum Dei sacerdote celebramus*; cf. *De Orat. domin.*, chap. 4). Already the Apostle (I Cor. 10:16) writes: "The chalice of benediction which we bless," that is, consecrate; in this the faith-

faithful in the celebration of the Eucharistic sacrifice is now made expressly prominent when the plural is used, as frequently occurs in the Canon. The participation of the faithful is explicitly expressed at the offering of the chalice because by the mingling of the water with the wine, the union of the faithful with Christ has just been symbolically represented, and this union is therefore now suitably expressed in the offering of the chalice. Some writers hold that the plural, "we offer," refers to the priest and the deacon, who in Solemn Masses offers the chalice with the celebrant and recites the prayer with him.[27]

We offer the chalice "for our salvation and for that of the whole world." Mass is, in the first place, a means of grace and salvation for the children of the Church, who especially receive in bountiful measure of the fruit of the sacrifice. But they who do not belong to the communion of the Church are by no means entirely excluded from the blessing of the sacrifice. The Church prays and offers that all may be saved and may attain unto the knowledge of the truth. Countless blessings daily flow from the altar and diffuse themselves over the vast expanse of the earth. In the Mass, as on the cross, Christ is "the propitiation for our sins, and not for ours only, but also for those of the whole world" (I John 2:2). If this "sacrifice for sin" were no longer left us, what else would remain for the world "but a certain dreadful expectation of judgment, and the rage of a fire which shall consume the adversaries?" (Heb. 10:27.) Although the Lord sees that the wickedness of men is great on the earth, and that all the thought of their heart is bent upon evil at all

---

ful are included, who assist at the sacrifice, and, by the Amen they say, make the prayers of the priest, as it were, their own.

[27] The deacon is at the same time the representative of the people and the consecrated assistant of the priest; in the first quality, he brings to the priest the matter of the sacrifice; in the second, he supports the priest in the oblation of the chalice and assists him, after the completion of the sacrifice, in the distribution of the sacrificial food, so that the last function has its foundation in the first (Scheeben, III, 607). Paratus debet esse diaconus progredi cum sacerdote ad sacrificium altaris, ad martyrium, ad evangelizandum. Experire certe utrum idoneum ministrum elegeris, cui commisisti Dominici (corporis et) sanguinis consecrationem—non ad conficiendum, sed ad assistendum. Quia sicut secretarius altaris particeps est confectionis Eucharistiae cum sacerdote; non quia sumat vel conficiat nec quod hos sine eo non possit fieri, sed quia celebrius et in majori reverentia conficitur corpus Domini cum praesentia, ministerio et testimonio illius (Petr. Cantor., *Verbum abbreviat.*, chap. 60).

times, yet He no longer says: "I will destroy man, whom I have created, from the face of the earth" (Gen. 6:5, 7); for He promised that no flood should henceforth come to destroy all flesh, and that He would no more curse the earth on account of man (Gen. 9:15). But why? Because the Lord God scents the sweet savor of the sacrifice (Gen. 8:21) that is offered daily on thousands and thousand of altars for the salvation of the whole world.

The Church offers Christ's sacrifice from the rising to the setting of the sun, every day and at every hour, without interruption and without end. As the sun moves around the earth, and as he advances in his course, shedding light and life, so also in the same round with him daily travels the Holy Sacrifice of the Mass, diffusing around the earth, as it is offered up, spiritual life in the Church and in its members. At the morning's dawn, priests ascend the altar to offer the Holy Sacrifice, hour after hour other priests succeed them, and to these, others still in every country wherein the Church has followers, and the offering of sacrifice goes on until the daily cycle is completed and to the last link is joined the first in the sacrificial chain and the perpetual sacrifice continues anew. This is the true eternal fire that is never extinguished, the sacrificial fire which burns day and night in the sanctuary in honor of the Almighty. This is the eternal high priesthood, the perpetually offered sacrifice of the high priest. Without ceasing does it go up to heaven, and without ceasing does God come down to the altar to become present in the Sacrament for our sakes, that we all together and each one in particular may be partakers of this sacrifice and of the whole plenitude of grace. Unceasingly does the Holy Sacrifice of the Mass fasten an eternally new bond between heaven and earth, between God and man. Truly the Holy Sacrifice of the Mass is a worship of God such as He is deserving of, a divinely ordained, true, and perfect divine service of adoration and subjection to God, of contrition and reconciliation, of praise and thanksgiving, and of the glorification of the Saviour invisibly and yet visibly enthroned among us on the altar; a divine service ever renewed and continued to the end of the world, when He shall come again in judgment amid the clouds of heaven with power and majesty. (Geissel.)

CHAPTER XXVIII

THE SELF-IMMOLATION AND THE EPIKLESIS

The Self-immolation

1. Bread and wine are now on the altar, set apart from profane use and dedicated to the service of the sacrifice; soon their substance will be changed, and under their appearances Christ's body and blood will be offered. In union with this divine sacrifice, we should offer ourselves with all that we are and have. Where Christ, the head, offers Himself, there the members of His mystical body must also be offered together with Him. Thus the Church prays that God would not only sanctify the elements of bread and wine just offered, but would also, by the Eucharistic sacrifice, make us wholly worthy to be presented to Him as an eternal sacrificial gift.[1] This self-offering of the Christian people has already been symbolically effected in the previous offering of the wine mixed with water; but now the self-offering is to be made especially for the purpose of awakening and enlivening sentiments of self-sacrifice, which are necessary for the proper offering of the sacrifice of the altar. For God favorably receives the sacrifice from our hands and for our salvation only when we present ourselves in the sanctuary animated with devout sentiments of self-immolation.

2. Therefore the priest, now in the name of all the faithful offering with him, recites the following prayer of offering, during which, with humble compunction, he makes a moderate inclination of the body and, to express fervent supplication, he supports his joined hands on the altar.

[1] Sanctifica, quaesumus Domine Deus noster, per tui sancti nominis invocationem hujus oblationis hostiam, et per eam nosmetipsos tibi perfice munus aeternum (*Secreta in festo ss. Trinit.*).

In spiritu humilitatis et in animo contrito suscipiamur a te, Domine; et sic fiat sacrificium nostrum in conspectu tuo hodie, ut placeat tibi, Domine Deus.	In a spirit of humility and with a contrite heart may we be received by Thee, O Lord; and grant that the sacrifice we this day offer in Thy sight, may be pleasing to Thee, O Lord God.

In order to fully appreciate the meaning of these words and to recite them in the proper spirit, we should remember by whom and in what place they were spoken for the first time. They are taken from a longer, humble, penitential prayer recited by the three young men in the Babylonian furnace. Faithful to God's law, they would not adore the statue of the king and therefore were cast into a burning furnace. Praising God, they walked about in the flames, which did not harm them in the least. They offered themselves as a propitiatory sacrifice for their sins and for those of their people in order to obtain mercy. "In a contrite heart and humble spirit let us be accepted. . . . So let our sacrifice be made in Thy sight this day, that it may please Thee" (Dan. 3:39 f.). In similar words the celebrant here prays that the Lord would graciously receive him and the faithful people, for the sake of their humble, penitential sentiments, as a spiritual sacrifice; and, if so accepted, then the Eucharistic sacrifice, when offered by them in the sight of God with these dispositions, will be graciously accepted by God from their hands.

The three young men were ready to offer their lives cheerfully in sacrifice to God by a bloody martyrdom; after their example we should present ourselves to God to suffer a life of perpetual sacrifice and an unbloody martyrdom. "As gold in the furnace He hath proved them, and as a victim of a holocaust He hath received them" (Wisd. 3:6). Thus should we also, filled with humility and compunction, offer ourselves to God as a holocaust in the furnace of suffering and tribulation, of persecution and temptations. A sacrifice to God is an afflicted spirit; a contrite and humbled heart He does not despise (Ps. 50:19). Yes, a heart penetrated with penitential love and sorrow, a mind bowed down with compunction will always be favorably received and accepted by the Lord. It is the best disposition that we should bring with us to the altar. When the Lord breathed forth His spirit amid the darkness that enshrouded Mount Calvary, many of the beholders were seized with such fear and sorrow that they returned to their homes striking their breast (Luke 23:48). Should not we also be penetrated with regret and contrition, with a penitential sorrow, as often as we celebrate in the Mass the remembrance of Christ's bloody death?

During this holy function we must offer ourselves with compunction of heart as a sacrifice; for when we commemorate the mystery of the passion of our Lord, we must imitate that which we celebrate. The Mass will be a sacrifice for us to God when we have made an offering of ourselves. But we should, moreover, after retirement from prayer, endeavor as far as we are able, with God's assistance, to keep our mind in recollection and renewed strength, so that passing thoughts may not distract it, nor vain joy find its way into the heart, and that our soul thus may not, by carelessness and fickleness, again lose the spirit of compunction it has acquired.[2]

Our entire life should be a cheerful, uninterrupted offertory. We should present ourselves in body and soul [3] as a living sacrifice, holy, pleasing to God (Rom. 12:1). Whatever moves and affects the soul in joy and sorrow, in prosperity and adversity, in distress and death, we place upon the altar during the Holy Sacrifice of the Mass, and we are sure of consolation and relief. Yes, all the children of the Church should unite in the offering, all the faithful should be incorporated into and offered along with the one great and eternal sacrifice, uniting with it all their own sacrifices, trials, and sufferings.

THE EPIKLESIS

The so-called epiklesis (invocation) [4] is found in all liturgies. But in the Greek and other Oriental liturgies it follows the act of con-

[2] S. Greg., *Dial.*, IV, chap. 59.
[3] Quid, fratres, nos offerimus aut quid retribuimus Domino pro omnibus quae retribuit nobis? Christus pro nobis obtulit hostiam pretiosiorem quam habuit, nimirum qua pretiosior esse non potuit—et nos ergo faciamus quod possumus, optimum quod habemus offerentes, quod sumus utique nosmetipsi. Ille seipsum obtulit: tu quis es qui teipsum offerre cuncteris? Quis mihi tribuat, ut oblationem meam dignetur majestas tanta suscipere? Duo minuta habeo, Domine, corpus et animam dico: utinam haec tibi perfecte possim in sacrificium laudis offerre! Bonum enim mihi longeque gloriosius atque utilius est, ut tibi magis offerar, quam ut deserar mihi ipsi. Nam ad meipsum anima mea conturbatur, in te vero exsultabit spiritus meus, si tibi veraciter offeratur (S. Bernard., *De Purific. B. M. serm.*, III, n. 3).
[4] By the word ἐπίκλησις (from ἐπικαλέω) = invocation, a liturgical prayer is designated, which implores the consecration of the sacrificial elements and

secration; in the Roman liturgy it has its place among the oblation prayers which precede the consecration. Simple, yet expressive and majestic, are the ceremonies and words of this invocation supplicating the Holy Ghost to bless and change the sacrificial elements. Just before, at the offering of himself, the priest took a posture of humility; but now he again raises his body and lifts up his head, and in an erect posture he solemnly invokes the Holy Ghost, while looking heavenward, raising, extending, and then immediately joining his hands before his breast. At the word *benedic* (bless) he makes the sign of the cross over the chalice and the host.[5] While this ceremony symbolically represents the blessing implored of the Holy Ghost and consecrates the gifts, the raising of the eyes and the motion of the hands denote longing and desire for the descent of the Holy Ghost from on high.

| Veni Sanctificator omnipotens aeterne Deus, et bene✠dic hoc sacrificium tuo sancto nomini praeparatum. | Come, the Sanctifier, O almighty and eternal God, and bless ✠ this sacrifice, prepared for the glory of Thy holy name. |

That this invocation is directed to the Holy Ghost is beyond doubt.[6] He is called *Sanctificator* (the Sanctifier) in the language of the Church to distinguish Him from the Father and the Son, inasmuch as the imparting of all sanctifying graces and charismatical gifts is ascribed to Him. From this prayer it is clearly evident that up to the present the sacrifice has been but "prepared" for the glorification of the divine name, the acknowledgment and praise of the infinite majesty and perfection of God. Only by honoring and adoring God do we obtain His gifts and graces; only in so far as

---

the imparting of the sacrificial fruits by the Holy Ghost, or at least through the Holy Ghost.

[5] In celebratione quisque calicem et oblata non circulo aut digitorum vacillatione, ut quidam faciunt, sed junctis et extensis digitis cruce signet sicque benedicat (*Pontif. Roman., Ordo ad Synodum*).

[6] Mitte, Domine, quaesumus, Spiritum Sanctum, qui et haec munera praesentia nostra tuum nobis efficiat sacramentum, et ad hoc percipiendum nostra corda purificet (*Sacrament. Leonian.*). In the Mozarabic Missal this prayer is as follows: Veni sancte Spiritus sanctificator: sanctifica hoc sacrificium de manibus meis tibi praeparatum (Migne, *P.L.*, LXXXV, 113). In the sacramentary manuscripts of the Middle Ages it is, for instance, given as follows: Veni sanctificator omnium, S. Spiritus, et sanctifica hoc praesens sacrificium ab indignis manibus praeparatum et descende in hanc hostiam invisibiliter, sicut in patrum hostias visibiliter descendisti.

we seek God's honor and glory do we secure our well-being and salvation. The concluding words implore the blessing of the Holy Ghost over the gifts of bread and wine. To understand this petition, three questions must be answered: What does *benedicere* (to bless) generally mean? What blessing is here asked? Why is this blessing expected only from the Holy Ghost?

Benedicere properly means to speak well, to say what is good. This can be done in many ways: if one already possesses the good that is said of him, then *benedicere* is to exalt, magnify, praise, or glorify the possessor; if a person (or thing) does not as yet possess the good, but if the speaker by his word wishes to procure it for him or to give it to him, then *benedicere* means speaking well for someone, wishing him something good. In this instance we must especially distinguish as to the one who speaks the words of blessing. The blessing word of God is efficacious and all-powerful, it is an actual benefit and infallibly imparts good to the creature. The liturgical blessing of the Church also is never without fruit, but it is always a "good wish imparting sanctification and good gifts,"[7] for Christ has commissioned her with full power to bless. Finally, the simple faithful also may bless, that is, impart good by desire and prayer,[8] but this private blessing is evidently not always crowned with success.[9]

In this place there is question especially of the blessing of consecration, which is to be effected by the descent of the Holy Spirit. No higher blessing can assuredly be imparted to the gifts prepared

[7] Benedictio est sanctificationis et gratiarum votiva collatio (S. Ambros., *De benedict. patr.*, chap. 2).

[8] Dividi solet benedictio etiam in ecclesiasticam et laicam. Ecclesiastica vim habet ex meritis et intercessione Ecclesiae, et ex institutione ejusdem Ecclesiae competit solum ministris sacris, videlicet episcopis vel aliis sacerdotibus. Benedictio vero laica vim habet ex merito personali eam conferentis: unde peti solet benedictio a viris sanctis vel etiam fundatur in auctoritate naturali, sicut ea quae confertur a parentibus suis filiis et utraque dici solet benedictio privata, quatenus confertur privata auctoritate; e contra benedictio ecclesiastica dicitur publica, quatenus confertur publica Ecclesiae auctoritate (Quarti, *De bened.*, I, sec. 1, dub. 2).

[9] Benedicere est bonum dicere. Contingit autem bonum dicere tripliciter. Uno modo enuntiando, puta cum quis bonum alterius laudat. Alio modo imperando, et sic benedicere per auctoritatem est proprium Dei, cujus imperio bonum ad creaturas derivatur; ministerium autem pertinet ad ministros Dei, qui nomen Domini super populum invocant. Tertio benedicit quis optando, et secundum hoc benedicere est bonum alicui velle et quasi bonum pro aliquo precari (S. Thom., *In Epist. ad Rom.*, chap. 12, lect. 3).

than that they be consecrated, changed into the body and blood of Christ by the almighty power of the Holy Ghost. The material elements of the sacrifice receive the most perfect blessing imaginable, in that they become Christ's body and blood offered in sacrifice, which again on their part are sources of blessing for us.[10] When the priest, with the sign of the cross, blesses and sanctifies the gifts on the altar, he prays for the gracious presence of the divine victim and for the plenitude of blessing flowing from His wounds. He implores this miracle of the Eucharistic consecration to be wrought by the Holy Ghost, the "almighty, eternal God," who, by reason of His unlimited power, can bestow and impart every blessing.

Why, finally, is the Third Person of the Deity, the Holy Ghost, invoked to change the material elements by His almighty blessing into divine sacrificial gifts? The proximate reason lies in the analogy which the consecration bears to the Incarnation. The great similarity and relation between the accomplishment of the Eucharist on the altar and the mystery of the Incarnation of the Son of God in the womb of the immaculate Virgin Mary are often commented on by the Fathers and are expressed also in the liturgy.[11] The Incarnation is, in a manner, renewed and enlarged in the Eucharistic consecration.[12] For the same reason the miracles of the Incarnation and consecration are ascribed to the efficacy of the Holy Ghost: [13] both

---

[10] The Eucharist is a blessing in its highest meaning.

[11] Thus, for example, on the feast of Corpus Christi the Christmas Preface and the concluding stanza, *Jesu, tibi sit gloria, Qui natus es de virgine*, are prescribed. Altari tuo, Domine, superposita munera Spiritus Sanctus assumat, qui hodie beatae Mariae viscera splendoribus suae virtutis replevit (*Sacrament. Gregor.*).

[12] St. Chrysostom (*De beato Philog.*, hom. 6) compares altar and crib, remarking that on them the body of Christ reposes, no longer wrapped in swaddling bands, but wholly reclothed by the Holy Ghost. An instrument customary in the Greek liturgy and known by the name star (ἀστήρ, ἀστερίσκος) also reminds us of the Incarnation. It consists of two intersecting arcs turned downwards. Assuredly the asterisk serves, in the first place, as a protecting cover for the Eucharistic bread, especially after the Consecration, that it may not be touched by the velum spread over it; at the same time it symbolizes by its appearance the star that stood over the place where the child Jesus lay. When, therefore, the priest has incensed the asterisk and placed it on the discus under the veil, he says: *et veniens stella adstitit ubi erat puer.*

[13] Quando congruentius quam ad consecrandum sacrificium corporis Christi sancta Ecclesia (quae corpus est Christi) Spiritus sancti deposcat adventum, quae ipsum caput suum secundum carnem de Spiritu sancto noverit natum? (S. Fulgent., *Ad Monim.*, II, chap. 10).

mysteries, being works of divine favor and love as well as works full of infinite purity and holiness, have a special resemblance to the peculiar character of the Holy Ghost, who is personal love and sanctity.[14] Therefore, although in reality all three divine persons [15] accomplish the act of consecration, it is most frequently ascribed to the power of the Holy Ghost.[16] As it is said in the Creed, that the Son of God "became incarnate by the Holy Ghost, of the Virgin Mary," we also acknowledge that the Holy Ghost, by His creative power as "Lord and Dispenser of life," changes the inanimate elements of bread and wine into Christ's body and blood. "How shall this be done," says the holy Virgin, "because I know not man?" The archangel Gabriel, answering, said to her: "The Holy Ghost shall come upon thee, and the power of the Most High shall overshadow thee" (Luke 1:34 f.). "And now you ask: How shall the bread become the body of Christ, and the wine, mingled with water, become the blood of Christ? And I also answer you: The Holy Ghost shall overshadow each and shall effect that which is beyond language and conception." [17]

"We invoke our merciful God, that He would send down the Holy Ghost upon the gifts before us, we invoke Him that He change the bread into the body of Christ and the wine into the blood of Christ. Whatever the Holy Ghost but touches is sanctified and changed. . . . The gifts which lie on the altar are holy after they

---

[14] Opus incarnationis manifestativum est divinae bonitatis et caritatis: sed hoc appropriatur Spiritui sancto. . . . In incarnatione fuit copiosissima divinae bonitatis effusio (S. Bonav., III, dist. 4, a. 1, q. 1). Quoniam liberalitas Spiritui Sancto appropriatur et sanctificatio Virginis, in qua peracta fuit Verbi conceptio, hinc est, quod licet opus illud sit a tota Trinitate, per appropriationem tamen dicitur Virgo concepisse de Spiritu sancto (S. Bonav., *Breviloq.*, IV, chap. 3).

[15] Sanctifica, quaesumus, Domine Deus noster, per Unigeniti tui virtutem hujus oblationis hostiam, et cooperante Spiritu sancto, per eam nosmetipsos tibi perfice munus aeternum (*Sacrament. Gregor.*).

[16] The golden or silver vessel for the preservation of the Holy of holies had often, in ancient Christian times, the form of a dove, and was therefore called *columba*, περιστερά, περιστέριον. This dovelike vessel indicated in a realistic manner that the blessed body of Christ, concealed therein, was formed by the Holy Ghost and was, at the same time, a symbol of Christ. Tu mihi, Christe, columba potens (Prudent., *Cathem.*, III, 166).
        Sanctusque columbae
        Spiritus in specie Christum vestivit honore.
                    (Sedulius)

[17] S. Joan. Damasc., *De fide orthod.*, IV, chap. 13.

have received the descent of the Holy Ghost." [18] The Holy Ghost, consequently, effects the presence of the body and blood of Christ, one that is full of grace. Hence it is certainly not without a deep signification that almost all the preparatory prayers of the priest for Mass, as given in the missal and recommended by the Church, invoke the Holy Ghost.[19]

[18] S. Cyrill. Hieros., *Catech. mystag.*, V, n. 7, 19.

[19] We mean the concluding prayers of the preparation: *Aures tuae pietatis. . . . Ure igne S. Spiritus*, etc. In the very ancient *Oratio s. Ambrosii* that has also been inserted in the Missal among the preparatory prayers of the priest, we read: Peto clementiam tuam, Domine, ut descendat super panem tibi sacrificandum plenitudo tuae benedictionis et sanctificatio tuae divinitatis. Descendat etiam, Domine, illa Sancti Spiritus tui invisibilis incomprehensibilisque majestas sicut quondam in patrum hostias descendebat, qui et oblationes nostras Corpus et Sanguinem tuum efficiat et me indignum sacerdotem doceat tantum tractare mysterium cum cordis puritate. This prayer is originally from St. Anselm (Or. 29).

CHAPTER XXIX

THE INCENSING AND THE WASHING OF THE HANDS

The Incensing of the Sacrificial Gifts

1. In a Solemn Mass the oblation and epiklesis are symbolically followed by the incensing, which has been observed in the Roman liturgy at this part of the Mass since the eleventh or twelfth century.[1] This incensing differs somewhat from the one that took place at the Introit of the Mass, since it has a richer rite and a more significant symbolism. When more closely studied, this grand ceremony is seen to be a poetical development and extension of the preceding Offertory.

First, by virtue of the sign of the cross and an impressive prayer for its blessing, the incense is made a sacramental, something holy, which has not only a holy meaning, but also an efficacious effect. While the priest puts the grains of incense on the live coals, he says:

Per intercessionem beati Michaelis Archangeli stantis a dextris altaris incensi, et omnium electorum suorum, incensum istud dignetur Dominus bene✢dicere, et in odorem suavitatis accipere. Per Christum Dominum nostrum. Amen.	Through the intercession of blessed Michael the archangel, standing at the right hand of the altar of incense, and of all His elect, may the Lord vouchsafe to bless ✢ this incense and receive it as an odor of sweetness. Through Christ our Lord. Amen.

---

[1] Romanus Ordo praecipit, ut incensum semper praecedat Evangelium, cum ad altare sive in ambonem portatur; non autem concedit, ut oblatio in altari thurificetur, quod et Amalarius in prologo libri sui de Officiis Romanos devitare fatetur, quamvis modo a pluribus, imo paene ab omnibus usurpetur (Microlog., *De eccles. observat.*, chap. 9). Cf. Krazer, sect. IV, art. 1, chap. 8, §251).

The prayers of the Church are always heard. In this instance she prays verbally and with the sign of the cross that the Lord would bless the incense and graciously accept it as a thing dedicated to His service.[2] To obtain a fuller answer to her petition, the Church has recourse to the intercession and mediation of the holy archangel Michael and all the elect of God. The name of St. Michael [3] occurs in the Confiteor and is again mentioned in this place because he is at the head of the angelic choirs and, at the same time, the heavenly protector of the Church on earth. It certainly is proper that the Church, at the moment when there is question of a favorable reception of her offering, symbolized by the incense, should invoke her great and powerful protector in heaven, St. Michael, for his assistance and intercession. This is all the more appropriate because, by incensing the sacrificial gifts, she would emulate the celestial choirs in paying homage to the divine Lamb on the throne; for when the earthly altar of the Church is enveloped in clouds of incense, it is in the eyes of all indeed a figure of the heavenly holy of holies, which is perpetually fragrant with the prayers of the blessed. St. Michael stands at the right hand of the altar of incense, that is, he presents before the face of God in golden censers the incense of prayer and sacrifice (Apoc. 8:3 f.).

The sacrificial gifts, the bread and the wine mixed with water, are first incensed by swinging the censer over them three times in the form of a cross and then three times in the form of a circle [4] while reciting the following prayer:

---

[2] Incense is also a material offering made to the Lord in connection with the Eucharistic sacrifice. This connection of the incensing with our sacrifice is, according to some, mentioned in Mal. 1:11, where the Hebrew word, rendered by *sacrificatur*, is properly *suffitur*.

[3] On account of the addition, *stantis a dextris altaris incensi*, which in St. Luke 1:11-19 is stated literally of the archangel Gabriel, there is to be found in many of the more ancient missals the name of Gabriel instead of Michael; therefore many liturgists feel that this prayer should be thus changed. But they are mistaken. For well established reasons the Church adheres to the name of Michael and wishes to invoke here the archangel Michael. The name of Michael is, consequently, not from oversight or by mistake placed in this benediction prayer (cf. S. R. C., September 25, 1705).

[4] Ducitur autem thuribulum primo per modum crucis, quia fructus gratiarum hujus sacrificii incruenti a sacrificio crucis tanquam a fonte proveniunt; secundo etiam ter ducitur circumcirca a dextris et a sinistris, ut indicetur, nos usquequaque adjuvari virtute sacrificii in prosperis et adversis (Quarti, *Comment. in Rubr. Miss.*, II, vii, 10).

THE INCENSING

| Incensum istud, a te benedictum, ascendat ad te, Domine: et descendat super nos misericordia tua. | May this incense which Thou hast blessed, O Lord, ascend to Thee, and may Thy mercy descend upon us. |

The rite and prayer constitute the symbolical representation of the previous offering. The separation and dedication of the sacrificial gifts consists in this, that they are enveloped in a holy atmosphere by the swinging of the censer, containing the fragrant, hallowed incense. The grains of incense, consumed in the fire and ascending heavenward as an agreeable sacrificial odor, also symbolically express the petition that the substance of the material elements, by the fire of the Holy Ghost, be changed into the divine victim, under the appearances of bread and wine.[5] The incense, ascending in clouds and descending upon the faithful and spreading round about, indicates that the Eucharistic sacrifice may be accepted for the salvation of the faithful and of the whole world.

2. By the incensing a hallowed circle has been drawn around the sacrificial gifts; the incensing is now continued and extended to the crucifix on the altar, or the Blessed Sacrament, to the relics or images of the saints, to the altar itself, to the celebrant together with his attendants, to the clergy and the people present. This incensing rite is but the further representation and development of the oblation ideas which were just before expressed in the prayer: "May this incense which Thou hast blessed, O Lord, ascend to Thee, and may Thy mercy descend upon us."

The burning, fragrant incense, which goes up in light clouds, symbolizes the Eucharistic sacrifice and the oblation prayers connected with it, in which the celebrant's interior dispositions and those of the devout participants manifest themselves.[6] This is clearly

---

[5] Sacrificia, Domine, tuis oblata conspectibus, ignis ille divinus absumat, qui discipulorum Christi Filii tui per Spiritum sanctum corda succendit (*Orat. secret. fer. VI p. Pent.*).

[6] Eucharistia vocatur incensum vel thymiama. Primo, quia continet Christi corpus quasi hostiam Deo in ara crucis igne caritatis incensam, quae quasi thymiama odorem suavissimum Deo exhalavit, quo ejus iram placavit eumque hominibus reconciliavit. Secundo, quia Eucharistia conficitur et conditur sacris precibus, quae sunt thymiama Deo. . . . Denique Eucharistia vocatur incensum, quia non tantum repraesentat, sed et re ipsa continet Christum in ara crucis pro nobis incensum, i.e. dolore et amore tostum Deoque sacrificatum. . . . Thymiama sunt ignitae orationes, suspiria et vota tam sacerdotum

evinced by the verses of the psalm which accompany the sacred ceremony of incensing. By the three swings of the censer (*ductu triplici*) Christ is honored, either in the figure of the crucifix or in the Blessed Sacrament.[7] Relics and images are incensed,[8] to honor the saints and, at the same time, to express thereby the desire that our sacrifice and prayers, supported by their powerful intercession, may be favorably received and made the more pleasing to God and profitable to ourselves. The words said while incensing the cross and altar are as follows (Ps. 140:2–4):

| Dirigatur, Domine, oratio mea, sicut incensum, in conspectu tuo: elevatio manuum mearum sacrificium vespertinum. Pone, Domine, custodiam ori meo, et ostium circumstantiae labiis meis: ut non declinet cor meum in verba malitiae, ad excusandas excusationes in peccatis.[9] | Let my prayer, O Lord, be directed as incense in Thy sight: the lifting up of my hands as the evening sacrifice. Set a watch, O Lord, before my mouth, and a door round about my lips. Incline not my heart to evil words, to make excuses in sins. |

---

quam fidelium, dum Eucharistiam vel consecrant et conficiunt, vel sumunt et manducant (Corn. a Lap., *In Malach.*, 1:11).

[7] When the Blessed Sacrament is not exposed, the cross on the altar forms the principal visible object and is, therefore, the first to be incensed after the offerings; *coram exposito* it should not be incensed in case it should be on the altar, according to the custom of some places. The Blessed Sacrament enclosed in the tabernacle is not incensed, but it is adored before and after the incensing of the crucifix by the genuflection of the celebrant and the *ministri*.

[8] As a distinction from the cross on the altar, they are incensed only *ductu duplici* (first those on the Gospel side, then those on the Epistle side); the inclinations of the head which precede are not made to them, but to the cross. Pictures painted on the wall of the altar are not incensed, but only pictures or statues placed on the altar (even though no relics are enclosed in them). If, besides the pictures of saints, relics are on the altar, the relics only, and not the pictures, are incensed. If at Christmastide the image of the divine Infant, and at Eastertide that of the risen Saviour, is exposed for public veneration in a prominent place on the altar (*principi loco super altari*), then it must likewise be incensed after the cross, *triplici ductu* (cf. S. R. C., February 15, 1873).

[9] *Dirigatur, Domine, oratio mea* = ascendat, coelos penetret, tibi perfecte complaceat; *sicut incensum* in Lege dirigebatur ad te et fumando ascendit ac tibi prae ceteris sacrificiis placuit, non propter seipsum, sed ex devotione offerentis; *in conspectu tuo* referri potest ad utrumque horum, videl. ut oratio dirigatur in conspectu Dei sicut incensum; dicebatur autem incensum oblatio quae tota incendebatur et comburebatur ad Dei honorem, per quod designatur obsequium perfectorum, qui se totos mancipant Deo seque totaliter abnegant et relinquunt. *Elevatio manuum mearum* = exaltatio desideriorum

THE INCENSING 579

David, an exile in the wilderness and therefore far removed from the sanctuary in Jerusalem, begs the Lord to receive his prayerful pleading, made with uplifted hands, with the same favor as He received the evening incense and food-offering which terminated the daily sacrificial service. But well aware that God willingly answers man's prayer only when it proceeds from clean lips and a pure heart, he utters the additional petition: Guard and protect my mouth, close my lips, that I sin not with my tongue, and if through weakness I have sinned in the past, grant by Thy powerful grace that at least my heart may not swerve from the straight path, and that it may not, for the purpose of self-justification, still add, through excessive pride, excuse to excuse for sin. Incomparably more profound is the meaning which these words of the psalm have in the mouth of the incensing priest. While fragrant clouds of incense envelop the altar and ascend on high, the celebrant implores most fervently that his sacrificial prayers and those of the faithful may, in union with Christ's most holy sacrifice, ascend direct to the throne of God as an odor equally agreeable and precious, and that they may draw down the divine good pleasure upon those who are praying and sacrificing.[10] To this petition the following one is also

---

meorum ad superna, directio operum meorum ad divina, erectio manuum mearum corporalium ex cordis elevatione procedens seu ordinata ad illam virtualiter sit coram te, Domine, *sacrificium vespertinum*, quatenus ita placeat tibi, sicut placebat sacrificium vespertinum seu ultimum quolibet die, quoniam videlicet offerebatur agnus ad vesperam, cujus immolatio erat figura immolationis Agni Dei sive Christi in cruce. Unde Christus in cruce pendens dicere poterat: "Elevatio manuum mearum sacrificium vespertinum." *Pone, Domine, custodiam ori meo* = da mihi gratiam custodiendi os meum, ne loquar vel taceam inordinate, sed, dum tempus est loquendi, prudenter atque utiliter loquar; dum vero tempus tacendi affuerit, moderate ac laudabiliter taceam. Pone quoque *ostium circumstantiae* = clausuram discretam *labiis meis* = ut tum et taliter labia mea ad loquendum aperiam et ad tacendum recludam, quando, quo loco et qualiter oportet aut expedit, ut sim in utroque discretus et fructuosus. *Non declines* [Missale: *ut non declinet*] = non inclinari seu moveri permittas *cor meum in verba malitiae* = ut verba maligna effundat, videl. *ad excusandas* = excusatorie proferendas *excusationes in peccatis* = mihi objectis et a me perpetratis (Dion. Carthus., *Comment. in Ps.*, 140).

[10] Declinante jam die in vesperum Dominus in cruce animam deposuit recepturus, non amisit invitus. . . . Illud ergo est sacrificium vespertinum, passio Domini, crux Domini, oblatio victimae salutaris, holocaustum acceptum Deo. Illud sacrificium vespertinum fecit in resurrectione munus matutinum. Oratio ergo pure directa de corde fideli tanquam de ara sancta surgit incensum. Nihil est delectabilius odore Domini: sic oleant omnes qui credunt (S. August., *Enarrat. in Ps.*, 140:5).

appropriately joined, that the Lord would Himself, by His grace, assist those present to attain and preserve the interior disposition which is necessary to render prayer acceptable to God. If prayer is to ascend in a manner agreeable to God as a spiritual odor of sacrifice, then it should proceed from a heart and from lips that are not profaned by worldly and sinful conversation, or that have, at least, by a sincere, humble, and contrite confession of sins been purified anew. He who has sinned must beware of alleging all kinds of pretexts and plausible reasons excusing his evil conduct. It is very difficult to govern and control perfectly the unruly tongue, which sins easily and in many ways; hence the priest prays for the assistance of God's grace, to which, however, must be added one's energetic cooperation.

If, in the previous act of incensing, the petition for a gracious acceptance of the sacrifice was symbolized by the smoking incense, then the act of incensing the celebrant, clergy, and people is principally a symbolic expression of the desire that the divine mercy may sweetly and plentifully descend on all assisting at Mass. Inasmuch as the fragrant clouds of incense penetrate everywhere and from the altar spread throughout the entire house of God, they symbolize the sweet fruit of the sacrifice and of prayer: divine mercy and grace. Grace is dispensed from the sacrifice, first to the priest, then through his ministrations to the faithful. This idea is conveyed in the ceremony of incensing, first the celebrant, then the clergy, and finally the faithful.[11] At the same time the incensing of persons cooperating in and assisting at the sacrifice contains a lesson and an admonition to them ever to be mindful of their priestly dignity, of their nobility as members of Christ and temples of the Holy Ghost, that by their conduct they may spread everywhere the good odor of piety and godliness. That this incensing is also to be understood as a mark of honor, as a religious distinction in favor of all those who are incensed, is self-evident from what has been said of the signification and use of incense in general.

[11] Ritus incensandi eos, qui Missae assistunt in choro et in ecclesia, laudabilis et conveniens est: tum quia laudabile est, moderatum honorem exhibere iis, qui Missae deserviunt et assistunt, tanquam Christi fidelibus; tum ob significationem, quia pie exprimitur, virtutum odorem a Christo derivari ad fideles officio ministrorum secundum illud (II Cor. 2:14): "Odorem notitiae suae spargit per nos in omni loco." Et ideo, ut docet S. Thom. (IIIa, q. 83, a. 5 ad 2), undique thurificato altari, per quod Christus designatur, thurificantur omnes per ordinem (Quarti, *De bened.*, IV, sect. 1, dub. 3).

When the priest returns the censer to the deacon, he says: *Accendat in nobis Dominus ignem sui amoris, et flammam aeternae caritatis. Amen.* ("May the Lord enkindle within us the fire of His love and the flame of eternal charity. Amen.") With these words the celebrant finally expresses the desire that Christ the Lord would, by the grace of His sacrifice, enkindle in everyone that inflamed and ardent love which is the real and deepest source whence rises aloft the offering of prayer.[12] And this wish the Lord will assuredly fulfill, since He Himself came to bring this pure, heavenly fire upon the earth; and He desires nothing more than that it be kindled in all hearts and that it continue to burn without ever being extinguished (Luke 12:49).

The Washing of the Hands

1. Before the priest puts on the sacred vestments, he should wash his hands in the sacristy: profound reverence for the divine mysteries, which should be celebrated with perfectly clean hands, dictates this regulation. Already at this washing, which is based mainly on propriety and practical reasons, the priest prays for a higher purification, that is, for purity of soul as well as of body, that he be found fit worthily to serve the Lord.[13] After the offering, or the incensing, of the sacrificial gifts, there is prescribed another washing of the hands, or rather, of the consecrated fingers. This washing dates from the earliest centuries, and its origin is traceable, not merely to reasons of necessity and propriety, but mainly to motives of higher consideration. After receiving in his hands the offerings of the people, the celebrant found it necessary to cleanse his hands again by washing them, especially the fingers which were to touch the Blessed Sacrament;[14] nevertheless, the symbolical

---

[12] Mystica sunt vas, thus, ignis, quia vase notatur: mens pia, thure preces, igne supernus amor.

[13] Da, Domine, virtutem (*strength of grace*) manibus meis (*to me at the washing of the hands*) ad abstergendam omnem maculam: ut sine polutione mentis et corporis valeam tibi servire (*Missal. Roman.*). Prior Gerhoch of Reichersberg (d. 1169), explaining psalm 25, remarks that at the washing of the hands *in praeparatione divinae servitutis*, the following prayer should be recited: Largire sensibus nostris, omnipotens Pater, ut sicut exterius abluuntur inquinamenta manuum, sic a te mundentur interius pollutiones mentium et crescat in nobis augmentum omnium sanctarum virtutum.

[14] Consummata oblatione sacerdos lavat manus, et tergit cum mundissimo linteolo, quod sibi soli ad hoc est deputatum, cavens postea ne aliud quid

signification of this action has ever been taken into consideration.[15]

The mystical sense of this rite of washing the hands is easy to comprehend. The hand has ever been considered the principal instrument, the privileged member, in which the power and activity of man are concentrated and by which, in a certain manner, the whole man is represented.[16] The outward washing of the hands, or rather, of the fingertips, consequently symbolizes the interior purification and cleansing of the whole man from all that sullies the soul and body; the circumstance of washing in reality only the tips of the consecrated fingers (both thumbs and both forefingers), is usually supposed to signify that the officiating priest should cleanse his heart and preserve it undefiled from even the slightest faults, even from the shadow of sin.[17] The Apostolic Constitutions (VIII, chap. 11) already present this washing of the hands as "a symbol of the purity of souls dedicated to God." St. Cyril of Jerusalem says that the washing of the hands evidently "designates the purity and blamelessness of our actions." [18] But "who can say: My heart is clean, I am pure from sin?" (Prov. 20:9.) For in the sight of God no man living shall be justified (Ps. 142:2). And yet the priest should appear at the altar for the Holy Sacrifice holy and spotless, pure and blameless, and without blemish in soul or body. Now, the further the holy action proceeds, the nearer the most holy moment

---

tangat cum digitis, quibus Domini corpus tangendum est (*Constit. Hirsaug. s. Gengenbac.* [eleventh century], I, chap. 84). Aliqua pretiosa tractare non consuevimus nisi manibus ablutis; unde indecens videtur quod ad tantum sacramentum aliquis accedat manibus etiam corporaliter inquinatis (S. Thom., IIIa, q.83, a.5 ad 1).

[15] Profound reverence for the holy mysteries made the washing of the hands a necessity at this place so long as the people were accustomed to bring offerings. Lavat sacerdos manus suas more priorum sacerdotum, ut extersae sint a tactu communium rerum atque terreno pane. Quae lavatio manus munditiam cordis significat per lacrymas et compunctiones (Amalar., *De eccles. off.*, III, chap. 19). Quod ideo ab antiquis Patribus decretum fertur, ut pontifex, qui coelestem panem accepturus est, a terreno pane, quem jam a laicis accepit, manus lavando expurget (*Ordo Rom. IV*, n. 9).

[16] Ablutio manuum sufficit ad significandam perfectam mundationem; cum enim manus sit organum organorum, omnia opera attribuuntur manibus (S. Thom., IIIa, q.83, a.5 ad 1).

[17] Cum sacerdos manus suas alias [i.e. ante Missam] laverit (ut intelligatur, quod sit a gravioribus mundus), nunc solum lavat digitorum extremitates, significans desiderium se purificandi etiam a culpis levioribus, praecipue si in aliquas esset lapsus post Missam inchoatam, et hoc spiritu lotio haec adhibetur (De Ponte, *De christ. hom. perfect.*, IV, tr.II, chap.12, § 1).

[18] *Catech. mystag.*, V, n. 2.

of consecration approaches, the more intensely does the priest feel his unworthiness, the more his desire for greater purity is increased. As an expression of this sentiment and disposition, he now washes his hands just as at the beginning of Mass, at the foot of the altar, he cleansed and prepared his soul by a contrite acknowledgment of his guilt.

2. The verses of the psalm that he recites in the meantime, express clearly the more profound meaning of the liturgical washing: the priest openly avows his purpose of celebrating the holy sacrifice with the utmost purity and devotion of heart (Ps. 25:6–12).

Lavabo inter innocentes manus meas: et circumdabo altare tuum, Domine.	I will wash my hands among the innocent: and I will compass Thy altar, O Lord.
Ut audiam vocem laudis: et enarrem universa mirabilia tua.	That I may hear the voice of Thy praise, and tell of all Thy wondrous works.
Domine, dilexi decorem domus tuae: et locum habitationis gloriae tuae.	I have loved, O Lord, the beauty of Thy house, and the place where Thy glory dwelleth.
Ne perdas cum impiis, Deus, animam meam: et cum viris sanguinum vitam meam.	Take not away my soul, O God, with the wicked, nor my life with bloody men.
In quorum manibus iniquitates sunt: dextera eorum repleta est muneribus.	In whose hands are iniquities: their right hand is filled with gifts.
Ego autem in innocentia mea ingressus sum: redime me et miserere mei.	But as for me, I have walked in my innocence: redeem me, and have mercy on me.
Pes meus stetit in directo: in ecclesiis benedicam te, Domine.	My foot hath stood in the direct way: in the churches I will bless Thee, O Lord.
Gloria Patri.	Glory be to the Father.

Among the innocent I will wash my hands. How can the priest pray thus? Does he not live in the midst of the world, where by reason of human frailty, carelessness, and attachment to earthly things, the luster of the soul's purity is in a greater or less degree most easily tarnished? Such is, in truth, the case, and a good priest feels convinced of it; but he is also daily intent on destroying within his heart the love of the world, sensuality, and all selfishness, in order that his soul may be purified more and more in the fountain of the precious blood of Jesus and by tears of penance and sorrow. Hence he may well protest that in his innocence he would wash his hands,[19] and thus with pure hands advance to the altar. Yes, it behooves those hands to be clean which he is to raise in supplication and prayer to God; clean must be the hands that are to touch, offer, and dispense the most holy, spotless victim.[20]

He loves the pomp and grandeur of the house of God; his heart clings to the place where the Lord dwells in His Eucharistic glory. He is consumed with zeal for the house of the Lord; he adorns it as worthily and as splendidly as possible, since the King of Glory does not disdain to dwell so silently near us and among us. The place where the Saviour has built His throne of grace is, in this wide, dreary world, the garden and favorite resort of the priest; thither does he flee to find consolation for his soul, peace and refreshment amid the woes, miseries, and turmoil of life. At the foot of the altar there flows for him a bright and clear stream of pure joys; he there spends the most delightful hours; he gathers there the most precious graces.

It is his care to lead a faultless and godly life; he seeks and cultivates an interior and familiar intercourse with the Lord "in the privacy of His tabernacle of grace"; he has nothing in common with a world forgetful of God, and he shuns its ways. Hence, abounding in confidence in God, he may beg of the Lord to preserve his soul and his life from the perdition which befalls all the godless, who through deceit and violence practice all manner of wickedness, trampling upon justice and the rights of their fellow men. Blameless and without stain he endeavors to live; hence he hopes that "deliverance and mercy" may be his share.

[19] Dicat devotus ac dignus Christi sacerdos: *Lavabo*, quando at celebrationem accessurus sum, *inter innocentes*, i.e. cum sanctis ac veris sacerdotibus N. L., quorum est nulli nocere, sed verbis et exemplis cunctis prodesse, *manus meas*, non solum corporales, quibus Christi sacramenta tractabo, sed etiam affectus, cogitationes et opera: istas lavabo in confessione, quoniam teste Scriptura omnia in confessione lavantur (Dion. Carthus., *In Ps.*, 25).

[20] Quodsi patena et calix non solum esse debent pretiosa, ex auro scilicet vel argento, sed etiam mundissima a quocunque pulvere et macula, eo quod sanctissimum corpus et sanguinem Salvatoris contingant, quanto erit magis rationi consentaneum, sacerdotes habere manus mundas a pravis operibus, linguam a verbis ineptis, et pectus suum a malis desideriis et cogitationibus, et sese purificare ab omni immunditia, etiam valde parva (De Ponte, *loc. cit.*, chap. 6, § 1).

Confident in God and assured of being heard, the priest, full of gratitude, exclaims: "My foot hath stood in the direct way," that is, snatched from the abyss of danger and sufferings, I stand on a firm and safe plain, or I dwell in the direct paths of grace and virtue leading to God. Both are gifts of the Lord; hence he promises to extol His favors and goodness in union with the pious all the days of his life.[21]

[21] Ecce ex psalmo isto sententioso et splendido audivimus, quid ad christianum perfectum pertineat. Si igitur aliquid horum in nobis invenimus, Deo gratias referamus et ad perfectionem feramur. Si autem praedictae perfectiones viri perfecti longe a nobis sunt, ingemiscamus, emendemus atque juxta verbum gloriosi Apostoli cum timore et tremore nostram operemur salutem (Dion. Carthus. [d. 1471], *In Ps.*, 25).

CHAPTER XXX

THE CONCLUDING PRAYERS OF THE OFFERTORY

Suscipe, Sancta Trinitas

AFTER the washing of the hands, which is performed at the Epistle side of the altar [1] the priest returns to the middle of the altar; full of confidence he raises his eyes to the crucifix, then lowers them again; he then bows with humility and reverence, places his joined hands on the altar, and recites in his suppliant posture [2] the following short oblation prayer:

Suscipe, santa Trinitas, hanc oblationem, quam tibi offerimus ob memoriam passionis, resurrectionis et ascensionis Jesu Christi Domini nostri: et in honorem beatae Mariae semper Virginis, et beati Joannis Baptistae, et sanctorum Apostolorum Petri et Pauli, et istorum, et omnium sanctorum: ut illis proficiat ad honorem, nobis autem ad salutem: et illi pro nobis intercedere dignentur in coelis, quorum memoriam agimus in terris. Per eundem Christum Dominum nostrum. Amen.	Receive, O Holy Trinity, this oblation, which we offer unto Thee, in memory of the passion, resurrection, and ascension of our Lord Jesus Christ, and in honor of the blessed Mary ever Virgin, of blessed John the Baptist, of the holy apostles Peter and Paul, of these and of all the saints, that it may be to their honor and to our salvation; and may they vouchsafe to intercede for us in heaven, whose memory we celebrate on earth. Through the same Christ our Lord. Amen.

[1] On this side, during the Middle Ages, there was often attached to the altar the sacrarium (*piscina, lavacrum, lavatorium, perfusorium*), which served not only to receive the remains of holy objects become useless, for instance, ashes, and to secure them against desecration, but, at the same time, answered for the washing of the hands of the priest at the Offertory and after Holy Communion.

[2] Quod sacerdos manus interdum jungit et se inclinat, est suppliciter et

THE CONCLUSION OF THE OFFERTORY

In this prayer [3] the previous oblation of the host and chalice is not simply repeated or continued, but developed and perfected by the incorporation of new aspects. While the first two oblation prayers were directed to the Father, and the invocation was made to the Holy Ghost, the Church now turns to the Holy Trinity and offers to it the sacrifice prepared on the altar. Host and chalice are here jointly offered, and that under a new aspect: it contains a short allusion to the relation which the Eucharistic sacrifice bears to the mysteries of the life of Christ, as well as to the saints of heaven.

The Mass is celebrated in memory of the entire work of the redemption, the principal parts of which are here expressly set forth, as they are immediately after the Elevation. In His passion [4] the immaculate victim was immolated; in His resurrection He was glorified, and in His ascension He was raised to the throne of God, in order to effect our redemption and to perfect our salvation. On the altar not only the sorrowful, but also the glorious mysteries of the life of Christ are represented and renewed. There Christ, who was dead and now lives eternally in heaven (Apoc. 1:18), offers Himself.

It is self-evident that the Sacrifice of the Mass can be offered only to the triune God,[5] not to the saints; the offering of it, however, not only serves to render supreme adoration and glory to God, but it also serves as an honorable commemoration (*in honorem*) [6] of

---

humiliter orantis, et designat humilitatem et obedientiam Christi, ex qua passus est (S. Thom., IIIa, q.83, a.5 ad 5).

[3] During the Middle Ages these prayers were often somewhat differently expressed, and were recited neither in all the churches nor at all Masses. In the eleventh century they were said, according to Micrologus, *non ex aliquo Ordine sed ex ecclesiastica consuetudine* (*De eccles. observ.*, chap. 11).

[4] Quoties celebratio corporis et sanguinis Domini agitur, non equidem Christum iterum occidimus, sed mortem ejus in ipsa et per ipsam celebrationem memoramus, estque ipsa celebratio passionis Christi quaedam commemoratio. Commemoratio autem passionis Christi ipsam passionem significat. Celebratio igitur corporis et sanguinis Domini passionis Christi est signum (Guitmund, *De corp. et sang. Dom. verit.*, II).

[5] Omne cujuslibet honorificentiae et sacrificii salutaris obsequium et Patri et Filio et Spiritui sancto, h. e. sanctae Trinitati ab Ecclesia catholica pariter exhibetur (S. Fulgent., *Ad Monim.*, II, chap. 5).

[6] The latest edition of the missal, approved by S. R. C., correctly gives the following reading: *in honorem*. According to the sense and form these words constitute a parallel clause to the preceding *ob memoriam* and are afterward paraphrased by the formula: *quorum memoriam agimus. In honorem*, there-

the saints, whose memory we celebrate at the altar. By an ecclesiastical ordinance, which dates back even to apostolic times, frequent mention is made of the saints during the celebration of Mass; by this, great honor and distinction are evidently shown them, since they are remembered at the altar and their names are honorably mentioned at the sacrifice. This we intend to express by saying that we offer this sacrifice "in their honor" (*in honorem*). But this prayer further says that the sacrifice is offered "to their honor." These words, indeed, signify the fruit accruing to the saints in heaven through the Holy Sacrifice; the Mass is also offered to obtain for the saints the spread of their veneration on earth. We therefore offer the sacrifice and pray that the saints may be ever more and more honored and glorified on earth.[7] This means that we offer sacrifice and pray, not so much in behalf of the saints, as for ourselves; for it is to our own benefit and advantage if greater honor be shown to the saints. Inasmuch as we honor and glorify the saints during and through the Holy Sacrifice of the Mass, we advance thereby our own welfare (*nobis ad salutem*), since in this way we obtain for ourselves the powerful intercession of the saints (*illi pro*

---

fore, = *memoriam venerantes*, as in the Canon, and is not tautological with the following: *ut illis proficiat ad honorem*, as is asserted by many following Lebrun, who gives the preference to the other reading, *in honore*, and would have it restored. We remark, on the contrary, that both formulas, *in honorem* and *in honore*, in vulgar Latin can have and often do have the same meaning. But in this prayer the reading *in honorem* is to be preferred, because it harmonizes more beautifully with the parallel *ob memoriam*. The sense of this expression, *in honorem*, is clearly paraphrased in the Postcommunion of the vigil of All Saints: Sacramentis, Domine, et gaudiis optatae celebratis expletis: quaesumus, ut eorum precibus adjuvemur, quorum recordationibus exhibentur. This controversy has been settled by a decree of the S. R. C. (dub. III): In Ordine Missae post Lavabo in Oratione "Suscipe sancta Trinitas" plures recentiores Rubricistae graves dicunt loco "in honorem B. M. semper V." esse legendum "in honore B. M." etc. Estne horum sententia sequenda et correctio hoc in loco Missalis facienda? R. Ad III. Legendum: in honorem (May 25, 1877).

[7] Sancti orationibus nostris non indigent, pro eo quod cum sint perfecte beati, omnia eis ad vota succedunt, sed nos potius eorum orationibus indigemus, quos, cum miseri simus, undique mala multa perturbant. Unde quod in plerisque orationibus continetur, prosit videl. vel proficiat huic sancto vel tali talis oblatio ad gloriam vel honorem, ita sane debet intelligi, ut ad hoc prosit, quod magis ac magis a fidelibus glorificetur in terris aut etiam honoretur, licet plerique reputent non indignum, Sanctorum gloriam (sc. accidentalem) usque ad judicium augmentari ac Ecclesiam interim sane posse augmentum glorificationis eorum optare (Innnocent. III, *Regest.*, V, ep. 121).

nobis intercedere dignentur in coelis). For, since we celebrate upon earth the memory of the citizens of heaven, we would thereby incline them to be more favorably disposed to interest themselves in our behalf with God. Moreover, the blessed rejoice when we offer Mass to God as a sacrifice of praise and thanksgiving in their name, that is, when we offer it to God to praise and thank Him for all the benefits, for the grace and the glory, they have received from Him.

The saints mentioned by name are the same as those mentioned in the Confiteor, with the exception of the archangel Michael, who, however, in Solemn Mass is named immediately before the blessing of the incense. Then is said: *et istorum et omnium Sanctorum* ("and of these and of all the saints"). Who are to be understood by "these" (saints)? According to the present context of the prayer, the most simple and natural meaning is to refer the demonstrative pronoun (*isti*) to the previously mentioned saints, that is, to regard it as comprising them all, so that the translation should be: "of the saints just mentioned and of all the saints." Formerly it may have been a word of the rubrics and may have signified that in this place still other saints may or should be mentioned, for example, those whose relics repose in the altar or are exposed upon it, or whose feast was celebrated, or who were honored as special patrons. But the purpose of this Eucharistic veneration "to their honor and our salvation," is accomplished "through Christ our Lord," the one Mediator, who crowns the blessed in glory and leads us to felicity.[8]

The *Orate Fratres* and the Secreta

1. The purer and the more perfect the disposition, recollection, and fervor of the priest and of the faithful present, so much the more acceptable does the sacrifice rise from their hands to the throne of God. In order to support and inflame each other mutually, the celebrant and the people uniting with him in the sacrifice keep up an active and lively intercourse with each other; hence the priest frequently salutes the people and invites them to pray with him, and the people join in through their representative, the acolyte or choir, in the priest's prayer. After the *Suscipe sancta Trinitas* has been concluded, the priest again summons all the faithful to unite

---

[8] Quidquid Sanctorum tuorum meritis adhibemus, ad tuam laudem recurrit et gloriam, qui in eorum semper es virtute mirabilis (*Sacrament. Leon.*).

with him in common prayer, in order that their common sacrifice may be so much the more favorably received by God. The priest kisses the altar, rises, and with downcast eyes turns toward the people, extending his hands and again joining them, and says, *Orate fratres* ("Brethren pray"), in a somewhat audible voice (*voce aliquantulum elata*), so as to be heard by the acolyte and those standing near by; then, while again turning to the altar, he continues in silence: *ut meum ac vestrum sacrificium acceptabile fiat apud Deum Patrem omnipotentem* ("that my sacrifice and yours may be acceptable to God the Father Almighty").[9]

The priest here addresses all the faithful as "brethren," [10] regardless of their state or sex. By their regeneration in baptism all Christians are children of God and of the Church; they form one great holy family of God, and they are all brethren one of another, to whom it is granted to say: "Our Father, who art in heaven." "All you are brethren" and "one is your Father who is in heaven" (Matt. 23:8 f.), says our Saviour. As brethren, all Christians should, above all at the Eucharistic sacrifice and communion, have but one heart and one soul, and pray for and with one another.

---

[9] Sacerdos versus ad populum orare moneat, conversusque ad altare secretam orationem dicat (Joann. Abrincens., *Lib. de offic. eccles.*). Erectus presbyter populum hortatur ad orandum, et ipse post finitam Secretam, Praefationem orditur in Canonem (Microl., *De eccles. observat.*, chap. 11). Accordingly, in the eleventh century this invitation to prayer was in general use; the oldest *Ordines Romani* have for it only the short formula, *Orate* (*Ordo II*, n. 9) or *Orate pro me* (*Ordo VI*, n. 10), while in *Ordo XIV* it runs thus: *Orate fratres*, and so forth. Since the words *ut meum ac vestrum* . . . form only an explanatory clause, that is, assign more minutely the purpose and object of the prayer (*Orate*), they were formerly not recited at all (as is still the case among the Dominicans and Carthusians), and later on only in silence.

[10] This mode of expression is genuinely Christian. *Fratres*, ἀδελφοί, *viri fratres, brethren, fraternitas*, ἀδελφότης, brotherhood; in the mouth of the apostles and Fathers these terms frequently designate the members of the Church, who were regenerated by the same sacrament (baptism) and are nourished at the same table (the Eucharist), and are united with one another by the bond of the same faith, hope, and charity (cf. Justin. Mart., *Apolog.*, I, chap. 65). Omnes qui jam de hoc mundo recesserunt sive qui adhuc versantur in mundo sive qui futuri sunt usque ad finem saeculi credentes in Christo fratres esse veraciter constat, utpote una baptismatis regeneratione in Christo renatos, unius matris Ecclesiae uberibus educatos, unius fidei vinculo tanquam dulcissimae fraternitatis affinitate connexos, ad unam eandemque coelestis regni haereditatem ab eodem piissimo Patre Deo pia adoptione vocatos. Debemus itaque omnia quae nobis accidunt fraterno affectu invicem communicare, i.e. in adversis pariter contristari et in prosperis communiter congratulari (Pseudo-Alcuin, chap. 18).

THE CONCLUSION OF THE OFFERTORY

In addressing the faithful the priest says: "my sacrifice and yours." The Eucharist is the sacrifice of the whole Church; it is not exclusively the priest's sacrifice, but the property of the faithful also.[11] In different ways and in different degrees they participate in the offering of the Eucharistic sacrifice, while the priest alone, in their name and for their benefit, completes the sacrificial action itself.[12] Thus priest and people are at the altar bound together in a communion of sacrifice; and they offer not only the host and chalice, but themselves also.

In compliance with the invitation of the priest, the acolyte [13] answers in the name of the faithful:

| Suscipiat Dominus sacrificium de manibus tuis ad laudem et gloriam nominis sui, ad utilitatem quoque nostram totiusque Ecclesiae suae sanctae. | May the Lord receive the sacrifice from thy hands, to the praise and glory of His name, to our benefit, and to that of all His holy Church. |

The priest answers in a low voice: *Amen* ("So be it"), whereby he expresses his assent to the devout desires of the faithful.

Although the faithful unite in offering the Holy Sacrifice, still they make mention here only of the act of the celebrant, inasmuch as they pray that the Lord would favorably receive this sacrifice from his hands. This is proper, for it indicates that the priest, as the servant and organ of Christ, alone performs the sacrificial act itself; for only his hands are anointed and consecrated to offer sacrifice.

---

[11] This idea is often expressed in the Secreta, for example: Suscipe munera populorum tuorum, munera exsultantis Ecclesiae; accepta tibi sit sacratae plebis oblatio. The expressions *munera, dona, oblationes, fidelium preces cum oblationibus hostiarum*, etc., in the original and actual sense referred to the material oblations of the people; they are still entirely true, although their signification has changed.

[12] Merito sacerdos ad populum dicit: *meum ac vestrum sacrificium*. Et laudandus esses, mi sacerdos, qui facta reflexione super ejusmodi verba, ex vera humilitate cogitares, esse complures e laicis praesentes, qui majori pietate ac puritate animi Deo offerunt hoc ss. sacrificium, quam tu, minister ordinarius et insignitus charactere sacerdotali. Sed haec in aurem (Sporer, *Theolog. sacrament.*, II, chap. 5, sect. 2, § 4, n. 3).

[13] As the rubrics give no precise rule, many rubricists insist that the server should answer at once; others, on the contrary, maintain that he should not do so until the priest has turned to the altar and finished his formula. The *Suscipiat* is of later origin and is not recited on Good Friday. Before the revision of the missal, in the sixteenth century, various formulas were in use (cf. Martene, *De antiq. Eccles. ritibus*, I, iv, 7).

Only from priestly hands, which exhale the mystical perfume of the chalice and the host, does the sacrifice ascend agreeably before God's holy face.[14] This prayer expresses the object and purpose of the Sacrifice of the Mass. On the one hand, the sacrifice is offered for the honor and praise of God, to adore and glorify His infinite majesty; on the other, it is offered to be for us and the whole Church an inexhaustible source of all goods and gifts.[15]

2. The *Orate fratres* here takes the place of the customary *Oremus* and introduces us to the prayer called the Secreta. As this was, in ancient times, the only oblation prayer in the Roman rite, the *Oremus* at the beginning of the Offertory answered as an introductory formula.[16] The prayer received the name, Secreta, from the manner of its recitation: from time immemorial [17] it has been

[14] Ut sacerdos pro causa, pro qua celebrat, exaudiri mereatur, taliter vivere sicque Deo dignissimo familiaris et carus esse conetur, ut mediator idoneus inter Deum et populum esse possit. Est nempe sacerdos inter Deum et populum medius, quoniam ea, quae populi sunt, scil. preces, vota et dona, repraesentat et immolat Deo. Ea quoque, quae Dei sunt, ut puta gratiam et sacramenta, impetrat, dispensat seu tribuit populo. Debet ergo sacerdos populo in omnibus esse exemplaris et Deo dilectus ac familiaris (Dion. Carthus., *Expos. Miss.*, a. 4).

[15] Sicut gloriam divinae potentiae munera pro Sanctis oblata testantur: sic nobis effectum, Domine, tuae salvationis impendant (*Secr. in festo ss. Mart. Viti, Modesti atque Cresc.*, June 15). Simul Christus semel se in cruce visibiliter obtulit Deo Patri pro nostra reconciliatione, gratia et salute, ita instituit se quotidie in hoc sacramento invisibiliter pro eisdem causis usque in finem saeculi immolandum, consecrandum, tractandum, sumendum, edendum ad maximum et excellentissimum Dei honorem, laudem et gloriam, totiusque suae ad nos dilectionis, pietatis, munificentiae commemorationem et regratiationem, ob multiplices quoque animarum nostrarum profectus, opes et gratias, ineffabiliter grandes et copiosas (Dion. Carthus., *Elementat. theolog.*, prop. 135).

[16] "Before the Secreta some priests say: *Dominus vobiscum, Oremus*, others do not, after saying it before the Offertory, and from then on the prayer is continued without interruption" (Berthold *Tewtsch Rational*, chap. 8, § 6).

[17] The former customary designation (for example, in the *Gregorian Sacramentary*), *Oratio super oblata* (*sc. panem et vinum*), only makes its oblation feature more striking, and does not make it apparent whether this prayer was originally (up to the ninth century) recited aloud or in a low tone. In the Ambrosian Ritual it is always said aloud. Beleth writes: Secreta dicitur, quia secrete pronuntiatur, cum tamen olim alta voce diceretur (*Ration.*, chap. 44). Compositio sacrificio sacerdos orationem sub silentio recitat (Honor. Augustod., chap. 40). "While the Offertory is sung, the priest reads the little Canon, called the silent Mass or the secret of the Mass, which is recited in a low tone until the Preface, especially the prayer Secreta. The great Canon is likewise considered a low Mass, before the words of consecration, which are said in perfect silence and with marked secrecy" (Berthold, *op. cit.*, chap. 8, § 2).

THE CONCLUSION OF THE OFFERTORY

said in an inaudible voice (*secreto*). Justly, therefore, is Secreta translated "silent prayer" or "silent dedicatory prayer." [18]

In regard to their construction, number, succession, and concluding form, the Secreta harmonize perfectly with the Collects which are said before the Epistle, but as to their contents the Secreta are entirely distinct from them. The Collects and Secreta are both prayers of petition, but the object prayed for is usually different.

The sacrifice is not referred to in the prayers of the Collects, which but ask some special grace connected with the mystery of the day; the Secreta, on the contrary, are oblation prayers, prayers that contain almost the same thoughts as those expressed in the *Offertorium*. Throughout the whole oblation rite, and hence in the Secreta also, are two closely connected petitions: the petition that the sacrificial gifts prepared on the altar be accepted, blessed, dedicated, sanctified, and consecrated; [19] then the petition that the abundant and manifold graces of the Sacrifice be bestowed.[20] Sometimes both petitions are united, sometimes each is separately presented; frequently God is implored for reconciliation, so that the propitiatory feature holds a prominent place. But this does not sufficiently characterize the contents of the Secreta. They belong to the changeable parts of the liturgy of the Mass; they are in intimate connection with the day's celebration, which has an influence on their form. The petitions contained in the Secreta are inspired by the day's special sacrificial celebration and in various ways are influenced, suggested, and supported by it. Hence in the Secreta the spirit of the mysteries of the ecclesiastical year are found incorporated and

[18] Secreta ideo nominatur, quia secreto (*silently*) dicitur. . . . Quod omnibus licet simul agere, i.e. gratias referre Deo, hoc acclamatur; quod ad solum sacerdotem pertinet, i.e. immolatio panis et vini, secreto agitur (Amalar., *De eccles. offic.*, III, chap. 20). This signification of the name is found throughout the Middle Ages. Utterly without foundation is the assertion that the prayers in question are called Secretae *eo quod super materiam ex fidelium oblationibus separatam et secretam recitantur*. The name *Arcana* also indicates the low tone.

[19] Secreta dicitur, eo quod secretam orationem dat episcopus super oblationem, ut velit respicere Deus super oblationem propositam, et deputare eam futurae consecrationi. Notum est enim, ideo secretam orationem facere super oblatam, ut possit ex ea fieri corpus Domini (*idem., Ecloga in Ord. Rom.*, n. 24).

[20] Sacerdos orat voce submissa, petens a Deo effectum et fructum acceptationemque oblationis exhibitae, benedictionem quoque oblatae materiae, sicut patere potest consideranti diversas Secretas (Dion. Carthus., *Expos. Miss.*, a. 14).

blended in the most beautiful harmony and variety with oblation petitions, which generally concern the same object. In spite of their great similarity in general, the Secreta are not uniform, but present in their arrangement and contents the most attractive and agreeable variety. The fruitful and inexhaustible eloquence of the heavenly wisdom of the Church is herein clearly manifested.

The Secreta for Pentecost is as follows:

Munera, quaesumus Domine, oblata sanctifica: et corda nostra sancti Spiritus illustratione emunda.	Sanctify, we beseech Thee, O Lord, these oblations, and purify our hearts by the light of the Holy Ghost.

The Secreta for the feast of Corpus Christi:

Ecclesiae tuae, quaesumus Domine, unitatis et pacis propitius dona concede: quae sub oblatis muneribus mystice designantur.	Mercifully grant Thy Church, O Lord, we beseech Thee, the gifts of unity and peace, which are mystically represented in these offerings.

The Secreta for the feast of St. Philip Neri:

Sacrificiis praesentibus, quaesumus Domine, intende placatus: et praesta, ut illo nos igne Spiritus sanctus inflammet, quo beati Philippi cor mirabiliter penetravit.	We beseech Thee, O Lord, to look favorably on this present sacrifice and to grant that the Holy Ghost may inflame us with that fire, wherewith in a wonderful manner He filled the heart of the blessed Philip.

After the priest has recited the Secreta reverently in silence, in ending the last prayer he raises his voice, saying aloud or singing: *per omnia saecula saeculorum* ("world without end"). To this majestic conclusion the acolyte or choir answers in the name of the people, *Amen*, that is, may what the priest has implored in secret of God be granted and fulfilled in every respect.[21]

---

[21] Officium, quod nos dicimus Offerenda, ab illo loco inchoatur, ubi sacerdos dicit *Dominus vobiscum*, et finitur, ubi excelsa voce dicit *Per omnia saecula saeculorum*. Ideo excelse novissimum profertur, ut audiatur a populo et populi responsione (sc. *Amen*) confirmetur oratio (Amalarius, *De eccles. offic.*, III, chap. 19). Sacerdos excitat attentionem populi dicendo: *Dominus vobiscum* et exspectat assensum dicentium: *Amen*. Et ideo etiam in his quae secrete dicuntur, publice praemittit: *Dominus vobiscum* et subjungit: *Per omnia saecula saeculorum* (S. Thom., IIIa, q.83, a.4 ad 6).

THE CONCLUSION OF THE OFFERTORY

When the priest sings, the faithful can assuredly do nothing better than to assent to the priest's words, even if they do not understand them, than to pray for what the priest prays, even if they do not exactly know what it is. This was done by the first Christians, especially at the time when the liturgy was handed down only by mere vocal tradition, and even for a long time after; they restricted themselves to answering "so be it" after the priest had prayed in silence, thus making an act of faith, really sublime in its simplicity; as if they said: we know not what is best for us, but God knows it; now the Church has prayed, for in her name and by her commission the priest has prayed; the Church has placed on his lips the prayers which he has recited, we assent thereto, whatsoever they may contain. We can desire nothing better than what the Church desires, we can say nothing better than what the Church utters, hence "so be it."

SECTION III

The Consecration

CHAPTER XXXI

THE PREFACE

THE Eucharistic celebration advances: we are drawing nigh to the most important part, the sacrificial action proper. The rite thus far explained was already exceedingly grand, holy, full of mystery; yet incomparably more sublime, more glorious, and more venerable are the prayers and actions that constitute the Consecration, the golden center of the whole liturgy of the Mass. First comes the Preface, which by its animated and grand soaring forms a worthy transition and introduction to the Canon, the innermost and mysterious sanctuary of the liturgical sacrificial celebration.

Holy Scripture informs us that Jesus Christ "gave thanks" to His heavenly Father before consecrating the bread and wine, before changing them into His body and blood. Who could fail to understand, even at the first glance, that the Church here also follows the example of her divine Lord and Master, in that she places before the act of consecration the Preface, an incomparably elevated chant of praise and thanksgiving to God? For the Preface bears the closest relation to the Consecration, with which liturgically it forms a whole.[1] As its position indicates and its name signifies,[2] the Preface

---

[1] The *Sacrament. Gelas.* has the inscription, *Incipit Canon actionis,* not after, but already before the Preface. The pronouncing of the words of consecration, the εὐχαριστεῖν in an eminent sense, forms the crown and conclusion of the εὐχαριστία, that is, of the liturgical thanksgiving contained in the Preface.

[2] Haec pars Missae vulgato nomine *Praefatio* dicitur, i.e. praelocutio ante

is the prologue, or the introduction, to the Canon, the prelude to and preparation for the accomplishment of the mystical action of sacrifice.

To trace the origin of the Preface [3] and its introduction into the sacrificial rite, one must go back to the days of the apostles; this apostolic origin of the Preface is evident from the testimony of the Fathers, and especially from the most ancient liturgies, not a single one of which can be found without a Preface. The oriental liturgies have had from the beginning until the present time but a single Preface. In the West, on the contrary, the number of Prefaces, even at an early date, increased to such a degree that before the time of St. Gregory the Great almost every formula of Mass contained a separate Preface.[4] It is probable that St. Gregory himself reduced this large number to ten. Under Urban II (1088 to 1099) the Preface for feasts of the Blessed Virgin was added.[5] Four prefaces

---

praecipuam orationem, sacrorum mysteriorum consummativam et in Canone contentam. Ut enim in principio operis ipsorum auctorum praefationes ponuntur, introductoriae ad totam operis materiam intelligendam, et in orationibus oratorum prooemia sunt et exordia ante causae narrationem, quibus captetur auditorum benevolentia reddanturque attenti ad ea, quae dicturus est orator: ita, si magna licet componere parvis, in hoc divinissimo celebrando sacrificio haec oratio quasi prologus quidam est et praelocutio sequentis Canonis, captans ipsius Dei in nos benevolentiam. In ea enim praeloquitur sacerdos gratias et laudes Deo, ut praeparatus hujusmodi laudatione aptius possit ac melius ad consecrandum Christi corpus pervenire (Clichtov., *Elucidator. ecclesiast.*, III).

[3] In the Mozarabic Missal it is called *inlatio* (*illatio*), either *ob donorum illationem seu hostiae oblationem* (Du Cange), or *quia ex verbis fidelium infert sacerdos, vere dignum et justum esse, Deo omnipotenti gratias agere, ipsumque laudare et praedicare* (Bona). In the old Gallican rite it is inscribed *Contestatio* or *Immolatio, quia in ea sacerdos audita voce populi vel cleri sive ministri asserentis dignum et justum esse Deo gratias agere, contestatur veram esse hanc populi assertionem; tum solemni gratiarum actione se et fideles disponit ad tremenda mysteria, quibus Christi corpus immolatur* (Bona, *Rer. liturg.*, II, x, 1). *Inlatio* and *Immolatio*, in all probability, were originally designations (titles) for the entire central portion of the Mass, which commences with the Preface and includes the sacrificial action.

[4] The *Sacrament. Leon.* contains 267 Prefaces, although those from January to April are wanting; of the *Gelasian.* only 56 still remain. Also from the time of St. Gregory the Great until the thirteenth century, it was customary to add to the missal numerous Prefaces, but usually only in the Appendix. Albinus (Alcuinus) Praefationes etsi non Gregorianas, ecclesiasticae tamen celebritati idoneas, collegit (Microl., chap. 60).

[5] According to the statement of a contemporary writer, it was sung for the first time at a Solemn Pontifical Mass by Pope Urban, during a synod held

have been added recently. Thus the Roman Missal now has fifteen prefaces.

According to their text and melody, the Prefaces belong to the most solemn, sublime, and touching chants of the Church; they are the purest poetry, flowing from the inspiration of the Holy Ghost. The Church is the divinely enlightened proclaimer of the Eternal, she is the bride of Christ ever in communication with Him, and this communication is a never-ending nuptial celebration in sacrifice and prayer. Therefore speech becomes on her lips a poem, a canticle, having throughout a poetical feature; her sacred poetry is also a sacred chant. In explaining the Preface, we distinguish three parts: the introduction, the body, and the conclusion. While the introduction always remains the same, the main part or body of the Preface changes according to the feasts and times of the ecclesiastical year.

1. **The introduction of the Preface.** The introduction consists of three versicles with corresponding responses.

V. Dominus vobiscum.	V. The Lord be with you.
R. Et cum spiritu tuo.	R. And with thy spirit.
V. Sursum corda.	V. Lift up your hearts.
R. Habemus ad Dominum.	R. We lift them up unto the Lord.
V. Gratias agamus Domino Deo nostro.	V. Let us give thanks unto the Lord our God.
R. Dignum et justum est.	R. It is meet and just.

The usual salutation and invocation of blessing, *Dominus vobiscum*, also introduces the Preface. Probably nowhere is this invocation more opportune than here, when the accomplishment of the holy mysteries is so near at hand. Priest and faithful at this moment greatly require the help of the Lord and assistance from on high.[6] Only when the heavenly breath of grace pervades the soul sweetly and powerfully, is the soul enabled to rid itself of earthly defilement, to raise itself above the baseness of earth and soar upward, in order to join in the chant of praise of the blessed spirits. Who will give

---

at Guastalla (1094). Its composition is sometimes attributed to Pope Urban II himself, sometimes to St. Bruno, founder of the Carthusians.

[6] *Dominus vobiscum:* tunc enim praesentia Dei et illuminatio gratiae ejus tanto amplius necessaria est, quanto ea, quae restant, magis ardua sunt (Dion. Carthus., *Expos. Miss.*, a. 14).

me the wing of the dove, that I may fly and be at rest (Ps. 54:7) in undisturbed contemplation of the sacrificial mysteries enacted on the altar? God only, from whom every good gift cometh. Recollection of mind and fervor of devotion are gifts of the Lord. Why does not the priest now turn toward the people when saluting them? After the *Orate fratres* he has, like Moses on Mount Sinai, entered into the holy cloud,[7] and therefore he henceforth communes "face to face" with the Lord; henceforth he has eyes and mind directed only to the altar, and the faithful will behold his countenance again only after the marvels of Consecration and Communion have been consummated.[8]

At the salutation, *Dominus vobiscum*, the priest reminds the people to raise their hearts,[9] and from the faithful comes the answer and assurance to the priest that it has been done.[10] At the words *Sursum corda* the priest raises his hands, in order by this gesture to manifest and accentuate the inward soaring of the mind and his desire to give himself wholly to the Lord. By this movement of the hands is expressed the longing for that which is above us, that which is heavenly and eternal. Thus the Church complies with the invitation of the Prophet: "Let us raise our hearts together with our hands to the Lord in the heavens" (Lam. 3:41). The hymn of the Church contains a like sentiment: *Mentes manusque tollimus* ("Minds and hands we raise to the Lord"). To the Saviour, who has preceded us to heaven and who is awaiting us on the heavenly throne, we cry

[7] Moses was beloved of God and men; . . . [the Lord] brought him into a cloud (Ecclus. 45:1, 5).

[8] Quando dicimus *Pax vobiscum* sive *Dominus vobiscum*, quod est salutatio, ad populum sumus versi. Quos salutamus, eis faciem praesentamus, excepto in uno, quod est in praeparatione hymni ante *Te igitur*. Ibi jam occupati circa altare, ita ut congruentius sit uno modo versos nos esse, quam retro adspicere, ad insinuandam intentionem devotissimam, quam habemus in offerendo sacrificio (Amalar., *De eccles. offic.*, III, chap. 9).

[9] In hoc sacramento et major devotio requiritur quam in aliis sacramentis propter hoc quod in hoc sacramento totus Christus continetur, et etiam communior, quia in hoc sacramento requiritur devotio totius populi, pro quo sacrificium offertur et non solum percipientium sacramentum, sicut in aliis sacramentis (S. Thom., IIIa, q.83, a.4 ad 5).

[10] Sicut sacerdos jussit eos sursum corda tenere, sic se habere profitentur (Raban. Maur., *De sacr. ordin.*, chap. 19). Audis quotidie, homo fidelis: "Sursum cor," et quasi contrarium audias, tu mergis in terram cor tuum (S. August., *Serm.*, CCCXI, chap. 15). Quotidie per universum orbem humanum genus una paene voce respondet, sursum corda se habere ad Dominum (*Idem, De vera relig.*, chap. 3).

out with holy enthusiasm: Be Thou, O Jesus, the desire of our hearts, and the object of our longing and striving.

Sursum corda ("Lift up your hearts").[11] The meaning of these words is most comprehensive: they signify that we should withdraw all the faculties of our soul from what is earthly and consecrate them exclusively to intercourse with God and divine things. We should turn our mind and spirit from worldly objects and close them to distracting thoughts, so as to be immersed with all our might and attention in holy meditations.[12] If the mind is penetrated with a higher light from above, then the will also will be incited to devotion. The heart becomes aglow with holy love of God and disengages itself from the bonds of worldly inclinations and desires that enchain it in the dust; it rouses itself from its sluggish indolence and tepidity that it may with holy ardor soar heavenward with all its powers.[13] However, serious effort on our part is required to raise

---

[11] Audi: "Sursum cor," sed *ad* Dominum, non *contra* Dominum. Omnes superbi sursum cor habent, sed contra Dominum. Si autem vis tu vere sursum cor habere, ad Dominum habe. Si enim ad Dominum habueris cor sursum, ipse tenet cor tuum, ne cadat in terram (S. August., *Serm.*, XXV, chap. 2). Nemo potest cogitare nisi de thesauro suo et quodam cordis itinere divitias suas sequi. Si ergo in terra obruuntur, ima petit cor; si autem in coelo reservantur, sursum erit cor. Si ergo volunt facere christiani, quod norunt se etiam profiteri (neque enim hoc omnes qui audiunt noverunt atque utinam non frustra noverint qui noverunt): qui ergo vult cor sursum habere, ibi, ibi ponat quod amat, et in terra positus carne, cum Christo habitet corde, et sicut ecclesiam praecessit caput ejus, sic christianum praecedat cor ejus. Quomodo membra itura sunt quo praecessit caput Christus, sic iterum resurgens iturus est quo nunc praecesserit cor hominis. Eamus ergo hinc ex qua parte possumus; sequetur totum nostrum, quo praecesserit aliquid nostrum. Domus terrena ruinosa est; domus coelestis aeterna est. Quo venire disponimus, ante migremus (*ibid.*, LXXXVI, chap. 1).

[12] Volens sacerdos populum ad divina mysteria praeparare, excitando eum ad laudem divinam, invitat eundem ad laudandum Altissimum; ideo addit: *Sursum corda.* Non enim laudare valemus Deum sincere ac digne, nisi contemplando divina, ad quod necesse est inferiora et sensibilia ista relinquere, mentisque oculum divinorum considerationi infigere, et hoc in praesenti officio summe requiritur, maxime in hoc loco, quoniam sacramentum istud totaliter divinum et spirituale ac abditum est (Dion. Carthus., *loc. cit.*).

[13] Quaedam corda sursum sunt, quaedam semetipsa deorsum demerserunt. Deorsum sunt illa corda, quae configurantur huic saeculo; sursum vero sunt illa, quae conversationem suam habent in coelo. Deorsum sunt, quae terrena sapiunt; sursum sunt, quae jugiter meditantur coelestia; secundum id ergo, cui per amorem conjungitur, cor hominis sursum ac deorsum esse judicatur. Et recte extra semetipsum esse dicitur, quando ad exteriora et transitoria haec expetenda dilabitur. Tunc autem ad semetipsum revertitur, quando ea quae ad suam salutem pertinent meditatur. Sunt ergo quaedam, quae amando

mind and spirit on high and keep them recollected and disengaged from what is earthly and perishable; human frailty and the inconstancy of man is so very great [14] that to persevere in undisturbed recollection and communion with God is possible only to a soul that daily endeavors to divest itself of all earthly dross and bonds, and labors to attain a permanent direction upward. Hence the words of the Apostle: "Our conversation is in heaven" (Phil. 3:20). What does this imply? That we should not grovel like worms in the dust, but like the birds in the air we ought to soar in spirit heavenward; we should not burden and oppress our hearts with the thoughts and desires, cares and pleasures of this life, but we should so divest ourselves of earthly things and of the love of perishable goods that our soul may aspire with ease to heaven, with lively hope and ardent desire. "Seek the things that are above; . . . mind the things that are above, not the things that are upon the earth" (Col. 3:1 f.)—that is the wisdom of Christian life. The *Sursum corda*, therefore, admonishes us, especially at the Sacrifice of the Mass, to have our mind occupied with heavenly things only and to be intent upon them. "No one should be present in such a manner, that, although he may say with the lips: 'We have lifted our hearts to the Lord,' his thoughts are directed to the cares of this life. We should indeed think of God at all times; but if this be impossible on account of human frailty, we should take it to heart most especially at least during the Holy Sacrifice." [15]

St. Martin is a striking example in this respect. The Church says of him in his office: "With eyes and hands raised toward heaven, he never let his mighty spirit slacken in prayer." His life of constant prayer and attention to the presence of God reached its highest degree of perfection during the celebration of Holy Mass. In a sacristy intended especially for his use, he carefully prepared himself for the divine service; when he afterward approached the altar, he appeared as an angel of the Lord, rapt in devotion and inflamed with love. Once when raising his hands during the Holy Sacrifice, they shone

---

et cogitando cor hominis deorsum premitur, scissumque per varia dissipatur, et sunt iterum quaedam, quae amando et meditando sursum elevatur et ad semetipsum colligitur (Hugo de s. Vict., *De vanitate mundi*, II).

[14] Quantis conatibus corda levare necesse est, quae quidem (ut miserabiliter satis in libro propriae experientiae legimus) et corruptio corporis aggravat et terrena inhabitatio deprimit (S. Bernard., *In Ascens. Dom. serm.*, V, n. 2).

[15] St. Cyril of Jerusalem, *Mystag. Catech.*, n. 4.

with crimsoned light and appeared adorned with precious jewels. At another time his head was environed with bright rays, as though his spirit had soared heavenward.[16]

The more estranged the soul becomes from frivolity and the distractions of the world, and the more she rises above all created things, the more clearly and profoundly also will she perceive that God is the eternal love and the source of all that is good: she thereby becomes penetrated with a lively sense of grateful praise to Him. To this sentiment the priest gives expression in the words: "Let us give thanks to the Lord our God." At the same time he joins his hands before his breast, and, when saying "our God" (*Deo nostro*), he raises his eyes and bows his head reverently toward the crucifix. The faithful reply in the person of the acolyte: "It is meet and just." [17] Countless are the benefits with which the Lord has overwhelmed us and for which we owe Him a debt of gratitude. If the heart is deeply moved with grateful love toward God, it breaks forth spontaneously into an exultant hymn of praise: the most solemn thanksgiving resounds in the jubilant strains of the *Te Deum*. The whole Preface is, consequently, but a magnificent rendition of the words: *Gratias agamus Domino Deo nostro!*

2. **The body of the Preface.** The priest, standing in a reverential posture with uplifted hands and elevated heart, continues (on ordinary days) to say or sing the following hymn of praise and thanksgiving.[18] This *Praefatio communis* is used for all Masses to which no special Preface is assigned.

[16] Cf. Sulpicius Severus, *Third Dialogue*, chap. 10, and *Second Dialogue*, chap. 2.

[17] The versicles of the introductory formula just explained date from apostolic times; proof of this is found in all the ancient liturgies and in the Fathers; for in these we meet the above introductory formula, and with a considerable degree of agreement in the words employed. St. Cyprian was already acquainted with the name Preface. Quando stamus ad orationem, vigilare et incumbere ad preces toto corde debemus. Cogitatio omnis carnalis et saecularis abscedat nec quidquam tunc animus quam id solum cogitet quod precatur. Ideo et sacerdos ante Orationem (*before the Canon*) Praefatione praemissa parat fratrum mentes dicendo: *Sursum corda*, ut dum respondet plebs: *Habemus ad Dominum*, admoneatur, nihil aliud se quam Dominum cogitare debere (S. Cypr., *De Orat. dom.*, chap. 31).

[18] Postea (*after the Oblation*) cantatur Missa a sacerdote, qui postquam loquitur ad populum de elevatione cordis ad Deum exhortaturque eos ad gratias agendas Domino, laudibus os implet rogatque ut ipse omnipotens Deus Pater, cui deserviunt coelestes potestates, sua gratia illorum vocibus jubeat humanas associari confessiones, quam deprecationem mox subsequitur

Vere dignum et justum est, aequum et salutare, nos tibi semper et ubique gratias agere: Domine sancte, Pater omnipotens, aeterne Deus: per Christum Dominum nostrum. Per quem majestatem tuam laudant Angeli, adorant Dominationes, tremunt Potestates. Coeli coelorumque Virtutes, ac beata Seraphim, socia exsultatione concelebrant. Cum quibus et nostras voces, ut admitti jubeas deprecamur, suplici confessione dicentes:	It is truly meet and just, right and salutary, that we should always and in all places give thanks to Thee, O holy Lord, Father Almighty, eternal God, through Christ our Lord: through whom the angels praise Thy majesty, the dominations adore it, the powers tremble before it, the heavens and the heavenly virtues, and the blessed seraphim, exultingly celebrate it in common. Together with whom we beseech Thee that we may be admitted to join our voices in suppliant confession, saying:

The priest resumes the words of the people, confirms and develops them, inasmuch as he calls special attention to the great importance and obligation of returning thanks to God: "It is truly meet and just, right and salutary, that we should always and in all places give thanks" to God the Lord. Four reasons are cited which clearly manifest the importance and necessity of gratitude.

a) That we give thanks is meet (*dignum*) with respect to God and ourselves: the practice of giving thanks acknowledges and glorifies the dignity of God, on the one hand; and, on the other hand, it enhances at the same time the dignity of man. For, when we return thanks to God, we acknowledge Him as the source of all good, we glorify His majesty and fatherly love, we magnify His greatness and goodness—we give to God what His dignity demands of us. This manifestation of our gratitude also contributes to our moral dignity, revealing the beauty and nobility of the soul. Gratitude is the sign of a noble heart, while ingratitude is the mark of a mean soul. Fervent thanksgiving belongs to Christian perfection. The more perfect and devout, the more humble and pure the soul, the more will it be filled with the spirit of gratitude. The saints, when

---

laus ex angelicis et humanis cantibus confecta (Raban. Maur., *De clericor. institut.*, I, chap. 33). Oratione secreta completa, sacerdos *Vere dignum* devota mente dulcique voce proferat (Joann. Abrinc., *De offic. eccles.*).

upon earth, never wearied thanking God, and unceasing thanksgiving is their blessed occupation in eternity.

b) To thank God is but just (*justum*): a claim and a duty of justice (in a wide sense). Gratitude is allied with justice: for it is the will and the endeavor to return and repay, as far as possible, the benefits received. He who possesses strict justice, will also entertain grateful sentiments: he will strive to reward the benefactor. God expressly exacts gratitude from us as a tribute which we owe to Him; frequently and strongly does Holy Writ inculcate this duty of proving ourselves grateful to the Lord our God. "In all things give thanks; for this is the will of God in Christ Jesus" (I Thess. 5:18). "Giving thanks always for all things, in the name of our Lord Jesus Christ to God and the Father" (Eph. 5:20).

c) To thank God is right (*aequum*): it is becoming and proper from reasons of propriety. After considering our relations to God, gratitude appears in the highest degree an act of equity, which performs more than what is required according to strict justice and law. Reflect on the excessive goodness of God toward you and the riches of His mercy wherewith He daily visits you; is it then requiring too much that your heart should be inflamed with an ardent, strong, and grateful love, that your lips should overflow with the praises of the divine goodness which accompanies you in all your ways? What is more proper and right than that, by a grateful return of love and fervent thanksgiving, you repay, as far as you are able, the favors you receive of God, who has no need of your gifts?

d) To thank God is, finally, salutary (*salutare*): it promotes the temporal and eternal welfare inasmuch as it enriches the soul with great blessings and precious graces.[19] Gratitude opens to us the treasures of the divine liberality. In so far as we sincerely thank God for benefits received, we draw down new and more special graces upon ourselves. God takes complacency in a grateful heart; nothing shall be wanting to it. Hence gratitude is salutary, profitable, and rich in blessings; while ingratitude is a scorching wind that dries up the spring of divine goodness, the dew of heavenly mercy, and the streams of grace. "The gifts of grace cannot abound or flow in

---

[19] Optima ratio impetrandi a Deo donum perseverantiae et pertingendi ad salutem et beatitudinem, est jugis gratiarum actio. Haec enim est inchoatio vitae coelestis, haec est stimulus ad iter hoc in coelum usque jugiter prosequendum; haec est tacita invocatio Dei, quae novam et continuam ab eo gratiam elicit et provocat (Corn. a Lap., *Comment. in Apoc.*, 7:12).

us, because we are ungrateful to the Giver; and because we do not return them all to the fountainhead. For grace will ever be given him who dutifully returns thanks. Be grateful, then, for the least, and thou shalt be worthy to receive greater things." [20]

To cultivate a spirit of gratitude toward God is, therefore, a practice "truly meet and just, right and salutary"; but how far must we go? what is the extent of this thanksgiving? This is made known by the words that we "should always and in all places" give thanks. There is no time or place in which we should not from the fullness of our heart say: *Deo gratias*. Even in the hour of tribulation and in the night of adversity, even when on the couch of suffering and in a home of direst poverty, gratitude towards God should never be silent on our lips or in our heart.[21] When St. Elizabeth on a cold winter's night wandered about, an outcast and forsaken, she entered a Franciscan church and had the *Te Deum* sung, to thank the Lord for the tribulations wherewith He had in His mercy visited her. Hence do you also repeat with the Psalmist: "I will bless the Lord at all times; His praise shall be always in my mouth" (Ps. 33:2).

The words "O holy Lord, Father Almighty, eternal God" refer to the First Person of the Deity: they express the majesty and glory of the Father, and should likewise incite us to fervent thanksgiving. But are we, poor, frail creatures, able appropriately and adequately to thank the holy, almighty, and eternal God? "Through Christ our Lord," answers the Church. Christ is our mediator: through Him do all gifts and graces descend upon us "from the Father of lights," and through Him must our gratitude and praise ascend to God.[22] This should be done especially during the celebration of Mass: we should place all our grateful sentiments and prayers in the Eucharistic chalice, by means of which we can present to God a

---

[20] *Imitation of Christ*, II, 10.

[21] Christiani non sumus nisi propter futurum saeculum: nemo praesentia bona speret, nemo sibi promittat felicitatem mundi, quia christianus est, sed utatur felicitate praesenti, ut potest, quomodo potest, quando potest, quantum potest. Cum adest, consolationi Dei gratias agat; cum deest, justitiae Dei gratias agat: Ubique sit gratus, numquam ingratus: et Patri consolanti et blandienti gratus sit; et Patri emendanti et flagellanti et disciplinam danti gratus sit; amat enim ille semper, sive blandiatur sive minetur (S. August., *Enarrat in Ps.*, 91:1).

[22] Eodem ordine debet gratiarum actio in Deum recurrere, quo gratiae a Deo in nos deveniunt, quod quidem est per Jesum Christum (S. Thom., *In Epist. ad Rom.*, chap. 1, lect. 5).

thanksgiving worthy and meritorious because it is infinitely perfect.

The Saviour enthroned at the right hand of God is as man the head also of all the angelic choirs. They constitute a part of the eternal kingdom of God, whose glorious King is Jesus Christ. The risen Saviour is exalted above every creature and placed "above . . . every name that is named, not only in this world, but also in that which is to come, and He hath subjected all things under His feet and He . . . hath made Him head over all the Church" (Eph. 1:21 f.). To Him "the angels and powers and virtues are made subject" (I Pet. 3:22).

According to the common teaching (founded upon Scripture and tradition), the angels are divided into nine distinct choirs.[23] Revelation gives no further particulars as to the peculiar nature or the special offices of the different orders of angels. We can, therefore, entertain only more or less probable opinions or conjectures concerning them.[24] To penetrate more deeply into the wonderful mysteries of the angelic world is reserved for the beatific vision in heaven. Yet already here below, how beautiful and attractive to the eye of faith is that grand, brilliant, angelic world! Like shining stars the angels surround the throne of the Most High; they bask in the rays of the divine glory and contemplate the abyss of the divine essence. Those sublime spirits overflow with light, love, and happiness; jubilation, praise, and thanksgiving ascend unceasingly from their midst up to the throne of God. The Preface reveals to us but a glimpse of that jubilant kingdom of the angels, for it declares:

---

[23] The gradations of the angelic world are principally based on natural perfections, but especially in the varied gifts of grace and offices of the angels. That among the angels generally there are higher and lower orders, is de fide; that there are but nine choirs of angels, no more and no less, is not so certain, still it is the teaching of tradition. Holy Scripture mentions nine choirs of angels, and since the ninth century we meet with the enumeration of them in the most ancient liturgies and in the Fathers. According to St. Gregory the Great (*Hom. in Evangel.*, XXIV) their order is: (1) angels; (2) archangels; (3) virtues; (4) powers; (5) principalities; (6) dominations; (7) thrones; (8) cherubim; (9) seraphim. The two lowest and the three highest are enumerated in the same order by all, while the four middle ones are differently grouped by others. In the Prefaces, all the choirs, with the exception of the principalities, are mentioned by name. In the *Ordo commendat. animae*, eight choirs are likewise mentioned, in which, however, the virtues are passed over. (Cf. Petavius, *De Angelis*, II, chaps. 3-5.)

[24] Quid inter se distent . . . dicant qui possunt, si tamen possunt probare, quod dicunt; ego me ista ignorare confiteor (S. August., *Enchirid.*, chap. 58).

"through whom the angels praise Thy majesty." The blessed spirits also present their homages to God "through Jesus Christ," their head.[25] Here "angels" does not refer to all the angelic spirits in general, as is otherwise frequently the case when angels are mentioned, but only to those angels who belong to the lowest choir.[26] As is evident from what follows, several choirs are to be mentioned by name. The dominations adore the majesty of the Creator (*adorant Dominationes*) as no mortal is capable of doing. The powers, those mighty spirits of heaven, tremble in profound humility and reverential awe (*tremunt Potestates*) before the grandeur of the divine majesty.[27] It is a joyous, blissful reverence that penetrates these glorious heavenly spirits.[28]

Moreover, "the heavens and the heavenly virtues and the blessed seraphim exultingly celebrate in common" the majesty of God. All

---

[25] Et "ipsum (Christum) dedit (Deus Pater) caput supra omnem Ecclesiam," scilicet tam militantem, quae est hominum in praesenti viventium, quam triumphantem, quae est ex hominibus et Angelis in patria (S. Thom., *In Epist. ad Ephes.*, chap. 1, lect. 8).

[26] The generic name *angelus* (ἄγγελος, *nuntius*) is employed in other Prefaces also to designate the lowest choir.

[27] Tremor autem nihil poenae, sed reverentiae castique timoris plurimum significat; constat enim, timorem castum et reverentialem haerere in coelitibus et "permanere in saeculum saeculi" (Ps. 18:10) et "tremere Potestates," in curia angelica non postremas, dum in luce atque oculis divinae majestatis humillime stratae et abjectae contremiscunt et pavent ad nutum ejus (Corder., *Comm. in libr. Job*, 26:11). Cum igitur in coelestibus tanta sit devotio laudantium, veneratio adorantium, tremor admirantium, consideret haec homo, cui dictum est: Quid superbit terra? (Flor. Diac., *De actione Miss.*, n. 27). Contemplare majestatem et item justitiam Dei altissimi, quatenus timorate in cunctis te habeas. Si enim columnae coeli pavent in conspectu ejus et si angelici spiritus cum reverentiali tremore Deo assistunt, intendunt, deserviunt, cum quanta sollicitudine atque custodia cordis, timoreque mentis nos pauperes Deo adstare et sacrificare oportet? (Dion. Carthus., *Expos. Miss.*, a. 4.)

[28] Divinam majestatem non solum Angeli, Dominationes et Potestates laudant, adorant, tremunt, sed etiam coeli et coelorum Virtutes et Seraphim concelebrant, i.e. in commune celebrant, concordi devotione et commune gaudio laudant (Flor. Diacon., *op. cit.*, n. 28). The expression *coeli* is often used to designate the angelic choir of the thrones, or it also means the heavenly abode, in which case by *virtutes caelorum* the heavenly spirits in general are understood (*hoc nomine omnes coelestes spiritus nonnunquam generaliter appellari solent* [ibid., n. 30]). Here five, or perhaps six, choirs of angels are mentioned; in other Prefaces *Angeli et Archangeli, Throni et Dominationes*, or *Angeli et Archangeli, Cherubim quoque ac Seraphim* are mentioned; and once (on Pentecost) all the angels are comprised in the words *supernae Virtutes atque angelicae Potestates*.

the choirs of angels are not specifically mentioned, but they are included in the word heaven (*coeli*),[29] for this word does not here denote the visible heaven, but the blessed citizens and princes of the invisible heaven in general. Then there are yet two choirs of angels expressly mentioned: the powers (*Virtutes*) and the seraphim (*Seraphim*). The latter constitute the highest choir of the angelic kingdom and are emphatically called blessed,[30] because they burn and glow with an incomparable love of God.

Thus the blessed hosts of heavenly spirits are eternally immersed in loving and praising the glory of God; they are never weary of celebrating and blessing the glory of their Creator. Now, in the sacred hour of the sacrifice, we rise and ascend in spirit above the lowliness of the earth and soar to the heights of the heavenly Jerusalem, there to join our voices in the angels' glorious hymn of praise. Of such an honor we are totally unworthy, our adoration being so very lowly and contemptible. But penetrated with this sentiment of our total unworthiness, we implore God that He would suffer us to join our feeble voices with the angelic choirs,[31] and in all humility we praise the glory of the triune God and the glory of the Redeemer in the *Sanctus*.[32]

3. The conclusion of the Preface.

Sanctus, Sanctus, Sanctus, Dominus Deus Sabaoth.	Holy, holy, holy, Lord God of hosts.
Pleni sunt coeli et terra gloria tua.	Heaven and earth are full of Thy glory.
Hosanna in excelsis.	Hosanna in the highest!
Benedictus qui venit in nomine Domini.	Blessed is He that cometh in the name of the Lord.
Hosanna in excelsis.	Hosanna in the highest!

[29] In the majority of Prefaces the choirs of angels not expressly mentioned are designated by the words *omnis militia coelestis exercitus*. Instead of *socia* (= allied) *exsultatione* (properly = exulting, rejoicing) *concelebrant* (= extol, glorify), once is given *una voce dicentes*. Omnes ordines majestatem Dei Patris per Christum juncta exsultatione aequaliter concelebrant (Raban. Maur., *De sacr. ord.*, chap. 19). Concentus in coelo angelicus totus est unisonus, totus consonus, quia projectus est inde antiquus ille disturbator coelestis harmoniae (Gerhoh. Reichersp., *In Ps.*, 25).

[30] They are called *beata Seraphim*, because, according to a general rule, indeclinable substantives are regarded as neuter.

[31] Haec est supplicatio nostra, ut ipse coelestis Pater per Christum Filium suum, per quem nos ei gratias de omnibus agimus, dignetur admittere voces nostras et jungere vocibus ordinum Angelorum (Raban. Maur., *loc. cit.*).

[32] Humility, which accompanies our chant of praise (*supplex confessio*),

THE PREFACE

This exceedingly sublime hymn of praise [33] is made up of words taken from Holy Scripture and consists of two parts. The first half contains the glorification of the Holy Trinity by the angels of heaven; the second half consists of the welcoming of the Saviour by the mouth of the faithful on earth.[34] With regard to the first part, this magnifying of the Lord God of hosts is termed the Thrice Holy (Trisagion) [35] or hymn of the seraphim, or of the angels (*Hymnus seraphicus* or *angelicus*); [36] and the second part of the hymn is designated the Triumphal Chant (*Hymnus triumphalis*). The Trisagion is found at least in part in all the liturgies; in ancient times it was sung also by the congregation.[37]

The first part of the hymn, with some slight alterations, is taken

---

is also manifested in the moderate inclination of the body when reciting the Thrice Holy. Cf. the original concluding stanza of the Saturday Vesper Hymn (of St. Ambrose), in which we read:

Te nostra *supplex gloria*
Per cuncta laudet saecula.

[33] The Second Council of Vaison (529) deemed it proper to renew the ordinance that this hymn must be sung at all Masses. Ut in omnibus Missis sive matutinis sive quadragesimalibus vel quae in defunctorum commemorationibus fiunt, semper *Sanctus, Sanctus, Sanctus* eo ordine, quo ad Missas publicas dici debeat: quia tam dulcis et desiderabilis vox, etiamsi diu noctuque posset dici, fastidium non potest generare (can. 1:1).

[34] Vox angelorum Trinitatis et unitatis in Deo commendat arcanum; vox hominum divinitatis et humanitatis in Christo personat sacramentum (Innocent. III, II, chap. 61). Circa consecrationem, quae supernaturali virtute agitur, excitatur populus ad devotionem in praefatione; unde et monetur *sursum habere corda ad Dominum*, et ideo, finita praefatione, populus devote laudat divinitatem Christi cum angelis dicens: *Sanctus, Sanctus, Sanctus*, et humanitatem cum pueris dicens: *Benedictus qui venit* (S. Thom., IIIa, q.83, a.4).

[35] Trisagion is also the name given to the enlarged biblical Thrice Holy: *Sanctus Deus, sanctus Fortis, sanctus Immortalis, miserere nobis* ("Holy God, holy Strong One, holy Immortal One, have mercy on us"). It is modeled after the psalm verse (41:3): *Sitivit anima mea ad Deum, fortem, vivum* ("My soul hath thirsted after the strong living God": God all-powerful and immortal) and it is only a paraphrase for Holy Father, Holy Son, and Holy Ghost. This Trisagion is recited in the ferial prayers of Prime and is sung in Latin and Greek in the liturgy of Good Friday. (Cf. S. Joann. Damasc., *Epistola de Hymno Trisagio*.)

[36] The designation, "Hymn of the Cherubim," also occurs; for they and all the other angels sing the Trisagion, although Isaias mentions only the Seraphim. (Cf. the Te Deum.)

[37] In the Pontifical this ordinance is ascribed to Pope Sixtus I (119–28): "when the priest begins the Canon (*actionem*) of the Mass, the congregation should sing the hymn: Holy, holy, holy is the Lord God of Sabaoth." In the Mozarabic liturgy we read that the Thrice Holy is that *aeterna laudatio, quae in coelestibus sine defectu psallitur ab Angelis et hic solemniter decan-*

from the grand description of a vision of the prophet Isaias (6:3): "And they [the seraphim] cried one to another, and said: Holy, holy, holy, the Lord God of hosts, all the earth is full of Thy glory."[38] St. John the apostle also heard the celestial canticle: "Holy, holy, holy, Lord God Almighty" (Apoc. 4:8). As is evident from the universal doctrine of the Fathers and from several passages of Holy Scripture itself, the thrice repeating of the word "holy" is intended, not merely to proclaim emphatically the holiness of God, but rather to indicate the threefold personality of God: it is a hymn of praise to the adorable Trinity.[39] Since in God's sanctity, His infinite perfection, beauty, and glory shine forth most resplendently, He is in the language of revelation and of the Church very often praised as "the Holy One." The divine holiness is uncreated, immense, unchangeable: the infinitely pure, luminous, spiritual being of God is holiness itself. God is the "only Holy One," and from God the supernal splendor of holiness is reflected over all the world of angels and of men: His is the type and the source of all created holiness.

In the holiness of the triune God is celebrated His interior and eternal glory, which of itself is invisible to us. This uncreated glory of the Lord of hosts is unveiled in the works of creation and redemption; for "heaven and earth," the sum of all creation, the visible and the invisible world, bear witness to the glory of God. "Heaven and earth are full of" His "glory," full of proofs of the power and greatness, of the goodness and mercy of God: hence they announce and proclaim His greatness, His unspeakably great glory.[40]

---

tatur a populis. Ubi expedita contestatione omnis populus *Sanctus* in Dei laudem proclamavit (S. Gregor. Turon., *De mirac. S. Martini*, II, chap. 14). The choir also sang with the people, and in many places the priest also, who in the Frankish capitularies of the eighth and ninth centuries was often forbidden to begin the Canon before the close of the hymn, for example: "*Te igitur*" *non inchoent sacerdotes, nisi post angelicum hymnum finitum;* and: *Ut Secreta presbyteri non inchoent antequam "Sanctus" finiatur, sed cum populo "Sanctus" cantent.* (Cf. Martene., *De antiq. Eccl. ritibus,* I, iv, 7.)

[38] The liturgical text is an address to God; according to the ancient biblical translation, it has, instead of *exercituum*, the Hebrew word *sabaoth*, which has been retained only in three passages in our Vulgate, and instead of the biblical *omnis terra*, it gives *coeli et terra.*

[39] Domine Deus dulcissime, sanctitas tua ineffabilis est: de qua quodammodo magis quam de aliis perfectionibus gloriaris. Seraphim ut te collaudent, ter sanctum vocant, non tantum ut personarum Trinitatem indicent, sed ut te omnino sanctum et pelagus sanctitatis insinuent (Alvar. de Paz, *De studio orationis,* Bk. III, Part III, dec. 6, contempl. 53).

[40] Tria laudant: personarum trinitatem, unitatis majestatem et provisionis

THE PREFACE

After the praise of the triune God follows the jubilant salutation of the Redeemer, who will soon appear mystically on the altar "in the fullness of mercy."[41] The hymn concludes with the triumphal chant with which the Saviour was welcomed by the multitudes as Prince of Peace and conqueror of death at His solemn entrance into Jerusalem, and with which He is now again saluted at His coming on the altar: "Hosanna in the highest! Blessed is He that cometh in the name of the Lord. Hosanna in the highest!" The original verse of the psalm from which this acclamation is taken, is somewhat different: "O Lord, save me! O Lord, give good success! Blessed be He that cometh in the name of the Lord" (Ps. 117:25 f.).[42] The first verse, which expresses the petition for salvation and success, was sung by the congregation at the procession on the Feast of Tabernacles; the other verse, which took up and continued the salutation or blessing of those who were entering the Temple, was said by the priests' choir. These words, however, are prophetically Messianic, for according to their highest purpose and meaning, they refer to Jesus Christ, who was announced by the prophets as "the one that was to come,"[43] and who came in the fullness of time "in

---

liberalitatem (quia usque ad ultimas creaturas, quae per terram intelliguntur, extendit diffusionem suae bonitatis). (S. Thom., *In Isa.*, chap.6, n.1.) Non perperam hunc locum intelliget, qui per coelos spiritus angelicos et per terram homines hic acceperit . . . nam et coelestes spiritus et homines Dei gloria implentur: illi quidem praesenti glorificatione, hi vero in spe et praevia dispositione (Clichtov., III).

[41] Since the first *Hosanna in excelsis* is, like the triple *Sanctus*, said with a moderate bow of the body, and is sung with it already before the Consecration, and not after it with the *Benedictus*, some consider it as an acclamation of homage and glorification to the triune God in the highest heavens. At the words *Benedictus qui venit*, the celebrant stands erect, not merely because he exults in going to meet the Redeemer about to descend on the altar at the Consecration, but also that he may make the prescribed sign of the cross more conveniently. The wording of other liturgies, however, undeniably excludes the aforesaid reference of the first *Hosanna* to the Blessed Trinity. Osanna Filio David, osanna in excelsis: benedictus qui venit in nomine Domini, osanna in excelsis (*Liturg. Mozarab.*).

[42] In the Hebrew, "me" is wanting, and *salvum fac* there is *Hoschianna*, whence the Greek expression ὡσαννά and the Latin *hosanna* originated (= to help). The designation *in nomine Domini* can be referred by the Psalmist to *qui venit* or to *benedictus*, but in the evangelical and liturgical text it must be combined with *qui venit*; for here it forms the clearer explanation and necessary supplement to the coming, upon which rests the emphasis. The Messias is glorified as the ambassador of God. (Cf. John 5:43.)

[43] Cf. the question of the disciples of John to Christ: *Tu es qui venturus*

the name of the Lord," that is, sent by the heavenly Father to redeem the world. The petition and the salutation found their application in the Messias in the mouth of the people who, enlightened from above, exultingly and in a loud voice saluted the Saviour entering Jerusalem with the words: "Hosanna to the Son of David! Blessed is He that cometh in the name of the Lord.[44] Hosanna in the highest!" In this text of the New Testament, "hosanna" is, according to its original signification, understood as a cry of supplication (help and blessing to the Son of David), and again as an acclamation of reverence and of exultation (hail to Him).[45] In comparing the passage of the psalm with the Gospel text, we find a difference in the wording, as well as a partly different meaning, which results from the application and reference of the biblical text in the Gospel.

The liturgical text departs somewhat from the biblical: "Hosanna in the highest! Blessed is He that cometh in the name of the Lord. Hosanna in the highest!" It is not taken directly from the psalm, but from the Gospel: hence it follows that it refers to the Saviour and His coming on the altar.[46] How profoundly significant is this formula of worship, this grateful and joyful praise of the Saviour, inserted at this part of the Mass, when He is about to reappear in our midst as a victim, as formerly He entered into Jerusalem to accomplish on the cross the bloody sacrifice![47] What is at this moment

---

es, an alium exspectamus? (Matt. 11:3.) *Veniens, venturus, exspectatus*, ὁ ἐρχόμενος, were well known designations of the Messias.

[44] Jesus Christ, who by the commission of God as well as for His glorification, came into the world, is in the fullest sense *benedictus* (blessed), because He is the source of all blessing and salvation for us and, therefore, infinitely worthy of all praise and glory. Hoc canticum consona voce resonabant, utique ex instructione et motione Spiritus sancti (Dion. Carthus., *In Matt.*, 21:9). Cf. Ps. 3:9.

[45] Expressing more than *vivat* (may he live), the *hosanna* corresponds to the Italian *evviva*.

[46] The liturgical text in the Apostolic Constitutions excludes every other signification: "Hosanna to the Son of David; blessed be He that cometh in the name of the Lord; God the Lord, He hath appeared to us. Hosanna in the highest!" (VIII, chap. 13.) That the words *Benedictus qui venit* cannot be understood as a blessing for those who assist at Mass, but are to be referred to the Eucharistic advent of the Saviour, is also evident from their rubrical destination, that they are to be sung by the choir only after the Consecration and Elevation (cf. *Cerem. Episc.*, II, viii, 70 f.).

[47] Ex Scriptura prophetica et evangelica completur plena laudatio, cum post laudem et gloriam sanctae Trinitatis adjungitur etiam gratiarum actio

more natural for us than exultingly to cry out: Highly praised be Christ, who, in obedience to the will of His heavenly Father, mystically descends upon the altar, daily to sacrifice Himself anew for the salvation of the whole world. This grateful praise is introduced and concluded by the acclamation of hosanna. What does the foreign Hebrew word *hosanna* here signify? In the language of the Church its original meaning (= help, save, redeem) was soon lost and is no longer clearly felt; for hosanna is a joyous, jubilant acclamation: Hail, glory, praise be to Him.[48] The grand liturgy of Palm Sunday illustrates and confirms this explanation. A few passages follow:

When the people heard that Jesus was coming to Jerusalem, they took branches of palms and went out to meet Him, and the children cried out, saying: This is He that is to come for the salvation of the people. He is our salvation and the redemption of Israel. How great is He whom thrones and dominations go forth to welcome! . . . Hail, O King, Creator of the world, who comest to redeem us!

The multitude go out to meet the Redeemer with flowers and palms, and as to a conqueror entering on his triumph, they render worthy homage to Him. With their mouth the nations praise the Son of God, and through the clouds of heaven voices resound to the praise of Christ: Hosanna in the highest!

Like the angels and the children will we also sing of the conqueror of death: Hosanna in the highest!

Praise, honor, and glory be to Thee, our King, Christ and Redeemer, unto whom the sweet and charming company of children poured forth their hosanna, their devout hymn of praise (*cui puerile decus prompsit Hosanna pium*). Thou art the King of Israel, Thou art the glorious Son of David. All praise be to Thee, O King, Thou that cometh in the name of the Lord. The multitude on high exalt Thee, the whole heavenly host, mortal man and all created things join in praising Thee. The Hebrew people went forth to meet Thee with palms: behold we also appear before Thee with petitions, prayers, and hymns. For Thy passion they

---

de adventu Salvatoris, qui unus in ipsa et ex ipsa Trinitate pro salute nostra homo factus in mundum venit et eandem salutem moriendo et resurgendo perfecit . . . unde rite illi gratias agentes dicimus *Hosanna*, i.e. salus in excelsis (Florus. Diacon., *op. cit.*, n. 41).

[48] In the votive Mass *de Passione Domini* the Church cries out to the Saviour: Tibi gloria, hosanna: tibi triumphus et victoria: tibi summae laudis et honoris corona. Alleluja. As *vox laetantis* (the expression of animated, exultant sentiment), hosanna was not translated into either Greek or Latin (cf. S. August., *De doctr. christ.*, II, xi, 16). In the Middle Ages even the verb *hosannare* (= to praise) was used.

brought Thee sacrifices of praise: behold we sing to Thee our canticle for Thy victorious dominion. These gave Thee pleasure, may our devotions also be agreeable to Thee, O good and gentle King, to whom good works are always pleasing.

The Trisagion is not sung by the priest (as is the Preface), but is recited in a half audible voice (*voce mediocri*).[49] When he joins in the angelic hymn of praise to glorify the Most Holy Trinity, he lowers his voice and with joined hands bows with humble reverence. At the joyful praise of the approaching Saviour, he again stands erect and signs himself with the cross,[50] not merely to conclude the hymn in due form, but also to indicate that Christ came as a victorious conqueror and Prince of Peace to establish His kingdom by means of the cross, and that He now comes down on the altar to renew mystically the sacrifice of the cross.

The wonderful hymn of the Preface is grand and its sublimity beggars description. As all "the angels and archangels, also the cherubim and seraphim do not cease to cry out as with one voice, saying: Holy, holy, holy, is the Lord God of hosts. Heaven and earth are full of Thy glory": in the same manner "does the Church throughout the earth acknowledge and praise Him, the Father of boundless majesty, His adorable, true, and only-begotten Son, as well as the Holy Ghost, the Comforter." St. Chrysostom exclaims:

O marvellous gifts of Christ! On high the angelic choirs sing glory to the Lord; on earth, after their example, men sing in church the same canticle in choirs. In heaven the seraphim sing aloud their Thrice Holy; on earth the same canticle resounds from the mouth of the assembled congregation.[51] Thus heaven and earth unite in a festive celebration;

---

[49] In Rome at an early period this hymn was no longer sung by the people, but by subdeacons (*Ordo Rom. I*, n. 16; *II*, n. 10), and later on (as is still the case) it was sung by the choir (*basilicarii; Ordo Rom. XI*, n. 20). While it was being sung, everyone bowed. Qui dum expleverint, surgit Pontifex solus et intrat in Canonem (*Ordo Rom. I*, n. 16).

[50] The liturgists of the Middle Ages often mention the rule of accompanying the recitation of the evangelical words with the sign of the cross. In omnibus verbis evangelicis signum crucis fieri oportet (Beleth., chap. 40). Hence Sicardus remarks, in reference to the concluding words of the Sanctus: Hoc sumptum est de Evangelio, unde cum cantatur, nobis signaculum crucis imprimimus (III, chap. 6).

[51] The same holy doctor of the Church says in a eulogy of the martyrs: "Because the martyrs showed the utmost love for the Lord, He kindly extends His hand to them; now they should rejoice at the heavenly glory and join the choirs of angels and unite in their mysterious hymns (Isa. 6:3). Among

it is a hymnal celebration of thanksgiving, of praise; it is a choir of common joy, which the unspeakable goodness of the Lord, in His great condescension to us, organized, and which the Holy Ghost assembled; on its harmony the heavenly Father dwells with complacency. Its melody is borrowed from heaven, being led by the hand of the Holy Trinity, to the end that those sweet and blessed notes, those chants of the angels, those canticles of praise, may never cease to resound.

4. **The proper Prefaces.** In addition to the ordinary Preface, the Roman Missal contains fourteen others which have a specific festal character, since various mysteries of the ecclesiastical year are therein prominently set forth as special motives of praise and thanksgiving.

The liturgy of the Church conspicuously sets forth our gratitude toward God; the sentiment of fervent thanksgiving for the salvation given us by Christ, for the grace of faith, the glory of the redemption, and the blessed hope of heaven, day after day finds its touching expression, as beautiful as it is joyful, in the Preface of the Mass. But when on the great feasts of the ecclesiastical year, the mysteries of sacred history, the great deeds and benefits of divine love seem to reveal themselves more vividly and brightly to the soul and to move the heart in the fullness of their beauty and glory; then it is that the hymn of thanksgiving and praise rises to the greatest heights of enthusiasm and jubilation.

The Church has proper Prefaces for the feasts of Christmas, the Epiphany, Easter, the Ascension, Pentecost, the Holy Trinity, the Sacred Heart, Christ the King, the Blessed Virgin, St. Joseph, and the apostles (and popes), for the seasons of Lent and Passiontide, and for the Requiem Mass. The Christmas Preface is used until Epiphany and for the feast of Corpus Christi and its octave.[52] The

---

these choirs they were counted already during their earthly life as often as they participated in the holy mysteries, in that they, with the cherubim, sang the Thrice Holy in praising the Lord. You, who belong to the consecrated, know the reason of this; so much the less should it surprise you, now that they have found their companions in heaven, that with greater confidence they take part in this hymn of praise."

[52] By a special exception from the general rule, during the octave of Christmas this Preface is to be taken also in such Masses as have a *Praefatio propria* (for example, on the feast of the apostle John, but not on his octave day, and in any votive Masses that may be said). Candlemas Day (*Purificatio B. M. V.*) has the Christmas Preface, inasmuch as this day, even in the West, is also a feast of the Lord; in the Greek rite it is even more prominently so, hence the name, *occursus, obviatio: quia venerabiles personae Simeon et Anna eo*

Easter Preface is used throughout the Easter season, except on feasts that have a proper Preface. The Preface for the Holy Trinity, which is one of the most recent, was prescribed by Clement XIII (1759) for all Sundays that have no special Preface; this Preface lacks poetic sentiment and bears the stamp of scholastic theology.[53] The Preface for Passiontide is a magnificent praise of the instrument of our salvation, and is therefore used in votive Masses or on feasts of the cross.[54] All the other Prefaces are used on the respective feasts and their octaves (if they have one) and in votive Masses commemorating the mystery or saint.

All of these Prefaces follow a certain pattern. All, except the Preface for feasts of the apostles and popes, are addressed to the Father;[55] all except the latter and the Easter Preface begin with the words: "It is truly meet and just, right and salutary, that we

---

die obviaverunt Domino, dum praesentaretur in templo (Microl., chap. 48). The feast of Corpus Christi, as well as the feast of the Holy Name of Jesus and the Transfiguration, have also the Christmas Preface.

[53] This Preface contains a majestic and sublime rendering of those words of the Athanasian Symbol: "This is Catholic faith, that we revere the one God in the Trinity and the Trinity in unity." The mystery of the Holy Trinity is the most profound and sublime mystery of our faith: to all created and finite minds the Trinity is absolutely unattainable and unfathomable. It was left to divine revelation alone to unveil the sublime truth, which we, with childlike and simple faith must accept and adhere to. Therefore Clement XIII prescribed for all Sundays that have no special Preface, the *Praefatio de Trinitate ad majorem splendidioremque tanti mysterii gloriam, ut fideles quoque, qui die Dominica Missae interesse debent, latius atque apertius ejusdem mysterii praeconia audientes, debitum et ipsi servitutis obsequium supremae impendant majestati.*

[54] In this Preface is appropriately expressed the antithetical relation between the tree (*lignum*, wood) of knowledge, by the fruit of which was perpetrated the fall of man, and the wood (tree, *lignum*) of the cross, on which the redemption was accomplished. The former tree, planted in the center of the Garden of Paradise, was intended for the blessing of humanity, and it became its curse. The latter tree, erected in the center of the globe, the gibbet of the curse ("for he is accursed of God that hangeth on a tree" [Deut. 21:23]), has become a blessing for all that believe in it. Cf. the beautiful Preface in the *Gregorian Sacramentary:* Christus per passionem crucis mundum redemit et antiquae arboris amarissimum gustum crucis medicamine indulcavit, mortemque quae per lignum vetitum venerat, per ligni trophaeum devicit, ut mirabili suae pietatis dispensatione qui per ligni gustum a florigera sede discesseramus, per crucis lignum ad paradisi gaudia redeamus.

[55] This is the only Preface whose words are addressed to Jesus Christ. The celebration of the feast of the apostles and their successors leads the Church to invoke the "eternal Shepherd" for the protection and defense of His faithful flock.

should always and in all places give thanks to Thee, O holy Lord, Father Almighty, eternal God." Then is mentioned the mystery for which we are particularly grateful. The Prefaces conclude with a joyful, heavenly praise of God's glory, in which we join ourselves to the angelic choirs. This inspiring conclusion, which forms an introduction to the glorious Sanctus, takes, with but two exceptions, one of the following forms:

Through whom [Christ] the angels praise Thy majesty, the dominations adore it, the powers tremble before it, the heavens and the heavenly virtues, and the blessed seraphim, exultingly celebrate it in common. Together with whom we beseech Thee that we may be admitted to join our voices in suppliant confession, saying:

And therefore with the angels and archangels, with the thrones and dominations, and with all the heavenly hosts, we sing a hymn [56] to Thy glory, saying without ceasing: [57]

Thus in union with the heavenly choirs of angels we exultingly sing that sublime hymn of praise, the Sanctus, and enter into the holy of holies, the Canon of the Mass.

[56] Already Walafrid Strabo distinguishes metrical and rhythmic hymns on the one hand (real hymns), and, on the other, hymns in a general (improper) sense. Among the latter he reckons the Preface with the Trisagion. Notandum hymnos dici non tantum qui metris vel rithmis decurrunt . . . verum etiam ceteras laudationes, quae verbis convenientibus et sonis dulcibus proferuntur. . . . Et quamvis in quibusdam ecclesiis hymni metrici non cantentur, tamen in omnibus generales hymni, i.e. laudes dicuntur (*De exord. et increm.*, chap. 26).

[57] Sine fine = sine cessatione, sine requie, sine intermissione, per quod significatur jugis et assidua illius excellentissimi hymni *Sanctus, Sanctus, Sanctus* . . . a nobis decantatio facienda. Quod cum in hac mortali vita perfecte a nobis expleri non possit, hoc verbo tacite et per subinsinuationem quandam expetitur aeternae beatitudinis consortium nobis demum concedi, in qua angelicis conjuncti choris sacra laudatione possimus hunc hymnum sine fine ac perpetuo decantare, quemadmodum et ipsae supernae virtutes atque angelicae potestates hymnum hunc gloriae Domini sine fine concinunt secundum illud verbum (Ps. 83): "Beati qui habitant in domo tua, Domine: in saecula saeculorum laudabunt te" (Clichtov., *Elucid. eccles.*, III, 3).

CHAPTER XXXII

THE CANON OF THE MASS

THE jubilant hosanna has now ceased.[1] Holy silence succeeds, for the Canon begins.[2] Cardinal Wiseman says of the Prefaces: "There could not be a more splendid introduction, with the hymn which closes them, to the divine rite that follows. Here we must pause; because the subject becomes too sacred for our pen; the ground upon which we are about to tread is holy, and the shoes must be loosed from the feet of him who will venture upon it."[3] These words of the devout prelate are a serious admonition to pray with all humility and love that the Lord "may lift the veil from our eyes," and that in some degree we may be enabled to behold and understand the mysteries concealed in the Canon: for the Lord giveth "wisdom to little ones" (Ps. 18:8).[4]

---

[1] According to a rubric (*Rubr. gener. Miss.*, tit. 20; *Ritus celebr. Miss.*, tit. 8, n. 6), that probably has no preceptive, but only a directive, character, the so-called Sanctus or Consecration candle is to be lighted on the Epistle side and to continue burning until after the Communion. This candle denotes the Eucharistic presence of the Lord and incites the faithful to devotion, love, and adoration. (Cf. S. R. C., December 30, 1881.)

[2] Post laudes et gratiarum actiones pro tanta gratia redemptionis nostrae, quae in illo divino mysterio agitur et commendatur, facto totius Ecclesiae silentio, in quo cessante omni strepitu verborum, sola ad Deum dirigitur intentio et devotio cordium, sociatis sibi omnium votis et desideriis, incipit sacerdos orationem fundere, qua ipsum mysterium dominici corporis et sanguinis consecratur. Sic enim oportet, ut in illa hora tam sacrae ac divinae actionis tota per Dei gratiam a terrenis cogitationibus mente separata et ecclesia cum sacerdote et sacerdos cum ecclesia spirituali desiderio intret in sanctuarium Dei aeternum et supernum. . . . Idcirco, ut ferunt, consuetudo venit in ecclesia, ut tacite ista obsecratio atque consecratio a sacerdote cantetur (*recited*), ne verba tam sacra et ad tantum mysterium pertinentia vilescerent (Pseudo-Alcuin., chap. 40).

[3] "On Prayer and Prayer-Books," *Essays*, II, 201.

[4] Blessed Otto of Cambrai (d. 1113) writes in the Preface to his *Expositio in Canonem Missae:* Praesumptionis argui timeo, quod ausus sum rem difficilem

THE CANON OF THE MASS

1. The name, origin, and antiquity of the Canon.[5] The word canon (Κανών)[6] in ecclesiastical language has many different meanings; but here, where it serves to designate the principal portion of the liturgy of the Mass, it signifies the standard formula, the fixed, invariable rule for the accomplishment of the essential act of the sacrifice. The Canon of the Mass, which begins after the *Sanctus* and ends before the *Pater noster*,[7] includes the consecration, or sacrificial act, and also those prayers and ceremonies that introduce the consecration and are most closely connected with it. It there-

---

contingere et extendere conatus in alta profunditate, scil. exponere Canonem altaris et probare tanta mysteria.

[5] The position of the Canon underwent many a change in the course of time. Until the ninth century it was in connection with the *Missa quotidiana* placed at the end of the cycle of the year's feasts. After this time it was placed at the beginning of the Sacramentary, being preceded by only a heading and a very short *Ordo Missae*. From the eleventh century it is more frequently found in the middle of the book, between Holy Saturday and Easter Sunday. Through the *Missale secundum consuetudinem curiae Romanae* it permanently retained that place after the thirteenth century. Since the Canon is the part of the missal the most used, it has been properly placed where it is most convenient for use, that is, in the middle of the missal. This practical feature decided its position. Moreover, the position between Holy Saturday and Easter Sunday may also indicate that the accomplishment of the Eucharistic sacrifice forms the vivifying center of the ecclesiastical year.

[6] Κανών originally denoted a straight staff and, therefore, the Mass rod or rule; metaphorically, then, any law, regulation or ordinance (*lex, regula, norma*). In ecclesiastical language the word *canon* (as also the adjective *canonicus*) has a manifold application. Thus, for example, it designates the entire collection of inspired revelation records, in so far as they constitute an authoritative or standard rule for the faith and morals of man; then divine tradition, which likewise forms a *regula fidei*; also the laws of the Church and the definitions of the Councils are called κανόνες. Furthermore, *canon* signifies the register of saints (hence *canonizatio*, the reception into it), also the list of the clerics who, belonging to a certain church (οἱ ἐν κανόνι = the clerics, hence the denomination *Canonici*), for the most part lived in common according to a determined rule. *Actio* dicitur ipse Canon, quia in eo sacramenta conficiuntur dominica. *Canon* vero eadem actio nominatur, quia ea est legitima et regularis sacramentorum confectio (Walafrid. Strabo, chap. 23). Moreover, other designations are, for example, *regula, legitimum, agenda, secretum Missae, prex, mystica prex, textus canonicae precis.*

[7] The Canon is limited in the *Rubr. generales* (tit. 12 et 13) and in the *Ritus celebr. Missam* (tit. 8 et 9); but in consequence of the continued superscription in the *Ordo Missae*, the Canon would extend from the Sanctus to the end of the Communion, that is, there would be question not only of a Canon of the Consecration, but also of a Canon of Communion; but this has never been customary. The word Canon, as a rule, is used without addition to designate the Canon of Consecration. (Cf. Cavalieri, V, xvi, 1.)

fore covers the divine sacrificial act with a mystical veil and encloses it in a most precious case. As the sacrifice which the eternal high priest offers on the altar to the end of ages, ever remains the same, in like manner the Canon, the ecclesiastical sacrificial prayer, in its sublime simplicity and venerable majesty, ever remains the same; only on the greatest feasts are a few additions made in order to harmonize with the changing spirit of the ecclesiastical year.[8]

The Church itself explains the origin of the Canon:

And since it is becoming that holy things be administered in a holy manner, and of all things this sacrifice is the most holy, the Catholic Church, to the end that it might be worthily and reverently offered and received, instituted many centuries ago the holy Canon, which is so free from error that it contains nothing that does not in the highest degree savor of a certain holiness and piety and raise up to God the minds of those who offer. For it consists partly of the very words of the Lord, partly of the traditions of the apostles, and also of pious regulations of holy pontiffs.[9]

On account of the want of reliable historical testimony, we are not able to state more accurately and minutely what parts of the Canon are of apostolic tradition and what are the later additions of holy popes.[10] Yet it is rather certain and generally admitted that Pope

---

[8] These changes are made in the *Communicantes* and *Hanc igitur*. The *Communicantes* receives a small addition on Holy Thursday, in the Masses of the octaves of Christmas, Epiphany, Easter, Ascension, and Pentecost, as well as in votive Masses of these feasts; the *Hanc igitur* on Holy Thursday (as well as the *Qui pridie*) and during the octaves of Easter and Pentecost also receives an addition of a few words. Ordinem precum in celebritate Missarum nullo nos tempore, nulla festivitate significamus habere diversum, sed semper eodem tenore oblata Deo munera consecrare. Quoties vero paschalis aut Ascensionis Domini vel Pentecostes aut Epiphaniae Sanctorumque Dei fuerit agenda festivitas, singula capitula diebus apta subjungimus, quibus commemorationem sanctae solemnitatis aut eorum facimus, quorum natalitia celebramus, cetera vero ordine consueto prosequimur. Quapropter et ipsius canonicae precis textum (*the Canon*) direximus subter adjectum, quem (Deo propitio) ex apostolica traditione suscepimus (Vigilii Papae [d. 555], *Epist. ad Profuturum episc. Bracarens.*).

[9] Trid., Sess. XXII, cap. 4.

[10] Praefationem actionis, qua populi affectus ad gratiarum actiones incitatur ac deinde humanae devotionis supplicatio coelestium virtutum laudibus admitti deposcitur vel ipsam actionem, qua conficitur sacrosanctum corporis et sanguinis dominici mysterium, quamque Romani canonem, ut in pontificalibus saepius invenitur, quis primus ordinaverit nobis ignotum est. . . . Actio sive Canon ex eo cognoscitur maxime per partes compositus, quod nomina sanctorum, quorum ibi communio et societas flagitatur, duobus in locis posita

St. Gregory I (590–604) completed the formula of the text of the Canon as we now have it.

"It is correct and a matter of fact to state that the text of the Canon of the present Roman Missal corresponds, in all that is essential, with that form in which it probably proceeded from the hands of Gregory I and in which it was handed down in the ancient manuscripts of the Roman Sacramentary. This fact, however, does not exclude the view that the development of the liturgy during the Middle Ages, which gradually encompassed the monumental edifice of the Gregorian-Roman rite of the Mass with the exuberant growth of numerous prayers, chants, and customs, did not stop entirely at the sanctuary of the Canon, but also here gave expression to the overflowing feelings by many well-meant, but not always appropriate, additions. The Roman Church has always cut down to right proportions at the proper time all the superfluous accessories produced by the piety of ages, and also, while preserving whatever possessed any durable value, to reform the liturgy in accordance with its ancient forms. Thus amid a wealth of prayers and rites she yet preserved that strictly logical clearness and preciseness which non-Catholics so greatly admire in the Roman liturgy. Hence the many changes and additions in the text of the Canon which were produced during the Middle Ages, have disappeared partly already since the thirteenth century, and wholly since the reform of St. Pius V in 1570." [11]

The Canon is, therefore, through its origin, antiquity, and use, venerable, inviolable, and sacred. If ever a prayer of the Church came into existence under the special inspiration of the Holy Ghost, it is assuredly the prayer of the Canon. It is permeated throughout by the spirit of faith and with the sweet odor of devotion; it is a holy work, full of force and unction. Its simple language, by its pithiness and its antique and Scriptural stamp, produces a touching effect on the mind of him who prays and offers the sacrifice; it charms the soul, just like the dimly lit, ancient, venerable basilicas of the Eternal City. It is a pleasure and a joy to the heart to still

---

reperiuntur. . . . Primam partem canonis praedicti ex eo vel maxime antiquam esse cognoscimus, quia in ea ordo apostolorum non ita est positus, sicut in emendatioribus evangeliis invenitur; quod ideo fortasse evenit, quia pars illa prius composita est, quam evangelia ad eam veritatem, quae nunc habetur apud Latinos, corrigerentur (Walafrid Strabo, chap. 23).

[11] Ebner, *Quellen und Forschungen*, p. 394.

utter the very same words at the altar which so many devout and holy priests throughout the entire Church and in all ages have always used in praying and offering the sacrifice. Already in the times of the martyrs and in the chapels of the catacombs these prayers of the Canon of the Mass were recited and sanctified.

2. **The silent recitation of the Canon.** The manner in which the Canon is to be recited deserves special notice and explanation. It is a strict ordinance of the Church that the Canon be said silently (*secreto*): in a voice so subdued that the celebrant may hear himself, but not be heard by those around him.[12] Historical testimonies and reasons drawn from the nature of the thing justify the most general assumption that it has been a custom from the earliest times [13] to pronounce in silence the words of consecration, as well as the whole Canon (excepting, of course, in the case of concelebration, which formerly was of more frequent occurrence). Still it is not merely the Church's scrupulous solicitude with which she preserves

---

[12] At the ordination of a priest, all the silent prayers of Mass are pronounced somewhat aloud (*aliquantulum alte*) by the ordaining bishop and the newly ordained co-celebrants. Ordinandi circa altare in genua provoluti disponuntur, et Episcopus quasi eos doceat Missam celebrare, lente ac paululum elata voce Secretas profert, non eas ut populus audiat, sed ut sacerdotes novissime initiati cum eo possint eas recitare, et verba consecrationis uno eodemque tempore cum Episcopo pronuntiare, ad exemplum Christi, qui voce, quae ab Apostolis audiri potuit, in ultima coena panem et vinum consecravit, ut eos, quos tunc sacerdotio initiabat, doceret consecrandi modum legitimumque ritum ad consummationem usque saeculi duraturum (Bened. XIV, *De ss. Missae sacrif.*, II, xxiii, 7).

[13] In the Greek and Oriental liturgies the words of consecration are said in a loud and high tone of voice, whereupon the people each time by Amen (= so be it) express their faith in the real presence of Jesus Christ in the Blessed Sacrament. Cardinal Bona was of the opinion that formerly in the Western Church also all heard the *sanctissima et efficacissima verba, quibus Christi corpus conficitur* (*Rer. liturg.*, II, xiii, 1), and he presumes that it is only since the tenth century that the silent recitation of the words of the institution has been prescribed. But the arguments he adduces are unreliable. The very ancient *Ordo Rom. II* (which probably dates from the seventh or eighth century), explained by Amalarius in his *Ecloga*, has the following rubric: Quae [sc. Praefationem et Trisagium] dum expleverint, surgit solus Pontifex et tacite intrat in Canonem. According to Mabillon it is prescribed in the oldest Roman *Ordines*: ut Pontifice Canonem recitante summum in choro teneatur silentium, et ministri perstent inclinati et silentes per totum Canonem. Canonem non incipiebat sacerdos nisi absoluto Trisagii cantu, ut scil. clerus et populus, sacerdote Canonem submissa voce recitante, in admiratione tanti mysterii quasi stupens sileret (*In Ord. Rom. comment.*, chap. 21).

the original traditions in performing the sacred mysteries, but there are other weighty reasons that move her to adhere so earnestly to the precept that the Canon be said in silence and that the Eucharistic sacrifice be accomplished without audible words. We will here cite the chief reason that demonstrates, not indeed the necessity, but the expediency and appropriateness of the recitation of the Canon in silence.

a) The silent recitation of the Canon betokens the consecration and sacrificial act to be an exclusively priestly function.[14] The prayers of the Canon, being liturgical, are therefore to be recited not merely mentally, but also vocally (*vocaliter*), that is, the words must be pronounced with the mouth. But this recitation of the Canon must be made softly, so as to be inaudible to those who are around, and yet audible to the priest himself. This last circumstance is to be noticed, since there is a difference in the recitation of the Canon and the Divine Office, for in the recitation of the latter it is not necessary that he who prays should hear himself. The silent recitation of the Canon is in contrast to the loud recitation of the preceding prayers.[15] Whereas the loud tone of voice invites those present to join with the priest, and reminds them that the prayers are said in common, the silent recitation appropriately indicates that here is a mystery, which the consecrated priest alone can accomplish, not the people.[16] To consecrate the material elements, to offer the body and blood of Christ, is a priestly privilege: the congregation present can contribute nothing to the accomplish-

---

[14] Canon secreto agitur, eo quod haec immolatio ad solum pertinet sacerdotem (Sicard., III, chap. 8).

[15] The rubrics distinguish a twofold or threefold tone of voice: *vox secreta* and *vox clara, alta, intelligibilis;* in the middle between the two (the silent and loud pronounciation) is the *vox paululum elevata, vox parum elata, vox aliquantulum elevata* (half aloud). The expression *vox submissa* (= falling, lowered, low) often designates moderately loud, sometimes silent pronunciation. In the Middle Ages the Canon was often called *Secretum vel Secreta Missae,* because it was recited *secreto* or *secrete* (= in silence). The word *secretus* (selected, set apart, separated) signifies, at the same time, that the priest recites the sacrificial prayer in silence and secrecy, because in it he in a special manner takes the part of mediator, raised above the people and separated from sinners.

[16] Sacerdos quaedam dicit publice, sc. quae pertinent et ad sacerdotem et ad populum, sicut sunt orationes communes; quaedam vero pertinent ad solum sacerdotem, sicut oblatio et consecratio, et ideo, quae circa haec sunt dicenda, occulte a sacerdote dicuntur (S. Thom., IIIa, q.83, a.4 ad 6).

ment of the sacrificial act. This is symbolically indicated by the silent recitation of the Canon. The priest does not here, as in the other portions of the Mass, commune with the people; he has entered into the holy of holies, there to commune with God alone and to pray and sacrifice for the whole Church. Moses was alone on the top of the mountain; he conversed with God and God answered him. Thus does the priest stand alone at the altar, when, as the representative and minister of Christ, the eternal high priest, he accomplishes and offers up the Holy Sacrifice for the entire Church.

b) The silent recitation of the Canon harmonizes very beautifully with the accomplishment and the essence of the mystery of the Eucharistic sacrifice. The material elements are changed into Christ's body and blood without either the senses perceiving it or the created mind being able to comprehend it; the real presence and sacrificial life of the Saviour under the sacramental species is concealed beyond all discernment. In every host there are miracles, as numerous as stars in the firmament, yet not the slightest trace of the wonders appears externally. With all this the ecclesiastical rite harmonizes perfectly. The holy silence is quite suited to indicate and to recall the concealment and depth, the incomprehensibility and ineffableness of the wonderful mysteries that are enacted on the altar.[17]

c) Silent prayer is related to religious silence, and therefore expresses the humility, reverence, admiration, and awe with which the Church administers and adores the mystery of the altar. "The Lord is in His holy temple; let all the earth keep silence before Him" (Hab. 2:20). The sight of the priest at the altar, communing in profound stillness with God alone, is, therefore, also an excellent means to arouse and promote in those who are present the proper dispositions with which they should admire, adore, and offer along with the priest, so grand and sublime a sacrifice. "How terrible is this hour!" Thus does the deacon cry out to the people in the Syrian liturgy. While the tremendous sacrifice is being accomplished on the altar, all present should be immersed in silent and devout contemplation of the divine mysteries. Now, precisely this mute silence that reigns at the altar during the most sacred moments of the sacrifice and directs attention to the mysteriousness of the sacrificial

---

[17] The Canon is recited *secreta voce ad significandum quod humana ratio nequaquam tantum mysterium plenarie capere potest* (Sicard., III, chap. 6).

act, forms the loudest summons to enter silently into ourselves, to be recollected in mind, and to stir our hearts to devotion.[18] The silent recitation of the Canon disposes the faithful to interior adoration and reverent celebration of the heavenly mysteries [19] by which God so graciously favors and blesses us poor mortals.

d) In addition to the principal reasons already mentioned, it must be remarked that the foreign language and the silent recitation serve to withdraw the sacred words of the Canon from ordinary intercourse and to protect them against every desecration.

e) Finally, a mystical reason may be alleged. The priest at the altar is the representative and image of the praying and sacrificing Saviour. Now, as on the Mount of Olives and on the cross Jesus prayed not only in loud tones, but also in a low voice and in the silence of His heart to His Father, so it is proper that the priest should also pray in a loud voice and in silent whisper when he renews on the altar the sacrifice of the cross.[20] The altar becomes not merely the cross, but also the crib; for at the moment of consecration the marvels of Bethlehem as well as those of Golgotha are renewed. While deep silence pervaded all things and the night was in the midst of its course, the almighty Word of God descended from His royal throne in heaven to the crib of Bethlehem; in like manner the King of Glory at the consecration comes down upon the altar amid the most profound silence.

3. **The meaning of the prayers of the Canon.** Prayer forms the liturgical accompaniment of the sacrifice. The Canon contains those prayers which most closely relate to the Eucharistic sacrifice. They are oblation prayers, which refer to the Consecration; for they contain in part petitions for the blessing and consecration of the

[18] Silentium laus est quaedam, tum interna animi Deum venerantis, tum externa, quia alios excitat ad Dei laudem, dum in sacris vident tantam modestiam et religionem (Corn. a Lap., *In Levit.*, 1:17).

[19] Secretis verbis Canon pronuntiatur etiam alio respectu, videl. ut habito circumquaque silentio ministri et circumstantes seipsos infra ipsum Canonem recolligant vimque et rationem tanti sacramenti advertant, quatenus eis proficiat (Hildeb. Turon., *Expositio Missae*). Silentium hoc compluribus altiori voce recitatis precibus interruptum nescio quid majestatis ac mysterii prae se fert, quod majorem venerationem conciliat, quod sacrum quendam horrorem excitat, quod devotam cordis compunctionem inspirat quodque vivo pietatis sensu adstantium animos penetrat (Languet, *De vero Eccl. sensu circa sacr. cerem. usum*, chap. 41).

[20] Oratio secreta sacerdotis commemoratio quaedam est secretae orationis Christi vel in horto vel in cruce (Suarez, disp. LXXXIII, sect. 1, n. 25).

sacrificial elements, in part an offering of the sacrificial body and blood of Christ, and in part supplications to obtain and to apply the fruits of the sacrifice. As to their contents, they harmonize with the foregoing prayers of the Offertory, and we behold in them a copy of the prayers of our divine Saviour. During His life and at His death He prayed continually. The longest and most solemn, fervent, and touching prayer of the Lord is the one which He uttered when He was about to accomplish is sacrifice on the cross; His prayer as high priest.[21] In it He makes known to whom, for whom, and for what purpose He would offer His sacrificial death; He supplicates for His disciples and for all who would believe in Him: for the entire Church militant. He besought the Father to fill all the faithful in time and in eternity with His saving gifts: to preserve them here below in unity, keep them in truth, and sanctify them by grace, that hereafter they might be transformed in beatitude and behold His glory.[22] Does not this prayer of the high priest resound throughout the Canon of the Mass, wherein the Church expresses what gifts of grace she would draw for herself and for all her children from the Holy Sacrifice? How powerful and effective do these petitions and intercessions of the Church become, as they ascend to the throne of mercy in union with the voice of the blood of Christ, which more loudly and more strongly cries to heaven than did the blood of Abel!

The Canon ushers in the holiest and most sacred moments of the sacrificial celebration; this part of the Mass, still more than any of the other portions, claims attention, devotion, and reverence.[23] The

---

[21] It is the most sublime prayer that ever proceeded from human lips: gentle emotion, mournful gravity, and a kind of devout melancholy are diffused throughout its composition in such a degree that it brings our high priest in an incomparable manner before the soul in the greatness of His divine liberality, as well as in the purity of a truly human affection: a high priest "who can have compassion on them that are ignorant and that err, because He Himself also is compassed with infirmity" (Heb. 5:2).

[22] Hoc ut tempore sacrificii postulemus, saluberrimum habemus nostri Salvatoris exemplum, qui hoc nos in commemoratione mortis ejus poscere voluit, quod nobis ipse, verus Pontifex, morti proximus postulavit . . . hoc ergo nobis poscimus, cum corpus et sanguinem Christi offerimus, quod nobis poposcit, quando se pro nobis offerre dignatus est Christus (S. Fulgent., *Contra Fabian.*, fragm. 28).

[23] Quamvis in toto officio Missae debeat celebrans omnibus viribus suis esse attentus atque sollicitus, tamen ab exordio Canonis debet *omnino recollectus* consistere et mente ad divina suspensus, in quantum humana fragilitas

heart should be occupied only with the divine function and be to all extraneous thoughts and cares as "a garden enclosed" and "a fountain sealed up" (Cant. 4:12). Above all, the passion and death of Christ should be devoutly meditated upon.[24] We are exhorted to this by the image of the Crucified, which is placed before the Canon in order that the painful and bloody death of Christ may be presented to our view in a striking manner. Some persons also recognize from the circumstance that the Canon commences with the letter T a certain special and divine intercession.[25] For the Tau (T) bears a resemblance to the cross,[26] and already in the prophets it is the seal of the elect who are spared the chastisements of God, or the sign of deliverance, life, and salvation, which the predestined bear on their foreheads. "Go through the midst of the city, through the midst of Jerusalem," thus says the Lord, "and mark Tau upon the foreheads of the men that sigh and mourn for all the abominations that are committed in the midst thereof" (Ezech. 9:4; cf. Apoc. 7:3).

---

fieri sustinet et Spiritus sancti clementia conferre dignatur, et ut talem gratiam a Deo in hac parte Missae mereatur recipere, sic tenetur ante celebrationem et postmodum vivere gratusque esse, quatenus tunc visitari atque illuminari sit dignus, nec est melior praeparatio ad celebrandum, quam ut sacerdos in omni vita sua sic conversari conetur, ut sit hujus Sacramenti condignus minister (Dion. Carthus., *Expos. Miss.*, a. 19).

[24] Notandum per totum Canonem Dominicae passionis commemorationem potissimum actitari. . . . Unde et ipse sacerdos per totum Canonem in expansione manuum non tam mentis devotionem quam Christi extensionem in cruce designat . . . congruum est ut manus expandamus infra Canonem, hoc tamen observato, ne quid digitis tangamus praeter Domini corpus (Microl., chap. 16). The *Ordo Rom. XIV*, chap. 71, also has after the Consecration the rubric: *Hic [Pontifex] ampliet manus et brachia.* According to our *Roman Missal*, on the contrary, the celebrant says most of the prayers of the Canon before and after the Consecration *extensis manibus ante pectus.* (Cf. Quarti, *In Rubr. Missal.*, II, tit. 9, sect. 1, dub. 1.)

[25] Inter Praefationem et Canonem in plerisque sacramentariis imago Christi depingitur, ut non solum intellectus litterae, verum etiam adspectus picturae memoriam dominicae passionis inspiret. Et forte divina factum est providentia, licet humana non sit industria procuratum, ut ab ea littera T Canon inciperet, quae sui forma signum crucis ostendit et exprimit in figura (Innocent. III, III, chap. 2).

[26] There are three kinds of crosses: (1) the *crux decussata*, that is, the transverse cross ✕; (2) the *crux immissa* +; and the *crux commissa* T. The last form is similar to the T and is, therefore, also called the T cross. Cf. *Catholic Encyclopedia*, IV, 517-38.

CHAPTER XXXIII

THE FIRST PRAYER OF THE CANON

Te igitur, clementissime Pater, per Jesum Christum Filium tuum Dominum nostrum, supplices rogamus ac petimus, uti accepta habeas, et benedicas, haec ✠ dona, haec ✠ munera, haec ✠ sancta sacrificia illibata; in primis quae tibi offerimus pro Ecclesia tua sancta catholica: quam pacificare, custodire, adunare, et regere digneris toto orbe terrarum: una cum famulo tuo Papa nostro N., et Antistite nostro N., et omnibus orthodoxis atque catholicae et apostolicae fidei cultoribus.

Commemoratio pro Vivis

Memento, Domine, famulorum famularumque tuarum N. et N. et omnium circumstantium, quorum tibi fides cognita est et nota devotio: pro quibus tibi offerimus, vel qui tibi offerunt hoc sacrificium laudis, pro se suisque omnibus: pro redemptione animarum suarum, pro spe

We therefore humbly pray and beseech Thee, most merciful Father, through Jesus Christ Thy Son, our Lord, that Thou wouldst accept and bless these ✠ gifts, these ✠ presents, these ✠ holy unspotted sacrifices, which, in the first place, we offer Thee for Thy holy Catholic Church, which Thou mayest vouchsafe to pacify, protect, unite, and govern throughout the world: together with Thy servant N. our pope, N. our bishop, as also all orthodox believers and promoters of the catholic and apostolic faith.

The Commemoration of the Living

Remember, O Lord, Thy servants and handmaids, N. and N., and all here present, whose faith and devotion are known to Thee; for whom we offer, or who offer up to Thee this sacrifice of praise for themselves and all pertaining to them, for the redemption of their souls, for the

FIRST PRAYER OF THE CANON

salutis et incolumitatis suae: tibique reddunt vota sua aeterno Deo, vivo et vero.

hope of their salvation and safety, and who pay their vows to Thee, the eternal God, living and true.

Infra Actionem

Communicantes et memoriam venerantes, in primis gloriosae semper Virginis Mariae, genitricis Dei et Domini nostri Jesu Christi: sed et beatorum Apostolorum ac Martyrum tuorum, Petri et Pauli, Andreae, Jacobi, Joannis, Thomae, Jacobi, Philippi, Bartholomaei, Matthaei, Simonis et Thaddaei: Lini, Cleti, Clementis, Xysti, Cornelii, Cypriani, Laurentii, Chrysogoni, Joannis et Pauli, Cosmae et Damiani: et omnium Sanctorum tuorum, quorum meritis precibusque concedas, ut in omnibus protectionis tuae muniamur auxilio. Per eundem Christum Dominum nostrum. Amen.

Within the Canon

In communion with and honoring the memory, first, of the glorious ever Virgin Mary, Mother of God and our Lord Jesus Christ; and also of Thy blessed apostles and martyrs, Peter and Paul, Andrew, James, John, Thomas, James, Philip, Bartholomew, Matthew, Simon and Thaddeus, Linus, Cletus, Clement, Sixtus, Cornelius, Cyprian, Lawrence, Chrysogonus, John and Paul, Cosmas and Damian, and all Thy saints; by whose merits and prayers grant that we may be defended in all things by the aid of Thy protection. Through the same Christ our Lord. Amen.

The above formula of prayer consists of three parts; all three parts are united and form a whole, one complete prayer, as is evident from the context and the single concluding formula, *Per eundem Christum Dominum nostrum.*[1]

1. a) The beginning of the prayer is introduced, or accompanied, by several ceremonies which serve to emphasize its contents in an impressive manner. Before presenting his petition to God, the priest raises his hands and eyes to express the elevation of his soul and to indicate that he is addressing the Father in heaven

---

[1] The prayers of the Canon have only the short concluding formula (three times *per eundem Chr. Dom. nostr.*, who shortly before is mentioned in the last member of the prayer, and twice *per Christ. Dom. nostr.*). In ipsa quinaria conclusione non incongrue quinaria Domini vulneratio intimatur (Microlog., *De eccles. observat.*, chap. 16).

and seeking help from God on high. But presently he lowers his eyes and hands, bows profoundly, and places his joined hands on the altar; in this posture he begins the Canon.² What posture of the body could be more appropriate for the priest at this moment, when with all humility and reverence he suppliantly addresses the Lord, who "is high above all nations . . . and looketh down on the low things in heaven and in earth" (Ps. 112:4, 6)? Before the words "that Thou wouldst accept and bless," the priest kisses the altar,³ and while he is saying, "these gifts, these presents, these holy unspotted sacrifices," with his hand he makes the sign of the cross three times over the oblation. As at the blessing at the end of Mass, the kissing of the altar and the sign of the cross have a close relationship with one another: both constitute a ritual whole in themselves, the symbolical significance of which is to be inferred from the prayer that is recited at the same time. The priest prays with great fervor for the blessing of the Eucharistic elements, and as they are designated by three different names, he makes at the same time the sign of the cross over the elements three times, that word and action may harmonize perfectly. The text, therefore, in this instance requires that the sign of the cross be conceived as a sign of blessing.⁴ If now the making of the sign of the cross over the sacrificial gifts is a true blessing, then the kissing of the altar that preceded should be conceived as an introduction to it. The priest indeed kisses the altar to evince his sentiments of reverence, homage, and subjection;

---

² The opinion of Quarti and Merati, that the words *Te igitur* are not to be said until after the inclination, is better founded than that of Gavanti and Cavalieri, that the Canon prayers are to be commenced at the same time as the elevation of the hands and eyes. (Cf. Bouvry, *Expositio Rubric.*, II, Part III, sect. 3, tit. 8.)

³ Hic osculatur sacerdos altare (Sicard. [d. 1215], *Mitral.*, III, chap. 6). Ancient writers do not mention this kissing of the altar. However, it was formerly (in some places even until the end of the fifteenth century) the custom, before beginning the Canon, to kiss the image of the Crucified (the cross) in the missal. The *Ordo Rom. XIV* (of the beginning of the fourteenth century) has the following rubric (chap. 53): Capellano praesentante sibi librum missalem, Pontifex osculetur imagines, quae debent esse depictae in eodem libro ante Canonem Missae. Subsequenter manibus junctis inclinatus ante incipiat submissa voce *Te igitur* etc. et cum dicet *uti accepta habeas*, erigat se et osculetur altare in parte sinistra prope hostiam.

⁴ Terna crucis signa sunt verae benedictiones, quibus Dei invocatur omnipotentia, ut oblata in corpus et sanguinem Christi convertat. Ternarius autem signorum crucis numerus hocce mysterium a S. Trinitate perfici indicat (Cavalieri, V, xvi, 4).

FIRST PRAYER OF THE CANON

but here by this kiss he would mainly renew and represent symbolically the union of love with Christ, because he draws from his relation with Christ all the power of blessing, which he then by the three signs of the cross [5] pours out, as it were, over the elements of sacrifice.

b) The opening words of the prayer, *Te igitur*, join what follows to what precedes and show how intimately the Canon is connected with the Preface, and also with the Offertory: because we have presented to Thee, O most merciful Father, thanksgivings, praises, and homages, we now again address ourselves to Thee with a petition. According to the example and admonition of the Saviour, the Church addresses this prayer to the Father; at the same time presenting her supplication in such a manner as to deserve to be answered. For she calls upon God as the "most merciful Father," she implores Him "through Jesus Christ," she supplicates with humility and earnestness.[6] God is addressed as the "most merciful Father" because, on account of His exceedingly great love and goodness, He

---

[5] At least since the eleventh century in the Canon, as at present, the sign of the cross is made over the oblations in seven places (altogether twenty-five times). (Cf. Innocent. III, *De sacr. alt. myst.*, V, chap. 14.) With the exception of the two signs of the Cross at the words *sacrosanctum Filii tui corpus et sanguinem* (*Supplices te rogamus*), all the others are mentioned already during the ninth century. (Cf. *Ordo Rom. II*, n. 10: In Canone sex ordines crucium observantur; Amalar. [d. about 847], *Eclog. in Ord. Roman. II*, n. 22.) Micrologus declares: Imparem numerum semper in dispensatione signorum super oblationem observamus, videl. unam crucem vel tres vel quinque faciendo, et hoc utique non sine certi causa mysterii. Nam in una et tribus unum et trinum Deum intimamus. In quinque autem quinquepartitam Domini passionem significamus (*De ecclesiast. observat.*, chap. 14). Attende quod *fere* in quolibet ordine per *imparem* numerum signacula disponuntur, quia corpus Christi unum permanens non scinditur (Sicard., *Mitral.*, III, chap. 6).

[6] Praeinducta verba Canonis igne divini amoris redundant ac igniunt, unde cum ardentissimo mentis affectu promenda sunt. Porro oratio *ardens* et *humilis* esse debet; nam desiderium pauperum, i.e. ardentem affectum humilium exaudivit Dominus: qui enim ardenter orat, valde cavere debet, ne propriis meritis innitatur vel confidat. Rursus, qui suis meritis non confidit, sed humiliter orat, omnino vitare habet, ne in orando pusillanimis efficiatur aut segnis. Ut ergo Spiritus Sanctus, qui utique *principaliter est auctor Canonis*, ad talem orationem nos incitaret, idcirco in ipso exordio Canonis duo verba praemisit, quorum alterum dilectionem inflammat, videlicet "*Pater*," alterum fiduciam exauditionis praestat propter bonitatem ejus, qui petitur, scilicet "*clementissime*," et ad designandam atque augendam interiorem cordis humiliationem inclinat se sacerdos ante altare praedicta verba dicendo (Dion. Carthus., *Expos. Miss.*, a. 19).

is ever inclined, not to judge and punish according to the full rigor of the law, but to have mercy and to spare, inasmuch as He remits in part or entirely the merited punishments.[7] "In God's works and judgments," St. Leo remarks, "all is full of true justice and merciful sweetness." [8] It is with filial confidence, therefore, that we pray to the "Father of our Lord Jesus Christ, the Father of mercies and the God of all comfort" (II Cor. 1:3), whose indulgent and forgiving love here below is without measure or limit; He is sweet and mild and plenteous in mercy to all that call upon Him (Ps. 85:5), and consequently ever attentive to the voice of our supplication. But all the more attentive will He be because we have offered our petitions "through Jesus Christ, His Son, our Lord." In His Son, Jesus Christ, God has had compassion upon us and given us the spirit of adoption, by which we call Him "Father" and in prayer may address Him as "our Father." Through His Son, "our Lord, Jesus Christ," the Father hears our petitions and bestows upon us all benefits.

As we draw near to the infinite majesty and holiness of the Eucharistic sacrifice, conscious of our wretchedness and sinfulness, we pray with humble dispositions and sentiments of heart (*supplices* [9]); for prayer penetrates more powerfully through the clouds to the throne of God, the more profoundly the one that prays abases himself interiorly and exteriorly. Finally, we present our petitions with fervor, with devout importunity and a holy vehemence; for the accumulated expressions *rogamus ac petimus* ("we pray and beseech") proceed from the greatness and earnestness of our desires.[10]

We beseech so persistently and imploringly because the object

[7] Ad *clementiam* pertinet, quod sit *diminutiva poenarum;* in hoc, quod diminuit poenas, clementia maxime videtur accedere ad caritatem, quae est potissima virtutum, per quam bona operamur ad proximos et eorum mala impedimus (S. Thom., II, IIae, q. 157, a. 1-4).

[8] *Serm.*, I (*de jejun.*), 10. mens.

[9] *Supplex* (from *sub* and *plico*, hence, strictly, bending the knee, kneeling down, hence) = to humble one's self, humbly imploring.

[10] Vehemens petendi affectus geminatione verbi deprecatorii exprimitur, scil. rogamus ac petimus. Accumulantur verba petitionem explicantia ad significandam ipsius affectus nostri magnitudinem (Clichtov., *Elucid. eccl.*, III, n. 4). Some writers endeavor to distinguish the signification of these two words. Rogatio ostendit humilitatem, petitio confidentiam; qui aliquid implorat, humilitatem debet ostendere et de impetratione confidere. Itaque supplices rogamus, confidenter petimus (B. Odo Camerac., *Exposit. in Canon.*, dist. 1).

of our ardent desire is so sublime and holy: the gracious acceptance and the blessing of the sacrificial elements of bread and wine prepared on the altar.[11] The purpose for which God is to "accept" the material gifts is expressed by the word "bless." By the blessing here implored is to be understood: first, the preparatory dedication of the bread and the wine to God, then the real consecration of these material gifts, and finally, the fullness of grace concealed under the consecrated elements and diffusing itself throughout the Church.[12] Now the Father is invoked, as was previously the Holy Ghost, "to bless" the elements of bread and wine, that is, to sanctify them beforehand for their exalted destiny, then to change them into the body and blood of Christ, and thus to make them for us the source of grace. For this copious blessing we must pray because it is a gift of the condescending love and a work of the almighty power of the triune God.[13]

The Eucharistic elements are designated and distinguished by three names,[14] inasmuch as we pray that God may accept and bless "these presents, these gifts, these holy unspotted sacrifices." Elsewhere, notably in the Secreta, each of these three words alone is often used to signify the sacrificial elements. They all indeed designate one and the same thing: the host and the chalice containing the

[11] Oblationem nostram, quaesumus, Domine, misericorditer acceptare et sanctificare digneris, ut ejus sanctificatione nobis salus proveniat et defensio sempiterna (*Sacrament. Gregor.*). *Acceptus* (graciously received) = welcome, agreeable, pleasing; *acceptum habere* = *acceptare*, to receive, to be contented with. Acceptabis (εὐδοκήσεις) sacrificium, oblationes et holocausta (Ps. 50:21). Sacerdotum est offerre et majestatem Dei invocare; Dei est autem dignanter suscipere et ea quae offeruntur benedicere (Florus Diac., *De actione Miss.*, n. 43).

[12] Petimus, ut Deus Pater benedicat haec dona, h. e. ut benedictionem suae virtutis et gratiae illis infundat, ut idonea sint tam digno sacramenta (Clichtov. *loc. cit.*, n. 5). Uti . . . benedicas, i.e. gratia et virtute coelesti perfundas atque sanctifices convertendo ea in corpus et sanguinem Christi (Dion. Carthus. *Exposit. Miss.*, art. 18). Petimus, ut Deus acceptet et benedicat haec dona ad totius Ecclesiae fructum et utilitatem (Suarez, disp.LXXXIII, sect.2, n.6).

[13] Efficacia verborum sacramentalium impediri potest per intentionem sacerdotis. Nec tamen est inconveniens quod a Deo petamus id quod certissime scimus ipsum facturum, sicut Christus (Joan., chap. 17) petit suam clarificationem (S. Thom., IIIa, q.83, a.4 ad 7).

[14] Quod subjungitur: haec dona, haec munera, haec sancta sacrificia illibata, non aliud atque aliud dicitur; sed res una pro sua magnitudine diversa appellatione laudatur et laudando commendatur. Ipsa sermonum repetitio tanti sacramenti est commendatio et piae devotionis excitatio (Flor. Diacon., *op. cit.*, n. 44).

wine. The elements of bread and wine are called "presents" (*dona*) and "gifts" (*munera*) in so far as they are simply regarded in the light of religious offerings, which we dedicate and present to our Lord; they are called "sacrifices" (*sacrificia*) even before the Consecration, in so far as they are prepared and destined soon to be consecrated into the true body and blood of Christ.[15] In consideration of their sublime destiny, the Eucharistic elements are not called simply "sacrifices," but "holy unspotted sacrifices" (*sancta sacrificia illibata*);[16] for it is the "Holy of holies," the Lamb without stain or blemish, that is offered under the appearances of bread and wine. Yet the matter itself of the sacrifice can be called "holy," inasmuch as it has previously been separated from profane use and dedicated to the service of God; it can likewise be designated as "unspotted" because in its selection and preparation religious care was taken that the sacrificial bread and wine should be faultless and without any foreign admixture.[17]

The sacrificial gifts designated are offered up to God for the

[15] Bread and wine vocantur sacrificia per anticipationem, quia sunt materia, ex qua conficiendum est sacrificium, et dicuntur sacrificia initiative, quia praeparantur in sacrificium (Quarti, II, tit. 9, sect. 2, dub. 1).

[16] The sacrificial gifts on the altar (*sacrificia*) are called *illibata*, inasmuch as in their natural state they are inviolable, uninjured, sound (that is, *sine defectibus*, as they are cited in the missal); *sancta*, inasmuch as, by a supernatural dedication, they are consecrated to God, they belong to God, and, therefore, as the property of God, they are holy, venerable, inviolate and not to be touched. Ex hoc verbo (sc. illibata) admonemur, ut appositus panis integer sit et nulla fractione vel laesura violatus (B. Odo Camerac., *Exposit. in Canon.*, dist. 1).

[17] Donum est, quod a superiore datur, munus, quod ab inferiore. Unde panis et vinum sunt *dona* a Deo nobis donata, *munera* a nobis Deo oblata; solemus enim illos munerare, a quibus aliquid volumus obtinere. Eadem sunt sacrificia *sancta*, scil. Deo dicata et ad sacrificium sanctum praeparata. *Illibata* sunt nec corporali gustu nec aliqua fractione vitiata, sed integra et intacta (Stephan. Augustod., *De sacram. altar.*, chap. 13). Dona *illibata*, quia ad litteram pura et integra esse debent propter significationem et reverentiam tanti sacramenti: non enim debet panis maculosus esse vel vinum permixtum, nisi cum modica aqua (Dion. Carthus., *Expos. Miss.*, a. 18). Dicuntur pluralitatis numero dona, munera et sacrificia, quoniam panis et vini, antequam consecrantur, alia et alia est substantia et una ab altera reipsa discrepans, quae substantiarum diversitas numero multitudinis apte exprimitur: nam hoc loco ipsa demonstrantur ante factam consecrationem. Ea vero consummata, interdum etiam adhuc nomine consimili et multitudinem indicante explicantur, et *sacramenta* aut *sacrificia* dicuntur, non quidem ob substantiarum (quae jam conversae sunt) varietatem, sed ob *specierum*, sub quibus tam sancta continentur mysteria *diversitatem* (Clichtov., *Elucid. eccl.*, III, n. 6).

welfare of the Church and her members. But since not the natural matter of bread and wine, but the body and blood of Christ alone are the real sacrifice of the Church and her fountains of grace, it is evident that this offering cannot exclusively have for its object the gifts of bread and wine, but must also be referred principally to that which they are soon to become, the sacrifice of the body and blood of Jesus Christ.[18] The full meaning of our prayer may thus be expressed: We beseech Thee, O Father, that Thou wouldst accept and bless these material gifts, which we present to Thee, in order that, by the blessing of consecration, they may become a heavenly, healing fountain for the Church.[19] It is, therefore, the sacrifice of the body and blood of Jesus Christ which we have especially in view when offering the bread and wine, and through which we implore and expect all the gifts of salvation.

Principally and "in the first place" (*in primis*) the Eucharistic sacrifice is offered for the "holy Catholic Church" of God;[20] hence from every Mass there flow to her abundant fruits and blessings. The heavenly Father is the Lord of the Church, and the Church is His property. He has purchased her with the precious blood of His Son; hence she belongs to Him, and she is bound to serve Him. As the Church of the "living God," she is "holy"; and the sacrifice of

---

[18] Per haec dona, ut nunc coram Deo proponuntur, nihil postulatur, sed per sacrificium, ad quod destinantur, et per Christum offerendum in eodem sacrificio (Quarti, *loc. cit.*).

[19] Non offerimus panem et vinum pro Ecclesia simpliciter et absolute, vel tanquam sacrificium principaliter finaliterque intentum, sed tali respectu et intentione, ut convertantur divina virtute in corpus et sanguinem Christi, sicque offeramus Patri coelesti sacrificium perfectum et sanctum, videlicet corpus et sanguinem Filii sui carissimi (Dion. Carthus., *Expos. Miss.*, a. 19). Cum dicimus, nos offerre panem Deo pro Ecclesia, sensus est, nos offerre Deo panem consecrandum et ex quo per consecrationem verum sacrificium Deo immolandum est pro ecclesia. (Bellarm., *De Missa*, II, chap. 21.)

[20] Intende *cur* celebres celebrareque debeas. Nempe *propter easdem causas, ob quas Christus se obtulit in cruce Deo Patri,* tu quoque eum offerre debes eidem in altari: h. e. primo et principaliter pro tota Ecclesia, pro infidelium conversione, pro fidelium reformatione, pro universorum salute, pro occurrentibus causis et necessitatibus quibuscunque, pro propinquis, commissis et benefactoribus tuis fidelibusque defunctis, et pro quibus ex speciali causa vis exorare, atque pro tui ipsius condigna emendatione in omnibus. Ut ergo utcunque pro viribus tuis existas idoneus deprecari et offerre pro tantis ac talibus causis, satage et indefesse conare teipsum Deo placitum exhibere, ei familiariter adhaerere, ipsum intra te amorose complecti, sinceriter contemplari omnique die magis ferventer diligere (Dion. Carthus., *De sacram. Euchar. serm.*, III).

the Mass is precisely that inexhaustible fountain of holiness, in the splendor of which the Church shines always more or less brightly. The holy Church of God is also "catholic," that is, universal, since she extends over the whole earth and continues to live and work throughout all ages, until time shall merge into eternity. She is that stately, majestic tree of life which affords shelter to the whole world, and under whose branches all nations have always been gathered.

Four graces are here implored for the Church by virtue of the Eucharistic sacrifice; we beg the Lord to grant to her and preserve her peace (*pacificare*), to protect and to shelter her (*custodire*), to give her unity and confirm her therein (*adunare*), to guide and to direct her (*regere*), and this "throughout the world," from the rising of the sun to the setting thereof.

a) We pray that the Lord may grant peace to His Church, complete interior and exterior peace. This peace, rich in blessings, facilitates the exercise of her great mission, which consists principally in imparting to mankind the treasures of divine truth and grace; it assists the Church to save souls, to consecrate and sanctify the temporal life in all its forms and relations. Peace is "the tranquillity of order" (St. Augustine) and enables us to "lead a quiet and peaceable life in all piety and chastity" (I Tim. 2:2). Hence the Church so often and so fervently prays: "Grant, O Lord, peace in our days; for there is no other that combats for us, than Thou our Lord and God." She ardently desires "to overcome all error and opposition in order to be enabled to serve the Lord with perfect freedom." But how can the Church be able to live long in peace in a world filled with unbelief and immorality? Her journey throughout the ages has always been a warlike pilgrimage. She is here below at all times the Church militant; she must strive and combat until she reaches the heavenly Jerusalem. Thus the Church must at all times be ready as "an army in battle array," and must persevere in combating the deceit and power of her numberless enemies, who are unceasingly intent on harassing and enslaving her, perverting and destroying her.[21] To whom then should she have recourse but to God, who is her safeguard and her helper?

---

[21] Ecclesia Dei, semper in procinctu posita, incessabili pugna contra inimicos dimicat (*Pontif. Roman., De ordinat. diaconi*).

b) Hence we implore that God may be pleased, amid all assaults and oppressions, to protect and defend His Church as the apple of His eye; that He vouchsafe to shelter her under the shadow of His wings, until the wicked shall have passed away (Ps. 16:8). We beseech the Lord to save the shepherd and the sheepfold from the rage of ravenous wolves, from the bite of venomous serpents. He has promised His Church protection and victory over all her adversaries. If God protects His people, His kingdom, His Church, what then can the gates of hell avail against them? We may, therefore, in time of persecution and tribulation cry out confidently: "Our God is our refuge and strength, a helper in troubles which have found us exceedingly. Therefore we will not fear when the earth shall be troubled and the mountains shall be removed into the heart of the sea. . . . Nations were troubled and kingdoms were bowed down; He uttered His voice, the earth trembled. The Lord of armies is with us, the God of Jacob is our protector" (Ps. 45:2 f., 7 f.).

c) The Church is strong and invincible in combat only through the union and harmony of her members; therefore we pray that God may unite His Church, that is, constantly preserve and confirm her in that grand unity, wrought through the firm cement of faith and love, which shows forth conspicuously the Church's supernatural majesty and glory, her inexhaustible fullness of life and power of victory. No earthly power is able to divide and split the marvelous unity of the Church, that supernatural communion of life and love binding together the children of the Catholic family; for this bond of union between the shepherd and the fold, and likewise between Catholics of all nations, has only the more closely and indissolubly been secured by the blood of martyrs and the sufferings of confessors. Before His passion the Saviour prayed especially for this very union of all the faithful among themselves and with God: Holy Father, "sanctify them in truth. Thy word is truth. As Thou hast sent Me into the world, I also have sent them into the world. And for them do I sanctify Myself: that they also may be sanctified in truth. And not for them only do I pray, but for them also who through their word shall believe in Me: that they all may be one, as Thou, Father, in Me and I in Thee: that they also may be one in us: that the world may believe that Thou hast sent Me" (John 17:17–21). He that separates himself from this living unity, is like a branch cut off and withered; he will go to destruction.

d) Finally we petition God that He would govern, guide, and direct His Church.[22] This He does through the pope, the bishops, and the priests. The increase, splendor, and beauty of the Church depend principally on the worthiness, fervor, and fidelity of her rulers and teachers. Therefore we pray God that He would give to His Church pastors prepared to sacrifice their ease and comfort, their liberty and their life for the sheep of Christ; shepherds who in word and act, in charity, faith, and chastity, show themselves an example to the faithful (I Tim. 4:12); shepherds who with humility, meekness, courage, and self-devotedness lead the flock confided to them in the ways of salvation and pasture them in the meadows of grace, at the fountains of the waters of life. Such shepherds are a joy to heaven and earth. But it behooves us to beseech God to send such laborers into His vineyard.

Thus do we, in the first place, offer our prayers and the sacrifice for the Church, for she is, indeed, our spiritual mother. The Lord shed His heart's blood for the Church, that He might present to Himself a glorious Church, not having spot or wrinkle or any such thing, but that she should be holy and without blemish, immaculate. Should we not, then, with filial devotedness love and reverence her, be zealous and make sacrifices for her cause, pray and labor for her, combat and suffer for her, live and die for her? In these points is revealed that sincere and devoted affection which blooms from a lively faith. Sacrifice and prayer offered principally for the Church, indirectly benefit the whole world; for in proportion as the Church is exalted and propagated, the wider and the more abundantly can she pour forth the gifts of salvation, the treasures of grace and truth, over all mankind.

The general fruit of the sacrifice falls the more copiously to the share of the individual members of the mystical body of Christ in proportion as they contribute to the common welfare of the Church; hence we have now a special offering and prayer for the pope and

---

[22] Ut in suis consiliis, dispositionibus, judiciis, decretis, institutis, actionibus nullo decipiatur errore et in omnibus tuo ducatur moderamine (B. Odo Camerac., *loc. cit.*).

for the chief pastor of the diocese in which the Mass is celebrated.[23] Then is added a general intercession for all those persons who not only preserve the true faith in their heart and confess it with their lips, but who, moreover, according to their ability defend and propagate it.

It is proper that throughout the entire Church the pope should be prayed for and the sacrifice be offered for him, for he is the vicar of Jesus Christ, the infallible teacher and supreme pastor of all the faithful, the head and father of all Christendom. The rays of the sun are not more intimately united to the sun itself, nor the branch to the trunk of the tree, nor the rivulet to its source, than are the pastors of the Church with their flocks connected with the pope. He has in his keeping all the treasures of salvation, and through him only are they accessible to us. "He gives admission to the pastures and to the sacred fountains of life" sings the Church. "Where Peter is, there is the Church," resounds throughout all ages.[24] The more noble the blessings for which we are indebted to the pope, the more, as head and support of the Church, he is persecuted and oppressed by the children of darkness, and the more childlike, faithful, and loyal should be our devotedness and attachment to him, the more fervent and persevering should be our prayers for him.

As all pastors with their flocks follow the pope, so should all the priests and the faithful of a diocese be attached to their bishop,[25] whom the Holy Ghost has appointed to feed them. Next to the pope, therefore, it is right and proper that in all the churches of a

---

[23] From the most ancient times it has been customary to name the pope and the bishop of the diocese in the prayers of the Canon. Until the eleventh century the prayer for the bishop was wanting in some manuscripts. Besides the pope and bishop, the name of the king or emperor was often added. Towards the end of the Middle Ages the names of temporal rulers were effaced from the manuscripts. With the exception of the never omitted prayer for the pope, the naming of the spiritual and temporal superiors was subject to continual changes during the Middle Ages. In Austria, by virtue of a papal privilege, the emperor was prayed for by name.

[24] Ubi Petrus, ibi ecclesia: ubi Ecclesia, ibi nulla mors, sed vita aeterna (S. Ambr., *Enarr. in Ps.*, 40:30).

[25] Antistes ($προεστώς$) from *antisto*, to stand in front, to have the preference, prominent = the head, especially the first and chief priest; hence the ancient Christian designation of a bishop. Antistes dicitur a verbo antesto (= emineo, excello), eo quod universum populum dignitate et honore superemineat (Pseudo-Alcuin., chap. 36).

diocese the ruling bishop should be commemorated by name,[26] that he may obtain strength and wisdom to exercise his sacred and difficult office according to God's will.

Finally, "all orthodox believers and promoters of the Catholic and apostolic faith" are prayed for. According to the definition of the word, such persons are here designated who not only are "orthodox believers" (*orthodoxi*),[27] that is, who not only confess the pure, genuine, unadulterated faith (in word and deed), but who, at the same time, are called and exert themselves to plant, nurture, and propagate the true faith, which is "catholic and apostolic" (*cultores fidei*).[28] Among them must be reckoned, first of all, the bishops and priests, because they are the pastors and teachers appointed by Christ for the edification of His mystical body and for the administration of divine service. Moreover, it corresponds to the context that, after mentioning by name the pope and the bishop of the diocese, the remaining hierarchical rulers and leaders of the Church of God should be remembered, in order that they may worthily exercise their pastorate for the honor of God and the salvation of

---

[26] The name of the bishop of the diocese in which a priest celebrates, is, in contradistinction from the pope, mentioned without an inclination; if his name is unknown, merely *antistite nostro* is said, by which the bishop in question is understood. However, in order that the name of the antistes be mentioned, he must really hold the episcopal chair, that is, he must have been named (chosen) and confirmed, and also have undertaken the government of the diocese; it is not requisite that he should be consecrated. An episcopally consecrated Vicar Capitular or Vicar Apostolic must not be named. The name of the Catholic ruler of the country may be inserted only in virtue of a special indult of the Holy See (S. R. C., March 20, 1862). If the papal or episcopal see is vacant, then the respective words (*una cum famulo . . .* or *et antistite nostro*) are omitted.

[27] *Orthodoxus*, having true faith, *qui de fide recte sentit* (from ὀρθός, *rectus*, and δόξα, *sententia*. Orthodoxi, i.e. rectae gloriae dicuntur, eo quod nullo errore depravati rectae fidei confessione Deum glorificant (Pseudo-Alcuin., c. 40). Orthodoxi, i.e. vita et doctrina gloriosi (B. Odo Camerac., *Exposit. in Canon.*, dist. 1).

[28] *Cultor* = *qui colit*, the worker, cultivator, nurse, worshipper. Rogamus pro his etiam, qui fidem excolunt vomere praedicationis et semine boni operis (Steph. Augustod., *De sacram. altar.*, chap. 13). Cultores fidei dicuntur, qui sarculo correctionis et sanctis documentis eam excolunt (Rob. Paulul., *De offic. eccl.*, II, chap. 29). *Fidei cultoribus*, non fidem tantum habentibus. Aliud est enim fidem habere et aliud fidem colere; fidem colit, qui studet et intendit secundum fidem vivere, cum multi fidem habeant, qui hoc non faciunt (B. Odo Camerac., *loc. cit.*). The expression *dei cultores* is found also in St. Fulgentius (*Pro fide catholica*, n. 2).

souls. But since the words "orthodox promoters of the catholic and apostolic faith" have a general meaning, there is nothing to prevent their reference and application also to all those of the faithful who, although not by the office of the apostolate and by preaching, but still in other ways contribute according to their ability to the propagation of the faith.[29] All Christians have in a wider sense a priestly and apostolic vocation; they can and should exercise the apostolate of prayer and alms, of labor and suffering, that the kingdom of faith in the world may be spread more and more and may flourish everywhere. Thus all the faithful should be actively employed in the extension and exaltation of the kingdom of God, and should labor for the salvation of souls, by striving to procure for others also the grace of the true and life-giving faith.

2. The second part of the first prayer of the Canon begins: "Remember, O Lord, Thy servants and handmaids, N. and N.": [30] have regard to their necessities with loving care, grant them Thy favor and mercy, give them grace and happiness, bless them. In this sense the word remember,[31] especially in connection with the

---

[29] Quamvis pro tota plebe christiana sit in Missa generaliter et primo orandum, tamen pro Summo Pontifice et proprio Pastore praecipue exorare oportet, deinde pro his, qui in populo christiano excellentius clarent et pluribus prosunt fidemque per suam sapientiam defendunt atque exponunt (Dion. Carthus., *Expos. Miss.*, art. 18).

[30] Tot famuli famulaeque Christi (S. August., *Epist.*, 36, n. 4). Elsewhere (for example, *Orate fratres*) mention is made of the stronger sex in the liturgy, when the feminine sex is included. Non est masculus neque femina: omnes enim vos unum estis in Christo Jesu (Gal. 3:28). Prius oblationes sunt commendandae (*in the Offertory*) et tunc eorum nomina quorum sunt (*the names of those who offer*) edicenda, ut inter sacra mysteria (*in the Canon*) nominentur (Innocent I [d. 417], *Ad Decentium*, n. 5). Quia in quibusdam codicibus invenitur N. littera, aliquorum fieri memoriam nominatim significatur. Unde quidam usu tenent hoc in loco memorandi quos cariores habent, subjugentes: "et omnium circumadstantium," ut facta memoria carorum absentium, fiat et adstantium (B. Odo Camerac., dist. 2).

[31] *Memento*, i.e. recordare, non quod in Deum cadat oblivio, sed ut per modum recordantis se habeat, reminiscendo misericordiae suae et subveniendo in omni tribulatione et necessitate et tribuendo dona gratiarum, quae postulantur ab ipso. Sed cum in Canone debeat intellectus sacerdotis maxime esse divinis infixus atque sensibilia deserens, mirum videtur, quod in hoc fit memoria hominum in carne viventium, cum talis memoria contemplationem impedire et evagationem inducere soleat. Et respondendum, quod hic fit rationabiliter vivorum memoria, sed ne talis memoria devotionem impediat vel distractionem inducat, caute agenda est, non nimis immorando considerationi personarum vel circumstantiarum et rerum, quae eas concernunt, sed potius in principio hujus memoriae debet sacerdos oculum cordis sui con-

term visit, is often said of God in Holy Scripture. "What is man that Thou art mindful of him, or the son of man that Thou visitest him?" exclaims David (Ps. 8:5). Elsewhere he prays: "Remember us, O Lord, in the favor of Thy people, visit us with Thy salvation" (Ps. 105:4).

According to the direction of the rubrics, the letters N. and N.[32] admonish the priest to mention in this place some persons by name and specially to include them in the sacrifice; the names themselves he can either mention in silence or merely think of and have present to his mind. The choice is left free to the celebrant: of the living he can here mention whomever he wishes.[33] Since the prayer of the

---

templationi Dei vehementer infigere, cogitando de Deo ea, quae devotionem atque fervorem caritatis magis accendunt, et tunc in tali mentis fervore Deum ardenter orando, ut se exaudire dignetur pro his, quos nominabit, ipsas vero personas cursorie meditando, sed bona, quae eis petit, intente et amorose rogando (Dion. Carthus., *Expos. Miss.*, a. 20).

[32] *Diptychum* (from δίς, twice, and πτύσσειν, to fold, δίπτυχος, folded in two or placed together) = *tabula duplicata vel duplex,* a writing tablet, consisting of two tablets or leaflets joined together by a hinge. By the liturgical diptychs, that were more or less large and precious, is generally understood the index of persons, whose names were publicly read at the Holy Sacrifice. There is a distinction made between the diptychs of the living (δ. ζώντων, *liber viventium*) and the diptychs of the dead (δ. νεκρῶν, *liber mortuorum*). In these diptychs were inscribed, among others, principally ecclesiastical and secular dignitaries, other persons of merit and distinction, signal benefactors of the Church, certain persons presenting Eucharistic offerings, and others. Regarding the time and place of the reading, and also the reader, the practice greatly varied in countries and epochs. In the Roman Church, from time immemorial, the names of the living were read at the above place in the beginning of the Canon, and those of the departed after the Consecration. The liturgical diptychs probably originated already in the second century, as in the third century they were already universally introduced; their use in the West continued until the twelfth century, and among the Greeks until the fifteenth. Adverte, diptycha sacra distinguenda esse a precibus, quae pro vivis et defunctis inter sacrorum solemnia fiunt. Finis et usus praecipuus diptychorum erat, ut retineretur catholica communio tum vivorum inter se, tum vivorum et mortuorum (Lesley, p. 1).

[33] Liturgists usually say that the priest may include in the Memento, not only members of the Church, but also unbelievers, heretics, schismatics, those who are excommunicated, and they state in proof of this assertion, that it is only a private prayer of the celebrant (thus write Gavanti, Merati, Cavalieri, De Herdt and others). But such a statement is vague and partly incorrect. As was formerly the public reading of the names from the diptychs, so also is now the silent commemoration that replaces it, a liturgical prayer of the Church, which as such possesses special impetratory power: the priest says this Memento by commission of the Church and, on his side, has only the choice of naming such or such persons whom the intercession of the

FIRST PRAYER OF THE CANON

Church, especially in connection with the sacrifice, is exceedingly powerful and efficacious, the zealous priest will not omit to render it profitable especially to all those to whom he is most closely bound, and to whom he is under obligations of justice, charity, or gratitude. This memento should not be too hastily ended, nor too much prolonged; hence it is advisable to make the memento more in detail before Mass so that at this part of the Mass it may be again renewed in general, briefly and fervently.

Then the priest proceeds in the name of the Church to beg God to be mindful of "all here present" (*omnium circumstantium*), that is, of all those who are present and are hearing the Mass. For this reason also the time spent in a devout manner at the foot of the altar during the celebration of the Holy Sacrifice, is a time of grace and salvation.[34] The words, God "knoweth the faith and devotion" of those who are recommended to His favor and mercy, confirm the petition offered, and designate the interior disposition which all, especially those who hear Mass, should have in order to share largely in the fruit of the sacrifice. The more perfectly the faithful present are penetrated with faith and devotion, the more susceptible will be their souls for receiving the blessings of the Holy Sacrifice, and the

---

Church should profit, and this, in like manner, is the case with regard to some prayers for the departed. Independently of other reasons, the public character of the Memento is evident from the full context. The words *Memento, Domine, famulorum* . . . contain an intercession which is offered likewise for "all present" (*et omnium circumstantium*), as well as for those named by the priest, and that by the Church herself by the mouth of the celebrant. The following relative clauses, *pro quibus tibi offerimus vel qui tibi offerunt*, also may be referred, not merely to the circumstances, but moreover to the persons whom the priest commemorates by name. In addition to this public intercession, that the priest makes as a minister of the Church, he may here, as a private person, pray for others, and that too for those who are excluded from the suffrages of the Church, or for whom the Holy Sacrifice of the Mass may not be applied, that is, for *excommunicati vitandi;* but these persons may not be included in the liturgical Memento. The priest may, therefore, in this place be satisfied with the public Memento or at the same time add private prayers. (Cf. Suarez, *De Censuris*, disp. IX, sect. 5, n. 4 f.; Coninck, *De Sacram. ac Censuris*, disp.XIV, dub.6.) Licet sacerdos celebret totam Missam ut publica persona ac nomine Ecclesiae, atque etiam "Memento," adhuc tamen potest interserere privatam supplicationem. Potest concipere affectum supplicationis apud Deum concomitantem actionem illam publicam in favorem vitandorum (Pasqualigo, *De sacrificio N. L.*, I, q. 145).

[34] Hinc evidenter apparet, quam sanctum sit ac salubre Missarum interesse mysteriis, cum sacrificium Eucharistiae pro circumstantibus offeratur specialiter (Innoc. III, *De sacr. altar. myster.*, III, chap. 6).

more bountifully will God pour into their souls heavenly graces. These sentiments of faith and devotion are awakened and nourished in proportion to the lively interest taken by the faithful assisting at the Mass in the celebration at the altar, and in proportion as they unite more closely in spirit with the celebrant.

Those who assist at divine worship, that is, the servants and handmaids of God mentioned,[35] are by the words, *pro quibus tibi offerimus vel qui tibi offerunt*,[36] represented under two aspects: first, as the ones "for whom we offer," and then as the ones who themselves also join in the sacrifice. Under both aspects the sacrifice is more salutary and beneficial to those present than to others who are not in such intimate connection with its offering; and the devout participation in the sacrifice by assisting at Mass and by being included therein, draws on the faithful present abundant blessings of grace. The words, "for whom we offer or who offer to Thee"[37] refer, therefore, to the same persons, but designate them in two different ways.

The priest and the faithful offer to the Lord the sacrifice of praise now prepared on the altar (*hoc sacrificium laudis*). The Mass is the infinitely perfect sacrifice of praise and adoration, which we offer to the glory of the Most High. When the wise man exhorts us: "Glorify the Lord as much as ever you can, for He will yet far ex-

---

[35] Pro quibus tibi offerimus vel qui tibi offerunt: pro quibus, inquam, famulis et famulabus tuis et omnibus circumstantibus fidelibus et devotis, tibi offerimus ut ministri et immediate, vel qui famuli tui et famulae, omnesque circumstantes fideles et devoti offerunt tibi spiritualiter et mediate (Clichtov., *Elucidat. eccles.*, III, n. 14).

[36] *Vel* here = *et*, and also. Micrologus remarks (chap. 13) that in *antiquioribus et veracioribus Sacramentariis*, the (later) addition, *pro quibus tibi offerimus*, is wanting and only the (original) words, *qui tibi offerunt*, are found. The cessation of the ancient custom of offerings appears to have occasioned the gradual reception of the words *pro quibus tibi offerimus*, which are by no means superfluous, as Micrologus holds. In a prayer of the Mozarabic Missal a distinction is made between the *offerentes*, that is, they who present the sacrificial gifts and have communicated, and the *adstantes*, that is, those who have merely assisted at the holy sacrifice. Deferatur in ista solemnia Spiritus Sanctus tuus, qui tam adstantis quam offerentis populi et oblata pariter et vota sanctificet (*fer. II Pasch.*).

[37] In quibus verbis patenter ostenditur, quod a cunctis fidelibus, non solum viris, sed et mulieribus sacrificium illud laudis offertur, licet ab uno specialiter offerri sacerdote videatur: quia quod ille Deo offerendo manibus tractat, hoc multitudo fidelium intenta mentium devotione commendat (S. Petr. Damian., "*Dominus vobiscum*," chap. 8).

ceed, and His magnificence is wonderful. Blessing the Lord, exalt Him as much as you can; for He is above all praise" (Ecclus. 43: 32 f.), we may boldly and cheerfully answer: here on the altar there is offered to God a praise worthy of His greatness, because it is infinite and divine, since it is the sacrifice of His only-begotten Son. When the Lord laid "the foundations of the earth," the morning stars praised Him, "and all the sons of God [the angels] made a joyful melody" (Job 38:4, 7); but the chant of praise of the heavenly hosts is not to be compared with the adoration, homage, and glorification that ascend from the altar to heaven. By the Eucharistic sacrifice of praise the name of the Lord is magnified "from the rising of the sun unto the going down of the same" (Ps. 112: 2 f.).

On the other hand, this sacrifice is at the same time the source whence flow forth all grace and mercy, salvation and blessing, peace and benefits of all kinds upon our poor earth; hence it is said, the faithful offer the sacrifice of the altar "for themselves and all pertaining to them." (*pro se suisque omnibus*).[38] Those present may, moreover, offer the Holy Sacrifice, not only for themselves, but also for others; the Church herself supports and recommends, as it were, the special intentions, inasmuch as she is here mindful even of those for whom the assistants on their part offer the sacrifice. It is an exercise of charity most pleasing to God to thus include in the Holy Sacrifice our own family, relatives, friends, and other persons, in order to draw down grace upon them. It is also to be expected of the goodness of God, that they who assist devoutly at Mass lose nothing of their own share in the fruit of the sacrifice when they make such intentions for the interests and wants of others.

In union with the priest, the faithful offer the Mass for themselves and for all those who are dear to them, as an atoning sacrifice "for the redemption of their souls" (*pro redemptione animarum suarum*)[39] and as a sacrifice of petition "for the hope of their salvation and safety" (*pro spe salutis et incolumitatis suae*).

The Eucharistic sacrifice effects the redemption of souls, inasmuch as it conveys and applies to them the graces of redemption

---

[38] *Pro* = for: in favor of, to the advantage and profit of.

[39] *Pro* = for; here expresses the object of the oblation, that is, the sacrificial fruit to be obtained. This is an exegesis, i.e., *expositio* (Sicard.), of the preceding words, *pro se suisque omnibus*.

acquired by the sacrifice of the cross, that they may be made perfectly pure and worthy "to enter the temple of eternal glory." The actual redemption of the individual man begins with regeneration in baptism; it is developed and completed under the influence of the grace of Christ during his whole earthly pilgrimage, and finally obtains its consummation at the glorious return of the Lord, when not only the soul, but also the body shall be delivered from all the misery of sin, snatched from temporal and eternal destruction, and transformed in glory. The expression, redemption of souls, is to be understood in the same sense as that of, salvation of the soul; the redemption and salvation of the body is herein included. This mode of speech is used to designate the soul as the essential object of redemption and as the actual subject of salvation; but through the soul and for the sake of the soul, sanctification and a state of glory will be imparted to the body also.[40] The soul will enjoy perfect happiness only when clothed with the glorified body. Although redemption in its full sense comprises not only deliverance from all evil, but also the bestowal of all that is good, yet here only the former is meant; the faithful offer the sacrifice "for the redemption of their souls," that is, to propitiate the irritated justice of God, and to be freed from every evil of guilt and punishment. That the Eucharistic sacrifice does also open to us the treasury of the divine goodness and liberality and procure us every good, is contained in the words: "for the hope of their salvation and safety," that is, for the obtaining of redemption and prosperity.[41] The word "salvation" (*salus*) here comprises all spiritual, supernatural gifts: grace in time and for eternity; the word "safety" (*incolumitas*) designates not merely health of body, but generally success and happiness in temporal things, in the goods (immaterial and material) belonging to the natural order. They too may be obtained by sacrifice and prayer, in so far as they serve for the attainment of eternal happiness.

The concluding clause: "and who pay their vows to Thee,"

[40] Licet corpus non sit *immediatum* subjectum gratiae, ex anima tamen redundat effectus gratiae ad corpus, dum in praesenti membra nostra exhibemus arma justitiae Deo (Rom., chap. 6), et in futuro corpus nostrum sortietur incorruptionem et gloriam animae (S. Thom., IIIa, q. 79, a. 1 ad 3).

[41] Hoc sacrosanctum sacrificium non solum liberat nos a malis, sed etiam accumulat nos bonis; non solum nos eripit a poenis, sed etiam auget gaudia salutis et incolumitatis. Salutis, inquam, aeternae animarum; incolumitatis, i.e., incorruptionis perpetuae corporum, et hoc est, pro quo offerimus tam pretiosum munus (B. Odo Camerac., *Expos. in Canon. Miss.*, dist. 2).

is a continuation of and a supplement to the preceding words: "who offer to Thee this sacrifice of praise." It accords with this verse of the psalm: "Offer to God the sacrifice of praise and pay thy vows to the Most High" (49:14). *Votum* does not always in the strict sense of the word signify a vow, but it has in the liturgical language a far more comprehensive meaning. It frequently occurs therein and at one time denotes the oblations on the altar, at other times, petition, supplication, resolutions—in brief, interior and exterior acts of religion.[42] Already at baptism we received precious gifts and glorious promises, and in return we solemnly vowed to die to the world and to sin, to live only for God and heaven. These holy vows [43] we pay at the Holy Sacrifice of the Mass, inasmuch as we offer not only the Eucharistic victim, but in union with it we offer ourselves also, our body and our soul, our prayers and our homage, our labors and trials, our sufferings and our joys, as gifts due to the Lord.[44] But by so doing we give "to the eternal, living, and true God" that only which we have previously received from Him; we but return to God that which He bestowed on us.

3. The concluding part of the first prayer of the Canon contains a list of saints and bears the heading *Infra actionem:* [45] during the sacrificial action or during the Canon; for *actio* here is a designation for sacrifice, or canon. Sacrifice in general is essentially an action,[46]

[42] Cf. the Secreta in *Dedicat. Ecclesiae*, in which we read: *dum haec vota praesentia reddimus*. In ancient missals is often found the expression *oblationum vota* as a designation of the sacrificial gifts. Voventur omnia, quae offeruntur Deo, maxime sancti altaris oblatio, quo sacramento praedicatur nostrum aliud votum maximum, quo nos vovimus in Christo esse mansuros, utique in compage corporis Christi (S. August, *Epist.*, 149, n. 16, *ad Paulin.*).

[43] Haec *vota* sunt desideria et sancta proposita colendi Deum, quae implemus et Deo reddimus praecipue hac oblatione sacrificii incruenti. Dicimur autem ea potius *reddere* quam donare Deo, quia per divinam gratiam illa concipimus et a Deo accipimus, et postmodum Deo ipsi offerimus et reddimus, quae accipimus (Quarti, II, tit. 9, sect. 2, dub. 2). In the *Sacrament. Gregor.* we read in a *Benedictio virginis:* Respice super hanc famulam tuam, quae tibi devotionem suam offert, a quo et ipsa idem votum assumpsit.

[44] Deo dona ejus in nobis *nosque ipsos* vovemus et reddimus (S. August, *De civit. Dei*, X, chap. 3 [al. 4]). Quisquis bene cogitat, quid voveat Domino et quae vota reddat, seipsum voveat, seipsum reddat: hoc exigitur, hoc debetur (*idem., Enarrat. in Ps.*, 115:8).

[45] This expression with the same signification is also in the *Ordo Rom. V*, n. 9. The *Ordo Rom. XIV*, chap. 71, has the inscription *Alia infra Actionem* also for the following prayer, *Hanc igitur oblationem*, because this, too, at times receives a special addition.

[46] In Greek δρᾶν, in Latin *agere, facere, operari*, are often used in the sense of

and the Eucharistic sacrifice in particular is the repetition of that which Christ did at the Last Supper and, consequently, the greatest, most sublime, and holiest action: *the action* in the highest sense of the word. The Mass is the unbloody representation and the mystical renewal of the sacrifice and redeeming act of Christ on the cross. The Eucharistic sacrifice is, therefore, a holy drama (*actio*), and from the sacrifice this same name, *actio* (action), had been transferred to the sacrificial prayer.[47] The superscription, *Infra actionem*, is, therefore, called "within the Canon." [48] But why is this title placed precisely above the *Communicantes?* On Holy Thursday and on five of the greatest feasts [49] the *Communicantes* is somewhat different, because it has an addition referring to the day celebrated; in this altered form it is placed immediately after the Preface and bears the superscription, *Infra actionem*, which there means that this formula of prayer is later on to be inserted and recited in the Canon. It seems that originally this superscription was placed only over those special *Communicantes* which were printed outside the Canon, and then later transferred to the ordinary *Communicantes* in the Canon.[50] In the latter place, at any rate, it is intended to refer to the special formula of prayer printed after the Preface, and to recall to our mind that on certain feasts this special formula is to be used instead of the general one in the Canon. These insertions have been customary since the beginning of the sixth century.

Communicantes et memoriam venerantes, thus begins the ordinary formula. These words, as a continuation of the preceding part of the Canon and its supplement, stand in the closest relation to the

---

offering (*sacrificare*) and are thus characterized as a special religious action. Thus Pope St. Leo wrote in the year 445 to Bishop Dioscorus of Alexandria, that it would be proper to repeat the Holy Sacrifice of the Mass, as the newly collected crowd filled the basilica in which the sacrifice was celebrated (*in qua agitur*).

[47] Actio, actio sacri mysterii, mysterium sanctissimae actionis = Canon. Infra actionem, i.e. inter verba ipsius Canonis, qui actio etiam nominatur a sacris auctoribus, quod in eo divina aguntur consecranturque et conficiuntur mysteria (Clichtov., *Elucid. eccl.*, III).

[48] Ancient missals have often the words *Infra Canonem*. The *infra* is here used in the sense of *intra*, as we say also *infra octavam* instead of *intra octavam*. (Cf. Lebrun, *Explication de la Messe*, IV, art. 4, § 1).

[49] Christmas, Epiphany, Easter, Ascension, and Pentecost.

[50] In the *Sacrament. Gelasian.* we find the superscription *Infra Actionem* not within the Canon, but only above the special *Communicantes* of the special Mass formulas.

FIRST PRAYER OF THE CANON

preceding words: [51] Those present offer up to Thee, O Lord, this sacrifice of praise and pay their vows unto Thee as members of Christ's mystical body and of the communion of saints (*communicantes*), who recognize their communion with the inhabitants of heaven by venerating their memory.[52]

The word *communicantes*, therefore, denotes that we are children of the Church, subjects of the kingdom of Christ, members of the great family of God—in a word, that we belong "to the communion of saints." This membership with the mystical body of Christ is here appropriately brought out because we would honor the memory of the blessed with the intention of rendering ourselves worthy of their intercession at the offering of the Holy Sacrifice. This fuller and deeper meaning [53] accommodates itself also to the context of the special formulas, in which the word *communicantes* is separated from the expression *memoriam venerantes* by an insertion; for example, at Easter the prayer begins thus: *Communicantes, et diem sacratissimum celebrantes Resurrectionis Domini nostri Jesu Christi secundum carnem: sed et memoriam venerantes:* that is, in spiritual communion with one another we celebrate the great day of the resurrection of our Lord Jesus Christ according to the flesh, and at the same time venerate the memory of the saints.

All the redeemed together constitute the kingdom of Jesus Christ;

---

[51] Dubitare potest de sensu illius verbi "Communicantes" et connexione ejus cum reliquis. Respondetur, totam hanc orationem esse unam unoque contextu legendam, ita ut sensus sit: tibi reddunt vota sua aeterno Deo, vivo et vero, communicantes vel inter se vel cum Sanctis tuis per societatem et conjunctionem, quam cum illis habent; quorum propterea memoriam venerantes per eorum intercessionem exaudiri petent (Suarez, disp. LXXXIII, sec. 2, n.7).

[52] Sequitur: *Communicantes et memoriam venerantes*. Ubi licet scriptores quasi capituli initium faciunt, eo quod in quibusdam solemnitatibus hic diversitas quaedam invenitur, jungitur tamen praemissis hoc modo: Offerunt pro se quisque, ipsi dico communicantes, in Ecclesiae communione per fidem manentes (Robert. Paululus, De offic. eccl., II, chap. 29).

[53] The signification of the word *communicantes* is often grasped in a manner too one-sided and limited. For instance, some say, that it merely signifies the relation of the faithful on earth with the saints of heaven, as is evident from what immediately follows, *memoriam venerantes;* others, on the contrary, are of opinion that this idea is excluded by the insertion made on certain days between *communicantes* and *memoriam venerantes*, so that *communicantes* is to be referred merely to the union of the faithful on earth, and particularly to those assembled at the divine service. (Cf. Bellarmin., *De Missa*, II, chap. 21).

among all these citizens, whether they have already happily reached their goal or are still combating on earth or making atonement in the place of purification, there is a living communication, a reciprocal interchange; good deeds and sufferings, merits and satisfactions, in short, all the fruits of grace are common property from which each draws and to which each contributes. It is precisely at the celebration of Mass that we are reminded of the privilege and happiness of belonging to so glorious a community, of being "fellow citizens with the saints and domestics of God" (Eph. 2:19). For after the priest has interceded for the Church militant and her members, he endeavors to add greater weight and efficacy to his supplications by invoking the saints. His mental vision is enlarged and directed to the heavenly Jerusalem. In happy consciousness of the intimate relationship he enjoys with the glorified saints, he celebrates their memory, as though to invite them, as kings and priests (Apoc. 5:10), to offer the sacrifice along with us, and by their powerful intercession and abundant merits to support our weak prayers, so that by the strength of their mediation we may experience God's help and protection in all situations and necessities (*ut in omnibus protectionis tuae muniamur auxilio*).

By name are mentioned: the Blessed Virgin Mary, the twelve apostles, and twelve martyrs; [54] finally, all the saints are mentioned in general.

a) First of all (*in primis*) we honor the memory of the "glorious ever Virgin Mary, Mother of God and our Lord Jesus Christ." As always, Mary is here rightly named in the first place; she is queen not merely of the apostles and martyrs, but of all the saints. Her name is not simply mentioned, but to it are added honorable qualifications that proclaim her grandeur, power, and dignity. She is called glorious, for as queen of heaven and of earth she is elevated above all the choirs of angels and saints in eternal bliss and glory. She was taken up to heaven, body and soul, and transfigured in glory; there she wears the most beautiful crown of honor and power. As on earth she excelled all creatures by the fullness of grace, so in the next life she surpasses all the citizens of heaven by the splendor and magnificence of her glory. Because she was on earth the most

---

[54] The order of names of the saints in the Canon shows an arrangement by pairs. Already in the enumeration of the apostles, and still more clearly in that of the martyrs, this division of names two by two is easily distinguishable.

humble, pure, devout, and loving, she is now in heaven the most glorious and the most happy. Then she is called "always a virgin" (*semper virgo*). This privilege is often commented upon. Mary is the Virgin of all virgins; she is the most venerable, glorious, and wonderful virgin; she is the model, guide, protectress of all virginal souls. By the virginity which she vowed to God, she was prepared to become the "Mother of our God and Lord Jesus Christ"; for assuredly it behooved the Mother of God to be and ever remain a virgin. The divine maternity was only the complete consecration and sealing of her incomparable virginity. Through the sole miracle of its kind she united "the joys of maternity with the honor of virginity." The divine maternity itself is of infinite dignity; for Mary gave birth to the Son of the Most High. This maternal dignity of hers is the intrinsic reason why Mary above all other creatures was endowed with the plenitude of grace and holiness, of glory and power. As the Mother of God she is the queen of heaven and earth, she reigns as mistress, with maternal power and love. Hence so frequently we cry to her: *Monstra te esse matrem* ("Show thyself a mother"); that is, show that thou art not merely our Mother who loves us so tenderly, but that thou art also and still more the Mother of God, all-powerful by thy intercession.

The victim of the sacrifice of the cross and of the sacrifice of the altar was given to us through the Virgin Mother, Mary; He is the fruit of her most noble body by the overshadowing of the Holy Ghost. She "stood by the cross of Jesus," and while her maternal tears were mingled with His blood and the sword of sorrow pierced her soul, she offered her crucified Son for the salvation of the world. She is justly called "the Queen of Martyrs." Her name, therefore, is inseparable from the sacrifice of Christ; the remembrance of Mary must always be united with that of Christ at His sacrificial celebration. Christ's holy flesh and blood offered in sacrifice on the altar come to us from the flesh and heart of Mary; from Mary, moreover, we should learn, with priestly disposition and self-devotedness, to offer the Lamb of God and ourselves at the foot of the altar.

b) After the Virgin Mother of God, twelve apostles are named in the Canon; the succession differs somewhat from the records of the apostles in Holy Scripture.[55] The apostles are those chosen mes-

[55] This enumeration probably originates from tradition, not from the Itala

sengers to whom the Lord imparted full powers as teachers, priests, and pastors, that as His representatives they might continue the work of the redemption. As the salt of the earth and light of the world, they were to establish in all places the kingdom of God, to extend and strengthen the Church. To prepare them for this mission, He was present with them more than with others, and He made them the immediate witnesses of His life, miracles, and doctrine, of His passion and resurrection; He promised them His assistance and sent them the Holy Ghost from on high. In obedience to the commission of their divine Master, the apostles went out into the whole world to teach and baptize all nations, to bring to them the blessings of religion and together with it true earthly happiness. "Their sound has gone forth into all the earth, and their words unto the ends of the world" (Ps. 18:5). Self-sacrifice was their office and calling, their life and their death. "For Thy sake we are put to death all the day long. We are accounted as sheep for the slaughter" (Rom. 8:36); but they rejoiced to endure shame and sorrow for the name of Jesus, and, after they had fought the good fight and finished the course (II Tim. 4:7), they gave up their life by the bloody death of martyrdom, and thus planted the Church in their blood. The apostles not only scattered the seed of the divine word, but they labored to bring it to maturity by watering it with the sweat of their brow and fructifying it by shedding their hearts' blood. Built and resting on the chief cornerstone, Christ, the apostles have thus become the foundation of the Church, which consequently is called apostolic. Of the life and death of most of the apostles we know very little.

c) Martyrdom of blood is the characteristic trait of the saints of the first four centuries; therefore twelve martyrs of these ancient times are now mentioned in the Canon. Among them are five popes, a bishop, a deacon, and five lay persons. Even at a very early period these saints were held in high esteem in Rome, and therefore were inserted in the Canon. First, five popes are mentioned: SS. Linus,[56]

---

version. St. Paul (in the liturgy the inseparable companion of St. Peter) is included in the list, and St. Matthias is here omitted, although he is mentioned in the commemoration of martyrs after the Consecration; thus the sacred number of twelve is retained.

[56] St. Linus, the first successor of St. Peter in the See of Rome, and therefore the second pope, is the same from whom St. Paul sends a salutation to Timothy. He was converted to Christianity by St. Peter, and, as a distinguished assistant of the Prince of the Apostles, he may frequently have supplied his place when the latter was obliged to leave Rome for a time in order

FIRST PRAYER OF THE CANON

Cletus,[57] and Clement,[58] the first three successors of St. Peter, and SS. Sixtus [59] and Cornelius.[60] Then is mentioned, St. Cyp-

---

to preach the Gospel elsewhere. He ruled the Church from 67 to 76 (?). He was decapitated and buried in the Vatican by the side of St. Peter. Under Pope Urban VIII a tomb was discovered there bearing the simple inscription: *Linus*. His feast occurs on September 23.

[57] St. Cletus (76–88?) succeeded St. Linus. It is believed that he erected a tombstone to St. Peter, who had ordained him priest. His feast falls on April 26.

[58] St. Clement is reckoned among the apostolic Fathers; he sat in the chair of Peter from 88 to 97 (?). St. Irenaeus writes of him: "In the third place after the apostles the Roman episcopate received Clement, who had seen the Princes of the Apostles, had associated with them, had listened to their sermons, and had the apostolic tradition before his eyes." St. Paul in his Epistle to the Philippians mentions him among his "fellow laborers, whose names are in the Book of Life" (4:2). According to the testimony of ancient writers, St. Clement was endowed with all the qualities of mind and heart that were requisite for the highest ecclesiastical dignities. The legend relates that the emperor Trajan banished him to the Taurian Chersoneus (Crimea), where he found two thousand Christians condemned to work in the marble quarries, who suffered greatly for want of water. Clement prayed, and on an adjacent hill appeared a lamb, from beneath whose right foot a spring of fresh water issued forth. This miracle brought about the conversion of many of the inhabitants. Then Trajan commanded St. Clement to be cast into the sea with an anchor fastened to his neck. The Christians on the shore fell upon their knees and prayed; and behold! the sea receded three thousand paces, and there appeared, built by the hands of angels, a marble temple in which the body of the saint together with the anchor was found. The mortal remains of the martyr are said to have been brought to Rome by the Greek missionaries, SS. Cyril and Methodius, during the pontificate of Pope Hadrian II, and placed in the very ancient basilica of St. Clement near the Coliseum, of which mention is already made by St. Jerome. His feast is celebrated on November 23.

[59] During the first three centuries there were two popes by this name. Sixtus I (115–25?) governed the Church during the reign of the emperor Hadrian, when the lot of the Christians was a hard and painful one; he suffered martyrdom and was buried in the Vatican near St. Peter. His feast occurs on April 6. Far better known is Sixtus II, a Greek by birth. His pontificate (257-58) fell during the stormy period of the Valerian persecution of the Christians. In spite of the Emperor's prohibition, he ventured to hold divine service in the catacombs. Discovered by the heathen soldiers and apprehended, he was dragged into the city before the tribunal and condemned; afterward he was again led back to the Catacomb of Praetextatus, in which he had previously celebrated the Holy Sacrifice, and was beheaded on or near his episcopal throne. The crown of martyrdom was granted to him on August 6. 258. His body now rests in the very ancient church situated on the Appian Way, *S. Sisto vecchio*. Scholars do not agree as to which pope is commemorated in the Canon.

[60] St. Cornelius, who had distinguished himself in all the grades of the Church service, ascended the Chair of Peter in the year 251; he accepted the

rian,[61] distinguished bishop of Carthage, and the celebrated deacon martyr, St. Lawrence.[62] Lastly, five laymen are commemo-

---

supreme dignity only by constraint. Under the tyrant, emperor Decius, St. Cornelius was in constant expectation of death. Under the emperor Gallus, in the year 252, a violent storm arose against the Christians in Rome; but they, with the Pope at their head, maintained the faith with such unanimity, fortitude, and strength as to excite universal joy and jubilation, and St. Cyprian could not sufficiently praise and admire them. St. Cornelius was banished to Centum Cellae (*Civitavecchia*), and there died a martyr on September 14, 252. On the same day six years later (258), St. Cyprian, bishop of Carthage, was martyred, hence both names are usually mentioned together. Their joint feast is celebrated on September 16.

[61] St. Cyprian was born in the beginning of the third century at Carthage. He was of distinguished rank, rich, very talented, and had received an excellent education. Only in a more mature age was he won over to the Catholic faith; his baptism took place about the year 246. He distributed his great wealth among the poor, made a vow of perpetual chastity, and spent his time in prayer and the study of the sacred sciences. From the very beginning of his conversion he was adorned with brilliant virtues. St. Cyprian was raised to the priesthood and was soon promoted to the episcopal See of Carthage (248). The ten years' episcopacy of the saint (248–58) fell during a time of most violent persecution and other external misfortunes. St. Cyprian fulfilled with indefatigable zeal his pastoral duties for the salvation of the faithful confided to his care and for the welfare of the whole Church. He combated for the unity and discipline of the Church against heretics and schismatics, and animated all to cheerful endurance of martyrdom. He himself was put to death by the sword in the public place of Carthage on September 14, 258.

[62] St. Lawrence is highly extolled by the Fathers and held in great veneration by all Christian nations. "As Jerusalem was glorified by Stephen, so is Rome renowned by its Lawrence from the rising to the setting of the sun," exclaims Pope St. Leo in a sermon on the feast of this saint. Spain is regarded as his native country; but he was brought up and educated in Rome. Sixtus II ordained him deacon and made him the first of the seven deacons of the Roman Church, wherefore he is also called the archdeacon of the pope. This was a most important office; for it included the administration of the treasures of the Church. Exceedingly glorious is the martyrdom of the young Levite. When Pope Sixtus II was being dragged to the catacombs for execution, Lawrence cried out to him: "Whither goest thou, Father, without thy son? Where art thou hastening, holy priest, without thy deacon? Never wert thou accustomed to offer the Holy Sacrifice without thy minister." And how singularly consoling are the words of the high priest to his deacon: " I am not forsaking thee, my son, greater combats await thee. Cease to weep, after three days thou wilt follow me." During those three days the deacon hastened through the city, distributed the goods of the Church to the needy, and in so doing he wrought several miracles. To the prefect of the city, who ordered him to deliver up the treasures of the Church, he presented the poor of Christ as the treasures of the Church. On this account the heathen became enraged, and subjected the young hero to many torments. St. Lawrence was scourged, struck with leaden balls, stretched on the rack, burned with red-

rated: SS. Chrysogonus,[63] John and Paul,[64] Cosmas and Damian.[65]

In the Roman Canon only martyrs are named before and after the Consecration.[66] They have merited this distinction by the bloody sacrifice of their life; they appear as the ripest and most glorious fruit of the sacrifice of Christ. They resembled the Saviour not only in life, but also in death. For Christ they lived, for Him they died; in return for the sacrifice of His love, they offered the sacrifice of the world and of themselves, amid untold torments and sufferings. The virtues of fortitude and patience, of faith and love, which they practised in an heroic degree, shone resplendent in them.

---

hot metallic plates. Afterward he was laid on a burning gridiron, whence he addressed the tyrant: "Behold, wretch, the power of my God; your heat for me is refreshing coolness, but it will end for you in inextinguishable fire." The illustrious deacon and martyr passed to the glory of God on August 10, 258. In the magnificent basilica of St. Lawrence erected above his grave by Constantine outside the walls, the relics of the two martyr deacons, Lawrence and Stephen, repose together in a marble sarcophagus beneath the high altar.

[63] St. Chrysogonus converted many heathens in Rome to Christianity; he was also the teacher of St. Anastasia and her counsel and consoler when on account of her faith she suffered many persecutions. He was arrested in Rome under Diocletian, and after a long imprisonment he was sent to Aquileja, where he was beheaded about the year 304. His feast occurs on November 24.

[64] John and Paul were brothers. As distinguished Romans, they were entrusted with high positions of honor at the court of St. Constantia, a daughter of Constantine the Great. The apostate emperor, Julian, tried to compel them to sacrifice to the idols and to enter his service; but such an order they rejected with contempt. For this reason Julian had them secretly decapitated in their own palace on June 26, 362.

[65] Cosmas and Damian were also brothers, descended from a distinguished race in Arabia; they practiced medicine in Roman territory without remuneration. Their learning, skill in healing, and devout mode of life won for them universal confidence and high esteem. Their acts of benevolence gained for the Christian religion many adherents. After enduring many torments, they were at last decapitated at Egaea, in Cilicia, probably in 297. Pope Felix IV (526-29) built at Rome the church of SS. Cosmas and Damian and brought to it the relics of the martyred brothers. Both are honored as patrons of physicians and of the science of medicine; their feast occurs on September 27.

[66] About the middle of the fourth century the period of martyrs came to an end. The latest of the martyrs here mentioned, SS. John and Paul (d. 362), were placed in the Roman Canon probably towards the end of the fourth century or in the beginning of the fifth century, and from that time the list of the saints mentioned in the Canon has been closed. Elsewhere since the sixth century many names were added to the *Communicantes*, particularly of saints that are specially honored in certain dioceses and convents.

CHAPTER XXXIV

SECOND AND THIRD PRAYERS OF THE CANON

The Second Prayer of the Canon [1]

Hanc igitur oblationem servitutis nostrae, sed et cunctae familiae tuae, quaesumus Domine, ut placatus accipias: diesque nostros in tua pace disponas, atque ab aeterna damnatione nos eripi, et in electorum tuorum jubeas grege numerari. Per Christum Dominum nostrum. Amen.

This oblation, therefore, of our service, and that of Thy whole family, we beseech Thee, O Lord, graciously to accept, and to dispose our days in Thy peace and to command us to be delivered from eternal damnation, and to be numbered in the flock of Thine elect. Through Christ Our Lord. Amen.

1. As in the beginning of the Canon, so here also we meet with the little word *igitur* (= therefore, consequently, accordingly, hence); it unites the second prayer to the first and designates it as a consequence or continuation of the first.[2] The same petitions are again

---

[1] This prayer now has an addition in four Mass formulas, which indicate the special intention for which the sacrifice is offered: on Holy Thursday, in commemoration of the institution of the Eucharistic mysteries; in Easter and Pentecost weeks, for the newly baptized; and at the consecration of a bishop, for the newly consecrated. Before the time of St. Gregory the Great, the *Hanc igitur* was a variable oblation and intercessory prayer, changing according to the character of the Mass formula. Hence in the Gelasian Sacramentary there are thirty-eight special formulas of the *Hanc igitur*, which do not, like the additions to the *Communicantes*, set off the thought of the feast, but contain petitions for the application of the fruits of the sacrifice to various events of this life.

[2] The recommendation of the sacrificial gifts and of those offering, or of those for whom the sacrifice is offered, which was interrupted by the *Communicantes*, is here resumed and is connected by the *igitur* with the petitions contained in this second prayer.

presented, but now with heightened confidence and intensified expression. We no longer stand there alone, alone in our poverty and wretchedness; for we have renewed our connection with the communion of saints, and in this communion we are enriched by the merits and prayers of our heavenly brethren. Hence, we venture with still greater confidence to turn to the Lord with the petition previously implored, that He would show Himself favorable, gracious (*placatus*), and with kind indulgence "accept" these sacrificial gifts from our hands.[3] Until now the same oblation is always meant: bread and wine, in so far as they are destined to be changed into the body and blood of Christ. The petition for the acceptance of the sacrificial elements, therefore, includes the petition for their transubstantiation:[4] the purpose for which they are to be accepted is the consecration. The Eucharistic oblation is here more minutely characterized as "this oblation of our service and that of Thy whole family." Unquestionably these words express the truth that the Eucharist is the offering of the whole Church,[5] that it is offered by all her members and for all her members.[6] The expression, "oblation of our service," may be applied to those who are present: to those who most intimately take part in the celebration of Mass; the addi-

[3] Quia hoc sacrificium tibi offerimus in corpore Ecclesiae communicando et memoriam Sanctorum venerando, hanc igitur oblationem, precamur, ut placatus accipias: ut scil., si peccatis nostris praepedimur, communione saltem sanctae Ecclesiae et Sanctorum tuorum veneratione placeris ad accipiendum, quod tibi offerimus, sacrificium (B. Odo Camerac., *Expos. in Canon. Miss.*, dist. 2).

[4] Sacerdos orat Deum, ut ipsam oblationem panis et vini accipiat ut materiam sacrificii futuri et eam videlicet benedicat et sanctificet (Bellarm., *De Missa*, II, chap. 22).

[5] In his verbis unitas Ecclesiae ostenditur, quando in illa oblatione communis servitus exhibetur Deo tam a sacerdotibus quam a cuncta familia domus Dei. Oratur itaque Deus, ut hanc oblationem, quam illi soli debita servitute defert Ecclesia, placatus accipiat et sic dies nostros, quibus inter diversa pericula vivimus, in sua pace disponat, finitoque hujus mortalitatis cursu, ab aeterna damnatione ereptos in electorum suorum grege annumerare dignetur (Pseudo-Alcuin., chap. 40).

[6] *Hanc igitur oblationem servitutis nostrae*, i.e. quam offerimus nos sacerdotes qui speciatim servi tui sumus, tuo cultui et obsequiis mancipati et hoc offerimus sacrificium, ut servitutis nostrae et subjectionis aliquod testimonium demus; nec tantum est oblatio nostra, qui tamquam ministri eam offerimus, *sed et cunctae familiae tuae*, i.e. totius Ecclesiae catholicae omniumque fidelium, qui per manus nostras et ministerium hanc offerunt, et quorum nomine eandem tibi offerimus (Antonius de Molina, *Instructio sacerdotum*, III, chap. 3).

tion, "and that of Thy whole family," to all the others, who are absent. Or we may consider the first clause as especially designating the consecrated ministers of the altar, in which case the family of God would refer to all the faithful, but in particular to those who by actual participation unite in the celebration of the Mass.

However, "the oblation of our service" may have a deeper meaning, which would signify more than the offering which "we Thy servants (*nos servi tui*) . . . offer unto" God, which is the expression used immediately after the Elevation. The Mass is called "the oblation of our service," that is, the offering that we and all the members of the Church make in order to acknowledge the absolute dominion of God over all that is created, and to express our profound submission to it.[7] As creatures we stand in a special relation of dependence toward God our Creator; the Mass now has principally for its object the giving to God of that veneration, homage, and acknowledgement—that religious worship—which is due to Him alone.[8] Sacrifice is the chief act of religion (divine worship).[9] Hence in this prayer we explicitly state that we offer "this oblation of our service," this divine sacrifice, to adore God and acknowledge His absolute dominion over us.

By virtue of the Eucharistic sacrifice we implore mercies and blessings for time and for eternity.[10] Earthly, temporal welfare con-

---

[7] This more profound meaning of the expression *oblatio servitutis nostrae* is evident also from other almost similar designations of the Eucharistic sacrifice, as they are found especially in the Secretae; for example, *nostrae servitutis munus; debitum nostrae servitutis; nostrae humilitatis oblatio*.

[8] Deo nos servitutem, quae λατρεία graece dicitur, sive in quibusque sacramentis sive in nobis ipsis debemus (S. Aug., *De civit. Dei*, X, chap. 3 [4]). Ipsa servitus graece λατρεία dicitur, quae soli vero Deo jure ac legitime non a perfidis, sed a catholicis fidelibus exhibetur . . . illa cultura quae λατρεία dicitur, maxime in sacrificiis invenitur (S. Fulgent., *Contra Fabian.*, frag. 12).

[9] *Cultus ac servitus Dei* reipsa non sunt actus religionis distincti: siquidem eodem actu religionis homo servit Deo et colit ipsum. Nam cultus respicit Dei excellentiam, cui reverentia debetur; servitus autem subjectionem hominis, qui ex sua conditione obligatur ad exhibendam reverentiam Deo, cum interim in omni actu religionis et excellentiam Dei et nostram erga Deum subjectionem protestemur, adeo ut ad haec duo pertineant omnes actus religionis, quia per omnes homo protestatur divinam excellentiam et subjectionem sui ad Deum (Tanner, *De relig.*, q. 1, dub. 2).

[10] Tria bona postulantur a Deo. Primum temporale; secundum perpetui mali devitatio; tertium perpetui boni adeptio. In horum trium bonorum postulatione profitetur Ecclesia, Deum esse universorum dominum et in triplicem mundi machinam extendi supremum ejus principatum. Per primum enim

sists in this, that God orders and directs our days in peace.[11] "*Diesque nostros in tua pace disponas*," do we pray, for we desire good and peaceful days that are not clouded by sufferings, combats, and persecutions, but always cheered and blessed with "the peace of God," "that, being delivered from the hand of our enemies, we may serve Him without fear in holiness and justice" (Luke 1:74 f.). We pray for temporal prosperity, in so far as it may be serviceable to the attainment of the one thing necessary and for possession of that "better part, which shall not be taken away from" us (Luke 10:42).

Our heavenly, eternal well-being includes our preservation from the greatest of all evils, eternal death (*ab aeterna damnatione nos eripi*), and the attainment to the supreme good, eternal life (*in electorum tuorum grege numerari*).[12] The number of those who are chosen for heavenly glory has been eternally and irrevocably determined by God, so that the number can be neither increased nor diminished; therefore the above petition can only refer to the execution of this divine decree and signify that God may be pleased to grant us the grace of final perseverance and admit us to heavenly bliss. This meaning is clearly expressed in a petition of almost the same import in the *Te Deum: Aeterna fac cum sanctis tuis in gloria numerari* ("May [Thy servants] be numbered among Thy saints in eternal glory").

As fruit to be derived from the sacrifice, therefore, we implore in the above prayer the peace of God for the days of our earthly life that we may attain the heavenly life; but we pray especially for the consummation of our redemption and eternal salvation. Full redemption consists in this, that we be forever snatched from eternal

---

profiteur, ipsum esse dominum in terris; per secundum in inferis; per tertium in coelis—et ubique omnia ipsius nutu disponi (Clichtov., *Elucid. eccl.*, III, n. 23). The three petitions, *pro pace temporum et ereptione ab aeternis suppliciis et consortio Sanctorum obtinendo*, were added by St. Gregory the Great (cf. Walafrid. Strab., chap. 23). Since in even earlier sacramentaries similar thoughts and expressions occur in this place, St. Gregory probably only made permanent the wording which until then had been changeable.

[11] Propter triplicem pacem ter oramus in Missa: "dies nostros in tua pace disponas," "da propitius pacem in diebus nostris," "dona nobis pacem," ut de *pace temporis* per *pacem pectoris* transeamus ad *pacem aeternitatis* (Innocent. III, chap. 11).

[12] *Numerari* = *numero aggregari*, received into the number. Consider the following prayer for a departed soul: Omnipotens sempiterne Deus . . . propitiare animae famuli tui, ut qui de hac vita in tui nominis confessione decessit, Sanctorum tuorum numero facias adgregari (*Sacrament. Gelasian.*).

ruin, to which the godless are doomed, and that we may for all eternity be possessed of that glory and happiness which God has prepared for those who love Him.

2. During this prayer the priest extends his two hands horizontally over the chalice and the host in such a manner that the right thumb is placed over the left one in the form of a cross. This imposing, or extending, of hands first appears in some missals toward the close of the fifteenth century; [13] it was afterwards universally prescribed by Pius V. This ceremony not only harmonizes with the tenor of the text, *hanc oblationem*, indicating the sacrificial elements in a just and reverential manner, but in addition contains a mystical meaning. The ritual laying on of hands frequently occurs in both the Old and the New Testaments, as well as in the liturgy. According to its fundamental signification, it is always a symbol of the transferring of one thing to another; for example, in the Mosaic worship the laying on of hands was a symbolical representation of the transferring of sin and guilt to the animal that was to be sacrificed, which vicariously had to suffer death instead of man. Here in the Mass the laying on of hands has a similar object; for it shows that Christ offers Himself on the altar, in our place, for our sake, and on account of our sins, thus fixing deeply in our mind the sacrificial character of the Eucharist. Moreover, it indicates that we should unite ourselves with this sacrifice, offering ourselves along with it.

The Third Prayer of the Canon

Quam oblationem tu Deus in omnibus, quaesumus, bene✠dictam, adscrip✠tam, ra✠tam, rationabilem, acceptabilemque facere digneris: ut nobis Cor✠pus et San✠guis fiat dilectissimi Filii tui Domini nostri Jesu Christi.	Which oblation do Thou, O God, we beseech Thee, vouchsafe to make in all things blessed ✠, approved ✠, ratified ✠, reasonable, and acceptable: that it may become for us the body ✠ and blood ✠ of Thy most beloved Son, our Lord Jesus Christ.

[13] Formerly it was often the custom, as it is now with the Dominicans and Carmelites, to bow profoundly at the recitation of this prayer. Hic inclinat se usque ad altare dicens: *Hanc igitur* .... (Amalar., *Eclog.*, n. 29). Presbyter humiliationem Domini usque ad crucem nos indicat, cum se usque ad altare inclinat dicendo (Microl., chap. 16). *Hanc igitur oblationem* dicendo sacerdos

1. This prayer is closely connected with the preceding one and forms the immediate transition and introduction to the act of consecration. In general its meaning is clear, but the meaning of the several designations given to the offering is obscure and difficult to understand. Since the foregoing preparation for the act of consecration ends with this prayer, it expresses for the last time in a simple, grand way the already oft-repeated petition to God for the blessing, or the changing of the bread and wine into the body and the blood of Christ.[14] Therefore we implore God that the elements lying on the altar and dedicated to Him be changed into heavenly sacrificial gifts. The Eucharistic Saviour is the perfectly "blessed, approved, ratified, reasonable, and acceptable" oblation which, by the power of God, is to replace the substance of bread and wine.[15]

Christ is the *oblatio in omnibus benedicta*, that is, the offering blessed in every respect, thoroughly and perfectly. The blessing here meant and to be imparted to the material elements is the very highest and the most sublime conceivable: the consecration, the changing of the elements into the glorious body and the precious blood of our Lord Jesus Christ.[16] We therefore beg God to bless the oblation of bread and wine, that is, to consecrate it and thereby

---

in quibusdam ecclesiis profunde se inclinat (Durand, VI, xxxix, 2). Christian antiquity and the Middle Ages make no mention of the stretching out of the hands in this place.

[14] Haec tertia periodus, quam ingredimur, maxime occupatur circa sacrificium, ut fiat perfectum et in aliam mutetur substantiam immortalem et incorruptam. . . . Transit ad partes a toto, ut universalis benedictionis partes imprecetur hostiae, cui universam benedictionem fuerat imprecatus, ut cum prius posuerit *in omnibus benedictam*, particulariter subjungat *adscriptam*, et *ratam*, et *rationabilem*, et *acceptabilem*, quae sunt partes omnimodae benedictionis (B. Odo Camerac., *Expos. in Can. Missae*, dist. 3).

[15] Praeinducta sacratissima verba exponuntur de eo, quod est res et sacramentum, videlicet de corpore Christi vel de ipso Christo, qui est hostia benedicta, adscripta, rata, rationabilis et acceptabilis (Dion. Cathus., *Expos. Miss.*, a.23). Solum Christi corpus et sanguis est hostia in omnibus benedicta, adscripta, rata, rationabilis acceptabilisque (B. Odo Camerac., *loc. cit.*).

[16] Oratio haec potest exponi, ut tota petitio referatur ad ipsius materiae consecrationem, nihilque aliud in summa petatur, quam ut ex pane corpus et ex vino fiat sanguis Christi, ut hoc modo ac per talem transmutationem oblatio ipsa panis et vini fiat *benedicta*; illa enim est summa benedictio et sanctificatio, quae in illam materiam supervenire potest, unde ipsamet consecratio benedictio solet a Patribus appellari (Suarez, LXXXII, ii, 10). Digneris hanc oblationem facere *benedictam*, i.e. convertere in carnem et sanguinem Christi, quae sunt hostia benedicta, h. e. omni carens macula culpae atque omni gratia adornata (Dion. Cathus., *loc. cit.*).

make it for us an inexhaustible source of every grace and blessing.

Christ is the *oblatio adscripta*.[17] This extremely obscure word can only with difficulty, or perhaps not at all, be explained in a perfectly satisfactory manner, as is evident from the different attempts at interpretation. Frequently *adscripta* is defined in the sense of acceptable, agreeable; but opposed to this meaning is the circumstance that then *adscripta* would have entirely the same signification as the following *acceptabilis*, which in so concise a prayer is by no means probable. Others understand *adscripta* as meaning consecrated or belonging to God. We translate *adscripta* by the word approved and thereby give our preference for an explanation according to which this word seems to coincide better with the whole context. Accordingly the oblation becomes *adscripta* when it corresponds to the ordinance and institution of Christ at the Last Supper.[18] In this manner, therefore, the same petition would be presented that frequently occurs elsewhere in different liturgies: that the elements of bread and wine may become *eucharistia legitima*, that is, legitimate Eucharist.[19]

If the oblation is so constituted as to be conformable to Holy Scripture, to the will and command of Christ (*Hoc facite*), then necessarily it is also an "*oblatio rata*," [20] that is, a true or valid sacrifice; for with this presupposition all the features and elements are at hand requisite for the existence and essence of the Eucharistic sacrifice.

The contents of the above three words (*benedicta, adscripta, rata*) are now stated more correctly and emphatically: the sacri-

---

[17] *Adscribere* = to ascribe or to attribute; to institute, to determine, to establish.

[18] Potest referri hoc verbum [*adscripta*] ad ea, quae de hac consecratione scripta sunt, ita ut postuletur, ut haec oblatio talis fiat, qualis scripta est et promissa illis verbis Christi: "Hoc facite"; adscriptum enim dici potest, quod est scripto conforme (Suarez, *loc. cit.*).

[19] Cf. also the prayer in the Pontifical for the consecration of a portable altar: Quaesumus omnipotens Deus, . . . qui inter ceteras creaturarum formas lapideum metallum ad obsequium tui sacrificii condidisti, ut legitimae libationi praeparetur altare, annue dignanter.

[20] *Ratus* (from *reor*) = intended; transferred to = determined, valid, true, legal. Quod nostro geritur ministerio, ratum habeas, ac si sine nobis manibus tuis idem ageretur (Robert. Paulul., *De offic. eccles.*, II, chap. 31). Praeterea postulatur, ut per consecrationem fiat *rata*, i.e. vera; non enim est haec vera sacrificalis oblatio, nisi consecratio valida sit et efficax; quomodo dicere solemus, sacramentum esse ratum, quando vere factum (Suarez, *loc. cit.*).

fice is called a spiritual or "reasonable oblation" (*oblatio rationabilis*).[21] In the various liturgies the Eucharist is often designated as "a spiritual sacrifice" or as "a reasonable and unbloody worship of God." This expression is borrowed from Holy Scripture (Rom. 12:1); in its liturgical use it refers as well to the manner of offering as to the sacrificial gift, and characterizes it as endowed with life, spirit, and reason, in contrast with the Old Testament offerings of irrational animals and inanimate things.[22] The Eucharist is, therefore, a "reasonable oblation," because on the altar is sacrificed the living Lamb of God, the God-man Jesus Christ, He who is indeed the eternal reason, the uncreated and personal wisdom of God.

If the Eucharistic sacrifice has these four qualities, it is then infallibly and in the highest degree also pleasing to God, dear, precious, and acceptable to Him (*oblatio acceptabilis*).[23]

The explanation of the obscure antecedent clause follows in the concluding words, "that it may become for us the body and blood of . . . Christ" (*fiat = transeat in*), which denote and implore quite unequivocally the change of substance of the matter of sacrifice.[24] In this respect this prayer is a kind of Epiklesis, since it also contains a petition for the consecration; however, there is no invoca-

[21] *Rationabilis* = endowed with reason, reasonable; according to reason. The word has reference to the divine Logos, who in and with His human nature is in the highest degree a spiritual and reasonable sacrificial gift: Christ's sacrificial body and blood are on the altar, not merely animated with a spiritual and reasonable soul, but, moreover, hypostatically united to the divine Word (*Logos*). Munus populi tui, Domine, placatus intende, quo non altaribus tuis ignis alienus nec irrationabilium cruor effunditur animantium, sed sancti Spiritus operante virtute sacrificium jam nostrum corpus et sanguis est ipsius sacerdotis (*Sacrament. Leonian.*).

[22] Petitur etiam, ut fiat *rationabilis*, i.e. rationalis hostia, quia per illam consecrationem fit, ut jam non simplex panis et vinum, nec sanguis hircorum aut vitulorum, sed Christus ipse, qui non solum rationalis est, sed aeterna sapientia et ratio, offeratur (Suarez, *loc. cit.*).

[23] Denique per eandem mutationem fit maxime acceptabilis haec oblatio, quia jam, non ex dignitate offerentium, sed ex re ipsa oblata, gratissima Deo est et accepta: nam per illam mutationem panis fit corpus illud, quod Deus adaptavit, ut veteribus repudiatis sacrificiis, eo placari posset (Suarez, *loc. cit.*).

[24] Posuerat in omnibus benedictam, subjungit quattuor species: adscriptam, ratam, rationabilem, acceptabilem. Sed haec omnia clausa erant, minus intellegebantur, minus patebant; aperuit ostium, patefecit totum, scil. ut nobis fiat corpus et sanguis Christi. Hic totum completur, hic totum perficitur, ut fiat corpus et sanguis Christi (B. Odo Camerac., dist. 3). Munera, Domine, oblata sanctifica, ut tui nobis Unigeniti corpus et sanguis fiant (*Sacrament. Gregor.*).

tion of the Holy Ghost, so the *Quam oblationem* must be considered a substitute for the Epiklesis, which is found in the Eastern liturgies, but not a true Epiklesis. The little word *nobis* ("for us") [25] adds a new idea; for it proves that the body and blood of Christ take the place of the bread and wine for our sake, for our salvation and blessing and advantage.[26] For us the Saviour offers Himself on the altar, to us He gives Himself in Holy Communion. *Totus mihi datus [Dominus] et totus in meos usus expensus est.*[27]

2. The above prayer is accompanied with five signs of the cross, three of which are first made over both sacrificial elements at one and the same time (at the words *benedictam, adscriptam, ratam*); [28] then one sign of the cross is made over each of the elements (at the words *Corpus et Sanguis*). These holy signs strengthen and visibly elucidate the text of the prayer spoken vocally; they symbolically express what the accompanying words signify. The signs of the cross are here symbols and means of blessing; they call down the divine blessing of consecration upon the bread and wine that they may be changed: that the bread may be changed into the same sacrificial body which hung on the cross, and the wine into the same sacrificial blood which was shed on the cross. The first three signs of the cross

---

[25] Fiat *nobis*, i.e., ad nostram salutem, ad nostrum cotidianum profectum, atque ad vitiorum nostrorum expurgationem omniumque spiritualium donorum multiplicationem (Dion. Carth., *Expos. Miss.*, a. 23).

[26] Sub hac oblatione non solum panis et vinum, sed Ecclesia ipsa in his significata intelligitur. Hinc 1. sacerdos nomine Ecclesiae orat, ut panis et vinum convertantur in corpus et sanguinem Christi; qua transsubstantiatione oblatio fit *benedicta*, quia Christus est victima a Patre sanctificata et benedicta, *adscripta*, quia Christus est victima divinae majestati penitus devota et addicta, *rata*, quia ipse est victima a Patre tamquam perfecta adprobata, *rationabilis et acceptabilis*, quia ipse est aeterna ratio et Deo Patri infinite placens, ad differentiam victimarum irrationalium, per se Deo non placentium, quae in antiqua lege offerebantur. 2. Sacerdos orat, ut nos ipsi in omnibus simus *benedicti* gratiis divinis, *adscripti* numero electorum in libro vitae (Apoc. 13:8; 17:8), *rati*, firmi et stabiles in Dei servitio, *rationabiles*, corpus et passiones rationi, rationem Deo subdendo (Rom. 12:1), et *acceptabiles*, digni, ut in vitam aeternam acceptemur; *ut nobis corpus et sanguis fiat D. N. J. Ch.*, scil. ut consecratio et oblatio nobis fiat fructuosa (Müller, *Theol. moral.*, III, tit. 1, § 16).

[27] S. Bernard., *In circumcis. Dom. serm.*, III, n. 4.

[28] Haec tria verba dicendo, super duo oblata simul ter signum crucis facimus, quod in omnibus consecrationibus familiare est et domesticum. Per virtutem enim crucis Domini multa credimus operari. Ideo ter, qui per virtutem crucis pariter Trinitas operatur (Robert. Paulul., *De offic. eccles.*, II, chap. 31).

by themselves symbolize the adorable Trinity, from whom proceeds the blessing of consecration, who sanctify the material elements and change them into the Eucharistic sacrifice.[29]

We can also see in the five signs of the cross that immediately precede and immediately follow the Consecration a symbol of the five sacred wounds,[30] which were particularly prominent on the body of Christ, and which, consequently, are also in the most intimate relation with the redeeming passion and death of the Lord. Precisely at the moment in which the altar, by the presence of the divine victim, becomes a mystical Mount Calvary, the sublime and sacred scene of the passion of the Saviour, crucified and covered with painful wounds, should present itself before the eyes and mind of priest and people in the most striking manner. "Christ, pierced on the cross, wounded in five different places, come, let us adore!"

---

[29] Fiunt tres cruces super oblatam materiam, dum dicit "benedictam, adscriptam, ratam" ad honorem supersanctae et adorandae Trinitatis et ad insinuandum, quod effectus orationis istius a tota beatissima Trinitate nobis donetur. Nam ipsa hanc ineffabilem conversionem panis in corpus et vini in sanguinem Christi facit (Dion. Carthus., *loc. cit.*).

[30] Nonnulli quinque signa referunt ad quinque Christi vulnera (Robert. Paulul., *loc. cit.*).

CHAPTER XXXV

THE CONSECRATION

ENGAGED in devout meditation and contemplation we have come through the vestibule and the sanctuary of the mystically constructed liturgy of the Mass; we have entered into the holy of holies and now stand in the very presence of God. Breathless silence prevails all around;[1] the Consecration, to which all that preceded served as a preparation, is approaching. The moment of consecration[2] is the most important and solemn moment, the most sublime and holy and fruitful of the whole sacrificial celebration; for at that moment is accomplished that glorious and unfathomably profound work, the Eucharistic sacrifice, in which all the marvels of God's

---

[1] Ad elevationem ss. Sacramenti pulsatur organum graviori et dulciori sono (*Cer. episc.*, I, xxviii, 9).

[2] Acutius intuere, o homo, qui sacerdotio fungeris: qua utique reverentia et devotione, qua humilitate ac dilectione te Dominum tuum in ipsa sacra hostia suscipere et amplecti, tractare contemplarique oporteat. Ipse equidem est, ante cujus te tribunal mox necesse est adstare, qui judicaturus est vivos et mortuos et saeculum per ignem. In manu illius universa tua salus sita est, eum Cherubim Seraphimque adorant, Throni ei sedes sunt. Sed jam, o metuende Dei Fili, o adorande Christe, o virtus et sapientia Patris, fac me in te sapientem et fortem, stabiliterque conversum: praesertim autem tunc me, o beate Salvator, tunc cor meum munias mentemque in te afficias, erigas atque convertas, dum ipsa tua divina sacerrimaque mysteria celebro, sacramenta contingo ac dilectionis tuae pignus passionisque memoriale accipio: tunc, o omnipotens Dominator, prae majestatis tuae contemplatione reverentiali timore concutiar, caritatis tuae contuitu inexstinguibiliter accendar totusque in te resolvar et configar: tunc te, Deus meus, splendida fide templer, tunc te sapiam affectuosissimeque complectar; anima mea tua ex praesentia excitetur ac liquefiat. Utinam te, Deus meus, amator auctorque salutis meae, qui te mihi tam multipliciter praestitisti: qui ex ipso tuae benignissimae mentis ardore sic nobis ubilibet conjungi dignaris, anima mea semper coram se et item se coram te constituat; utinam tibi grata, utinam in te sic custodita consistat, ut ad tui participationem celebrationemque tuorum mysteriorum magis incessanter idonea, purior ardentiorque reddatur (Dion. Carthus., *De munificentia et beneficiis Dei*, a. 25).

love are concentrated as in a focus of heat and light. The change of the bread and wine into Christ's body and blood can proceed only from Him who "alone effects what is wonderful": it is an act of creative omnipotence. But for this act of almighty power there is required a human act, human cooperation on the part of an ordained priest.

At his ordination the priest received the supernatural power to effect, by pronouncing the words, "This is My body, . . . This is My blood," Eucharistic consecration; that is, these words, recited by the priest with the proper intention, change the prepared elements of bread and wine into the body and blood of Christ. At the Last Supper, Christ was the sole priest offering sacrifice; at the altar He is the principal sacrificer. Whereas in the Cenaculum He offered Himself without the assistance of others,[3] He now offers Himself on the altar by the hands and mouth of the visible priest. The priest is His organ and minister. "The priest acts as the representative of Christ when he pronounces those words; but it is the power and grace of God. 'This is My body,' he says. These words transform the gifts placed before him."[4] These words clearly manifest the manner in which the priest performs the act of consecration; all he does indicates plainly that he takes the place of Christ, speaks and acts in the person of Christ in accomplishing the Eucharistic sacrifice. That this may be manifest, he is directed by the Church to imitate as faithfully as possible by word and deed Christ's model act of consecration. The Church's liturgical act of consecration is nothing else than the repetition and re-enactment of the first celebration of the Lord's Supper in the Cenaculum at Jerusalem. The priest narrates the first offering and institution of the unbloody sacrifice by Jesus Christ, and while relating this, he performs the corresponding actions: he imitates the Lord as far as possible, and does the same

---

[3] When we impartially read the biblical accounts regarding the first celebration and the institution of the Eucharist, we cannot but marvel that already in ancient times and again quite recently it could be asserted that our divine Saviour did not change the bread and wine by the words of the institution ("This is My body; This is My blood"), but that He had by the preceding benediction, or merely by an interior act of the will, changed them into His body and blood. The only well-grounded and tenable thesis in the Bible and in tradition is that the Lord performed the first Eucharistic consecration *ritu sacramentali* by the words of the institution, and thus by His example left the norm for all succeeding consecrations.

[4] S. Chrysost., *De prodit. Judae hom.*, I, n. 6.

as Christ did. He pronounces over the bread and wine the effective words of consecration in the person of Christ (*quasi ex persona ipsius Christi loquentis*) [5] with the intention of changing the gifts at present lying on the altar and thereby of offering up in sacrifice the body and blood of Christ.[6] Plain and simple are the words of the liturgical text, as is best suited for a thing that is ineffably sublime and divine.

1. The Consecration of the host.

Qui pridie quam pateretur accepit panem in sanctas ac venerabiles manus suas, et elevatis oculis in coelum ad te Deum Patrem suum omnipotentem, tibi gratias agens, bene✠dixit, fregit, deditque discipulis suis, dicens: Accipite, et manducate ex hoc omnes:

Hoc est enim Corpus meum.

Who, the day before He suffered, took bread into His holy and venerable hands, and with eyes lifted up toward heaven, unto Thee, O God, His almighty Father, giving thanks to Thee, did bless, ✠ break, and give to His disciples, saying: Take and eat ye all of this:

For this is My body.

Three evangelists (Matt. 26:26-28; Mark 14:22-24; Luke 22:19 f.) and the Apostle of the Gentiles, Paul (I Cor. 11:23-26), have informed us of the act of consecration. These four holy authors, though not in perfect accord as to the very words, yet agree perfectly as to the matter itself: all relate what the Saviour did at that

---

[5] Verba consecrationis dicuntur et recitative et formaliter seu significative. Sacerdos enim et commemorat, quae verba Christus in ultima coena dixerit et, intendens ea applicare materiae praesenti, ac facere, quod significant, simul exercet actum suae potestatis. Atque hinc est, quod propriissime dicatur conficere in persona Christi, quia non tantum utitur potestate a Christo accepta, sed eam exercet ejus personam repraesentans, et loquens ejus verbis, quasi esset ipsemet Christus (Sylvius, III, q.78, a.1, q.3).

[6] Hoc sacramentum directe repraesentativum est dominicae passionis, qua Christus ut sacerdos et hostia Deo se obtulit in ara crucis. Hostia autem quam sacerdos offert, est una cum illa quam Christus obtulit secundum rem, quia Christum realiter continet; minister autem offerens non est idem realiter, unde oportet, quod sit idem repraesentatione, et ideo sacedos consecrans prout gerit personam Christi, profert verba consecrationis recitative ex persona Christi, ne hostia alia videatur. Et quia per ea quae gerit respectu exterioris materiae, Christi personam repraesentat, ideo verba illa simul et recitative et significative tenentur respectu praesentis materiae, quae est figura illius, quam Christus praesentem habuit, et propter hoc dicitur convenientius: "hoc est corpus meum," quam: "hoc est corpus Christi" (S. Thom., IV, dist.8, q.2, a.1, sol.4 ad 4).

THE CONSECRATION

solemn moment and what priests were to do in His name and in commemoration of Him unto the end of the world. Not one of them has omitted anything essentially necessary for the accomplishment of the consecration and of the sacrifice; but with regard to accessories, the statements of the evangelists are not equally complete. Let us compare the liturgical formula at the consecration of the host and of the chalice with the biblical text, and we shall find that the Canon contains several words (*in sanctas ac venerabiles manus suas, et elevatis oculis in coelum ad te Deum Patrem suum omnipotentem . . . aeterni testamenti . . . mysterium fidei*) that are wanting in Holy Scripture. These additions of the liturgy have emanated from a divine and apostolic tradition and are, therefore, as incontestably true and certain as are the words of the inspired authors.[7]

Qui pridie quam pateretur.[8] How touching and solemnly impressive is that scene which these words recall to our mind! The Lord chose the eve of His bitter passion and death, the night on which He was betrayed (I Cor. 11:23), to give us by the institution of the Eucharist the most wonderful proof of His love.[9] With desire He had longed for this hour. Before shedding His blood in torrents on the painful way of the cross, He would pour out for us ungrateful creatures the abundance of His grace, all the treasures of His love in the sacrament of the altar, that we might never forget what He has done and suffered for us.[10]

---

[7] Quod additur "aeterni" et iterum "mysterium fidei," ex traditione Domini habetur (S. Thom., IIIa, q.78, a.3 ad 9).

[8] On Holy Thursday the insertion is here made: Qui pridie, quam pro nostra omniumque salute pateretur, hoc est, hodie.

[9] Venit Jesus ministrare Apostolis et praecipue hodie dilexit. Sciens enim quia transiret de mundo ad Patrem et quod ituri essent post eum . . . recedens ab eis et iter sequendi (sc. humilitatem in ablutione pedum) ostendit eis et cibum quo vescerentur in itinere, reliquit, i.e. viam dedit et viaticum. Sub forma enim panis et vini corpus suum et sanguinem ad edendum dedit et conficiendum reliquit. . . . Christus in cruce fuit pretium, in deserto est viaticum, in coelo erit praemium. Hic est cibus grandium, qui munit contra adversa et confert bona, servat collata (Hildeb. Turon., *Serm.*, XXXIX).

[10] Christo non suffecit semel pro nobis immolari in cruce per mortis perpessionem, sed hanc quotidianam et perennem sui immolationem in mysterio (sc. in Missae officio) ejus infinita sapientia adinvenit, ejus immensa clementia ordinavit, ejus caritas summa praefixit, qua et Dei Patris honorem generisque humani procuravit opem, gratiam ac salutem, quod totum sic fieri decentissimum exstitisse ratio dictat desuper illustrata: quae quanto plus illustratur, tanto limpidius intuetur, quam rationabile seu potius superrationabile, miseri-

"He took bread into His holy and venerable hands": saying these words, the priest also takes the host into his hands. Holy and sanctifying, venerable and adorable beyond all expression are the hands of Christ. How often has He raised them in prayer to His Father, and extended them over men to bless them! How these hands were transpierced on the cross with the most intolerable heat of pain! How are thy hands constituted, O priest of the Lord? They are indeed holy and venerable by the consecration thou hast received; but are they also holy and venerable by the abundance of virtuous actions, by the odor of a devout life, and by exemplary conduct? With holy oil [11] were thy hands anointed and consecrated to the service of God and the salvation of souls; day and night shouldst thou elevate them to heaven, to praise thy Lord, to call down upon men His mercies and blessings. Are thy hands innocent and pure? Are they worthy to touch, to offer, and to distribute to others the immaculate Lamb of God?

"And with His eyes lifted up toward heaven, unto Thee, O God, His almighty Father, giving thanks to Thee, did bless" the bread. While the priest pronounces these words, he performs the corresponding ceremonies, so as to imitate as far as possible what the Saviour did at the institution of the Eucharist. For a moment the priest looks up at the crucifix on the altar, and then bows his head, thereby to signify and to express Christ's thanksgiving; he makes over the host the sign of the cross, thus appropriately to represent the blessing of the Saviour, since we do not know after what manner it was imparted.[12]

Christ's looking up to His almighty Father, as also the giving of thanks and the blessing of the bread, not only indicates the great-

---

cordissimum, sapientissimum, amorosissimum fuerit istud, ut et quotidie dominicae passionis quasi recenter memores simus, caritatisque Dei ac pietatis suae et liberalitatis ad nos assidue recordemur recordandoque inflammemur et meritum Christi abundantius participemus, consequendo effectus sacramenti istius (Dion. Carthus., *De sacram. altar. serm.*, II).

[11] Unctio sancta in manibus sacerdotum infunditur, ut S. Spiritus, qui per oleum designatur, in operibus consecrationis eorum descendat (Hildeb. Turon., *Serm.*, CXXXII). Manus sacratae et sacrantes tremenda mysteria (S. Bernard., *Tract. de mor. et offic. episcop.*, chap. 2, n. 4).

[12] When it is said that the Saviour blessed the little ones or the bread and the chalice, we may conceive that the Lord Himself preceded His Church in using the sign of the cross for liturgical purposes (Oswald, *Eschatologie* [ed. 2], p. 238).

ness and sublimity of the mystery He was about to accomplish, but served at the same time as a fitting preparation for the consecration. Not Holy Scripture, but tradition, informs us that the Saviour looked up to heaven, as He had done in the desert when He miraculously multiplied a few loaves. Thanksgiving and blessing [13] are here to be distinguished from the consecration, as well as from each other, even though they may have been performed by Christ with the same prayer. For thanksgiving refers to God, the author of all good; but the blessing, to the gifts to be changed. This thanksgiving and this blessing were not the ones customary at the paschal supper, but were far more significant.

Christ did indeed adhere to the Old Testament paschal rite as to the selection of time for the institution and the matter of the Eucharist, as also to its breaking and distribution and the thanksgiving and blessing, but He gave to this thanksgiving a more sublime meaning and to the blessing a more exalted end, inasmuch as He thanked His heavenly Father for the benefits bestowed on His holy humanity and on the entire human race in general, and in particular for the great grace of the holy Sacrament, decreed from eternity and now about to be instituted by Him. By blessing bread and wine, He prepared both for the sacramental consecration at hand; as Man and high priest He prayed for this wonderful consecration which He as God, together with the Father and the Holy Ghost, was about to perform.[14]

"He broke and gave to His disciples, saying: Take and eat ye all of this." The Church in the celebration of the sacrifice follows her divine Lord and Master step by step; however, the breaking of the sacramental species and the distribution of the Eucharistic bread cannot take place until after the Consecration, while the majestic thanksgiving prayer of the Preface and the manifold blessing of the sacrificial matter have already an appropriate place before the Consecration. The priest, in the midst of a solemn silence that shuts out from him all the noise of the world, humbly bowing down at the altar, pronounces "in the person of Christ," with the deepest atten-

[13] Haec benedictio fuit bona super panem precatio, et divinae beneficentiae super illum invocatio, qua Christus elevatis oculis in coelum petebat ejus sanctificationem et transmutationem mox futuram; unde, quamvis Evangelistae nunc benedictionem, nunc gratiarum actionem nominent, quia Christus eas conjunxit, diversae tamen sunt, et inter se et a consecratione. Benedictio enim ad symbola refertur, gratiarum actio autem ad Deum (Sylvius, III, q. 78, art. 1, quaer. 2).

[14] Franz, *Die Eucharistische Wandlung*, I, 37.

tion, devotion, and reverence, the mighty words: [15] *Hoc est enim Corpus meum* ("For this is My body"). With reverential awe at the power given him, the priest pronounces these divine words, which bear along with them the power of changing the substance of the bread. And now there is no longer bread on the altar, but under the appearances that remain of bread, Christ's body is truly present. In a moment the power of God has wrought a series of miracles, more magnificent and glorious than all the wonders of creation. The tiny host now contains in itself infinitely more treasures, riches, and glory than are to be found on the vast expanse of the globe.[16] By virtue of the words of consecration, Christ's body becomes present, veiled under the appearance of bread. Here indeed is His glorified

---

[15] Haec verba cum summa attentione, reverentia et veneratione integre distincteque sunt proferenda, quoniam illa sacerdos quasi ore Christi (ut ita dixerim) eloquitur et illa loquens Christi fungitur officio. Quocirca in illis recte et decenter enuntiandis summa adhibenda est cura et animadversio (Clichtov., III, n. 29). The *enim* (= for, namely), elucidating and consolidating the preceding invitation (*accipite et manducate*), is found only in St. Matthew in the formula of the consecration of the chalice, but it was appropriately placed also in the formula of the consecration of the bread. Ipse summus ac generalis vicarius Christi, beatissimus Petrus, ex familiari et secreto Spiritus sancti instinctu addidit verbum "enim" et hoc ex rationabili causa ad designandam continuationem et ordinem ad praecedentia verba et gesta (Dion. Carthus., *De sacram. altar.*, a. 32).

[16] Credere firmiter debes et nullatenus dubitare, secundum quod docet et praedicat catholica fides, quod in hora expressionis verborum Christi panis materialis atque visibilis advenienti vivifico et coelesti pani, velut vero Creatori honorem deferens, locum suum, scil. visibilem speciem accidentium, pro ministerio et sacramentali servitio relinquit, quo desinente esse, miro et ineffabili modo in eodem instanti ista sub illis accidentibus veraciter exsistunt: *primo*, illa purissima Christi caro et sacrum corpus, quod fabricante Spiritu Sancto, tractum fuit de utero gloriosae Virginis Mariae, appensum in cruce, positum in sepulcro, glorificatum in coelo. *Secundo*, quia caro non vivit sine sanguine, ideo necessario est ibi sanguis ille pretiosus, qui feliciter manavit pro mundi salute in cruce. *Tertio*, cum non sit verus homo absque anima rationali, propterea est ibi illa anima gloriosa Christi, excedens in gratia et gloria omnem virtutem et gloriam et potestatem, in qua repositi sunt omnes thesauri divinae sapientiae (Col. 2:3). *Quarto*, quia Christus est verus homo et verus Deus, ibi consequenter est Deus in sua majestate gloriosus. Haec omnia quattuor simul et singula, tota simul sub speciebus panis et vini perfecte continentur, non minus in calice quam in hostia nec minus in hostia quam in calice, nec in uno suppletur defectus alterius, sed in ambobus invenitur integrum propter mysterium, de quo est grandis sermo (Heb. 5:11). Sufficit credere, Deum verum et hominem sub utraque contineri specie, cui assistunt Angelorum frequentia et Sanctorum praesentia (S. Bonav., *Tr. de praepar. ad Miss.*, chap. 1, §3, n. 1).

body, which shines in the glory of heaven: a body immortal, impassible, with the precious blood flowing through it, vivified by the most holy soul, united to the eternal Godhead; therefore in the host Christ is present, whole and entire, with His divinity and humanity. The same God-man who lives and reigns in heaven in inconceivable majesty and beauty, is now mysteriously present in our very midst under foreign, sacramental appearances. The gates of heaven open and in the company of invisible choirs of angels the King of heaven descends upon the altar. The earth becomes a paradise; the priest holds his Creator, Redeemer, and Judge in his hands. What then is more natural than that we should fall down on our knees before Him in holy fear and rapturous joy? [17]

The bread has been changed into the sacrificial body of Christ; the wine has now still to become the sacrificial blood of Christ.

2. The Consecration of the chalice.

Simili modo postquam coenatum est, accipiens et hunc praeclarum Calicem in sanctas ac venerabiles manus suas: item tibi gratias agens bene✛dixit, deditque discipulis suis dicens: Accipite et bibite ex eo omnes:	In like manner, after He had supped, taking also this excellent chalice into His holy and venerable hands, and giving thanks to Thee, He blessed ✛ and gave to His disciples, saying: Take, and drink ye all of it:
Hic est enim Calix Sanguinis Mei, novi et aeterni testamenti: mysterium fidei: qui pro vobis et pro multis effundetur in remissionem peccatorum.	**For this is the chalice of My blood, of the new and eternal testament: the mystery of faith: which shall be shed for you and for many for the remission of sins.**
Haec quotiescumque feceritis, in mei memoriam facietis.	As often as you do these things, you shall do them in remembrance of Me.

---

[17] Quando sacerdos sacram Hostiam manu tenens genua flectit, Dominum hunc adorare debet adeo profunda reverentia, ut cor suum usque ad ipsam abyssum humiliet, quasi desiderans in terrae profundum descendere ob tantae majestatis reverentiam. Et memor, quod Angeli descendant e coelo, et huic Domino in sacrificio adsint, cogitare debet, in eo momento se circumdari Angelorum exercitu, et simul cum illis adorare et laudare communem omnium Dominum et Creatorem. Et quando ipsam Hostiam sacram sursum elevat, id faciet, nunc cum sensu doloris et lacrymis, memor, Dominum eundem propter ipsius peccata fuisse in cruce elevatum et ab omnibus contemptum;

"In like manner, after He had supped, taking also this excellent chalice into His holy and venerable hands." At these words the priest takes up the chalice in his hands and slightly elevates it, following the example of Christ. After the Old Testament paschal supper was over, the Lord consecrated the bread, and immediately afterward followed the consecration of the chalice. The Saviour took into His hands "this excellent chalice": [18] evidently not the very chalice of the celebrant, but a chalice of like contents and of similar destination as the chalice which is before the eyes of the priest and which he holds in his hands. The identity existing between the chalice used at the Last Supper and the chalice on the altar, therefore, principally refers to the sacrificial matter therein contained, which is and must be everywhere essentially the same. This identity is perfect only after the Consecration; then there is present in the chalice on the altar the very same blood that was present in the chalice at the Last Supper. "This is the chalice of My blood," said the Redeemer in the supper room; in the person of Christ the priest repeats these same words at the altar.

The Saviour also blessed the chalice with thanksgiving, as He had previously blessed the bread. He then pronounced over the blessed wine those holy words which the priest now in His stead pronounces over the chalice to change the material element into the divine blood of Christ: *Hic est enim Calix Sanguinis mei* ("For this is the chalice of My blood"); that is, this is My blood which is contained in the chalice. The expression, "chalice of My blood," indi-

---

nunc idem faciet affectu quodam gaudii et gratitudinis, quod ipsam Hostiam elevet, ut honos ipsi Domino deferatur, et ab omnibus adoretur, quasi in compensationem praeteritorum contemptuum. Alias potest etiam in memoriam revocare, quod idem Dominus dixit: "Ego si exaltatus fuero a terra, omnia traham ad meipsum" (Joan. 12:32), et eundem Dominum orabit, ut dignetur ipsius cor ad coelum elevare, ubi ipse ad dextram Patris sedet (De Ponte, *De christ. hom. perfect.*, IV, tr. II, chap. 12. § 3).

[18] *Hunc* autem calicem dicens sacerdos, qui celebrat, non eum demonstrat calicem secundum numerum, quem manibus tenet, . . . sed ad intellectum demonstrat similem secundum speciem, non quidem secundum speciem substantiae aut figurae, . . . sed similem quantum ad usum et liquoris continentiam. Sicut enim in hoc calice, quo sacerdos consecrationem vini perficit, continetur vinum aqua mixtum, ita et in eo calice, quem Christus accepit, continebatur vinum aquae permixtum, ut uno animo sentiunt omnes. Quare nomine calicis non intellegendum est hic solum vas potorium, sed id ipsum cum vino contento in eo (Clichtov., *Elucid. eccl.*, III, n. 30). *Idem* calix est in mysterio, quem Christus in manibus tenuit, quamvis in materia metalli alius sit (Honor. Augustod., *Gemm. anim.*, I, chap. 106).

cates that Christ's blood becomes truly present on the altar, the heavenly drink of the soul. According to the common opinion, these words alone constitute the essential formula for the consecration of the chalice; for they signify and effect the presence of the blood of Christ under the appearances of wine.[19] The remaining words: the blood "of the new and eternal testament, the mystery of faith, which [blood] shall be shed for you and for many unto the remission of sins," are appropriately added. It is generally accepted that they were once spoken by the Lord Himself; moreover, they explain the dignity and effects of this sacrifice.[20]

In the chalice is the blood of the "new and eternal testament." At the foot of Sinai the Old Covenant, whose promises were only earthly and which was to continue but for a time, was concluded with the blood of animals. But by Christ's sacrificial blood, which is in the chalice, the New Covenant of grace was established and sealed, one that is to be eternal: first, because the gifts and blessings appertaining to it are heavenly and imperishable; secondly, because the new covenant will ever remain in force and its validity will endure to the consummation of the world. The Eucharistic blood of the Lord is at the same time the most precious treasure of this new and eternal covenant of grace.

The concluding words, "which shall be shed for you and for

[19] Haec forma: *Hic est calix sanguinis mei*, est forma certa, forma congrua; sed utrum sit tota, an quod sequitur sit de integritate (*essential*), dubium est; creditur tamen, quod est tota. Tamen quod sequitur non est frustra additum, nec debet aliquid resecari. Quod autem ista sit forma certa, patet per hoc, quod ipsam tenet Romana Ecclesia, quae fuit ab Apostolorum principibus edocta. . . . Est etiam congrua, quia in hoc sacramento significatur sanguis Christi ut effusus in pretium et ut administratus in potum; sanguis autem neutrum dicit de se expresse, sed per conjunctionem cum *calice*, quia sanguis in calice ut effusus et potandus proponitur. Ideo calix in Scriptura significat aliquando passionem (Matt. 20:22); significat et potus refectionem (Ps. 22:5). Propter hunc duplicem tropum melius dicitur calix sanguinis quam sanguis per se. . . . Est etiam tota et perfecta; sufficiens enim est ad significandum transsubstantiationem vini in sanguinem Christi. Unde quod additur est de bene esse, quia in sequentibus describuntur effectus sanguinis in hoc sacramento significati et in passione effusi (S. Bonav., IV, dist. 8, p. 2, a. 1, q. 2).

[20] Dicendum est, omnia illa verba esse prolata a Christo. Haec est communis sententia et mihi certa (Suarez, disp. LX, sect. 3, n. 2). Licet haec verba non spectent ad essentiam formae, tamen pertinent ad ejus integritatem, estque hic sensus communis totius Ecclesiae Latinae, quae in Missa et forma consecrationis calicis ea quasi a Christo dicta et ab Apostolis praecepta, eodem tenore ac modo quo cetera, scribit et pronuntiat (Corn. a Lap., *In Matt.*, 26:28).

many for the remission of sins," [21] characterize the sacrificial blood of Christ as the very source of atonement, pouring forth its floods of grace for the remission of sin for all mankind. The exclamatory phrase in the middle, *mysterium fidei* ("the mystery of faith"), indicates the unsearchable depth of the Eucharistic sacrifice. That the God-man did shed His blood for us on the cross, and that He again sheds it for us in a mystical manner on the altar, is a divine achievement which includes in itself the sum of the most unheard-of wonders, all of which can be acknowledged and believed as true only in the light and power of faith. Christ's sacrificial blood in the chalice is a mystery of faith in the fullest sense of the term.[22]

After the priest has pronounced the words of consecration, he again genuflects to venerate the infinitely precious and adorable blood of Christ in the chalice. At the same time [23] he pronounces the words: "As often as you do these things, you shall do them in remembrance of Me." With these words the Saviour instituted the Christian priesthood and the perpetual sacrifice of the New Law as a commemorative celebration of His redeeming passion and death.[24]

[21] Qui pro vobis, sumentibus scilicet, et pro multis = aliis. Illi multi vel intelleguntur omnes electi vel omnes omnino; nam pro omnibus sufficienter effusus est sanguis Christi, pro electis vero etiam efficaciter (Sylvius, III, q. 78, art. 3).

[22] Per prima verba cum dicitur: "Hic est calix sanguinis mei," significatur ipsa conversio vini in sanguinem; per verba autem sequentia designatur virtus sanguinis effusi in passione, quae operatur in hoc sacramento, quae quidem ad tria ordinatur: Primo quidem et principaliter ad adipiscendam aeternam hereditatem (Heb. 10:19), et ad hoc designandum dicitur: "novi et aeterni testamenti." Secundo ad justitiam gratiae quae est per fidem (Rom. 3:23), et quantum ad hoc subditur: "mysterium fidei." Tertio autem ad removendum impedimenta utriusque praedictorum, sc. peccatum (Heb. 9:14), et quantum ad hoc subditur: "qui pro vobis et pro multis effundetur in remissionem peccatorum" (S. Thom., IIIa, q. 78, a. 3).

[23] In the Middle Ages they were frequently said only *post elevationem calicis*. Deponendo calicem dicat haec verba: *Haec quotiescumque etc.* (*Ordo Rom. XIV*, chap. 53).

[24] Verba praetacta, videlicet *Haec quotiescumque* . . . , ut ait Bernardus, omni affectu plenissima sunt, et fidelem ac vere christianum animum vehementer inflammant, suntque a sacerdote celebrante cum ingenti devotione ac mentis sapore promenda, et proh dolor! miserabilem sacerdotem, qui haec verba sine memoria ineffabilis atque eximiae dilectionis atque acerbissimae mortis Christi pronuntiat atque sine cordiali affectu effundit: imo veraciter haec verba non solum tempore celebrationis, sed frequentissime nobis sunt cogitanda, revolvenda et amplectenda. His quippe verbis jubemur a Christo, non sine actuali devotione celebrare, sed cum diligenti divinorum beneficiorum recordatione (Dion. Carth., *Expos. Miss.*, a. 29).

THE CONSECRATION

By the separate consecration of the host and of the chalice, Christ's body and blood are rendered present under the appearances of bread and wine. The twofold consecration is a mystical shedding of blood and places before our eyes in a most lively manner the bloody death of Christ on the cross.[25] The sacrifice on the altar is, indeed, painless; for the Saviour is no longer passible and can no longer suffer death. But His divinely human heart is here inflamed with the same love of sacrifice and is moved by the same obedience to His Father as when He was on the cross. This love and this obedience urged Him to sacrifice Himself mystically on the altar under the twofold sacramental appearances. It is at the moment of consecration that the sacrifice is accomplished, offered to God, and placed in the hands of us poor mortals. This entire act of consecration is performed so quietly and so mysteriously, that no one perceives anything of the wonderful transformation wrought by the priest's words in the host and in the chalice. The priest pronounces a few inaudible words, and the essence of the bread and wine has disappeared: their place is taken by Christ's body and blood, the whole Christ, the victim of Golgotha. For the senses alone nothing has happened, nothing is changed; for the appearances of bread and wine, upheld by the power of God, have remained to serve as veil and covering for the bright majesty of the King of Glory, who with us and for us is present as victim on the altar.[26] To fathom the height and the depth of the Eucharistic consecration is beyond even the wisdom of the cherubim; worthily to praise the miracles of mercy contained in this same Eucharistic consecration, even the love of the seraphim of heaven is wholly insufficient. Truly, no moment commands greater reverence, no moment is more holy or more beneficial than that in which the Eucharistic sacrifice is accom-

---

[25] Sanguis seorsum consecratus a corpore expressius repraesentat passionem Christi, et ideo potius in consecratione sanguinis fit mentio de passione Christi et fructu ipsius, quam in consecratione corporis (S. Thom., *loc. cit.*, ad 7).

[26] There He is, indeed; He is present; the word has had its effect; there Jesus is as truly present as He was when on the cross, where He appeared for us by the sacrifice of Himself (Heb. 9:26); as truly present as He is in heaven, where He again appears for us before the face of God (Heb. 9:24). This consecration, this holy ceremony, this worship full of blood, and yet unbloody, where death is everywhere, and where, nevertheless, the victim is alive, is the true worship of Christians; falling under the senses and spiritual, simple and august, humble and magnificent at the same time (Bossuet, *Médit. sur l'Évang.*, I, 63e jour).

plished and the altar becomes a mystical Mount Calvary surrounded by adoring angels.[27]

3. The Consecration, especially in the more or less solemn rite of the elevation and adoration of Christ's body and blood, appears as the sublime center and pinnacle of the whole Mass.[28] Immediately

[27] Saint Hildegard, that great seer of the twelfth century, writes (*Scivias*, II, 6): "I saw also, when the priest, robed in the sacred vestments, advanced to the altar to celebrate the divine mysteries, that suddenly a great radiance and a retinue of angels came down from heaven, encircling the entire altar, and remaining there until the mystery was accomplished and the priest had retired from the altar. But when the Gospel of peace had been read, and the sacrificial gifts, which were to be consecrated, had been placed on the altar, and the priest sang the praise of almighty God, which is as follows: 'Holy, holy, holy is the Lord, God of Sabaoth,' and thus began the unspeakable mysteries: then descended suddenly a fiery lightning of indescribable brilliancy from the open heavens down upon the sacrificial gift, flooding it entirely with its brightness, as the light of the sun lights up every thing which it penetrates with its rays. And while the fiery lightning illumined in this manner the oblations, it carried them in an invisible way upward into the privacy of heaven, and brought them down again upon the altar; as a man draws his breath inwardly and then exhales it outwardly, thus did that sacrificial gift, after it had become the true body and the true blood of Christ, although to the eyes of men they appeared as bread and wine. And as I saw that, there appeared at the same time the signs of the birth, passion, and burial, as well as the resurrection and ascension of our Saviour, the incarnate God, as in a mirror, as they took place in the Son of God when upon earth," that is, Christ becomes present on the earthly altar as high priest, together with the whole work of redemption. (Cf. Schmelzeis, *Das Leben und Wirken der hl. Hildegardis*, pp. 371 ff.)

[28] The adoration of the Eucharistic body and blood of Christ during the sacrificial celebration was always customary in the Church (cf. Muratori, *Dissertat. de reb. liturg.*, chap. 19). Carnem Christi in mysteriis adoramus (S. Ambr., *De Spir. sancto*, III, xi, 79; cf. S. Aug., *Enarr. in Ps.*, 98:9). This adoration in the course of time differed ritually. According to the Roman *Ordines* and the writers of the Middle Ages, up to the twelfth century mainly the bowing (*inclinatio*) of the head, or of the body, was prescribed as the expression of adoration. Inclinato capite pontifex vel diaconus salutat Sancta (*Ordo Rom. I*, n.8). Pontifex inclinato capite ad altare primo adorat Sancta (*Ordo Rom. II*, n. 4). During the entire Canon the clerics maintained an adoring posture: *inclinati* (*Ordo Rom. I*, n. 16; *II*, n. 10; *III*, n. 15). Acclines manent orationi intenti (*Consuet. Cluniac.*, II, chap. 30). Post finitum hymnum: Sanctus . . . inclinant se circumstantes, venerando divinam majestatem cum angelis et Domini incarnationem cum turba et inclinati perseverant, usque dum finiatur omnis praesens Oratio (*the Canon*) (Hildeb. Turon., *De expos. Missae*). Not until the end of the Canon were the host and chalice elevated by the priest and the deacon and shown to the people for adoration. Cum dicimus: "Per omnia saecula saeculorum," corpus cum calice levamus et statim in altari deposita cooperimus (Microl., chap. 17). The heresy of Berengarius

after pronouncing the words of consecration, the priest in all reverence elevates the host and then the chalice in order to hold up to the view of the assembled congregation the divine sacrificial victim for their adoration, while he himself keeps his eyes riveted on the body and blood of Christ. The principal object of the elevation is adoration; as the celebrant genuflects before and after the elevation, adoring with faith and humility, thus also all who assist at the Mass should be moved at the sight of the Blessed Sacrament to render to the God and Saviour therein concealed due adoration through their humble and reverent deportment, as well as by the interior oblation of themselves to Him. After the birth of Christ, heaven and earth sent adorers to the crib at Bethlehem; after the consecration heavenly adorers again surround the Eucharistic Saviour on the

---

(d. 1088) may have been the external occasion for the introduction of the rite of the elevation immediately after the consecration. It first appeared after the twelfth century in France; in the thirteenth century the practice was widespread, because it was well calculated publicly and solemnly to confess the faith in transubstantiation and in the real presence of Christ in the Blessed Sacrament. In many churches for a long time the host alone was raised; in others the chalice was also elevated (in some places veiled with the pall, in others uncovered). The *Ceremoniale Roman.* (*Ordo Rom. XIII*) published under Gregory X (d. 1276) has the rubric: In elevatione corporis Christi . . . prosternant se ad terram et adorent reverenter in facies cadendo et sic prostrati stent usque ad "per omnia . . ." ante "Agnus Dei" (n. 19). The *Ordo Romanus XIV* (chap. 53) describes the rite more accurately. After the priest has said the words of consecration over the bread: ipse primo adoret inclinato capite sacrum divinum corpus; deinde reverenter et attente ipsum elevet in altum adorandum a populo . . . inclinato paululum capite adoret sacrum Domini sanguinem et elevet adorandum a populo . . . nec oportet, quod vel corpus vel sanguinem diu teneat elevatum, sed post brevem moram deponat, ita tamen quod elevationes et depositiones faciat cum debita reverentia et maturitate. Accordingly, in the fourteenth century the celebrant did not genuflect at or after the consecration.

With the elevation, the practice of ringing a small bell for those present and the large bell for those absent was also introduced. In elevatione utriusque [sc. hostiae et calicis] squilla pulsatur (Durand., IV, lxi, 53). Ivo of Chartres says that we ring the bell: quando illa singularis hostia pro nobis redimendis in ara crucis oblata per novi sacerdotii ministros in Domini mensa quotidie consecratur (*Epist.*, 142). Campanula in Missis pulsanda est etiam in Oratoriis privatis (S. R. C., July 18, 1885). The Elevation rite is rendered more impressive in *Missa solemni* by the use of lights and incense. Several acolytes appear with torches, and the thurifer incenses the host and chalice while they are being elevated. The burning of the light as well as the consuming of the incense is a token and expression of devout adoration and worship rising heavenward. The incensing at this place occurs already at the close of the fourteenth century.

altar: "Heaven opens at the words of the priest, and the choirs of angels surround the altar," [29] to admire and to adore the divine mysteries. What then is more proper than that man also should, in unison with the celestial spirits, render to the divine victim present their most profound testimonies of homage and worship?

This elevation of the body and blood of Christ is truly the commemoration of the death of the Lord (I Cor. 11:26): it places before our eyes the raising up of Christ on the cross upon Golgotha. As once on Mount Calvary, so Christ here on the altar, as the great mediator, as the true victim, and as the eternal high priest, is elevated between heaven and earth to reconcile God and man, inasmuch as He moves the heavenly Father to mercy and forgiveness, and moves sinful man to love and compunction.

[29] S. Greg., *Dial.*, IV, chap. 58.

CHAPTER XXXVI

THE FIRST PRAYER AFTER THE CONSECRATION

BY the consecration, the Eucharistic sacrifice is essentially accomplished. But as the sacrificial action, as simple as it is sublime, was appropriately introduced and prepared by various rites, it must also be properly developed and worthily concluded; hence appropriate prayers and ceremonies follow the sublime moment of the Eucharistic consecration, when an immense treasury of graces was thrown open to us on the altar. First there follows an oblation prayer in three parts.

Unde et memores, Domine, nos servi tui, sed et plebs tua sancta, ejusdem Christi Filii tui Domini nostri tam beatae passionis, necnon et ab inferis resurrectionis, sed et in coelos gloriosae ascensionis: offerimus praeclarae majestati tuae de tuis donis ac datis hostiam ✠ puram, hostiam ✠ sanctam, hostiam ✠ immaculatum: panem ✠ sanctum vitae aeternae, et calicem ✠ salutis perpetuae.

Supra quae propitio ac sereno vultu respicere digneris: et accepta habere, sicuti accepta habere dignatus es munera pueri tui justi Abel, et sacrificium

Wherefore, O Lord, we Thy servants, and likewise Thy holy people, calling to mind the blessed passion of the same Christ Thy Son, our Lord, together with His resurrection from the grave and also His glorious ascension into heaven, offer unto Thy excellent majesty, of Thy gifts and presents, a pure ✠ victim, a holy ✠ victim, an immaculate ✠ victim: the holy ✠ bread of eternal life and the chalice ✠ of everlasting salvation.

Upon which do Thou vouchsafe to look with favorable and gracious countenance, and accept them as Thou didst vouchsafe to accept the gifts of Thy

Patriarchae nostri Abrahae: et quod tibi obtulit summus sacerdos tuus Melchisedech, sanctum sacrificium, immaculatam hostiam.

Supplices te rogamus, omnipotens Deus: jube haec perferri per manus sancti Angeli tui in sublime altare tuum, in conspectu divinae majestatis tuae: ut quotquot ex hac altaris participatione sacrosanctum Filii tui cor✠pus et san✠guinem sumpserimus, omni benedictione ceolesti et gratia repleamur. Per eundem Christum Dominum nostrum. Amen.

just servant Abel and the sacrifice of our patriarch Abraham and that which Thy high priest, Melchisedech, offered unto Thee, a holy sacrifice, an unspotted victim.

We humbly beseech Thee, almighty God, command these things to be carried by the hands of Thy holy angel to Thine altar on high, in the presence of Thy divine Majesty, that as many of us as shall, by partaking at this altar, receive the most sacred body ✠ and blood ✠ of Thy Son, may be filled with every heavenly blessing and grace. Through the same Christ our Lord. Amen.

These three parts of the Canon constitute but a single prayer, which has the customary conclusion; the intimate relation of the parts of the prayer and the gradual development of the whole cannot be mistaken. In general it contains the presentation to God of our sacrificial gifts and the supplication that He graciously accept them; it terminates with the wish that the most abundant benedictions of grace may be poured out from the altar upon all who participate in the sacrificial banquet.

The *Unde et memores*

After the consecration, the Lamb of God is on the altar in a state of sacrifice, immolated by the two-edged sword of the mighty words of consecration. Assuredly the Lord dieth no more, nor can He die; He is exalted above death and the pangs of death; but nevertheless He here submits, under the sacramental species, to a mystical death, inasmuch as He renders present His separated body and His blood and conceals them under the cover of inanimate things. While He places Himself by the separate consecration in this state on the altar, He consecrates Himself to His Heavenly Father

FIRST PRAYER AFTER THE CONSECRATION

as a sacrifice of praise, of propitiation, of thanksgiving, and of petition. His Eucharistic heart burns with the same fire of sacrificial love which at one time consumed Him as a holocaust on Calvary.

But on the altar He is also *our* sacrifice, He is in *our* hands: we are to offer Him. This is done already at the consecration; for the sacrificial act essentially includes the oblation of the gift.[1] The offering already contained in the sacrificial action itself may still be more clearly expressed and made repeatedly under different aspects and for different purposes through words and ceremonies. The Offertory prayers previous to the consecration do not refer to the Eucharistic elements exclusively, but also refer to the victim about to be present. Immediately after the consecration similar oblation petitions again occur; they do not belong to the essence of the sacrifice, yet in a certain sense they add to its greater perfection.[2] The immolated, sacrificed Lamb of God, His body and blood, lie before us on the altar; these infinitely precious gifts we now present to the divine majesty, principally to commemorate the Redeemer and His work, as well as to gain the fruits of the sacrifice.[3]

1. This offering is made, chiefly by consecrated priests, then by the rest of the faithful united with them: "We, Thy servants, as

---

[1] Adverte duplicem esse oblationem. Una est intrinseca sacrificio. Omne enim sacrificium est oblatio, et haec quidem oblatio non est alia actio ab ipsa, quae dicitur sacrificium, sed eadem ut in Deum ordinatur. Altera est, quae ab ipso sacrificio disjungitur; et haec est, qua expressius et distinctius sacrificium ipsum factum aut faciendum in Deum ordinamus et mente et voce. Et haec est, quae fit post consecrationem illis verbis: *Unde et memores . . .* et ante consecrationem illis: *Suscipe, sancta Trinitas . . .* (Tolet., *In Summ. s. Thom. De sacrif. Missae*, controvers. 5).

[2] Deposito Calice et adorato, prosequitur sacerdos sacram actionem Canonis, et facta *reali* et *substantiali* oblatione victimae per consecrationem, eandem confirmat et perficit repetita oblatione *verbali*, nempe oratione, quae incipit: "Unde et memores . . ." et aliis subsequentibus, additis etiam sacris ritibus in eundem finem: quae omnia accidentalem addunt perfectionem et majorem ornatum sacrificio, qualis tum maxime decet, dum in altari jam praesens est victima seu hostia vivens, sancta et Deo placens, videlicet ipse Christus sub accidentibus panis et vini (Quarti, II, ix, 1).

[3] Quod sacerdos etiam tunc (sc. post consecrationem) orat, ut Deus acceptum habeat sacrificium, non est quia essentialis oblatio sacrificii non sit jam peracta, sed quia adhuc habemus praesentem rem oblatam, et per illam possumus plura semper beneficia impetrare, et iterum atque iterum Deum deprecari, ut et majorem in ipsum reverentiam ostendamus, et ut ad plura beneficia nobis conferenda sacrificium nostrum acceptet ac denique, ut effectus sacrificii propter demeritum nostrum non impediatur (Suarez, disp. LXXV, sect. 5, n. 15).

also Thy holy people." The plural, "Thy servants," recalls the time when priests still concelebrated Mass [4] with the bishop, and accordingly proves the antiquity of the prayer.[5] Priests are in a special manner "servants of God"; but as they are to serve Him through love and with joy, they are also called "friends of God." In His farewell discourse the Lord spoke to His disciples these words, which the bishop, after the ordination, addresses to the newly ordained: "I not now call you servants; . . . but I have called you friends" (John 15:15).[6] Thus does the Lord by an unmerited favor elevate priests to the rank of bosom friends and intimate associates, but priests will ever remain "His servants." This service is in itself a very great honor and distinction, to which the Lord freely chose

[4] For many centuries priests celebrated the Eucharistic sacrifice in common with the bishop, especially on great feasts. Mos est Romanae Ecclesiae, ut in confectione immolationis Christi adsint Presbyteri et simul cum Pontifice verbis et manibus conficiant (Amalar., *De eccles. offic.*, I, chap. 12). Consueverunt presbyteri Cardinales Romanum circumstare Pontificem et cum eo pariter celebrare, cumque consummatum est sacrificium, de manu ejus communionem recipere (Innoc. III, *De sacro altar. myster.*, IV, chap. 25). In the Roman liturgy this rite of concelebration is now limited to the Masses at which takes place the ordination of priests and the consecration of bishops; in the Greek liturgy it still frequently occurs. (Cf. Bona, *Rerum liturg.*, I, xviii, 9.)

[5] Primum de praelatis; alterum de subjectis agere non dubitatur (Microlog. c. 13). The expression *servi* is not to be confined to priests alone, but according to circumstances it is also to be referred to those in lesser orders. As in the prayer *Hanc igitur*, we have here also a grouping together of clerics and the laity; the former (the officials of the house of God) constitute the hierarchical, the latter the laical, priesthood. As members of the congregation and of the house of God, all Christians have, in a wider sense, a priestly character (I Pet. 2:5), and they exercise it chiefly at the Eucharistic celebration, in which by closest adherence to the liturgy they in common offer the sacrificial body and sacrificial blood of Christ, as well as their own subjective sacrifice. Non solum sacerdotes et clerus (qui secundum diversos gradus divinis occupantur officiis) offerunt, sed etiam audientes, qui votis et orationibus assistunt cooperantes (B. Odo Camerac., dist. 2).

[6] Nonne per charismata gratiarum, per sapientiae claritatem, per virtutum decorem, per puritatem internam, per custoditam, fructuosam et contemplativam coram Deo conversationem, per odium vitiorum, per ardentem Deitatis amorem efficeris non solum servus Dei, imo et filius adoptivus, secretus amicus, heres regni coelestis, increatae Sapientiae sponsus, amantissimus Dei et tamquam consiliarius ac secretarius Creatoris? Intuere, quam deificum et praeclarum consistat, cum Deo assidue miscere colloquia in orationibus ac laudibus ejus, ipsum quoque tibi loquentem audire in lectionibus Scripturarum, in inspiratione occulta, in manifestationibus abditorum (Dion. Carthus., *De laude vitae solitariae*, a. 12).

them and called them through His grace. Priests should administer and dispense the mysteries of God like good and faithful servants, leading a life befitting their vocation and office. The ministers of the Church are indeed, by their ordination, dignity, and power, exalted above the laity; but they are thereby none the less obliged to serve in love and humility, with devotedness and self-sacrifice, the flock that has been entrusted to them, they must labor, suffer, and care for the salvation and temporal welfare of their flock, after the example of "the Son of Man, [who] is not come to be ministered unto but to minister, and to give His life a redemption for many" (Matt. 20:28).

The words, "Thy holy people," denote the high dignity of the faithful regenerated by the sacrament of baptism; they are a people of God (*plebs tua*), and as such a "holy people" (*plebs sancta*).[7] The faithful are a people belonging to God; for God has purchased them and acquired them with the great price of Christ's blood. They form a community which, in a very special manner, is dedicated to God as His peculiar property. The members of the Church are designated as a "holy people" inasmuch as God has singularly favored them and abundantly poured out on them the spirit of sanctification, whereby they are enabled to lead a virtuous and holy life. Then indeed shall the children of the Church truly be the holy people of God if, by word and deed, by their whole conduct, they endeavor to serve God and to glorify Him, since for this has He called and transplanted them out of the darkness of the world into the wonderful light of His heavenly truth and grace. God gave us His Son, and He gives Him again daily on the altar, that "He might redeem us from all iniquity, and might cleanse to Himself a people acceptable, a pursuer of good works" (Tit. 2:14).

At this offering, priest and people are mindful also of "the blessed passion, resurrection, and ascension of Jesus Christ," because the Lord Himself commanded it. To these preceding words of Christ uttered by the priest, *in mei memoriam facietis*, the words *Unde et memores* ("wherefore also calling to mind") refer.[8] The Eucha-

---

[7] In like manner Christians are called: *gens sancta, populus acquisitionis* (I Pet. 2:9); frequently in the liturgy: *sacrata plebs; plebs Domino dicata; populus sanctus Dei*.

[8] Peracta consecratione in omnibus Liturgiis Christi mandatum commemoratur praecipientis, ut ipsum sacrificium in ejus memoriam peragamus: "Haec quotiescumque feceritis, in mei memoriam facietis." Quis enim auderet ad

ristic sacrifice is the living commemoration and mystical accomplishment of the entire work of redemption; Christ as high priest and as victim is present on the altar with all the fruits and merits of the redemption. In the Holy Sacrifice of the Mass, not only His passion and death,[9] but also the life of His glory is mystically represented and renewed. Three great mysteries are here made prominent: before all, the sufferings of Christ in His sacrifice and death on the cross, as the essence and center of the work of redemption; then the joyful resurrection and glorious ascension, which constitute the conclusion and crown of the work of redemption.[10] The passion, so full of pain and torment for the Saviour, is here designated as "blessed" (*tam beata passio*),[11] by reason of the blessed effects and sweet fruits which it produced for us men. Thus the Church in a passion hymn also calls the hard wood of the cross and the cruel nails "sweet" (*dulce lignum, dulces clavi*). Since the merci-

---

altare Dei accedere et augustissimum mysterium celebrare, nisi Dominus tanti sacramenti institutor praecipisset? Propterea Ecclesia Domini mandato obsequens sequentia verba recitari constituit: *Unde et memores, Domine, nos servi tui, sed et plebs tua sancta,* fidelis scilicet et in Ecclesiae gremio consistens; sancta, non quidem actu, cum non omnes sancti sint, sed vocatione, debito et professione; quae vel praesens adest sacrificio vel in unitate Ecclesiae ubique degens particeps est sacrificii (Bona, *Rer. liturg.*, II, xii, 3).

[9] Illius ergo panis et calicis oblatio mortis Christi est commemoratio et annuntiatio, quae *non tam verbis quam mysteriis ipsis* agitur, per quae nostris mentibus mors illa pretiosa altius et fortius commendatur (Florus Lugdun., *De actione Missar.*, n. 89). Cf. Algerus, *De sacram. corp. et sang. Domin.*, I, chap. 16.

[10] Nominantur potius hic ista tria Christi opera: passio, resurrectio, ascensio, quam alia in dispensatione carnis assumptae ab eo facta, quoniam plus ceteris faciunt ad complementum redemptionis et glorificationis humanae. Passio namque Christi pretium nostrae redemptionis exsolvit et mortem destruxit. Resurrectio ejusdem perditam reparavit vitam nobisque resurgendi spem et fiduciam suggessit. Ascensio vero in coelum paradisi patefecit introitum quantum ad ejus ingressum et nobis eandem ingrediendi viam monstravit (Clichtov., *Elucidat. eccles.*, III, n. 35).

[11] Nulla nobis sit de Christi cruce confusio, quia habemus de ejus passione victoriam: sicut enim sempiternus Dei Filius non sibi, sed nobis est natus, ita immaculatus Dei Agnus non sibi, sed nobis est passus (Maxim. Taurin., *Homil.*, LXXXIII). Haec dominicae dispensationis arcana (*the mysteries of the redemption*) et semper nos animo decet retinere et intentius solito ubi beatissimae passionis sacramenta conficiuntur, ubi mors Salvatoris nostri, quam citissimae resurrectionis virtute in aeternum conculcavit, mysticis in altari renovatur officiis (Bed. Venerab., II, hom. 4). Tam beatae, h. e. tam excellenter beatificantis [passionis], quia mortuos a vinculis mortis absolvit (Albert. M., *Summa de offic. Missae*, tract. III, chap. 13).

ful Saviour has left us on the altar such a wonderful memorial of His redeeming life and death, we should during the celebration of the Holy Sacrifice most fervently meditate upon and venerate these great mysteries.[12]

At the institution of the Eucharist, the Lord Himself said to the apostles: "Do this in remembrance of Me!" so that this sublime and venerable Sacrament might be to us an excellent and singular memorial of the immense love wherewith He loved us. This is the sweetest memorial, the most salutary memorial, by means of which we renew the joyful remembrance of our redemption. This is the glorious commemoration that fills the souls of the faithful with a salutary joy, infuses into our hearts felicity, at the same time sweetly moving to tears. For we rejoice in the remembrance of our deliverance; but inasmuch as we renew the passion of Jesus Christ, through which we received our deliverance, we can scarcely restrain our tears.[13]

We offer the sacrifice to the most exalted and glorious majesty of the heavenly Father: *offerimus praeclarae majestati tuae*. But where shall we find the offering for the God of majesty? Since every good and perfect gift comes from above, from the Giver of all that is good, we cannot offer anything to God but from His "presents and gifts" which He had previously imparted to us.[14] "Thine, O Lord, is magnificence and power and glory and victory: and to Thee is praise. For all that is in heaven and in earth is Thine: Thine is the kingdom, O Lord, and Thou art above all princes. All things are Thine, and we have given Thee what we received of Thy hand" (I Par. 29: 11, 14). The "presents and gifts" (*dona et data*) here men-

---

[12] Commemorantur tria opera Christi, videlicet passio ejus, cujus memoria caritatem inflammat; resurrectio, quae fidem confortat; ascensio, quae spem nostram corroborat. Quod enim in Christo capite nostro factum credimus, in nobis perficiendum speramus. Dum vero sacerdos haec verba dicit, debet quidem celeriter, non tamen superficialiter, imo cordialiter recordari passionis Christi, non sine compassionis affectu, resurrectionis quoque et ascensionis cum exsultatione mentali, contemplando mentaliter, quomodo ex clauso sepulcro surrexit, anima ex limbo inferni ad corpus redeunte, et qualiter nubes in ascensione accepit eum ab oculis discipulorum (Dion. Carthus., *Expos. Miss.*, a. 32).

[13] Cf. the Bull of the Institution of the feast of Corpus Christi by Urban IV, August 11, 1264.

[14] Deus, qui cum muneribus nullis indigeas ipse nobis munera cuncta largiris, accipe propitius, quae de tuis donis tibi nos offerre voluisti, non solum nostrae reputans devotioni quae tua sunt, sed etiam per haec nos ad coelestia regna perducens (*Sacrament. Leon.*, XXIV).

tioned, by means of which we offer a sacrifice to God, are the natural elements of bread and wine, taken from the noblest fruits and productions of God's creation.[15] For these earthly "presents and gifts" of God are changed by the consecration into the gift of the Eucharistic sacrifice, into the bread of life and the chalice of salvation, which we likewise received from God, and which we again offer to the divine Majesty.

Our sacrifice is worthy of the greatness and goodness of God; it is an infinitely precious and perfect sacrifice. For indeed we present the "clean oblation" predicted by the prophet Malachias (1:11), on which there cannot possibly fall the least shadow of blemish. Jesus Christ is in Himself the unspeakably pure, holy, and unspotted victim (*hostiam puram, hostiam sanctam, hostiam immaculatam*), and consequently the inexhaustible source whence purity, holiness, and spotlessness are poured forth into every susceptible human heart.[16] The Eucharistic victim is, moreover, partaken of; His sacrificial body is a sacrificial food, and His sacrificial blood is a sacrificial drink; both together form a holy sacrificial repast. Hence we offer the bread of heaven, which nourishes unto eternal life, and the precious chalice, whence issues everlasting salvation.[17]

2. Even after the consecration the sign of the cross is made over the sacrificial gifts.[18] These signs of the cross after the consecration

---

[15] Among the "God-given gifts and presents" we may also at the same time understand the Eucharistic victim. Sensus est: offerimus tibi hostiam puram, panem sanctum et calicem salutis, quae ex creaturis tuis a te datis et donatis, ex pane scil. et vino per consecrationem habemus. Sic exponit Innocentius. Possunt etiam referri omnia ad ipsam Eucharistiam sive ad Christum ut in Eucharistia existentem; rectissime enim dicitur Christus Dei datum et donum (Bellarm., *De Missa*, II, chap. 24). Dicitur haec hostia offerri ex Dei donis et datis, vel quia ex pane et vino effecta est, vel certe, quia Christum ipsum continet, qui nobis a Deo datus est (Suarez, disp. LXXXIII, sect. 2).

[16] Christus est hostia pura, electos suos purificans; hostia sancta, dilectos suos sanctificans; hostia immaculata, maculas nostras purgans; panis vitae aeternae, angelos et homines reficiens, et calice sui praeclari sanguinis inebrians et perfundens (S. Bonav., *Expos. Miss.*, chap. 4).

[17] In the Mozarabic liturgy the Eucharist is also frequently designated as *panis* (sc. *quem lignum crucis coxit*) and as *calix*, or *vinum* (sc. *quod torcular passionis expressit*). It has a similar designation in a prayer of the old Gallican rite: *immolatus panis et sanguis*.

[18] In three places (in all ten times) it is made with the hand over the sacrificial gifts, and in two places (in all eight times) with the host (six times over the chalice and twice outside the chalice).

have always been regarded as difficult to explain; hence various interpretations have been given.

The use of the sign of the cross in ecclesiastical worship is very extensive; it is employed, not merely as a holy symbol to express various mysteries and truths, but even as a means to produce supernatural effects and to impart blessings; it is a sign efficacious as well as profoundly significant. Since the sign of the cross, on account of its profound contents, is so extensively employed for liturgical purposes, it is self-evident that it is not always and everywhere used in the same sense; and often in the same place it may even have several purposes.[19] First, the distinction between the sign of the cross made before the consecration and that made after the consecration can be shown. Very often the cross is a sign of blessing; such is the case before the consecration, where it is a significant and at the same time an effective sign of blessing: it consecrates the material elements of bread and wine to their high destiny, and at the same time indicates and implores their perfect sanctification through the consecration. But evidently this object cannot be ascribed to the sign of the cross after the Elevation: there are no longer present on the altar material elements susceptible or in need of blessing, but only Christ's body and blood under the appearances of bread and wine. Jesus Christ, the source of all blessings, cannot be blessed by the priest; therefore the signs of the cross made over the oblation after the consecration can in nowise have the signification and power of effective signs for blessing Christ, who is present.[20] The signs of the cross after the consecration again have different meanings and ends, which will be best shown by explaining the prayers and acts connected with them.

In our present prayer the Eucharistic sacrifice is named five

[19] We must always follow the fundamental rule that text and ceremony are to be explained in harmony with each other; for word and act constitute a ritual whole, since they belong to each other, mutually complete one another, and reciprocally cast light on one another. This is the case in the rite of the Mass, in which frequently occurs the sign of the cross.

[20] In sacramento altaris benedictio sacerdotis fertur super terminum a quo, i.e. super panem, non super terminum ad quem, i.e. corpus Christi (S. Thom., *In I ad Cor.*, chap. 10, n. 4). Notandum quod consignatio facta super panem et calicem ante consecrationem quasi oratio est, ut consecratio compleatur; post consecrationem vero iterata consignatio consecrationis jam adimpletae quaedam est testificatio (Robert. Paulul., *De offic. eccles.*, II, chap. 32).

times, and at each mention of it a cross is made over the consecrated elements. The sign of the cross is indeed but a passing action, yet it possesses the form and expression of a holy image: it is like the crucifix, and like it, it ever reminds us of Christ's passion and death. The cross, therefore, has always and everywhere this reminding feature, especially at the celebration of Mass, which is the renewal of the sacrifice of the cross.[21] When the gifts of the Eucharistic sacrifice are named, the symbol of the cross appropriately accompanies the words to represent also to the eye that on the altar the same body and the same blood are offered which were once sacrificed on the Cross. This symbolical interpretation does not exclude other meanings. The essence of our prayer is the offering (*offerimus*); now, if the signs of the cross figuratively express what the words signify, then they can also rightly be conceived as a symbolical dedication and surrendering up to God of the Eucharistic victim. Yet these crosses in a certain respect can here be understood as signs of blessing.[22] They may be regarded as a symbol of that plenitude of grace and blessing which gushes forth from the sacrificed body and blood of Christ over His mystical body, that is, the Church. This thought is warranted because the Church is united to Christ and offered together with Him on the altar, and consequently she is blessed to a certain extent by these signs of the cross. Finally, the five signs of the cross may be considered a symbol of the five wounds of our crucified Saviour.[23]

[21] Mentio mortis adest, ubicumque perennibus escis
Imprimit uncta manus mystica signa crucis.
(Hildeb. Turon., *Vers. de myster. Missae.*)
Quid est inter ipsa mysteria rebus sacratis vel sacrandis signum crucis superponere, nisi mortem Domini commemorare? Unde et Dominus formam consecrandi corporis et sanguinis sui tradens, ait inter cetera: "Hoc facite in meam commemorationem" (Ivonis Carnotens., *Serm.*, V).

[22] "The blessings made over the body of Jesus Christ with the sign of the cross, do not regard that divine body, but those who are to receive it; or if they regard it, it is to indicate the blessings and graces with which it is filled and which He desires to impart to us liberally, if our want of fidelity does not prevent Him; or, in fine, if we wish to consider it in that light, Jesus Christ is blessed in all His members, who are offered in this sacrifice as forming but one and the same body with the Saviour, in order that the grace of the Head be abundantly bestowed upon them" (Bossuet, *loc. cit.*).

[23] Quinaria cruce signamus, non ut eum, a quo omnis sanctificatio, sanctificemus, sed ut vulnera pendentis in cruce—duo manuum, duo pedum, quin-

The *Supra quae*

Immediately after the above offering very appropriately follows the petition that God would vouchsafe to look with a propitious and gracious countenance upon our sacrificial gifts and vouchsafe to accept them, as formerly He received the typical offerings of Abel, Abraham, and Melchisedech. But must not such a petition appear strange? Does not the eye of the heavenly Father rest with eternal love and infinite complacency on Jesus Christ, the pure, holy, and unspotted victim of our altars? How then can the oblation of the body and blood of Christ be placed on the same level with the figurative offerings of ancient times? To solve this difficulty, we must examine more closely the aspect under which the Eucharistic sacrifice is here regarded.

In so far as Christ on the altar offers Himself, the Eucharistic sacrifice is ever absolutely pleasing to God; to beg for a favorable acceptance of the sacrifice of Christ from this standpoint, or even to place it on the same plane with the ancient sacrifices, is out of question, and consequently such cannot be the meaning of our prayer. Here the Eucharistic oblation is considered under another aspect. At the moment of consecration, Jesus Christ as high priest offers Himself up through the Holy Ghost and the ministry of the visible priest to the honor of His heavenly Father and for our salvation, and at the same time He places His sacrificial body and blood in the hands of the Church. The Church now presents to the majesty of the Father, as her sacrifice, the divine victim mystically immolated, while including the sacrifice of her own self as a gift in union with the infinitely meritorious sacrificial body and blood of Christ. The petition for the favorable reception refers, therefore, to the Eucharistic oblation in so far as the Church comes to the foreground as offering it together with herself. For the value of an offering depends not alone on the quality of the gift, but also and principally on the dignity and holiness of the person who offers it. The more pure and perfect his intention in sacrificing is, the more agreeable is his homage in the sight of God. "The Lord had respect to Abel and to his offerings" (Gen. 4:4), that is, the first was the cause of the second: the gift of Abel was pleasing to God because Abel him-

---

tum lateris—flebiliter et devote recolamus (Stephan. Augustod., *De sacram. altar.*, chap. 17).

self was pleasing to Him.[24] This principle is applicable also to the offering at the altar, in so far as the Church, the priest, and the faithful are regarded as those who offer. Naturally this is not to be understood as though our disposition could impart a higher value to the sacrificial gift infinitely precious in itself, but it means only that God ever prefers to receive it from hands that possess the greater purity and holiness. Since we are often wanting in the proper dispositions, in piety, purity of heart, fervor of devotion, let us make humble supplications to the Most High, that He be not offended on account of our sinfulness, and reject not the Eucharistic gifts from our unworthy hands, but that He look upon and graciously accept them presented by us, that they may, not only as the sacrifice of Christ but also as our sacrifice, bring down upon us bountiful blessings and a superabundance of grace.[25]

For the clearer understanding of such petitions, we must further consider that the Church participates still in another way in the sacrifice of the altar: together with her head, Jesus Christ, she offers herself as a gift dedicated to God; the real body of Christ and the mystical body of Christ are thus combined in one sacrifice. This mystery is symbolized at the Offertory by the pouring of some water into the wine in the chalice; accordingly, the priest already then prayed "in a spirit of humility and with a contrite heart," that we be received by God as a sacrifice well pleasing to Him; he then summoned the faithful to pray that his sacrifice and theirs "may be acceptable to God the Father Almighty." Therefore, since we place ourselves with all our works and prayers, desires and concerns, as a

[24] With respect to the sacrifices offered by Abel and Cain, St. Cyprian writes: Non munera eorum Deus, sed corda intuebatur, ut ille placeret in munere, qui placebat in corde (*De Orat. domin.*, chap. 24).

[25] Clarum est, quod sacerdos novae legis non orat sacrificium seu sacramentum altaris sic Deo placere, quemadmodum ei placuerunt sacrificia horum trium virorum [Abel, Abrahae, Melchisedech], quoniam illa sacrificia nec gratiam continebant nec placita Deo erant nisi ex devotione offerentium meritisque eorum, sed sacrificium novae legis, videlicet sacramentum corporis et sanguinis Christi, gratiarum plenitudinem continet et per seipsum Deo acceptum est, ejusque oblatio fructuosa est non solum ex meritis offerentis, sed propter dignitatem oblati. Orat ergo sacerdos oblationem suam seu sacramentum altaris Deo placere non quantum ad seipsum seu rem oblatam, quae per se sancta ac Deo placita existit, sed quantum ad offerentem, quatenus sacerdotis actio atque devotio Deo sic placeat, sicut placuit antiquorum patrum devotio, sicque effectum et gratiam hujus sacramenti consequi mereatur (Dion. Carthus., *Expos. Miss.*, a. 33).

FIRST PRAYER AFTER THE CONSECRATION   693

sacrificial gift upon the altar, the reason is easily understood why, with lively sentiments of our worthlessness and unworthiness, we implore that God would deign to look with mercy on us and on our sacrifice. Such petitions frequently occur in the liturgy of the Mass, and we shall meet them again at the conclusion of the sacrifice. They are perfectly justifiable, inasmuch as we offer the Eucharistic sacrifice and ourselves in union with it. To do this worthily, we should possess perfect sanctity, but as this is wanting to us, we recommend our sacrifice to the favor and indulgence of God, that it may be more agreeable to Him and more salutary to us. When, therefore, we are assembled around the altar, may God never look down upon us with reproach and resentment, but may He always regard us and our gifts "with a favorable and gracious countenance." [26]

The next petition, that the heavenly Father would favorably accept this our sacrifice as He accepted the sacrifices of Abel, Abraham, and Melchisedech, is explained from the same point of view.[27] Here these sacrifices are by no means compared with the Eucharistic sacrifice as far as Christ is its priest and gift; there is an infinite distance between them. The comparison is made between us and those devout patriarchs. We pray that our oblation may be agreeable and pleasing to the eyes of God as were the sacrifices of those saints of ancient times.[28] Now this is nothing else than praying for the fulfillment of that which the prophet Malachias (3:3 f.) at one time predicted: "He shall purify the sons of Levi [the priests], and shall refine them as gold and as silver, and they shall offer sacrifices [the Eucharistic oblation] to the Lord in justice. And the sacrifice of Juda and of Jerusalem [that is, of the Christian Church] shall please the Lord, as in the days of old and in the ancient years," when

---

[26] *Vultus* = glance, mien, feature, inasmuch as it is the indication of the interior sentiment of the mind; often emphatic = angry, threatening countenance, look of anger (cf. Ps. 33:17); *propitius* = inclined, disposed, favorable, graciously inclined; *serenus* = serene, bright, clear, brilliant, radiant. We also pray God not to be angry, dark, severe, but favorable, mild, graciously to look down on our oblation. Cf. Ps. 30:17; 66:2.

[27] Licet hoc sacramentum ex se ipso praeferatur omnibus antiquis sacrificiis, tamen sacrificia antiquorum fuerunt Deo acceptissima ex eorum devotione. Petit ergo sacerdos, ut sic hoc sacrificium accepetetur a Deo ex devotione offerentium, sicut illa accepta fuerunt Deo (S. Thom., IIIa, q.83, a.4 ad 8).

[28] Fit in canone Missae mentio de oblatione Abrahae et Abel magis propter devotionem offerentium, quam propter figuram rei oblatae (S. Thom., IV, dist. 8, q. 1, a. sol. 2 ad 6).

holy men, as Abel, Abraham, and Melchisedech, offered sacrifices pleasing to God. The Lord was pleased to accept their gifts because they were presented to Him with perfect dispositions, and because they at the same time prefigured the sacrifice of Jesus Christ.[29]

There is no doubt regarding the typical character of the sacrifices mentioned. If the sacrifices of Abel and Abraham are principally figures of the bloody sacrifice of the cross, they must, indeed, in this connection with Melchisedech's sacrifice, be also considered as figures of the unbloody sacrifice of the altar. Such a conception corresponds to the view of Christian antiquity, as it is often expressed by the Fathers and in the various liturgies.[30]

The devout and faithful Abel offered to God the firstlings of his flock. In all probability God manifested His special pleasure by sending fire from heaven to consume Abel's sacrifice. According to the expression of the Lord Himself (Matt. 23:35), Abel is designated as the just (*justus*) and as the servant (*puer*) of God. Full of faith and humble simplicity, he offered a lamb to the Lord, and this sacrifice is intended to prefigure the sacrifice of that true and immaculate Lamb daily immolated on the altar.[31] Inasmuch as Abel was infamously slain by his brother Cain, he was, by suffering death innocently, one of the principal figures of the propitiatory sacrifice of Jesus Christ (Heb. 12:24). "In him," St. Ambrose says, "the redemption of the world and the sacrifice of Christ are announced." [32]

---

[29] Post consecrationem rogamus Patrem, ut super dona praedicta respiciat et accepta habeat. Sed cum Patri Filio nihil sit acceptius, quem propitio et sereno vultu semper sibi Deum aequalem intuetur: quid aliud oramus, nisi ut mediante et interpellante Filio nobis Deus fiat placabilis, et propitius et per eum, qui sibi placet, ei placeamus? Itaque oramus eum per haec sacrificia nobis miserendo placatum fieri, sicut misertus est patribus nostris propitiando eorum sacrificiis. Unde attendenda est haec comparatio in sola similitudine, non in quantitate, nec est referenda ad sacrificia, sed ad offerentium vota. Plus valet res, quam figura. Omnibus sacrificiis praecellit Eucharistia; est autem talis similitudo, ut recte offerendo similes simus patribus nostris, qui recte obtulerunt (Steph. Augustod., *De sacr. altar.*, chap. 17).

[30] Tuae laudis hostiam jugiter immolamus, cujus figuram Abel justus instituit, celebravit Abraham, Melchisedech sacerdos exhibuit, sed verus Agnus et aeternus Pontifex Christus implevit (*Sacrament. Leonian.*, IV).

[31] Deus, qui legalium differentiam hostiarum, unius sacrificii perfectione sanxisti: accipe sacrificium a devotis tibi famulis, et pari benedictione, sicut munera Abel, sanctifica; ut quod singuli obtulerunt ad majestatis tuae honorem, cunctis proficiat ad salutem (*Secret. Dom. VII p. Pent.*).

[32] In isto [Abel] mundi redemptio annuntiatur, ab illo [Cain] mundi ruina.

Abraham, "our patriarch" [33] since he was chosen by God as the first father of all the faithful, stands forth prominent as an example of heroic obedience and faith. God commanded him "to immolate his son Isaac in sacrifice, and already had Abraham bound his long-desired child of promise, placed him on the pile of wood, and had raised the sword above him; but at the decisive moment the Almighty restrained the father's arm and instead of the son allowed him to sacrifice a ram to Him" (Laurent). This sacrifice of Abraham is often represented in the catacombs, together with other biblical events symbolizing the priesthood and the sacrifice of the New Law, as a figure of the Eucharistic sacrifice. Abraham did indeed sacrifice his son, but Isaac's blood in reality was not shed; Abraham received him from death for a parable (Heb. 11:19), that is, as a figure of the risen Saviour, who as a Lamb "as it were slain" (Apoc. 5:6) offers Himself on the altar in an unbloody manner. The Sequence of Corpus Christi places the sacrifice of Abraham on a par with the manna and the paschal lamb; for it declares that the Eucharist "was prefigured when Isaac was sacrificed." [34]

The offering of food, the sacrifice of bread and wine, which the faithful and royal priest Melchisedech presented to the Most High, is the most luminous and most striking figure of the Eucharistic sacrifice; [35] for this reason it is justly styled holy and spotless (*sanctum sacrificium, immaculatam hostiam*).[36] Melchisedech himself is

---

In hoc Christi sacrificium, in illo diaboli parricidium (*Exhortat. virgin.*, n.36, chap.6).

[33] Dicitur Abraham Patriarcha, i.e. princeps patrum, non quia non habuerit patrem, sed quia sibi facta est promissio de paternitate gentium (S. Thom., *In ep. ad Heb.*, chap.7, lect.2).

[34] Est et sine cruore sacrificium. Norunt hoc, quod dico, quicunque initiati sunt, ac propterea sine sanguine transactum est illud (*the sacrifice of Isaac by Abraham*), quoniam istius (*the unbloody sacrifice*) figura esse debebat (S. Chrysost., *Oratio in S. Eustathium*). Cf. Petav., *De Incarnat.*, XII, xiii, 7.

[35] Melchisedech obtulit sacrificium in pane et vino, et in eisdem speciebus modo offertur et celebratur sacramentum altaris: ergo cum non possit expressius figurari quam in simili secundum speciem, videtur, quod tunc praecessit figura expressissima (S. Bonav., IV, dist.8, p.1, a.1, q.3).

[36] The addition, *sanctum sacrificium, immaculatam hostiam*, ascribed to Leo the Great, grammatically cannot be conceived as in apposition with *Supra quae* and be referred to the Eucharistic sacrifice; it belongs to *quod obtulit summus sacerdos tuus Melchisedech*. Vocat hic littera Canonis sacrificium ipsius Melchisedech *sanctum sacrificium et immaculatam hostiam*, non quidem quantum ad se absolute, sed collatione facta ad sacrificium novi testamenti, quod significat et cujus expressior erat figura quam ceterae

a figure of the eternal high priest, Jesus Christ; his priesthood as to dignity and importance is not inferior to that of Aaron, but rather superior to it, hence he is called the high priest of God (*summus sacerdos tuus*).[37] "It is Jesus Christ whom the high priest Melchisedech prefigured, who did not offer to God the sacrifices of the Jews, but the sacrifice of that mystery which our Saviour consecrated in His body and blood." [38]

These patriarchs offered their merely figurative, imperfect sacrificial gifts with sentiments so devout and pure that God regarded them with favor and grace. We pray that we may now offer the perfect sacrifice of the New Law with far greater piety and devotion, to the end that the Most High may also regard it with pleasure and graciously accept the gift from our hands.

The *Supplices te rogamus*

The third part of the first prayer after the consecration, beginning with the words, *Supplices te rogamus*, contains the concluding petition, by which we beseech God to command our sacrificial gifts to be carried by the hands of the angels to His altar on high, in the presence of His divine Majesty, that, by partaking of the sacrificial food, we may be filled with all heavenly blessing and grace. This petition is clothed in words full of mystery, for it is manifest that there can be no question of a local transfer of the body of Christ from the altar to heaven. The text of this prayer recalls a celestial vision of St. John (Apoc. 8:3 f.): "And another angel came and stood before the altar, having a golden censer; and there was given to him much incense, that he should offer of the prayers of all saints upon the golden altar, which is before the throne of God. And the smoke of the incense of the prayers of the saints ascended up before God, from the hand of the angel." [39]

---

oblationes, et idcirco nostri sacrificii conditiones illi attribuuntur tanquam imagini (Clichtov., *Elucidat. eccl.*, III, n. 39).

[37] Melchisedech sacerdos *summus* dicitur, qui inter sacerdotes illius temporis habebatur (B. Odonis Camer., *Expos. in Canon.*, dist. 3).

[38] S. Leo, *Serm.*, IV [vel V] *in annivers. assumpt. suae*, A similar petition is also found in the Pontifical: Sicut Melchisedech sacerdotis praecipui oblationem dignatione mirabili suscepisti, ita imposita huic novo altari munera semper accepta ferre digneris (*De eccl. dedicat.*).

[39] Ex hoc loco Apocalypsis et similibus colligunt viri docti, peculiarem esse Angelum, qui sacerdoti celebranti assistat, eum juvet et dirigat, ejus preces

First we humbly beseech God to "command these [sacrificial gifts] to be carried" to His altar on high. To these sacrificial gifts (*haec*), which are to be carried up from the earthly to the heavenly altar, belongs not only the mystical body of Christ, that is, the faithful with all they are and have (their prayers, labors, sufferings, and combats), but, moreover, the Eucharistic sacrificial body and blood of our Lord in so far as we offer them.

These sacrificial gifts are to be borne into "the presence of the divine Majesty" [40] and presented in such a manner that He may not reject them, but may regard and accept them with pleasure. But this will be the case only if the eye of God detects nothing displeasing in those who offer them, but beholds them so pure and so holy as to deserve to be united and presented with the most holy sacrifice of Christ.

Yet our life is not so blameless, nor our heart so pure, nor our dispositions so perfect. Glancing at the consecrated host and chalice so near to us, the thought of the unspeakable holiness of the gift which becomes ours at the moment of consecration, arouses us to a consciousness of our own unworthiness. Penetrated with such humble sentiments, therefore, most ardently do we implore almighty God that He would "by the hands of His holy angel" carry from this earthly altar the present sacrificial gifts into the presence of His divine Majesty. When thus offered by the hands of angels, they cannot be otherwise than most highly pleasing to Him in every respect.

It is not strange that we should implore the ministry and assistance of an angel to present our oblation for the purpose of making it more acceptable to God and salutary to us. It is a tradition originating in ancient Christian times and frequently expressed by the Church, that the angels who participated in the work of redemption from beginning to end are also present at and take part in the celebration of the holy sacrificial mysteries.[41] As St. Chrysostom says: "The

---

et hostias Deo offerat, sive is Angelus sit custos celebrantis, sive custos altaris et templi, ad hanc custodiam et sacrificiorum oblationem peculiariter a Deo deputatus (Corn. a Lap., *In Apoc.*, 8:3).

[40] "To bring our offerings up to God, to raise them up to heaven, where He may receive them, or to cause them to reach His throne, means in the ordinary language of Scripture, to present them to Him in such a manner and with so pure a conscience, that they may be pleasing to Him" (Bossuet, *Explication de quelques difficultés sur les prières de la Messe*).

[41] Semper angelus credendus est adesse immolationi corporis Christi (Joann. Abrinc., n. 22).

priest is himself at that solemn moment surrounded by angels, and the choir of the heavenly powers unite with him; they occupy the entire space around the altar, to honor Him who lies there as a sacrifice." [42] Then the Saint describes a vision in which was seen a multitude of angels, who, robed in dazzling white garments and with head deeply bowed, surrounded the altar as warriors standing in the presence of their king. The blessed vocation of the heavenly spirits consists in glorifying God by praise and in assisting man to attain salvation. Where could this twofold object be better fulfilled than during the Holy Sacrifice? Hence hosts of angels collect about the altar to procure for God honor on high and for man peace on earth. Between the angels and the Holy Eucharist there exist, undoubtedly, intimate relations which to our weak vision here below remain always shrouded in a mysterious obscurity.

Christian tradition not only speaks of the presence of many angels at the celebration of the holy mysteries, but also often mentions a certain angel specially commissioned to carry our prayers and sacrifices before the throne of God.[43] Tertullian says that it is highly irreverent to sit in church "before the face of the living God while the angel of prayer is still standing there." [44] St. Ambrose tells us that we cannot doubt that "an angel assists" when Christ is sacrificed on the altar.[45] Thus the text of the Canon also mentions but one angel. Does it not appear that the Church herself would thereby indicate that God entrusts an angel with the special mission of bringing the oblation of the priest and people into His presence? More detailed and accurate information relative to this angel of the Sacrifice of the Mass is not granted to us.[46] Many saints and servants of God had a particular devotion to the angel here mentioned, without being able or willing to decide as to his name. Some believe him to be

---

[42] *On the Priesthood*, VI, 4.

[43] Sicut Angeli intelliguntur Deo offerre orationes nostras et petitiones, similiter et desideria, non propter ignorantiam Dei, sed propter commoditatem nostram; quia suis sanctis affectibus puris nos adjuvant et merita nostra in conspectu Dei replicant, ut ex eorum puritate sancta et affectione ferventi ratione dignitatis nuntii sint acceptabilia—sic intellegendum est offerre *sacrificia*, quia sacris mysteriis assistentes una nobiscum precantur, ut nostra munera sint accepta, et una nobiscum reverentur sanctissimum corpus Christi, sicut in coelo (S. Bonav., IV, dist. 11, p. 1, dub. 4).

[44] *On Prayer*, chap. 16.

[45] *In Luc.*, I, n. 28.

[46] *Angelus assistens divinis mysteriis* (S. Thom., IIIa, q. 83, a. 4 ad 9).

the guardian angel of the church and the altar, or that of the priest, who most effectually assists, directs, and enlightens him during the celebration of the holy mysteries.[47] Others suppose—and this appears probable—that it is St. Michael, who is honored as the guardian angel of the Eucharist and of the Church militant.[48] It is not easy to correctly judge the value of such pious opinions; the majority of them have their foundation in divine things which can be more readily conjectured than explained. With the angels, multitudes of other heavenly spirits unite in humble adoration at the sacred mysteries; hence many writers perceive in this petition of the Canon a supplication to obtain the assistance of all the angels in general.[49]

We therefore pray that our sacrificial gifts may, through the assistance of the angels,[50] ascend on high in the presence of the

[47] Angelus is, cujus manibus sacer ille minister
In sublime geri munus utrumque rogat,
Angelus est ejus, vel quos reverenda vetustas
Desursum missos dicit adesse sacris.
(Hildeb. Turon., *Versus de Myst. Missae*.)

[48] S. Michael ecclesiam visitat et ante ejus altare stat, habens thuribulum aureum, i.e. caritatem praecipuam ad fideles, per quam eorum spiritualia sacrificia colligit Deoque offert; cui dantur incensa multa, quando Ecclesia ejus suffragia petit suasque preces per manus illius Deo offerri precatur. Quod et ille diligenter exsequitur, offerens preces et actus fidelium super altare aureum illud coeleste in patria, super quod beati laudes et preces offerunt Domino (Dion. Carthus., *In Apoc. Enarr.*, chap. 8, art. 9).

[49] Singulare nomen "sancti angeli tui" pro plurali positum et significantiam habere pluralem, ab expositoribus censetur (Clichtov., *Elucid. eccles.*, III, n. 41). Forte singulare posuit pro plurali, angeli pro angelorum (Robert. Paulul., *De offic. eccles.*, II, chap. 34).

[50] There is no reason in this instance for departing from the ordinary signification of the word, and finding in *sanctus Angelus* anything more than a created angelic spirit. According to the ancient language of the Church, the name *Angelus* (= *nuntius, missus, legatus*) often, indeed, serves to designate the second and third persons of the Godhead; but the contents of the prayer do not require such a signification, even though it might be admissible in a certain sense. In this case there is a question not of a consecrated, but only of a mediatorial action, and only the latter might, therefore, be ascribed to the God-man or to the Holy Ghost, if we thus understood *Angelus*. Thus the expression *per manus sancti Angeli* is conceived as strengthening *per Christum Dominum*, which gives a good meaning; in the latter instance the mediatorial action of the angels rests on Christ. The liturgy of the Apostolic Constitution likewise (VIII, chap. 13) has: "Again and again let us beg of God, through His Christ and by His sacrifice, offered to God our Lord, that the good God may accept the same as an agreeable odor on His heavenly altar, through the mediation of His Christ." This prayer has also some con-

divine Majesty, and there receive a gracious acceptance. Still this does not exhaust the profound meaning of this mystical prayer. It also supplicates God that our oblation may be carried by the hands of angels from the earthly altar to His "altar on high." Since there can be no question of a real altar in heaven, the question arises, what is to be here understood by this "altar on high"? A heavenly altar is mentioned in the Old Testament (Isa. 6:6) and in the New Testament (Apoc. 8:5 f.), as well as by the Fathers. Thus writes St. Irenaeus: "In heaven there is an altar, to which our gifts and prayers are raised." [51] The symbolism of the heavenly altar is not always the same. By an altar is properly understood the place destined for the offering of sacrifice, the holy place of sacrifice. Is there in heaven a place of sacrifice? Who offers there? A sacrifice in its real signification, as we have it here on earth, does not exist in heaven. But Christ appears there as high priest and mediator before the face of God, and, interceding for us, He presents to Him His wounds and His bloody death in order to apply to us the fruits of redemption. The blessed too are priests of God (Apoc. 5:10; 20:6), for they minister to Him day and night and through Christ offer without intermission the sacrifice of praise and thanksgiving. The altar in the holy of holies in heaven is, therefore, not a material place of sacrifice, but it symbolizes the heavenly sacrifice: the incense of praise, homage, and thanksgiving, which the glorified Church in union with her glorified head, Jesus Christ, offers eternally to the triune God. This prayer accordingly designates the union of our

---

nection with the oriental Epiklesis (Invocation), in as far at least as the latter in part proposes the imploring of the sacramental gifts of salvation; now if we would refer the word *Angelus* to the Holy Ghost, we would then regard Him in this place as mediator of the accomplished sacrifice, so as to make it most meritorious to us. But some have gone still further and have understood by the action here solicited of the *Angelus* (Holy Ghost) a consecrating activity (*perferri in sublime altare = transmutari in corpus et sanguinem Christi*), so that this prayer would be a real Epiklesis, that is, a petition that "God would transform the bread into the sacred body, and that which is contained in the chalice into the precious blood of His Christ, changing both through His Holy Spirit." But as this interpretation does violence to the text and brings into the Roman Canon of the Mass an almost insoluble difficulty (that is, the Epiklesis) of the Greek and Oriental liturgies without sufficient reason, and contradicts the convictions of the assembled Church at the Council of Florence (1439), as well as the traditional views of liturgists and dogmaticians of all ages, we must reject it as untenable.

[51] *Adv. haeres.*, IV, xviii, 6.

earthly sacrifice with the heavenly sacrifice of the Church triumphant. But as the latter is always in the presence of the divine Majesty, entirely pleasing and agreeable in the sight of God, so will our offering, supported and recommended by its union with the precious sacrifice of heaven, also be admitted into the presence of God and be favorably received by Him.[52] But how this union of the Church militant on earth and of her sacrifice with heaven is properly to be understood, the human mind is unable to fathom: a holy obscurity remains and shall ever remain over this prayer so rich in mysteries. The liturgists of the Middle Ages give expression to this sentiment when they exclaim with the deacon Florus: "These words of mystery are so profound, so wonderful and inconceivable, . . . that we ought rather to revere them with humility and a holy awe than attempt to interpret them." [53]

In this prayer we implore almighty God to come to the assistance of our weakness and impotence, not only by looking graciously upon us and our gifts, but even by uniting our oblation, through the ministry of the angels, with the sacrifice of heaven and, in consequence, permitting it to ascend as a pleasing odor in His presence.[54]

---

[52] Jube haec i.e. corpus et sanguinem Christi, preces quoque ac vota nostra, perferri i.e. portari, non substantialiter, sed repraesentative per modum commemorantis atque orantis, per manus sancti Angeli tui, i.e. per obsequium Angeli, qui divinorum celebrationi interesse credendus est: imo secundum Ambrosium adest coelestis militia et secundum Bernardum angelorum adest exercitus. Quam reverenter ergo nos ibi habere oportet! In sublime altare tuum, i.e. in ipsum coelum empyreum, in quo tu specialiter habitare, sedere, regnare et exaudire cognosceris, et dum sancti angeli illuc perveniunt, vota nostra, preces et opera bona tibi offerunt: in conspectu divinae majestatis tuae i.e. coram facie tua, ita ut tu ipse ea aspicias nec vultum tuum avertas a nobis (Dion. Carthus., *Expos. Miss.*, a. 34).

[53] Haec verba mysterii tam profunda, tam mira et stupenda quis comprehendere sufficiat? Quis inde digne aliquid loquatur? Magis veneranda sunt et pavenda quam discutienda. . . . Sic cogitanda sunt, ut aliquid quo nihil sit melius atque sublimius illa cogitatione conemur attingere (*De actione Missae*, n. 66).

[54] Sicut videmus in causis terrenis, quod qui nescit loqui coram praetore, conducit advocatum, qui loquatur et alleget pro ipso; sic in spiritualibus intellegendum, quod cum nos nec perorare, imo quasi nec balbutire sciamus coram Deo, quod Angelus tanquam advocatus et allegator magnus in illa superna curia assumit verbum et orationem nostram proponit. Si autem quaeritur, per quem modum habeat esse, dico, quod loqui nostrum et oratio nostra est desiderium alicujus rei vel petitio formata secundum desiderium; et quando desiderium nostrum ex mera et vera et ardenti dilectione est, tunc fortiter clamamus in auribus Dei et tunc optime peroramus. Et quoniam af-

Pope St. Gregory the Great undoubtedly alludes to the mysteries contained in this petition when he writes: "What believing soul can doubt that at the hour of the sacrifice heaven opens at the word of the priest, and choirs of angels assist at this mystery of Jesus Christ; that here the highest is combined with the lowest, the earthly united with the heavenly, the visible and invisible become one?"

The concluding clause of the prayer expresses the object of the petition. For the Church implores so ardently for a gracious acceptance of her sacrifice that it may produce the greatest possible fruit in all those who communicate sacramentally or spiritually.[55] The more closely we enter into relation with the sacrifice, which is borne from the earthly to the heavenly altar, the more abundant heavenly graces and blessings flow to us as the wholesome fruit of the sacrifice. If God allows our sacrifice to ascend up in the presence of His divine Majesty, then it opens to us His heavenly treasures, so that we become rich in all things and shall be in want of no grace.[56]

The accompanying ceremony is in perfect harmony with the tenor of the prayer. According to a very ancient rubric,[57] the priest

---

fectiones nostrae sunt tepidae, et affectiones Angelorum ferventissimae et magis elevatae ad ipsum; desiderando pro nobis quod nos desideramus, cum accedant ad Deum familiarius et proximius, dicuntur sibi offerre, et quod Deus vidit nos primo petere et approbare per os nostrum, secundo magis approbat per os et desiderium Angelorum (S. Bonav., IV, dist. 45, dub. 7).

[55] Id unum petit Ecclesia cum Daniele (3:40), "ut fiat sacrificium nostrum in conspectu Dei et placeat illi," h. e. ut ad Deum deferatur oratio, actio et oblatio nostra, atque in conspectu Dei in coelo compleatur, quod in terrestri altari peragitur, et ex praestantia coelestis victimae et ex acceptatione sacrificii nostri in nos deinde omnis benedictio descendat. Hoc subsequentia verba confirmant. Vota nempe nostra ascendere ad Deum cupimus, "ut quotquot ex hac altaris participatione sacros. Filii tui corpus et sanguinem sumpserimus, omni benedictione coelesti et gratia repleamur." In altari est corpus et sanguis Christi: ex illo sumendum est nobis; sed rogandus divinus ejus Pater, ut actio hominum peccatorum tam sanctam hostiam offerentium ab eo clementer accipiatur: tunc enim omnis benedictio coelestis et gratia e coelesti isto convivio et sacrificio est nobis speranda (Muratori, *De rebus liturgicis dissertatio*, chap. 21.

[56] Tunc a Deo (hostia) quasi acceptatur, quando Deus nobis propitiatur et coelestis benedictio nobis ab eo mittitur (B. Odo Camer., *Expos. in Can. Missae*, dist. 3).

[57] Sacerdos quando dicit "Supplices te rogamus," humiliato capite inclinat se ante altare (*Ordo Rom. II*, n. 10). Cf. Amalarius, III, chap. 25; Microlog., chap. 16. In many places the hands were placed over the breast in the form of a cross at the same time. Sacerdos dicendo *Supplices* . . . stat inclinatus

FIRST PRAYER AFTER THE CONSECRATION

pronounces the petition of the principal clause with a profound inclination of the body to indicate the humility and fervor with which he implores almighty God to grant such great things.[58] Before the words, *ex hac altaris participatione* ("by partaking at this altar"), the priest reverently kisses the altar which he mentions in the prayer, so as to unite himself with the sacrificial Lamb thereon immolated. He then stands erect, and at the words "body and blood" he makes the sign of the cross over each of them to indicate also to the eye that this same body and blood were once offered on the cross. At the words *omni benedictione coelesti* ("with every heavenly blessing"), the priest makes the sign of the cross on himself to apply the overflowing benediction of the altar to himself and to the congregation, and to show that every blessing of the Eucharist comes to us through the cross. That the sacrifice ascends from earth to heaven, and the blessing of Heaven descends upon us, we are indebted to the one fountain of all grace, to our one and perfect mediator between heaven and earth; hence the petition concludes with the words: "Through the same Christ our Lord. Amen."

---

cancellatis (*crossed thus*: ✕) manibus ante pectus (Durand., IV, xl, 4). Cum dicit *Supplices* . . . , manibus cancellatis ante pectus, ita quod dextrum brachium sit supra sinistrum, inclinet ante altare (*Ordo Rom. XIV*, chap. 53). The Carmelites, Carthusians, and Dominicans still observe this rite. Some missals of the Middle Ages have in this place a special rubric; for example, Hic orat apud se quod voluerit, deinde dicit: *Jube haec*. Hic orat apud se inclinatus quae velit. *Jube*. (Gerbert., *Vetus Liturg. alemann.*, I, 363.) Cf. Berthold, *Tewtsch Rational*, chap. 15.

[58] Supplicamus tibi, curvamur ante te, obnixius deprecamur, ostende omnipotentiam, extende manum validam, ut quae propitio ac sereno vultu respicis, etiam ad invisibilia et sublimia tua perferantur et conspectui majestatis admittas. Hic necessitas incurvationis, hic opus supplicationis, hic incumbit consummatio totius nostri laboris, ut haec hostia perferatur in sublime altare tuum (B. Odo Camerac., *Expos. in Canon. Missae*, dist. 3).

CHAPTER XXXVII

THE SECOND PRAYER AFTER THE CONSECRATION

1. Inasmuch as our sacrifice is carried by the hands of angels from the earthly to the heavenly altar and united with the homages of the blessed, and thus presented before the throne of God, it becomes in a most sublime sense a fountain of living waters that descend in a full stream (Cant. 4:15) upon the earth and into the flaming abyss of purgatory, to refresh and revive the suffering children of the Church. Hence the Church feels urged to beg specially for the application of the spiritual waters of salvation. This she does, in the first place, in the concluding petition of the previous prayer, in behalf of all who by Communion will partake of the sacrifice; but she is still mindful of her children, whether they are suffering in the abode of purification or are still pilgrims on earth. She therefore not only prays for the communicants, but also intercedes (*Memento etiam*) for the departed, that they may quickly be admitted into heaven, and she implores for all those present (*Nobis quoque*) participation in the glory of the saints.

Memento etiam, Domine, famulorum famularumque tuarum N. et N., qui nos praecesserunt cum signo fidei, et dormiunt in somno pacis. Ipsis, Domine, et omnibus in Christo quiescentibus, locum refrigerii, lucis et pacis, ut indulgeas, deprecamur. Per eundem Christum Dominum nostrum. Amen.	Remember also, O Lord, Thy servants and handmaids, N. and N., who have gone before us with the sign of faith, and sleep the sleep of peace. To these, O Lord, and to all who rest in Christ, grant, we beseech Thee, a place of refreshment, light, and peace. Through Christ our Lord. Amen.

The Church's practice of offering the Holy Sacrifice for the departed and of praying for them during its celebration, dates from apostolic times and is an apostolic ordinance,[1] as the ancient liturgies and the writings of the Fathers clearly prove. The present silent recitation of the Memento of the Dead had its origin probably in the twelfth century, when the custom was discontinued of reading publicly the names of the departed for whom a special commemoration was to be made.[2] The liturgical commemoration for the departed is in many respects different from that for the living. This distinction is evident even from their position in the Mass: the one is placed before and the other after the Consecration.[3] As members of the Church militant on earth, the living may and ought to unite with the priest in offering the sacrifice, and offer themselves in the sacrifice. This is most fittingly done before the accomplishment of the real sacrificial action, that is, before the Consecration. The departed, however, are no longer able to unite in offering, but merely partake of the fruits of the sacrifice which we apply to them; hence it is most proper to be mindful of them when the sacrificial victim is resting on the altar. The Church neither offers nor prays for the reprobates in hell, nor for the blessed in heaven, but only for the suffering souls who, amid the pains of purgatory, await their final and complete redemption. Corresponding to this intention, the

---

[1] In Machabaeorum libris legimus, oblatum pro mortuis sacrificium; sed etsi nusquam in Scripturis veteribus omnino legeretur, non parva est universae Ecclesiae, quae in hac consuetudine claret, auctoritas, ubi in precibus sacerdotis, quae Domino Deo ad ejus altare funduntur, locum suum habet etiam commendatio mortuorum (S. August., *De cura pro mort. gerenda*, chap. 1, n. 1).

[2] This prayer (as also the *commemoratio pro vivis*) was in former times often inscribed: *Oratio super diptycha*, or *Oratio post nomina*. Post illa verba, quibus dicitur *in somno pacis*, usus fuit antiquorum, sicut etiam usque hodie romana agit Ecclesia, ut statim recitarentur ex diptychis, i.e. tabulis nomina defunctorum atque ita post lectionem nominum subjungerentur verba sequentia: *Ipsis*, videlicet quorum nomina memorantur, et ceteris *omnibus in Christo quiescentibus indulgeas locum refrigerii*, ubi non sentitur ardor poenarum (Pseudo-Alcuin., chap. 40).

[3] Both Mementos received various additions, inasmuch as express mention was made of various states and classes of persons. Also their position was long subject to change; for it often happened that the Memento of the Dead was joined to the Memento of the Living before the Consecration. One writer gives as the reason for its present position: Hic pro defunctis in Christo quiescentibus orat Ecclesia, ut iis haec prosint sacramenta, ubi notare poteris nomina quae volueris. Et quidem congrue haec interseritur memoria transeuntium, "qui in Domino moriuntur." Finita est enim memoria mortis Domini et sequitur mors nostra; Christus praecessit et nos ejus vestigia sequimur (*Sicard.*, III, chap. 6).

formula [4] of the Church in the Memento of the Dead refers only to the souls in purgatory.

2. "Remember also, O Lord, Thy servants and handmaids, N. and N., who have gone before us with the sign of faith, and sleep the sleep of peace." Here [5] the priest should commemorate some of the departed by name, that is, he should recall or even mention them in order to recommend them in a special manner to the favor and mercy of God. While so doing, he must keep his eyes fixed on the Blessed Sacrament, whereas at the Memento of the Living only a slight inclination of the head (*demisso aliquantulum capite*) is prescribed, and the eyes need not be fixed on the host.[6] The selection of the names is left to the priest, who should in this place comply with obligations of gratitude and love toward those of the dead who during life were related to him or in any manner associated with him. But since the Memento is made in the name of the Church, the celebrant must adhere to the ordinance expressed in the text itself. For the Church prays here in a special manner for those "who have gone before us with the sign of faith, and sleep the sleep of peace," that is, those who as true believers and as members of the Church have departed this earthly life in communion with the Church.[7] Accordingly, here all are excluded from being mentioned by name who have died outside the pale of the Church, as was formerly the case when names were read out from the diptychs.[8]

---

[4] A monumental commentary on these prayers and, at the same time, a proof of their great antiquity is established by the ancient Christian epitaphs, the various forms of which (acclamations, salutations, wishes, petitions) contain principally the words *refrigerium, lux, pax*, by which the bliss of heaven, under different aspects, is expressed. In the "lapidary prayers" of these tumular inscriptions the survivors wish to their departed: refreshment, light, peace, admission into paradise and the communion of saints, life in God, in Christ, and in the Holy Ghost. Entirely similar expressions are met with in the prayers of the *Sacrament. Gelasian.;* for example: *locus lucidus, locus refrigerii et quietis refrigerii sedes, quietis beatitudo, luminis claritas, lucis et pacis regio.*

[5] That is, not at the letters N. and N., but after the words *in somno pacis*. During the first thousand years they wrote, instead of N., the letters *ill.* diagonally.

[6] In Memento pro vivis tenentur oculi demissi vel clausi ad vitandam mentis distractionem; hic vero intenti ad Sacramentum teneri debent, quia ex Christi praesentia major devotio excitatur (Quarti, II, ix, 2).

[7] St. Cyril of Jerusalem writes (*Catech. mystag.*, V, chap. 2): "During the Holy Sacrifice we make intercession for all collectively who among us [that is, in the bosom of the Church, as members of the Church] are departed." This has been at all times the practice of the Church.

[8] In his private intention the priest may offer the Mass for others and here

SECOND PRAYER AFTER THE CONSECRATION

To move the Lord to pity and to indulgence, the Church calls her suffering children in purgatory the servants and handmaids of God, and stresses that they have departed from this world with the sign of faith. By the sign of faith is here to be understood, in the first place, the indelible character imprinted on the soul in the sacrament of baptism, whereby the faithful are distinguished from unbelievers.[9] Baptism is, indeed, called the sacrament of faith; by it men become united to Christ and incorporated into the Church. Furthermore, by the sign of faith is also to be understood the profession by word and deed, by a Christian life, by devotion to the Church, by the reception of the sacraments. Faith received in baptism must necessarily be a living faith in which one must persevere until death if it is to lead to salvation.[10] All who have passed into eternity with such a faith "sleep the sleep of peace": they died in peace with the Church, united interiorly and exteriorly to it.[11] Death in the grace and love of God, in living communion with Christ and the Church, may be designated as a peaceful slumber, inasmuch as the weary pilgrim of earth reposes in the grave far removed from all the sufferings and labors of life, and awaits

---

pray for all without distinction. Facile stat, ipsum sacerdotem talem ceremoniam [sc. Memento] ut personam publicam perficere et [futurum] sacrificium ex persona Ecclesiae Deo offerre, et tamen simul ut privatum illud ipsum offerre Deumque per ipsum pro aliquo deprecari (Coninck, *De sacr. et censur.*, disp. XIV, dub. 6).

[9] Orat pia Mater Ecclesia non solum pro vivis, sed etiam pro defunctis et eos sacrae oblationis intercessione commendat certissime credens, quod sanguis ille pretiosus, qui pro multis effusus est in remissionem peccatorum, non solum ad salutem viventium, verum etiam ad absolutionem valeat defunctorum, qui cum signo fidei praecedunt. . . . Signum fidei pro charactere christianitatis accipitur, quo fideles ab infidelibus discernuntur (Innoc. III, V, chap. 5).

[10] In like manner the Church prays at the blessing of a cemetery, that the Shepherd of eternal glory may not cease "to impart to the bodies that repose in this place, continual inviolability, that all the baptized who to the end of their life persevere in the Catholic faith (*quicunque Baptismi sacramentum perceperint et in fide catholica usque ad vitae terminum perseverantes fuerint*), and after the completion of the earthly pilgrimage commit their bodies to rest in this cemetery, at the sound of the angel's trumpet, united in body and soul, may be admitted to the eternal rewards of the joys of heaven." (Cf. *Pontif. Roman., De coemeterii benedictione.*)

[11] *In pace; vixit in pace; vitam duxit in pace; in pace morienti; decessit in pace fidei catholicae; credidit fide, dormit in pace; requiescit in pace; requiescit in somno pacis*: these and similar formulas on ancient Christian graves indicate that the departed lived in the orthodox faith and died in communion with the Church. This applies especially to places in which a heresy or schism prevailed.

a blissful awakening, a glorious resurrection of the body.[12]

The intercession for the dead continues. Not merely upon "these" (*ipsis*) who have just been mentioned, but upon "all who rest in Christ" [13] the blessing of the redeeming blood from the altar is to flow.[14] The Church forgets none of her children; she is full of maternal care and solicitude for all; in particular she ceases not to pray for her suffering children in purgatory, until they have reached their heavenly Father's house. As in this Memento, so likewise in other liturgical formulas of prayer, the special intercession for individual departed souls is united with supplicaton for all the faithful departed.[15]

But how can the Church, for those who sleep in peace and rest in Christ, still implore for "a place of refreshment, light, and peace?" [16]

---

[12] In Holy Writ, the Fathers, and the liturgy, death (of the just) is often called *dormitio, somnus,* and the dead are called *dormientes*. That death is but a passing sleep, is also signified by the name *coemeterium* (κοιμητήριον, *dormitorium,* place of slumber), by which the Church from the most ancient times designates the (blessed) burial-place. Cymiterium recubitorium vel dormitorium est mortuorum, qui et ideo ab Ecclesia dormientes dicuntur, quia resurrecturi non dubitantur (Walafr. Strabo, *De rebus ecclesiast.,* chap. 6). Prudentius (*Cathemer.,* X, 56) calls the body of a Christian resting in the vault a *res non mortua, sed data somno,* as the Lord Himself said of the departed daughter of Jairus: *Non est mortua puella, sed dormit* (Matt. 9:24).

[13] With reference to the Apoc. 14:13, *Amodo jam dicit Spiritus, ut requiescant a laboribus suis,* as it says of them *qui in Domino moriuntur,* the departed are often called *quiescentes* (*in Christo*), but in the Mozarabic Missal they are called *pausantes,* according to the Greek appellation. We likewise meet the words: *quietoria, requietionis loca, sedes requietionis,* as designations of the Christian cemetery. In the *benedictio coemeterii* the Church prays that the consecrated place may be *dulcis requies et pausatio mortuorum*. By the words *aeternae pausationis solatium* in the Mozarabic liturgy, eternal rest is implored for the departed (on the feast of St. Eulalia of Emerita, Dec. 10). In Purgatorio etiam est requies propter certitudinem de salute, suffragia vivorum et consolationem Angelorum. Mors justo est requies, somnus, cessatio a labore et dolore, recreatio (Corn. a Lap., *In Sap.,* 4:7).

[14] Non sunt praetermittendae supplicationes pro spiritibus mortuorum, quas faciendas pro omnibus in christiana et catholica societate defunctis . . . sub generali commemoratione suscepit Ecclesia, ut quibus ad ista desunt parentes aut filii aut quicunque cognati vel amici, ab una eis exhibeatur matre communi (S. August., *De cura pro mortuis gerenda,* chap. 4).

[15] Cf., for example, the Requiem Mass, in which the Introit, Tract, Offertorium, and Communio refer to all the departed, even though the sacrifice is offered for one individual soul.

[16] Apte instituta est haec oratio, ut iis solis conveniret, qui in Purgatorio degunt: hi enim et pacem ac quietem eo sensu habent, quod jam certi sint

The suffering souls indeed enjoy peace and rest, inasmuch as they are removed from the discord and turmoil of this sinful and deceitful world; but as long as they must remain at a distance from the vision of God in a place of silent suffering, their peace and rest are still imperfect; therefore, we implore for them full and eternal peace in heaven. When the just soul has reached purgatory, she sees before her but two objects, suffering and joy. The greatest bitterness is there mingled with the most serene peace. These souls are full of a pure and strong love of God, full of patient contentment and resignation to God's holy decrees. They praise purgatory as an invention of His mercy; but, at the same time, they are consumed with the flames of longing for God, with the fire of pains, and with the pains of fire. Full of quiet sorrow they linger in the place of their banishment, weeping tears at the thought of the heavenly Jerusalem, because their exile in a foreign country is prolonged. In a manner inexplicable to us, they are at one and the same time filled with a holy suffering and a holy joy. In contrast with the painful exile of purgatory, heaven is indeed a blissful place of refreshment (*refrigerii*),[17] light, and peace.[18]

---

de futuro aeternae beatitudinis praemio, et liberi a tentationum ac concupiscentiae bello; est tamen, unde iis ulterius et refrigerium ac pacem deprecemur, quia et flammis torquentur et quamdiu a divino, quem toti inhiant, conspectu arcentur, omnimoda pace frui non possunt (Tournely, *De Eucharist.*, II, x, 3).

[17] *Refrigerium* = refreshment; often occurs in the ancient Christian Latin and designates that which is, contains, and affords refreshment, recreation, regalement, alleviation, relief, solace, rest, comfort, joy, felicity—hence the state of the blessed after death.

Refrigerium here denotes a twofold refreshment. In the first place it signifies (from *refrigerare* = to make something cold, to cool it) the ceasing of *poena sensus*; that is, the extinguishing of the heat of purgatory. This is shown also by the following petitions from the Mozarabic Missal: *animam pietate tua refrigerii rore perfundas; animam coelestis roris perfusione refrigera.* *Refrigerium* also frequently denotes refreshment by food and drink: *Inopes refrigerio isto juvamus,* writes Tertullian of the agape (*Apolog.*, chap. 39). Therefore we may here understand the remission of *poena damni*, that is, the cessation of the temporary exclusion from the beatific vision. Heavenly bliss is often represented under the figure of a nuptial celebration and a joyful banquet. Cf. the concluding formulas of the liturgical blessing at meals: *Mensae coelestis participes faciat nos rex aeternae gloriae. Ad coenam vitae aeternae perducat nos rex aeternae gloria.* Many epitaphs also contain the word; for example: *in refrigerio anima tua; cujus spiritum in refrigerium suscipiat Dominus; Antonia anima dulcis tibi Deus refrigeret.*

[18] The formula *in pace* is frequently met with on ancient Christian graves:

At the concluding formula, "Through the same Christ our Lord," the priest not only joins his hands, but also bows his head. The inclination of the head at these words is singular, as otherwise it is nowhere prescribed when the name "Christ" occurs without the addition of Jesus. It must, therefore, be grounded on the text of the prayer itself and have some mysterious signification.[19] Christ bowed His head on the cross when He died, and then descended into the kingdom of the dead, there to console the devout who lived before His coming. According to medieval commentators, the priest would now call to mind the death of Christ by bowing his head, since he here prays and implores for all who rest in Christ that the atoning blood, flowing from the Eucharistic sacrifice as from a fountain, may flow into purgatory to alleviate and abridge the sufferings of the poor souls.

---

for instance: victori in pace; vale in pace; in pace Domini dormias; tecum pax Christi; Gaudentia suscepeatur in pace; te in pace Christus faciat; semper vive in pace; cum Deo in pace; pax cum angelis; Laurinia melle dulcior quiescas in pace; Gensane pax ispirito tuo; dormit in somno pacis; pausat in pace; in pace requievit; quescit in pace aeterna; susceptus in pace; accercitus in pacem; natus in pace; mater dulcissima in pace Christi recepta; letaris in pace; in pace delicium; vivis in gloria Dei et in pace Domini nostri.

[19] This bowing cannot be occasioned by either the preceding *deprecamur* (as de Vert asserts), or by the following *Nobis quoque peccatoribus* (as Gavantius supposes); for in that case the action would be combined with the words in question. In hoc ego magis peculiare dicerem adesse mysterium, et est, quod ibi sermo est de Christo, in quo mortui quiescunt, et omnibus in Christo quiescentibus; quare cum Christus mortem nostram moriendo destruxerit repraesentat sibi sacerdos Christum morientem, qui inclinato capite emisit spiritum. In memoriam igitur et venerationem illius gestus, quo Christus mortuus est, sacerdos inclinat caput, nisi mavis dicere, inclinationem fieri in commemorationem descensus, quem ad inferos fecit Christi spiritus pro liberandis mortuis (Cavalieri, III, xi, 4). Cf. Quarti, III, ix, 2.

CHAPTER XXXVIII

THE THIRD PRAYER AFTER THE CONSECRATION

1. The Memento of the Dead is for the living a solemn and touching *Memento mori*. It reminds us of those who on this earthly pilgrimage "have gone before us" (*nos praecesserunt*) [1] and have arrived in the land of eternity. We will soon follow them. The short years pass away rapidly, and we are walking in a path by which we shall not return (Job 16:23). We are strangers and newcomers upon earth, as were all our fathers before us. "Our days upon earth are as a shadow, and there is no stay" (I Par. 29:15). Soon we shall be standing on the brink of the grave. As these thoughts come up, what is more natural than for us to desire that the Lord would receive us into the eternal dwellings of light? Therefore this petition most appropriately follows the Memento of the Dead.[2]

---

[1] These words are also found on epitaphs; for example: quae nos praecesserunt in somno pacis; in pace precessit; precessit nos in pace; praecessit ad pacem. In the Mozarabic Mass for the vigil of Pentecost the departed are called *nostri, qui jam a seculo precesserunt*.

[2] Originally this prayer was a special supplication for the priests and clerics assisting at the altar, or for the whole clergy in general, and may now still be suitably and principally recited for this intention. The clergy are in a strict and eminent sense God's servants (*famuli*). Sicut patet in Canone Missae, cum dicitur *Nobis quoque peccatoribus*, statutum est, quod sacerdos offerat etiam pro se, quod non fieret, nisi esset infirmitate peccatorum, quibus est circumdatus, non oppressus. Si enim sit in mortali peccato, non debet celebrare (S. Thom., *In epist. ad Heb.*, chap. 5, lect. 1).

The contents and connection of the Canon prayers after the Consecration are concisely and clearly shown by St. Thomas. Sacerdos accedit ad ipsam consecrationem, in qua (1) petit consecrationis effectum (*Quam oblationem* . . .); (2) consecrationem peragit per verba Salvatoris (*Qui pridie* . . .); (3) excusat praesumptionem per obedientiam ad mandatum Christi (*Unde et memores* . . .); (4) petit hoc sacrificium peractum esse Deo acceptum (*Supra quae* . . .); (5) petit hujus sacrificii et sacramenti effectum: primo quidem quantum ad ipsos sumentes (*Supplices te* . . .), secundo quantum ad mortuos (*Memento etiam* . . .), tertio specialiter quantum ad ipsos sacerdotes offerentes (*Nobis quoque* . . .). S. Thom., IIIa, q. 83, a. 4.

Nobis quoque peccatoribus famulis tuis, de multitudine miserationum tuarum sperantibus, partem aliquam et societatem donare digneris, cum tuis sanctis Apostolis et Martyribus: cum Joanne, Stephano, Matthia, Barnaba, Ignatio, Alexandro, Marcellino, Petro, Felicitate, Perpetua, Agatha, Lucia, Agnete, Caecilia, Anastasia, et omnibus sanctis tuis: intra quorum nos consortium, non aestimator meriti, sed veniae, quaesumus, largitor admitte. Per Christum Dominum nostrum.

To us also, Thy sinful servants, who hope in the multitude of Thy mercies, vouchsafe to grant some part and fellowship with Thy holy apostles and martyrs: with John, Stephen, Matthias, Barnabas, Ignatius, Alexander, Marcellinus, Peter, Felicitas, Perpetua, Agatha, Lucy, Agnes, Cecilia, Anastasia, and all Thy saints: into whose company admit us, we beseech Thee, not weighing our merits but granting us pardon. Through Christ our Lord.

The first three words, *nobis quoque peccatoribus* ("To us also, Thy sinful servants"), are the only words in the Canon that are said in a slightly raised tone of voice, that is, half aloud (*elata parum voce*); the priest at the same time strikes his breast.[3] Both the tone of voice and the striking of the breast indicate to the celebrant with what great sorrow and compunction he is to acknowledge his sinfulness, and admonish all the faithful present to unite with the officiating priest in these same penitential sentiments which animate him, since he recites this prayer also for them and in their name.[4] We acknowledge and confess ourselves in all humility to be but poor sinners, for we thereby draw on ourselves God's favor and mercy.

[3] Dicentes: *Nobis quoque peccatoribus*, vocem paululum elevamus, ut ex gemitu cordis in silentio procedat gemens oris confessio. . . . Cum dicitur: *Nobis quoque peccatoribus*, solet rumpi silentium, paululum expressa voce proferendo, ut veniat nobis in mentem latronis confessio et pietas Domini de cruce dicentis: "Hodie mecum eris in paradiso" (Luke, chap. 23). (Steph. Augustod., chap. 17.) Percussura pectoris poenitentiae est et luctus indicium (Amalar., III, chap. 26).

[4] Ut facilius exaudiatur sacerdos captetque Dei benevolentiam, peccatorem se et alios vivos (quos eodem pronomine quo se signat et includit) pronuntiat, quoniam nihil aeque divinam majestatem inflectit ad impendendam hominibus misericordiam, quam humilis peccatorum recognitio atque confessio, qua quis se indignum fatetur ex se ipso divinis beneficiis, sed totam suam fiduciam collocat atque reponit in Dei misericordia (Clichtov., *Elucidat. eccles.*, III, n. 24).

THIRD PRAYER AFTER THE CONSECRATION 713

To obtain admittance into the kingdom of heaven we must pray for it and place all our confidence in the greatness and abundance of the divine mercies (*de multitudine miserationum tuarum sperantibus*).[5] Animated with this sentiment we beg God to mercifully grant us "some part and fellowship" with His holy apostles and martyrs.[6] The imperishable inheritance of the kingdom of heaven is prepared for all the redeemed; but the individual man will share therein according to the measure of his merits and virtue. All the happiness of the citizens of heaven proceeds from God's eternal and infinite glory. Our inheritance, our share in the land of the living will be God Himself: the clear vision, the ravishing love, and the blissful enjoyment of God. "For what have I in heaven, and besides Thee what do I desire upon earth? For Thee my flesh and my heart hath fainted away; Thou art the God of my heart, and the God that is my portion forever" (Ps. 72:25 f.). The possession of the Supreme Good will, therefore, be imparted to us in union with the other blessed; the fellowship of all the other citizens of heaven is a fresh source of the purest, sweetest joys.[7]

---

[5] Cf. Miserere mei Deus, secundum magnam misericordiam tuam, et secundum *multitudinem miserationum tuarum* dele iniquitatem meam (Ps. 50:1 f.). *Misericordia* = mercy, compassion as a virtue or disposition (*habitus*); on the contrary, *miseratio* = the feeling sympathy, the pardoning as actualization and proof (*actus*) of a merciful disposition (*usus sive effectus misericordiae* [S. Thom.]). Hence the Lord in the Psalms is often called *misericors et miserator: sc. misericors in affectu benignitatis intus abscondito et sibi naturaliter insito, miserator in effectu foris conspicuo* (Gerhoh. Reichersp., *In Ps.* 24). Misericordia prout in Deo esse censetur non est nisi bonitas ejus piissima; miseratio autem Dei est effectus misericordiae ejus. Multae ergo possunt esse miserationes Dei, quoniam multa sunt opera pietatis divinae, sed misericordia Dei non est nisi una, quae est divina essentia (Dion. Carthus., *In Ps.* 24). Major est multitudo Dei miserationum, quam multitudo omnium peccatorum (Gerhoh. Reichersp., *loc. cit.*). Omnipotens sempiterne Deus, qui abundantia pietatis tuae et merita supplicum excedis et vota: effunde super nos misericordiam tuam, ut dimittas quae conscientia metuit, et adjicias quod oratio non praesumit (*Dom. XI post Pent.*).

[6] The words "God give you a portion and a share with His saints" occur already in a letter of St. Polycarp to the Philippians (chap. 12), written about the year 107, and are probably taken from the apostolic liturgy.

[7] Quarto consistit [vita aeterna] in omnium beatorum jucunda societate, quae societas erit maxime delectabilis, quia quilibet habebit omnia bona cum omnibus beatis; nam quilibet diliget alium sicut seipsum et ideo gaudebit de bono alterius sicut de suo. Quo fit, ut tantum augeatur laetitia et gaudium unius, quantum est gaudium omnium. Ps. 86:7: Sicut laetantium omnium habitatio est in te (S. Thom., *In Symbol. Apostol. expos.*, n. 39).

2. Of the saints of heaven some apostles and martyrs are mentioned by name in the *Nobis quoque*—fifteen in all (eight male and seven female saints), who all underwent the violent death of martyrdom. At the head of the list is St. John the Baptist,[8] as the enumeration of the male saints is regulated by the time of their martyrdom. St. John suffered a martyr's death even before Christ died on the cross; he was beheaded because he had severely censured the adulterous union of Herod with Herodias. After St. John, mention is made of St. Stephen, who leads [9] the brilliant host of Christian martyrs that after the death of the Saviour shed their blood for divine truth. He was one of those seven wise and pious men who were ordained as the first deacons [10] by the apostles; before all the others he is praised in Holy Scripture as a man "full of faith and of the Holy Ghost, . . . full of grace and fortitude, [who] did great wonders and signs among the people" (Acts 6:5, 8). Following St. Stephen comes St. Matthias,[11] who, after the ascension of the Lord, was by the will of God called to the apostolate in place of the traitor, Judas. St. Barnabas,[12] the fourth martyr mentioned in this prayer, was also

[8] S. R. C., March 27, 1824. The opinion, very general during the Middle Ages, that the apostle and evangelist John is here named a second time, is no longer tenable.

[9] The name μάρτυς (= *testis*) is given to St. Stephen for the first time by St. Paul (Acts 22:20). By the Fathers he is styled: *primitiae martyrum; vertex martyrum; martyrum princeps; triumphatorum martyrum dux; qui primus martyrii fores aperuit; qui primus choro martyrum aditum patefecit; phalangis martyrum antesignanus;* πρωτομάρτυς. Cf. Nilles, *Kalendarium manuale,* I, 232.

[10] In the Greek liturgy he is called ἀρχιδιάκονος, and in the *Roman Pontifical, dux ac praevius* of the other deacons. As deacon, with loving solicitude he exercised the charge of caring for the poor and the sick; he likewise, with great wisdom and power, preached the doctrine of Christ to the Jews. They obstinately resisted him, and in their fury they stoned to death this courageous preacher of the truth, whom they hated. In the sixth century the principal part of his body was taken to Rome and placed beside the remains of St. Lawrence in a splendid marble sarcophagus under the high altar of the Basilica of St. Lawrence outside the Walls. His feast is celebrated on December 26.

[11] It is said that he was beheaded with an axe, and that St. Helena brought a portion of his relics to Treves. His head is preserved in the Church of *S. Maria Maggiore* in Rome; his feast occurs on February 24 or (in leap year) 25.

[12] St. Barnabas was a Levite and came from Cyprus. He was originally called Joseph; the apostles gave him the name Barnabas (= Son of Consolation) to indicate that he consoled and encouraged others by his supernatural enthusiasm and power of speaking. St. Barnabas is regarded by many only as an assistant and companion to the apostles, as one resembling the apostles;

an apostle called to the apostolate after Christ's ascension. The Scriptures call him a "good man and full of the Holy Ghost and of faith" (Acts 11:24).

In this catalogue of saints are mentioned martyrs from every walk of life. We have here a celebrated bishop, a pope, a priest, and an exorcist. St. Ignatius of Antioch [13] was a pupil of the apostles and the second successor of St. Peter in the see of Antioch. St. Alexander I [14] was the fifth pope after St. Peter. St. Marcellinus was a priest and St. Peter [15] an exorcist of the Roman Church. Among the female saints we commemorate two young mothers, SS. Felicitas

---

but many more and better reasons favor the opinion that Barnabas, like St. Paul, was an apostle in the strict sense of the term. "In consequence of a supernatural revelation, Paul and Barnabas were ordained with prayer and the imposing of hands, and furnished with all authority; they were to complete the Apostolic College" (Hergenröther, *Handbuch der allgemeinen Kirchengeschichte*, I, 71). After having been consecrated bishop at Antioch, he made (44 or 45 A.D.) an extended missionary tour with St. Paul; later on he separated from him and labored chiefly in his native island, Cyprus, where his renowned apostolate was crowned with martyrdom (between 53 and 76 A.D.). Toward the end of the fifth century the body of the saint was discovered in a cave at Salamis in Cyprus. His feast occurs on June 11, the day of his death.

[13] Under the emperor Trajan he was sentenced to death, dragged in chains to Rome, and there in the Colosseum, on December 20, 107, exposed to the wild beasts, which tore and ate his body so that only the larger and harder bones remained. This greatly celebrated bishop burned with an ardent desire for martyrdom, as is evident from the letters which on the way to Rome he wrote to different communities: "You cannot prove your tender love for me better than by allowing me to consecrate myself in sacrifice. . . . Well is it for me if I would perish to the world so that I may arise for God. Allow me to become the food of beasts, that through them I may attain to God. I am the wheat of God and must be ground by the teeth of beasts, so as to become the pure bread of Christ. Fire and cross, multitudes of wild beasts, the tearing of the body, the cutting into pieces of my limbs, the grinding of my bones—in brief, whatever of tortures the devil can invent, let all come upon me, if I but gain Jesus Christ. All the delights of earth I account as nothing, as nothing all the kingdoms of the world; better is it for me to die for Jesus Christ than to reign over all the bounds of the earth."

[14] On May 3, 115 (?), this holy pope was beheaded outside Rome together with the priests Eventius and Theodulus. His body now reposes in the Church of St. Sabina at Rome. His feast occurs on May 3.

[15] St. Peter, while in prison, had delivered the daughter of the jailer, Artemius, from an evil spirit, whereupon the whole family of Artemius was converted and baptized by the priest Marcellinus. SS. Peter and Marcellinus were then frightfully tortured and led outside the city for execution as far as the so-called Black Forest (*Silva nigra*), where they themselves cleared the place in the thickets and then bowed their heads under the sword. On account of

and Perpetua; [16] four chaste virgins, SS. Agatha, Lucy, Agnes, and Cecilia; [17] and a holy widow, St. Anastasia.[18] In commemorating these virgins and holy women who suffered cruel martyrdom for Christ, the Church acknowledges and extols the divine power that "has granted even to the weaker sex the triumph of martyrdom." [19] These illustrious martyrs mentioned in the Mass are but a few of that "great multitude, which no man could number, of all nations and tribes and peoples and tongues," which St. John saw "standing before the throne and in the sight of the Lamb, clothed with white robes and palms in their hands. . . . These are they who are come out of great tribulation, and have washed their robes and have made them white in the blood of the Lamb" (Apoc. 7:9, 14).

3. With these and all the rest of the saints, whose number and names the all-seeing eye of God alone knows, we desire to be eternally united in heaven.[20] This petition is expressed at the beginning of the prayer, and is now at the conclusion repeated in different words; we implore admittance into the community of heaven, and for such a fellowship with the saints we do not rely on our own merit, but on the merciful indulgence of God.[21] The communion

---

their martyrdom the place was afterward called the White Forest (*Silva candida*). Their feast is kept on June 2.

[16] The two youthful heroines, Felicitas and Perpetua, suffered at Carthage in North Africa. The former was a slave, the latter of noble birth. They were confined in a dark prison filled with smoke and filth, where, amid the taunts of her jailers, Felicitas gave birth to a child. In the year 202, during the persecution of the emperor Severus, the young women were cruelly scourged and then cast before a wild cow; finally they were beheaded. Their feast occurs on March 6.

[17] For these four virgins see footnote 26 at the end of this chapter.

[18] St. Anastasia, according to a Roman legend, suffered from the cruelty of her pagan husband, Publius; after his death she gave herself over to practices of charity and mercy.

[19] *Orat. Eccles.*

[20] Quidnam nobis de nostra quantacumque scientia provenire possit, quod non sit minus hac gloria, qua inter Dei filios numeramur? Parum dixi: nec respici in ejus comparatione potest orbis ipse et plenitudo ejus, etiamsi totus cedat unicuivis in possessionem. Ceterum, si nos ignorantia Dei tenet, quomodo speramus in eum quem ignoramus? Si nostri, quomodo humiles erimus, putantes nos aliquid esse cum nihil simus? Scimus autem nec superbis nec desperatis partem esse vel societatem in sorte Sanctorum (S. Bernard., *In Cantic. serm.*, XXXVII, n. 5).

[21] Novit Ecclesia, Deum non nisi intercedentibus meritis tribuere beatitudinem; sed nec illud ignorat, ut in Sanctorum admittamur consortium, non

THIRD PRAYER AFTER THE CONSECRATION

of life and of goods with the saints (*consortium Sanctorum*) consists in this, that we may become associates (*consortes*) in their heavenly bliss and glory and obtain some part (*sors*) of the blessed inheritance which will be granted to all who are born again of the Holy Ghost.[22] Thus the Apostle writes (Col. 1:12): "Giving thanks to God the Father, who hath made us worthy to be partakers of the lot (*sortis*) of the saints in light." And in the Book of Wisdom (5:5) it is said of the pious: "Behold! how they are numbered among the children of God, and their lot (*sors*) is among the saints." We do not ask for the glory of the saints by reason of our own merits, but we confide in the merciful and gracious bounty of the Lord.[23]

The happiness of heaven is assuredly a gift of divine mercy.[24] It is in itself a mark of the goodness of God that we can even merit heaven, and His bounty bestows upon us a far richer reward than we

---

modo necessariam esse gloriam, sed etiam gratiam et veniam peccatorum, quae sine meritis nostris dantur tantummodo per Christum Dominum nostrum; ipsa nostra merita dona esse misericordiae Dei et gratiae, nobisque misericordia Dei opus esse vel in earum actionum examine, quas bonas existimamus (Bened. XIV, *De Missae sacrif.*, II, xviii, 2).

[22] Often in the liturgy, especially in the prayers for the departed, eternal bliss is designated as *consortium Dei, consortium Sanctorum; consortium perpetuae beatitudinis, consortium lucis aeternae*.

[23] *Non aestimator meriti, sed veniae largitor* = in that Thou wilt not consider, make account of, regard, what we deserve, that is, our trifling merits, or also our misdeeds, to influence Thy judgment according to them, but in abundant measure to impart to us merciful indulgence and forgiveness. The word *meritum* can be taken here as = *malum meritum, demeritum, meritum supplicii*: the guilt, the transgression, as *merere* often = an evil, to deserve or to draw on one's self punishment. Omnipotens aeterne Deus, misericordiam tuam ostende supplicibus, ut qui de meritorum (= peccatorum) qualitate diffidimus, non judicium tuum, sed indulgentiam sentiamus (*Sacrament. Gregor., Dom. XIX post Pent.*). Cum pro nostris meritis jugiter mereamur affligi, tu tamen judicium ad correctionem temperas, non perpetuam exerces ad poenam (*ibid., Dom. XXII post Pent.*). Quia de meritorum qualitate diffido, ad misericordiam tuam confugio, ut impetrem per tuam misericordiam, quod non merui per meam justitiam, immo quod ex toto demeruisse convincor, si delictorum meorum fueris memor et misericordiae tuae immemor (Gerhoh. Reichersp., *In Ps.* 24). Cum praesens est veniae largitor, magis confidit exaudiri devotus peccator (Stephan. Augustod., chap. 9).

[24] Vita aeterna non ut debitum rependitur hominibus, sed ut gratia et misericordia. "Gratia Dei vita aeterna," inquit Apostolus (Rom. 6:23). Haec meritis quidem nostris redditur, sed merita ipsa sunt dona gratiae et misericordiae Dei, Deusque merita nostra remunerans, remuneratur dona sua, "cumulans sua dona coronis," inquit S. Prosper, carmine de ingratis (Pouget, *Inst. cathol.*, II, Part III, sect. 2, chap. 7, § 22, n. 25). Cum Deus coronat *merita nostra*, nihil aliud coronat quam munera sua (S. August., *Epist.*, 194, chap. 5, n. 19).

actually deserve. If we consider the succession of all the graces from the first to the last, including the grace of final perseverance, must we not gratefully acknowledge that our life is adorned with a rich wreath of divine mercies? Yes, our rescue from eternal perdition is a free gift of God's merciful goodness and predilection; His mercy goes before us (Ps. 58:11), accompanies us (Ps. 22:25), and follows us all the days of our life (Ps. 22:6). Out of mercy God sent us His Son as a Redeemer; out of mercy He has promised us life eternal; out of mercy He has rescued us from the depths of a life of sin incurred through our own fault, and placed us in the kingdom of His light; out of mercy He has preserved us from innumerable sins and pardoned all those committed; out of mercy He knocks at our hearts, admonishes and warns us, directs our destiny in such a manner, and so grants us a chain of powerful graces as to enable us to remain faithful until death and bear off the crown of life. But action must correspond with the desire. If we wish for the glory of the saints, we must share their labors and sufferings. Through many tribulations only can we enter with all the saints into the joy of the Lord,[25] for if with them we suffer and die for Christ, with them also shall we be glorified.[26]

[25] "I enjoy great peace, a sweet contentment. . . . The most bitter portion of the chalice of the passion our Lord has drunk. For us there remain but some drops. Let us praise His infinite love which forestalls us with so much sweetness. I have always recited with an elevated heart this wonderful prayer of our holy liturgy: 'that Thou vouchsafe to grant us some part and fellowship with Thy holy apostles and martyrs.' Well, then, our dear Lord has heard me. I, too, like His most faithful friends, have been adorned with the glorious ignominy of our Master. Hence again, let us praise God. . . . I will suffer all; but I will remain united to Pius IX, to the Apostolic See, and until my last breath will I defend the liberty of the Church." Thus wrote Don Antonio de Macedo Costa, bishop of Para in Brazil, from his captivity, 1874 (cf. *Stimmen aus Maria-Laach*, VI [1874], 380).

[26] Two cities of Sicily, Palermo and Catania, contest the honor of St. Agathas' birthplace. It is certain that under the emperor Decius, in 251, she bore the crown of martyrdom at Catania. This holy virgin was renowned far and wide for her nobility and wealth, as well as for her beauty and virtue. Already in her childhood she had chosen Jesus for her spouse, and she clung to Him with undivided love. Accused of being a Christian, she was dragged before the heathen judge, Quintianus. This villain endeavored by many mean artifices to overcome her chaste mind and her courage. But, like a rock in the ocean, the virgin remained unmoved and unshaken; as the dust beneath her feet she accounted all that the world could offer. In prison her tortured breasts were miraculously healed by St. Peter. Afterward the wretched tyrant gave orders that the saint be rolled on sharp potsherds and glowing coals.

Again brought back to prison, the saint prayed: "Lord, Thou who hast created me and preserved me since my childhood, who hast delivered my heart from the love of the world and protected my body from perdition, who hast made me triumph over tortures and bonds, over iron and fire, I pray Thee, receive my spirit from this earth into the bosom of Thy mercy." After her death her tomb, made glorious by God with many miracles, became the refuge of the Christians and even of the heathens. There also was kept the wonderful veil that was not burned, but only somewhat crimsoned, when the saint was thrown into the fire. Exactly one year after her death the neighboring volcano of Etna burst forth in torrents of fire, which moved toward the city of Catania and threatened its destruction; then the inhabitants ran in terror to her tomb, took the veil, and held it in the direction of the stream of lava. At that very instant the lava took another course toward the ocean and the city was saved. February 5 is her feast day.

St. Lucy suffered martyrdom about 304, in the great persecution of Diocletian against the Christians. She came from Syracuse, was of noble lineage, and at an early age vowed perpetual chastity to the Lord. According to her acts, which are not at all reliable, her mother was miraculously restored to health at the tomb of St. Agatha. Thereupon Lucy sold her ornaments and her goods in order to give the proceeds to the poor and the sick. Accused of being a Christian, she appeared before the tribunal of the heathen judge, Paschasius, but refused to offer sacrifice to the idols when commanded to do so. Because she had said: "They that live chastely and devoutly are a temple of God, and the Holy Ghost dwells in them," they wished to drag her to a brothel; but the Lord rendered her as immovable as a pillar, so that no power could move her. Then a funereal pyre was built around her and ignited; but the flames left her untouched. Finally a sword was thrust through her neck; but she lived until she had received the Viaticum from a priest and had consoled the Christians who were standing around. Her feast is kept on December 13.

St. Agnes, the child of wealthy and distinguished parents, was the most celebrated virgin martyr of Rome. Truly responding to her name, as St. Jerome writes, she passed her childhood in spotless purity and lamblike innocence ($ἀγνή$ = the chaste or pure; *agnus* = lamb). A hundred years after her death St. Ambrose said: "Even at the present day many Roman maidens cherish the example of St. Agnes as though she were still dwelling and living among us, animating themselves thereby to a perpetual preservation of purity." She gained the double crown of virginity and martyrdom at the tender age of twelve. The accounts of her death do not agree, but it is certain that she was buried a short distance from the city on the Via Nomentana in the villa of her parents. Her tomb became glorious; for on the spot arises one of the loveliest and most renowned churches of Rome, *S. Agnese fuori le mura*. There annually on the anniversary of her death (January 21) two white lambs are laid on the altar and blessed during the singing of the Agnus Dei. They are again blessed by the pope and then entrusted to the Benedictine nuns of St. Agnes to be cared for. From their wool are made the palliums, which the Holy Father, after having placed them for one night on the tomb of the Princes of the Apostles, blesses and sends to the archbishops as a sign of their precedence over the bishops.

St. Cecilia was a maiden of noble origin; from her earliest childhood she had wholly dedicated herself to the service of God by the vow of chastity.

According to her acts, which are not reliable, she was commanded by her parents to marry a wealthy and distinguished young man named Valerian, who was a heathen. She consented only after receiving the assurance, through her guardian angel, that God would preserve her virginity even after her marriage. By prayer and penance Cecilia prepared for this worldly nuptial day, and when at the wedding feast the nuptial hymn was sung "amidst the sound of musical instruments (*cantantibus organis*), Cecilia secretly sang in her heart to the Lord: 'Keep Thou my heart and my body immaculate, that I may not be confounded' " (*Brev. Roman.*). Shortly afterward she converted her husband, Valerian, and his brother, Tiburtius. Cecilia was commanded by Almachius, the pagan prefect of the city, to be suffocated in the bathroom (*Caldarium*) of her own palace. She survived this ordeal, whereupon the tyrant sent the executioner to her, who struck her thrice without severing her head; for three days she continued to live, giving consolation and counsel to all who came to the palace. She ordered that her house should perpetually serve as a church, and finally breathed forth her angelic soul. She was laid in a coffin of cypress wood, in the same posture in which she died, and was interred in the Catacombs of St. Callistus. In the year 821 her holy body was discovered by Paschal I, who placed it under the high altar in the *S. Cecilia in Trastevere*. Almost eight hundred years later (in 1599) Cardinal Sfondrati found the body of the holy martyr still incorrupt in precisely the same posture in which she lay on the floor of her house. Thus she still reposes, enveloped in her rich attire and in a penitential garment, on which the glorious traces of her blood are still visible. She probably died about the year 230; her feast is celebrated on November 22. St. Cecilia is honored as the patroness of Church music, of poets and musicians.

CHAPTER XXXIX

THE CONCLUSION OF THE CANON

THE foregoing prayer closes with the ordinary formula, "through Christ our Lord," but no Amen follows, so that the intimate connection between these concluding words and the beginning of the following prayer may be clearly shown.[1]

Per quem haec omnia, Domine, semper bona creas, sancti✠ficas, vivi✠ficas, bene✠dicis, et praestas nobis. Per ip✠sum, et cum ip✠so, et in ip✠so est tibi, Deo Patri ✠ omnipotenti, in unitate Spiritus ✠ sancti, omnis honor et gloria. Per omnia saecula saeculorum. R. Amen.	By whom, O Lord, Thou dost always create, sanctify ✠, vivify ✠, bless ✠, and bestow upon us all these good things. Through Him ✠ and with Him ✠ and in Him ✠ is to Thee, God the Father ✠ Almighty, in the unity of the Holy ✠ Ghost, all honor and glory: world without end. R. Amen.

The sacrificial prayer of the Canon thus closes with a beautiful and solemn prayer accompanied by expressive ceremonies. It is di-

[1] The concluding formulas of the preceding Canon Prayers have received the *Amen* only since the twelfth century; previously it was placed at the end of the whole Canon after the words *per omnia saecula saeculorum*, and that as a response of the people. Hic elevat Oblatam cum calice dicens: *Per omnia saecula saeculorum*. Responsio: *Amen* (Microl., chap. 22). Assensum quaerit Ecclesiae sacerdos, dicens sonora voce *Per omnia saecula saeculorum*. Supplet populus super orationem ejus locum idiotae et respondet *Amen* (I Cor., chap. 14), hac una participem voce se faciens omnium charismatum, quae sacerdos multiplici sacramentorum diversitate studuit impetrare. Jam ergo quasi mutato habitu, quo utebatur, dum sacra mysteria tractaret, mutat vocem (Ivon. Carnot., *Serm.*, V). With regard to the conclusion of the preceding prayer said in silence, Blessed Albertus Magnus makes the judicious remark: Est conclusio, ad quam nullus respondet *Amen* (sicut in aliis Secretorum conclusionibus) nisi Angeli, qui in ministerio esse dicuntur (*Tract.*, III, chap. 9).

vided into two parts sharply differing from each other. In the first we confess that the Eucharistic sacrificial gifts have been prepared and given to us by God through Jesus Christ; in the other part we declare that by the sacrifice of Christ supreme honor and glory are given to the triune God. Here at the close of the Canon the whole significance and efficacy of the Sacrifice of the Mass are again summarized, for Jesus Christ, the divine high priest, appears on the altar as mediator between God and men (I Tim. 2:5): on the one hand, to bless and enrich men with the plenitude of the gifts of salvation; on the other, most perfectly to honor and glorify the eternal majesty of God.

1. The words, "all these good things" (*haec omnia bona*), designate principally the Eucharistic elements of bread and wine which were on the altar before the Consecration and still come before the mind of the priest as if present. And this can happen since their appearances have remained after the Consecration as a sacramental covering for the body and blood of Christ. The natural elements of bread and wine are the created gifts of God, and on the altar they are changed from earthly gifts into heavenly ones, and then given to us for our enjoyment and sanctification. At the last word (*praestas*, bestow) we should, therefore, think about the consecrated elements on the altar: the sacrificial body and blood of Christ consecrated from bread and wine. By "all these good things" are to be understood partly the natural goods of bread and wine, partly the supernatural goods of the body and blood of Christ; the former He "creates, sanctifies, vivifies," but the latter, the body and blood of Christ, He bestows upon us in Communion, or as a sacrificial gift, which we should offer to Him.

Through His Son, Jesus Christ, God the Father "dost always create"—as in the beginning of the world, so also now—all the products of nature, hence the most noble nourishing plants, wheat and grapes; for year after year He causes herbs to grow for the use of man, so that He may bring forth bread out of the earth and wine that cheers the heart of man (Ps. 103:14 f.).[2]

These created gifts of nature, the Almighty then changes through

---

[2] Per Christum omnipotens Deus Pater *haec bona omnia*, quae sacris altaribus consecrantur, non solum in exordio mundi creavit, condendo quod non erat . . . , sed etiam semper eadem bona creat propagando et reparando, ut per annos singulos et novae segetes et nova vina nascantur (Florus Diacon., n. 73).

the same Jesus Christ into the heavenly sacrificial gifts of the Eucharist, a change of substance, which is here apprehended and represented under a threefold aspect: it is the most perfect sanctification (*sanctificas*), vivifying (*vivificas*), as well as blessing (*benedicis*) of the material substances of bread and wine.³ By the consecration, the bread and wine are sanctified in the highest degree; for their substances vanish, and in their stead there are present the most holy body and blood of Christ in union with His soul and infinitely holy divinity, while the appearances of bread and wine still remain; but they likewise receive in this sacramental connection a sanctified character.⁴ Furthermore, by the consecration the dead, lifeless elements of bread and wine are vivified,⁵ that is, changed into the living and enlivening bread (*panis vivus et vitalis*) of the body of Christ and into the life-streaming drink of His blood. The Eucharistic Saviour is, indeed, the eternal Living One, who, as the Son of the living God, hath life in Himself (John 5:26) and is the source of all supernatural life for His creatures (John 1:4). Finally, the bread and wine are in the fullest sense of the term blessed by the consecration,⁶ that is, not merely made a blessed food, as, for example, the bread and wine blessed on certain feasts, but even changed as to their entire substances into Christ's sacrificial body and blood.⁷ The altar gifts

³ Quoniam corpus Christi est sanctum et benedictum, idcirco per hoc quod Deus Pater convertit haec omnia (sc. panem et vinum) in corpus et sanguinem Christi, dicitur ea sanctificare, vivificare et benedicere (Dion. Carthus., *Expos. Miss.*, a. 36).

⁴ Panis ille quem videtis in altari, sanctificatus per verbum Dei, corpus est Christi; calix ille, imo quod habet calix, sanctificatum per verbum Dei, *sanguis est Christi* (S. August., *Serm.*, CCXXVII [*ad Infantes de Sacramentis*]).

⁵ In the Mozarabic liturgy (*in Dom. I post Octav. Epiphan.*) the substantial change of the Eucharistic elements is expressed by the following words: Coelesti benedictione creatura visibilis animatur. Again (*In Ascensione Domini*): Visitet et vivificet ea (sc. munera) Spiritus tuus sanctus, qui per vaporem incendii Heliae prophetae holocaustum adsumpsit.

⁶ In the ordination rite of priests the Church prays: In obsequium plebis tuae panem et vinum in corpus et sanguinem Filii tui immaculata benedictione transforment.—Verba, in quibus consistit vis consecrandi, dicuntur benedictio tum ratione benedictionis praecedentis, tum quia ad eorum prolationem Dominus benedicit, quia convertit in corpus, quod super omnia benedixit, ditando perfectis donis gratiarum animam, et sanctificatione et puritate carnem illam sanctissimam (S. Bonav., IV, dist. 10, p. 2, dub. 3).

⁷ The three words, *sanctificas, vivificas, benedicis*, are understood still in another way. By *sanctificatio* is meant the preparatory sanctification of the sacrificial matter through the oblation; by *vivificatio*, its change by the consecration, and by *benedictio*, the fulfillment of the sacrificial gifts with all

thus sanctified, vivified, and blessed, that is, consecrated, are bestowed upon us (*praestas nobis*) by God through Jesus Christ as a sacrifice and sacrament, as food for the soul, as our most sacred and most precious gift.

A still richer and more profound meaning of the above words may be discovered if we regard the elements which lie on the altar, bread and wine according to visible appearances, as the representatives of all the other products of nature; then God, or Jesus Christ, appears as the author and dispenser of all the collective goods of the natural and supernatural order. Such a view is quite proper if we consider that formerly at certain times and on special feasts there was a blessing immediately before this prayer,[8] by which various objects, chiefly articles of food, for example, water, milk, honey, grapes, beans, fruit, were blessed by a special formula here inserted. When such blessed objects lay near the altar, they could, but in a somewhat different sense, be also comprised among "all these good things" that God ever creates, sanctifies, vivifies, blesses, and bestows upon us through Jesus Christ. Even now the bishop, according to a strict ordinance, annually on Holy Thursday blesses at this place in the Canon the holy oil for the sick.

The somewhat ambiguous expression, "through Him, and with Him, and in Him," may be explained in different ways; and in this singular expression regard must ever be had to the twofold nature of Jesus Christ. Through Jesus Christ (*per ipsum*) the Father and the Holy Ghost are honored and glorified in an infinitely sublime man-

---

heavenly blessing. Hac oratione Ecclesia profitetur, maximum Eucharistiae beneficium a Deo sibi esse collatum, a quo panis et vinum, elementa eucharistica consecranda, creantur; creata, cum altari admoventur, sanctificantur; sanctificata vivificantur, cum in corpus et sanguinem Christi transsubstantiantur; vivificata benedicuntur donisque Spiritus sui sancti affatim replentur, atque ita benedicta nobis indignis servis suis fruenda traduntur (Lesley, S. J. [Migne, LXXXV, 553]).

[8] The Gelasian Sacramentary has here (*in Ascensa Domini*) the rubric: Inde vero modicum ante expletum Canonem benedices fruges novas, after which comes the following benediction formula: Benedic, Domine, et has fruges novas fabae, quas tu, Domine, rore coelesti et inundantia pluviarum ad maturitatem perducere dignatus es, ad percipiendum nobis cum gratiarum actione in nomine D. N. J. Ch. Per quem haec omnia. . . . This blessing of the first fruits, before the concluding prayer of the Canon, was never general, but prescribed only by individual bishops. A *Sacramentarium vetus* of the eleventh century admits the words *Per quem haec, Domine, semper bona creas, sanctificas, vivificas, benedicis et nobis servis tuis largiter praestas* even into the *benedictio palmae et olivae*. (Cf. Migne, CLI, 843.)

ner, inasmuch as the God-man offers Himself on the altar and through Him alone can all creatures render to God perfect homage and adoration. At the same time and jointly with Jesus Christ (*cum ipso*)[9] the Father and the Holy Ghost receive all honor and praise, for Jesus Christ is true God and, therefore, "together" with the other divine persons "adored and glorified" (*simul adoratur et conglorificatur*); moreover, the Eucharistic sacrifice of praise and adoration is offered to all the persons of the Most Holy Trinity. Finally, in Jesus Christ (*in ipso*)[10] the Father and the Holy Ghost also are glorified, since all three divine persons, by reason of the unity of their essence, are eternally in each other, and, consequently, the veneration of one is not to be separated from the veneration of the other two. If we consider Jesus Christ according to His human nature as our head and our mediator, then we render to the triune God all honor and glory "through Him" and "with Him," in that we are in union with Him in the offering of the sacrifice, and "in Him," in so far as we are included in His sacrifice and are jointly offered with it.

2. The accompanying ceremony harmonizes perfectly with the text of the prayer. The three signs of the cross prescribed at the words, "sanctify, vivify, bless," symbolize not the present sanctification, but the accomplished sanctification, vivifying, and blessing of the oblation which took place at the moment of consecration,[11] and, at the same time, also indicates the fullness of life and of blessing contained in the Eucharistic sacrificial gifts and thence flowing out over the whole Church.

Now the rite of the sign of the cross changes. The sacred sign is no longer made merely with the hand of the priest, but with the sacred body of the Lord.[12] When pronouncing the words "through

---

[9] *Cum ipso*, quia Filius a Patre separari non debet, sed simul cum eo venerari. Honor enim uni personae impensus toti Trinitati adorandae saltem implicite exhibetur (Dion. Carthus., *Expos. Miss.*, a. 36).

[10] *In ipso*, i.e. omnis honor et gloria est tibi Patri atque Spiritui sancto seu in unitate Spiritus sancti in Filio tuo, quia omnis, qui Filium Dei vere cognoscit, ex eius cognitione Deum Patrem glorificat atque honorat (*ibid.*).

[11] Signa tria crucis quae hic fiunt, operatione Trinitatis per virtutem crucis ostendunt facta esse quae praemissa sunt. Signa enim facta hucusque post consecrationem non consecrationem operantur, sed ejus faciunt commemorationem sive testificationem (Robert. Paulul., *De offic. eccles.*, II, chap. 36).

[12] The rite at this point was somewhat different in the Middle Ages. The practice of forming the cross here *cum oblatis, cum corpore dominico, cum*

Him and with Him and in Him," the sign of the cross is made three times with the sacred host over the chalice; and when mention is made of the Father Almighty and of the Holy Ghost, the holy sign is made twice between the chalice and the breast of the priest. One reason for these signs of the cross may be that here all three divine persons are mentioned separately and consecutively; the Son three times, hence a threefold sign of the cross is made with the host over the chalice, because His adorable blood is contained therein; but when mention is made of the Father and the Holy Ghost, the last two signs of the cross take place outside of the chalice. While the priest pronounces the words *omnis honor et gloria* ("all honor and glory"), he holds the host and the chalice in his hands, raising them slightly. This slight elevation (*elevatio minor*) of the sacrificial gifts is far more ancient than the greater one (*elevatio major*) at the Consecration. Originally this minor elevation was a more solemn invitation to all to render their homage of adoration to the Most Holy; [13] according to the rite of that age, the minor elevation can be considered an emphasis on the words, "all honor and glory," that is, as symbolically indicating the glory which day after day ascends from the altar and its sacrificial gifts to the eternal throne of the Holy Trinity. This supreme praise is rendered to the Most High, not merely as long as this world will continue to last, but "forever and ever" (*per omnia saecula saeculorum*). By this majestic conclusion, recited aloud or sung, the solemn silence of the Canon is broken in order that the people, by answering *Amen*, may make known their assent to all that the priest alone has performed. Thus the Canon terminates in an enthusiastic doxology, which is the glorious crown of the ancient sacrificial prayer.

---

hostia, was in all probability brought about chiefly by the circumstance, that at the Elevation, which here took place, the chalice was touched with the host. Cum oblata tangitur calix. Novissima crux cum oblatione celebratur (Amalar., *Eclog.*, n. 22). Cf. *Ordo Rom. I*, n. 16. Notandum quod cum alia signa sola manu sacerdotis fiant, ista fiunt de corpore Christi. Hic enim ipsa Christi crucifixio repraesentatur, quasi Christus quem praesentem credimus sic pro nobis in ligno crucis est extensus (Robert. Paulul., *op. cit.*, II, chap. 37).

[13] In many places, for example, in Belgium, a threefold sign is here given with the little bell; this custom, being of ancient origin, may be tolerated. (Cf. S. R. C., May 14, 1856.)

SECTION IV

The Communion

THE Communion is the last principal part of the sacrifice of the Mass. The Eucharist is, indeed, according to its very nature and object, a food-offering and a sacrificial food. It is a food-offering, for the divine Lamb is, in the Consecration, mystically immolated and offered on the altar, that those who offer may partake of Him. The essential sacrificial act must precede its reception as food in Communion, as it consists precisely in the preparing of the sacrificial repast. Christ's body and blood are sacrificed that they may, under the separate appearances of bread and wine, be placed on the altar. Only by Communion does the Eucharistic sacrifice attain its destination as a food-offering, and as such it is thereby rendered complete. Because of this connection of the sacrifice of the altar with the Communion of the celebrant, this Communion constitutes, although not an essential, yet an integral part of the Eucharistic sacrifice; it would be incomplete if Communion were not joined to it. According to divine and ecclesiastical law, the celebrant at least must eat and drink of the sacrificial body and blood which have been previously offered by him in sacrifice to God, that by such participation he may enter into the most intimate communion of sacrifice with Christ. "The chalice of benediction, which we bless, is it not the communion of the blood of Christ? And the bread, which we break, is it not the partaking of the body of the Lord?" (I Cor. 10:16.)

Therefore the Eucharist is also sacrificial food and sacrificial drink; the Eucharistic repast is a sacrificial repast, because it is the precious fruit of the sacrifice of the altar. It is only by a sacrificial act that the sacramental food of life can be prepared. To the sacrificial act is attached the sacrificial repast; the Communion is a participation in the preceding and accomplished sacrifice. But as Christ must Himself become previously a victim in order to become our food of grace, thus also must we previously offer ourselves to Him in worship so as to be worthy of the Eucharistic sacrificial repast.[1]

The Eucharist is both a sacrifice and a sacrament; but as sacrifice and sacrament it acts in different ways and produces different effects of grace, so that the fruits of the sacrifice are to be distinguished from the fruits of Communion. As the faithful, "a holy and royal priesthood," unite in offering the Eucharistic sacrifice, they should also by sacramental Communion unite themselves with and participate in the sacrifice offered, in order thus to receive the fruits of the sacrifice in greater abundance. The Communion is the sacrificial repast, the perfect conclusion of the sacrificial action.

The Communion forms the center of the following part of the liturgy of the Mass: the prayers which precede the Communion may be regarded as a preparation; those which follow, as thanksgiving.

---

[1] Ipsa participatio corporis et sanguinis Domini, cum ejus panem manducamus et calicem bibimus, hoc utique nobis insinuat, ut moriamur mundo et vitam nostram absconditam habeamus cum Christo in Deo carnemque nostram crucifigamus cum vitiis et concupiscentiis suis. Sic fit, ut omnes fideles qui Deum et proximum diligunt, etiamsi non bibant calicem corporeae passionis, bibant tamen calicem dominicae caritatis, quo inebriati membra sua, quae sunt super terram, mortificent et induti Dominum J. Chr. carnis curam non faciant in desideriis neque contemplentur quae videntur, sed quae non videntur (S. Fulgent., *Contra Fabian.*, frag. 28).

CHAPTER XL

THE PATER NOSTER

1. The Lord's Prayer has from the time of the apostles [1] formed a constituent part of the sacrificial celebration, in the East as well as in the West. It is recited aloud, or sung, and is placed at the beginning of the Communion [2] in the same manner as the Preface introduces the Canon, or Consecration. The position of the Pater Noster in the liturgy of the Mass is very appropriate; for according to its contents it can be referred partly to the sacrifice, partly to the Communion, forming a beautiful transition between these two parts and connecting them with each other. In the Pater Noster we pray for the sanctification of God's divine name, for the coming of the

---

[1] St. Jerome dates the use of the Our Father at the sacrificial celebration to an ordinance of the Lord Himself. Sic (Christus) docuit discipulos suos, ut quotidie in corporis illius sacrificio credentes audeant loqui: Pater noster, qui es in coelis . . . (*Adv. Pelag.*, III, n. 15). The same is found in all liturgies, but it was and is not recited in all in the same manner. Among the Greeks it is said in a low tone by the priest, while the entire congregation recite it aloud. In the Mozarabic rite the people respond to the priest, who recites or sings it aloud, in the following manner: Pater noster, qui es in coelis. R. *Amen.* Sanctificetur nomen tuum. R. *Amen.* Adveniat regnum tuum. R. *Amen.* Fiat voluntas tua sicut in coelo et in terra. R. *Amen.* Panem nostrum quotidianum da nobis hodie. R. *Quia Deus es.* Et dimitte nobis debita nostra, sicut et nos dimittimus debitoribus nostris. R. *Amen.* Et ne nos inducas in tentationem. R. *Sed libera nos a malo.* In Christian antiquity the Our Father was regarded as really and exclusively the "prayer of the faithful"; for the baptized alone had the right to address God as their Father. Recall the so-called *traditio* (delivery) and *redditio* (return) of the *Oratio dominica* (and the symbol) in the old baptismal practice. The Our Father is also called *legitima et ordinaria oratio, prex legitima.* (Cf. Tertull., *De orat.*, chap. 10.)

[2] Previous to the time of St. Gregory the Great it was not recited (as is still the case in the Ambrosian and Mozarabic rites) until after the breaking of the host; this pope gave it its present position immediately after the Canon (*mox post precem*).

divine kingdom, and the fulfillment of the divine will; then the granting of our daily bread; and finally, the forgiveness of our debts, preservation from temptation, and deliverance from evil. The first three petitions are concerned with the glory of God; but the last three have for their object man's salvation. The first three petitions are connected with the last three by the fourth petition, which refers to the supernatural bread of the soul as well as to the earthly bread of the body. We obtain the honor of God and the salvation of the world principally through the Eucharistic bread of heaven, the sacred body of Christ.[3]

In the Roman rite the Pater Noster is introduced by the *Oremus* [4] and an unchangeable preamble.[5] In this prayer we express our reliance on the wholesome precepts and divine instruction (*Praeceptis salutaribus moniti et divina institutione formati*), as though we would excuse ourselves that "we make bold" (*audemus*) to call the Lord of heaven and earth "our Father" and invoke Him as "Father." But Christ himself commanded us to repeat this prayer with heart and lips, saying: "Thus therefore shall you pray" (Matt. 6:9):

[3] Sequitur Oratio dominica cum appositionibus congruis. Una enim praecedens eam fiduciam praedicat, qua Dominum creatorem Patrem dicere praesumamus; altera subsequens explicat, quomodo et a quibus malis per Dominum nos liberari petamus. Quae Oratio dominica, quia prius quam cetera in consecratione sacrificiorum assumpta est, in expletione ejusdem sacratissimae actionis digne ponitur, ut per hanc purificati qui communicaturi sunt, quae sancte confecta sunt, digne ad salutem veram percipiant (Walafrid. Strabo, chap. 23).

[4] Cur hanc solam Orationem praecedit adhortatio, cum plures in hoc Canone faciamus et ad nullam hortati sumus? Quia illae sunt inferiores et humana ratione compositae; haec perfecta et a solo Deo formata (B. Odo Camer., *In Can.*, dist. 4). Dignum profecto fuit, ut tota haec tam sacrosancta actio Dominica oratione concluderetur, et petitiones fidelium, quas vel propter futuram vel propter praesentem vitam nos Dominus docuit, per eandem passionis ejus commemorationem efficacius commendarentur. Admonetur ergo tota Ecclesia et dicitur a sacerdote *Oremus* et orat Ecclesia cum sacerdote, non voce, sed corde: labia clausa sunt, sed patet conscientia; silentium est, clamat pectus, sed auribus ille audit qui miseretur (Florus Diac., n. 75).

[5] In all liturgies the Pater Noster is introduced by a preface; in the Mozarabic and the ancient Gallican rites it continually varies according to the course of the ecclesiastical year. The Milanese liturgy has but twice (on Holy Thursday and Easter Sunday) an introduction differing somewhat from that of the Roman liturgy. St. Cyprian already alludes to this preamble: Qui (sc. Dominus) inter cetera salutaria sua monita et praecepta divina, quibus populo suo consulit ad salutem, etiam orandi ipse formam dedit, ipse quid precaremur, *monuit* et *instruxit* (*De orat. Domin.*, chap. 2).

THE PATER NOSTER

Pater noster, qui es in coelis; sanctificetur nomen tuum. Adveniat regnum tuum. Fiat voluntas tua, sicut in coelo et in terra. Panem nostrum quotidianum da nobis hodie. Et dimitte nobis debita nostra, sicut et nos dimittimus debitoribus nostris. Et ne nos inducas in tentationem R. Sed libera nos a malo. Amen.	Our Father, who art in heaven, hallowed be Thy name; Thy kingdom come; Thy will be done on earth as it is in heaven. Give us this day our daily bread; and forgive us our trespasses, as we forgive those who trespass against us. And lead us not into temptation. R. But deliver us from evil. Amen.

Tertullian says (*De Orat.*, chap. 1) that the Lord's Prayer is as brief and concise in words as it is full of thought, and then he designates it as "an abbreviation of the whole Gospel," which, "together with the special theme of the prayer" (the adoration of God and petitions for man), "contains almost the whole sum of the doctrine and law of Christ." This glorious prayer is so profound in its signification, so rich in mysteries, so powerful in its efficacy, and so ingenious in its arrangement, that no one is able to conceive or express it.[6] There are innumerable explanations, more or less complete, of the Pater Noster; hence we content ourselves to give a mere sketch of its immeasurably rich contents,[7] and in so doing we shall adhere to the masterly interpretation of the Angelic Doctor.

The introduction of the prayer awakens confidence; but this is principally brought about by contemplating that love of God which desires our every good; hence we say: "Our Father"; then, after considering His greatness and majesty, by virtue of which He can bestow on us every good, we say: "who art in heaven." [8] The prayer

---

[6] De hujus orationis expositione, laude et efficacia tanta jam a sanctis atque catholicis doctoribus dicta sunt, ut paene taedio sit ea perlegere. Verumtamen nec digna nec sufficientia dicta sunt nec usquam dicentur. Tanta nempe est hujus gloriosae orationis profunditas in sensu, fecunditas in mysteriis, efficacia in effectu, artificialitas in processu seu ordine, ut nemo capere queat vel eloqui (Dion. Carthus., *In Matt.*, chap. 6).

[7] In orationis dominicae expositione multa a sanctis Patribus dicta leguntur; sed quia mens orantis tot ea hora capere non potest, nos de singulis petitionibus pauca dicere volumus, ut qui orat intellegere possit quid petat et intellegens devotior fiat (Robert. Paulul., *De offic. eccles.*, II, chap. 38).

[8] Quamvis oratio ista communiter dirigenda sit ad totam Trinitatem, quae est unus Deus et Pater noster ratione creationis et justificationis seu naturae et gratiae: nam naturam et gratiam a Deo trino sortimur; in Missa tamen specialiter ad Patrem dirigitur, sicut orationes in Canone praecedentes et oratio proxime sequens (Dion. Carthus., *Expos. Miss.*, a. 37).

itself contains not only all that we should ask for, but the succession one after another of the seven petitions shows the order which we should observe in imploring the various goods from God; it therefore regulates our affections, inclinations, and desires.

Evidently the first object of our desires is God Himself, who is the end of our whole being. But our desires aspire to God in a twofold manner: as we desire the glory for God Himself, and as we desire the glory of God for ourselves. Accordingly, the first petition reads, "hallowed be Thy name," whereby we implore the glorification of God; the second, "Thy kingdom come," whereby we ask that we may arrive at the participation in the glory and beatitude of His heavenly kingdom.

The two following petitions refer to what is conducive to the attainment of our last end. For this it is necessary, above all, that we merit eternal happiness by obediently keeping the divine commandments; but since we are unable to accomplish this by our own strength, we beg the necessary assistance of grace from on high with the words: "Thy will be done on earth as it is in heaven." A further means for the attainment of the end of our being is our daily bread, in so far as the bread of the soul is here understood, that is, chiefly the holy Sacrament of the altar, the devout daily reception of which is profitable to man, and in which, as in their source, all the other sacraments are included. On the other hand, in so far as the bread of the body is here understood, by which is meant all that serves for the maintenance of life, the fourth petition, "Give us this day our daily bread," implores the Father for all that is necessary for the attainment of our natural end.

The last three petitions beg God to remove all impediments which could hinder us in the attainment of our last end. The first and greatest of these impediments is sin, which directly excludes us from the kingdom of heaven; hence we pray: "Forgive us our trespasses, as we forgive those who trespass against us." We further implore God to remove from us the temptation to sin, which incites us to oppose the will of God and renders its fulfillment difficult: "And lead us not into temptation"; that is, do not permit us to be overcome by temptation, but strengthen us to gain the victory over it. In the last petition we cry. "Deliver us from evil," and continue this petition in the following prayer.

This last petition is made in the name of the faithful by the acolyte or choir,[9] after which the priest concludes the Pater Noster by saying, in a low voice, *Amen*.[10] This *Amen* from the lips of the priest, who is mediator between God and man, has in this place a peculiar significance. It does not express consent and desire, as at other times, but is, so to speak, the answer that God gives, that He has received the petition of the people. The Pater Noster is recited aloud,[11] or sung, in order that all present may join in the prayer with devout hearts and in childlike confidence,[12] to which they are also incited by the *Oremus* said before the prayer. This divine prayer, so full of power, inspiration, and holiness, should indeed at all times be recited with profound devotion,[13] but especially during the celebration of Mass, when before our eyes on the altar He reposes who taught and commanded us thus to pray.[14]

[9] Hoc septimum chorus succinit, in quo se orasse cum sacerdote ostendit. Ad hoc enim fuerat invitatus, cum sacerdos ante orationem Dominicam diceret *Oremus*. Deinde subjungit sacerdos *Amen* ad petitionum omnium praemissarum confirmationem (Robert. Paulul., II, chap. 29).

[10] In orationis dominicae particula finali populus tamquam infirmus petiit a malo liberari. Cui sacerdos compatiens dixit *Amen*, desiderans dicti populi liberationem secundum unam, aut petitionis susceptionem affirmans secundum aliam ejus expositionem (Gabr. Biel, *Exposit. Canon. Miss.*, lect. 79).

[11] Alta et distincta voce dicitur, ut et populus et postea loco ipsius chorus ultimam petitionem quasi quendam orationis Dominicae epilogum recitare et sic in ejus partem venire potuerit (Krazer, sect. 4, art. 1, c. 12, § 273). In ecclesia ad altare Dei quotidie dicitur ista Dominica oratio et *audiunt* illam fideles (S. August., *Serm.*, LVIII, n. 12).

[12] In the Gelasian and Gregorian Sacramentaries the *Amen* is omitted after the Our Father. Later (probably not until after the eleventh century) it was taken up in the rite, but recited only in a low tone (*submissa voce*) by the priest, as the people, or the acolyte, at the close of the Embolism, which really concludes the petitions of the Our Father, express by a loud *Amen* their faithful and devout assent, the confirmation and recommendation of these petitions. In the Hours of the breviary the *Amen* is, on the contrary, to be added only when the entire Pater Noster is recited in silence (*totum secreto*), for example, at Compline before the Confiteor; it is always omitted when the Our Father throughout is recited aloud (*totum clara voce*), for example, in the ferial prayers of Lauds and Vespers; or when it is recited in silence, but commenced and concluded aloud, for instance, in the dominical prayers of Prime and Compline.

[13] Hanc sacratissimam orationem ex divinae ac sempiternae Sapientiae fonte immediate manantem devotissime proferamus, et tanto devotius, quanto frequentius, ne frequentia incuriam pariat atque fastidium, sed eam saepius iterando crescamus semper in ejus effectu seu gratia, per quam ardentius solito repetatur (Dion. Carthus., *In Matt.*, chap. 6).

[14] Oratio Dominica cum singulari et maxima devotione dicenda est in Missa, ubi Christus auctor ejus tam dignanter atque mirabiliter ac verissime praesens

2. The last petition of the Pater Noster is enlarged upon by the priest; this appendix or addition to the Lord's Prayer is commonly called the Embolism.[15]

Libera nos, quaesumus, Domine, ab omnibus malis, praeteritis, praesentibus et futuris: et intercedente beata et gloriosa semper Virgine Dei genitrice Maria, cum beatis Apostolis tuis Petro et Paulo, atque Andrea, et omnibus Sanctis, da propitius pacem in diebus nostris: ut ope misericordiae tuae adjuti, et a peccato simus semper liberi, et ab omni perturbatione securi. Per eundem Dominum.	Deliver us, we beseech Thee, O Lord, from all evils, past, present, and to come; and by the intercession of the blessed and glorious ever Virgin Mary, Mother of God, together with Thy blessed apostles Peter and Paul, and Andrew, and all Thy saints, graciously give peace in our days, that aided by the help of Thy mercy, we may be always free from sin and secure from all disturbance. Through the same Lord.

Why do we dwell so long on the petition for deliverance from every evil? Because this earth on which we, as exiled children of Eve, are still sojourning, is a land of spiritual and corporal evils that sprout from the poisonous root of sin. The life of mortal man overflows with hardships and miseries, sorrows and cares, dangers

---

est, et qui eam taliter dicit, ineffabilem fructum reportat (*idem, Expos. Miss.*, a. 37).

[15] *Embolismus*, ἐμβολισμός from ἐμβάλλω, I add = inserted; substantive = insertion, middle links, addition. Authors of the Middle Ages usually translate: *superaugmentum, excrescentia*. Sequitur in altum praefatio Dominicae orationis et oratio Dominica cum embolismo (*Ordo Rom. II*, n. 11). Sequitur embolismus, i.e. superaccrescens: superaccrescitur enim ultimae petitionis repetitio et expositio (Sicard., III, chap. 6). On Good Friday this prayer is said aloud *in tono orationis Missae ferialis;* the Ambrosian rite always prescribes that it should be recited aloud or chanted. The silent recitation of the Embolism is prescribed already in the fourth Ordo: Dicit domnus papa, interveniente nullo sono, hanc orationem: *Libera nos*. . . . Bishop Bonizo of Piacenza (d. 1088) is of the opinion that St. Gregory the Great ordered the silent recitation of the Embolism. Beatus Gregorius constituit, ut sequens oratio, quae sic incipit: "Libera nos, Domine, ab omnibus malis," quae ante eum alta voce decantabatur, secrete diceretur (*Lib. de Sacramentis*). It seems, however, that the silent recitation serves to represent the Embolism as an ecclesiastical addition to the Lord's Prayer. Facta confirmatione Dominicae orationis dicendo *Amen*, totus textus qui sequitur pro venia peccatorum orat et pro pace (B. Odo Camer., *In Can.*, dist. 4).

and temptations. "Many are the afflictions of the just; but out of them all will the Lord deliver them" (Ps. 33:20). As long as we remain on earth, encompassed with infirmity and subject to suffering and spiritual combat, it is ever necessary for us to pray for deliverance [16] from all evils, past, present, and to come. Of past evils, sins often continue to abide in their painful consequences, in their unhappy results and fruits, which we wish to be totally removed. In the present we are pressed down by evils from within and without, from all sides, and from these we wish to be delivered. The future is frequently enveloped in darkness, and in its bosom conceals a host of threatening evils, from which we would beg to be spared.

The infinitely holy and just God often permits painful sufferings and tribulations to befall us, not merely for our trial and purification from all inordinate attachment to the world, but also as a chastisement for our sins and imperfections. Therefore we earnestly beseech the Lord not to chastise us in His wrath and indignation (Ps. 6:2), but to regard us with the eyes of His favor and be propitious to us, and to give us true peace in our days.[17] We here pray in the first place for interior peace of soul, which consists in this, that by the powerful assistance (*ope* [18]) of the divine mercy we may ever keep ourselves free from sin and thus persevere in the blessed love and friendship of God and rejoice in the sweet consolations of His grace. Then we pray for exterior peace of life, which consists in this, that by God's help and merciful protection we may be ever secure from all disturbances, disorders, and persecutions, by which in our frailty we are easily drawn from the right path of salvation and led into evil. If the days of our life are not darkened by fears from within and combats from without (II Cor. 7:5), that is, by

---

[16] *Liberare*, to loosen, to deliver us from something that, as it were, chains or binds us; here in the full sense = to deliver from evils present and to preserve (protect, guard) us from impending evils (*inde se recte dicunt liberari, quo per liberatores suos non sunt permissi perduci* [S. August.]). In consuetudine latinae linguae liberari duobus modis dicitur et maxime in eo consuevimus audire hoc verbum, ut quicumque liberatur, intelligatur periculum evadere, molestiis carere (S. August., *Serm.*, CXXXIV, n. 2).

[17] Exaudi nos, Deus salutaris noster, et dies nostros in tua pace dispone, ut a cunctis perturbationibus liberati, tranquilla tibi servitute famulemur (*Sacram. Gregor.*). Ecclesia deprecatur pacem in diebus nostris, quod et post nos alii et post ipsos alii usque ad finem saeculi similiter orabunt (Pseudo-Alcuin., chap. 40).

[18] *Ope* from the obsolete *ops* = every assisting means; power, vigor, strength, assistance, support.

the bitterness of sin and the misery of contention, then we enjoy the blessings of interior and exterior peace,[19] whereby we taste already beforehand some drops from the fountain of heavenly, eternal peace. To obtain the inestimable gift of this desirable peace the more easily and in greater abundance, we have recourse to the intercession "of the glorious ever Virgin Mary, Mother of God, together with the blessed apostles Peter and Paul, and Andrew,[20] and all the saints." For the sake of such intercessors, our supplications will be answered, and the superabundant riches of the divine mercy will be imparted to us.

While the priest prays, "Graciously give peace in our days," he makes the sign of the cross on himself with the paten [21] to express symbolically the desire of participating in that peace which Christ brought us by His cross and by the sacrifice of His body; for in a few moments the host is placed on the paten.[22] The kissing of the paten [23]

[19] Populus fidelium in hujus saeculi peregrinatione, tamquam in Babylone captivus et supernae patriae suspirans, orat etiam pro pace temporali, ne impediatur a spirituali, ut, remotis per Dei pietatem omnibus adversitatibus, quietam et tranquillam vitam agat Ecclesia. Hoc autem paucissimis, sed eminentissimis Sanctis nominatis exorat (Pseudo-Alcuin., chap. 40).

[20] These three apostles are also in the first place in the list of the saints before the Consecration. As the brother of St. Peter, the Prince of the Apostles, St. Andrew was ever held in great veneration in Rome and his feast kept with marked solemnity. (Cf. *Ordo Rom XI*, n. 76.) In the Middle Ages the celebrant could according to his pleasure mention here other saints, especially the Patrons of the Church. Aliorum Sanctorum nomina annumerare non debemus, nisi quos in Canone invenimus antiquitus descriptos, excepto post "Pater noster" in illa oratione, ubi juxta Ordinem quorumlibet Sanctorum nomina internumerare possumus (Microl., chap. 13). Cf. *Ordo Rom IX*.

[21] In the Middle Ages the paten was kissed previous to the sign of the cross in many places. Vide quod sacerdos cum osculata patena se in ultima clausula signat (Sicard., III, chap. 6). Cf. Durand., IV, l, 4.

[22] In the most ancient times the breads offered were consecrated on the paten, later on the corporal, and only the fraction of the host took place on the paten; already during the Middle Ages the present rite originated of placing the host on the paten before and after the breaking over the chalice (*ut facilius tolli possit*). Patenam sacerdos de manu diaconi suscipit et in altari, ut fractionem super eam faciat, deponit. Nos tamen hanc fractionem ad cautelam faciamus super calicem (Robert. Paulul., II, chap. 39).

[23] According to the (three) oldest Roman *Ordines* the paten was not kissed in this place by the celebrant, but only by the archdeacon; first in the *Ordo Rom. V*, n. 10 (of the eleventh century) appears the rubric: Patenas diaconus episcopo osculandas praebeat. The present rite is found in *Ordo Rom. XIV*, c. 53: Pontifex patenam accipiens cum dextra manu, quando dicit "intercedente b. Dei genitrice . . ." faciat sibi cum ipsa patena signum crucis (*a com-*

is a sign of love and reverence toward this "new sepulchre" of the holy body of Christ.[24]

---

plete sign of the Cross), et quando dicit "da propitius . . ." osculetur ipsam patenam in superiori ejus parte (*on the upper end or rim*). The present rubric, *Patenam ipsam osculatur*, is more accurately explained by a decree: Patena in extremitate seu in ora congruentius osculanda est (S. R. C., July 24, 1683).

[24] In Spain many priests communicated immediately after the Pater noster, or after the Embolism, and only afterward gave the blessing to the congregation. To oppose these innovations the Fourth Council of Toledo (633) prescribed, ut post Orationem dominicam et conjunctionem panis et calicis benedictio in populum sequatur et tunc demum sacramentum corporis et sanguinis Domini sumatur. After the summons *Humiliate vos benedictioni* and the salutation (*Dominus sit . . .*), the formula of blessing was pronounced, to the individual petitions of which the people answered *Amen*. The ancient Gallican rite had also at this place a similar imparting of the blessing. The benediction formulas were manifold. In Spain bishops and priests used the same formula, but the priest was not permitted to impart the blessing in presence of a bishop. In Gaul priests made use of a shorter formula than bishops, which was not subject to change; it was as follows: Pax, fides, caritas et communio corporis et sanguinis Christi sit semper vobiscum. It appears that in Germany likewise, at least in some places, at Pontifical Mass the episcopal blessing was solemnly imparted before the Communion. The Roman rite, as well as the Greek and Oriental liturgies, ignores the above benediction. Cf. the remarks of Lesley, S. J., on the Mozarabic Missal (Migne, LXXX, 592); Gerbert., *Vetus Liturg. Alemann.*, Part I, disp. I, chap. 3, n. 39.

CHAPTER XLI

THE FRACTION OF THE HOST AND THE MINGLING OF THE CONSECRATED ELEMENTS

THE breaking of the host is connected with the concluding formula belonging to the Embolism: *Per eundem Dominum nostrum Jesum Christum Filium tuum, qui tecum vivit et regnat in unitate Spiritus sancti Deus per omnia saecula saeculorum. R. Amen.* While the priest says in silence, "Through the same our Lord Jesus Christ, Thy Son," with both hands he holds the host over the chalice and reverently breaks it in half, one half of which he lays with his right hand on the paten; and while he continues, "Who liveth and reigneth with Thee," from the other half he breaks from below a particle and holds it firmly in the right hand. He proceeds: "in the unity of the Holy Ghost, God," and at the same time joins the other half in the left hand with that on the paten in such a way that the host again appears entire and round; at the last words, "World without end," the priest raises his voice, and then says aloud: *Pax ✠ Domini sit ✠ semper vobis✠cum* ("May the peace ✠ of the Lord be ✠ always with ✠ you"), while with the small particle he makes the sign of the cross three times over the chalice. After the acolyte has given to this salutation the answer: *Et cum spiritu tuo* ("And with thy spirit"), the priest drops the particle of the host into the chalice, and while doing so he says silently: [1]

Haec commixtio et consecratio Corporis et Sanguinis Domini nostri Jesu Christi fiat accipientibus nobis in vitam aeternam. Amen.	May the mingling and the consecration of the body and blood of our Lord Jesus Christ be unto us that receive it effectual for life everlasting. Amen.

[1] In the Mozarabic rite the prayer for the mingling is as follows: Sancta sanctis (τὰ ἅγια τοῖς ἁγίοις) et conjunctio corporis (et sanguinis) D. N. J. Ch. sit sumentibus (= edentibus) et potantibus nobis ad veniam, et defunctis fide-

THE FRACTION OF THE HOST

The liturgical Fraction of the host and the mingling of the consecrated elements is a rite very simple, but exceedingly rich in holy mysteries. This small portion of the Eucharistic celebration is of profound significance and of the highest importance, as is seen from the fact that this rite of the breaking and the mingling, although greatly modified, is found to agree in its essential features in the liturgies of all countries and times. Even if this rite in former times was occasioned by natural reasons, still the fraction and the mingling have a higher symbolical signification, in the explanation of which it must not be forgotten that the breaking and mingling of the consecrated elements are intimately connected.

1. The great importance of the Fraction of the host is already indicated by the fact that the bishop, after the ordination of the newly ordained priests, urges them to carefully study the entire rite of the Mass before they celebrate, especially the Consecration, the Fraction, and the Communion. Although here the Fraction of the host is mentioned together with the Consecration and the Communion, still it would be erroneous to describe it as an essential or even as an integral part of the Eucharistic sacrificial action.[2] The Fraction is, indeed, very significant in the constitution of the sacrificial celebration, but in no wise does it touch upon the essence or integrity of the sacrifice. The peculiar importance of this breaking of the host is manifold. At one time it is done in imitation of what the Lord did at the Last Supper, when He broke the Eucharistic bread before distributing it; hence in the early ages the Eucharistic sacrifice and Communion celebration were designated by the name of the breaking of bread (*fractio panis;* cf. Acts 2:42; 20:7, 11; I Cor. 10:16). Consequently the liturgical breaking of the host has a profound significance in a twofold connection, first, with the preceding sacrificial action; secondly, with the Communion which follows.

The host is broken in order more vividly to represent in a liturgical

---

libus praestetur ad requiem; in the Ambrosian Missal: Commixtio consecrati corporis et sanguinis D. N. J. Ch. nobis edentibus et sumentibus (= potantibus) proficiat ad vitam et gaudium sempiternum.

[2] Fractio hostiae consecratae et quod una sola pars mittatur in calicem, respicit corpus mysticum, sicut admixtio aquae significat populum et ideo horum praetermissio non facit imperfectionem sacrificii, ut propter hoc sit necesse aliquid reiterare circa celebrationem hujus sacramenti (S. Thom., IIIa, q.83, a.6 ad 6).

manner the Eucharist's character as a sacrifice; for the breaking symbolizes in an expressive way Christ's violent and bloody death on the cross, inasmuch as it indicates that wounding and lacerating that caused the separation of His soul from His body, which resulted in His sacrificial death.[3] In the breaking of the host, Christ is figured as the Lamb that was slain and bruised for our sins (Isa. 53:5). The breaking of the host, therefore, expresses the same mystery that is represented by the separate consecration of the two species. The host, moreover, is broken over the chalice.[4] This rite may be founded especially on great reverence towards the Blessed Sacrament, so that any loose particles may fall into the precious blood;[5] but nevertheless the breaking has a mystical signification.[6] The breaking of the Eucharistic bread over the chalice is intended to indicate that the blood contained in the chalice proceeds from the broken (wounded and mangled) body of Christ, and therefore belongs to it and with it constitutes but one sacrifice and one sacrificial gift.[7]

That the Fraction of the Eucharistic species has also a connection with Communion, as a preparation and introduction to it, is universally acknowledged; for "to break bread" means the same as to prepare it for food, to present or distribute it for participation.[8]

[3] Sicut species sacramentales sunt sacramentum corporis Christi veri, ita fractio hujusmodi specierum est sacramentum dominicae passionis, quae fuit in corpore Christi vero (S. Thom., IIIa, q.77, a.7).

[4] In the eleventh century the host was broken on the paten. Archidiaconus patenam osculatam dat uni ex diaconibus tenendam, ad confractionem in ea faciendam. Unde sacerdos sine ministro sacrificans ad eundem locum eam de sub corporali absconditam resumit et osculatam in altari deponit, ut hostiam in ea confringat (Microl., chap. 17).

[5] Super calicem frangitur, ne minutiae spargantur, sed in ejus concavitate caute recipiantur (Durand., *Ration.*, IV, chap. 51).

[6] Confractio et commixtio corporis Domini tantis mysteriis declarata antiquitus sanctis Patribus fuit, ut dum sacerdos oblationem frangeret, videbatur quasi Angelus Dei membra fulgentis pueri cultro concaedere et sanguinem ejus in calicem excipiendo colligere (S. Germanus, *Expositio brevis antiquae Liturgiae Gallicanae* [Migne, LXXII, 94]).

[7] Fractio significat passionem Domini . . . frangitur autem supra calicem propter reverentiam Sacramenti, ne aliqua ejus particula aliorsum prosiliat . . . praeterea ad significandum, quod in fractione, h. e. in vulneratione corporis Christi, sanguis, qui in calice continetur, continue fluxit de corpore (Gabr. Biel, *Expos. Can. Miss.*, lect. 80).

[8] "The breaking of the body takes place at the sacred banquet; on the cross it did not occur, but rather the contrary, since it is said: 'Neither shall you break a bone thereof' (Exod. 12:46). What He did not suffer on the cross, He suffers for thy sake at the Holy Sacrifice, and He permits Himself to be

THE FRACTION OF THE HOST

But this connection ought to be more deeply and more fully understood. The Fraction characterizes the Eucharistic bread of life as a sacrificial food; for it means that the body of Christ broken for us, that is, sacrificed, is given in Communion to be eaten. Our Lord Himself promised: "The bread that I will give, is My flesh for the life of the world" (John 6:52). Inasmuch as Christ gave His body for us in His bloody death of the cross, and daily on the altar gives it in a mystical sacrificial death,—which twofold giving is symbolized by the liturgical breaking of the host—He makes it a sacrificial food, which is administered and partaken of in Holy Communion.

According to the Roman rite the consecrated bread, at least since the ninth century, is divided into three parts; [9] all three parts are consumed by the celebrant, the two larger together, the smallest with the sacred blood, into which it was dropped. Formerly the practice was somewhat different. As the hosts were much larger, one of these three parts was subdivided into several particles and used in different ways: [10] distributed to those present, sent to the

---

broken that He may satiate all" (St. Chrysostom, *Homilies on I Cor.* [10:27], XXIV).

[9] In the Mozarabic liturgy the host is broken into nine parts, which are named after the chief mysteries of redemption: (1) *Corporatio* (Incarnation); (2) *Nativitas* (Nativity); (3) *Circumcisio* (Circumcision); (4) *Apparitio* (Apparition); (5) *Passio* (Passion); (6) *Mors* (Death); (7) *Resurrectio* (Resurrection); (8) *Gloria* (Glorification); (9) *Regnum* (Kingdom). The first seven parts are placed on the paten in such a manner as to form a cross, while the two remaining portions are placed to the right at the foot of the cross (*ultra rotas*, that is, outside of the marks in the form of a ring affixed to the paten for the other seven particles).

```
      1
  6   2   7
      3
      4   8
      5   9
```

[10] Sacerdos rumpit hostiam ex dextro latere juxta Ordinem ad designandam dominici lateris percussionem. Deinde majorem partem in duo confringit, ut tres portiones de corpore dominico efficere possit. Nam unam in calicem, faciendo crucem, mittere debet, cum dicit: *Pax Domini* . . . , ad designandum corporis et animae conjunctionem in resurrectione Christi. Alteram vero ipse presbyter necessario sumit ante calicis participationem juxta dominicam institutionem. Tertiam autem communicaturis sive infirmis necessario dimittit (Microl., chap. 17). Diaconus sacerdoti offerat patenam, in qua sacerdos corpus Domini tripliciter dividat, quarum partium *unam* sacerdos calici immittens *Pax Domini* alta voce dicendo, protinus subdat secrete: "Fiat commixtio corporis et sanguinis Domini nobis accipientibus in vitam aeternam." Alia se, diaconum subdiaconumque communicet. Tertiam viati-

absent, or put into the chalice at the next sacrificial celebration.[11] Participation in the same Holy Sacrifice was regarded as a sign and pledge of ecclesiastical Communion; hence popes and bishops sent to other bishops, or priests too, parts of consecrated hosts, which the recipients dropped into the chalice and consumed.[12] This division of the the host into three parts was symbolically interpreted in various ways. The three parts were, for example, referred to the Holy Trinity, or to the earthly life, the sacrificial death, and the eternal glory of Christ; but generally and principally to the mystical body of Christ, the Church: the three parts of the host were interpreted to refer to the Church militant, suffering, and triumphant; and there were other interpretations.[13]

2. There is an immediate and intimate connection between the Fraction of the host and the mingling of the Eucharistic species.[14] If we pay attention to this connection, the object and

cum, si opus fuerit, in patena usque ad finem Missae reservet; si autem opus non fuerit, tertiam sacerdos aut unus ministrorum accipiat (Joann. Abrincens. [d. 1079], *De offic. eccles.*).

[11] A particle previously consecrated was preserved and united to the precious blood at the following sacrifice, to represent, in all probability, the continual succession of the sacrifice, as well as the unity of the last with the present celebration.

[12] This custom existed in Rome until about the ninth century. There the pope on Sundays and feast days sent to those priests who had charge of divine service at the churches within the city, the Eucharist as a symbol of communion with the ecclesiastical head, and as a sign that they were empowered to celebrate. To more distant churches, situated outside the city, the Eucharist was not permitted to be borne, through reverence for the holy mysteries and also because the priests in those places had already permission to celebrate the Holy Sacrifice. The name "*fermentum,*" whereby these consecrated particles were designated by Popes Melchiades, Siricius, and Innocent I, has received various interpretations. Cf. the Brief [*epistola regularis*] of Pope Innocent I [402-17] to Decentius, bishop of Gubbio; Mabillon, *In Ord. Rom. comment. praevius,* chap. 6.

[13] Fractio hostiae tria significat: primo quidem ipsam divisionem corporis Christi, quae facta est in passione; secundo distinctionem corporis mystici secundum diversos status; tertio distributionem gratiarum procedentium ex passione Christi (S. Thom., IIIa, q. 83, a. 5 ad 7).

[14] Ancient writers have various designations for this universally prescribed rite, for example: commixtio corporis et sanguinis Domini; conjunctio panis et calicis; immissio panis in vinum v. calicem; officium consecrationis. Hac oratione (*the Embolism*) expleta, commiscens sacerdos Dominicam oblationem, ut calix Domini totam plenitudinem contineat sacramenti, tamquam per ejusdem mysterii copulationem imprecatur Ecclesiae pacem, dicens: *Pax Domini* . . . (Pseudo-Alcuin., chap. 40). Immissionem panis in vinum cerno apud quosdam varie actitari, ita ut aliqui primo mittant de sancta in calicem

meaning of the rite of mingling will easily be seen from the symbolism of the Fraction. In the separate consecration under two species, as well as in the liturgical breaking of the host, Christ's body and blood appear as though they were separated from each other; but from the fact that the consecrated elements are united with each other by the mingling, it is thereby symbolically expressed that in reality on the altar the body is not without the blood, and the blood not without the body, but under each species the whole Christ is present as one sacrificial gift and one sacrificial food.[15] Furthermore, as the mystical separation of the body and blood of Christ by the consecration and Fraction represents His bloody

---

et postea dicant: *Pax Domini* . . . ; econtra aliqui reservent immissionem, usque dum pax celebrata sit et fractio panis (Amalar., III, chap. 31). In Rome for a considerable time (perhaps until the ninth century) it was customary to unite the sacred body and blood of Christ twice in the chalice when celebrating Mass. The first mingling, when a previously consecrated host, or a host received from another place, was used, took place at the salutation of peace (*Pax Domini* . . . .) after the Our Father; the second mingling, for which was used a particle broken from the host just consecrated, did not take place until the Communion. (Cf. *Ordo Rom. I*, n. 18, 19, 22; *II*, n. 12 f.) Hence Amalarius, in his explanation of the Roman rite, speaks of a *bis positus panis in calicem* (*De eccles. offic.*, III, chap. 31). But when the custom of sending the Eucharist to other churches as a sign of union ceased, only one immission of a particle into the chalice was retained, the first one at the kiss of peace. Only when the Pope officiated, the union of the sacramental species at this point was omitted, taking place after the consuming of the sacred body. This variation continued until about the fifteenth century, when at the Pontifical Mass of the pope the universal and still existing mingling rite came into use. (Cf. *Ordo Rom. IV* and *XIV*. Innocent. III, *De sacr. alt. myst.*, VI, chap. 9). According to the *Ordo Rom. I*, n. 8, as the pope advanced to the altar, the Eucharist (*Sancta*) was carried before him in an open case by two acolytes. This particle, preserved from the previous consecration, was dropped into the precious blood after the salutation of peace, *Pax Domini*. . . . Ex his conjicere licet, recentiorem morem Eucharistiam praeferendi Pontifici, cum aliquo proficiscitur, forsitan manasse non solum ex communi primorum christianorum more, qui peregrinantes Eucharistiam secum gestare solebant, sed etiam ex veteri consuetudine deferendi sacrosancta mysteria ante Pontificem, cum ad Missarum solemnia celebranda ad altare procederet, qui tamen ritus in primo tantum Romani Ordinis libello praescribitur, non in aliis. Nam secundus libellus praecipit, ut Pontifex, cum venerit ad altare, "primo adoret Sancta," quae proinde ibidem antea exstitisse necesse est (Mabillon, *In Ord. Rom. comment. praev.*, chap. 6).

[15] Fit haec permixtio: primo ad notandum, quod Christi corpus non fuit sine sanguine nec sanguis sine corpore; secundo ad designandum, quod unum sacramentum conficitur ex speciebus panis et vini; tertio corporis et sanguinis post trinum crucis signum permixtio est animae ad corpus reditio (Durandus, IV, li, 17).

sacrificial death, so the mystical union of the body and blood of Christ by this mingling symbolizes His glorious resurrection, in which His body and blood were again united and vivified.[16] If we consider both of these meanings together, we can then say that the liturgical act of mingling is intended to represent the Eucharistic Saviour as the undivided and living victim on the altar. As the breaking of the host can be referred to the Communion, so likewise can the mingling; for the union of the Eucharistic body and blood contains an allusion to the fact that the whole Christ, and indeed the gloriously risen Christ, is the bread of life for the world. Thus the Fraction and the mingling of the two elements announce in a mystical but eloquent manner that Christ suffered death for us and now lives eternally (Apoc. 5:12, 14).

3. After the breaking of the host and before the mingling, the priest makes three signs of the cross over the chalice with the small piece of the host broken off in his right hand,[17] at the same time saying: "May the peace of the Lord be always with you." The fact that this salutation of peace is made precisely between the symbolical fraction and mingling, signifies that Christ by His redeeming death and glorious resurrection has become the author and source of true peace; likewise does the sign of the cross over the chalice,

[16] Per particulam oblatae immissae in calicem ostenditur corpus Christi, quod resurrexit a mortuis (Joann. Abrinc., *De officiis ecclesiast.*). *Pax Domini* . . . dicens, sacerdos vel episcopus ter super calicem cum particula signat et infundit calici, quia cunctis in coelo et terra pacificatis ad corpus rediit anima Jesu Christi. Quidam infundunt, antequam dicant *Pax Domini* . . . , quod etiam non vacat a mysterio, quia post resurrectionem manifestum est pacem datam hominibus bonae voluntatis (Sicard., III, chap. 8).

[17] As may be seen from the most ancient Roman *Ordines*, as early as the ninth century the sign of the cross was made three times over the chalice with a small particle, but not until the dropping of the (second) particle (immediately before receiving the precious blood), when the present prayer at the mingling (*Fiat commixtio et consecratio* . . .) was recited. (Cf. *Ordo Rom. I*, n. 19; *II*, n. 13.) According to *Ordo IV* no prayer was then said: Quando communicat domnus apostolicus, partem sibi mordet et reliquam in calice mittit, faciens crucem de ea tribus vicibus super calicem nihil dicens. Crux quae formatur super calicem particulae oblatae, ipsum nobis corpus ante oculos praescribit, quod pro nobis crucifixum est. Ideo tangit quattuor latera calicis, quia per illud hominum genus quattuor climatum ad unitatem unius corporis accessit et ad pacem catholicae Ecclesiae (Amalar., III, chap. 31). Cum dicitur: *Pax Domini* . . . inter calicem fit triplex signaculum crucis ad laudem et honorem ss. Trinitatis, quae misit Agnum qui per crucem salvavit mundum et fecit pacem hominum et angelorum (Stephan. Augustod., *De sacram. altar..* chap. 18).

containing the precious blood, allude to the fact that the peace of God was purchased for us by the holy cross and the blood shed thereon, for through the blood of the cross Christ has made peace, "both as to the things that are on earth and the things that are in heaven" (Col. 1:20). Moreover, in this connection the sign of the cross illustrates and completes the meaning of the previous Fraction, inasmuch as it more particularly characterizes the immolation of the divine victim symbolized thereby as a sacrifice accomplished on the cross. Finally with regard to the mingling that follows, the signs of the cross made with the host over the chalice express that the glory of the resurrection was given to the Saviour as a reward for His ready self-humiliation even to the death of the cross.

4. The dropping of the small particle of the host into the most precious blood is designated in the accompanying prayer as the mingling (*commixtio*) and consecration (*consecratio*) of the body and blood of Christ. It is most difficult to determine precisely the sense and signification of the word *consecratio*, since this passage has various readings in the liturgical documents.[18] Liturgical writers have attempted numerous explanations.

The words *haec commixtio et consecratio* have been frequently understood in a concrete sense: may these mingled and consecrated [19] sacrificial gifts of the body and blood of Christ be effectual to us for life everlasting.[20] This conception is assuredly favored by the

---

[18] Commixtio consecrati corporis et sanguinis; haec sacrosancta commixtio corporis et sanguinis; conjunctio corporis et sanguinis; haec commixtio corporis et sanguinis; fiat commixtio et consecratio corporis et sanguinis; fiat commixtio et consecratio corporis et sanguinis D. N. J. Ch. nobis accipientibus vita aeterna; haec sacra commixtio corporis et sanguinis D. N. J. Ch.

[19] Both expressions are also correctly used in another sense (= *commixtum et consecratum*); for example, in Lev. 27:29 we find *consecratio* = dedicated.

[20] The words consecration of the body and of the blood signify here merely the consecrated body and blood (Lebrun, V, art. 5). Respondeo, consecrationem hic objective sumi pro rebus consecratis, non formaliter pro actu, quo res consecrantur (Tournely, *Tract. de Euchar.*, II, x, 2). In support of this conception are adduced the words of the holy deacon Lawrence to Pope Sixtus II, when the latter was led to martyrdom: Experire, utrum idoneum ministrum elegeris. Cui commisisti dominici sanguinis consecrationem, cui consummandorum consortium sacramentorum, hic sanguinis tui consortium negas? (S. Ambr., *De offic. ministr.*, I, chap. 41.) *Sanguinis consecratio* here is conceived as = *sanguis consecratus*, the distribution of which was a function of the deacon. But the reception of the precious blood forms, as Micrologus asserts (chap. 19), the *complementum communionis*, and the Holy Communion in general, as the sacrificial banquet, is the termina-

circumstance that not the act of mingling or of consecration, but the mingled and consecrated elements are for us the source of life; [21] but this explanation does not altogether suffice. Perhaps *commixtio et consecratio* are best explained according to the Ambrosian rite, which has: *Haec commixtio consecrati corporis et sanguinis* ("This mingling of the consecrated body and blood of Christ").

Therefore the mystical rite of the breaking of the host and its mingling with the blood in the chalice brings vividly before our eyes the death and resurrection of the divine victim, who has become for us in the Eucharistic sacrifice and in the sacrificial banquet the inexhaustible source of a heavenly life (*fiat accipientibus nobis in vitam aeternam*).

The body of Christ, born as the divine victim for the sins of the world, was also the heavenly grain of wheat sown by the Holy Ghost in the virginal earth; it was the heavenly grape on the virgin vine which sprung up under the breath of the Holy Spirit. In order to become our sacrifice for the atonement of sins, the body of Christ was to die and shed its blood upon the altar of the cross: the heavenly grain of wheat was to die in the earth; the heavenly grape was to be trodden down. To become food and drink for the nourishment of our life of grace, the body of Christ was again to resume its vitality: the heavenly wheat was to be ground and baked into the life-giving bread; the heavenly juice of the grape was to

---

tion of the sacrificial mysteries, so that we can say the deacon shares (*consortium*) in the *consummatio*, that is, in the accomplishment of the Eucharistic sacrifice. This interpretation may of course be accepted, but it does not appear to exhaust the full sense of the expression *consecratio sanguinis dominici*. The deacon is ordained mainly, *ut proxime assistat sacerdoti sacra facienti sitque ejus in tanti mysterii celebratione adjutor* (Menardus), and in the *Pontif. Roman.* he is called *comminister et cooperator corporis et sanguinis Domini*; hence a certain participation not merely in dispensing Holy Communion, but also in the celebration of the sacrifice can and must be ascribed to him. In this sense, then, is the deacon admitted "to the consecrating and offering of the blood of the Lord, to the accomplishment of the holy mysteries." (Cf. Bona, *Rerum liturg.*, I, xxv, 4, cum notis et observationibus R. Sala.)

[21] Commixtio et consecratio dicuntur fieri in nostram salutem, non quod ipsa actio commiscendi et consecrandi nos salvet, sed quia res ipsae commixtae et consecratae, dum a nobis devote suscipiuntur, multum prosunt ad salutem; unde hic dicimus: fiat summentibus nobis in vitam aeternam (Bellarm., *De Missa*, II, chap. 27). Non ex ipsa commiscendi cum sanguine corporis actione salutem et vitam exspectamus, sed ex corpore et sanguine Christi, quae commiscentur a nobis, ut post adumbratam passionem, adumbremus et resurrectionem, quae ad justificationem nostram cum ipsa passione suo modo concurrit (Tournely *loc. cit.*).

be pressed and fermented into the inebriating wine of life. Thus life and death were to be swallowed up in Christ, in order to make Him our life's bread and drink. He was to be dead and yet live, He was to be alive and yet die. How was this to be effected? This was accomplished at the Last Supper. This continually takes place in the Mass, where, by virtue of the words of Christ, His blood is represented separated from His body, as the blood of the immolated victim shed once for all on the cross, but where in virtue of the blessed immortality of the risen Christ, His living body is permeated with His living blood, to be to us the nourishment and refreshment of eternal life.[22]

[22] Laurent, *Christol. Predigten*, I, 284.

CHAPTER XLII

THE AGNUS DEI AND THE KISS OF PEACE

THE Holy Eucharist is the sign of unity, the bond of charity, the symbol of concord,[1] that is, the sacrament of peace; for peace is one of the principal effects of the reception of the Eucharist, but at the same time it is also a necessary requisite for participation in the Eucharistic sacrifice and banquet of love. At the table of the Lord the bond of love and concord should be formed ever more closely between the faithful, until they have "but one heart and one soul" (Acts 4:32); "for we, being many, are one bread, one body, all that partake of one bread" (I Cor. 10:17). Peace must reign in the heart into which the "God of peace and love" enters and takes up His abode. Therefore after the Pater Noster there are such frequent and fervent prayers for the great gift of peace in preparation for the Communion. In the Embolism we meet with the urgent supplication: "Graciously give peace in our days" (*da propitius pacem in diebus nostris*), and at the Fraction the three signs of the cross are accompanied with the salutation of peace: "May the peace of the Lord be always with you" (*Pax Domini sit semper vobiscum*); at the Agnus Dei we now implore the Lamb of God lying on the altar to give us peace (*dona nobis pacem*), and in the prayer immediately following, this petition is continued, as we implore the Lord to impart peace to His entire Church and preserve it; and finally, the peace prayed for so urgently is sealed by a holy kiss.

The Agnus Dei

Pope Sergius I (687–701) is said to have been the first to order the singing of the Agnus Dei by the clergy and the people at the

---

[1] Trid., Sess. XIII, cap. 8.

THE AGNUS DEI

breaking of the host.[2] The original rite differs in some respects from the present one, which was developed from the eleventh to the thirteenth century.[3] At this time we meet everywhere the threefold repetition of the Agnus Dei,[4] and instead of concluding, as previously, each with the same petition, *miserere nobis* ("have mercy on us"), the third petition, *dona nobis pacem* ("grant us peace"), began to be substituted. The last petition was occasioned by many calamities and disturbances that had befallen the Church.[5] The reason for it lies in the relation of the Agnus Dei to the imparting of the kiss of peace, or to the reception of Holy Communion.[6]

[2] Hic statuit, ut tempore confractionis dominici corporis, *Agnus Dei, qui tollis peccata mundi*, a clero et populo decantaretur (*Lib. Pontific.*). Now, since the Agnus Dei occurs already in the *Sacrament. Gregor.*, Mabillon (*In Ord. Rom.*, chap. 8, n. 7) infers that it was said already before the time of Sergius, but only by the choir, as was again the case soon after Sergius. (Cf. *Ordo Rom. I*, n. 19; *II*, n. 13.) In Missa Sabbati sancti, quae veteri more etiam nunc celebratur, omittitur *Agnus Dei* cum Antiphonis ad *Offertorium* et ad *Communionem*, quae primarii non esse instituti Walafridus Strabo et alii observarunt (Mabillon, *loc. cit.*).

[3] The most ancient Roman *Ordines* and the earliest liturgical writers say nothing with regard to the repetition of the Agnus Dei. Gradually the rite became fixed and general of singing, or reciting it three times. Agnus Dei ter canitur (Beleth). At the same time the practice was also introduced of saying the third time *dona nobis pacem*. Bis repetitur *Miserere nobis* et tertio variatur per *Dona nobis pacem* (Beleth). On Holy Thursday alone was an exception made during the Middle Ages, probably because the kiss of peace was not given. In coena Domini ter debet dici cum *Miserere nobis* (Beleth, chap. 48). According to Durandus the Roman *schola cantorum* still observed in the thirteenth century the ancient custom of singing three times *miserere nobis*, which is done at present only in the Basilica of St. John Lateran (cf. IV, chap. 52). Usually the choir sang it: Chorus psallat *Agnus Dei* (Joann. Abrinc.); chorus clamat ad Jesum et postulat: *Agnus Dei . . .* (Innoc. III); sometimes also the people (cf. Pseudo-Alcuin., chap. 40; Sicard., III, chap. 8). Quidam sacerdotes dicunt *Agnus Dei* manibus super altare depositis . . . alii vero stant manibus junctis, parum super altare inclinati (Durand., IV, chap. 52). Pontifex, junctis ante pectus manibus, dicit *Agnus Dei* submissa voce cum ministris adstantibus (*Ordo Rom. XIV*, chap. 53).

[4] Generally in former times the priest, as a general custom, did not recite what the choir sang and what was recited by the assistant ministers (deacon, subdeacon, lector), as he directed his attention either to the singing or to the reading, or was in the meantime engaged in other liturgical functions.

[5] Postmodum autem multis et variis adversitatibus et terroribus Ecclesiae ingruentibus, coepit ad Dominum clamare de tribulatione: *dona nobis pacem*. Et ut clamor ejus facilius audiretur, in ipsa duxit immolationis hora clamandum (Innoc. III, *De sacr. alt. myst.*, VI, chap. 4).

[6] Postquam ad communicandum et ad percipiendum corpus perventum fuerit, pacis osculum sibi invicem tradunt, cantantes: *Agnus Dei, qui tollis*

SACRIFICE OF THE MASS

Agnus Dei, qui tollis peccata mundi, miserere nobis.	Lamb of God, who takest away the sins of the world, have mercy on us.
Agnus Dei, qui tollis peccata mundi, miserere nobis.	Lamb of God, who takest away the sins of the world, have mercy on us.
Agnus Dei, qui tollis peccata mundi, dona nobis pacem.	Lamb of God, who takest away the sins of the world, grant us peace.

In the foregoing Fraction and mingling of the sacrificial elements, Christ is mystically placed before our eyes as the victim immolated by shedding His blood and again gloriously risen to life; therefore this humble supplication of the Agnus Dei, in which the priest addresses himself to the Saviour concealed and offered under the Eucharistic species, appropriately concludes with the twofold cry for mercy and the single cry for peace.[7] The priest at the same time strikes his breast three times to express his sinfulness and compunction.[8]

---

peccata mundi, miserere nobis, ut pacifici sacramentum perficientes, in filiorum Dei numero (remissis delictis omnibus) mereantur copulari (Raban. Maur., *De clericor. institut.*, I, chap. 33).

[7] Sequitur vox Ecclesiae supplicans Agno largitori pacis et misericordiae. Ter cum eodem principio cantatur et duplici fine terminatur; itaque orat: *miserere nobis*, dando veniam; *miserere nobis*, conservando justitiam; *dona nobis pacem*, quae superat omnem sensum et intellegentiam. Miserere captivis, miserere peregrinis, da nobis finem laboris; miserere peccatoribus, miserere exsulibus, da requiem laborantibus; tribue peccatorum remissionem, perduc ad patriae certam mansionem, da post laborem pacem et requiem (Stephan. Augustod., chap. 18). *Agnus Dei* ter cantatur, ut verus Agnus, cujus carnem et sanguinem sumimus, nobis propitietur. Primo rogamus, ut nobis misereatur peccata relaxando; secundo, ut nobis misereatur devotos sibi faciendo; tertio, ut nobis pacem donare dignetur, quae hic initium habet in sanctis, et in beata vita perficietur (Robert. Paulul., II, chap. 40).

[8] Ad *Agnus Dei* sacerdos manus jungit et caput inclinat, ut nimirum non tantum verbis, sed etiam actione statum supplicantis exprimat: manibus autem altare non tangit ad majorem erga Christum in illo quiescentem venerationem. Elata voce illud recitat ad excitandam populi attentionem eumque exstimulandum, ut simili oratione ac pectoribus percussione Dei misericordiam imploret. Post primum *Agnus Dei*, deposita sinistra, ne sola pendula maneat, super corporale usque ad tertium *Agnus Dei*, postremis dexterae digitis pectus percutit in signum compunctionis, dum bis profert, *miserere nobis*, itemque dum inquit *dona nobis pacem*, quum cordis compunctio sit optima dispositio ad pacem obtinendam. In Missis defunctorum sacerdos non percutit sibi pectus, dum pronuntiat *dona eis requiem*, ut nempe significet, se in

THE AGNUS DEI

In the Old Law a lamb was one of the usual animals of sacrifice, and all these sacrificial lambs were types of Jesus Christ, the one true Lamb, who took away the sins of the world, who atoned for them by His blood. The designation of Christ as a Lamb expresses His sacrificial character, at the same time denoting His purity and freedom from guilt; but prominently it refers to the gentle patience and voluntary resignation with which He subjected Himself to the most painful sufferings and death.[9] The name, "Lamb of God" (*Agnus Dei*), not merely signifies that Christ, by the will of God and for His honor, became a sacrifice slain for the world; but moreover, it includes the deeper meaning that He is the well-beloved Son of God, that the fullness of the divinity dwells in Him.[10] In reality Christ is the sacrificial Lamb that takes away the sins of the world, only because He is the beloved Son, in whom God is well pleased. As a lamb Christ was promised in the Old Law (Isa. 53:7); as a lamb He was pointed out in the New Law by John the Baptist and extolled by the apostles (John 1:29; I Pet. 1:19). With marked preference St. John in his mystical Apocalypse calls the Son of God a lamb (about twenty-seven times). In a mystical ecstasy he beholds Jesus as the Lamb that was slain and that purchased souls for God out of all tribes and nations, that washed them clean in His blood and thereby made of them a royal-priestly people; as the Lamb that with His blood strengthens the Church militant, making it victorious in its combats with Satan; as the Lamb worthy to receive power and divinity and wisdom and strength and honor and glory and

---

hisce Missis pro defunctis specialiter celebratis ipsorum magis quam sui memorem esse (De Carpo, *Biblioth. liturg.*, I, a. 50, n. 202).

[9] Agnus propter innocentiam, mansuetudinem, obedientiam et immolationem vocatur Christus (Dion. Carthus., *In Apoc.*, 5:6).

[10] The addition of "God" is variously explained, for example, the divine Lamb; the Lamb belonging to God, His property; the Lamb destined by God for sacrifice; the Lamb submissive or pleasing or dedicated to God. (Cf. Haneberg-Schegg, *Das Evangelium nach Johannes*, I, 125.) This formula of prayer (taken in part from Holy Scripture, John 1:29) has a wealth and profundity of meaning. In the first place, it discloses the entire sublimity of the nature and mission of Jesus Christ, since the highly significant designation of Agnus Dei characterizes the Saviour as the Son of God, as the divine sacrificial Lamb given by God and again offered to Him, who innocently, meekly and freely underwent the death of the Cross; in the next place, it exalts the sin-effacing, world-redeeming power and efficacy of His sacrificial death; finally, it contains a humble, sorrowful, contrite appeal for mercy and for the obtaining of peace.

benediction; as the Lamb to whom all creation and all the choirs of angels present praise and adoration.

As the lamb in Holy Scripture is a consistent symbol of Christ, and as the citizens of heaven bless the Lamb without ceasing, so also does the Church love to invoke Jesus Christ in a simple, touching manner as the "Lamb of God." Throughout all ages there continues ever to resound in her liturgy of the Mass this fervent supplication to the divine, eternal, sacrificial Lamb, who has taken upon Himself the sins of the world and effaced them. As often as she administers Holy Communion to the faithful, she exhorts them in the words of St. John the Baptist (*Ecce Agnus Dei! ecce qui tollit peccata mundi!*) to consider the wealth of grace contained in this heavenly sacrificial food. Almost all her litanies conclude with this solemn invocation to the Lamb of God: "spare us, . . . hear us, . . . have mercy on us."

The Church has ever been accustomed to represent the divine Saviour both under the figure of the Good Shepherd and under the symbol of the lamb: both images are intimately connected with each other. Jesus Christ is the Good Shepherd, who Himself became our sacrificial Lamb on the cross, and who daily becomes the same again on the altar; He is the Good Shepherd, who gave His life for us and who, with His living flesh and heart's blood, nourishes us for an eternal life of blessedness.

From the sacrificial Lamb present on the altar there streams forth salvation and redemption, the favor and blessing and peace of God. This Lamb, that was slain from the beginning of the world and that will be slain until the end of the world, we should adore and invoke during Mass, in order that we may obtain the fullness of mercy and peace, whereby we shall be prepared for admittance to the "royal banquet of the lamb." [11]

In Requiem Masses the petition of the Agnus Dei—perhaps since the eleventh century, certainly since the twelfth—is quite different, inasmuch as we twice implore the divine sacrificial Lamb to "grant

---

[11] Sancta Mechtildis: "Eia mi Domine, modo mihi aliquid ex praesentibus Missae verbis dona, unde anima mea spiritualiter consoletur." Cui Dominus: "Ecce jam mihi canitur ter *Agnus Dei:* in primo me offero Deo Patri cum omni humilitate et patientia mea pro vobis; ad secundum, offero me cum omni amaritudine passionis meae in plenam reconciliationem; ad tertium, cum toto amore divini Cordis, in supplementum omnium quae homini desunt bonorum" (S. Mechtild., *Lib. special. grat.*, III, chap. 19).

THE PRAYER FOR PEACE

rest" to the suffering souls in purgatory, and the third time we implore for them "eternal rest" in heaven.[12]

THE PRAYER FOR PEACE

As the Agnus Dei, so also are the following prayers until the Communion addressed, not to the Father, but to the Saviour present in the Blessed Sacrament. The longing for peace is so ardent that the priest, bowing humbly and looking intently upon the sacred host lying on the paten, continues to beg for this precious gift for the whole Church.[13]

Domine Jesu Christe, qui dixisti Apostolis tuis: Pacem relinquo vobis, pacem meam do vobis: ne respicias peccata mea, sed fidem Ecclesiae tuae: eamque secundum voluntatem tuam pacificare et coadunare digneris: qui vivis et regnas Deus per omnia saecula saeculorum. Amen.	O Lord Jesus Christ, who saidst to Thy apostles: Peace I leave with you, My peace I give unto you, look not upon my sins, but upon the faith of Thy Church; and vouchsafe to grant her peace and unity according to Thy will: who livest and reignest God world without end. Amen.

The human heart longs for peace and finds no rest until it has found true peace. For "so great," says St. Augustine, "is the gift of peace, that even in worldly and mortal things nothing more pleasant can be heard, nothing more desirable can be longed for, and nothing better can be found." [14] These words apply both to that

---

[12] The Ambrosian rite has the Agnus Dei only in Requiem Masses. The formula is the same as in our missals; but the third time the petition is enlarged by an additional clause: "Dona eis requiem sempiternam et locum indulgentiae cum Sanctis tuis in gloria."

[13] Micrologus (in the eleventh century) does not know of this prayer; while Durandus (in the thirteenth century) mentions it. According to the Roman rite, the kiss of peace was formerly imparted after the salutation: *Pax Domini sit semper vobiscum*, without the preceding special prayer for peace. The Mozarabic and the ancient Gallican liturgies have an *Oratio ad pacem* which varies according to the Mass. In many Oriental missals we find likewise a similar prayer (*oratio ante pacis osculum, oratio osculi pacis, oratio amplexus*, εὐχὴ τοῦ ἀσπασμοῦ). Infertur oratio pro osculo pacis, ut caritate omnes reconciliati invicem digne sacramento corporis et sanguinis Christi consocientur (S. Isid., *De ecclesiast. offic.*, I, chap. 15).

[14] *De civit. Dei*, XIX, chap. 11.

interior peace of soul with God and with one's self, and that exterior peace with one's neighbor.[15]

Interior peace is the state of a soul enjoying spiritual well-being and prosperity, to which belongs, first of all, the consoling consciousness that by the remission of sin we are reconciled to God and united to Him by the holy bond of a mystical friendship, by which we may confidently expect the plenitude of all the gifts and blessings that flow from this abundant source of grace. This peace of God, which surpasseth all understanding (Phil. 4:7), comprises, therefore, all the beneficial and refreshing effects of divine truth and grace, all the precious fruits of supernatural faith, hope, and love in the sanctified soul, which is the dwelling place of God; this disposition of the heart is a gift that the Holy Ghost imparts. But here below this peace is more or less imperfect,[16] because it is mingled with sorrow and pain; perfect and unperturbed it will be only above in heaven, where all woe shall cease.[17] The more a man rids himself of attachment to the world and recollects his heart in God, the more he mortifies and overcomes his passions, the more he lives a life of faith and grace: the more also will he taste the consolation and sweetness of that interior peace which the Lord pours out, as a stream, on humble and self-sacrificing souls (Isa. 66:12). True piety is joy and peace in the Holy Ghost; it is godliness.

This is the peace which Christ left to His own, and which the world can neither give nor take away (John 14:27). Such peace of heart the world cannot bestow, for it has and offers only treasures that do not satiate: earthly goods, vain honors, and sensual pleasures. All these things are but apparent goods, they are vanity and vexation of spirit (Eccles. 2:17), and consequently they cannot impart true peace, but only a transitory, counterfeit peace. Sensual pleasure

[15] Continet pax Christi 1. amicitiam cum Deo; 2. tranquillitatem animi et serenitatem in tentationibus et persecutionibus; 3. mutuam inter ipsos homines concordiam (Corn. a Lap., *In Joann.*, 14:27).

[16] Hic (*on earth*) talis est pax nostra, ut solatium miseriae sit potius quam beatitudinis gaudium (S. August., *De civ. Dei*, XIX, chap. 27).

[17] Dicendum, quod cum *vera* pax non sit nisi de bono, sicut dupliciter habetur verum bonum, sc. perfecte et imperfecte, ita est duplex pax vera. Una quidem perfecta, quae consistit in perfecta fruitione summi boni, per quam omnes appetitus uniuntur quietati in uno, et hic est ultimus finis creaturae rationalis, secundum illud (Ps. 147:14): "Qui posuit fines tuos pacem." Alia vero est pax imperfecta, quae habetur in hoc mundo; quia etsi principalis animae motus quiescat in Deo, sunt tamen aliqua repugnantia et intus et extra, quae perturbant hanc pacem (S. Thom., IIa IIae, q. 29, a. 2 ad 4).

"goeth in pleasantly, . . . but in the end it will bite like a snake and will spread abroad poison like a basilisk" (Prov. 23:31 f.). The world, tossed about and turbulent like a restless ocean, is unwilling to understand what conduces to its peace (Luke 19:42); at present this knowedge is concealed from its eyes and it lives in a false peace.[18] But the world cannot rob us of the peace of God, which is deeply rooted in the heart and is elevated above earthly conditions and external influences. This peace comes from heaven and leads to heaven; it is affected neither by the alluring pleasures nor by the oppressive sufferings of this transitory life. If mind and heart are firmly centered in God, then they will also remain calm and tranquil and serene amid the storms of persecution, temptation, and distress.[19] To such a holy peace St. Theresa exhorts us:

> Let nothing trouble thee,
> Nothing afright thee;
> All things pass away:
> God is immutable.
> Patience obtains all.
> He that possesses God
> Can want for nothing;
> God alone suffices.

[18] Dicendum, quod pax consistit in quietatione et unione appetitus. Sicut autem appetitus potest esse vel simpliciter boni vel boni apparentis, ita etiam et pax potest esse et vera et apparens. Vera quidem pax non potest esse nisi circa appetitum veri boni, quia omne malum, etsi secundum aliquid appareat bonum, unde ex aliqua parte appetitum quietat, habet tamen multos defectus, ex quibus appetitus remanet inquietus et perturbatus. Unde pax vera non potest esse nisi in bonis et bonorum. Pax autem, quae malorum est, est pax apparens et non vera; unde dicitur (Sap. 14:22): In magno viventes inscientiae bello, tot et tam magna mala pacem appellant (S. Thom., IIa IIae, q.29, a.2 ad 3).

[19] Orat Archiapostolus, ut pax nobis multiplicetur, i.e. abundanter ac multipliciter divinitus detur et conservetur, videlicet pax pectoris, quae est tranquillitas mentis in Deo, pax temporis, quae est quies ab exterioribus impugnationibus, et pax aeternitatis, quae est tranquillissima quies beatorum in patria imperturbatumque gaudium eorum in Deo. Quantumcumque autem forinsecus impugnemur aut corporaliter molestemur, semper tamen pro posse conemur pacem pectoris conservare, ut tranquilletur in Deo cor nostrum et spiritaliter gaudeat in adversis. De qua pace ait Psalmista: "Pax multa diligentibus legem tuam." Qui enim divinae legis praecepta amorose custodiunt, mentis inquietudinem vincunt in omni eventu, in prosperis scilicet et adversis in Deo se figunt ac bene agendo gloriantur in Domino: estque in eis corpus subditum animae, sensualitas rationi, ratio Deo, ex qua optima ordinatione consurgit et manet in eis pax pectoris, quae ab Augustino vocatur tranquillitas ordinis (Dion. Carthus., *In I Pet.*, 1:2).

Exterior peace consists in concord and union with our neighbor; therefore it presupposes a meek, gentle, accommodating disposition, even towards those who injure or oppress us: "With them that hated peace, I was peaceable" (Ps. 119:7). A peaceful disposition, free from irritation, aversion, and bitterness, should reign among Christians; "of one mind, having compassion one of another, being lovers of the brotherhood" (I Pet. 3:8), they should live together. Unity of sentiment should animate us to a sincere participation in one another's welfare and joy and sorrow, and to true, sincere fraternal love. For this unity among His disciples the Saviour prayed on the night before His death: "The glory which Thou hast given Me, I have given to them, that they may be one, as We also are one; I in them and Thou in Me, that they may be made perfect in one" (John 17:22 f.). And the Apostle of the Gentiles exhorts us: "If it be possible, as much as is in you, have peace with all men" (Rom. 12:18); "Follow peace with all men" (Heb. 12:14). How beautiful and edifying it is to see so strong a bond of union and harmony bind together all the members of the Church! It gives joy, consolation, strength, amid all the trials and persecutions at the hands of a hostile, godless world. *Ubi caritas et amor, Deus ibi est* ("Where there is charity and love, there God is"), the Church chants at the washing of the feet on Holy Thursday.

This peace, interior and exterior, Christ acquired by His death and bequeathed to us as a precious heritage. "Peace I leave with you, My peace I give unto you; not as the world giveth, do I give unto you" (John 14:27). To this promise and legacy of the Saviour we here appeal when we implore peace for the Church militant, that all "with humility and mildness, with patience, supporting one another in charity, [be] careful to keep the unity of the Spirit in the bond of peace" (Eph. 4:2 f.). At the same time we petition the Lord to rescue His Church from all the hostility, violence, and persecution to which she is exposed in the world. Why should the Lord not listen to such supplication? Is it not altogether in accord and in compliance with His holy will (*secundum voluntatem tuam*)? Does He not wish that the Church should live in peace and concord? For He underwent the painful death of reconciliation to destroy the wall of separation and to gather into one body the dispersed children of God. In humble fear that his own sinfulness should be an impediment to the granting of this petition, the priest implores that the Lord would not look with anger upon him, the unworthy minister of the Church, but behold rather the worthiness and holiness of His beloved spouse, the Church (*ne respicias peccata mea, sed fidem Ecclesiae tuae*), in order to impart to her and increase in her the gift of peace and concord.

The Kiss of Peace

In the Epistles we frequently meet the admonition to the Christians, that with the kiss of love, or with the holy kiss,[20] they should salute one another (I Pet. 5:14; Rom. 16:16; I Cor. 16:20). This salutation took place after the Epistles were read in the assemblies for divine worship. Thus it came to pass that the holy kiss formed a constituent part of the Eucharistic celebration from the days of the apostles, as a symbol and confirmation of Christian love that dwells with peace in all. In the Roman rite the kiss of peace (*Pax*) has always been placed before the Communion;[21] in the Oriental Church,

---

[20] The *osculum* was always and everywhere regarded as a sign and expression of love, veneration, friendship, peace, reconciliation, gratitude, and joy. In Christianity, and especially by its reception into the liturgy, it received a supernatural character and a higher consecration. The *osculum sanctum*, of which the apostles speak, does not proceed merely from natural affection, but from *caritas*, from Christian brotherly love, which it would nourish and strengthen: this spiritual, divine love which has for its root Christian faith, and which is poured out by the Holy Ghost into our hearts and, therefore, appears, not as the work of nature, but of grace. The liturgical *osculum* (kiss of peace and the kissing of the hand of the celebrant at Solemn Mass by the assistants) is given to persons and to things. As the hand is an emblem of power, of protection, of help and of blessing in general, kissing the hand symbolizes the veneration and esteem bestowed upon some one on account of the authority and blessings conferred upon him. This *actus reverentialis* is certainly appropriate toward the person who celebrates the Eucharistic sacrifice, this act of omnipotent love, and who holds in his consecrated hand the Most Holy, who administers Holy Communion and blesses all present. Erat osculum non solius communionis, sed et omnium ecclesiasticarum functionum signaculum et sigillum, quod in omnibus Sacramentis adhiberi solebat (Bona, II, xvi, 7).

[21] Pope Innocent I writes to Decentius, Bishop of Gubbio, that the kiss of peace is not to be given until after the completion of the holy mysteries, that is, immediately before Communion. "You assert that some persons recommend the kiss of peace to the congregation before the completion of the mysteries (*ante confecta mysteria*, that is, before the Consecration), or the priests mutually give it, when necessarily it should be given only after all is over, that by it may be revealed that the congregation give their consent to all that has been done in the mysteries and celebrated in the church, and to

on the contrary, as well as in the Mozarabic and Gallican liturgies, it is placed already before the Consecration.[22] Moreover, the mode and manner of imparting the *Pax* varied at different times and in different churches.[23] Since the end of the thirteenth century, the real kiss (*osculum oris*) [24] was gradually omitted, and only the embrace (*amplexus*) formerly connected with it has been retained. In consequence of this, the *Pax* also began to be imparted in another way: by kissing the so-called *Osculatorium*, a small tablet to which was affixed the picture of the Saviour or of a saint. Later on, however, the general imparting of the *Pax* ceased and it was, as is the case at present, limited almost entirely to the Solemn Mass, at which only the clergy assisting in the sanctuary receive the kiss of peace by embracing one another. On special occasions dignitaries of the laity are permitted to receive the kiss of peace through the *Osculatorium*.[25]

---

prove by this sign of the concluding kiss of peace the completion of the celebration of reconciliation (*finita esse pacis concludentis signaculo demonstrentur*)."

[22] In many churches it was (with reference to Matt. 4:23: *si offers munus tuum ad altare* etc.) given only before the Oblation (S. Justin. M., *Apol. II*, n. 65), that is, immediately before the Preface (*Constit. Apostol.*, II, chap. 61).

[23] At the salutation of peace (*Pax Domini* . . .) the celebrant made the sign of the cross over the chalice three times and then dropped the (reserved) particle into it, after which he gave the *Pax* to the archdeacon. Sed archidiaconus pacem dat episcopo priori, deinde ceteris per ordinem et populis (*Ordo Rom. I*, n. 18). Archidiaconus pacem dat episcopo priori, qui et ultra dabit juxta se stanti ac deinde per ordinem ceteri, atque populus osculantur se invicem in osculo Christi (*Ordo Rom. III*, n. 16). Veniens presbyter accipiat pacem ab episcopo, eandem ceteris oblaturus (*Ordo Rom. V*, n. 12). Pontifex osculato altari (*after the prayer for peace*) convertat se ad capellanum et det ei pacem dicendo *Pax tecum*, quam ille recepturus prius inclinet reverenter ante Pontificem absque genuflexione; deinde recepta pace respondet *Et cum spiritu tuo* et osculetur pectus Pontificis; . . . postea det pacem diacono, et diaconus subdiacono . . . et sic pax diffunditur per circumstantes (*Ordo Rom. XIV*, chap. 53).

[24] Innocent III and Durandus affirm that kissing on the mouth was still the custom in the thirteenth century. Sacerdos praebet osculum oris ministro . . . pacis osculum per universos fideles diffunditur in ecclesia (Innoc. III, VI, chap. 5). Sacerdos facta commixtione et finita oratione accipit in quibusdam ecclesiis pacem ab eucharistia sive ad ipso corpore Domini, vel secundum alios ab ipso sepulchro, i.e. calice vel altari et mox praebet oris osculum ministro, sc. diacono (Durand., IV, chap. 53).

[25] In solemn Requiem Masses the kiss of peace is omitted, since St. Thomas remarks (IIIa, q.83, a.4), sacrificium offertur non pro pace praesenti, sed pro requie mortuorum. In the liturgy for the dead the Church is entirely engrossed in her care for the departed and, therefore, omits in all Requiem

THE KISS OF PEACE

The celebrant imparts the kiss of peace (*Pax*) to the deacon, who gives it to the subdeacon. Before giving the *Pax*, the priest, together with the deacon, kisses the altar to salute Christ and His saints in love and reverence, and thus to confirm and renew their mystical relation to the heavenly Church. For this connection is the necessary condition and source of the holy union and Christian fraternal love which should reign among the members of the Church militant, and which finds its expression and seal in the kiss of peace. In so far, therefore, as the kiss of peace is still in use, it has its proper place after the prayer for peace, and it serves as a preparation for the actual or spiritual reception of the Sacrament of charity and concord.[26] This holy kiss "reconciles and unites souls to one another, promising an entire oblivion of all offenses. It is a sign that the minds are again reconciled with one another, and that all remembrance of injustice suffered in the past is banished from the heart."[27]

Masses also the preceding petition for peace for all present (*dona nobis pacem*) and the prayer for peace (*Domine J. Chr. . . .*) for the entire Church. Inasmuch as the *osculum pacis* is at the same time a symbol of joy and enhances the solemnity, it is likewise appropriately omitted in solemn Requiem Masses. The opinion that the kiss of peace is omitted in solemn Requiem Masses because in them Holy Communion is not administered, is now untenable; for according to the general decree of S. R. C., June 27, 1868, it is permitted to administer Holy Communion with previously consecrated particles even in black vestments, during as well as immediately before and after the Requiem Mass. On Holy Thursday the Church omits the *osculum pacis*, to express her sorrow and abhorrence of the deceitful kiss of Judas, as on Good Friday she omits the genuflection at the prayer for the Jews, because they reviled the Saviour on the day of His death by scornful genuflections.

[26] Liturgists of the Middle Ages often regard not only the eulogia (*hostiae non consecratae—panis benedictus sanctae communionis vicarius*) and the *Oratio super populum*, but also the kiss of peace as a kind of surrogate (substitute) for the general Communion of the congregation, which at that epoch had ceased for a considerable time to take place daily. Contra hunc primae institutionis defectum triplex est remedium. Primum est pacis osculum ideoque in gallicana ecclesia datur in omni Missa nisi defunctorum; secundum est panis benedictus, qui eulogia dicitur, qui quia in Quadragesima propter abstinentiam dari non debuit, institutum est tertium remedium, sc. Oratio super populum, cui praedicitur: "Inclinate capita vestra Deo" (Sicard., III, chap. 8). Cf. Beleth., chap. 48; Durand., IV, liii, 3.

[27] St. Cyril of Jerusalem, *Catech. Mystag.*, V, n. 3.

CHAPTER XLIII

THE LAST PREPARATORY PRAYERS FOR COMMUNION [1]

THE two prayers following the prayer for peace serve as a proximate preparation for Holy Communion. The moment is now at hand for the most intimate, blessed union of the priest with the body and blood, soul and divinity of the Eucharistic victim. Boundless, indescribable treasures of salvation and grace are concealed in the Eucharist; why then do we not daily become richer in the goods of heaven? Why do we remain so destitute of solid virtue, so full of imperfection, weakness, and frailty? No doubt this is due, for the most part, to our short, careless, and lukewarm preparation and thanksgiving for Communion. The Lord would pour out upon us the plenitude of blessing, but we check the current of His liberality because we do not more carefully prepare and guard the soil of our heart, because we are so slothful and distracted even during those sacred moments when the King of heaven and earth enters into our soul and abides there. On the contrary, the greater our solicitude,

[1] Ante-Tridentine missals have many kinds of private prayers for the priest before and after Communion. (Cf. Martene, *De antiq. Eccles. ritib.*, iv, 9.) Micrologus (in the eleventh century) and Radulphus de Rivo, Dean of Tongres (in the fourteenth), mention only the prayer: *Domine J. Chr., qui ex voluntate Patris. . . . Orationem, quam inclinati dicimus, antequam communicemus, non ex Ordine, sed ex religiosorum traditione habemus, scil.* hanc: *Domine J. Chr., qui ex voluntate Patris. . . . Sunt et aliae multae orationes, quas quidem ad pacem et communionem privatim frequentant, sed diligentiores antiquiorum observatores nos in hujusmodi privatis orationibus brevitati studere docuerent potiusque publicis precibus in officio Missae occupari voluerunt* (Microlog., chap. 18). Cf. Radulph. Tungren., *De canonum observantia*, chap. 33. In *Ordo Rom. XIV* (chap. 71) the other Communion prayer (*Perceptio corporis. . . .*) is also inserted. Clichtoveus (d. 1543) mentions the three Communion prayers of our Missal and adds: *et alias pro arbitrio et pia devotione aut ritu suae ecclesiae dicere potest qui Missam celebrat*.

PREPARATION FOR COMMUNION

the more ardent our fervor, before, during, and after Communion, the more bounteous will be the measure of the gifts of grace wherewith the Saviour will enrich our poverty.

1. Holy Communion draws near; we must make the final preparation for the reception of so great a gift. Hence the priest continues to pray, while with eyes fixed on the victim lying before him he contemplates the great mystery about to take place within him.

Domine Jesu Christe, Fili Dei vivi, qui ex voluntate Patris, cooperante Spiritu sancto, per mortem tuam mundum vivificasti: libera me per hoc sacrosanctum Corpus et Sanguinem tuum ab omnibus iniquitatibus meis et universis malis, et fac me tuis semper inhaerere mandatis, et a te nunquam separari permittas: qui cum eodem Deo Patre et Spiritu sancto, vivis et regnas Deus, in saecula saeculorum. Amen.[2]	O Lord Jesus Christ, Son of the living God, who, by the will of the Father and through the cooperation of the Holy Ghost, hast by Thy death given life to the world, deliver me by this, Thy most sacred body and blood, from all my iniquities and from all evils; and make me always adhere to Thy commandments and suffer me never to be separated from Thee. Who with the same God the Father and the Holy Ghost livest and reignest God, world without end. Amen.

This prayer, as solid and comprehensive as it is brief and simple, must principally be referred to the approaching Communion, but not exclusively so; for the words, "by this, Thy most sacred body and blood," together with the petition that follows, have so general

[2] In the three prayers before Communion, which are equally addressed to the Second Person of the Trinity, Jesus Christ, the peculiar and varying concluding formula (*conclusio*) is worthy of notice. The prayer for peace concludes with the rarely occurring short formula: *qui vivis et regnas Deus per omnia saecula saeculorum*, in which the addition *Deus* forms a departure from the rule. As in the above prayer the Father and the Holy Ghost are mentioned, this is signified in the prolonged concluding formula, but in a peculiar way: *qui cum eodem Deo Patre et Spiritu sancto vivis et regnas . . .* (in Clichtoveus: *qui cum eodem Patre vivis et regnas in unitate ejusdem Spiritus sancti . . .* ; the *Ordo Rom. XIV* has still a different conclusion). The third prayer (*Perceptio . . .*) alone has the regular longer concluding formula, as is customary in the Collects. As Communion prayers that were originally private and intended especially for the priest, since they date from a period in which the general Communion of those present had ceased, these prayers have this peculiarity that the petitions in the singular number refer to the celebrant only (*libra me, fac me, prosit mihi . . .*).

a meaning that they may at the same time be referred to the Sacrifice of the Mass, and likewise be understood of the fruits of the sacrifice, as is the case also with the prayer after the Communion. The petition for gaining the fruits of the Eucharistic Communion and sacrifice is highly appropriate here, for we may assume that the priest who celebrates worthily, obtains at least a portion of the sacrificial fruits which fall to him at the moment in which the sacrifice is completed, that is, during the act of Communion.[3]

St. Peter once addressed to the Lord this solemn profession of faith: "Thou art Christ, the Son of the living God" (Matt. 16:16). He saw only His humanity and confessed His divinity; therefore he was called "blessed" by the Lord and his faith was praised and rewarded. On the altar Christ's divinity and humanity are both concealed from mortal vision, and yet the priest confesses both with a firm faith at the moment he receives the God-man, "Lord Jesus Christ, Son of the living God." He confesses not only the divine dignity of Jesus Christ, but also His most sublime, divine and human act: the restoring to a new life of a world dead in sin, by His propitiatory sacrificial death for our redemption (*per mortem tuam mundum vivificasti*). With special predilection the Church extols this wonderful mystery: Jesus Christ, who is life, the source and the author of all life, suffered death and by His death destroyed our death, that is, regained for us the life of grace and glory.

The work of redemption was accomplished by Christ according to the will of His Father, "through the cooperation of the Holy Ghost."[4] The Father did not spare His only-begotten Son, but placed upon Him the sins of the world and presented to Him the bitter chalice of the passion; through love for the Father, Christ became

[3] Probabile est, celebrantem bene dispositum tunc sacrificii fructum, saltem aliquem percipere, quando percipit fructum sacramenti, h. e. in communione, quando sacrificium jam perfecte completur (Sylvius, III, q. 83, art. 1, quaer. 2, concl. 4 ad 8).

[4] Qui sacrosanctam Christi Domini meditatur incarnationem, ejusque miras operationes et amarissimam passionem propter nos homines, et propter nostram salutem ac instructionem, nonne statim gratias aget toti sanctissimae Trinitati mysterium hoc operanti, et singulis specialiter personis? Patri quidem, qui "sic dilexit mundum, ut Filium suum unigenitum daret," qui ut servum redimeret, tradidit Filium; Filio etiam, qui tam arduum et difficile, propter amorem creaturae, munus redemptoris suscepit: et Spiritui sancto, qui principaliter, tamquam amoris principium, ad hoc mysterium concurrisse dicitur (Philipp. a ss. Trinitate, *Summa theol. mystic.*, I, Part I, tr. 1, disc. 3, art. 5).

obedient, obedient even unto the death of the cross (Phil. 2:8). The Holy Ghost, who had formed His sacred body in the womb of the immaculate Virgin, at the same time breathed into Him the most ardent love of sacrifice, in order that He might sacrifice Himself for us unto death; for by the Holy Ghost has Jesus Christ offered Himself unspotted unto God the Father (Heb. 9:14).[5]

Christ's redeeming death is mystically renewed and perpetuated on the altar; for as often as we eat the Eucharistic bread and drink of the Eucharistic chalice, we show the death of the Lord until He come (I Cor. 11:26). What graces do we here implore in virtue of the body and blood of Jesus Christ, sacrificed for us and about to be received by us? On the one hand, deliverance from all that oppresses us; on the other, the granting of all that may conduce to our happiness. The first petition refers more to the sacrifice than to the sacrament of the Eucharist; for as a sacrifice of propitiation and petition does the Eucharist chiefly effect for us deliverance from all our sins and from all evils (*ab omnibus iniquitatibus meis et universis malis*). The second petition, however, refers rather to the sacrament than to the sacrifice of the Eucharist; for as a sacrament it is mainly a powerful means of keeping the divine commandments and of being indissolubly united to Christ (*fac me tuis semper inhaerere mandatis et a te numquam separari permittas*). Among the effects of the Eucharist, final perseverance in good is also reckoned. Frequent, devout Communion is, according to the Fathers and doctors, to be regarded as a mark of predestination. For he who often and worthily communicates will avoid sin, increase in the love of God, become enriched with good works, and advance in the way of divine commandments, and thus he will be preserved from the loss of eternal salvation. The Eucharistic food is the bread of the strong; it re-

---

[5] The Father willed, decreed, ordained the passion and death of His Son; the Son executed this divine plan of salvation in that He assumed human nature and voluntarily suffered death: this mighty sacrifice of His life on the part of Christ was an act of obedience which emanated from His love of the Father and of the salvation of mankind; but this love and this obedience of His human will were infused by the Holy Ghost. Hoc ipsum quod Christus obedivit, processit ex dilectione quam habuit ad Patrem et ad nos (S. Thom., *In Epist. ad Rom.*, chap. 5, lect. 5). Christus passus est ex caritate et obedientia, quia et praecepta caritatis ex obedientia implevit et obediens fuit ex dilectione ad Patrem praecipientem (S. Thom., IIIa, q. 47, a. 2 ad 3). Causa quare Christus sanguinem suum fudit, fuit Spiritus sanctus, cujus motu et instinctu, scil. caritate Dei et proximi, hoc fecit (S. Thom., *In Epist. ad Heb.*, chap. 9, lect. 3).

freshes and strengthens the earthly pilgrim on his painful journey to the eternal home in heaven. "Suffer me never to be separated from Thee." How touching is this petition at the moment in which the soul celebrates the most intimate espousals with her divine bridegroom! "What can the world without Jesus impart to thee? To be without Jesus is a bitter hell; to be with Jesus, a sweet paradise." We cannot do without Jesus; we need Him at every step. There is something delightful in this feeling of utter dependence on Him. No loss can be comparable to the loss of Jesus; no sorrow, to the sorrow of being separated from Him by grievous sin. Worthy Communion strengthens us to avert this misfortune.

2. The second prayer in preparation for Communion, as simple as it is efficacious, refers directly and exclusively to Holy Communion.

Perceptio Corporis tui, Domine Jesu Christe, quod ego indignus sumere praesumo, non mihi proveniat in judicium et condemnationem, sed pro tua pietate prosit mihi ad tutamentum mentis et corporis, et ad medelam percipiendam: qui vivis et regnas cum Deo Patre in unitate Spiritus sancti Deus, per omnia saecula saeculorum. Amen.

Let not the partaking of Thy Body, O Lord Jesus Christ, which I, though unworthy, presume to receive, turn to my judgment and condemnation; but by Thy mercy may it be unto me a safeguard and a healing remedy both of soul and body; who with God the Father, in the unity of the Holy Ghost, livest and reignest God, world without end. Amen.

Here the priest first humbly confesses his own unworthiness; then with fervor he petitions the Saviour to avert from him the misfortune of an unworthy Communion and apply to him the plentiful blessings of a worthy Communion. The priest reflects on this great miracle about to take place. "The bread of angels becomes the food of man. O miracle! wonderful thing! the poor, the servant, the lowly, receives his Lord" (*Hymn. Eccl.*). Hence the priest humbly acknowledges that he is not worthy to receive the most holy body of our Lord (*quod ego indignus sumere praesumo*).[6] Well does he know the admonition of the Apostle: "But let a man prove himself,

---

[6] Praesumptio interdum accipitur pro abundanti fiducia (Dion. Carthus., *Expos. prol. Sent.*). *Praesumere* = to presume, to venture.

and so let him eat of that bread and drink of the chalice" (I Cor. 11:28); therefore, he guards against approaching the table of the Lord laden with grievous sin: "Whosoever shall eat this bread or drink the chalice of the Lord unworthily, shall be guilty of the body and of the blood of the Lord; . . . for he that eateth and drinketh unworthily, eateth and drinketh judgment to himself" (I Cor. 11: 27, 29). Such an unworthiness as would make the Communion sacrilegious is not alone intended by this acknowledgment of the priest. The unworthiness here referred to presupposes, rather, the state of grace (freedom from mortal sin). It expresses the want of perfect worthiness, of that perfect purity, reverence, love, and devotion which are a becoming requisite for the entirely worthy reception of the ineffably sublime and holy sacrament of the altar. The frailty of human nature and the weakness of the human will are so great that our disposition almost invariably remains defective, that is, it is less perfect than it could and should be. If a man has done all in his power, if he has prepared himself as carefully as possible, then indeed we say, and justly, that he is worthy to receive Holy Communion. But this does not prevent his regarding and confessing himself as unworthy of so great a grace; it is precisely this humble avowal of his own unworthiness that is required to make him in some degree worthy of Holy Communion. In sentiments of holy and salutary fear he should at all times prepare himself, and that so much the more carefully, the oftener he has the grace and happiness to approach the Eucharistic banquet.[7]

To receive the Blessed Sacrament with impure mouth and heart,

---

[7] Dico, quod ceteris paribus multo melius sit ex caritate et zelo boni communis accedere, quam ex humilitate et timore cessare, praesertim cum sacramentum istud sit sacramentum totius caritatis, liberalitatis ac gratiae, medicinaque animae. Et dato, quod quis tam meritorie quoad *se* abstineret, sicut accederet: tamen multo fructuosius est accedere per comparationem ad alios: quia devote accedens multipliciter succurrit non sibi dumtaxat, sed et toti ecclesiae, et vivis ac mortuis, specialiter quoque adstantibus et eis, pro quibus sacrificat ac deposcit. Quamvis autem nullus sit absolute dignus celebrare aut communicare per considerationem ad infinitam dignitatem Christi, et quoad suae deitatis majestatem nec non etiam per respectum ad suae assumptae humanitatis sanctitatem et honorabilitatem, tamen secundum quandam proportionabilitatem dignus est homo, si cum debita diligentia, custodia, humilitate, munditia et fervore se praeparet atque accedat. Verumtamen, qui accedunt quotidie, studeant tanto ferventius quanto frequentius tanta mysteria pertractare et coram Altissimo jugiter mundi ac fructuosi consistere (Dion. Carthus., IV, dist. 12, q. 5).

that is, to make an unworthy Communion, is one of the most grievous of sacrileges, and consequently it draws down on the guilty person a severe chastisement from God. Full of humble distrust in himself, on account of his weakness and infidelity, the priest implores the Lord to keep far away from him the outrage and curse of a sacrilegious Communion, that he may not be judged and condemned (*non mihi proveniat in judicium et condemnationem*).[8] Such a request on the part of the priest is so much the better founded since, being permitted to partake daily of this precious heavenly food, greater is the danger for him that frequent reception of the Blessed Sacrament may, through routine, beget carelessness and tepidity, and thus more easily pave the way to an unworthy Communion.

Confiding in the paternal goodness of the Saviour, the priest continues to pray that the Holy Communion may become rather a source of blessing to him (*sed pro tua pietate prosit mihi*). The word *pietas* designates the divine condescension, goodness, mildness, mercy toward man.[9] How unutterably great does this condescending goodness and mercy of the Saviour appear in the crib, on the cross, and on the altar! Everywhere He conceals His majesty and shows Himself only as the Good Shepherd and heavenly physician who has come to seek and to heal us, as well as to inflame our hearts with childlike, grateful love. Now the priest prays that the Lord, by this merciful goodness, may be pleased to grant that His holy body may be profitable to those who receive it as "a safeguard and a healing remedy both of soul and body" (*ad tutamentum*

---

[8] *Judicium* (κρίσις, κρῖμα) is often = *condemnatio* (κατάκρισις), for example, I Cor. 11:29: *judicium sibi manducat et bibit*, but here it can be taken in the sense of a legal proceeding, a process, and be distinguished from *condemnatio* = final condemnatory judgment. Cf. the petition in the Office of the Dead: *dum veneris judicare, noli me condemnare*. Or also: *judicium* = judicial condemnation; *condemnatio* (from *damnum*, damage, loss, injury) = the sentence of the judge, punishment, chastisement. Da quaesumus Domine, ut tanti mysterii munus indultum non condemnatio, sed sit medicina sumentibus (*Sacrament. Gelas.*). Similar petitions are found in other liturgical formulas.

[9] The expressions *pius* and *pietas* are, after the example of Holy Scripture (cf. II Par. 30:9; Ecclus. 2:13), in the liturgy (especially in the prayers) by a particular preference applied to God. Cf., for instance, *in festo s. Matthiae*: "Deus . . . tribue . . . ut tuae circa nos pietatis semper viscera sentiamus." Quos tuos efficis, Domine, tua pietate circumtege (*Sacrament. Leonian.*). Haec (sc. pietas) perfecta virtus in hominibus, haec plena in Deo laus est. (S. Ambros., *In Ps. 118 Serm.*, XVIII, n. 46).

mentis et corporis et ad medelam percipiendam); these words include the whole wealth of the sacramental grace of the Eucharistic banquet.[10] The life of a true Christian is a continual combat between grace and nature, between spirit and flesh, between virtue and vice. Without intermission we must struggle against the visible and the invisible enemies of our soul; for we are surrounded by the weaknesses and temptations of sensual nature, by the attacks and allurements of this sinful world, by the snares and deceits of the devil. In this warfare of salvation the Holy Eucharist is, on the one hand, a strong and powerful weapon of defense by which we are enabled to victoriously overcome all assaults; and on the other, it is a salutary medicine to heal anew the injuries suffered and the wounds received.[11]

Holy Communion preserves and protects the life of grace in the children of God, for one of its effects is preservation from mortal sin. The Lord Himself declared that whoever would eat of the Eucharistic bread, should not die (John 6:50); that is, he should not die the death of sin. The world drinks in sin like water; the enemy lies in ambush and everywhere dangers threaten, so that we must work out our salvation in fear and trembling. How consoling, therefore, is the thought that in the "bread of the strong" we have so powerful a means of protection against the danger of sinning, of being separated from God and forfeiting His grace! Thus the Eucharist protects the life of grace principally in this way, that, as a supernatural food, it imparts perfect health of soul and refreshment of heart. It strengthens the spiritual life; for it increases sanctifying grace, awakens and fortifies the supernatural virtues, above all, charity, but also faith and hope, purity and devotion, humility and

---

[10] Similar petitions often occur, especially in the Postcommunions, for example: per coelestia alimenta contra omnia adversa muniamur; perceptione sacramenti ab hostium liberemur insidiis; hoc sacramentum sit fortitudo fragilium, sit contra omnia mundi pericula firmamentum; sacri dona mysterii in nostrae proficiat infirmitatis auxilium; per haec sacramenta, quidquid in nostra mente vitiosum est, ipsorum medicationis dono curetur. Sentiamus, quaesumus Domine, tui perceptione sacramenti, subsidium mentis et corporis: ut in utroque salvati, coelestis remedii plenitudine gloriemur (Postcomm., *Dom. XI post Pent.*). Sit nobis, Domine, reparatio mentis et corporis coeleste mysterium (*Dom. VIII post Pent.*).

[11] Sacramentum hoc est vigorosissima medicina contra reliquias vitiorum, contra concupiscentiam saevientem, contra venialia quotidianasque culpas, et contra mortalia peccata oblita, et singulari modo valet contra universa animae vulnera (Dion. Carthus., *De sacram. altar.*, a. 7).

meekness, patience and perseverance. Thus it impels to good works, bestows upon us earnestness and fervor to consecrate and devote ourselves with generosity to the service of God. Holy Communion at the same time brings a stream of heavenly joy and bliss into the well disposed heart of the recipient. Already here below, the Eucharistic banquet refreshes the soul with a foretaste of the happiness of heaven, with sweetness and peace and serenity, with that vigor whereby we overcome all the dangers and obstacles to salvation. The soul that is still weak and tepid may become strong and healthy by means of the heavenly medicine of the holy sacrament of the altar, which cleanses from venial sins, destroys rebellious sensuality, weakens inclinations and aversions, diminishes the perverse love for the world and for one's self. The Holy Eucharist, therefore, possesses in the highest degree power to conduct us to eternal glory. It is the pledge of future glory and an unfailing guarantee of celestial bliss. It is the fountain of living waters that issue forth from life eternal. Hence the Church teaches us to pray: "Grant, O Lord, we beseech Thee, that we may be satiated with the eternal enjoyment of Thy divine glory, prefigured by the temporal reception of Thy precious body and blood."

The Eucharist protects and strengthens the supernatural life of the soul, but to the body also do its effects of grace extend. The soul is the recipient of grace and salvation; through the soul and for the sake of the soul supernatural gifts are also imparted to the body.[12] If, therefore, in Holy Communion sanctifying grace, together with the infused virtues and the gifts of the Holy Ghost, is increased, and if sacramental graces of light and strength are also imparted, that we may remain in Christ and Christ in us, that in time we may persevere in the life of grace and in eternity attain to the life of glory, then the body too is benefited thereby, at least indirectly, because the superabundance of grace in a certain degree flows from the soul into the body. Holy Communion, by inflaming the

---

[12] Quia sacramenta operantur salutem quam significant, ideo secundum quandam assimilationem dicitur quod in hoc sacramento corpus offertur pro salute corporis et sanguis pro salute animae, quamvis utrumque ad salutem utriusque operetur, cum sub utroque totus sit Christus. Et licet corpus non sit immediatum subjectum gratiae, ex anima tamen redundat effectus gratiae ad corpus, dum in praesenti membra nostra exhibemus arma justitiae Deo (Rom., cap. 6) et in futuro corpus nostrum sortietur incorruptionem et gloriam animae (S. Thom., IIIa, q. 79, a. 1 ad 3).

heart with ardent love and heavenly aspirations, by imparting more abundant grace for energetic resistance against the attacks of the enemy, diminishes at least indirectly the sensuality of the body. But we may go still further and assume that the most holy and pure body of Christ suppresses also directly the temptations and inclinations to concupiscence in the body of the worthy communicant. In so far as the miraculous Eucharistic food thus preserves the body pure and chaste, it disposes and preserves it for the glorious resurrection. Since in Holy Communion we receive Christ's body and blood into our heart, we are not merely spiritually united with Him by faith, charity, and grace, but also corporally united with Christ; and as a consequence, in a more perfect sense we become members of the body of Christ, bone of His bone and flesh of His flesh, as it were one body and one blood with Christ (*concorporei* and *consanguinei*).[13] Since by Christ's body and blood the personality of the devout communicant is elevated and ennobled, consecrated and sanctified, Christ loves and cherishes it as His own, for it is in a special manner espoused to Him. The eternal glorification of the body is, consequently, already here below prepared and established through the sanctification imparted to mortal flesh by the heavenly Eucharistic food. By Holy Communion, therefore, the soul and body of man are healed of every weakness and frailty, and are preserved and safeguarded for life eternal.[14]

[13] Cf. S. Cyrill. Hierosol., *Catech. mystag.*, IV, chap. 1.

[14] Actualis consecutio gloriae peculiari quadam ratione est et dicitur effectus hujus sacramenti. Id quod non solum ad animae, sed etiam corporis beatitudinem referendum est, ut eo scil. novo titulo unionis cujusdam corporis nostri cum corpore Christi, dignius praeparentur corpora communicantium ad dotes corporales in resurrectione futuras, idque veluti participatione quadam et incohatione quasi in semine, qua justis etiam in hac vita communicatur agilitas quaedam et vigor ad studiosa opera simulque mundities ex assistentia divini auxilii et aliud quid simile dotibus, per quod caro, imminuto in dies fomite, promptius obediat spiritui et quasi spiritualis reddatur, eo fere sensu, quo I Cor., cap. 15, post resurrectionem corpus dicitur fore spirituale quoad effectum, quia perfecte obediet spiritui. Eodemque sensu in *Catech. Rom.*, II, cap. 4, q.41, dicitur sacrae Eucharistiae summam vim esse ad aeternam gloriam comparandam hujusque sacramenti gratia fideles, dum hanc vitam degunt, summa conscientiae pace et tranquillitate perfrui, ejusque virtute recreatos non secus atque Elias, qui subcinericii panis fortitudine ambulavit usque ad montem Dei Horeb, cum ex hac vita migrandi tempus advenit, ad aeternam gloriam et beatitudinem ascendere (Tanner, disp. V, q.7, dub.1, n.8).

CHAPTER XLIV

THE HOLY BANQUET

THE preceding prayers the priest recites with a humble inclination of the body and with eyes fixed on the sacred host (*oculis ad Sacramentum intentis*); now the preparation for Communion is concluded in the following manner.[1]

The Conclusion of the Preparation for Communion

The priest longs to be fed with the fat of wheat and filled with honey out of the rock (Ps. 80: 17); he yearns for the strength of the true manna; therefore he adores the Blessed Sacrament by genuflecting and manifests, while rising again,[2] the desire and longing of his heart in the words: *Panem coelestem accipiam*[3] *et nomen*

---

[1] Sacerdos ante perceptionem corporis et sanguinis Christi debet dicere orationes a s. Patribus institutas; deinde meditari debet in incarnatione, in passione, in virtute hujus Sacramenti, dicens: *Panem coelestem.* . . . Hoc dicens se ipsum incitat ad devotionem, reducens ad memoriam, quid est quod sumere debet, quia panem qui de coelo descendit, et qualiter sumere debet, quia nomen Domini invocando, ut sic cum majori sumat reverentia et timore. Dicendo vero subsequenter: *Domine, non sum dignus*, ex humilitate suam profitetur indignitatem (Durand., IV, liv, 10). This is the most ancient notice of the liturgical use of the above mentioned formulas of prayer before the Communion of the celebrant. The *Ordo Rom. XIV*, chap. 53, remarks after the recitation of the Prayer for Peace and the imparting of the kiss of peace: junctis manibus dicat reverenter illas orationes: *Domine J. Chr., Fili Dei vivi* . . . et alias orationes, quae dicendae sunt ante sumptionem corporis prout habentur in libro (*in the missal*).

[2] Adoratio hic signanter praescribitur tamquam actus proxime disponens ad communionem. Deinde surgens dicit "Panem coelestem accipiam . . ." ad explicandam famem et fervens desiderium hujus panis coelestis, quo mirifice disponitur anima ad percipiendam ex eo perfectam nutritionem et pinguedinem spiritus (Quarti, II, x, 4).

[3] *Accipere* = to take in the hand, to seize and = to partake of, to eat. In Evangelio legitur quod Christus accepit panem et calicem; non est autem intellegendum quod acceperit solum in manibus, ut quidam dicunt, sed eo

THE HOLY BANQUET

Domini invocabo ("I will take the bread of heaven, and will call upon the name of the Lord"), that is, I will magnify the Lord and praise Him (cf. Ps. 115:4). Then he takes the host and paten in the left hand and, slightly inclining his body, strikes his breast three times with the right hand, saying each time:

Domine, non sum dignus, ut intres sub tectum meum: sed tantum dic verbo, et sanabitur anima mea.	Lord, I am not worthy that Thou shouldst enter under my roof; but only say the word, and my soul shall be healed.

The profound humility and unshaken confidence of the priest preparing for Communion could not be expressed more strikingly and, at the same time, more simply than by the threefold repetition of words spoken by the centurion of Capharnaum, to whom the Lord had said that He would enter his house and cure his sick servant (Matt. 8:5–14).[4] Humility and confidence at this moment take possession of the soul. If the priest considers the greatness and holiness of the Eucharistic Lord, now about to enter into him, then he is profoundly humbled because of his unworthiness. Filled with fear, he would exclaim with St. Peter: "Depart from me, for I am a sinful man, O Lord!" (Luke 5:8.) Yet at the sight of the condescending love and goodness of the Saviour, who on the altar con-

---

modo accepit quo aliis accipiendum tradidit; unde cum discipulis dixerit: Accipite et comedite, et iterum: Accipite et bibite, intellegendum est quod ipse accipiens comederit et biberit (S. Thom., IIIa, q. 81, a. 1 ad 1).

[4] These words of the centurion whom Jesus praised, the Church has taken in such a manner to heart, that she always places them in the mouth of her children before Holy Communion, the corporeal visit of our Saviour; on the one hand, to confess her unworthiness for a like visitation, and, on the other, to express her confidence that by a single word of His gentle power, He will deliver them from their unworthiness. Dicendo se indignum, praestitit dignum, non in cuius parietis, sed in cujus cor Christus intraret. Neque hoc diceret cum tanta fide et humilitate, nisi illum, quem timebat intrare in domum suam, corde gestaret (S. August., *Serm.*, LXII, n. 1). Non sum dignus qui sub tectum meum intres. Tecto non recipiebat, corde receperat. Quanto humilior, tanto capacior, tanto plenior. Colles enim aquas repellunt, valles implentur (*ibid.*, *Serm.*, LXXVII, n. 12). Per centurionem figurati sunt timorati ac humiles christiani, qui Christi opem desiderant, sed eum intra se communicando vel celebrando recipere vehementer verentur, unde cum spirituali receptione Sacramenti multoties contentantur. Et quamvis hoc interdum sit bonum, melius tamen est ex fervore et spe pietatis divinae Sacramentum recipere. Semper etiam expedit, cum centurione Christi dignitatem propriamque vilitatem perpendere et intimo corde fateri (Dion. Carthus., *In Matt.*, chap. 8).

ceals His glory in order to attract us, he is again encouraged and animated with joyful confidence.

O sweet and amiable word in the ear of a sinner, that Thou, O Lord my God, shouldst invite the poor and needy to the communion of Thy most sacred body! But who am I, O Lord, that I should presume to come to Thee? Behold, the heaven of heavens cannot contain Thee; and Thou sayest: "Come you all to Me." What means this bounteous condescension and this so friendly invitation? How shall I dare approach, I, who am not conscious of any good in me on which I can presume? . . . I sigh and grieve that I am yet so carnal and worldly, so unmortified in my passions, so full of the motions of concupiscence; so unguarded in my outward senses; so often entangled with many vain imaginations; so much inclined to exterior things, so negligent as to the interior; so easy to laughter and dissipation, so hard to tears and compunction; so prone to relaxation and to the pleasures of the flesh, so sluggish to austerity and fervor; so curious to hear news and to see fine sights, so remiss to embrace things humble and abject; so covetous to possess much, so sparing in giving, so close in retaining; so inconsiderate in speech, so little able to hold my peace; so disorderly in my manners, so impetuous in my actions; so greedy at meat, so deaf to the word of God; so eager for rest, so slow to labor; so wakeful to hear idle tales, so drowsy to watch in the service of God; so hasty to make an end of my prayers, so wandering in my attention; so negligent in saying the Divine Office, so tepid in celebrating, so dry at the time of receiving; so quickly distracted, so seldom quite recollected in Thee; so easily moved to anger, so apt to take offense at others; so prone to judge, so severe in reprehending; so joyful in prosperity, so despondent in adversity; so frequent in good resolutions, and so backward in carrying them out.[5]

Thus does the priest bewail his imperfections and weaknesses. Yet he also has unlimited confidence in Jesus Christ, who, as St. Agatha said, by His word alone can cure all maladies. Whilst acknowledging his unworthiness, he at the same time confidently implores that the Lord, by a mere word of His omnipotence (*tantum dic verbo*) would perfectly heal and restore his diseased soul, make it worthy for God's entrance into the lowly tabernacle of the human heart. Already before Mass the priest prayed: "O Lord, be Thou merciful to me. Heal my soul (*sana animam meam*); for I have sinned against Thee" (Ps. 40:5).

[5] *Imitation of Christ*, IV, i, 2 f.; vii, 2.

The Receiving of the Host

"The marriage of the Lamb is come, and his wife [the soul] hath prepared herself. . . . Blessed are they who are called to the marriage supper of the Lamb" (Apoc. 19:7, 9). Holy Communion is the greatest joy and happiness of this life; it is heaven upon earth and in the heart. Therefore "rejoice O my soul, and give thanks for so noble a gift and so singular a comfort left to thee in this vale of tears. For as often as thou repeatest this mystery and receivest the body of Christ, so often dost thou celebrate the work of thy redemption and art made partaker of all the merits of Christ. For the charity of Christ is never diminished, and the greatness of His propitiation is never exhausted." [6]

The priest takes the sacred host in his right hand and blesses himself [7] with Christ's sacrificial body, pronouncing at the same time these words: *Corpus Domini nostri Jesu Christi* [8] *custodiat animam meam in vitam aeternam. Amen.* ("May the body of our Lord Jesus Christ preserve my soul unto life everlasting. Amen.") Then with profound humility and reverence, with fervent devotion and ardent love, he receives the heavenly bread of life which God in His sweetness has provided for the poor and hungry (Ps. 67:11).[9]

The prayers said when the priest receives Christ's body and blood express the plenitude of the fruits of Communion. The preservation of the soul to eternal life includes that of the body also as a necessary consequence: for the sake of the soul and by the soul, the body, too, is preserved to life eternal; the salvation of the soul is likewise the

---

[6] *Ibid.,* IV, ii, 6.

[7] Corpus et sanguinem Domini sumpturus se cum illis ante faciem cruce signat. Sicut enim prius cruces faciendo active tamquam minister illa sanctificavit, sic se eis nunc cruce signando passive petit sanctificari (Durand, IV, liv, 11).

[8] An sacerdos seipsum signans cum hostia et calice consecratis ante sumptionem sanctissimi Sacramenti ad verba, *Jesu Christi,* debeat caput inclinare? Resp.: Affirmative, juxta Rubricas (S. R. C., September 24, 1842).

[9] Deinde sacerdos communionem sumit, quam cum magno affectu et reverentia summa accipere debet, non festinando, sed beneficia Christi ardentissime recolendo, videlicet incarnationem, passionem, dilectionem ejus ad nos, tantam dignationem ac liberalitatem, qua sic dignatur esse nobiscum et sumi a nobis. Debet etiam Christum fiducialiter alloqui eumque intime exorare pro his, quae vehementius cupit adipisci ab ipso, tam pro se quam pro carioribus sibi, deprecando Christum, ut dignetur se omnino convertere et stabilire semperque confortare in ipso (Dion. Carthus., *Expos. Miss.,* a. 38).

salvation of the body. The divine power of the Eucharist protects the soul against all dangers to salvation, inasmuch as it preserves, strengthens, and perfects in it the life of grace. To them who eat His glorious body, Christ gives the fat, the unction, the fullness of the life of the spirit (*se manducantibus dat spiritus pinquedinem*).[10] United most intimately with the Eucharistic Saviour, the soul experiences how sweet the Lord is (Ps. 33:9); she is quickened, refreshed, and encouraged: she finds strength and vigor, comfort and peace, amid the temptations and sufferings of life. "Thou didst feed Thy people with the food of angels, and gavest them bread from heaven prepared without labor, having in it all that is delicious and the sweetness of every taste, for Thy sustenance shewed Thy sweetness to Thy children" (Wisd. 16:20 f.). Pious thoughts, affections, and resolutions fill the breast of the communicating priest during the short pause that the rubrics prescribe for the silent meditation on the sublime and wonderful grace that has been bestowed upon him.[11] The Church expresses this injunction most beautifully in the following words: *quiescit aliquantulum in meditatione Ss. Sacramenti* ("he rests a short time in meditation on the Most Blessed Sacrament").

The Receiving of the Chalice

The celebrant must receive the Sacrament under both species; this is necessary for the completion of the sacrifice, which he accomplishes by the consecration of the two elements.[12] After the

---

[10] *Offic. ss. Corp. Christi.* "When thou beholdest the pure and immaculate body of the God-man lying before thee on the altar, say to thyself: Through this body I am no longer dust and ashes, no longer a captive, but free; through this body I hope to obtain heaven and all it contains; eternal life, the lot of the angels, the society of Christ. This body pierced through with nails, death could not retain; in the presence of this crucified body the sun was enveloped in darkness; because of it the veil of the temple was rent, the rocks were split, and the whole earth shook; this is the body, covered with blood, pierced with a lance, from which issued for the entire universe two fountains of salvation, blood and water" (St. Chrysostom, *Homilies on the First Epistle to the Corinthians*, XXIV).

[11] Sumat duas partes hostiae cum omni devotione et reverentia, et dum habet in ore sacrum Domini corpus, teneat manus ante pectus junctas in modum orantis (*Ordo Rom. XIV*, chap. 53).

[12] Ex parte ipsius sacramenti convenit quod utrumque sumatur, scil. et corpus et sanguis, quia in utroque consistit perfectio sacramenti, et ideo quia ad sacerdotem pertinet hoc sacramentum consecrare et perficere, nullo modo debet corpus Christi sumere sine sanguine (S. Thom., IIIa, q. 80, a. 12).

receiving of the body of Christ, therefore, follows the receiving of the precious blood. He prepares to receive the chalice [13] by uncovering it, genuflecting before it, putting into it the fragments of the sacred host which may have been gathered up by the paten, and at last holding it with the right hand; meanwhile he recites some verses of the Psalms (115:12 f.; 17:4):

| Quid retribuam Domino pro omnibus, quae retribuit mihi? Calicem salutaris accipiam et nomen Domini invocabo. Laudans invocabo Dominum, et ab inimicis meis salvus ero. | What shall I render to the Lord, for all the things that He hath rendered to me? I will take the chalice of salvation and I will call upon the name of the Lord. Praising I will call upon the Lord, and I shall be saved from my enemies. |

While the priest in silent adoration reflects for some moments on the inconceivable love and liberality of God, on the boundless riches and joys of the Eucharistic banquet, "in which Christ is received, the remembrance of His passion celebrated, the soul inundated with grace, and an earnest of future glory given to us," [14] his heart overflows with gratitude and he cries out in holy enthusiasm: "What shall I render to the Lord, for all the things that He hath rendered to me?" [15] The infinite God with infinite love bestows upon me an infinite gift; for in Communion Jesus offers Himself to me with His glorious divinity and humanity. Although He is almighty, He could not give me more; although He is omniscient, He knows not how to give me more; although He is most wealthy, He has not more to give. While in silence the priest considers how he might

---

[13] In the thirteenth century the rite in this place was somewhat different. Junctis manibus inclinans sanguini dicat: *Quid retribuam . . . et dicens: Calicem Domini accipiam* (et non prius) accipit et elevat calicem de altari. Postea vero dicens: *Laudans invocabo Dominum* se signat cum illo, quo versu expleto sanguinum sumit (Durand., IV, liv, 11). Dicat illos versus: *Quid retribuam . . . Calicem . . .* et alia dicenda ante sumptionem sanguinis, prout in libro habentur (*Ordo Rom. XIV*, chap. 53 [in the fourteenth century]).

[14] *Antiph. II Vesp. ss. Corp. Christi.*

[15] Versiculus iste cum ingenti devotione dicendus est, quatenus tota mente optemus Deo esse grati, ejus beneficia memoriter atque frequenter recolendo eaque Domine humiliter confitendo, ipsum pro eis ferventer amando (Dion. Carthus., *In Ps.*, 115:3).

suitably thank the Lord for His boundless goodness,[16] he collects the particles on the corporal, and then, taking the chalice in his right hand, he breaks out into words which betoken his elevated sentiments of gratitude: "I will take the chalice of salvation and I will call upon the name of the Lord. Praising I will call upon the Lord, and I shall be saved from my enemies." While considering what we may give to the Lord, we find nothing else than what He had previously given us. Thus the priest affirms his gratitude by taking the chalice with its infinitely precious contents, to offer it for the glorification of the divine name and to drink it while gratefully magnifying the Lord.

God has no need of our gifts (Ps. 15:2); the most acceptable thanksgiving to His loving heart is for us to esteem His benefits, to receive them with desire and fervor,[17] and to employ them in His honor with fidelity and zeal. Therefore the priest returns thanks for the heavenly bread of life by extending his hand for new gifts, the chalice of salvation.[18] At the same time his heart overflows with grateful sentiments of divine praise and glorification, and he is animated with unshaken confidence toward God that he shall find in the chalice salvation, safety, redemption. The Lord has prepared the

---

[16] Subsistens aliquantulum in considerandis bonis, quae cum sacratissimo Christi corpore accepit, in eam postea sententiam magno effectu erumpit: *Quid retribuam Domino pro omnibus, quae retribuit mihi?* cum in hoc solo Sacramento omnia contineantur, eo quod sit summum bonum, in quo omnia bona latent. Et sacrum Calicem accipiens, quasi respondeat sibi interroganti: *Calicem,* inquit, *salutaris accipiam et nomen Domini invocabo.* Sanguinem scilicet pretiosissimum, qui in hoc salutis meo Calice continetur, accipiam in gratiarum actionem pro innumeris bonis, quae cum sanctissimo suo Corpore mihi est largitus. Et quoniam cum ipso Sanguine eadem bona recipio, ac propterea est singulare omnino beneficium, pro utroque laudabo semper sanctum ejus nomen et cupio, ut totus mundus ipsum laudet ac benedicat et cum Angelorum hierarchiis novum illud canticum cantet in honorem hujus sacrificii, quod ejus mortem repraesentat: "Dignus est Agnus, qui occisus est (et hic immolatus) accipere virtutem et divinitatem et sapientiam et fortitudinem et gloriam et honorem et benedictionem in saecula saeculorum. Amen" (Apoc. 5:12). (De Ponte, *De christian. hom. perfect.*, IV, tr. II, chap. 14.)

[17] Prima gratitudo et gratiae repensio est beneficium gratanter (*with joy*) recipere (Dion. Carthus., *In Ps.*, 102:2).

[18] Ad sacra mysteria celebranda trahat te gratiarum actio pro omnibus beneficiis temporalibus et spiritualibus tibi et aliis impensis, cum nihil habeamus Deo retribuere pro omnibus quae retribuit nobis, aliud quam calicem salutaris accipere et sacrificare hostiam laudis (Ps. 115:3 f.), i.e. Jesum Christum (S. Bonav., *Tr. de praep. ad Miss.*, 1, § 4, n. 15).

THE HOLY BANQUET

Eucharistic table against all that afflict us (Ps. 22:5); in this joyful banquet lies the mystery of strength and fortitude, by which the faithful soul victoriously bears all exterior and interior trials and triumphs gloriously over Satan, the world, and the flesh.

"The chalice of benediction, which we bless, is it not the communion of the blood of Christ?" (I Cor. 10:16.) Appropriate and fearful utterance! For the Apostle would thereby say: the blood in the chalice is identical with that which flowed from the side of Jesus, and this we drink. He calls it a chalice of benediction, because while holding it in our hands, we praise and magnify Christ, we admire with astonishment His unutterable gift, and thank Him that He has not only shed this blood to redeem us from sin, but that He has, moreover, imparted the same to us.[19]

The priest now makes the sign of the cross over himself with the chalice, pronouncing the words of benediction: *Sanguis Domini nostri Jesu Christi custodiat animam meam in vitam aeternam. Amen.* ("The Blood of our Lord Jesus Christ preserve my soul unto life everlasting. Amen.") Then with desire, fervor, and joy he drinks the precious blood, which streams forth unto eternal life. At this moment his heart exults. The sacrificial chalice bestows new devotion and the ardor of love and spiritual joy. "It imparts to the soul a fountain of well-being which overflows to the body, so that heart and flesh rejoice in the living God and cease to desire aught that is carnal." Exceedingly glorious, excellent, and noble is the inebriating sacrificial chalice. Therein shines the Eucharistic blood, the holy blood which once coursed through and animated the mortal members of the Saviour; that divine blood which, in His painful passion and death, was shed upon the earth from His lacerated body and pierced heart; that adorable blood which in heaven above flows through the corporeal heart of Jesus; that precious blood which, as the price of our redemption, streams forth over the earth in the ever-fresh fountain of the Sacrifice of the Mass and in the sevenfold stream of the sacraments.

THE COMMUNION OF THE FAITHFUL

Immediately after having received the precious blood,[20] the priest prepares to administer the Eucharistic bread to the faithful who are

[19] St. Chrysost., *Homilies on I Cor.* (10:16), XXIV.
[20] "The Communion of the people within the Mass shall take place immediately after the Communion of the celebrating priest (unless, for a reason-

prepared to receive it. The faithful, or the server alone in the name of the faithful, recite the Confiteor, humbly acknowledging their sinfulness and unworthiness to receive this precious heavenly gift. The priest then turns to the people and says the following prayers.

Misereatur vestri omnipotens Deus, et dimissis peccatis vestris, perducat vos ad vitam aeternam. R. Amen.	May almighty God be merciful to you and, forgiving you your sins, bring you to life everlasting. R. Amen.
Indulgentiam, ✠ absolutionem, et remissionem peccatorum vestrorum, tribuat vobis omnipotens et misericors Dominus. R. Amen.	May the almighty and merciful Lord grant you pardon, ✠ absolution, and remission of your sins. R. Amen.

By these prayers and this absolution [21] the priest would remove the last traces of sin and imperfection in the souls of the faithful, and thus make them more worthy to receive the spotless body of Christ. We can note how the Church, in the entire liturgy of the Mass, strives to make her children ever more pure and holy, free from every stain, thus to prepare them to receive with perfect dispositions the divine victim sacrificed on the altar. Finally, just before Christ's body is given to the faithful, the priest turns to them and,

---

able cause, it take place immediately before or after the private Mass), for the prayers which are said after the Communion in the Mass apply not only to the priest but also to the people" (*Rituale Rom., Tit.* IV., chap. 2, n. 11). The faithful should receive Holy Communion, not before or after Mass, but during Mass, whenever that is possible. "The faithful exercise their priesthood, that is, take that active participation in the holy sacrifice, desired by Christ and the Church, in no other way than in the sacrificial meal after the sacrifice has been offered" (Parsch, *The Liturgy of the Mass*, p. 306). The practice by many pious souls of receiving Holy Communion before Mass in order to make a long thanksgiving during the whole Mass, is an abuse to be discouraged wherever possible, for it degrades the Holy Sacrifice to a mere devotional exercise.

[21] "The practice of saying the Confiteor, the absolution formula, the Agnus Dei, and the more recent *Domine non sum dignus*, came into the Mass during the fourteenth century, from the rite of Communion for the sick and from the Communion rite outside of Mass. In the Communion of the sick, this practice is well founded, because the Communion rite for the sick represents an abbreviated Mass, which begins with the Confiteor and closes with the blessing by the priest" (*Ibid.*, p. 311). Although the ritual expressly states that the blessing is to be omitted after the distribution of Holy Communion in the Mass, "because the priest will give it at the end of the Mass," the introductory prayers have been retained and are obligatory.

to excite their devotion and love, holds up before them the sacred host, saying while he does so: *Ecce Agnus Dei: ecce qui tollit peccata mundi* ("Behold the Lamb of God; behold Him who taketh away the sins of the world"). Then three times the priest says, still holding aloft the host:

Domine non sum dignus, ut intres sub tectum meum: sed tantum dic verbo, et sanabitur anima mea.	Lord, I am not worthy that Thou shouldst enter under my roof; but only say the word, and my soul shall be healed.

Behold the Lamb who was sacrificed on the cross for the sins of the world. By His bitter passion and death Christ atoned for all sins; this same death has just been renewed on the altar, and now this sacred body once sacrificed on the cross is given to the faithful to apply to them all the graces of redemption. O precious gift! O sacred body of Christ now become our sacrificial food! Who is worthy to receive this heavenly bread which contains God Himself? "Lord, I am not worthy that Thou shouldst enter under my roof." With such sentiments of humility and unworthiness, the faithful receive the sacred body of Christ, which the priest places on their tongues [22] with the words: *Corpus Domini nostri Jesu Christi custodiat animam tuam in vitam aeternam. Amen.* ("May the body of our Lord Jesus Christ preserve thy soul to life everlasting. Amen.") [23]

[22] The rite for administering Communion to clerics and to the laity differed greatly in various times and places. Until the seventeenth century the faithful received the Blessed Sacrament standing, but with a reverential, bowed posture of the body. "The custom of placing the sacred Host on the bare hand of the men and upon a cloth (*dominicale*) spread over the hand of the women, was observed until after the beginning of the Middle Ages; as late as the nineteenth century, a council at Rome was legislating against the practice" (*Ibid.*, p. 308). Until the fourteenth century the laity communicated under both species during Mass; but already from the thirteenth century the practice was gradually discontinued: it is now observed only at the High Mass of the Pope, when the *ministri sacri* (deacon and subdeacon) receive Communion under both species. After the sixth century the precious blood was received through a chalice tube (*calamus, fistula, pugillaris, pipa, canna*). In the Middle Ages frequently a portion of the consecrated blood was poured into a ministerial chalice filled with wine, or in many places the host was dipped into the precious blood. In very early times the communicants would touch their fingers to their still moist lips and then to their eyes, forehead, nostrils, and ears, thus to sanctify all their senses with Christ's precious blood (cf. St. Cyril of Jerusalem, *Mystag. Catech.*, V, 22).

[23] This is the usual formula for administering Holy Communion; but if

Now Christ has entered into intimate union with the faithful soul. Only after partaking of the Eucharistic sacrificial banquet are the priest and faithful perfectly one with the divine victim. This sacrificial meal belongs to the sacrifice; it is the fruit and the effect of the holy sacrifice; only by partaking in this sacrificial meal can they fully participate in the sacrifice and derive from it its full effects.

The Church ardently wishes that her children should often by sacramental Communion participate in the Sacrifice of the Mass.

With parental affection [she] admonishes, exhorts, prays, and beseeches through the bowels of the mercy of our God, that [all Christians be] . . . mindful of so great a majesty and such boundless love of our Lord Jesus Christ, . . . that they may believe and venerate these sacred mysteries of his body and blood with such constancy and firmness of faith, with such devotion of mind, with such piety and worship, that they may be able to frequently receive this super-substantial bread, and that it may truly be to them the life of the soul and the perpetual health of their mind; that being invigorated by its strength, they may be able, after the journey of this miserable pilgrimage, to arrive in their heavenly country, there to eat, without any veil, the same bread of angels which they now eat under sacred veils.[24]

They who do not receive sacramentally, should unite themselves to the Eucharistic Saviour at least by a spiritual communion,—by

---

Communion is given *per modum viatici*, the priest says: Accipe frater (*vel soror*) viaticum corporis D. N. J. Ch., qui te custodiat ab hoste maligno et perducat in vitam aeternam. Amen. At the Communion of the newly ordained, the bishop says: Corpus D. N. J. Ch. custodiat *te* in vitam aeternam; and each priest answers: Amen. In former times various formulas were in use, for example, Corpus Christi. R. Amen. Sanguis Christi. R. Amen. Corpus D. N. J. Ch. conservet animam tuam. Corpus et sanguis D. N. J. Ch. conservet et custodiat te in vitam aeternam. Corpus D. N. J. Ch. custodiat corpus tuum et animam tuam in vitam aeternam. Perceptio corporis Domini nostri sit tibi vita et salus et redemptio omnium tuorum peccatorum. Corpus et sanguis D. N. J. Ch. in vitam aeternam te perducat et in die judicii ad sanctam requiem te resuscitet. Corpus D. N. J. Ch. sit tibi salus animae et corporis. Corpus D. N. J. Ch. sanguine suo intinctum conservet animam tuam in vitam aeternam. Amen. In the ancient Communion rite the *Amen* of this administering formula was a responsory, whereby the communicant expressed his faith in the real presence of Christ in the Blessed Sacrament. In toto orbe terrarum pretium nostrum accipitur: *Amen respondetur* (S. Aug., *Ennarr. in Ps.*, 125, n. 9). Habet magnam vocem Christi sanguis in terra, quum eo accepto ab omnibus gentibus *respondetur Amen* (*Idem.*, *Contra Faust.*, XII, chap. 10). Cf. Pseudo-Ambr., *De sacrament.*, IV, v, 25.

[24] Trid., Sess. XIII, cap. 8.

lively faith, compunction, sincere humility, ardent love, fervent desire—for spiritual communion also obtains for the soul many precious graces.

The Purification of the Chalice and the Ablution of the Fingers [25]

In the smallest particle of the sacramental species the whole Christ is present. Numerous liturgical practices and ordinances are founded on the belief in this truth, all of them aimed to prevent the slightest profanation of the smallest portion of the sacred host or of a single drop of the Eucharistic blood. After the Consecration, therefore, the thumb and forefinger must continually be held together,[26] and as often as they touch the sacred host, be purified over the chalice. For this reason the fragments on the corporal and paten must be so carefully collected after Communion, and the chalice and hands well cleaned. In this matter great care and attention have always been

---

[25] *Purificatio* in liturgical books designates not only the cleansing of the chalice, and the mouth also, but likewise the wine with which the priest rinses the chalice after receiving the precious blood, and even the wine which may be given to those who communicate after they have received the sacred host. By *ablutio* is understood the wine and water whereby the fingers that held the host are cleansed from any particle of the sacred host that may be attached to them, and the chalice rinsed a second time. Celebrans, sumpta purificatione, lavat digitos et sumit ablutionem (*Cerem. Episc.*, II, xxix, 8). By the purification and ablution it is intended to prevent as securely as possible every profanation of the Blessed Sacrament. This object is, however, obtained, since by a strict adherence to the prescribed rite hardly any particle of the consecrated species can yet remain. Practically unimportant is the question, whether the rest of the consecrated wine still remaining in the chalice is drunk with the fluids poured in, or whether it is so altered by being mixed with the wine and water, that the real presence of Christ ceases therein. The Church nowhere prescribes more water than wine to be taken at the ablution, but it is recommended by many authors, in order more securely to effect the destruction of holy species that might still be in the chalice. We should take notice, moreover, that the Church very unwillingly and quite seldom grants that the ablution be taken with water only. Verisimile est et pietate conforme asserere, colligi ab angelis fragmenta, quae remanent, praesertim minutiora, quae conspici non possunt, nec consequenter humana diligentia custodiri et colligi (Quarti, *Comment.*, II, x, 7).

[26] Sacerdos digitos jungit post consecrationem, scil. pollicem cum indice, quibus corpus Christi consecratum tetigerat, ut si qua particula digitis adhaeserit, non dispergatur, quod pertinet ad reverentiam sacramenti (S. Thom., IIIa, q.83, a.5 ad 5).

exerted;[27] thus already St. Cyril of Jerusalem exhorts: "Have the utmost care that no part of the Eucharistic species be lost. For, tell me, if anyone gave you grains of gold, would you not guard them with the greatest circumspection and be most solicitous that none of them be lost and that you thereby suffered no loss? How much more cautious must you be not to lose a crumb of that which is incomparably more valuable than gold and precious stones."[28]

The present purification and ablution rite, which is minutely ordered and prescribed, was established and developed only during the course of the Middle Ages.[29] While the priest, filled with profound reverence toward the Blessed Sacrament, performs the exterior act of cleansing the chalice and his fingers, his mind and heart are recollected in meditation on the heavenly sacrificial banquet, which has so wonderfully refreshed and strengthened him; for he makes use of two similar prayers to implore the blessed effects of

[27] Archidiacono nimis caute procurandum est, ne quid in calice aut patena sanguinis vel corporis Christi remaneat (*Ordo Rom. IV*, n. 12).

[28] *Mystag catech.*, V, 21.

[29] With respect to the purification of the chalice and paten, as well as the ablution (washing) of the mouth and fingers after Holy Communion, we have no information dating from the first ten centuries. The *Ordo Rom. IV* (written probably at the beginning of the eleventh century) mentions (n. 13) that the bishop at this point washes his hands; the *Ordo X* of a later period remarks (n. 15) in reference to Good Friday and Requiem Masses: perfusionem facit Pontifex in calice et ipse sumit et postea lavat cum aqua in bacilibus (*vessels or basins*). In the Middle Ages the chalice was generally purified with wine, and the purification drunk; the fingers, on the contrary, were usually rinsed with water and the ablution thrown into the sacrarium. Post contrectata et sumpta Sacramenta sacerdos . . . manus lavat et in locum sacrum huic cultui deputatum ipsa aqua vergitur (Ivonis Carnot., *Serm.*, V). Post sumptum Eucharistiae sacrificium sacerdos abluit et perfundit manus, ne quid incaute remaneat ex contactu divinissimi Sacramenti. . . . Ablutionis autem aqua debet in locum mundum diffundi honeste, ut altitudo Sacramenti reverentius honoretur (Innocent. III, IV, chap. 8). For the purification of the fingers, as a rule, another chalice was used. Sanguine sumpto, recipiat Pontifex modicum de vino in calice, infundente illud subdiacono, et illud sumat ad abluendum os suum. Postea dicendo illas orationes, *Quod ore . . . et Corpus tuum . . .* , tenens super calicem digitos utriusque manus, quibus tetigit hostiam, abluat ipsos modicum, subdiacono iterum infundente vinum, et antequam illud sumat, abluat iterum eos digitos cum aqua, quam infundat capellanus cum pelvibus, et ipsa aqua projiciatur in loco mundo. Pontifex, ablutis digitis praedicto modo cum aqua, abstergat os cum panno tersorio. . . . Postea sumpto vino quod erat in calice, tergat os suum eodem panno (*Ordo Rom. XIV*, chap. 53). This rite of the first half of the fourteenth century is almost similar to that prescribed later on by Pius V for general practice, which is still in use.

THE PURIFICATION OF THE CHALICE 783

Holy Communion. This is all the more proper since, according to an established opinion, during the whole period of the corporal presence of Christ in the heart of the communicant, the sacramental grace is being ever increased, provided that the communicant produces constantly new and, at the same time, more perfect acts of devotion.[30] Hence the two following prayers are intended to foster and augment the actual disposition of the celebrant, that he may become susceptible to further outpourings of grace.

1. Immediately after consuming the precious blood, that is, without making a short meditation,[31] as is allowed or prescribed after the reception of the sacred body, the priest has wine poured[32] into the chalice, while he recites the following prayer, which is found already in the most ancient sacramentaries[33] and is still to be seen in our missal as a Postcommunion:

| Quod ore sumpsimus, Domine, pura mente capiamus: et de munere temporali fiat nobis remedium sempiternum. | What we have taken with our mouth, O Lord, may we receive with a pure mind; and from a temporal gift may it become for us an everlasting remedy. |

By these words we beseech God the Father to grant us a twofold grace: in the first place, that our sacramental Communion may be also a worthy Communion, rich in grace through the greatest pos-

---

[30] The present *capiamus*, in opposition to the transitory or past reception (*sumpsimus*) of the host, seems to indicate this permanent efficacy of the Eucharistic sacrament as well as the requisite cooperation of the communicant.

[31] S. R. C., September 24, 1842.

[32] Vinum ratione suae humiditatis est ablutivum et ideo sumitur post susceptionem hujus Sacramenti ad abluendum os, ne aliquae reliquiae remaneant, quod pertinet ad reverentiam Sacramenti . . . et eadem ratione perfundit vino digitos, quibus corpus Christi tetigerat (S. Thom., IIIa, q. 83, a. 5 ad 10). Calicis purificatio fit solo vino ob reverentiam pretiosi sanguinis, cujus gutta quaepiam, uti plerumque accidit, ad imum calicis fluit. Ablutio sumitur ex eadem parte, per quam pretiosus sanguis absorptus est, ne scil. sacrae ejusdem reliquiae circa labia calicis remaneant. Hic advertendum est, in ablutione digitorum minime fas esse adhiberi, sine Apostolica dispensatione, sola aqua. (Cf. Indultum S. R. C., January 15, 1847; De Carpo, *Biblioth. liturg.*, I, a. 52, n. 207.)

[33] In the *Sacrament. Leonian.* we read: Quod ore sumpsimus, Domine, quaesumus, mente capiamus et de munere temporali fiat nobis remedium sempiternum. Micrologus remarks (chap. 19) that in this place the prayer *juxta Romanum Ordinem sub silentio* is to be recited; the other: Corpus tuum . . . he does not mention, while the *Ordo Rom. XIV* (in the fourteenth century) alludes to it.

sible purity of soul; and, in consequence of this disposition, may the participation in the temporal celebration of the Eucharist produce in us lasting and imperishable effects, that is, may it conduct us to eternal life.[34] In Communion we truly receive into our mouth the human nature of Christ, we truly eat His flesh and truly drink His blood (*Quod ore sumpsimus*); but in order that by this sacramental union with Christ and by His corporal indwelling we may draw grace upon grace, we must receive this sublime and heavenly guest, embrace and hold Him fast with a heart that is pure and chaste, disengaged from attachment to whatever is temporal and perishable, and penetrated with heavenly love and desire for that which is eternal and imperishable (*pura mente capiamus*).[35]

By the temporal gift the Eucharist is to be understood as a sacrifice and as a sacrament; the gift of the Eucharist is, therefore, called temporal mainly [36] because sacrifice and sacrament are instituted and necessary only for time, for the duration of our temporal life, for the days of our earthly pilgrimage, but not for eternity and for the life to come, where the full possession and enjoyment of all heavenly gifts without sacramental veils shall be bestowed upon us.[37] The Eucharist, moreover, may be designated as a temporal

---

[34] Post perceptionem sacramenti petit sacerdos, ut hoc mysterium, quod sub venerandis signis corporaliter est sumptum, spiritualiter etiam sumatur et cum debita puritate mentis ipsius sacramenti fructus et virtus percipiatur, quoniam nihil prodest, quinimo plurimum obest sumptio sacramentalis, nisi eidem conjuncta sit perceptio spiritualis et gratiae illius participatio. Secundo postulat idem, ut de hoc munere temporali, participatione scil. sacrorum mysteriorum sub visibilibus signis ad tempus et pro vitae hujus curriculo data fiat illi et omnibus sumentibus ore et spiritu remedium sempiternum contra vitia et tentationes, ut hoc cibo et potu confortati non excidamus umquam virtute, sed perducamur ad vitam aeternam (Clichtov., *Elucidat.*, III, n. 82).

[35] Cf. similar petitions in the Postcommunions, for example: quod ore percepimus, pura mente sectemur; quae sedula servitute donante te gerimus, dignis sensibus tuo munere capiamus; quod ore prosequimur, contingamus et mente, quae temporaliter agimus, spiritualiter consequamur; quod ore contingimus, pura mente capiamus.

[36] At the same time we can also think of the temporal, earthly, material elements, bread and wine, which are offered to God and consecrated in the Eucharist. Plebis tuae munera, quaesumus, Domine, propitius intende, et quae sanctis mysteriis exsequendis temporaliter nos offerre docuisti, ad aeternam nobis proficere fac salutem (*Sacram. Leon.*).

[37] Quia hoc sacramento non est in aeternum mors Christi annuntianda, sed tantum donec veniat, quia postea nullis mysteriis egebimus, constat illud transitorium esse signum et temporale, quo tantum egemus nunc, dum videmus per speculum et in aenigmate (Alger., I, n. 57).

THE PURIFICATION OF THE CHALICE

gift in so far as the sacrifice is accomplished in a short time and the Sacrament is present within us for but a few minutes, so long as the species remain within us. Although a temporal gift, the Eucharist is yet to become for us an eternal remedy [38] and a means of obtaining eternal salvation.[39] For it has the power to redeem our life from perdition, to heal all spiritual and corporal frailty, to enrich us with every gift, whereby it becomes for us the guarantee and pledge of a blessed eternity.

2. The prayer for the washing of the fingers is as follows:

Corpus tuum, Domine, quod sumpsi, et Sanguis, quem potavi, adhaereat visceribus meis, et praesta: ut in me non remaneat scelerum macula, quem pura et sancta refecerunt sacramenta: qui vivis et regnas in saecula saeculorum. Amen.	May Thy body, O Lord, which I have received, and Thy blood which I have drunk, cleave to my inmost parts; and grant that no stain of sin may remain in me, whom the pure and holy mysteries have refreshed: who livest and reignest world without end. Amen.

Here we beseech [40] the Lord that His transient sacramental presence may produce in the depths of our soul lasting and profound interior effects, that it may obtain for us in a special manner perfect purity from all that is sinful. Christ's body and blood remain in us so long as the sacramental species are not destroyed, they remain also afterward within us (*adhaereat visceribus meis*) [41] by the

---

[38] *Remedium* = a remedy for something, a healing remedy, a helpful means; *remedium sempiternum* = *salutis aeternae remedium*.

[39] This same thought is expressed in various Postcommunions: Quod temporali celebramus actione, perpetua salvatione capiamus; quod temporaliter gerimus, aeternis gaudiis consequamur; quae nunc specie gerimus, rerum veritate capiamus; quod temporaliter gerimus, ad vitam capiamus aeternam; quod est nobis in praesenti vita mysterium, fiat aeternitatis auxilium.

[40] As this prayer is in the singular and presupposes that holy Communion has been received under both kinds, it appears to be intended and destined for the celebrant, while the preceding prayer (as well as the Postcommunion) is applicable to all who have received Communion.

[41] Petit sacerdos, quod ipsius sumpti sacramenti virtus adhaereat immaneatque visceribus ejus, non quidem corporalibus, sed spiritualibus ipsius animae, quae sunt memoria, intellectus et voluntas. . . . Postulat autem Missam celebrans ipsum quod sumpsit sacramentum adhaerere suis visceribus, non quidem secundum substantiam et rei adhaerentiam, quemadmodum cibus sensibilis adhaeret stomacho, sed secundum virtutem et efficaciam, per quam memoria intellectualis jugem habeat divinorum beneficiorum coelestiumque bonorum

sacramental power and grace which purify, ennoble, and sanctify the faculties of the soul and the inclinations of the heart, so that it is no longer we that live, but Christ that liveth in us (Gal. 2:20). As the branch is connected with the vine, so in like manner Communion causes us to remain in Christ and continually to draw from Him grace and life, in order that we may be ever faithful in the love and service of God. In that our Eucharistic Saviour remains and acts in us like a glowing coal,[42] we become perfectly cleansed from every stain of sin; all that is impure is consumed within us. The garment of sanctifying grace is so brilliantly white and so resplendent that no imperfection, no breath of evil may tarnish its purity (*in me non remaneat scelerum macula*).[43] These spiritual miracles of purification and sanctification are produced by the pure and holy mysteries (*pura et sancta sacramenta*)[44] of the Eucharist, which ever continue to refresh, rejuvenate, quicken, renew (*refecerunt*),[45] the

---

recordationem, intellectus rectam eorum quae credenda sunt et agenda cognitionem, voluntas vero promptam et ardentem bonorum et Deo placentium operum prosecutionem. Neque id quidem in transitu et perfunctorie, sed permanenter et indesinenter (Clichtov., *Elucid. eccles.*, III, n. 82). *Viscera*, in the first place = entrails (in Holy Scripture often regarded as the seat of the affections), then = the interior, the inmost part of the heart.

[42] In the primitive Church the incarnate Son of God (*Verbum incarnatum*) was called, especially in the Blessed Sacrament, a glowing coal (*carbo ignitus, pruna ignita*); for the Eucharist is a food of fire which purifies and inflames (cf. Isa. 6:6).

[43] Deus, qui sumitur, ignis consumens est omnem peccati scoriam exurensque spirituali et sacro incendio omnes noxios humores vitiorum in anima. Ipse itidem lux est clarissima illuminans tenebras nostras et omnem iniquitatis caliginem infusione sui luminis effugans (Clichtov., *Elucidat. eccles.*, III, n. 83).

[44] The designation of the Eucharistic sacrifice and sacrament by the plural *sacrificia* and *sacramenta* is usually explained and justified with reference to the two divisions of the sacramental species; but in this we should notice, that the word *sacramenta* in the liturgy is often used in a wider sense = *mysteria*, that is, mysteries. The stricter (specific) signification in which it is now used to designate the seven means of grace in the Church, became customary only since the Middle Ages. For the Eucharistic mysteries we frequently in the Postcommunions come across similar expressions, for example, *mysteria, divina sacramenta, sancta, sacri dona mysterii, sancta vel sacra munera, dona coelestia, salutis nostrae subsidia, mystica vota et gaudia, coelestia sacramenta et gaudia, salutaria dona, votiva sacramenta, coeslestia alimenta, magnifica sacramenta, munera sacrata*.

[45] Refecerunt haec sacramenta animae viscera quantum ad effectum ab eis causatum et derelictum ex digna eorum sumptione. Sic enim refecerunt rationem et intellectum in sinceritate cognitionis illuminando, voluntatem per amorem et dilectionem inflammando, memoriam ad passionis rememorationem

higher life of the soul so that it may not wither away and be lost.[46]

O dearest Lord Jesus, what great sweetness hath a faithful soul perfectly devoted to Thee, that feasteth with Thee at Thy banquet, where there is no other meat set before her to be eaten but Thyself, her only beloved and most to be desired above all the desires of her heart. And to me indeed it would be delightful to pour out tears in Thy presence with the whole affection of my heart, and like the devout Magdalen, to wash Thy feet with my tears. But where is this ardor of devotion, where is this stream of holy tears? Surely in the sight of Thee and of Thy holy angels, my whole heart ought to be inflamed and to weep for joy. For I have Thee in the Sacrament truly present, though hidden under another form. For to behold Thee in Thine own divine brightness, is what mine eyes would not be able to endure, neither could the entire world subsist in the splendor of the glory of Thy majesty. In this, therefore, Thou condescendest to my weakness, that Thou hidest Thyself under the sacramental species. I truly have and adore Him whom the angels adore in heaven; but I as yet in faith, they by sight and without a veil. I must be content with the light of true faith and walk therein till the day of eternal brightness break forth and the shades of concealing forms pass away. But when that which is perfect shall come, the use of sacraments shall cease; for the blessed in heavenly glory stand not in need of the medicine of the sacraments. For they rejoice without end in the presence of God, beholding His glory face to face; and being plunged from brightness into the brightness of the incomprehensible Deity, they taste the Word made flesh, as He was from the beginning, and as He remaineth forever.

O how sublime and how venerable is the office of priests, to whom it is given to consecrate by sacred words the Lord of majesty, with their lips to bless, with their hands to hold, with their mouths to receive Him, and also to administer to others. O how clean ought those hands to be, how pure that mouth, how holy that body, how unspotted the heart of the priest, into whom the Author of purity so often enters! From the mouth of the priest, who so often receives Jesus Christ in His Sacrament, nothing but what is holy, no word but what is good and profitable, ought to proceed. His eyes, which are used to behold the body of Christ, ought to be simple and chaste; his hands, which are used to handle the

---

excitando, suavitatem quandam et laetitiam spiritualem in toto homine efficiendo (Gabr. Biel, *Expos. Canon. Miss.*, lect. 83).

[46] Sacrosancti corporis et sanguinis D. N. J. Chr. refectione vegetati, supplices te rogamus Deus, ut hoc remedio singulari et ab omnium peccatorum nos contagione purifices et a periculorum munias incursione cunctorum (*Sacram. Leon.*).

Creator of heaven and earth, should be pure and lifted up to heaven in prayer. . . . O almighty God! come with Thy grace to our assistance, that we priests may serve Thee worthily and devoutly, in all purity and good conscience. And, if we cannot live yet perfectly free from every fault, as our calling demands, grant us at least the grace duly to bewail the sins which we have hitherto committed; and in spirit of humility, and the resolution of a good will, to serve Thee more fervently for the time to come.[47]

[47] *Imitation of Christ*, IV, xi, 1 f., 6 ff.

CHAPTER XLV

THE THANKSGIVING

THE moments which immediately follow the reception of Holy Communion are exceedingly blessed and precious and rich in grace and devotion; for in astounding condescension the sweet and gracious Jesus now dwells, with all the treasures of heaven, in the inmost sanctuary of the poor human heart. It is then especially requisite [1] for us to forget the world and its pleasures, to avoid all levity, in recollection and silence to direct all the powers and faculties of the soul to the heavenly guest, to embrace Him with devotion and ardent love, to glorify, adore, and petition Him—in short, to offer a joyful and heartfelt thanksgiving for the unutterably marvelous grace of Holy Communion. Heavenly, imperishable food has been presented to us, Christ's most sacred body and His most precious blood. As the soul is here filled with the marrow and fatness of celestial gifts and consolations, she should overflow with gratitude, and with joyful lips praise and magnify the Lord (Ps. 62:6). This thanksgiving, by which the Eucharistic stream of grace is more copiously poured into the heart, the Church leaves to the fervor and devotion of the individual. Hence for public worship she has prescribed only a very short and simple celebration after Communion, which is called the thanksgiving.[2]

---

[1] Decet post communionem in omnibus mente et corpore custoditum ac modestum consistere nec minus esse sollicitum ad Christum grate tenendum quam ante exstiterat ad eum digne suscipiendum. Unde multi arguendi videntur, qui post communionem et Missae consummationem tam faciliter se foras effundunt atque in exterioribus occupantur, nisi necessitas postulet (Dion. Carthus., *Expos. Miss.*, a. 38). Expleto officio, ferventi ac devotissimo corde gratias age, gratus permane atque in omni conversatione tua esto sollicitus, ne offendas: esto timoratus et custoditus, ne susceptam gratiam perdas, ne fructum amittas adeptum, et sic tota vita tua sit praeparatio ad celebrandum continua (Dion. Carthus., *De sacr. serm.*, III).

[2] Tota missae celebratio in gratiarum actione terminatur, populo exsultante

Here we find the Communio and the Postcommunion, to which on the ferial days of Lent the *Oratio super populum* is added.

THE COMMUNIO

The antiphon which is read out of the missal by the priest after Communion, on the Epistle side [3] of the altar, is called the Communio. Like the Offertory before the oblation, this antiphon is an abbreviated chant, that is, a remnant of that longer psalm chant which in former times (from the days of the apostles until about the twelfth century) accompanied the administration of the Eucharist to the clergy and laity. The psalm verses which were sung by the choir alternately with a frequently repeated antiphon, received the name Communio (Communion hymn) because they accompanied the act of Communion and were intended to intensify the devotion of the communicant.[4] Since the twelfth century [5] these psalm verses

---

pro sumptione mysterii (quod significat cantus post communionem), et sacerdote per orationem gratias offerente, sicut et Christus celebrata coena cum discipulis, hymnum dixit ut dicitur Matth. c. 26 (S. Thom., IIIa, q. 83, a.4).

[3] On the Epistle side, as the less worthy side of the altar, the less important portions of the Mass are read, that is, those parts which precede the first Gospel and follow the Communion; on the Gospel side and in the middle of the altar *tamquam in partibus dignioribus altaris*, on the contrary, are performed those prayers and ceremonies which by their intimate connection with the accomplishment of the sacrifice have a more profound signification. (Cf. Quarti, II, xi, 1.)

[4] Mox ut Pontifex coeperit in senatorio (*that is, at the place destined for the more distinguished men*) communicare, statim schola incipit Antiphonam ad Communionem per vices cum subdiaconibus et psallunt usquedum, communicato omni populo, annuat Pontifex ut dicant "Gloria Patri" et repetito Versu (antiphon) quiescunt (*Ordo Rom. I*, n. 20). Facta confractione debent omnes communicare, interim cum et Antiphona cantatur, quae de Communione nomen mutavit, cui et Psalmus subjungendus est cum "Gloria Patri," si necesse fuerit (Microl., chap. 18). In the Ambrosian rite this antiphon to be recited after Communion is called *Transitorium: scil. quia tunc sacerdos ex cornu Evangelii transit ad partem Epistolae.*

[5] Cantus quem communionem dicimus, quem post cibum salutarem canimus, gratiarum actio est, juxta illud: "Edent pauperes et saturabuntur et laudabunt Dominum, qui requirunt eum" (Ps. 21:27). (Rupert. Tuit., *De divin. offic.*, II, chap. 18.) Since this time it received in many places also the name postcommunio, which later on was exclusively used to designate the last prayer. Antiphona, quam usitato nomine vocamus Postcommunionem (Hildeb. Turon. [d. 1134], *Lib. de expositione Missae*). Antiphona, quae Postcommunio a pluribus nuncupatur, ideo sic appellata est, quoniam post com-

THE THANKSGIVING

were gradually omitted at the administration of Communion, and sung afterward, so that they constituted a portion of the liturgical thanksgiving. Later on this hymn was abridged and reduced to the Antiphon which at present, notwithstanding its altered position and application to the thanksgiving, still retains the original name (Communio). The custom, introduced at an early date and universally adopted in the East as well as in the West, of enhancing the celebration of Communion by the singing of psalms, had undoubtedly its origin in the supper room at Jerusalem, where the Lord and His apostles at the Last Supper concluded a hymn (Matt. 26:30) before they proceeded to the Mount of Olives.

As a rule the Communion verse is taken from Holy Scripture, usually from the Psalms, but also frequently from the other books. Occasionally it is of ecclesiastical origin, or consists of a characteristic saying of the saint commemorated. As to its contents the Communion antiphon does not refer to the reception of the Eucharist, as might be presumed from its name and position, but to the particular celebration of the day. In harmony with the remaining variable parts of the rite of the Mass, it serves to bring the mystery of the feast, or the idea of the ecclesiastical time, or the subject of the Mass being celebrated, more prominently into view. But rarely is the text so arranged that a reference to Holy Communion could therein be discovered. Rather, the same fundamental tones, which were often heard in the Introit and during the progress of the Mass, return in the concluding chant of the Communion antiphon and in the Postcommunion.

The Postcommunion

1. The Communion antiphon and the usual salutation, *Dominus vobiscum: Et cum spiritu tuo*,[6] constitute the introduction to the

---

municationem sive in signum, quod communicatio expleta est, concinitur (Durand., IV, lvi, 1). Afterward (chap. 57, n. 1) he observes: Sacerdos elevatis manibus ultimam orationem, quae proprie Postcommunio vocatur, exsequitur.

[6] Departing from the present rite, the celebrant, when intoning the Gloria, formerly turned toward the people, while he omitted doing so at the *Dominus vobiscum* after Communion. Placet regula Joannis Diaconi ex epistola ad Senarium: "Illud firma mente custodio, quod non a majoribus tradita custodiret Ecclesia, nisi certa sui ratio poposcisset; nec ea possumus dicere inania videri ac frivola, quia eorum minime rationem accepimus." Si tamen conjecturis indulgere licet, ideo Pontifex "hymnum angelicum" praecinens con-

last prayer, which, from its position after the Communion of all, received the name, Postcommunion.[7] Like the Collect and Secreta, the Postcommunion is also a prayer of petition, but in it the following characteristic distinction is to be made and emphasized. While in the Collect the idea (the subject) of the ecclesiastical celebration is exclusively expressed, and in the Secreta the remembrance of the sacrifice of the Mass takes precedence, there is frequently in the Postcommunion a reference to the reception of the Eucharist. The petition presented in the last prayer is based, at one time on the subject of the day's celebration, at another on the celebration of the sacrifice, again, on participation in the sacrificial banquet, and even on all these motives combined. The gifts implored are of various kinds. They comprise all that may be beneficial to our welfare and salvation for time and for eternity. Chiefly do we pray for a plenteous outpouring of all the fruits of the sacrifice and of the Communion celebration. What is more opportune at this moment than the ardent desire that the sacrificial body and blood of Christ, which we have received, may bring forth the fruit of virtue and sanctity? The Postcommunions are always recited by the priest in the plural number, that is, for all and in the name of all who have taken part in the Mass, either by actual (sacramental) Communion, as was generally the case in ancient times, or at least by spiritual communion.[8]

---

vertebat se ad populum, ut eum ad laudandum Deum invitaret. Ideo vero salutationem illam postremam pronuntiabat versus altare, quod ad fideles communione seu corpore et sanguine Christi Domini tum refectos verba dirigeret, quibus proinde non jam apprecantis optantisve, sed gratulantis more Dominum inesse hac salutatione contestabatur (Mabillon, *In Ord. Rom.,* chap. 21).

[7] Other ancient designations are, for example, *ultima benedictio* (this last word often = *oratio sacerdotis*), *oratio ad complendum* (*complenda*, inasmuch as in the first ten centuries it formed the conclusion of the sacrificial celebration, as only the dismissal [*Ite missa est*] followed it). Finita Antiphona surgit Pontifex . . . et veniens ante altare dat Orationem ad complendum, directus ad Orientem. Nam in isto loco, cum *Dominus vobiscum* dixerit, non se dirigit ad populum (*Ordo Rom. I*, n. 21). Collectae quae dicuntur ad complendum (Rupert. Tuit., II, chap. 19). Sequitur oratio, quae post communionem vocatur, in qua sacerdos orat pro his, qui ad communionem eucharistiae accessere (Sicard., III, chap. 8). Sacerdos salutato populo orationem dicat; cui iterum saltanti populum, diaconus "Ite missa est" tempore suo aut "Benedicamus Domino" succinat. Clero respondente "Deo gratias" officium finiat (Joann. Abrinc., *De offic. ecclesiast.*).

[8] Sequitur oratio sive orationes post communionem dicendae, quae eodem numero et ordine orationibus ante lectionem sive pro secreta ante praefa-

THE THANKSGIVING

On the Second Sunday of Advent we pray:

Repleti cibo spiritualis alimoniae, supplices te, Domine, deprecamur: ut hujus participatione mysterii, doceas nos terrena despicere, et amare coelestia.

Having been filled with the food of spiritual nourishment, we humbly beseech Thee, O Lord, that by the participation in this mystery Thou wouldst teach us to despise earthly things and to love those that are heavenly.

On the Feast of St. Catherine of Siena:

Aeternitatem nobis, Domine, conferat, qua pasti sumus, mensa coelestis: quae beatae Catharinae Virginis vitam etiam aluit temporalem.

May eternal life, O Lord, be conferred on us by the heavenly food with which we have been fed, and which nourished even the temporal life of the blessed virgin, Catherine.

On the Feast of St. Aloysius:

Angelorum esca nutritos, angelicis etiam, Domine, da moribus vivere: et ejus, quem hodie colimus, exemplo in gratiarum semper actione manere.

Grant us, O Lord, who have been nourished with the food of angels, also to live the lives of angels, and by the example of him whom we this day celebrate, always to abide in thanksgiving.

2. Although a prayer of petition differs and must be distinguished from a prayer of thanksgiving, yet the Postcommunion, which is a prayer of petition, is justly considered as a thanksgiving after Communion, and is designated as a thanksgiving.[9] By this appellation,

---

tionem dictis debent respondere. Quae utique orationes non pro his, qui communicaturi sunt, sed qui jam communicaverunt, juxta proprietatem sui nominis agunt. Ergo et ante ipsas communicare non neglegant, quicumque earundem orationum benedictione foveri desiderant (Microl., chap. 19). Iste orationes pro communicantibus institutae sunt, quando omnes vel plerique, quia aderant sacrificio, communicabant; nam et ipsum communionis vocabulum improprie hic usurparetur, nisi plures de eodem sacrificio participarent. Quamvis autem mos ille desierit, nihil tamen in orationibus immutatum est, sed ideo retentae sunt, ut sciamus, quid olim factum sit, et ex ipso precationum tenore ad pristinum fervorem excitemur (Bona, *Rer. liturg.*, II, xx, 11).

[9] Participato tanto Sacramento, gratiarum actio cuncta concludit (S. August., *Epis.*, 149, n. 16 [*ad Paulin.*]). Sequuntur orationes, in quibus fit per-

petition and thanksgiving are not exchanged for one another, but it merely expresses that the petition which is contained in the Postcommunion serves also to manifest and confirm the grateful sentiments of our heart toward God. Our gratitude is displayed in this, that we honor the greatness and goodness of our gracious Benefactor, esteeming His gifts, employing them faithfully, and striving as far as possible to make a return for them. Toward God we can render in various ways a grateful acknowledgment of benefits received, not only by actual prayer of thanksgiving or formal words of thanksgiving, but also by many other acts; for example, acts of praise and adoration, of offering and glorification, yes, even of petition. The prayer of petition is, in the first place and according to its intrinsic nature, an act of veneration and glorification of God, inasmuch as God is thereby acknowledged as the source and dispenser of all gifts.[10] Accordingly, by filial and confident petition after Communion, homage is offered to the divine Majesty, and this homage is the principal gift which we present to the Lord, who has no need of our goods (Ps. 15:2), in return for the grace of Communion. These fervent and humble petitions, therefore, can justly be regarded as the outcome and testimony of our grateful disposition, and, consequently, they may be accounted as thanksgiving after Communion. Therefore as heartfelt thanksgiving for benefits received is the best claim for obtaining new favors (*de perceptis muneribus gratias exhibentes beneficia potiora sumamus*); so, vice versa, confiding petition after Communion is an acceptable thanksgiving for the sublime grace of the body and blood of Christ, which has been received.[11] Even that marvelous hymn of thanksgiving, the

---

ceptorum beneficiorum commemoratio et gratiarum actio (Ivonis Carnot., *Serm.*, V). In ultima oratione sacerdos rogat et gratias agit de sacramenti perceptione, dicens collectas pro numero Secretarum (Durand., IV, chap. 57). Ultima pars Missae sequitur, quae dicitur gratiarum actio atque incipit a communione. Vocatur autem communio quasi participatio, quam ideo canimus, ut per eam cum Sanctis divinae gratiae participes efficiamur. Appellatur etiam completio, quoniam per illam Missa, ut sic dicam, completur (Joann. Beleth., chap. 49).

[10] Quamvis orans praeconia Dei in suis orationibus formaliter non exprimeret tamen ipsa oratio est Dei laudatio: quoniam orans eo ipso, quod oret Deum, fatetur, ac praesupponit insufficientiam propriam, et omnipotentiam, providentiam atque clementiam Dei, quem non invocaret, nisi crederet eum potentem ad adjuvandum et omnium provisorem ac pium ad succurrendum (Dion. Carthus., *De orat.*, a. 31).

[11] Cf. the *Postcom. Dom. XVIII post Pent.:* Gratias tibi referimus, Domine,

THE THANKSGIVING

Te Deum, peals out in the most touching and hopeful petition, as, in general, almost all the prayers of the Church resolve into petition.

THE *Oratio super populum*

1. On the ferial days of Lent after the Postcommunion there follows a prayer for the people; it is directly introduced by an *Oremus* and the exhortation: *Humiliate capita vestra Deo* ("Bow your heads before God").[12] Concerning the origin and object of this prayer, a variety of opinions have been adduced.[13] The following appears to be the most simple and correct. According to the ancient rite of the Roman Church, the *Oratio super populum* was not recited, as at present, only on the days of Lent, but every day, even on great feasts: it belonged to the ordinary prayers of the Mass. At that period, when the present benediction at the end of Mass had not yet been introduced, this prayer was intended to invoke God's blessing, protection, and assistance on the assembled congregation before they were dismissed from the house of God by the *Ite missa est* after

---

sacro munere vegetati: tuam misericordiam deprecantes, ut dignos nos ejus participatione perficias. Per Dominum.

[12] The *inclinatio capitis* must be made not merely at the *Oremus*, but it must also accompany the words *Humiliate capita vestra Deo* (S. R. C., December 12, 1879).

[13] Micrologus says (chap. 51), that the *Oratio super populum* is intended for those who do not communicate, while the *Postcommunio* is destined exclusively for the communicants. That, namely, those persons, who on the ferial days of Lent did not communicate, might not be dismissed without prayer or blessing, the above prayer has been added in their behalf, *in qua non de communicatione, sed de populi protectione specialiter oratur*. This ordinance was made expressly for the season of Lent, *quia cum majorem conflictum in jejuniis et orationibus contra spiritales nequitias sumimus, necessario nos instantius Deo commendare debemus*. On Sundays it is not said, either because the prescribed genuflection is omitted, or rather because all present should have received Holy Communion. Honorius of Autun beholds in the *Oratio super populum* a substitute for the otherwise customary distribution of the so-called eulogia, which during Lent (*proper jejunium*) did not take place (cf. Gemma animae, I, chap. 67). The occurrence of this prayer in Lent may also be regarded as a reminder of the ancient observance, which now is customary only on Holy Saturday, and which consisted in combining Vespers with the Mass sung after None; the *Oratio super populum* was at the same time a concluding benediction and prayer at the end of Vespers preceding the formula of dismissal, as even now the *Oratio super populum* and the prayer of Vespers in Lent are alike (Quadt, Die Liturgie der Quatembertage, p. 113).

the celebration of the Eucharist. These very ancient prayers are intended as a supplication for the divine benediction, not merely by their contents, but still more by the accompanying ceremony, for from the earliest times the liturgies require a humble bow to be made by the faithful whenever they receive a blessing. St. Gregory the Great restricted the *Oratio super populum* to the ferial days of Lent. This ancient prayer was retained in the Masses for Lent because this period of the ecclesiastical year has in many respects preserved the ancient Roman rite; then, too, it is characteristic of this great and solemn season of penance to implore more frequently and more urgently the protection and assistance of Heaven, so as to enable us to support courageously the combat against the enemies of our salvation. The original object of the *Oratio super populum*, which formerly was said every day, is, consequently, to be distinguished from the reason of its being exclusively restricted to the penitential season of Lent.[14]

2. With what enthusiasm should not the love of our God and Redeemer be praised for the banquet of grace, for the food and drink of life, which He dispenses to us on the altar: for the bread, which is His body, and for the blood, which issues forth from His sacred heart. Yes, upon the marble of our altars there is found a wondrous food and a wondrous drink, prepared for the poor pilgrims who in pain and sorrow tread the rugged and stony path, and walk amid the cruel thorns and brambles of this life. To the shadow of the altar they retire as to a haven of rest. Exhausted and weary by reason of the weakness of their nature, amid the pressure of temptation and the bitter warfare of this life, they seek in this nourishment solace, refreshment, and strength. Hence the heart of the Church expands with joy and gratitude and exults in beholding this sacred,

---

[14] The forty days of Lent are, according to the Fathers and the spirit of the liturgy, a time of combat of the Christian army against Satan, the world, and the flesh. Cf. the expression *praesidia militiae Christianae* in a prayer for Ash Wednesday. Amalarius mentions the prayer in question in reference to the Postcommunion *ulterior ultima benedictio, in qua milites Christi commendantur pugnae contra antiquum hostem.* He then adds: Sacerdos noster, prudens agonotheta et pugnator, quantum in majore periculo videt milites fore, tantum munit eos amplius sua benedictione. Arma nostra contra diabolum sunt humilitas et ceterae virtutes. Vult sacerdos noster, ut nostris armis vestiti simus: propterea jubet per ministrum, ut humiliemus capita nostra Deo, et ita tandem infundit super milites protectionem benedictionis suae (*De eccles. offic.*, III, chap. 37).

mystical nourishment on the altar, our life's food. By fervent prayers and chants the Church urges her children to praise unceasingly the treasure of grace, the boundless wealth bestowed upon them in these gifts. Well aware that the praise and gratitude of men are at all times inadequate to the dignity and grandeur of these gifts, the Church presents herself in supplication at the portals of heaven, she appears at the celestial court and invites all the angels and saints to unite with her in praise, adoration, and thanksgiving (Eberhard).

CHAPTER XLVI

THE CONCLUSION

AFTER the Postcommunion that reciprocal salutation is said again [1] which throughout the celebration of Mass has so often been repeated in order to maintain between priest and people an active, lively intercourse: *Dominus vobiscum. Et cum spiritu tuo.*[2] By the sacrifice and communion our relations with God have become more close and intimate; hence the priest, before the conclusion of the holy action, desires for all present that the Lord, by His grace, protection, and assistance, would be with them during the course of the day, in joy and in sorrow, in fatigue and in labor; that, as the Good Shepherd, He would conduct and pasture them, be their staff and support; that He would remain with them when the day draws to a close and the evening appears, so that they "may watch with Christ and rest in peace."

[1] It is peculiar to the soul, repeatedly to pronounce that with which she is strikingly and profoundly impressed. The repetition of the *Dominus vobiscum*, accordingly, signifies that the most ardent wish of the Church is that the Lord may always remain with us. This applies especially at the conclusion of Mass, when the *Dominus vobiscum* is in a particular manner a petition, that we may be nourished and strengthened by the sacramental or spiritual Communion and the sacrificial fruits, in communion with Christ, that is, in His grace and love, that we may persevere unceasingly in His peace and service; for only he that abides in Christ and Christ in him, produces much fruit (John 15:5), because he does nothing without Christ, but all with and through Christ.

[2] Hoc tantum bonum sibi invicem optant et postulant (et sacerdos Ecclesiae et Ecclesia sacerdoti), ut sicut ejus gratia illuminatur, ejus praesentia confortatur, ejus protectione munitur, semper eum manere nobiscum, quemadmodum est pollicitus, sentiamus (Florus Diacon. [d. about 860], *De actione Missarum*, n. 13).

The Dismissal

According to the character of the celebration of the Mass, there now follows the concluding formula: *Ite missa est* or *Benedicamus Domino* or *Requiescant in pace*.[3]

From the earliest times it was customary at the Christian assemblies for divine worship, to liturgically announce the dismissal at the close of the holy action.[4] In the East and West there were different formulas of dismissal;[5] it is probable that to the Roman Church the formula *Ite missa est* ("Go, it is the dismissal") was at all times peculiar. As is evident from the translation given, the word *missa*, from which the whole sacrificial celebration has received its name of Mass,[6] occurs here again in its original signification (*missio = dimissio*).[7] In the eleventh century [8] the present rule was adopted, that the faithful were solemnly dismissed only on days of a festive or joyful character, that is, the formula of parting, *Ite missa est*, was used only when the hymn *Gloria in excelsis* was recited.[9] The *Ite*

[3] "Ite missa est" dicitur versus populum, quia dimittitur; "Benedicamus Domino" versus altare, quia ibi peculiari modo Dominus adest; "Requiescant in pace" item versus altare quia sermo est de absentibus (Gravant., *Thesaur.*, II, tit. 11 ad Rubr. 1). When the deacon sings this concluding formula, the celebrant must likewise say the *Benedicamus Domino* and the *Requiescant in pace*, but not the *Ite missa est*, because the latter has not the character of a prayer, but is only a formula for dismissing the people (S. R. C., September 7, 1816).

[4] Post communionem et post ejusdem nominis canticum, data benedictione a sacerdote ad plebem (*that is, after the recitation of the Postcommunion*), diaconus praedicat Missae officium esse peractum, dans licentiam abeundi (Raban. Maur., *De clericor. instit.*, I, chap. 33).

[5] In the Apostolic Constitutions (VIII, chap. 15): "Go in peace"; in the liturgy of St. James: "In the peace of Christ let us go"; in the liturgy of St. Chrysostom: "Let us go in peace"; in the Ambrosian rite: *Procedamus in pace*; in the Mozarabic: *Solemnia completa sunt in nomine D. N. J. Ch., votum sit acceptum cum pace.*

[6] On the name, "Mass," see the note at the end of this chapter.

[7] Finitis vero omnibus, adstanti et observanti populo absolutio datur, inclamante diacono: "Ite missa est." Missa ergo nihil aliud intellegitur, quam dimissio, i.e. absolutio, quam celebratis omnibus tunc diaconus esse pronuntiat, cum populus a solemni observatione dimittitur (Florus Diaconus, *De actione Missarum*, n. 92).

[8] The three oldest *Ordines Romani*, written before the tenth century, mention without any distinction of days or Masses only the concluding formula, *Ite missa est*. R. *Deo gratias*. (Cf. *Ordo Rom. I*, n. 21, 24; *II*, n. 15; *III*, n. 18.)

[9] Semper cum "Gloria in excelsis" etiam "Te Deum" et "Ite missa est" recitamus (Microlog., *De observat. eccles.*, chap. 46).

missa est, therefore, since the Middle Ages has been regarded as a characteristic mark of the joyful days of the ecclesiastical year, and to this aspect also corresponds the circumstance that in the singing thereof, it resounds in joyous tones.

On other days which bear the character of sorrow and penance, the dismissal was not announced; but instead of the *Ite missa est*, the *Benedicamus Domino* ("Let us bless the Lord") was substituted, whereby all were encouraged to praise God. This usage originated from the fact that on those days of penance and prayer the people were not permitted to leave the house of God immediately after the conclusion of the Mass, but had to remain there [10] for the canonical hours or the celebration of the stations which followed directly after the sacrifice.[11] Hence arose the present prescriptions, that those Masses whose character does not admit of the *Gloria in excelsis* should be concluded by the more grave and supplicatory *Benedicamus Domino*.[12] To these two formulas, of which the first directly and the other at least indirectly announce the close of the sacrificial celebration, the people answer by the mouth of the acolyte: *Deo gratias* ("Thanks be to God"), for a sentiment of gratitude should now fill the people, since they have been admitted to mysteries so sublime and enriched with graces so precious.[13]

As Requiem Masses are a service of mourning for the departed,

---

[10] For this reason in the Middle Ages the first Mass of Christmas Eve was often concluded, not as now with the *Ite missa est*, but with *Benedicamus Domino*, whereby the congregation was exhorted not to leave the church, but to assist at Lauds, which followed immediately after the first Mass. (Cf. Microl., chap. 34; Joann. Beleth, chap. 49; Durand., IV, lvii, 7.)

[11] Crederem, tunc omissam dimissionem, cum fideles peracta Missa non statim abirent, sed permanebant in Ecclesia, donec recitatis canonicis precibus et statione soluta abire fas erat (Bona, *Rer. liturg.*, II, xx, 3).

[12] Already Micrologus remarks (chap. 46) that in Advent and Lent, instead of *Ite missa est*, the *Benedicamus Domino* should be sung *pro tristitia temporis insinuanda* (to show the penitential sorrow of these days). The frequently used liturgical formula, *Benedicamus Domino*, to which is regularly given the answer *Deo gratias*, is itself a magnifying of the Lord, and contains, at the same time, a summons to praise the Lord. In the Middle Ages it was also called *Versus clusorius*, because with the *Deo gratias* all the canonical hours are concluded.

[13] Deo gratias, i.e. Deo dicamus agamusque gratias de Missae consummatione et sacrorum mysteriorum completione, ne merito nobis impingatur et exprobretur ingratitudo. Est enim gratiarum actio cum in ceteris a Deo perceptis bonis, tum in hoc excellentissimo dono sacrificii salutaris apprime necessaria et nequaquam praetermittenda (Clichtov., III, n. 84).

many prayers and ceremonies are omitted in them which either designate the participation of the living in the sacrificial fruit or denote joy and solemnity. For the last reason already, in Requiem Masses the dismissal of the people is not accompanied by the joyful and festive *Ite missa est*. Besides, those present are not to depart at once, but should continue in prayer until the suffrages, which as a rule take place for the departed after Requiem Masses, are completed. Already in the twelfth century [14] it was the general custom to conclude divine worship for the departed with the devout and prayerful wish: *Requiescant in pace* ("May they rest in peace").[15] A more comprehensive and suitable formula of conclusion could not be found; for it includes all the gifts which we would procure by the sacrifice for the suffering souls,[16] and which we can in general implore: eternal rest and heavenly peace in the bosom of God. The *Amen* ("So be it") given as reply by the acolyte, unites the wishes of the people with those of the priest, so that the combined supplication may be more readily and promptly answered.[17]

Formerly, until about the twelfth century, the Holy Sacrifice was concluded with one of these formulas; for the three following parts —the *Placeat*, the Blessing, and the beginning of the Gospel of St.

[14] Diaconus Missae finem imponit decantans "Benedicamus Domino" vel "Ite missa est" in diebus festivis vel "Requiescant in pace" ut in mortuorum exsequiis (Stephan. Augustod., *De sacram. alt.*, chap. 18). Dicitur in Missis pro defunctis "Requiescant in pace," quod ex sola consuetudine generali natum est (Joann. Beleth., chap. 49).

[15] This formula is an abridgment of the more detailed one, which frequently occurs in the Office of the Church: Fidelium animae per misericordiam Dei requiescant in pace. In it is found a harmony with the biblical words: In pace in idipsum dormiam et requiescam (Ps. 4:9), that is, "in peace in the self same I will sleep (= with all the saints of God) and I will rest" in gentle slumber, full of hope in a glorious resurrection to come. Whether Mass is celebrated for one or for more departed souls, the plural number *Requiescant* always refers to all the suffering souls; for the Church is accustomed in her liturgy to unite her intercession for departed individuals most intimately with her intercession for all the faithful departed.

[16] In Missa (etiam pro uno defuncto) semper "Requiescant" dicendum (S. R. C., January 22, 1678).

[17] In Missa pro defunctis celebrata dicitur haec conclusio: "Requiescant in pace," ut finis hujus Missae respondeat principio, in quo eis aeterna requies postulatur. Quoniam enim totum illud officium peculiariter ordinatur pro requie defunctis impetranda, ideo ipsis placida requies postulatur in Missae principio, medio et in fine. Et hic respondet pro populo chorus aut minister: "Amen," i.e. fiat quod petitur piaque nostra desideria compleantur (Clichtov.. III, n. 84).

John—are later additions which gradually found acceptance, but which were not until the sixteenth century universally prescribed.

The *Placeat*

While the priest rests his joined hands on the altar, he prays [18] with head bowed and in silence:

Placeat tibi, sancta Trinitas, obsequium servitutis meae, et praesta: ut sacrificium, quod oculis tuae majestatis indignus obtuli, tibi sit acceptabile, mihique, et omnibus, pro quibus illud obtuli, sit, te miserante, propitiabile. Per Christum Dominum nostrum. Amen.	May the performance of my homage be pleasing to Thee, O Holy Trinity; and grant that the sacrifice which I, though unworthy, have offered up in the sight of Thy Majesty, may be acceptable to Thee, and may, through Thy mercy, be a propitiation for myself and all those for whom I have offered it. Through Christ our Lord. Amen.

Originally the *Placeat* was a private prayer recited by the priest at the close of the holy celebration, but previous to his leaving the altar; since the tenth century it is to be found in different missals.[19] Wherever the concluding blessing was introduced, this prayer was

---

[18] Primum condescensionem et acceptionem Dei circa obsequium jam in officio altaris exhibitum expostulat ipse sacerdos. Deinde supplex orat, quod hoc sacrificium divinae majestatis oculis oblatum sit illi acceptabile . . . ex parte offerentis, ut quantulacumque ejus devotio acceptetur a Deo; sit etiam idem sacrificium et ipsi offerenti et omnibus christianis tam vivis quam defunctis, pro quibus illud obtulit, propitiabile, utile et salutare ad diluenda peccata et consequendam gratiam. Et quo facilius exaudiatur sacerdos, haec supradicta deposcit sibi praestari non ex suis meritis et operibus justitiae quae fecerit, sed ex divinae misericordiae magnitudine et miseratrice ejus bonitate. Similiter eadem petit sibi indulgeri per Chr. D. N., in cujus nomine quidquid petere volumus est postulandum et quidquid postulatum fuerit haud dubie ut promisit impetrabitur: cui pro expleta expositione familiari ipsius sacri Canonis sit laus, honor et gloria in saecula saeculorum. Amen (Clichtov., III, n. 86).

[19] Finitis omnibus osculatur sacerdos altare, dicens: "Placeat tibi, sancta Trinitas . . ." (Microlog., chap. 22). We find in many missals up to the sixteenth century the rubric, that the prayer *Placeat* should be recited *finita Missa* or *post Missa*.

said after it;[20] only since the fifteenth century has it been placed before the blessing.

This prayer is a brief repetition, or an epitome, of the oblation petitions, which before as well as after the Consecration form a constituent portion of the liturgy of the Mass. In the name of and for the glorification of the triune God the Holy Sacrifice was begun, continued, and completed; to the Blessed Trinity it is now once more and for the last time recommended.[21] Impressed with the consciousness of his frailty, sinfulness, and unworthiness, the priest first implores that the sacrifice offered by him and the homage of profound submission thereby rendered [22] may be graciously accepted by the Holy Trinity; he then begs that, in consequence of the divine pleasure taken in the sacrifice and in virtue of the divine mercy, reconciliation and grace may flow from the altar to all for whom it was offered. In order to understand the last petition, it is to be remarked that God does not always impart at once all the sacrificial fruits after the accomplishment of the act of sacrifice, but many of them He frequently bestows at a later period, when, where, and as it pleases Him, in conformity with the impenetrable designs of His wise and merciful providence.

[20] This ordinance is still found in *Ordo Roman. XIV*, of the fourteenth century. Even some missals of the sixteenth century have the concluding benediction before the *Placeat*.

[21] Sanctae Trinitati, cui unam debemus et individuam per omnia servitutem, sicut unum sacrificium offerimus, sic unam quoque gloriam fideli devotione cantamus. Nam quia unam naturam constat esse sanctae Trinitatis, dignum est ut una gloria Patri et Filio et Spiritui sancto dicatur a fidelibus in hymnis et psalmis (S. Fulgent., *Contra Fabian.*, fragm. 34).

[22] The worship and veneration (*obsequium*) of which there is question here, is more minutely characterized as such by the addition *servitutis*, as is due by the totally dependent creature toward the Creator, because of His absolute dominion, and as in sacrifice it principally finds its expression; that is, as a worship of servitude and adoration due to God alone ($\lambda\alpha\tau\rho\epsilon\acute{\iota}\alpha$). *Obsequium servitutis* would, therefore, as to its meaning be the same as *oblatio servitutis*. The Vulgate often translates (John 16:2; Rom. 9:4; 12:1) $\lambda\alpha\tau\rho\epsilon\acute{\iota}\alpha$ by *obsequium*. In the *Sacram. Leonian.* the Eucharistic gifts are called *piae devotionis obsequia*. We find there also the following prayer: Repleti, Domine, munificentia gratiae tuae, benedictione copiosa, et pro nostrae servitutis obsequiis et pro celebritate Sanctorum, coelestia dona sumentes, gratias tibi referimus. Trinitati exhibemus servitutis obsequium (S. Fulgent., *Contra Fabian.*, fragm. 12).

The Blessing

As a recapitulation [23] of the preceding oblation prayers, the *Placeat* is at the same time a suitable preparation for the blessing which immediately follows; [24] for every blessing proceeds from the sacrifice, and the celebrant is the minister through which the divine blessing is imparted. After the *Placeat* the priest kisses the altar and then pronounces aloud the blessing: *Benedicat vos omnipotens Deus, Pater et Filius ✠ et Spiritus sanctus. R. Amen.* ("May almighty God bless you: the Father, the Son ✠, and the Holy Ghost. R. Amen.") The act which accompanies and completes the text is as simple as it is impressive: in pronouncing the first words (*Benedicat vos omni-*

---

[23] Sacerdos velut in quodam compendio petitiones priores recolligit, humiliter petens pro se aliisque omnibus, pro quibus sacrificium illud obtulit, exaudiri (Gabr. Biel, *Expos. Can.*, lect. 89).

[24] The present blessing at the end of Mass can not be shown to have been in use during the first ten centuries. In the ninth century some commentators do indeed mention a similar *benedictio*, but they understand thereby the concluding prayer (the *Postcommunio* or the *Oratio super populum*). The three oldest Roman *Ordines* mention that the celebrant at the end of Mass, not at the altar, but on returning to the sacristy, to the petition of the different ranks of the officiating clerics for the blessing (*Jube domne benedicere*), repeated each time the words *Benedicat nos* (or *vos*) *Dominus*, to which they responded *Amen*. (Cf. *Ordo Rom. I*, n. 21; *II*, n. 15; *III*, n. 18.) Since the tenth century many bishops no longer gave the blessing before the Communion (as was the custom in a number of places), but only at the end of Mass, and gradually the priest also began to bless the congregation after the sacrificial celebration, which according to Micrologus (chap. 21) already in the eleventh century they could not omit without great scandal (*absque gravi scandalo*). The words and actions of the benediction rite during the whole of the Middle Ages were neither fixed nor uniform. Some priests often blessed with a threefold sign of the cross, while others made merely one or even four signs of the cross; in so doing frequently the chalice or paten or a cross was held in the hand. Already in the fourteenth century (*Ordo Rom. XIV*, chap. 71) the formula now in use is found; on the other hand, we read in Clichtoveus (III) still in the sixteenth century, the following formula of blessing: Coeli benedictione benedicat et custodiat vos divina majestas et una deitas: Pater et Filius et Spiritus sanctus. Amen. Only at the revision of the missal, under Pius V and Clement VIII (d. 1605), was the different rite of the episcopal and priestly blessing fully regulated and universally prescribed, as Pope Clement interdicted priests from blessing with three signs of the cross even in *Missa solemni*. Only since that time may the bishop make, even in low Masses, a threefold sign of blessing, when he introduces the usual formula with some versicles (*Sit nomen Dom.* . . . with the so-called German cross on the breast and *Adjutorium nostrum* . . . with the so-called Latin cross); for *benedictio solemnis* the mitre is placed on the head and the crosier in the left hand of the bishop.

THE BLESSING

potens Deus), the priest raises his eyes and hands toward heaven, whence all good gifts come to us; then he turns to the faithful who are present and, at the mention of the triune God (*Pater et Filius* ✠ *et Spiritus sanctus*), makes over them the sign of the cross.

To comprehend the full import of the kissing of the altar here prescribed, it must be considered in its twofold relation: to the preceding prayer, *Placeat*, and to the imparting of the blessing which follows. In the first place, the kissing of the altar concludes the prayer *Placeat*, inasmuch as symbolically it strengthens and confirms the petition therein expressed.[25] In the *Placeat* the celebrant begs for a gracious acceptance of the sacrifice which is accomplished and for an abundant bestowal of the sacrificial fruits, that the union with Christ and His saints, renewed by the sacrifice and sacrificial banquet, may be confirmed and completed. This petition is now crowned by the kissing of the altar, which concludes the prayer. For it is not intended merely to manifest homage and reverence toward the Church triumphant; but rather, according to its profound signification, it is a figure, expression, and pledge of the holy communion of love, in which we live with Christ and His saints, and which at the altar, by the sacrificial celebration, has once again been ratified and strengthened. Like the *Placeat*, with which the altar kiss forms a whole, the latter has, then, a relation to the blessing, which it introduces. The kissing of the altar, therefore, renews the mystical union with Christ. But precisely from this living and mysterious union with Christ, whose representative he is, the priest draws the power and efficacy to pour out upon the assembled people, in the name of the triune God and by means of the words and signs of blessing, the plenitude of the graces of our salvation. Moreover, as the kissing of the altar, independently of the blessing and in connection with the *Placeat*, still retains its essential meaning with respect to the conclusion of the sacrificial celebration, it is prescribed even when the concluding blessing is omitted, that is, in Requiem Masses. In these Masses those who are present (the living) are not blessed, in order to indicate that all the sacrificial fruits are reserved for the benefit of the departed.

From the rite prescribed for the blessing, we see that the priest

---

[25] Per altaris osculum, quod in fine Missae fit, intelligitur sacerdos omnia praecedentia approbare et eis toto mentis affectu assentire (Durand., IV, xxix, 7).

blesses in the name and by the commission of the Church; he implores of almighty God the fullness of heavenly and earthly blessings upon the faithful; while, by making the sign of the cross [26] over those who are present, he indicates the source of all blessings and symbolically represents the fulfillment of the benediction pronounced. From the triune God proceed all the blessings of the creation and redemption; by His almighty power (*omnipotens Deus*) He can impart every blessing. The priest implores the blessing of the triune God who has created, redeemed, and sanctified us: the blessing of the Father, who gave His only-begotten Son for the world, and to whom the Son has even now presented the infinitely precious sacrifice; the blessing of the Son, who, for love of man and the redemption of mankind, endured the poverty of the crib and the ignominy of the cross, and who, day after day, renews the humiliation of His sacrificial life and death on the altar; the blessing of the Holy Ghost, who prepared the sacrificial body of the Saviour in the womb of the Virgin Mary, and whose heavenly ardor changes earthly elements into the body and blood of Christ.

To bless as well as to offer sacrifice is the vocation of the priest.[27] After he has offered on the altar the Lamb of God to the Most High, he raises his hands in order to bless the people. But his prayer of sacerdotal blessing is more than a devout wish of happiness; it is at all times efficacious and has the guarantee of being answered. The priest pronounces the words and God bestows the blessing, for God blesses by his mouth and by his hand.[28]

[26] Crux est signum Christi, quod nobis est fons omnis benedictionis et gratiae. Quocirca a Christo et Apostolis manavit traditio, ut, dum cui benedicimus, manibus in formam crucis deductis id faciamus (Corn. a Lap., *In Luc.*, 24:50).

[27] Benediximus nos episcopi et praelati vobis, o subditi, de domo Domini, i.e. de Ecclesia Christi praedicando vobis verbum salutis, ministrando vobis sacramenta N. L., orando quoque pro vobis et gratiam nobis divinitus datam, sicut caritas exigit, communicando. Benedictio proprie dicitur collatio gratiae Dei; gratiam autem non confert nisi Deus. Quomodo ergo unus nostrum alteri benedicere seu gratiam communicare potest nisi instrumentaliter, non principaliter? Ideo subditur: *Deus Dominus et illuxit nobis*, i.e. Deus, qui est Dominus noster, ipse et illuxit nobis, illuminando corda nostra Spiritu sancto et gratiam splendidam nostris mentibus infundendo, dando quoque vobis auctoritatem ligandi atque solvendi, ministrandi sacramenta, praedicandi evangelica verba, consecrandi et benedicendi—ex quibus idonei sumus ad benedicendum vobis (Dion. Carthus., *In Ps.*, 117:25).

[28] Sacerdotes benedicunt exorando, Deus largiendo (Florus Diac., n. 43). Fit mirabilis operationis divinae effectus, ut per sacerdotum ora Deus ipse

THE BLESSING

The concluding blessing is so efficacious because it is an ecclesiastical blessing, which can never be fruitless and inefficacious provided that the recipient present no obstacle. The liturgical blessing is especially a powerful petition of the Church: a petition which is always answered and granted by God, since, on the one hand, it is supported by the authority and holiness of the Church, and, on the other hand, it is based on the infinite merits of Jesus, on His precious blood and loving promises. Already in the Old Law, the Lord spoke in this manner to Moses (Num. 6:23, 27): "Say to Aaron and his sons [the high priests and the priests]: Thus shall you bless the children of Israel. . . . They shall invoke My name upon the children of Israel, and I will bless them." Should not this divine promise have far greater value in the Church of Christ, which is an institution and a kingdom of blessings, of salvation and redemption for the whole human race, in fact, for all creation? But as the full efficacy of the sacramentals, to which this blessing appertains, depends also in part on the worthiness of the dispenser and of the receiver, therefore during this holy act of blessing both priest and people should be animated and filled with faith, confidence, humility, and devotion.

This concluding blessing will appear in a new light if we conceive it, according to the precedent of the liturgists of the Middle Ages, as a figure of that blessing which the Saviour bestowed upon His disciples on the Mount of Olives at His departure out of this world,[29] and which He will again impart to those who are His own when He returns to judge the world.[30] Such a conception is solidly established; for it cannot be denied that points of resemblance occur. The liturgical sacrificial celebration is frequently considered as the

---

benedicat . . . deprecatur quidem pro salute hominum pia sacerdotis intentio, et praestat eam divinae pietatis devotio, sicque fit, ut caritas quae exhibet in sacerdote deprecationem, ipsa praestet a Domino integram sanitatem (Raban. Maur., II, chap. 55).

[29] Haec ultima benedictio significat illam benedictionem, quam Christus ascensurus in coelum discipulis dedit; unde ea facta sacerdos se ad orientem vertit quasi se Christo ascendenti commendans (Durand., *Ration.*, IV, lix, 4).

[30] Post hoc sacerdos dicit: "Ite, missa est" et populum benedicit. Quod signat quod veniet Dominus in judicio et se nobis ostendet et fidelibus suis dabit benedictionem suam et tunc laeti vadent ad mansiones suas, de quibus dicitur in Joanne (14:2): "In domo Patris mei mansiones multae sunt." Ad quas mansiones nos perducat ipse Pontifex et Sacerdos, qui cum Patre et Spiritu Sancto vivit et regnat. Amen (S. Bonav., *Expos. Missae*, chap. 4).

representation of the entire sacrificial life of Christ, from the Incarnation to the Ascension;[31] or, even more comprehensively, as a representation of the history of salvation from the beginning to the end of the world. In this aspect the blessing at the end of the celebration of the Mass, by which Christ's work of redemption is mystically renewed, reminds us naturally of the last blessing given by the Saviour after the work of redemption was objectively accomplished; in like manner the concluding blessing at Mass contains an indication of the last and greatest of all blessings, which the Lord will impart at the end of time, when the redemption of the world will be entirely completed.

From the top of Mount Olivet the Saviour, in the presence of His Mother and His disciples, ascended to heaven; and as He ascended He blessed them with uplifted hands (Luke 24:50), making over them, as we may presume, the sign of the Cross. What devout thoughts and sentiments will be awakened in us if we consider the blessing at the end of Mass as a repetition of this solemn blessing given by the divine Saviour! And how greatly must the devotion and joy of our heart be increased if we behold in this blessing at the conclusion of the sacrificial celebration a figure of that perfect blessing which, at the consummation of the time of grace, will be imparted to all the elect at the Last Judgment! The full blessing which Christ acquired by His blood is reserved for us in eternity, where God shall wipe away all tears from our eyes, where death shall be no more, nor mourning, nor crying, nor sorrow shall be any more, for the former things are passed away (Apoc. 21:4). "Come, ye blessed (*benedicti*) of my Father, possess you the kingdom prepared for you from the foundation of the world" (Matt. 25:34), will the Saviour cry out to His own, leading them to eternal glory, where they shall be blessed with imperishable goods and unspeakable joys. Christians are called that they may inherit a blessing (I Pet. 3:9)—a spiritual, heavenly, eternal blessing.

Since already here on earth God has showered upon us His blessings and in eternity will make us happy with the infinite plenitude of His blessing, we also, as the favored children of the heavenly

---

[31] Missae officium tam provida reperitur ordinatione dispositum, ut quae per Christum et in Christum, ex quo de coelo descendit usquedum in coelum ascendit, gesta sunt, magna ex parte contineat et ea tam verbis quam signis admirabili quadam specie repraesentet (Durand., IV, i, 11).

Father, should shed blessings around us. Compassionate and active love of our neighbor, mercy and benevolence, goodness and friendliness, should be reflected in our whole life, so that whatever we do may be upright and noble, and consolation and happiness, peace and joy may enter into the hearts of all those around us. We should spend our life on earth doing good. As the apostles, after receiving the blessing on the Mount of Olives, "went back into Jerusalem with great joy, . . . praising and blessing God," (Luke 24:52 f.), so should we, filled with holy joy, return to our daily occupations; and our life, sufferings, labors, prayers, and joys should thenceforth be an uninterrupted praise of God and a perpetual thanksgiving for the ineffable riches of the sacrificial blessing which has been bestowed so undeservedly upon us.[32]

THE LAST GOSPEL

The final conclusion of the Eucharistic sacrificial celebration is always the reading of a portion of the Gospel. In votive and Requiem Masses and usually [33] at other times also, the last Gospel is the beginning of the Gospel according to St. John (1:1-14). The reading of St. John's Gospel at this place was universally prescribed by a decree of Pius V. Previously it was merely a custom introduced during the thirteenth century and observed only in some places, to recite in a low voice or aloud this section of the Gospel, which was ever held in high repute, either at the altar or when retiring from the altar or while taking off the sacred vestments.

[32] St. Chrysostom endeavors to draw the faithful from sinful conversations, by reminding them of the grace and dignity which they obtained by participating in the holy mysteries. "Therefore, do nothing, say nothing that is earthly. God has elevated you to a heavenly rank: why do you again debase yourselves? Do you not behold here the sacred vessels? Do they not always serve one only purpose? Would any one venture to employ them for aught else? But you are holier than these vessels, yea, far holier. Why do you defile and contaminate yourselves? You stand in heaven and you slander? You dwell among angels, and you slander? The Lord has favored you with the kiss of peace, and you slander? So greatly has God adorned your mouth, by angelic praises, by a more than angelic food, by His kiss, by His embrace, and do you slander? Act not thus, I beseech you!" (*Homilies on the Epistle to the Ephesians*, XIV.)

[33] Except the third Mass of the feast of Christmas (*Ult. Evang. fest. Epiph.*), and the low Masses on Palm Sunday (*Ult. Evang. e bened. palm.*), and the feast day Masses which are celebrated on Sundays or on the ferial days and vigils that have a special Gospel (*Ult Evang. de Dom., Fer. major. et Vigil.*).

As Moses received the Law from God amid thunder and lightning, so in like manner, as tradition informs us, St. John wrote the beginning of his Gospel in the midst of thunder and lightning. Rightly, therefore, was he called by Jesus the Son of Thunder, since from the dark cloud of mysteries in fruitful showers he pours out the floods of wisdom which he had drunk from the heart of the Master. As the eagle, like an arrow, flies with open eyes toward the sun, thus does St. John soar directly upward to the light of the loftiest mysteries of God; . . . consequently, among the Evangelists he is designated by the eagle. (Laurent.)

The profound, magnificent contents of St. John's Gospel are in most beautiful harmony with the mysteries of faith celebrated on the altar. All the rays of revelation scattered in the Holy Books regarding Jesus Christ, are here found gathered into a focus. The virginal Evangelist announces, in his majestic flight, the eternal divinity of the Son; he calls Him the Creator of the universe, he exalts Him as the uncreated Light and Life, as well as the Source of all supernatural light and life, that is, as the Author of the order of grace. He then declares His incarnation [34] and magnifies the Incarnate as the only-begotten Son of the Father, in whom the glory of the divinity, the fullness of truth and grace, appeared visibly to man. This Gospel, therefore, depicts the divinity and the divine efficacy of Jesus Christ; it shows in what manner all the blessings of creation and redemption proceed from Him. It may also be appropriately applied to the Eucharistic Saviour; for the sacrifice and the Sacrament of the altar is truly a memorial of all the mysteries of the Incarnate Word. To the eye of faith, the glory of His divinity is revealed on the altar under foreign appearances; thence He pours out light and life, truth and grace into all susceptible hearts. But on the altar the world and darkness do not recognize Him; many do not receive Him; hence they do not become children of God, but remain in the shadow and night of death.

The sacrificial celebration was introduced by the longing cry of the Old Testament: "Send forth, O Lord, Thy light and Thy truth!" It could not be concluded in a more worthy and more sublime manner than with the powerful and dignified words of the New Testament: "The Word was made flesh, and dwelt among us;

[34] To adore the incarnate Son of God and honor the mystery of His Incarnation as the foundation of our forgiveness by and union with God, that is, our adoption, a genuflection is made at the words: *Et verbum caro factum est.*

and we saw His glory, the glory as of the Only-begotten of the Father, full of grace and truth." And the faithful, highly favored and strengthened anew by the celebration of the Holy Sacrifice, answer by the mouth of the acolyte: *Deo gratias* ("Thanks be to God"). Thus the Holy Sacrifice and the Communion celebration conclude with a simple expression of gratitude. And, in fact, this assuredly is the place in which joyfully to exclaim: "Thanks be to God for His unspeakable gift." (II Cor. 9:15.) For unutterably precious and glorious is the gift of God which we have received from the altar; inexhaustible and indescribable are the blessings that flow to us from the sacrifice and Communion.[35]

The *Deo gratias* is an admonition to the priest to continue for some time in silent and devout thanksgiving.[36]

[35] Frequently (at least in five Mass formulas) the Church recites the following Postcommunion: Repleti, Domine, muneribus sacris; da quaesumus, ut in gratiarum semper actione maneamus.

[36] The thanksgiving inserted in the missal by the Church (the *Canticum trium puerorum*, the psalm 150, the Our Father with several versicles and the three prayers) in the main dates from the Middle Ages; for already in the eleventh century Micrologus writes (chap. 22): Sacerdos sacris vestibus se exuens cantat "Hymnum trium puerorum" ... psalmum quoque "Laudate Dominum in sanctis ejus" in gratiarum actionem subjungens, cum "Pater noster" et versibus ad hoc competentibus, concludit eam cum oratione illa: "Deus qui tribus pueris." Soon after (chap. 23) he mentions the prayer *Actiones nostras*. The *Ordo XIV* of the fourteenth century has all the constituent parts of our *gratiarum actio* with the exception of the third prayer, *Da nobis*, which we do not come across at this point until the fifteenth century. The history and the figurative representation of the three youths in the fiery furnace, was for the Christians in the dark ages of persecution a source of comfort and encouragement. Likewise the canticle of praise intoned by the youths miraculously preserved amid the flames, was at all times highly prized and frequently used in the liturgy. According to Alcuin (*De Psalm. usu*, 1, n. 12) it is: omnibus laudibus laudabilior et Deo pro omnibus amabilior—melle et favo dulcior—hymnus hymnorum, in quo succincte et affatim melius quam in omnibus laudatur Deus. In consideration of the Mass and Communion celebration, in which the Lord has done such great things in him, the priest is filled with sentiments of joy, of jubilation, and of gratitude; hence he calls upon the entire creation, heaven and earth, all creatures, animate and inanimate, rational and irrational, to unite in his prayer of praise and thanksgiving, with him and for him to glorify the triune God, because of the blessings wherewith he and the whole world have again been favored from the altar. This same invitation to join in jubilant praise of God is continued in psalm 150, in which all voices, all the manifold praises of the other Psalms again meet in unison and exalted accord. *Omnis spiritus laudet Dominum*, "Let every spirit praise the Lord." The main object and chief fruit of the Eucharist is unquestionably *quaedam integritatis restauratio, quae con-*

812   SACRIFICE OF THE MASS

Thou oughtest not only to prepare thyself by devotion before Communion, but also to carefully keep thyself therein after receiving the Sacrament; neither is carefully guarding thyself afterward less required than devoutly preparing thyself before; for vigilance afterward

---

tinetur tum cupiditatum restinctione pro vita mortali, tum praeparatione ad gloriosam resurrectionem et immortalitatem pro vita futura (Franzelin). Hence the priest implores of God in the first and third prayers, that He would by the powerful breath of His grace suppress and extinguish in us the fire of concupiscence and of the passions, as He once changed the burning heat for the three youths in the furnace and the blessed Lawrence on the gridiron into a refreshing coolness. In the second prayer, he begs for the sanctification of his entire conduct, for self-sacrificing abandonment to God and to His service, as also the help of grace always to pray, to suffer and to labor for the salvation of souls. The first prayer is generally annexed in the liturgy (for example, on the Ember Saturdays) to the hymn of the three youths. The prayer of St. Lawrence was added, *quia hujus sacrificii fuit insignis minister et specialis advocatus offerentium sacrificium ad impetrandam puritatem et ne exurantur flamma vitiorum, eo vel maxime, quia ejus Oratio concordat cum prima Oratione, qua idem effectus ex sacrificio postulatur, et specialiter congruit hymno recitato trium puerorum, quibus mitigavit Deus flammas ignium* (Quarti, II, tit. 12). Yet the fervent priest is not satisfied with this short thanksgiving after the *sacrum convivium* of the Eucharist, as he knows the gift of God (John 4:19) and esteems it, and since he knows what has been presented to him by God (I Cor. 2:12). In silent meditation he is immersed in the unfathomable and, therefore, impenetrable mysteries he has just accomplished: his soul is thereby incited to interior and vocal acts of gratitude, of adoration, of astonishment, of praise, of self-annihilation, of petition, of atonement and of intercession. In the German mystics there are few prayers after Holy Communion. The reason may be because the German mystics understood full well and demanded of others, that after receiving the Blessed Sacrament the affections should be drawn from our inmost loving heart rather than from books. In consideration of this *excellentissima dilectio, summa dignatio, pietas maxima, misericordia infinita*, which the Saviour confers on the priest in the sacrament of the altar, a longer more fervent thanksgiving after Mass is for him an act of necessary homage and grateful love; at the same time it is, if well performed, a source of blessing and grace for the life and labors of the priest, that is, a specially powerful means of his own sanctification as well as of the salvation of the souls entrusted to his care. On the contrary, to leave the altar and to speak immediately after of worldly affairs without urgent necessity, and to occupy the mind with temporal cares, frivolity and distraction, infidelity and ingratitude directly after the holiest and most tremendous action, leads easily to that dangerous state of tepidity, which often passes into hardness and impenitence of heart (cf. Apoc. 3:15 f.). Then only will the Most Blessed Sacrament be for the priest *contra omnia mundi pericula firmamentum,* if he, as a man of mortification and prayer, overcomes the opposition of corrupt nature, in order that day after day he may bestow sufficient time and due care on the preparation for Mass as well as on the thanksgiving after Mass. (Cf. *Collect. Lacens.,* V, 165, 675, 902; Quarti, II, xi, 1–5; St. Teresa, *The Way of Perfection,* chap. 35.)

is the best preparation for again obtaining greater graces. For what renders a man very much indisposed to receive them, is to devote himself at once with all his soul to exterior things which claim his heart. Beware of much talk, remain in secret, and enjoy thy God; for thou hast Him, whom all the world cannot take from thee.

Who will help me, O Lord, to find Thee alone, that I may open my whole heart to Thee and enjoy Thee as my soul desireth? . . . This I pray for, this I desire, that I may be wholly united to Thee and may withdraw my heart from all created things, and, by Communion and the frequent celebrating of the Sacrifice of the Mass, may learn even more to relish heavenly and eternal things. Ah! Lord God, when shall I be wholly united to Thee and absorbed in Thee and altogether forgetful of myself? Thou in me, and I in Thee; grant that we both thus continue as one. . . . Verily, Thou art my peace-maker, in whom is sovereign peace and rest; outside of whom is labor and sorrow and endless misery. . . . What creature under heaven is so loved as the devout soul into whom God cometh, that He may feed her with His glorious flesh? . . . O infinite love, singularly bestowed upon man! But what return shall I make to the Lord for this grace, and for this so indescribable a love? There is nothing that I can give Him that will please Him better than my heart, and this will I wholly consecrate to Him and unite most intimately with His heart. Then all that is within me shall rejoice exceedingly when my soul shall be perfectly united to my God; then will He say to me: If thou wilt be with Me, I will be with thee; and I will answer Him: Vouchsafe, O Lord, to remain with me, and I will willingly be with Thee. This is my only desire, that my heart may be united to Thee.[37]

To the divine Lamb, who was sacrificed for us and who, with His blood, hath purchased us from all tribes and languages and peoples and nations, be praise and honor and benediction and thanksgiving and power and glory for all eternity. Amen.[38]

[37] *Imit. Christ.*, IV, xii, 4; xiii.
[38] Cf. Apoc. 5:6, 9; 19:14.

NOTE

THE NAME "MASS"

INNUMERABLE graces, incomprehensible wonders and mysteries are contained in the Holy Sacrifice of the Mass. This holy sacrifice is too great, too precious, and too glorious to be adequately expressed in words or to receive an appropriate name: it surpasses all created knowledge, it is unspeakably grand and sublime. Since the mind of man is too limited and his language too feeble to express perfectly the mystery of the Eucharistic sacrifice, there have been even from the most ancient times a number of titles bestowed upon it, each of which, however, brings into prominence but some aspect of the mystery, yet not one of them exhausts its unfathomably deep and rich contents.[1] Among these names that of *Missa* (Mass) deserves a more particular explanation, since it is the one most generally employed since the early part of the Middle Ages to designate the Eucharistic sacrifice.

The word *missa* (= *missio*, i.e. *dimissio*)[2] denotes the solemn

---

[1] Nomen dictum quasi notamen (*characteristic, mark*), quod nobis vocabulo suo res notas efficiat. Nisi enim nomen scieris, cognitio rerum perit (S. Isid., *Etymolog.*, I, V, 1). Such names are, for example: *collecta, dominicum, memoriale, communio, oblatio,* λειτουργία, εὐχαριστία, θυσία, λατρεία, σύναξις, μυσταγωγία, οἰκονομία. Cf. Bona, *Rer. liturg.*, I, chap. 3.

[2] Altogether untenable and therefore to be rejected is the etymological tracing of the word *missa* from the Hebrew (Deut. 16:10, *missah* = *tributum, oblatio*), or from the Greek (μύησις = *initiatio, mystica doctrina*), or from the German (*Mess* = *festum, congregatio*). *Missa* is also not to be taken as a participle of *mitto*, to which the substantive *concio* or *congregatio* (*concio vel congregatio missa*, i.e. *dimissa est*) or *oblatio* (*oblatio missa*, i.e. *transmissa est ad Deum*) would have to be supplied; *missa* is rather a later Latin substantive for *missio*, as similar derivative words often occur, for example: *remissa* = *remissio*; *collecta* = *collectio*; *ingressa* = *ingressio*; *oblata* = *oblatio*; *accessa* = *accessio*; *confessa* = *confessio*. As a substantive, *missa* was used in many meanings. It designated in the first place the dismissal at the close of divine service and also of secular assemblies; for the holy Bishop Avitus of

THE NAME "MASS"

dismissal or the departure of those present after the conclusion of divine service; this signification it even now retains in the well known concluding formula: *Ite, missa est* ("Go, it is the dismissal"). As long as the old baptismal and penitential discipline was in force, a twofold dismissal took place at the Eucharistic sacrifice: the catechumens and the penitents were permitted to assist along with the faithful at the readings or discourses, but were formally dismissed after the Gospel, or the sermon; [3] the faithful only were allowed to assist at the celebration of the sacrifice, and to them also the dismissal was formally announced at the conclusion of the service. The rite of the dismissal with blessing and prayer was called *missa;* the term at first found its way into the language of the people, and later on was written and introduced into the public liturgical service which was introduced and concluded with the dismissal.

The name *Missa*, which in the beginning signified only the people's dismissal from divine service, was thus transferred to the celebration of divine worship itself. This without doubt occurred already at an early period; but when this first happened cannot be historically ascertained. A certain proof for the use of the expression *missa* in the meaning of the liturgical celebration of the divine sacri-

---

Vienne writes (about the year 500) to the Burgundian king, Gundobald, that it was customary in churches and in judgment-halls to cry out *missa est* when the people were dismissed (*in ecclesiis palatiisque sive praetoriis missa fieri pronunciatur, cum populus ab observatione dimittitur*). Furthermore, the word *missa* was employed to designate the entire *Officium divinum*, as well as the separate readings and prayers during it; for example, *missae matutinae*, was the name given to Matins; Vespers were called *missae vespertinae*. In the Middle Ages we meet the word *missa* in the signification of feast and annual fair, since celebration of the sacrifice was the principal part of the festivity, and since the people flocked together at the festivals for buying and selling. The view already advanced and recently defended by Müller in his pamphlet, *Missa, Ursprung und Bedeutung der Benennung*, that *missa* is an ancient Latin sacrificial name and originally signified the same as *oblatio*, is unfounded. Cf. Bellarmin., *De Missa*, I, chap. 1; Benedict. XIV, *De sacr. Miss. sacrif.*, II, chap. 1; P. Rottmanner, O. S. B., in the *Tübinger Quartalschrift*, 1889.

[3] Missa (*dismissal*), tempore sacrificii, est quando catechumeni foras mittuntur, clamante levita: "Si quis catechumenus remansit, exeat foras," et inde missa, quia sacramentis altaris interesse non possunt, qui nondum regenerati noscuntur (S. Isidor., *Etymol.*, VI, chap. 19, n. 4). Missa (*the dismissal*) catechumenorum fiebat ante actionem Sacramentorum: missa (*the dismissal*) fidelium post confectionem et participationem eorundem Sacramentorum (*mysteries*) (Flor. Diac., *De expos. Miss.*, n. 131).

fice is first met with in the writings of St. Ambrose (d. 397);[4] from his manner of speaking, it is evident that the word *missa* was at that time not a newly coined expression, but a traditional designation of the celebration of the Eucharistic sacrifice.

The transfer of the expression *missa* to designate the most holy and sublime sacrifice is at first sight strange indeed, but is, however, susceptible of explanation. At the period when the name *Missa* was first applied to the celebration of the Eucharistic mystery, the strictest discipline of secrecy was in force. This mode of calling the Holy Sacrifice was well fitted to conceal the holy mysteries from the uninitiated. Therefore the dismissals in use at that period are not to be regarded as implying "unessential rulings of Church discipline," but as important acts which were conducted with a certain degree of solemnity. After an appropriate prayer of thanksgiving and a blessing, the dismissal was liturgically announced by the deacon's exclaiming: *Ite, missa est.* The first dismissal, which was intended for the uninitiated, characterized the subsequent celebration as mysterious, and gave those who remained to understand what purity was required to assist at the sacrifice and to receive the sacrificial food. Not less venerable was the liturgical dismissal of the faithful; they were thereby admonished not to depart from the house of God without permission and not to return to the daily duties of their calling until they had rendered unto God the honor and adoration due to Him and had been enriched with the fullness of heavenly gifts and blessings.[5]

[4] Sequenti die (erat autem Dominica), post lectiones (sc. sacrae Scripturae) atque tractatum (sc. expositionem lectionis vel concionem), dimissis catechumenis, symbolum aliquibus competentibus in baptisteriis tradebam basilicae. Illic nuntiatum est mihi comperto quod ad Portianam basilicam de palatio decanos (= lictores) misissent et vela suspenderent, populi partem eo pergere. Ego tamen mansi in munere, *Missam* facere coepi. Dum offero, raptum cognovi a populo Castulum quemdam (S. Ambr., *Epistol.*, 20, n. 4 f.).

[5] "The Latins have given this name (*Missa*) to the sacrifice because, when the time of the offering was reached, the catechumens, the penitents, and the possessed, and at the end all the faithful, were dismissed by a solemn proclamation. . . . This solemn exclusion of these three kinds of persons inspired the people with an exalted idea of the holy mysteries, because it showed them how great a purity is required for assisting thereat, and much more still for participating therein. The dismissal of the faithful at the end of the service was not less venerable, because it gave them to understand that they should not go out of the church without leave, and that the Church did not dismiss her children until she had filled them with veneration for the majesty of the

In addition to this explanation, the most common and reliable, there is still another that deserves mention, one which was held in esteem especially by the liturgists of the Middle Ages. It runs thus: the Eucharistic sacrifice is called *Missa* because in it there is a sending forth (*missa = transmissio*) from earth to heaven and from heaven to earth. The Church sends up to the throne of God by the ministry of the priest the Eucharistic sacrifice and prayers and the necessities and desires of the faithful; God in return sends down upon men the riches of heavenly grace and blessing. Or we may put it this way: Christ is sent into the world by the Father as a sacrifice, and in turn He is sent back again to heaven by the faithful as a sacrifice, in order to reconcile us to the Father and to procure for us all blessings.[6] This signification of *missa* is implied by the very nature of the thing, and thus far undoubtedly contains truth; but this point of view probably did not determine the selection of the expression *missa* to designate the holy sacrifice: in other words, the faithful of the first ages did not choose the word *missa* to express that in the sacrifice the above-mentioned mission or sending forth from God to man and from man to God takes place; only later was this explanation given to the word.[7]

---

holy mysteries and the graces accompanying their reception; so that they returned to their ordinary occupations, bearing in mind that the Church, which had dismissed them, admonished them thereby to perform them as religiously as their vocation called for, and with the spirit with which they were filled" (Bossuet, *Sur les prières de la Messe. Oeuvres complètes*, IV [Bar-le-Duc 1870], q. 447).

[6] Sacrosanctum altaris mysterium idcirco missa dicitur, quia ad placationem et solutionem inimicitiarum quae erant inter Deum et homines, sola valens et idonea missio est (Rupert. Tuitiens., *De divin. off.*, II, chap. 10). Dicitur autem Missa a mittendo, et repraesentat legationem inter homines et Deum; Deus enim mittit Filium suum Christum in altare, et iterum mittit Ecclesia fidelis eundem Christum ad Patrem, ut pro nobis intercedat (S. Bonavent., *Expos. Miss.*, chap. 2). Missa dicitur, quia in hoc officio repraesentatur missio Christi a sinu Patris in mundum redimendum, i.e. incarnatio, et missio Christi a mundo ad Patrem placandum, scilicet passio (Sicardus, *Mitral.*, III, chap. 1).

[7] Prima etymologia verior videtur, altera ad pietatem propensior (Benedict. XIV, *De Miss. sacrif.*, II, chap. 1, n. 5).

SOURCES

Albertus Magnus, *Summa de officio Missae.*
Amalarius Metensis, *De officiis ecclesiasticis libri IV* (Migne, P. L., CV, 985–1242).
Arias, Francis, S.J., *Thesaurus inexhaustus bonorum, quae in Christo habemus,* 1652.
Arriaga, Rodríguez de, S.J., *Disputationes theologicae in Summam s. Thomae,* 1643–55.
Auber, M. l'abbé, *Histoire et Théorie du Symbolisme religieux,* 1870, 4 vols.
Bacuez, L., *Du divin sacrifice et du prêtre qui le célèbre,* 1888.
Baldassari, Anthony, *La sacra Liturgia,* 1715.
Becanus, Martin, S.J., *Summa theologiae scholasticae,* 1640.
Bechoffen, John, O.S.A., *Quadruplex Missalis expositio, literalis scil., allegorica, tropologica et anagogica,* 1512.
Beleth, Jean, *Rationale divinorum officiorum* (Migne, P. L., CCII, 14–166).
Bellarmine, Robert Cardinal, S.J., *De controversiis fidei adversus huius temporis haereticos,* 1601.
Benedict XIV, *De sacrosancto Missae sacrificio* (Migne, *Theologiae cursus completus,* vol. 23).
Bernard, M., *Cours de Liturgie Romaine,* 1884.
Berthold (of Chiemsee), *Tewtsch Rational über das Ambt heiliger Mess,* 1535.
Bickell, Gustav, *Messe und Pascha,* 1872.
Biel, Gabriel, *Sacri canonis Missae tam mystica quam literalis expositio,* 1515.
Bona, John Cardinal, O.C., *Rerum liturgicarum libri duo,* 1763.
—— *De sacrificio Missae tractatus asceticus,* 1846.
Bonaventure, St., *Opera omnia,* 1883–91.
Bossuet, *Oeuvres complètes,* 1870.
Bourbon, A., *Introduction aux cérémonies Romaines,* 1864.
Buathier, J. M., *Le sacrifice dans le dogme catholique et dans la vie chrétienne,* 1889.

SOURCES

Cavalieri, John M., O.S.A., *Opera omnia liturgica seu Commentaria in authentica S. R. C. decreta*, 1764, 5 vols.

Clichtoveus, Jodocus, *Elucidatorium ecclesiasticum, ad officium Ecclesiae pertinentia planius exponens et quatuor libros complectens*, 1548.

Collectio Lacensis. *Acta et decreta sacrorum conciliorum recentiorum*, 1870–90, 7 vols.

Coninck, Giles de, S.J., *De sacramentis accensuris*, 1624.

Contenson, Vincent, O.P., *Theologiae mentis et cordis*, 1875.

Corblet, J., *Histoire dogmatique, liturgique et archéologique du sacrement de l'Eucharistie*, 1885.

Denys the Carthusian, *Opera minora*, 1532, 2 vols.

Duchesne, Louis, *Origines du culte chrétien*, 1889.

Dufrène, P. J., S.J., *Sacerdos numini eucharistico devotus*, 1754.

Durandus, William, *Rationale sive Enchiridion divinorum officiorum*, 1561.

Du Saussay, Andrew, *Panoplia sacerdotalis seu de venerando sacerdotum habitu libri 14*, 1653.

Eberhard, Matthew, *Kanzelvorträge*, 1877.

Ebner, Adalbert, *Quellen und Forschungen zur Geschichte und Kunstgeschichte des Missale Romanum im Mittelalter*, 1896.

Einig, P., *Tractatus de ss. Eucharistiae mysterio*, 1888.

Florus (deacon of Lyons), *Opusculum de expositione Missae* (Migne, P. L., CLX, 1053–70).

Fornici, I., *Institutiones liturgicae*, 1852.

Franzelin, John Cardinal, S.J., *Tractatus de ss. Eucharistiae sacramento et sacrificio*, 1873.

Gautier, L., *Histoire de la poésie liturgique du moyen âge. Les Tropes*, 1886.

Gavanti-Merati, *Thesaurus sacrorum rituum*, 1763, 2 vols.

Gerbert, M., O.S.B., *Vetus Liturgia Alemannica*, 1776.

Gouda, William de, O.F.M., *Expositio mysteriorum Missae et verus modus rite celebrandi*.

Grancolas, J. J., *Traité de la Messe et de l'Office divin*, 1713.

Guyetus, C., S.J., *Heortologia sive de festis propriis locorum et ecclesiarum*, 1726.

Hazé, I. H., *De sensu ceremoniarum Missae brevis explicatio*, 1869.

Hefele, Karl Joseph, *Beiträge zur Kirchengeschichte, Archäologie und Liturgik*, 1864, 2 vols.

Henno, Francis, O.F.M., *Theologia dogmatica, moralis et scholastica*, 1718.

Herdt, Pierre de, *Sacrae Liturgiae praxis*, 1883.

Hergenröther, Philip, *Die Eucharistie als Opfer*, 1868.

Hildebert, *Liber de expositione Missae; Versus de mysterio Missae* (Migne, *P. L.*, CLXXI, 1153–95).
Hildegard, St., *Scivias sive visionum ac revelationum libri III* (Migne, *P. L.*, CXCVII, 383–738).
Hittorpius, M., *De divinis catholicae Ecclesiae officiis ac ministeriis varii vetustorum aliquot Ecclesiae Patrum ac Scriptorum libri*, 1568.
Honorius of Autun, *Gemma animae sive de divinis officiis et antiquo ritu Missarum, etc.* (Migne, *P. L.*, CLXXII, 543–737).
―― *Sacramentarium, seu de causis et significatu mystico rituum divini in ecclesia officii liber* (*ibid.*, pp. 737–806).
Hugo, Cardinal, O.P., *Expositio Missae*, 1507.
Innocent III, *De sacro altaris mysterio libri IV* (Migne, *P. L.*, CXLVII, 773–914).
Ioannes, Episcopus Abrincensis, *Liber de officiis ecclesiasticis* (Migne, *P. L.*, CXLVII, 15 ff.).
Jakob, G., *Die Kunst im Dienste der Kirche*, 1885.
Jobin, *Études sur les lampes du Saint-Sacrement et le luminaire ecclésiastique*, 1870.
Kenrick, Francis P., *Theologia dogmatica*, 1858.
Kneip, N., *Erklärung des heiligen Messopfers*, 1876.
Knoll, Albert, O.F.M. Cap., *Institutiones theologiae theoreticae*, 1865.
Krazer, August, O.P., *De apostolicis necnon antiquis Ecclesiae occidentalis liturgiis liber singularis*, 1786.
Kreuser, *Das Heilige Messopfer geschichtlich erklärt*, 1854.
Lambrecht, *De sanctissimo Missae sacrificio*, 1875.
Lapini, P. F., *La Liturgia studiata nelle sue relazioni colle scienze sacre*, 1889.
Laurent, J., *Christologische Predigten*, 1860.
Lebrun, Pierre, *Explication littéraire, historique et dogmatique des prières et des cérémonies de la messe*, 1860.
Le Courtier, F. J., *Manuel de la Messe ou Explication des prières et des cérémonies du saint sacrifice*, 1864.
Lehmkuhl, August, S.J., *Theologia moralis*, 1888.
Lohner, T., S.J., *Instructio practica primo de Missae sacrificio*, 1717.
Lüft, J. B., *Liturgik*, 1844–47.
Lugo, John Cardinal de, S.J., *Tractatus de venerabili Eucharistiae sacramento* (Migne, *Theologiae cursus completus*, vol. 23).
Mabillon, Jean, O.S.B., *De Liturgia Gallicana libri III* (Migne, *P. L.*, LXXII, 99 ff.).
―― *In Ordinem Romanum commentarius praevius* (Migne, *P. L.*, LXXVIII, 851 ff.).

Menne, Xavier, *Das Allerheiligste Sakrament des Altars als Opfer*, 1876.
Michael (bishop of Mersburg), *Ein Vergissmeinnicht*, ed. by Hasak, 1884.
Micrologus, *De ecclesiasticis observationibus* (Migne, P. L., CLI, 973–1022).
Müller, Ernest, *Theologia moralis*, 1876.
Müller, Michael, C.SS.R., *The Holy Mass; the Sacrifice for the Living and the Dead*, 1874.
Muratori, *De rebus liturgicis dissertatio* (Migne, P. L., LXXIV, 847 ff.).
Noël, *Instructions sur la Liturgie*, 1861, 5 vols.
Odo of Cambrai, *Expositio in Canonem Missae*, (Migne, P. L., CLX, 1053–70).
Olier, M., *Explication des cérémonies de la grand' Messe de paroisse*, 1858.
Olivier, J. H., *Solutions théologiques et liturgiques touchant le saint sacrifice de la Messe*, 1873.
Orsi, O.P., *Dissertatio theologica de invocatione Spiritus sancti in Liturgiis Graecorum et Orientalium*, 1731.
Oswald, J. H., *Die dogmatische Lehre von den Sacramenten*, 1877.
Pasqualigo, Z., *De sacrificio Novae Legis quaestiones theologicae, morales, juridicae*, 1662, 2 vols.
Patroni, R., *Lesioni di sacra Liturgia ossia Esposizione letterale, mistica, storica e ceremoniale della Messa*, 1881.
Piazza, C. B., *L'Iride sacra*, 1682.
Platelius, J., S.J., *Synopsis totius cursus theologici*, 1688.
Pouget, *Institutiones catholicae in modum catecheseos*, 1764, 2 vols.
Probst, Ferdinand, *Liturgie der drei ersten christlichen Jahrhunderte*, 1870.
—— *Verwaltung des Hohepriesterlichen Amtes*, 1881.
—— *Die ältesten römischen Sacramentarien und Ordines*, 1892.
—— *Die Liturgie des vierten Jahrhunderts und deren Reform*, 1893.
—— *Die abendländische Messe vom 5ten bis zum 8ten Jahrhundert*, 1896.
Quadt, M. W., *Die Liturgie der Quatembertage*, 1869.
Quarti, P. M., *Rubricae Missalis Romani commentariis illustratae*, 1727.
Rabanus Maurus, *De clericorum institutione libri III* (Migne, P. L., CVII, 295–419).
Raffray, M. X., *Beautés du culte catholique*, 1858.
Renaudotius, Eusebius, *Liturgiarum orientalium collectio*, 1847, 2 vols.
Rigler, P. P., *Pastoralis liturgica seu intelligentia et regula ministerii liturgici*, 1864.
Romsée, T., *Opera liturgica*, 1838.

Rupert of Deutz (*Tuitiensis*), O.S.B., *De divinis officiis libri XII* (Migne, P. L., CLXX, 13–332).
Sanchez, G., S.J., *Spiritualis thesaurus Missae*, 1620.
Sarnelli, P., *Lettere ecclesiastiche*, 1716.
Sauter, O.S.B., *Das hl. Messopfer*, 1894.
Scouville, Philip, S.J., *Sancta sanctorum sancte tractandi sive religiose sacrificandi methodus*, 1713.
Sicard of Cremona, *Mitrale sive de officiis ecclesiasticis Summa* (Migne, P. L., CCXIII, 13–434).
Sporer, O.F.M., *Theologiae moralis sacramentalis Pars II. De sacerdotio, sacrificio et sacramento Eucharistiae*, 1688.
Stella, F., *Institutiones Liturgicae*, 1895.
Stentrup, F., S.J., *De Verbo incarnato*, 1882–89, 4 vols.
Stephen of Autun, *Tractatus de sacramento altaris* (Migne, P. L., CLXXII, 1273–1308).
Stöckl, A., *Das Opfer nach seinem Wesen und nach seiner Geschichte*, 1861.
Suarez, F., S.J., *Commentaria ac disputationes in tertiam partem s. Thomae; De sacramento Eucharistiae et de Missae sacrificio*, 1861.
Sylvius, F., *Commentarius in tertiam partem s. Thomae Aquinatis*, 1622.
Tanner, Adam, S.J., *Theologia scholastica*, 1627.
Tapfer, A., *Analytico-literalis expositio incruenti Missae sacrificii secundum ritum Romanum*, 1828.
Thalhofer, V., *Das Opfer des Alten und Neuen Bundes*, 1870.
—— *Handbuch der katholischen Liturgik*, 1883–90.
Thomas Aquinas, St., *Summa theologica*.
Toletus, Francis Cardinal, S.J., *In Summam theologiae s. Thomae Aquinatis enarratio*.
Tournely, H., *Cursum theologicus scholastico-dogmaticus et moralis*, 1752.
Triplex expositio (literalis, mystica et practica) totius Missae, 1866.
Ulloa, John de, S.J., *Theologia scholastica*, 1719.
Valentia, Gregory de, S.J., *Commentaria theologica*, 1609.
Van der Burg, *Brevis elucidatio totius Missae*, 1860.
Vasquez, G., S.J., *Commentaria ac disputationes in tertiam partem s. Thomae*, 1631.
Walafrid Strabo, *Liber de exordiis et incrementis quarundam in observationibus ecclesiasticis rerum*, 1890 (Migne, P.L., CXIV, 919 ff.).
Wiseman, Nicholas Cardinal, "On Prayer and Prayer-Books," *Essays on Various Subjects* (vol. 2).
Zaccaria, F., S.J., *Onomasticon rituale selectum*, 1787.
—— *Bibliotheca ritualis*, 1776.

Index

INDEX

Abel: figure of Christ, 694; sacrifice of, 26, 691, 693 f.; St. Ambrose on, 694
Ablutio, 781 note
Ablution of the fingers, 781 note, 785 f.: amount of water, 781 note; development of the rite, 782 note; prayer at, 785 f. and notes
Abraham, sacrifice of, 691, 693-95: depicted in the catacombs, 118-20; figure of the Eucharist, 118-20; Laurent on, 695
Absolom and David, 397
Absolutio, 409 f. notes
Absolution before Communion of the faithful, 778
Accendat in nobis, 581
Acceptabilis (*oblatio*), 663 and note
Accipere, 770 note
Acolytes, 392 note
Actio (canon), 647 f. and note
Adam and Christ, 31
Adjutorium nostrum, 402 and note
Adoramus te, 443
Adorare, 441 f. note
Adoration
  as act of religion, 9 f.
  of Christ's humanity, 9 f. note
  Christ's infinite sacrifice of, 58
  church decoration and, 263 f.
  in the Collects, 464
  due to God Alone, 9 f., 443
  duties of angels and saints, 164
  at the Elevation, 678-80 and note
  an end of sacrifice, 18 f.
  of the Eucharistic Christ, 678-80 and note
  excellence of, 13 f.
  infinite: by the Mass, 165-67, 173, 220 f.
  Mass as sacrifice of, 145 f., 149, 165-68, 173, 195 f., 644 f.
  necessity of, 6, 9 f.
  Old Testament sacrifice of, 26 f. and note
  in our life, 168
  symbolized by incense, 419, 421 f.

Adoration (*continued*)
  symbolized by the candle, 299
  in the word alleluja, 498 f.
Adscriptio (*oblatio*), 662 and notes
Adstantes, in the Mozarabic rite, 644 note
Advent, 219
  Collects during, 476
  Gloria sung during, 440 note
  joyful character of, 496
  Lent and, 496
  penitential spirit of, 496
  spirit during, 356
Aequum (in the Preface), 604
Agatha, St., 716, 718 f. note: and St. Lucy, 719 note; on service of God, 337
Agnes, St., 716, 719 note: St. Ambrose on, 719 note; on treasures of grace, 461; on virginity, 251
Agnus Dei, 100, 748-53
  in the Ambrosian rite, 753 note
  development of, 749 and notes
  kiss of peace and, 749
  peace petitioned in, 748
  in Requiem Masses, 752 f.
  striking of the breast, 750
Alb, 323-26: decorations on, 323 f. note; symbolism of, 318, 324-26; worn by all clerics, 330 note; worn in choir, 330 note
Albigensians, 360 note
Alexander, St.: inscription on tomb of, 120
Alexander I, St. (pope), 715 and note
All Saints, Creed recited on feast of, 530
All Souls' Day, 209: purple vestments on, 346 note
Alleluja, 496-501
  added to the Introit, 429
  during Eastertide, 489, 493, 497, 499 f.
  expression of joy, 491-93, 496 f., 498 note, 499-502
  farewell to the, 497 and note
  on feast of the Ascension, 500 f.

825

Alleluja (*continued*)
   the Gradual and the, 491-93, 496 f.:
      during Easter week, 500 f.
   in the Greek liturgy, 498 note
   in liturgy for the dead, 498 note
   meaning of the word, 498 f.
   old customs concerning, 497 note, 498
      note
   St. Jerome on, 498 note
Aloysius, St.: Postcommunion on feast
   of, 793
Alphonsus Liguori, St.: on the *Gloria Patri*, 401; intercession of Christ, 193 f.; intercession of the angels, 194
Altar
   breast of St. Lucian as, 271
   in the figurative sense, 25
   in heaven, 700, 702
   in the human heart, 280 f. and note
   of the Last Supper, 271
   sacrifice and, 20: in Christianity, 82; the Fathers on, 105; in heaven, 700
   spiritual, 280 note
   "table of devils," 101 f.
Altar, Christian
   beauty of, 263, 272: Laurent on, 265
   candles on, 286 and notes
   in the catacombs, 272
   consecration of, 229, 231, 274-78, 283, 422: loss of, 273 note, 274, 275 f. note; St. Gregory of Nyssa on, 274 note
   crib and, 625: St. Chrysostom on, 572 note
   crucifix on, 287 f.
   destruction of, 272
   dressing and decoration of, 283-95
   elevation of, 274
   enclosing of relics, 276-78
   erection of, 272
   form of a tomb, 272 f.
   frons of, 286
   holiness of, 274 note, 281 f., 424, 455 note
   holy of holies, 415 n., 424
   immovable, 272 f. and note, 275 note
   incensing of; see Incensing
   kissing of; see Kissing of the altar
   Laurent on, 265
   loss of consecration, 273 note, 274, 275 f. note
   a Mount Calvary, 143, 239, 274, 278, 287, 665
   names for, 270 note
   necessity of, 270 f.
   parts of, 273

Altar, Christian (*continued*)
   portable, 273 f. and note, 275 note, 276 note
   privileged, 160 note, 208
   pulpit and, 365, 480
   refuge of virgins, 254 and note
   sepulcher of, 273 and note: violation of, 276 note
   sides of, 430 note: parts of the Mass read on, 790 note
   of stone, 272 f. and note, 279
   stripping of, 285
   symbol of Christ, 179 f. and note, 285, 456
   symbolism of, 278-81
   a table, 271 ff.
   title of, 275 note, 289 note
   veneration for, 455 note
   of wood, 271 f.
Altar bell, 310 f. and notes
Altar cards, 288 and note, 290 note
Altar cloths, 283-85: Laurent on, 265; St. Optatus on, 284; symbolism of, 285
Altar steps, 274 note
Altar stone, 273 f. and notes: crosses in, 554 f. and note; symbol of Christ, 455
Altarpiece, 289 note
Amalarius, number of Collects, 473 note
Amalek, Moses' victory over, 471
Ambo, 483 and note, 489
Ambrose, St.
   angels at Mass, 112, 698
   death of Abel, 694
   incensing the altar, 419 note
   martyrdom and the Mass, 277
   the Mass a sacrifice, 112 f.
   relics in the altar, 277
   St. Agnes, 719 note
   virginity, 254 note, 280 note
Ambrosian rite, 373 note
   Agnus Dei in, 753 note
   compared with the Roman, 373 note
   the dismissal, 799 note
   Dominus vobiscum in, 413 note
   Embolism in, 734 note
   Introit in, 428 note
   Kyrie eleison in, 433 note
   lessons in, 482 note
   Pater noster in, 729 note, 730 note
   prayer at the mingling of the elements, 746
   Secreta in, 592 note
Amen, 469 f. and notes, 595: at the end of the Canon, 721 note, 726; at the

INDEX

Amen (continued)
  Pater noster, 733 and note; at the *Requiescant in pace*, 801; after the Secreta, 594 f.; at the sign of the cross, 395
Amice, 319-23: kissing of, 320; *parura* on, 324 note; symbolism of, 318, 320-23
Amictus, 319 note
Ampula, 309 note
Anastasia, St., 655 note, 716 and note
Anastasius I, St. (pope): standing at the Gospel, 518 f. note
Andrew, St.: Acts of, 106 and note; invoked in the Embolism, 736 and note; the Mass a sacrifice, 106
Angel of the Mass, 698 f. and note
Angela of Foligno, Blessed, 517
Angelic Hymn, 437, 440 notes, 450, 459; *see also* Gloria
Angels, 406
  appearance in white, 347
  at Bethlehem, 510
  choirs of, 606 and note
  at Christ's ascension, 501
  Creed recited on feasts of, 530
  duties of, 530, 698
  the Gloria sung by, 440 f.
  God praised by, 164, 166, 440 f., 443, 606-8
  guardian, 699
  images of, 289 note
  implored in the *Supplices te*, 696-99, 701 f.
  intercession of, 194
  King of, 606 f.
  man's equality to, 337
  purity of, 349
  St. Gregory on, 680
  singing of alleluja, 498
  singing of the Sanctus, 614 f. and note, 617
  Suso on, 350
  before the throne of God, 696
  united with the saints, 614 f. note
  white vestments and, 349
Angels present at Mass, 697-99 and notes
  at the Consecration, 678 and note
  St. Ambrose on, 112, 698
  St. Chrysostom on, 391, 697 f.
  St. Gregory on, 702
  St. Hildegard on, 678 note
  Tertullian on, 698
Angelus, 607, 699 f. note
Animetta, 305 note
Annunciation, feast of, 527 f. note
Anointing of kings, 231

Anselm, St.: Author of *Oratio s. Ambrosii*, 574 note
Antependium, 286 and note
Antiphon: at the foot of the altar, 395 f.; of the Introit, 428 f. and notes
Antiphona, 395 note
Antiphonarium, 374 note
Antistes, 639 note; *see also* Bishop
Apostles
  authors of the Apostles' Creed, 525
  bishops as successors of, 459 f.
  Creed recited on feasts of, 530
  death of, 652
  Mass celebrated by, 359 note, 370 f.
  mentioned in the *Nobis quoque*, 714 f. and notes
  named in the Canon, 629, 650 note, 651 f. and note
  origin of the Preface, 597
  prayers for the dead, 704 f.
  preaching of, 652
  Preface for feasts of, 616 and note
  self-sacrifice of, 251
Apostles' Creed, 525
Apostolic Constitutions
  the dismissal, 799 note
  Gloria in, 438 note
  Gradual chants, 489 f.
  liturgical rite in, 371 note
  the Mass a sacrifice, 116
  Sanctus in, 612 note
  Supplices te and, 699 note
  washing of the hands, 582
Appearance, exterior: at the altar, 381 f.
Application of the fruits of the Mass, 202 note, 204-14; *see also* Fruits of the Mass, Ministerial fruits
Appreciation for the Mass, 162
Arabian language, 359 note
Aramean, used on the cross, 359 note
Arcanum, discipline of, 105, 816
Archangels, 666 note
Archangelus, 405 note
Armenian language, 359 note, 364 note
Armenian rite, unleavened bread use in, 545 note
Artemius and St. Peter, 715 note
Ascension, feast of: the Alleluja 500 f.; Collect on, 476; white vestments on, 349
Ascension of Christ: blessing at, 807 f.; commemorated in the *Unde et memores*, 285 f.; joy over the, 500 f.; part in redemption, 65 note; renewed in the Mass, 587
Asceticism, self-sacrifice and, 235 f.

828 INDEX

Ash Wednesday, 229
Ashes, blessing of, 229 f.
Asterisk in the Greek rite, 572 note
Athanasius, St.: indwelling of the Holy Ghost, 561
Atonement
  as an act of religion, 10
  Christ's sacrifice of, 30 ff., 52 f., 57 ff., 67
  an end of sacrifice, 18 f.
  expressed by sacrifice, 58
  infinite, 67
  Mass as sacrifice of, 146, 149 f., 173-86, 195 f., 763: in ancient liturgies, 175 f.; for averting punishments, 184 f.; the Fathers on, 176; necessity of, 186 f.; for remission of sin, 176-81; for remission of temporal punishment, 181-84, 208
  Memento of the Living and, 646
  necessity of, 10, 221
  Old Testament sacrifice of, 27 and note, 174
  petition and, 177 ff., 186, 208
Attendance at Mass: degrees of, 127; dispositions for, 624 f.; manner of, 144
Attendants at Mass
  benefit for, 160 f.
  commemorated at Mass, 643 f.
  conduct of, 110
  fruitful participation of, 643 f.
  participation in the fruits, 152
  requirements for, 106
  special sacrificial fruit, 200 ff., 559
Aufer a nobis, 415
Augustine, St.
  chants at Mass, 488
  Church offered at Mass, 141
  the Eucharistic sacrifice, 113
  exterior and interior worship, 380
  Gradual chants, 490
  mystical body, 141
  peace, 753: definition of, 636
  prayers for the dead, 176
  progress of the Church, 241
  propitiatory character of the Mass, 176
  time for granting petitions, 190
Austria, emperor of, 629 note
Avarice and church decoration, 266
Averting of God's wrath, 184 ff., 194, 566
Avignon, the popes in, 425, 427
Azymus panis, 545 note

Babylonian Captivity, 364 note
Balaeus (the Syrian): on the Eucharist, 108; prayers for the dead, 207
Balteus, 326 note
Banquet, sacrificial; *see* Eucharist, Sacrificial banquet
Baptism, 228, 707: beginning of salvation, 647; promises at, 647; remission of punishment and, 183; symbolized by water from Christ's side, 549
Barnabas, St., 714 f. and note
Basil, St.: liturgy of, 175; the Mass a sacrifice, 117
Basin for the hands, 310 note
Beata passio, 686
Beatific vision, 713: merited by Christ, 60 f.
Beauty of liturgical worship, 220, 223, 261-66, 375 f., 379
  Bossuet on, 376 f. note
  Faber on, 375
  Laurent on, 265
  Nepotian and, 269
  Oswald on, 376
  Wiseman on, 375 f.
Bede, St.: on martyrs and confessors, 250
Bee, symbol of virginity, 295
Beeswax, 294 f. and notes
Bells: for the altar, 310 f. and notes; blessing of, 229, 331 note; Laurent on, 265; ringing of, 310 note
Benedicamus Domino, 799-801 and notes
Benedicere, 441 f. note, 571 and note
Benedicimus te, 442 f. and note
Benedict, St.: Amen at the Gospel, 521; death of, 347 f.
Benedict VIII (pope), adoption of the Creed, 527
Benedictio, 441 f. and note
Benedictio constitutiva, 267 note, 316
Benedictio invocativa, 267 note
Benedictus qui venit, 612 and notes: sign of the cross at, 614 and note
Benefactor of a gift, 169
Berengarius, 678 f. note
Bernard, St.: ingratitude, 176; substitution of graces, 190
Berno of Reichenau (abbot), 526
Berthold, on the Secreta, 592 notes
Bethlehem, singing of angels at, 440 f. and notes
Bible; *see* Scripture
Biretta, 390 note
Bishop of the diocese, named in the Canon, 639 f. and notes
Bishops
  blessing at the end of Mass, 460, 804 note
  and blessing of vestments, 316 note

Bishops (*continued*)
  consecration of, 194, 229: concelebration at, 684 note; the *Hanc igitur*, 656 note
  government of the Church by, 638
  Pax vobis, 459 f. and notes
  powers of, 231, 460
  prayers for, 638-40 and notes
  putting on the maniple, 330 note
  representatives of Christ, 459
  stole worn by, 333 f. and notes, 336
  successors of the apostles, 459 f.
Black garments of the clergy, 357 note
Black vestments: symbolism of, 357 f.; use of, 346 notes, 355 note, 357 f.
Blessed in heaven, 68: God praised by, 164, 166; reward of, 808; *see also* Saints
Blessed Sacrament, incensing of, 422 f. and note, 577 f. and note
Blessed Virgin, 405
  Assumption of, 492
  in the *Communicantes*, 650 f.
  Creed recited on feasts of, 529 f.
  Dominus vobiscum and, 456 note
  Epistles in Masses of, 486
  glories of, 650 f.
  God praised by, 164
  honored in the Mass, 222
  Incarnation of Christ and, 572 f.
  invoked in the Embolism, 736
  maternity of, 651
  merits of, 417
  model of priests, 133 f., 233
  offering of, 147
  sorrows of: in the *Stabat matter*, 506 and note
  splendor of, 349
  Suso on, 349
  titles of, 349
  virginity of, 651
  virtues of, 650 f.
  white vestments on feasts of, 349
Blessing (*see also* Consecration [a sacramental])
  of bells, 229, 331 note
  by bishops, 460
  of bread: at the consecration, 670; at the Last Supper, 670
  of candles, 229 f., 294 note: on Candlemas Day, 296
  of a cemetery, 229, 707 note
  by Christ: at the Ascension, 807 f.; at the Last Judgment, 807 f.; at the Last Supper, 670; with the sign of the cross, 670 note

Blessing (*continued*)
  consecration and, 267 note
  the Consecration as a, 723 f.
  of the corporal, 305 note, 307
  effected by the sign of the cross, 689, 690 note
  effects of, 267 note
  efficacy of, 571, 806
  at the Embolism, 737 note
  at the end of the Canon, 724 and note
  after the Epistle, 484 note
  of fire, 296
  of first fruits, 724 note
  of food, 229
  of the golden rose, 291 f. and note
  before the Gospel, 484 f.
  of holy oil, 229 f., 724
  implored in the *Quam oblationem*, 661, 664 f.
  of incense, 229, 422 f. and notes: at the Offertory, 575 f.
  of lambs, 719 note
  of liturgical objects, 267 f. and notes
  Mass as a source of, 645
  meaning of the word, 571 and note
  in the Old Testament, 807
  of the pall, 305 note, 307
  of palms, 62, 230, 613 f.: vestments worn at, 330 f. note
  at the receiving of the chalice, 777
  at the receiving of the host, 773
  symbolized by signs of the cross, 690 and note
  thanksgiving and, 671
  of vestments, 315 f. and notes
  of water, 229 f.: at the Offertory, 560
  of wine: at the Consecration, 674; at the Last Supper, 674
Blessing at the end of Mass, 801 f., 804-9
  by a bishop, 460, 804 note
  ceremonies at, 804 f. and note
  efficacy of, 806 f.
  figure of Christ's blessing, 807 f.
  historical development, 802 f., 804 note
  kissing of the altar and, 805
  omitted in Requiem Masses, 560, 805
  the *Placeat* and, 802 f. and note, 805
  position of, 802 f. and note
Blessings: in the missal, 230; sacramentals, 228 f.
Blood: Chrysostom on the offering of, 111; symbolized by red, 351-53
Blood of Christ, 777 (*see also* Body and blood)
  in the chalice, 674-77
  offered at the Offertory, 564

Blood of Christ (*continued*)
  receiving of, 774-77
  St. Chrysostom on, 777
  seal of the New Covenant, 99 f.
  senses sanctified by, 779 note
  shed in the chalice, 96-99
  shed on the altar, 130-32, 135-39
  source of grace, 69
  symbolized by wine and water, 549 f., 562
"Blood of the covenant," 99 f.
Blue vestments, 346 and note
Body: benefited by the Eucharist, 768 f.; inclination of: see Inclination; salvation of, 773 f.
Body and blood of Christ
  care for, 781 f.
  at the conclusion of the Canon, 722 f.
  gift of thanksgiving, 171
  life-giving, 723
  matter of the Eucharistic sacrifice, 123
  object of oblation prayers, 536 f. and note, 556 f., 563 f., 634 f.
  offered after the Consecration, 683-88
  offered in the *Supplices te*, 697
  present on the altar, 677-80, 682 f.
  sacrificed at the Consecration, 130-32, 135-40, 675-77
  St. Gregory of Nyssa on, 129
  separated at the Consecration, 130 f., 135-39
Body of Christ, 779
  offered at the Offertory, 556 f. and note
  receiving of, 773 f.
  sacrificed at the Last Supper, 94-101
  St. Chrysostom on, 774 note
  in state of sacrifice, 130-32, 135-39
  symbolized by linen, 307
Bona (cardinal), use of unleavened bread, 546 note
Bonaventure, St.: intercession of the saints, 404
Books, liturgical, 374 and note
Booz and the *Dominus vobiscum*, 456 note
Borgia, St. Francis: on flowers, 291
Bossuet: blessing after the Consecration, 690 note; the Consecration, 677 note; the dismissal, 816 f. note; grandeur of the liturgy, 376 f. note; the *Supplices te*, 697 note
Bowing; see Inclination
Brass, chalices of, 301 note, 302 and note
Bread (*see also* Host)
  blessed (Eulogia), 540 note, 759 note, 795 note

Bread (*continued*)
  blessing of: at the Consecration, 670; at the Last Supper, 670
  breaking of; see Breaking
  consecration of, 668-73
  leavened, 545 f. and notes
  matter of the Eucharist, 545-47, 551 f. and note
  offering of, 553-59: before Mass, 553 note
  petitioned in the Pater noster, 732
  preparation of, 551
  unleavened, 545-47 and notes: symbolism of, 546 f.; used at the Last Supper, 546
Bread and wine
  blessing of, 633 f.
  Christ's use of, 543
  designated at the end of the Canon, 722, 724
  elements of the Eucharist, 542-52
  fitness of, 543 f.
  incensing of, 576 f.
  Laurent on, 543 f., 746 f.
  matter of the Eucharistic sacrifice, 123
  object of the oblation prayers, 536 f. and note, 556 f., 563 f., 657
  offered by Melchisedech, 78, 85 f.
  offered in the *Unde et memores*, 688
  offering of, 553 f. and note
  preparation of, 551 f., 634
  products of man's labor, 543 f.
  representatives of nature's products, 724
  "temporal gifts," 784 note
"Breaking of bread," 102
Breaking of the host, 671, 738-47
  over the chalice, 736 note, 740
  importance of, 739
  Laurent on, 746 note
  in the Mozarabic rite, 741 note
  nonessential, 127
  on the paten, 736 note, 740 note
  peace petitioned at, 748
  prayer at, 738
  the rite of, 738, 741 f. and notes
  St. Chrysostom on, 740 note
  symbolism of, 739-43, 748
Breast, striking of: at the Agnus Dei, 750; at the Confiteor, 408 f.; at the *Nobis quoque*, 712; symbolism of, 408 f.
Breviary: missal and, 431; prayer of the Church, 156
Bridge: blessing of a, 229; Mass as a, 145
Buccale, 310 note
Bulgarian language, 359 note

INDEX   831

Burial: in black vestments, 357 f.; of children, 358 note
Bursa, 308 note
Burse, 308 f. and notes

Cain, 692 note, 694
Calamus, 779 note
Calix, 301 note
Callistus, Catacombs of St., 118-20, 720 note
Calvary, 50 f.: redemption accomplished on, 140; relation of the Mass to: *see* Relation; source of grace, 69; symbolized by the altar: *see* Altar; *see also* Sacrifice of the cross
Campanula, 310 note
Candle at the Consecration, 618
Candles
  blessing of, 229 f., 294 note: on Candlemas Day, 296
  efficacy of blessed, 296 note
  Laurent on, 265
  light of, 297
  number of, 286, 294 note
  offered at ordinations, 539 note, 541 note
  paschal, 294 note: symbolism of, 297
  position of, 286 and notes
  purpose of, 223
  at Solemn Mass, 300 note
  stearine, 294 note
  symbol of Christ, 295, 297, 300
  symbolism of, 294 f.
  use of, 293 f. and notes
  of wax, 293-95 and notes
Candlemas Day: blessing of candles, 296; Christmas Preface used on, 615 note
Canon
  changes in, 620 and note
  conclusion of, 721-26: the *Amen,* 721 note; ceremonies at, 725 f. and notes
  the Consecration; *see* Consecration
  Council of Trent on, 620
  culmination of the Mass, 216
  first prayer of, 628-55; *see also:* Communicantes, Memento of the Living, *Te igitur*
  grandeur of, 596
  introduction to, 617 f.
  martyrs mentioned in, 652-55
  meaning of the name, 619 and notes
  meditation on Christ's death, 627
  Offertory and, 626, 631
  origin of, 620-22
  position in the missal, 619 note

Canon (*continued*)
  prayers after the Consecration, 681 ff.: St. Thomas on, 711 note
  prayers of, 625 ff.: concluding formula of, 629 note; and high-priestly prayer of Christ, 626; and Offertory prayer, 626
  recitation of, 618, 622-25: in Oriental rites, 622 note
  sacredness of, 621 f., 626 f.
  second prayer of, 656-60: additions to, 656 note; ceremonies during, 660
  T at the beginning of, 627
  third prayer of, 660-65: ceremonies accompanying, 664 f.
Canon cards, 288 and note, 290 note
Canon major, 538
Canon minor, 538
Canon of Communion, 619 note
Cardinals, *Patres purpurati,* 350 note
Carmelites, Mass rite of, 375 note
Carthusians, Mass rite of, 375 note: the *Orate fratres* in, 590 note
Casula, 339 note
Catacombs
  language used in, 363
  paintings in, 471
  purpose of, 117
  sacrificial character of the Mass, 117-20
  of St. Callistus, 118-20, 720 note
  of St. Priscilla, 118
  use of lights in, 295
Catechumens: dismissal of, 815 f. and note; introduction to the Mass of, 430
Catherine, St.: Postcommunion on feast of, 793
Catholic worship, Eucharistic, 220
Cattle, blessing of, 229
Cecilia, St., 716, 719 f. note: on virginity, 251
Celebrant of the Mass; *see* Priest at Mass
Celestine I, St. (pope): introduction of the Introit, 431 note; *Legem credendi,* 115
Cemetery: blessing of, 229, 707 note; origin of the name, 708 note
Ceremonies at Mass
  beauty of, 376
  classes of, 379 f.
  Council of Trent on, 378
  esteem for, 381 f.
  expressive of prayerful spirit, 225
  forms of worship, 379 f.
  instituted by the Church, 261 f.

Ceremonies at Mass (*continued*)
  meaning of, 378-81: Blessed Thomasius on, 378 note
  in the name of the Church, 126, 157
  nonessential, 127
  observance of, 381 f.
  purpose of, 378-81
  sacramental character of, 381
  St. Augustine on, 380
  symbolical, 378, 380 f. and note
  symbols of Christ's passion, 239
Chaldaic language, 359 note
Chalice
  consecration of, 302 f.: loss of, 303 and note
  kinds of, 301 note
  material used in, 301 note, 302
  names for, 301 note, 302 note
  offering of; *see* Offering of the wine
  position of, 563 note
  purification of, 781-85: development of the rite, 782 note; prayer at, 783 f.
  receiving of, 774-77
  "of salvation," 563 f.
  symbolism of, 304, 308
  uncovering of: at Communion, 775
  used at the Last Supper, 301 note
Chalice tube, 779 note
Chanting: of the Epistle, 482 note, 483 note; of the Gospel, 482 note
Chants of the Mass, 225 f., 430-32, 488-509
  beauty of, 376
  Church year and, 490
  effects of, 488
  after the Epistle, 488-509
  historical development, 430 f.
  Laurent on, 265
  the Preface; *see* Preface
  purpose of, 488
  St. Augustine on, 488
  Scripture text used in, 430 note
  selection of, 431
Charity
  the Church and, 242 ff., 265
  effects of, 340 f.
  the Eucharist and, 767
  qualities of, 340
  source of zeal, 341
  symbolized by light, 299
  symbolized by the chasuble, 339-42
  works of, 22 f.: Hettinger on, 254 f.; *see also* Works of mercy
Chastisements, the averting of, 184 f., 194

Chasuble, 339-42: historical development of, 339 and note; symbolism of, 319, 339-42; wearing of, 340 note
Cherubim, 606 note, 615: the Consecration and the, 677; "Hymn of the," 609 note
Children: burial of, 358 note; Mass offered for, 205; unbaptized, 210
Children of God, 69
Choir, duty of the, 488
Chrism, in the consecration of the chalice, 303
Chrismale, 284
Christ
  Adam and, 31
  benedictus, 612 note
  birth of: renewed on the altar, 625
  blessing by: at the Ascension, 807 f.; at the Last Judgment, 807 f.; at the Last Supper, 670; with the sign of the cross, 670 note
  blood and water from side of, 549 f. and notes
  blood of; *see* Blood of Christ
  body of; *see* Body of Christ
  Church's source of life, 85
  Collects addressed to, 467
  Creed recited on feasts of, 529 f.
  death of; *see* Death of Christ, Sacrifice of Christ
  divinity of, 810
  entrance into Jerusalem, 611-13
  extolled in the Gloria, 446 f.
  generosity of, 238
  gift offered at Mass, 688
  glorified body of, 84
  glorious mysteries of, 348 f.: renewed in the Mass, 586 f.
  Good Shepherd, 752
  goodness of: continued in the Church, 242; shown in Communion, 766
  in the Gospel, 484 f.
  hands of, 670: extended, 471
  hate for, 41
  head of human race, 31 f.
  high priesthood of; *see* Priesthood of Christ
  holiness of, 147 f., 155, 448 f.: in the Eucharist, 238; symbolized by unleavened bread, 547
  the Holy One, 448 and note
  humanity of, 9 f. note, 37-39, 41
  humiliation of, 59
  humility of: in the Eucharist, 237 f., 263
  images of, 578 note: in the missal, 627

INDEX 833

Christ (continued)
  impassibility of, 677
  impeccability of, 37
  incarnation of; see Incarnation
  infirmities of, 38 f., 40
  innocence of, 32, 43 f.
  intercession of, 72-78, 189 f., 193 f.
  joyful mysteries of, 348
  as king, 77, 216 f.
  kingdom of, 649 f.
  Lamb of God, 100 f., 106, 751 f.
  life of; see Life of Christ
  light of the world, 298 f.
  love for, 33: in the Catholic Church, 143
  love of, 32 f., 42, 51 f., 63: manifested in the Eucharist, 102-4, 238
  the mediator, 36 f., 72-78, 198, 467 f., 479: at the conclusion of the Canon, 722; in heaven, 700; by intercession for us, 189 f., 193; in the Preface, 605
  merits of; see Merits
  ministry of: Eberhard on, 216 f.
  mode of blessing, 670 note
  mysteries of; see Mysteries
  mystical body of; see Mystical body
  natures of: symbolized by water and wine, 551
  obedience of, 40, 58, 677, 763 note: in the Eucharist, 237
  offerer of the Last Supper, 667 f.
  offerer of the Mass; see Offerer of the Mass
  offices of: represented in the Mass, 216 f.
  our representative, 31, 33
  patience of: in the Ecuharist, 238; symbolized by the lamb, 751
  perfection of, 447-49
  piercing of side of, 549 f. and notes
  prayers of, 73 f., 626
  Preface addressed to, 616 note
  prefigured: by Abel, 694; by Isaac, 695; by Melchisedech, 696
  presence of: after communion, 783, 785 f., 789; on earth, 84; in the Eucharist, 84, 281 f., 672 f., 675-69, 681; in heaven 84
  priest and victim, 40, 46 f. and note, 49
  priest of the sacrifice of the cross, 46 f., 49, 55
  priesthood of; see Priesthood of Christ
  purity of: symbolized by the lamb, 751; symbolized by unleavened bread, 547
  Redeemer of mankind, 25 f., 31-34

Christ (continued)
  relics of, 276 note, 289 note
  represented by the priest, 125 f., 155, 625: at the consecration, 667 f.
  resurrection of; see Resurrection
  sacrifice of; see Sacrifice of Christ
  sacrificial spirit of, 683
  sorrowful mysteries of, 351: renewed in the Mass, 586 f.
  sorrows of, 38, 50 ff.
  source of holiness, 484 f.
  source of salvation, 26
  sovereignty of, 446, 448 f.
  sufferings of, 31 f., 38, 50 ff., 59: model for us, 63 f.; offered in the Mass, 165 f.; part in redemption, 65
  symbolized by: the altar, 279 f. and note, 285, 456; the altar stone, 455; the candle, 295, 297, 300; the Gospel book, 521 note; the lamb, 751 f.; light, 298 ff., 519 f.
  as teacher, 216, 479 f., 484: at the Gospel, 519
  thanksgiving of: at the Last Supper, 670 f., 674
  Transfiguration of, 347
  union with, 764: after Communion, 786; through the Eucharist, 562 and note, 769; St. Cyril on, 562 note; symbolized by water and wine 550 f., 560-62, 565
  victim of the sacrifice of the cross, 45 f., 49, 55
  victim sacrificed at Mass; see Victim of the Mass
  virtues of, 37 and note
  will of, 151
  wounds of: retained in heaven, 74 f.; symbolized by five signs of the cross, 665, 690 and note
Christian life
  a battle, 327 f.
  joys and sorrows in, 256-58
  nourished by the Eucharist, 233 f., 236 f., 253-58
  an offering of self, 569
  a pilgrimage, 327 f., 477 f., 636
  a sacrifice, 234-37, 241 f., 244-58
  St. Chrysostom on, 809 note
  symbolized by incense, 521
  a time of labor, 327 f.
  a warfare, 767
Christianity: founded on Christ's sacrifice, 82; Judaism and, 81; perfection of, 81 f.; perpetual sacrifice in, 80-85, 103, 121; vestibule to heaven, 81 f.

Christmas, 219
  brightness, of, 348
  Collects of, 475
  genuflection at the Creed, 527 f. note
  Preface for, 615 and note
  three Masses on, 222
  white vestments on, 348
Chrysogonus, St., 655
Chrysostom, St.
  altar and crib, 572 note
  angels present at Mass, 391, 697 f.
  angels united with the saints, 614 f. note
  blood of Christ, 777
  breaking of the host, 740 note
  conduct at Mass, 110
  the Consecration, 667
  dignity of the Christian life, 809 note
  dignity of the priesthood, 110
  Eucharistic presence, 774 note
  holiness required of the priest, 391
  Mass for the dead, 111
  offering of blood, 111
  oneness of the Eucharistic sacrifice, 110 f.
  real and spiritual altars, 280 note
  singing of the Sanctus, 614 f. and note
Church, the
  application of the Mass, 157
  "catholic," 636
  civilization and, 243 f.: Eberhard on, 244
  continuation of Christ's life, 242
  custodian of the Eucharist, 125 f., 141 f.
  death in union with, 706 f.
  efficacy of blessings by, 807
  government of, 638
  holiness of, 156 f., 233 f., 252-55
  life of: Hettinger on, 256 f.; a sacrifice, 241 f., 244-58
  martyrdom and, 353
  Mass offered by, 125 ff., 141 f., 156 f., 199, 657: as sacrifice of praise, 166; in the *Supra quae*, 691-93
  Mass offered for, 141, 197-200, 205, 565, 635-39, 657
  means of salvation, 215
  offered in the Mass, 141 f., 692
  offered with Christ, 141 f.
  peace implored for, 636, 756
  perpetuity of, 636
  persecution of, 245-49
  from pierced side of Christ, 549 f.
  prayer offered for, 635-38
  prayers of, 366
  progress of, 241

Church (*continued*)
  protection implored for, 637
  regulation of liturgical worship, 261 f.
  represented by the priest, 125 f., 156, 199, 202, 458: at the final blessing, 806; at the Offertory, 564 f.
  St. Michael, defender of, 406
  symbolized by altar cloths, 285
  symbolized by the three particles, 742
  as a tree, 354
  triumph of, 247 f.
  unity of; see Unity
  vestibule to heaven, 81 f.
  warfare of, 636
  works of mercy and, 242-45, 265
Church triumphant, sacrifice of, 701
Churches
  beauty of, 262, 264 f.: Laurent on, 265
  care for, 269, 584
  consecration of, 229, 231, 275-78
  neglected, 266
  patron of, 532 and note
Cincture, 326-29: color of, 314 and note; material for, 314 and note; symbolism of, 318, 326-28
Cingulo puritatis, 326 note
Circuminsession, 434, 725
Civilization, the Church and, 243 f.: Eberhard on, 244
Clavus (on the alb), 323 note
Cleanliness
  of corporal and pall, 306
  of the cruets, 310
  divine worship and, 266 f.
  Nepotian and, 269
  of the purificator, 308 note
  of the sacred vessels, 302
Clement I, St. (pope), 653 note
Clement VIII (pope), 374
Clement XIII (pope), Preface for the Holy Trinity, 616 and note
Clement, Basilica of St., 483
Clementine Liturgy, 371 note
Clergy, incensing of, 580
Cletus, St. (pope), 653 note
Cluny, preparation of the hosts at, 552
Collecta, 452 note, 453-55, 461
Collects, the, 452-78
  during Advent, 476
  on Ascension, 476
  of Christmas, 476
  the Church year and, 463 f., 475-78
  conclusion of, 467-70
  contents of, 463-65
  Divine Office and, 454
  excellence of, 474 f.

INDEX

835

Collects (*continued*)
  on feasts of the saints, 476
  form of, 463 ff., 467 f.
  kneeling at, 462
  during Lent, 476 f.
  mode of saying, 470-72
  the name *Collecta*, 452 note, 453-55
  number of, 473 f. and note
  for Pentecost, 465
  after Pentecost, 477 f.
  Pichenot on, 454 note
  position of, 452
  Postcommunion and, 792
  prayer of petition, 463-65
  public prayer, 454, 460 f.
  saints' names in, 486 note
  Secreta and, 593
  translation of, 474
  uniformity of, 464
  value of, 474 f.
  to whom addressed, 466 f.
  Wiseman on, 474 f.
Colors, liturgical, 345-58
  combination of, 346
  historical development, 345 and note, 355 note
  light and the, 346 f.
  number of, 345 f. and note
  purpose of, 345
  symbolism of, 347-58
Columba, 573 note
Comes, 374 note
Commixtio, 745 f. and note; *see also* Mingling
Communicantes, 629, 647-55
  Blessed Virgin invoked in, 650 f.
  for Easter, 649
  meaning of the word, 649 and notes
  saints invoked in, 650-55
  superscription of, 647 f. and notes
  variations in, 648 note
Communio, the, 790 f. and notes
Communion, 535, 727 ff.
  bell at the, 310 and note
  under both species, 779 note
  continuation of the divine presence, 783, 785 f., 789
  distributed in Requiem Masses, 759 note
  Domine non sum dignus, 771 f., 779
  effects of, 767-69, 774 f.
  of the faithful, 777-81: Confiteor before, 778 and note; during Mass, 777 f. note; nonessential, 128; rite of, 779 and note
  foretold in the psalms, 92 f.

Communion (*continued*)
  formula for administering, 779 f. and note
  frequent, 763 f.: Council of Trent on, 780
  fruits of the Mass and, 728
  genuflection before, 770
  historical development, 431
  hymn at, 790 f. and note
  Imitation of Christ on, 787 f.
  joy at receiving, 768, 773, 775, 777, 796 f.
  longing for, 770
  before Mass, 777 f. note
  outside of Mass, 778 note
  necessity of, 760 f.
  prayers before, 760-69: conclusion of, 761 note; historical development, 760 note; inclination during, 770
  preparation for, 728 ff., 760-72
  of the priest, 773-77: ceremonies at, 773, 775; on Good Friday, 128; necessity of, 128, 727; nonessential, 128; pause after, 783
  rite of administering, 799 and note
  sacrificial banquet, 128 f., 727 f.; *see also* Sacrificial banquet
  for the sick, 778 note
  spiritual, 780 f.
  thanksgiving after, 789, 793 f., 796
  time for administration of, 230 note
  unworthy, 764-66
  as Viaticum, 780 note
Communion of saints, 417, 649 f., 657: sacrifice of, 700 f.
Compline: *Adjutorium nostrum* at, 402 note; Oration at, 454 note; Pater noster at, 733 note
Compunction: expressed by striking of the breast, 750; at the *Nobis quoque*, 712; St. Gregory on, 569; symbolized by the maniple, 332
Concelebration, 152, 684 and note: recitation of the Canon during, 622 and note
Confessors: Creed omitted on feasts of, 531; purity of, 250; St. Bede on, 250; self-sacrifice of, 250 f.; white vestments on feasts of, 350
Confidence: before Communion, 771 f.; in divine mercy, 214
Confiteor, the, 401-9: before Communion of the faithful, 778 and note; inclination at, 408; prayers after, 411-17; saints mentioned in, 405-7; striking of the breast, 408 f.

Consecratio (at the mingling of the elements), 745 f. and note
Consecration (a sacramental), 228
 of an altar, 229, 231, 274-78, 283, 422: loss of, 273 note, 274, 275 f. note; relics enclosed, 276-78; St. Gregory of Nyssa on, 274 note
 of a bishop, 194, 229: concelebration at, 684 note; *Hanc igitur* at, 656 note
 blessing and, 267 note
 of the chalice, 302 f.: loss of, 303 and note
 of churches, 229, 231, 275-78
 of the paten, 302 f.
Consecration, the, 535, 666-80
 accomplished by the Holy Ghost, 370, 571-74: St. Cyril on, 573 f.; St. Damascene on, 573
 as a blessing, 723 f.
 blessing of bread at, 670
 Bossuet on, 677 note
 of the chalice, 673-77: ceremonies during, 674, 676
 effects of, 723
 essence of the Mass, 127-32, 135-40, 677 f., 681 ff.
 first prayer after, 681-703; see also: *Supplices te rogamus, Supra quae, Unde et memores*
 of the host, 668-73: ceremonies during, 670 f., 673
 Incarnation and, 572 f.
 miracles at, 624, 672, 676
 oblation prayers after, 683-88
 of only one substance, 139
 prayers after, 681 ff.: St. Thomas on, 711 note
 preparation for, 661
 priestly power of, 667
 sacrificial act, 127-32, 135-40, 675-77, 682 f.
 St. Chrysostom on, 667
 St. Hildegard on, 678 note
 second prayer after; see Memento of the Dead
 signs of the cross at, 670, 674
 silence at, 666
 sublimity of, 666 f., 671
 third prayer after; see *Nobis quoque*
 of the wine, 673-77: ceremonies during, 674, 676
 words of, 667-69 and notes, 672-77: at the Last Supper, 95-98; Laurent on, 747; St. Gregory of Nazianzus on, 136; a spiritual sword, 105, 131, 136, 138, 682

Consecration candle, 618
Constantia, St., 655 note
Contrition, Mass and, 177, 179, 187
Conversation: control of, 322; purity of, 512 f., 580, 787
Coofferentes, 200 f.
Cope and wearing of the maniple, 331 note
Copper chalices condemned, 301 note, 302 and note
Coptic language, 359 note
Cornelius, St. (pope), 653 f. note
Coronation of the pope, 23
Corporal, 304-8: blessing of, 305 note, 307; handling of, 306 note; Laurent on, 265; made of linen, 265; symbolism of, 306-8
Corpus Christi, feast of: Christmas Preface used on, 615, 616 note; institution of, 505; Secreta for, 594; Sequence for, 503 note, 505 f.; white vestments on, 348
Corpus tuum, Domine, 785 f.
Cosmas, St., 655 note
Council of Trent; see Trent
Covenant; see New Testament, Old Testament
Covering for the head, 390 note
Creation: through Christ, 722; God praised by all, 163 f.
Creator, God as, 4 f.
Creatures: God praised by, 163 f.; religious use of, 12; sanctification of all, 228 f.
Creed, the, 524-34
 adoption of, 526 f.
 in the Greek liturgy, 528
 manner of recitation, 527 f.
 in the Mozarabic rite, 526 and note
 position of, 526 note, 528
 text of, 524 f.
 when recited, 529-33
Crib: adorers at, 679; altar and, 572 note, 625; cross and, 40 f.; St. Chrysostom on, 572 note
Cross of Christ
 altar of the world, 44
 crib and, 40 f.
 road to glory, 528
 sacrifice of; see Sacrifice of Christ, Sacrifice of the cross
 source of all blessings, 115
 veneration for the, 50 f., 54
Crosses, kinds of, 627 note
Crucifix, 137
 on the altar, 287 f. and notes

INDEX

Crucifix (*continued*)
  blessing of, 229
  incensing of, 423, 577 f. and note
  reminder of Calvary, 287 f.
  St. Philip Benitius on, 288
  unveiling of, 49 f.
Cruets, 309 f. and notes
Crux commissa, 627 note
Cultores fidei, 640 and note
Cultus, 4 note
Cum ipso, 725
Cushion for the missal, 289
Cymbalum, 310 note
Cyprian, St., 654 and note
  bread and wine, 86
  lay participation in the sacrifice, 564 note
  the Mass a sacrifice, 112
  Mass for the dead, 112
  the priesthood, 111 f.
  priesthood of Christ, 86
  reading of the Gospel, 483 note
  sacrifice of Cain and Abel, 692 note
  use of water and wine, 548 f.
Cyril, St.: conversion of the Slavs, 359 note; and relics of St. Clement, 653 note
Cyril of Jerusalem, St.
  elevation of mind, 601
  Holy Ghost and the Consecration, 573 f.
  kiss of peace, 759
  the Mass a sacrifice, 109
  Memento of the Dead, 706 note
  prayers for the dead, 176
  propitiatory character of the Mass, 176
  reverence for the Eucharist, 782
  union with Christ, 562 note
  washing of the hands, 582
Cyril, liturgy of St., 116
Cyrillonas, on the Eucharist, 107 f.

Da, Domine, virtutem, 581 note
Damasus I, St.: and St. Jerome, 481
Damian, St., 655 note
Damned, the, 210, 705
Darkness, symbolism of, 297
David: Absalom and, 397; in psalm 140, 579
Deacon: the *Flectamus genua*, 462 note; ordination of, 483 note; reading of the Gospel, 483 note, 484 note, 511, 512 note; singing of the dismissal, 799 note; wearing of the stole, 333 f. and notes, 336

Dead, the
  black used in the liturgy for, 357 f.
  candles used at Office for, 294 note
  diptychs of, 642 note, 705 f. and note
  Memento of; see Memento of the Dead
  names for, 708 notes, 711 note
  prayers for, 176, 184, 358: Balaeus on, 207; during Mass, 704 f., 708-10; origin of, 704 f.; St. Cyril on, 176, 706 note
Dead, Masses for the, 106, 194, 200, 207-10, 559
  on All Souls' Day, 209
  apostolic origin of, 111
  Balaeus on, 207
  the Memento of the Dead and, 704
  publicly celebrated, 209
  repetition of, 150
  St. Augustine on, 176
  St. Chrysostom on, 111
  St. Cyprian on, 112
  St. Cyril on, 176
Dead languages, 359 note, 363 f. and note
Death: remembrance of, 711; symbolized by black, 357 f.; in union with the Church, 706 f.
Death of Christ, 34, 48
  commemorated before Communion, 762 f.
  commemorated in the *Unde et memores*, 685-87
  effects of, 174
  end of His meritorious action, 66 f.
  meditation on, 239 ff.; during the Canon, 627
  natural phenomena at, 240
  price of redemption, 59-63, 65 f., 140, 174
  prophecies concerning, 43
  represented in the Mass, 143, 217, 238 f., 763; see also Relation of Mass and Calvary
  a Sacrifice, 34
  symbolized by an inclination, 710 and note
  symbolized by the Fraction, 740, 743 f., 746
Dedication of a church, 530
Denis the Carthusian, on the *Veni Creator Spiritus*, 505 note
Deo gratias, 486 f.: at the dismissal, 800; after the Last Gospel, 811
Deus qui humanae, 561 f.
Devil, dominion of, 228 f.
Diaconate, powers of the, 231

Didymus (the Blind), St.: on the Eucharist, 109
Dies irae, 507 f.: author of, 503 note
Differences between Mass and Calvary, 139-42
Dignity of man, 56
Dignum (in the Preface), 603 f.
Diocletian (emperor), 655 note, 719 note
Dionysius, St. (of Alexandria): celebration of Mass, 232
Diptychum, 642 note
Dirigatur, Domine, 578-80 and note
Dismissal, the, 795, 799-801 and notes: Bossuet on, 816 f. note; of the catechumens, 815 f. and note; *Dominus vobiscum* before, 798 and note; and the name "Mass," 814-16 and note; in various liturgies, 799 note
Dispositions required: for grace, 151; for obtaining our petitions, 192; for sacrifice, 27; for sharing in the Mass, 366
Divine nature, our participation in the, 461
Divine Office, the
  the Collect and, 454
  conclusion of the Oration in, 467
  Dominus vobiscum in, 456 note
  Oremus in, 468 note
  Pater noster in, 733 note
  recitation of, 623
Doctors of the Church, 531 and note
Dogma and worship, 368 and note
Dominations, 606 note, 607 and note
Domine non sum dignus, 771 f., 779
Dominica in Albis, 501 note
Dominicae virides, 354 and note
Dominicans, Mass rite of, 375 note: *Orate fratres* in, 590 note
Dominus vobiscum, 414 f. and note, 456-60
  in Ambrosian rite, 413 note
  before the Collect, 457
  before the dismissal, 798 and note
  in the Divine Office, 456 note
  efficacy of, 460
  at the foot of the altar, 413 f. and note
  at the Gospel, 514 f.
  in the Mozarabic rite, 413 note
  number of times recited during Mass, 413 note, 456
  before the Offertory, 539
  origin of, 456 note
  before the Preface, 598 f.
Dona, 634

Doxologia major, 399 note; *see also* Gloria
Doxologia minor, 399 f. note; *see also* Gloria Patri
Doxology: at the end of the Canon, 725 f.; greater: *see* Gloria; lesser: *see* Gloria Patri

Eagle, symbol of St. John, 810
East, praying toward the, 472 and note
Easter
  Communicantes for, 649
  joy of, 349, 599-501
  Hanc igitur on, 656 note
  Preface for, 616
  Sequence for, 503 f.: author of, 503 note
  white vestments on, 349
Easter week, liturgy during, 501 and note
Eastern liturgies, 372: recitation of the Canon in, 622 note; use of incense in, 418 note, 419 and note; *see also* Greek liturgy
Eastertide, 219: joy of, 499-501
Eberhard
  Christ as teacher in the Eucharist, 216 f.
  Church and civilization, 244
  esteem for the Eucharist, 232
  life of Christ, 216-18
  the Mass and Calvary, 239 f.
  the Mass and self-sacrifice, 249 f.
  meditation on the passion, 240
  nature at Christ's death, 239 f.
  the oblation of the elements, 538
  places for celebrating the Eucharist, 232
  universality of the Mass, 367 f.
Ebner, on the Canon, 621
Ecce Agnus Dei, 779
Ecclesia collecta, 425, 453
Ecclesiastical year; *see* Year
Effects of Communion, 767-69, 774 f.
Effects of the Mass, 763: dependent on God's will, 151-53, 155; dependent on man's disposition, 151; limited extensively, 153-55; limited intensively, 150 f.; for those present, 152
Efficacia of the Mass, 145 note
Efficacy of Old Testament sacrifices, 28 ff.
Efficacy of the Mass, 146-62
  Christ as chief offerer, 147-55
  comprehensive, 226 f.
  derived from Calvary, 140 f.

INDEX

Efficacy of the Mass (*continued*)
 ex opere operantis, 161
 ex opere operantis ecclesiae, 160
 ex opere operato, 147 f., 155, 161
 High Mass, 157
 holiness of Christ and, 147 f., 155
 holiness of the Church and, 156 f.
 infinite, 147-50, 155, 161
 as offered by the Church, 156-60
 as offered by the priest, 160 f.
 Requiem Mass, 158-60
 restricted in application, 150-55
 Solemn Mass, 158
 universal, 226 f.
 votive Mass, 158-60
Egypt, exodus from, 62
Electric lights, 294 note
Eleison, 433 note
Elements of the Eucharist, 537 f., 542-52, 722: Laurent on, 746 f.; names for, 633 f.
Elevatio major, 726
Elevatio minor, 726
Elevation, the, 678-80 and note: bell at, 310 and note; at the end of the Canon, 726; in the Mozarabic rite, 526 note
Elizabeth, St. (of Hungary): thanksgiving by, 605
Ember days, 356: *Flectamus genua*, 462; purpose of, 486
Ember Saturdays: lessons on, 482 note, 486 and note; Tract on, 494 note
Ember Wednesday, lessons on, 482 note, 486 and note
Embolism (*Libera nos*), the, 734-37
 in the Ambrosian rite, 734 note
 breaking of the host and, 738
 ceremonies during, 736
 on Good Friday, 734 note
 peace petitioned in, 735 f., 748
 silent recitation of, 734 note
 various practices at, 737 note
Emperor, named in the Canon, 639 note
Ends of the Mass, 145 f., 149, 163-69: atonement, 173-87, 195 f.; petition, 146, 149, 183 f., 188-96; praise and adoration, 163-68, 173, 195 f.; thanksgiving, 168-73, 195 f.
Ephrem, St.: on the Eucharist, 107; on the priesthood, 107
Epiklesis, the, 569-74: in the Mozarabic rite, 570 note; *Quam oblationem* as kind of, 663 f.; sign of the cross at, 570, 572; *Supplices te* and, 699 f. note

Epiphanius, St.: shape of the host, 551 note
Epiphany: time after, 354 f.; white vestments on, 348
Epistle, the, 481-87
 ambo for, 483 and note
 in Ambrosian and Mozarabic rites, 482 note
 conclusion of, 486 f.
 Gradual chants and, 490 f.
 during Lent, 486
 manner of hearing, 484 note
 manner of saying, 482-84 notes
 Old Testament in, 485 f.
 origin of the name, 482 and note
 reader of, 483 f. and note
 relation to the Gospel, 485
 selection of, 481 f.
 subordinate to the Gospel, 483-85
 superscription of, 482 f. note
Epistle side, parts of the Mass read on, 790 note
Epistola, 482 and note
Epistolarium, 374 note
Equity, thanksgiving and, 604
Essence of the Eucharistic sacrifice, 122-32: double consecration, 127-32, 135-40, 677 f., 681 ff.; St. Thomas on, 134 note
Esteem for the Mass, 162, 232: and Church decoration, 264 f.
Et cum spiritu tuo, 458 and note: before the dismissal, 798 and note
Eternal life, a reward, 70
Ethiopian language, 359 note, 364 note
Eucharist, the
 adoration of, 678 f. and note
 appreciation for, 162
 beauty of, 262-65, 375-77, 379
 celebrated by the apostles, 359 note, 370 f.
 in the celebration of feasts, 222
 center of Catholic worship, 219-32
 Christian charity and, 245, 254 f.
 comfort for souls in purgatory, 207-10
 devotion to Christ's passion and, 136 f.
 effects of; *see* Effects
 efficacy of; *see* Efficacy of the Mass
 elements of, 537 f., 542-52, 722: Laurent on, 746 f.; names for, 633 f.
 ends of; *see* Ends of the Mass
 essence of; *see* Essence
 esteem for, 162, 232, 264 f.
 "eternal remedy," 785 and note
 excellence of, 220 f., 262 f.

840 INDEX

Eucharist (*continued*)
    fountain of grace, 192-94
    fruits of; *see* Fruits of the Mass
    fulfillment of Old Testament sacrifices, 146
    God's wrath averted by, 184 ff., 194, 566
    graces obtained in, 191-94
    holiness of the Church and, 253
    institution of, 135, 676: Franz on, 671
    a liturgical action, 365
    love for, 144
    matter of the sacrifice of, 123, 537 f., 542-52
    means of giving thanks, 168, 171, 173
    means of grace, 226 f.
    a memorical sacrifice, 131 f., 134 ff.
    mysteries in, 624
    not an instruction, 365, 377
    offered by Christ, 123-26, 138, 147 f., 155, 667: ancient liturgies on, 116; as sacrifice of petition, 188 f.; as sacrifice of praise, 165 f.; as sacrifice of thanksgiving, 170 f.; St. Ambrose on, 113
    offered by the Church, 125 ff., 141 f., 156 f., 199, 657: as sacrifice of praise, 166; in the *Supra quae*, 691-93
    offered by the faithful, 683-85: in the *Supra quae*, 692 f.
    offered by the priest, 683-85: in the *Supra quae*, 697 f.
    offered for man's salvation, 149 ff.
    offered for non-Catholics, 197, 565, 642 f. and note
    offered for the Church, 141, 197-200, 205, 565, 635-39, 657
    offered for the faithful, 196-202, 204-6, 558
    offered in honor of the saints, 587-89 and note
    offered in name of the Church, 125 ff., 140 f., 156 f.
    offered to God, 149, 587, 725 f.
    pagan sacrifices and, 101 f.
    painless sacrifice, 140
    patristic terms for, 105
    perpetuity of, 90, 103: Eberhard on, 367 f.; Geissel on, 566
    place for celebration of: Eberhard, 232; Wiseman, 376
    power of: derived from Calvary, 140
    prefigured by Melchisedech, 695 f.
    priest's regard for, 232 f.
    principal parts of, 535, 727

Eucharist (*continued*)
    property of the Church, 125, 141 f., 166, 205, 591
    purpose of, 140, 195, 559, 592, 722
    redemption renewed in, 654, 686 f.
    remission of sin by, 176-81
    remission of temporal punishment by, 181-84, 208
    repeated for the dead, 208
    repetition of the Last Supper, 667-74
    representation of Christ's life, 807 f.
    reverence for, 782
    relation to the sacrifice of the cross, 131 f., 134-44; *see also* Relation
    as a sacrament; *see* Communion
    the sacraments and, 226-31
    sacrifice and sacrament, 728
    sacrifice of adoration, 145 f., 149, 165-68, 173, 195 f., 644 f.
    sacrifice of atonement, 146, 149 f., 173-86, 195 f., 763; *see also* Atonement
    sacrifice of petition, 146, 149, 188-96: for benefit of poor souls, 208; in honoring the saints, 211-14; remission of temporal punishment, 183 f.
    sacrifice of praise, 145 f., 149, 165-68, 173, 195 f., 644 f.: in honor of the saints, 211
    sacrifice of thanksgiving, 146, 149, 168, 170-73: in honor of the saints, 211
    sacrificial banquet, *see* Sacrificial banquet
    sacrificial character of; *see* Sacrificial character
    St. Cyril on reverence for, 782
    saints in heaven and, 210-14
    saints nourished by 252 ff., 289
    school of Christian perfection, 237-41
    self-sacrifice and, 253-55
    souls in purgatory and; *see* Dead, Mass for the
    source of blessing, 645
    source of Catholic life, 233-38, 240 f., 252-58
    source of grace, 226-31, 645
    source of mercy, 645
    source of peace, 645
    source of piety, 223-25, 237 f.
    spiritual sacrifices and, 253 note
    strength in suffering, 248 f.
    support against temptations, 767, 774
    symbol of unity, 748
    symbolized by incense, 577
    symbolized by the blood from Christ's side, 228, 549
    teaching office of Christ and, 216 f.

INDEX

Eucharist (*continued*)
  temporal benefits from, 192-94
  temporal gift, 784 f. and note
  "tree of life," 145
  truth and, 480
  unbloody sacrifice, 139 f. and note
  union with Christ, 562 and note
  value of; *see* Value of the Mass
  worship of latria, 149
Eucharistia legitima, 662
Eulogia (blessed bread), 540 note, 759 note, 795 note
Evangelarium, 374 note
Evangelists: account of the Last Supper, 668 f.; Creed recited on feasts of, 531
Evangelium, 510
Eventius, St., 715 note
Evil, deliverance from, 730, 732, 734 f. and note
Ex opere operantis, 161
Ex opere operantis ecclesiae, 160
Ex opere operato, 147 f., 155, 161, 196: *fructus ministerialis,* 204; *fructus specialissimus,* 202 note; impetratory fruits, 188; remission of temporal punishment, 183
Excommunicated persons, 199, 206, 642 note
Excommunicati vitandi, 206
Exorcism, a sacramental, 228
Explanation of the Mass, 365 f., 377 f.: Amberger on, 377; prescribed, 361
Exsequiae, 358
Exterior acts of religion, 11 ff.
Exterior and interior worship, 380
Eyes: elevation of, 629; fixed on the host: at the Memento of the Dead, 706; at the prayers before Communion, 770

Faber: beauty of liturgical worship, 375; hymns, 505
Faith: enkindled by the Eucharist, 224, 237; Geissel on, 533 f.; necessary for sharing in the Mass, 366; symbolized by light, 299
Faithful, the
  apostolate of, 641
  benefits of the Mass, 160 f.
  Communion of; *see* Communion
  dispositions required of: for Mass, 624 f.; for obtaining petition, 192
  graces enjoyed by, 209
  holiness of, 250, 685
  incensing of, 580
  Mass offered by, 644 f., 683-85: in the *Supra quae,* 692 f.

Faithful (*continued*)
  Mass offered for, 196-202, 204-6, 558
  offered with the Eucharist, 141 f.: in the *Supplices te,* 697
  participation in Mass, 160 f., 196-202, 461
  plebs sancta, 685
  prayed for in the *Te igitur,* 641
  priesthood of, 24 f., 125, 127, 684 note: restricted, 125; St. Leo on, 114
  represented by the priest, 126 f., 591: at the Offertory, 564 f.; at the self-immolation, 567
  singing of the Sanctus, 609 f. and note
  spiritual altars, 280 note
  symbolized by water at the Offertory, 550 f., 560, 562, 565
  symbolized by wheat and grapes, 141
  temples of God, 280
Fall of man, 25, 56, 543, 562: effects of, 56 f.; tree of knowledge, 616 note
Fasting, 357: in Collects of Lent, 477; the *statio* and, 426 and note
Father, God the, 466 f., 555 f., 605: Collects addressed to, 466 f.; Mass offered to, 687; in the Preface, 605; Prefaces addressed to, 616; *Te igitur* addressed to, 631
Fathers of the Church, sacrificial character of the Eucharist, 104-15
Feast of Tabernacles, 611
Feasts, rank of, 473 f.
Felicitas, St., 715 f. and note
Feriae in albis, 501 note
Feriae legitimae, 494 f. note
Fermentum, 742 note
Filiola, 305 note
Fingers, ablution of, 781 note, 785 f.: amount of water, 781 note; development of the rite, 782 note; prayer at, 785 f. and notes
Fingers, washing of; *see* Washing
Fire, blessing of, 296
"Fire" (the Eucharist), 107 and note
Fish, symbol of the Eucharist, 118 f.
Flectamus genua, 462 and note
Florus (the Deacon), *Supplices te,* 701
Flowers
  artificial, 290 f. and notes
  Laurent on, 265
  Paradise and, 291
  purpose of, 223
  St. Francis Borgia on, 291
  Suso on, 293
  symbolism of, 291 ff.
  use of, 290 f. and notes

Food, blessing of, 229
Forgiveness of sin: effected by the Eucharist, 763; petitioned in the Pater noster, 732
Form of liturgical objects, 262
Forty Hours' Devotion, 346 note
Fractio panis, 739
Fraction of the host; see Breaking of the host
Francis, St. (of Assisi): purity required of priests, 133
Francis Borgia, St.: on flowers, 291
Francis de Sales, St.: sign of cross, 394
Franz, institution of the Eucharist, 671
Fratres, 590 note
Fructus (of the Mass), 145 note
Fructus generalis, 197-200
Fructus individualis, 202
Fructus ministerialist, 204-14; see also Ministerial fruit
Fructus specialis, 200 ff.: application of, 202 note
Fructus specialissimus, 202 and note
Fruits of the field: blessing of, 229
Fruits of the Holy Ghost, 191: merited by Christ, 60
Fruits of the Mass, 195
  application of, 161, 202 note, 204-14; see also Memento of the Dead, Memento of the Living
  applied by the Church, 157 ff.
  atonement, 205
  Communion and, 728
  derived from Calvary, 140 f.
  determined by the Church, 157 ff.
  ex opere operantis, 161
  ex opere operantis ecclesiae, 160
  ex opere operato; see *Ex opere operato*
  excommunicated persons and, 199
  general, 197-200
  impetratory, 188-94
  implored for the Church, 635-39
  individual, 202 f.
  limited, 160 f.
  ministerial, 204-14; see also Ministerial
  non-Catholics and, 197, 565
  participants in, 196-214, 638-48
  petitioned before Communion, 762 f.
  restricted in application, 150-55
  satisfactory, 173-86
  sinners and, 199
  special, 152, 200 ff.
  subordinate, 159
  for those present, 152
  very special, 202 f.

Gabriel, St. (archangel), 405 note: blessing of incense, 576 note
Galea salutis, 320 f.
Gallican Church, 360 note
Gallican rite, 372 f. note
  blessing at the Embolism, 737 note
  kiss of peace, 758
  Mozarabic rite compared with, 372 f. note
  name for the Eucharist, 688 note
  Pater noster in, 730 note
  Preface in, 597 note
Gaudentius, St.: the Mass a memorial sacrifice, 113 f., 135
Gaudete Sunday, rose vestments on, 345 note
Geissel: on faith, 533 f.; perpetuity of the Mass, 566
Gelasius I, St. (pope): introduction of the Introit, 431 note; Sacramentary of, 374, 473
Gens sancta, 685 and note
Genuflection: at the Communion, 770, 775; at the Consecration, 673, 676; at the Creed, 527 and note; at the Last Gospel, 810
Georgians, use of Greek, 364 note
Gift: giver and recipient of a, 169; value of a, 169
Gift offered at Mass, 122 f., 138, 147 f., 155: as sacrifice of petition, 190; as sacrifice of praise, 165; as sacrifice of thanksgiving, 171; St. Ambrose on, 113; the *Unde et memores*, 688 and note
Gifts: of the Holy Ghost, 60; at the Offertory, 581, 582 note; used in sacrifice, 16
Glass: chalices of, 301 note, 302; cruets of, 310; vestments with threads of, 315 and note
Gloria, the, 437-51
  in the Apostolic Constitutions, 438 note
  Christ extolled in, 446 f.
  composition of, 438 and note, 440
  devotion while reciting, 450 f.
  Gloria Patri and, 400
  historical development of, 438 f. and notes
  hymn of praise, 440-43, 447-51
  Ite missa est and, 799 f.
  joy expressed by, 439, 443 f., 447-51
  manner of recitation, 449 f.
  in Oriental liturgies, 438

INDEX

Gloria (*continued*)
  the *Pax vobis* and, 459
  petition expressed in, 441, 446 f.
  St. Philip Neri's death and, 451
  Te Deum and, 437 f. notes, 439, 799 note
  thanksgiving expressed by, 441, 443-45
  when sung, 439 and note
  Wiseman on, 436, 451
Gloria in excelsis Deo, 440-42
Gloria Marianum, 438 note
Gloria Patri, 399-401: in the Mozarabic rite, 400 note; omission of, 401, 429; St. Alphonsus on, 401; St. Mary Magdalen de Pazzi and, 401
Gloria tibi, Domine, 515 and note, 522
Glorificamus te, 443
Glorificare, 441 f. note
Glorification of God, 6 f., 10: an end of sacrifice, 18; at the end of the Canon, 725 f.
Glorious mysteries of Christ, 348 f.
Glory: grace and, 562 and note; stole as garment of, 336, 338
Glory of God, 443-45, 610: Church decoration and, 263 f.; exterior, 444 f.; interior, 444; petitioned in the Pater noster, 729, 732
God
  adoration of, 443
  ceremonies honoring, 379 f.
  as Creator, 4 f.
  dignity of, 603
  dominion of, 658
  the Father; *see* Father
  fatherhood of, 555 f.
  gifts of, 169 f.
  glory of; *see* Glory of God
  goodness of, 604
  greatness of, 442, 645
  holiness of, 442: expressed in the Sanctus, 610
  infinite worship of, 149
  justice of, 184 f., 208
  "living and true," 556
  love for: inflamed by the Eucharist, 172 f., 224 f., 237 f.; inflamed by the *Sursum corda*, 600-602; St. Paul of the Cross on, 172; symbolized by the chasuble, 340 f.
  mercy of, 208, 437, 632
  mercy and power of, 410 f.
  nature of: symbolized by light, 298
  object of religion, 8 f.
  omnipotence of, 5 f., 9 f., 442

God (*continued*)
  our relation to, 4 ff., 9 f.
  perfections of, 4-6, 9 f., 13 f.
  praise of; *see* Praise of God
  presence of, 168, 414
  providence of, 151, 179 f., 183: in granting petitions, 190, 192
  redemption and love of, 562 f.
  service of: *Imitation of Christ* on, 337; St. Agatha on, 337
  sons of, 69
  source of all good, 602
  sovereignty of, 5 f., 9, 13 f.: expressed by sacrifice, 15, 17
  union with, 253
  will of, 208
  worthy of all praise, 163, 165
  wrath of, 184 ff., 194, 566
Gold: cloth of (for vestments), 315, 346; cruets of, 310; symbolism of, 304 note; used in sacred vessels, 301 note, 302
Golden rose, blessing of the, 291 f. and note
Golgotha; *see* Calvary
Good Friday, 222 f.
  black vestments on, 357
  blessing of incense omitted, 422 note
  candles used on, 294 note
  double Orations on, 463
  Embolism on, 734 note
  Flectamus genua, 462
  Gradual omitted, 489, 492, 494 note
  Improperia, 246
  Mass of the Presanctified, 128
  mourning on, 357
  Suscipiat omitted on, 591 note
  Tract on, 489, 492, 494 and note
  Trisagion, 609 note
  unveiling of the cross, 49 f.
  wearing of the maniple, 330 note
Good Shepherd, 752
Good works: the Eucharist and, 768; necessity of, 69 f.; as satisfaction for sin, 59
Goodness of God, 604
Gospel, 510-23
  delivery of, 514-22
  at the end of Mass, 809-11 and notes
  ending of, 521 f. and note
  Gradual chants and, 490 f., 509 and note
  incense at, 511, 519-21 and note
  introductory formula, 514-17
  life of Christ in, 484 f., 511

844 INDEX

Gospel (*continued*)
lights at, 511, 519 f.
manner of reading, 482 f. notes, 518
meaning of the word, 510
preparation for reading, 511-14
prominence of, 483-85, 517 f.
read by lectors, 483
relation to the Epistle, 483-85
in Requiem Masses, 522 note
reverence for, 511
by St. John, 810
selection of, 481 f. and note, 517 and note
sign of the cross at, 516 and note
standing at the reading of, 484 note, 518 f. and notes
Gospel book: incensing of, 422; kissing of, 521 f. and note; sign of the cross on, 516 and note; symbol of Christ, 521 note; veneration for, 521 f. note
Gospel side, parts of the Mass read on, 790 note
Grace
applied in the Mass, 140 f., 645 f.
dispensation of, 70 f.
dispositions required for, 151
effect of Christ's sacrifice, 55 f., 60, 67 f.
before the Fall, 68 note
glory and, 562 and note
Mass as source of, 191-94, 226 f., 645
means of, 70 f.
merited by Christ, 140 f., 189
necessary for prayer, 457
original loss of, 56
petitioned before Communion, 763
preserved by the Eucharist, 767
restoration to, 57, 60 f.
sacraments as means of, 226-29
St. Agnes on, 561
superabundance of, 55 f., 68
symbolized by flowers, 292
symbolized by light, 297, 299 f.
withheld, 178-81
Gradual, the, 489-93
Alleluja and, 491-93, 496 f.: during Easter week, 500 f.
Church year and, 490 f.
of Easter week, 501
historical development, 489 f.
omission of, 489, 492 f.
origin of the name, 489 and note
other names for, 489 note
of the Requiem Mass, 490 note
Scripture readings and, 490 f.

Gradual (*continued*)
structure of, 490
Tract and, 492 f., 494 note, 496
Graduale, 374 note, 489 and note
Grapes: cultivated only with labor, 543 f.; Laurent on, 746 f.; symbol of the faithful, 141
Gratiarum actio, 464 f. and notes
Gratias agimus, 443 f.
Gratitude; *see* Thanksgiving
Greek: pronunciation of, 443 note; used in the Mass, 359 note, 364 note, 434 f.; used on the cross, 359 note, 362
Greek Chapel, altarpiece in, 118
Greek liturgy
Alleluja in, 498 note
the asterisk in, 572 note
Creed in, 528
leavened bread used in, 545 f. and note
Pater noster in, 729 note
recitation of the Canon, 622 note
use of incense in, 418 note, 419 and note
Green vestments, 353-55: symbolism of, 353 note, 354 f.; use of, 346 note, 354
Gregorian Sacramentary, recitation of the Gloria, 438 f. and note
Gregory, St. (of Nazianzus): requirements for the priesthood, 110; words of consecration, 136
Gregory, St. (of Nyssa): body and blood of Christ, 129; consecration of an altar, 274 note; institution of the Eucharist, 129
Gregory I, St. (pope)
angels at Mass, 680, 702
the Canon and, 621
chants at Mass, 431
compunction, 569
intercession of Christ, 193
Kyrie eleison, 433 note
the Mass a memorial of Christ's death, 135 f.
number of Prefaces, 597
Offertory chant regulated by, 540
Oratio super populum and, 796
petition for eternal goods, 193
regulations concerning the stations, 426
Sacramentary of, 374, 473
Grief, symbolized by black, 357
Guéranger, the Sequences, 503
Guilt: forgiveness of, 409-12; punishment and, 57

INDEX

Hadrian II (pope), 653 note
Hanc igitur, 656-60: additions to, 656 note; ceremonies during, 660
Hands
 on the altar: at the *Placeat,* 802
 of Christ, 670
 extending of, 470-72: at the Gloria, 449; at the *Hanc igitur,* 660
 joining of: at the Confiteor, 408
 position of: at the Collect, 470-72; during the Creed, 527; before the Preface, 599, 602
 of the priest, 670, 787 f.
 raising of: before the Preface, 599; at the *Te igitur,* 629
 significance of, 582
 washing of, 581-85: Apostolic Constitutions on, 582; on the Epistle side, 586 note; prayer at, 583-85; St. Cyril on, 582
Happiness of heaven, 713, 717 f.
Hate for Christ, 41
Head: covering for, 390 note; inclination of: *see* Inclination
Heart: an altar, 25, 280 f.; of Christ, 549 f. and notes; purity of, 514
Hearts, elevation of, 599-601
Heaven: happiness of, 713, 717 f.; longing for, 355-57; saints in: *see* Saints
Hebrew
 alleluja, 498
 the *Amen,* 469 f. and note
 hosanna, 611 note, 612 note, 613 and note
 used in the Mass, 435
 used in Old Testament liturgy, 364 note
 used on the cross, 359 note, 362
Helen, St.: and St. Matthias, 714 note
"Helmet of salvation," 320 f.
Henry II (emperor), 527
Heresy and national language, 360 and note, 369
Heretics, Mass offered for, 206
Herod and St. John, 714
Hettinger: life of the Church 256 f.; the Mass and self-sacrifice, 253-55
High Mass, greater value of, 157 f.
High priesthood of Christ; *see* Priesthood of Christ
Hilary of Poitiers, St., 438
Hildegard, St.: angels present at Mass, 678 note; the Consecration, 678 note
Hispano-Gallican liturgy; *see* Mozarabic rite

Holiness
 of the altar, 274 note, 281 f., 424, 455 note
 of Christ, 147 f., 155, 448 f.: in the Eucharist, 238; symbolized by unleavened bread, 547
 of the Church, 156 f., 233 f., 252-55
 of the faithful, 250, 685
 of God, 442: expressed in the Sanctus, 610
 God's presence and personal, 168
 necessity of, 69 f.
 of the priesthood, 328 f.: *Imitation of Christ* on, 787 f.
 required of the priest, 161, 233: *Et cum spiritu tuo* and, 458 f., St. Chrysostom on, 391
 spirit of sacrifice and, 250
 symbolized by flowers, 292
 symbolized by unleavened bread, 547
 symbolized by white, 347, 350
Holocaust sacrifices, 26 f. and note
Holy Chapel at Turin, 306
Holy Ghost
 author of the Scriptures, 480, 484
 Collects not addressed to, 467
 consecration effected by, 370, 571-74: St. Cyril on, 573 f.; St. John Damascene on, 573
 cooperation in redemption, 762 f. and note
 development of the liturgy, 370, 374, 376
 Incarnation accomplished by, 370, 572 f., 763
 indwelling of, 561
 invoked in the Epiklesis, 570-74
 invoked in the *Veni Sancte Spiritus,* 504 f.
 symbolized by red, 353
Holy Innocents, 277: feast of, 353, 355 note
Holy of holies, 415
Holy orders, 194: administration of, 230; the Mass and, 229 ff.; perpetuity of, 125; powers of, 231
Holy Saturday: allelujas on, 497; blessing of fire, 296; blessing of water, 230; *Flectamus genua,* 462; Mass without Introit, 429 and note
Holy Thursday
 blessing of holy oils, 230, 724
 Hanc igitur on, 656 note
 kiss of peace omitted on, 759 note
 natalis calicis, 301 note

Holy Thursday (*continued*)
  Qui pridie on, 669 note
  stripping of the altars, 285
Honor, stole as garment of, 335, 337
Hope
  enkindled by the Eucharist, 224, 237
  necessary for sharing in the Mass, 366
  in the season after Pentecost, 477
  symbolized by green, 353 note, 354 f.
  symbolized by light, 299
  symbolized by the amice, 321
Hosanna in excelsis, 611-13 and notes: in Mozarabic rite, 611 note
Hosannare, 613 note
Host
  breaking of; *see* Breaking
  care for, 781 f.
  consecration of, 668-73
  offering of, 553-59: before Mass, 553 note
  preparation of, 551 f. and note
  receiving of, 773 f.
  reverence for, 781 f.
  size and shape of, 551 note
  "unspotted," 556 f. and notes
  see also Bread
Houses, blessing of, 229
Human heart, an altar, 25
Humanity of Christ, 37-39, 41: adoration of, 9 f. note; on the cross, 46, 49, 55
Humeral veil, 309 note
Humiliate capita vestra Deo, 795 and note
Humiliation of Christ, 59
Humility
  before Communion, 771 f.
  fostered by the Eucharist, 237
  Imitation of Christ on, 772
  pleasing to God, 568
  the Sanctus and, 608 f. note
  signified by kneeling, 462
  symbolized by violet, 355
  in the *Te igitur*, 632
Hymns, kinds of, 617
Hymnus, 437 note
Hymnus angelicus, 437 note; *see also* Gloria
Hymnus angelicus (Sanctus), 609
Hymnus seraphicus, 609
Hymnus triumphalis, 609
Hypostatic union, 37

Igitur, 656
Ignatius, St. (of Loyola): sorrows of Christ, 51
Ignatius, St. (martyr), 715 and note

Images
  of the angels, 289 note
  of Christ, 578 note: in the missal, 627
  incensing of, 422, 424, 577 f. and note
  of saints, 289 f. and notes: Laurent on, 265
Imitation of Christ
  devotion after Communion, 787
  dignity of the priesthood, 787 f.
  gratitude, 604 f.
  human imperfections, 772
  Incarnation and the Mass, 241
  joy over Communion, 773
  the Mass and Calvary, 241
  priest in vestments, 343 f.
  self-sacrifice, 235 f.
  service of God, 337
  thanksgiving after Mass, 812 f.
  value of the Mass, 162
Immaculata hostia, 556 f. and notes, 695 note
Immolatio, 597 note
Immovable altar, 272 f. and note, 275 note: loss of consecration, 273 note, 274, 276 note
Impeccability of Christ, 37
Impetratory power of votive and Requiem Masses, 158-60
Improperia of Good Friday, 246
In honorem, 587 f. and note
In ipso, 725
In spiritu humilitatis, 568
Incarnation, 31
  accomplished by the Holy Ghost, 370, 572 f., 763
  consecration and the, 370, 571-74
  Eucharist and, 241
  Imitation of Christ on, 241
  priesthood and, 35 f.
  represented in the Mass, 218
  symbolized by the asterisk, 572 note
  symbolized by water and wine, 562
Incense
  blessing of, 229, 422 f. and notes: at the Offertory, 575 f.
  at the Gospel, 511, 519-21 and note
  kind to be used, 419 note
  Laurent on, 265
  at the Offertory, 575-81
  in the Oriental liturgies, 418 note, 419 and note
  in pagan worship, 419 note
  purpose of, 223
  sacrifice of, 419, 420 note
  St. Ambrose on, 419 note
  symbol of adoration, 419, 421 f.

INDEX 847

Incense (continued)
  symbolism of, 420 f., 423 f., 576 f., 580: at the Gospel, 520 f.
  use of, 422-24
  used in *Missa cantata*, 418 note
  used in the Old Law, 418 f., 420 note
Incensing
  of the altar, 418, 422-25: at the beginning of Mass, 423 ff.; historical development, 418 note, 419 and note; at the Offertory, 577-79; St. Ambrose on, 419 note
  of the bread and wine, 576 f.
  of celebrant, clergy, and the faithful, 580
  of the crucifix, Blessed Sacrament, and relics, 422 and note, 424, 577 f. and note
  at *Missa cantata*, 418 note
  Pseudo-Denis on, 418 note
Incensum istud, 577
Inclination
  after ascending the altar, 415
  at the Confiteor, 408
  after the Confiteor, 412, 414
  at the Consecration, 670 f., 678 note
  during the Creed, 527 f.
  to the cross, 390 f. note
  at the Gloria, 449
  at the *Hanc igitur*, 660 note
  at the Memento of the Dead, 710 and note
  at the Memento of the Living, 706
  at mention of the pope, 640 note
  at the *Oratio super populum*, 795 note
  at the *Placeat*, 802
  at the prayer for peace, 753
  at the prayers before Communion, 770
  before the Preface, 602
  at the Sanctus, 608 f. note, 614 and note
  at the self-immolation, 567
  at the *Supplices te*, 703
  at the *Suscipe, Sancte Trinitas*, 586
  at the *Te igitur*, 630
Incolumitas, 646
Individuals, salvation of, 68
Indulgence: plenary, 208; of the privileged altar, 160 note
Indulgentia, 410 note
Indulgentiam (prayer), 410 f. and notes
Infirmities of Christ, 38-40
Infra actionem, 647 f. and notes
Ingratitude, 169, 171 f., 603 f.: St. Bernard on, 178
Inlatio, 597 note

Innocence: of Christ, 32, 43 f.; stole as robe of, 335, 336 note, 337 f.; symbolized by the alb, 324 f.; symbolized by the chasuble, 342; symbolized by white, 347, 350
Innocent I, St. (pope): kiss of peace, 757 note; origin of the Roman rite, 373
Innocent III (pope), author of *Veni Sancte Spiritus*, 503 note
Inscription on the cross, 359 note, 362, 435
Institution: of the Christian priesthood, 95, 98 f.; of the Holy Sacrifice, 94-100
Instructional character of the Mass, 361, 365, 377
Instructions on the Mass, 361, 365 f., 377 f.
Instruments of the Passion, 352: symbolized by the vestments, 318 f.
Intercession: of Christ, 72-78, 189 f., 193 f.; of the angels, 194; of the saints: *see* Saints
Interdicted priest, 160
Interior life, symbolized by the amice, 322 f.
Introibo ad altare Dei, 395 f., 398
Introit, 428-32
  in the Ambrosian and Mozarabic rites, 428 note
  Communio and, 791
  historical development of, 430 f. and note
  liturgical year and, 431 f.
  Offertory chant and, 541
  omission of, 429 and note
  other Mass chants and, 430, 432
  selection of, 431 f.
  Wiseman on, 432
Introitus, 428 notes
Introitus regulares, 429 note
Irenaeus, St.: altar in heaven, 700; the Mass a sacrifice, 106 f.; on St. Clement (pope), 653 note
Irrational creatures, as substitute for man, 30
Isaac, sacrifice of, 695
Isaac (of Antioch), on the Eucharist, 108
Isaias, cleansing of lips of, 513
Itacism, 433 note
Itala versions, used in the Mass chants, 430 note
Ite missa est, 795, 799-801 and notes: and the name "Mass," 799, 815 f.

848   INDEX

Jacopone da Todi, 503 note
James, liturgy of St., 109, 116: the dismissal, 799 note; propitiatory character of the Mass, 175
Jansenists, 360 note
Jerome, St.
  lights at the Gospel, 519
  Mary Magdalen's name, 531
  response: *Amen*, 469 note
  selection of biblical passages, 481
  the singing of alleluja, 498 note
  symbolism of light, 296
Jerusalem: Christ's entry into, 611-13; Tobias' vision of, 498
Jews, Mass offered for, 206
John, St. (apostle): at the foot of the cross, 239; and the Lamb, 751; sublimity of the Gospel by, 810
John, St. (of Avila): preparation for Mass, 388
John VIII (pope), use of Slavonic at Mass, 359 note
John the Baptist, St., 406 f. and note, 714 and note: Collect on Nativity of, 476; and the Lamb of God, 751 f.
John Damascene, St., 573
John and Paul, SS., 655 note
Joseph, St.: devotion to, 407 note; omitted in the Mass, 407 note
Josephites, 360 note
Joy, 412
  of Advent season, 496
  of the angels: at Christ's ascension, 501; at Christ's birth, 510
  through the cross, 528
  on Easter, 349
  expressed in the Alleluja, 491-93, 496 f., 498 note, 499-502
  expressed in the Gloria, 439, 443 f., 447-51
  expressed in the Gradual, 491 f., 509
  expressed in the hosanna, 613
  expressed in the *Ite missa est*, 799 f.
  on feast of the Ascension, 349
  reception of Communion and, 768, 773, 775, 777, 796 f.
  sorrow and, 256 ff.
  of souls in purgatory, 709
  symbolized by: bright colors, 347; flowers, 292; the kiss, 757 note, 759 note; the maniple, 332 f.; white vestments, 348
Joyful mysteries of Christ, 348
Jube domne benedicere, 512-14 and note
Jubere, 513 note
Jubilatio (Sequence), 502
Jubilus (Sequence), 502

Judas, avarice of, 266
Judaism: Christianity and, 81; renunciation of, 101
Judicium, 766 note
Julian (emperor), 655 note
Justice: of God, 184 f.; thanksgiving and, 604; mercy and, 632
Justification, in Old Testament, 26, 29
Justin, St.: reading of biblical passages, 481; response: *Amen*, 469 note
Justum (in the Preface), 604

King, named in the Canon, 639 note
Kingship of Christ, 77: exercised in the Mass, 216 f.
Kiss: in the Scriptures, 757; significance of, 757 and note, 759 note
Kiss of peace, 748, 757-59 and notes: Agnus Dei and, 749; omission of, 758 f. note; St. Cyril on, 759; substitute for Communion, 759 note
Kissing: of the amice, 320; of the Gospel book, 521 f. and note; of the maniple, 320 note, 330; of the paten, 736 f. and notes; of the vestments, 320 and note
Kissing of the altar, 416 f.
  at the final blessing, 804 f.
  after the Gloria, 455 f. and notes
  at the kiss of peace, 759
  at the *Orate fratres*, 590
  relics of the saints and, 276 note
  sign of the cross and, 630 f.
  at the *Supplices te*, 703
  at the *Te igitur*, 630 f. and note
Kneeling, signification of, 462
Knowledge required for participation, 365 f.
Kyrie, 433-37: in the Ambrosian rite, 433 note; a Greek prayer, 434 f.; never omitted, 433 note, 435; St. Gregory on, 433 note; Wiseman on, 436

Labor: symbolized by the maniple, 322; symbolized by the stole, 335 f.
Lace on vestments, 314 and note, 323 f. note
Laetare Sunday: blessing of golden rose, 219 f. and note; vestments used on, 345 note, 355 note
Laity: handling of sacred vessels, 303 and note; priesthood of, 24 f., 125, 127, 684 note; St. Leo on, 114; washing of purificators, 315 note; *see also* Faithful

Lamb, symbol of Christ, 751 f.
"Lamb of God," 100 f., 106, 751 f. and note
Lambs of St. Agnes, 719 note
Languages used at Mass, 359-69: dead languages, 359 note, 363 f. and note; by early Christians, 359 note; number of, 359 note; in Oriental Churches, 364 note
Lanx, 310 note
Last blessing; *see* Blessing at the end of Mass
Last Gospel, 809-11 and notes
Last Judgment, blessing by Christ at, 807 f.
Last Supper, the, 94-100, 103
  breaking of the host and, 739
  chalice used at, 301 note
  manifestation of love, 102-4
  model of Mass rites, 370 f.
  perpetuated in the Eucharist, 98, 104, 667-74
  prayer of Christ at, 627
  preparatory prayer at, 553 f. and note, 596
  a sacrifice, 95 ff.
  sacrifice of the cross and, 94-98, 102-4
  St. Gregory of Nyssa on, 129
  St. Leo on, 114
  thanksgiving at, 553 f. note, 596, 670 f., 674
  water mixed with wine at, 548 f.
Latin
  Catholic unity and, 367 ff.
  a dead language, 359, 363 ff.
  dignity of, 363, 365
  fixed language, 363-65
  genius of, 363 f.
  language of the Mass, 359-69
  official Church language, 364
  opponents of, 360 and note
  reasons for use of, 362-69
  used on the cross, 359 note, 362
Lauda Sion, 505 f.: author of, 503 note
Laudamus te, 441 f. and note
Laudare, 441 f. note
Lauds, Pater noster at, 773 note
Laurent
  Abraham's sacrifice, 695
  beauty of liturgical worship, 265
  Christ's blood on the altar, 747
  elements of the Eucharist, 746 f.
  fitness of bread and wine, 543 f.
  Gospel by St. John, 810
  heavenly bodies of light, 297
  Office of Corpus Christi, 505
  red vestments, 350

Laus, 441 f. note
Laus tibi Christi, 521 f.
Lawrence, St. 266: distribution of sacred vessels, 309 note; life and death of, 654 f. note; prayer of, 812 note; and St. Stephen, 654 f. note, 714 note
Lectio, 482
Lectio libri Sapientiae, 482 note
Lector, 483 and note
Lent, 219
  Advent and, 496
  Collects during, 476 f.
  Epistles during, 486
  feriae legitimae, 494 f. note
  Oratio super populum during, 795 f. and note
  penitential character of, 496 f.
  Tract during, 494 f.
  spirit during, 356 f., 796 note
Leo I, St. (pope)
  Christ's perfect sacrifice, 42 f., 79
  holiness of Christ's sacrifice, 49
  justice and mercy of God, 632
  the Last Supper, 114
  Old Testament sacrifices, 114 f.
  priesthood of the laity, 114
  redemption by the death of Christ, 48 f., 62
  Sacramentary of, 374, 473
  sacrifice of Melchisedech, 696
  St. Lawrence, 654 note
  universality of Redemption, 44
Lessons at Mass: in Ambrosian and Mozarabic rites, 482 note; and Gradual chants, 490 f.; number of, 482 and note
Lex credendi, 115, 368 notes
Lex orandi, 368 notes
Levate, 462 and note
Levites, rejection of the, 87 f.
Libera nos, 734-37
Liberare, 735 note
Lidwina, St.: death of, 348
Life
  Christian; *see* Christian life
  divine: participation in, 561 f.
  preciousness of, 351
  symbolized by incense, 521
  symbolized by green, 353 note, 354
Life of Christ
  continued in the Church, 242, 256 f.
  in the Gospels, 484 f., 511
  our model, 234
  relived in the Church, 256 f.
  represented in the Mass, 217-19, 807 f.: Eberhard on, 218
  a sacrifice, 40-42

850 INDEX

Light
  of candles, 297
  at the Gospel, 511, 519 f.
  Laurent on, 297
  liturgical colors and, 346 f.
  qualities of, 297, 299
  St. Jerome on, 296
  St. Paulinus on, 296
  at Solemn Mass, 300 note
  symbol of Christ, 298 ff., 519 f.
  symbol of the divine nature, 298
  symbolism of, 294-300
  use of, 293 ff. and notes
Linen: altar cloths of, 283-85; preparation of, 307; symbolism of, 285, 307, 324 f.
Linus, St. (pope), 652 f. note
Lips, purity of the, 512 f., 580: *Imitation of Christ* on, 787
Litaniae, 426 f. and note
Litaniae majores, 356, 427
Litaniae minores, 427
Litanies: conclusion of, 752; order of saints in, 407 note
Litany of the Saints, 426
Liturgies; *see* Rites
Liturgy of St. Basil, 175: the Mass a sacrifice, 117
Liturgy of St. Cyril, 116
Liturgy of St. James, 109, 116: the dismissal, 799 note; propitiatory character of the Mass, 175
Liturgy of the Church: beauty of, 220, 223; Eucharist as center of, 219-32; purpose of, 219, 231; regulated by the Church, 261 f.
Living: diptychs of, 642 note; Memento of the: *see* Memento of the Living
Loins, girding of, 327 f.
Longing: during Advent, 356; for Communion, 770; for heaven, symbolized by violet, 355-57; of souls in purgatory, 709
Lorum (on the alb), 323
Love
  for Christ, 33: in the Catholic Church, 143
  of Christ, 32 f., 42, 51 f., 63: manifested in the Eucharist, 102-4, 238
  for Christ's sacrifice, 143 f.
  for God: enkindled by the Eucharist, 172 f., 224 f., 237 f.; inflamed by the *Sursum corda*, 600-602; symbolized by the chasuble, 340 f.
  martyrdom and, 351 f., 353 note
  necessary for sharing in the Mass, 366

Love (*continued*)
  in the New Testament, 82
  power of, 341
  redemption and God's, 562 f.
  source of prayer, 581
  suffering and, 351 f.
  symbolized by red, 351-53
  symbolized by the chasuble, 339-42
  symbolized by the kiss, 757 and note, 759
Lucy, St., 716, 719 note
Lucian of Antioch, St. (martyr), 271

Mabillon, use of unleavened bread, 545 f. note
Magdalena, 532 note
Magnificat, 164: and the *Gloria Patri*, 400
Malachias, prophecy of, 86-90: the Fathers on, 105; St. Iranaeus on, 106 f.
Man
  as creature of God, 6, 9 f.
  dignity of, 56, 562
  after the Fall, 56 f.
  fall of, 543, 562: tree of knowledge and, 616 note
  needs of, 192, 194
  sinfulness of, 184 ff., 233: in the *Nobis quoque*, 712
  submission of, 658
  wretchedness of, 170, 437, 767: *Imitation of Christ* on, 772
Maniple, 330 ff.: historical development of, 330 and notes; kissing of, 320 note, 330; symbolism of, 318 f., 330 note, 331 f.; wearing of, 330 f. note
Manipulus, 330 note
Manutergium, 310 note
Marcellinus, St., 715 and note
Marriage, 194
Martin, St.: the celebration of Mass by, 601 f.
Martyrdom
  Christ's sacrifice and, 277
  of early Christians, 120
  the Eucharist and, 248 f.
  glory of, 24, 251
  love and, 351 f., 353 note
  Mass offered in thanksgiving for the grace of, 112
  Mass offered on the anniversary of, 112
  sacrifice and, 24
  seed of the Church, 353
  symbolized by red, 351-53
  unity of the Church and, 637
  virginity and, 352, 353 note

INDEX

Martyrs
  Creed omitted on feasts of, 531
  listed in the *Nobis quoque*, 714-16 and notes, 718-20 note
  mentioned in the *Communicantes*, 652-55
  natural death of some, 352 note
  Queen of, 651
  red vestments on feasts of, 352
  relics of, 416 and note: in the altar, 276-78 and notes, 455 and note
  resemblance to Christ, 655
  St. Bede on, 250
  self-sacrifice of, 250 f.
  virgins and, 352, 353 note
  virtues of the, 655
Mary; *see* Blessed Virgin
Mary Magdalen, St., 239: anointing of Christ's feet, 264, 266; Creed recited on feast of, 531 f.; in the Easter Sequence, 503 f.; name of, 532 and note; St. Jerome on, 532
Mary Magdalen di Pazzi, St., 401
Mass, the name, 799, 814-17: Bossuet on, 816 f. note
Mass of the Catechumens, preparatory character of, 388 ff.
Mass of the Presanctified, 128; *see also* Good Friday
Material: for liturgical objects, 262; for vestments, 314 f.
Matrimony, 194
Matter of the Eucharist, 123, 537 f., 542-52
Matthias, St., 714 and note: omitted in the *Communicantes*, 652 note
Maximus, St.: on praying with hands extended, 471
May, dedicated to Mary, 349
Mechtilde, St.: on virtue, 237 f.
Medicine, blessing of, 229
Mediatorship of Christ, 36 f., 72-78; *see also* Christ, the mediator
Meditation on the Passion, 240
Meekness, fostered by the Eucharist, 237
Melchisedech: priesthood of, 77 f., 85 f., 105; sacrifice of, 85 f., 105, 691, 693-96; St. Augustine on, 113; St. Leo on, 696
Melchites, use of Greek, 364 note
Memento, 641 note
Memento of the Dead, 704-11: inclination at, 710 and note; names mentioned in, 706 and notes; position of, 642 note, 705 and note; St. Cyril on, 706 note

Memento of the Living, 628 f., 641-47: graces implored in, 645 f.; names mentioned in, 642 f. and note, 705 note; position of, 705 and note; public character of, 642 f. note; for whom made, 643-45
Mercy
  of God, 437, 713, 717 f.
  justice and, 632
  the Kyrie a plea for, 433-37
  Mass as source of, 645
  petitioned after the Confiteor, 410-12
  petitioned in the Gloria, 446 f.
  petitioned in the *Te igitur*, 632
  power of God and, 410 f.
  works of, 242-45, 254 f., 265: Eberhard on, 242 f.; Hettinger on, 254 f.
Merit: of Christ's sacrifice, 60; satisfaction and, 60 note
Merits of Christ, 60
  applied in the Mass, 140 f., 173 f.
  gained on the cross, 148, 173
  infinite, 67 f.
  intercessory value of, 189
  not augmented by the Mass, 173
  remission of temporal punishment, 181
Methodius, St.: conversion of the Slavs, 359; relics of, 653 note
Michael, St. (archangel), 405 f.: angel of the Mass, 699; in the blessing of incense, 576 and note; in the Offertory of the Requiem Mass, 542 note; titles for, 406 note
Milanese rite; *see* Ambrosian rite
Mind, elevation of, 600-2
Mingling of the elements, 738 f., 742-46
  Laurent on, 746 f.
  in the Mozarabic rite, 738 f. note
  nonessential, 127
  prayer at, 738, 745 f.
  signs of the cross at, 744 f. and note
  symbolism of, 743 f.
Ministerial fruit, 204-14
  application of, 204 f.
  for children: baptized, 205; unbaptized, 210
  for the dead, 207-10
  for the faithful of the Church, 205
  for non-Catholics, 205 f.
  not for *excommunicati vitandi*, 206
  not for the damned, 210
  saints in heaven and, 210-14
  for sinners, 205
Minor orders, 231
Miracles at the Consecration, 624, 672, 676

Miseratio, 713 note
Misereatur, 409 f. and note
Misericordia, 713 note
Missa, 799, 814-17
Missa cantata, use of incense at, 418 note
Missa pro populo, 202
Missa solemnis, 418 note
Missal, the
  blessings in, 230
  breviary and, 431
  cushion for, 289
  development of, 374 f. and note
  prayers of; *see* Prayers
  revision of, 374 f. and note
  stand for, 289
  the stations in, 426
Missioners, self-sacrifice of, 254
Monica, St., 176
Moral virtues: sanctifying grace and the, 3; theological virtues and, 8
Mortal sin, Mass and the remission of, 176-80
Mortification
  as act of sacrifice, 22 f.
  Christian perfection and, 235 f.
  Christ's sacrifice of, 40 f.
  in Collects of Lent, 477
  fostered by the Eucharist, 236 f.
  Imitation of Christ on, 235 f.
  symbolized by the cincture, 327 ff.
Moses, 99: hands extended, 471; priests at Mass compared with, 599
Mourning, symbolized by black, 357 f.
Mouth, holiness of the priest's, 512 f., 787
Mozarabic rite, 372 f. note
  breaking of the bread in, 741
  the Creed in, 526 and note
  designations for the Eucharist, 688 note
  the dismissal, 799 note
  Dominus vobiscum in, 413 note
  the Epiklesis, 570 note
  the Gallican rite and, 372 f. note
  Gloria Patri in, 400 note
  Hosanna in excelsis, 611 note
  Introit in, 428 note
  kiss of peace, 758
  lessons in, 482 note
  mingling of the elements, 738
  names for the dead, 708 note, 711 note
  oblation prayer for the wine, 560 note
  offerentes and *adstantes,* 664 note
  Oremus in, 414 note
  Pater noster in, 729 notes, 730 note

Mozarabic rite *(continued)*
  prayer for peace, 753 note
  Preface in, 597 note
  Sanctus in, 609 note, 611
Multiplicity of Masses, 162
Munda cor meum, 512 f.
Munera, 634
Munere temporali, 784 f. and note
Mysteries of Christ
  celebrated by the Mass, 222, 586 f.
  glorious, 348 f.
  joyful, 348
  represented in the Church year, 219
  represented in the Mass, 216-19
  St. Hildegard on, 678 note
  sorrowful, 351
  in the *Unde et memores,* 685-87 and note
Mysterium fidei, 676
Mystical body of Christ, 31 f., 126
  in the *Communicantes,* 649 f.
  Mass offered for, 199 f.
  members as living altars, 280 note
  offered at the Mass, 141, 692
  offered in the *Supplices te,* 697
  St. Augustine on, 141
  symbolized by altar cloths, 285
  symbolized by water and wine, 550 f., 560, 562, 692
  symbolized by wheat and grapes, 141
  union through Communion, 769

Nature, products of: blessing of, 724 and note; represented by bread and wine, 724
Neophytes, 501
Nepotian, cleanliness of, 269
Neuma (Sequence), 502
New Covenant; *see* New Testament
New Testament: divine character of, 484, 486 f.; establishment of, 99 f.; instituted by Christ's sacrifice, 82; sacrifice in, 83; supported by a perpetual sacrifice, 82
Nicene-Constantinopolitan Creed, 525 f.
Nobis quoque, 711-20: petition of, 713, 716-18 and note; saints mentioned in, 714-16 and notes, 718-20 note; striking of the breast, 712; tone of voice, 712
Non-Catholics, Mass offered for, 197, 206, 209, 565, 642 f. and note
North, symbol of darkness, 518
Notker, St., 502
Numerus impar, 474

INDEX 853

Obedience: of Christ, 40, 58, 237, 677, 763 note; fostered by the Eucharist, 237; in observing the rubrics, 381; required for salvation, 69
Oblatio, 16 f. and notes
Oblation: after the Consecration, 683-85; Eberhard on, 538; material object of, 536 f. and note, 556 f., 563 f., 633-35, 657; preparation for, 536-52; *see also* Offering
Oblation prayers: of the Canon, 625 f.; nonessential, 127; repeated in the *Placeat,* 803 f.
Obsecratio, 464 f. and notes
Obsequium, 803 note
Octave, Creed recited during an, 533
Odor suavitatis, 564 and notes
Offerer of the Mass, 123-27, 138, 147 f., 155, 667: ancient liturgies on, 116; as sacrifice of petition, 188 f.; as sacrifice of praise, 165 f.; as sacrifice of thanksgiving, 170 f.; St. Ambrose on, 113, 124
Offerimus tibi, 563
Offering of ourselves, 647
Offering of the consecrated elements, 683-88
Offering of the host, 553-59: act of, 554 f.; prayer at, 555-59
Offering of the wine, 560-66: act of, 563; before Mass, 553 note; in the Mozarabic rite, 560 note; prayer at, 563-65 and note; purpose of, 565 f.
Offertorium, 538-41, 539 note: at ordinations, 539 note, 541 note
Offertory, 535
 blessing of incense, 575 f.
 Canon and, 626, 631
 concluding prayers of, 586-95
 development of prayers of, 538 and note
 Dominus vobiscum at, 539
 gifts offered at, 540 and note, 544, 581, 582 note
 material object of, 536 f. and note, 556 f., 563 f.
 Oremus at, 539
 preparation for the Consecration, 535 f., 553 f.
 procession at, 539 f. and note
 for Requiem Mass, 541 f. and note
 washing of the hands at, 581-85; *see also* Washing of the hands
Offertory chant, 538-41: composition of, 541; Introit and, 541

Offices of Christ, represented in the Mass, 216 f.
Oil, blessing of, 229 f., 724
Oil lights, 294 note
Old Catholics, 360 note
Old Slavonic, 359 note
Old Testament
 beauty of vestments in, 312
 blessing in, 807
 divine character of, 484, 486 f.
 ending of, 79 f.: St. Leo on, 114
 establishment of, 99 f.
 fulfillment of, 79 f., 484
 holy of holies in, 415
 incense used in, 418 f., 420 note
 in the lessons, 482 and notes, 484-86
 liturgical language in, 364 note
 preparation for Christianity, 81
 sacrifices in; *see* Sacrifice in the Old Law
 salvation in, 26, 29
 spirit of penance, 486
 used in the Epistles, 485 f.
Olive, branches of, 62
Omnipotence of God, 5 f., 9 f., 442
Omnium circumstantium, 643
Oneness of the Eucharistic sacrifice, 110 f.
Ope, 735 and note
Optatus, St.: on altar cloths, 284
Oramus te, 416 f.
Orante, in the catacombs, 119
Orarium, 333 and note, 335 notes
Orate fratres, 589-92
Oratio, 452 note, 464 f. and notes
Oratio s. Ambrosii, 574 note
Oratio super oblata, 592 note
Oratio super populum, 795-97 and notes: said at Vespers, 454 note
Orders, religious: active, 253; for charity, 242, 265; contemplative, 252 f.; founders of, 533 note
Ordination to the priesthood, 194, 229
 candles offered at, 539 note, 541 note
 concelebration at, 684 note
 on Ember days, 486
 formula for Communion, 780 note
 Fraction of the host and, 739
 recitation of the Canon, 622 note
Ordines Romani, 374 note
Oremus, 414, 460-63: before the Collect, 460 f.; in the Mozarabic rite, 414 note; at the Offertory, 539; at the *Oratio super populum,* 795 and note; before the Pater noster, 730

Organ, Laurent on, 265
Oriental liturgies, 372: recitation of the Canon in, 622 note; use of incense in, 418 note, 419 and note; *see also* Greek liturgy
Origen, praying toward the east, 472 note
Orthodoxus, 640 and note
Osculatorium, 757
Osculum, 757-59 and notes
Ostiarius, 487

Paenula, 339 note
Pagan sacrifices, and the Eucharist, 101 f.
Pagans, Mass offered for, 206
Pall, 305-8: blessing of, 305 note, 307; handling of, 306 note; symbolism of, 306-8
Palla, 305 note
Pallium (of archbishops), 719 note
Pallium, 305 note
Palm Sunday, liturgy of, 613 f.
Palms, blessing of, 62, 230, 613 f.: vestments worn at, 330 f.
Panem coelestem accipiam, 770 f.
Panis benedictus, 540 note
Paradise, flowers and, 291
Paramenta, 315 note
Pardon, longing for, 174
Parsch, Communion of the faithful, 778 f. notes
Participants in the fruits of the Mass, 196-214, 638-46
Participation in Mass, 160 f.: active, 461; by Communion, 778 note, 780; degrees of, 127; more fruitful, 643 f.; necessity of instruction for, 361, 365 f., 377
Parts of the Mass, 535, 727
Parura, 328 note
Pasch, the, 100 f.
Paschal I (pope), 720 note
Paschal candle, 294 note: symbolism of, 297
Paschal lamb, figure of the Eucharist, 100 f.
Passion of Christ, 246
"blessed," 686
commemorated in the *Unde et memores*, 685-87
instruments of the, 352, 686
meditated on during the Canon, 627
meditation on, 239 ff.
recalled by the Mass, 239 f.; *see also* Relation of Mass to Calvary

Passion of Christ (*continued*)
remission of temporal punishment, 181
repeated in the Church, 246-49
symbolized by red, 351 f.
symbolized by the sign of the cross, 394
symbolized by the vestments, 239, 318 f.
Passiontide: *Gloria Patri* omitted in the Masses of, 401, 429; Preface for, 616 and note; psalm 42 omitted, 401
Passover, Jewish, 62
Pastors, prayers for, 638 f.
Paten
bread consecrated on, 736 note
breaking of the host over, 736 note, 740 note
consecration of, 302 f.
design of, 302
held by the subdeacon, 559 note
kissing of, 736 f. and notes
material used in, 301 note, 302
after the Offertory, 559 note
sign of the cross with, 736 and note
symbolism of, 304, 308
Patena, 302 notes
Patena chrismales, 302 note
Patens, donated by St. Urban I, 301 note
Pater noster, the, 729-37
in the Ambrosian rite, 729 note, 730 note
Amen after, 733 and note
contents of, 729-33
in the Divine Office, 733 note
the Embolism, 734-37
in the Gallican rite, 730 note
in the Greek liturgy, 729 note
manner of recitation, 729 note, 733
in the Mozarabic rite, 729 f. notes
position of, 729 and note
preface to, 730 and note
Preface to Communion, 729
Tertullian on, 731
Patience, fostered by the Eucharist, 237
Patronus altaris, 275 note
Patronus ecclesiae, 532 and note
Patronus loci, 532 and note
Paul, St.
Apostle of the Gentiles, 407
invoked in the Confiteor, 407
invoked in the Embolism, 736
linked with St. Peter, 407 f., 652
St. Barnabas and, 715 note
St. Linus and, 652 note
Paul of the Cross, St.: goodness of God, 172

INDEX 855

Paulinus, St. (of Nola): on the Eucharist, 119; use of light, 296
Pause after Communion, 774 f., 783
Pax (kiss of peace), 757-59 and notes
Pax Domini, 738, 744 f., 758 notes
Pax vobis, 459 f. and notes
Peace
  effect of the Eucharist, 748
  exterior, 756
  implored for the Church, 756
  implored in the *Libera nos*, 735 f., 748
  implored in the Gloria, 446
  implored in the *Hanc igitur*, 659
  implored in the *Te igitur*, 636
  interior, 754 f.
  kiss of, 748, 757-59 and notes: Agnus Dei and, 749; omission of, 758 f. note; St. Cyril on, 759; substitute for Communion, 759 note
  Mass as source of, 645
  in the Memento of the Dead, 709 and note
  the *Pax vobis* and, 459 f.
  petitioned after the Pater noster, 748
  petitioned at the Fraction of the host, 748
  prayers for, 636, 753-57: omitted in Requiem Masses, 758 f. note
  proclaimed by the angels, 440 f.
  sacrament of, 748
  St. Augustine on, 636, 753
  St. Theresa on, 755
  salutation of, 738, 744 f., 758
  symbolized by the kiss, 757 note
Peace offerings, 27 and note, 92 note
Pelvicula, 310
Penance
  as act of sacrifice, 23
  Benedicamus Domino and spirit of, 800 and note
  in the Collects of Lent, 476 f.
  expressed in the Tract, 493 f.
  of Lenten season, 496 f.
  Mass and grace of, 177, 179, 187
  Old Testament lessons and, 486
  pleasing to God, 568
  signified by kneeling, 462
  symbolized by striking the breast, 408
  symbolized by violet, 355-57
Pentecost: birthday of the Church, 353; Mass celebrated on, 370
Pentecost, feast of
  Collect for, 465
  Creed recited on, 529 f.
  Epistle and Gospel of, 485
  Hanc igitur on, 656 note

Pentecost, feast of (*continued*)
  red vestments on, 353
  Secreta for, 594
  Sequence for, 504 f.: author of, 503 note
  time after, 355, 477 f.
Per intercessionem beati Michaelis, 575
Per ipsum, 724 f.
Pera, 308 note
Perceptio corporis, 764-69
Perfection, Christian, 234-38
Perfection of the Mass, 124
Perfections of God, 4-6, 9 f.
Perpetua, St., 715 f. and note
Perpetuity of the Mass, 90, 103: Eberhard on, 367 f.; Geissel on, 566
Persecution: of the Church, 245-49; of early Christians, 120 f.; Mass celebrated amid, 232
Peter, St. (of Alcantara), 521
Peter, St. (apostle)
  altar of wood, 271
  Artemius and, 715 note
  founder of the Roman rite, 373 f.
  invoked in the Confiteor, 407
  invoked in the Embolism, 736
  St. Paul and, 407 f., 652 note
Peter Chrysologus, St.: on praying with arms extended, 471
Peter Claver, St., 255
Peter Damian, St.: author of *Victimae paschali*, 503 note
Petition
  as act of religion, 10
  atonement and, 177 ff., 186, 208
  Collects as prayers of, 463-65
  dispositions for obtaining, 192
  an end of sacrifice, 18 f.
  expressed in the Gloria, 441, 446 f.
  expressed in the Secreta, 593 f.
  expressed in the Tract, 493, 497
  importance of, 464
  Mass as sacrifice of, 146, 149, 188-96: for benefit of poor souls, 208; in honoring the saints, 211-14; remission of temporal punishment, 183 f.
  necessity of, 10, 221, 464
  object of, 188-94
  Old Testament sacrifice of, 27 and note
  in the Pater noster, 729-33
  in the *Placeat*, 803
  Postcommunion as prayer of, 793-95
  thanksgiving and, 794 f.
Pewter: chalices of, 301 note, 302; cruets of, 310
Philip Benitius, St.: on the crucifix, 288

Philip Neri, St.: Gloria and death of, 451; on love of God, 342; Secreta for the feast of, 594
Pichenot, the Collect, 454
Pictures: blessing of, 229; of saints: *see* Images
Pietas, 766 and note
Piety, fostered by the Eucharist, 223-25, 237 f.
Pilgrimage, life a, 477 f.
Pius, 766 note
Pius V, St. (pope), 3', 375 note
Placeat, the, 801-3 and notes: the blessing and, 802 f. and note, 805
Place for the celebration of Mass: Eberhard on, 232; Wiseman on, 376
Place of sacrifice; *see* Altar
Planeta, 339 note
Plebs sancta, 685
Poena-satispassio, 182
Poetry: *Dies irae*, 506 note, 507; marks of true, 506 note
Polycarp, St.: letter of, 713
Pope, the
coronation of, 230 f.
guidance of the Church by, 638
named in the Canon, 639 and note
office of, 639
participant in the Mass, 198, 638 f.
prayers for, 638 f. and note
Popes: mentioned in the *Communicantes*, 652 f. and notes; Preface for feasts of, 616 and note
Portable altar, 273 f. and note, 275 note: loss of consecration, 276 note
Postcommunion, 791-95: contents of, 792; name applied to the Communio, 790 note; prayer of petition and thanksgiving, 793 f.; recited in the plural, 792
Postulatio, 464 f. and notes
Posture during prayer, 461 f., 470-72: Tertullian on, 462 note, 470
Poverty: and church decoration, 266; Mass celebrated amid, 232
Power and mercy of God, 410 f.
Power of the Mass, derived from Calvary, 140; *see also* Efficacy of the Mass
Powers (angelic choir), 606 note, 607 f. and note
Praefatio communis, 602-8
Praise, Mass as sacrifice of, 145 f., 149, 165-68, 173, 195 f.: expressed in the Memento of the Living, 644 f.; in honor of the saints, 211; *see also* Adoration

Praise of God
by the angels, 606-8
duty of all creatures, 163 f.
duty of the priest, 442
at the end of the Canon, 725 f.
expressed in the Collects, 464
expressed in the Gloria, 440-43, 447-51
expressed in the Preface, 596, 614
expressed in the Sanctus, 612-15
expressed in the thanksgiving after Mass, 811 note
infinite by the Mass, 165-68, 173, 220 f.
necessity of, 221
offered in heaven, 700 f.
in our life, 168
Ruysbroek on, 166
Suso on, 164 f.
in the word alleluja, 498 f.
Prayer
an act of religion, 13
Christ and, 73 f., 626
efficacy of Christ's, 74
enhanced by the Eucharist, 221
means of self-perfection, 357
necessity of grace for, 457
offered for the Church, 635-38
of petition, 190-92
posture during, 461 f., 470-72: Tertullian on, 426 note, 470
public, 460 f.
qualities of, 193
sacrifice and, 13, 23, 73 f.
symbolized by incense, 420 f.
Prayers
for bishops, 638-40 and notes
for the dead, 176, 184, 358: Balaeus on, 207; during Mass, 704 f., 708-10; origin of, 704 f.; St. Cyril on, 176, 706 note
kinds of, 462 note, 464 f. and notes
of the Missal: blessings, 230; in honor of the saints, 212-14 and notes; of petition, 191 note, 192; for reconciliation, 186 note
for the pope, 638 f. and note
for temporal rulers, 639 note
Prayers at Mass, 225 f.
beauty of, 376
difficult to translate, 363 f., 366
difficult to understand, 366
excellence of, 366, 376
in name of the Church, 126, 157
for reconciliation, 186
thanksgiving expressed by, 171
tone of recitation, 592 note
Wiseman on, 375 f.

INDEX

857

Prayers at the Foot of the Altar, 390-417
  antiphon of, 395 f.
  conclusion of, 411-17
  the Confiteor, 401-9
  development of, 390 note
  Gloria Patri, 399-401
  psalm 42, 397-99
  sentiments of the priest during, 391 f., 398 f., 402 f.
  sign of the cross, 392-95
Preface, 596-617
  angels mentioned in, 606-8 and notes
  of the Blessed Virgin, 597 f. note
  for Christmas, 615 and note
  conclusion of, 608-15
  for Easter, 616
  for feasts of the apostles, 616 and note
  in the Gallican rite, 597
  grandeur of, 596, 598, 614
  for the Holy Trinity, 616 and note
  hymnus gloriae, 437 note
  introduction to, 598-602
  in the Mozarabic rite, 597 note
  origin of, 597 f.
  for Passiontide, 616 and note
  Pater noster and, 729
  poetry of, 598
  praise expressed in, 596, 614
  thanksgiving in, 596, 602-5, 615
  Wiseman on, 618
Prefaces: common characteristics of, 616 f.; number of, 597 f., 615; proper, 615-17 and notes
Preparation for Mass, 387-89: recommended prayers, 388 f. note; St. John of Avila on, 388
Presbyter, 382 note
Presence of Christ: after Communion, 783, 785 f., 789; on earth, 84; in the Eucharist, 84, 281 f., 672 f., 675-79, 681; in heaven, 84
Presence of God, 168, 414
Priest
  blessing by, 806
  devotion to Mary, 133 f.
  the Eucharist and, 232 f.
  hands of, 670
  holiness of; *see* Priest at Mass
  interdicted, 160
  love for God and neighbor, 341
  meaning of the word, 34 note
  a mediator, 36, 126, 454, 456
  office of, 34 and note
  powers of, 231
  praise a duty of, 442

Priest (*continued*)
  purity of; *see* Purity
  of the sacrifice of the cross, 46 f., 49, 55
  zeal of, 341
Priest at Mass, 160 f.
  Communion of; *see* Communion
  dispositions required of, 161, 568 f., 582-84, 589: after Communion, 783
  faults of, 558
  holiness required of, 161, 233: *Et cum spiritu tuo* and, 458 f.; St. Chrysostom on, 391
  host offered by, 557
  incensing of, 424, 520 note, 580
  Mass offered by, 683-85: in the *Supra quae*, 692 f.
  Mass offered for, 558
  Moses compared with, 599
  recitation of the Canon, 623-25
  representative of Christ, 125 f., 155: at the Consecration, 667 f.; shown by tones of voice, 625
  representative of the Church, 125 f., 156, 199, 202, 458: at the final blessing, 806; at the Offertory, 564 f.
  representative of the faithful, 126 f., 591: at the Offertory, 564 f.; at the self-immolation, 567
  "servant of God," 684
  unworthiness of: expressed in the *Placeat*, 803
  very special fruit due to, 202 f.
Priesthood
  of the laity, 24 f., 127, 684 note: restricted, 125; St. Leo on, 114
  of Melchisedech, 77 f., 85 f.: the Fathers on, 105; St. Augustine on, 113; in the *Supra quae*, 691, 693-96
  necessity of, 20
  office of, 34 and note, 36
  sacrifice and, 20, 34: in Christianity, 82, 105
Priesthood, Christian
  Blessed Virgin and, 133 f., 233
  dignity of, 125, 685: *Imitation of Christ* on, 787 f.; in sacrificing, 132 ff.; St. Chrysostom on, 110; St. Cyprian on, 111 f.; St. Leo on, 115
  education of, 265
  holiness required for, 133 f., 161, 233, 328 f.: *Imitation of Christ* on, 787 f.; St. Chrysostom on, 391
  institution of, 95, 98 f., 676
  labors of, 685
  perpetuity of, 125
  powers of, 125, 132-34, 231, 667

Priesthood, Christian (*continued*)
  purity required of, 133, 328 f.: St. Chrysostom on, 319; *see also* Purity
  requirements for, 106: St. Chrysostom on, 110; St. Cyprian on, 111; St. Gregory of Nazianzus on, 110
  sacrifice and, 82: the Fathers on, 105
  sublimity of, 337
  universality of, 89
  virginal, 244
  works of mercy and, 244 f.
Priesthood of Christ, 33-38, 71-78
  in the Church, 77 f.
  eternal, 71 f., 78
  exercised at Mass, 123-26, 216 f.
  in heaven, 74-77, 700
  interceding for us, 189 f., 193 f.
  participation in, 35
  perpetual, 124 f.
  pre-eminence of, 34 ff.
  prefigured by Melchisedech, 77 f., 85 f., 105, 113: in the *Supra quae*, 691, 694-97
  uniqueness of, 78
  vocation to, 35
Priests: prayed for in the *Te igitur*, 638, 640; stole worn by, 333 f. and notes, 336
Prime: *Adjutorium nostrum* at, 402 note; Oration at, 454 note; Pater noster at, 733 note
Principalities, 606 note
Priscilla, Catacomb of St., 118
Privileged altar, 160 note, 208
Pro, meanings of, 645 notes
Profession of religious, 231
Prophecies: concerning Christ's death, 43; concerning the Mass, 85-94
Prophecy of Malachias, 86-90: the Fathers on, 105; St. Irenaeus on, 106 f.
Propitiation; *see* Atonement
Propitius, 693 note
Prosa (Sequence), 502 note
Providence of God, 151 f., 179 f., 183: in granting petitions, 190, 192
Prudentius, kinds of prayer, 462 note
Psalms
  21: 90-93
  25: 583-85
  42: 396-99: omission of, 401 and note
  83: 389 note
  84: 389 note
  85: 389 note
  112: 389 note
  115: 389 note
  140: 578-80 and note

Pudens, St., 271 and note
Pudentiana, St.: church of, 271 and note
Pulpit, altar and, 365, 480
Punishment: averting of, 184 f.: guilt and, 57; remission of temporal, 181-84, 208; remitted by Christ, 181; for sin, 735
Purgatory, souls in, 358, 650, 707
  disposition of, 183, 207
  Mass for, 744-6
  need for the Mass, 207-10
  prayers for, 496
  satispassio of, 182
  state of, 709 and note
Purificatio, 781 note
Purification, feast of the, 615 note
Purification of the chalice, 781-85: development of the rite, 782 note; prayer at, 783 f.
Purificator, 308 and notes: washing of, 306 note
Purity
  attainment of, 324 f., 328 f.
  beauty of, 328 f.
  of Christ: symbolized by the lamb, 751; symbolized by unleavened bread, 547
  after Communion, 784, 786-88
  of confessors, 250 f.
  fostered by the Eucharist, 767, 769
  invoked before the Gospel, 512-14
  necessity of, 582-84: at the foot of the altar, 403
  petitioned in the thanksgiving after Mass, 812 note
  required of the priest, 133, 328 f.: St. Chrysostom on, 391
  supplication for, 415
  symbolized by the alb, 324-26
  symbolized by the chasuble, 342
  symbolized by the cincture, 328 f.
  symbolized by unleavened bread, 547
  symbolized by white, 347 f., 350
  washing of the hands and, 581-84
  of virgins, 251 f.
Purple, 350 note; *see also* Violet

Quam oblationem, 660-65: ceremonies accompanying the, 664 f.; petition for the consecration, 661 f.
Queen of Martyrs, 651
Qui pridie, 668-72
Quid retribuam Domino, 775 f.
Quod ore sumpsimus, 783 f.

INDEX

Rain, prayers for, 194
Raphael, St. (archangel), 405 note
Rata (oblatio), 662 and note
Rationalbilis (oblatio), 663 and note
Reader of the Epistle, 483 f. and note
Real Presence, 84, 281 f., 672 f., 675-79, 683
Recipient of a gift, 169
Recollection: Christian perfection and, 235; after Communion, 789; required for exterior works, 245; St. Gregory on, 569
Reconciliation, longing for, 174
Red and white, 350
Red purple, 350 note
Red vestments, 350-53: use of, 346 note, 351-53
Redemptio, 61 note
Redemption
through Christ's death, 43 ff., 59-63, 65 f., 140, 174
effected by the Mass, 645 f.
Holy Trinity and work of, 763 and note
of the individual, 646
love of God and, 562
of mankind, 25
object of Christ's sacrifice, 48 f.
objectively fulfilled, 68
in the Old Law, 26, 29
renewed in the Mass, 686 f.
signified by the sign of the cross, 493 f.
subjectively accomplished, 68-71
superabundance of, 67
universality of, 44 f.
Refrigerium, 709 and notes
Reischl, on word of God, 520, 522
Relation of Mass to Calvary, 131 f., 134-44, 215 f., 226
Council of Trent on, 134
differences, 139-42 and note
Eberhard on, 239 f.
errors concerning, 142 f.
five wounds of Christ, 665
Imitation of Christ on, 241
infinite value of both, 147
meditation on, 239 ff.
the passion symbolized at Mass, 239
St. Thomas on, 134 note
a source of devotion, 136 f.
symbolized by the vestments, 318 f.
in the words of institution, 94-98, 135
Relics
in the altar, 273 and notes, 276-78 and notes, 416 and note, 455 and note: St. Ambrose on, 277

Relics *(continued)*
of Christ, 276 note, 289 note
esteem for, 278
incensing of, 422, 424, 577 f. and note
of the saints, 533 and note: used on the altar, 289 and note, 290 note
Religio, 3 note
Religion
acts of, 7 f. and notes, 11 ff.
definition of, 3 f. and notes
requisites for, 4
sacrifice and, 3, 658
virtue of, 3-15: effects of, 4; as a natural virtue, 3 note; object of, 8 f.; pre-eminence of, 8 f., 13; as a supernatural virtue, 3 f. and notes
Religious: self-sacrifice of, 252-55; works of charity and, 244 f.
Religious life, a sacrifice, 24, 252-55
Religious orders: active, 253; for charity, 242, 265; contemplative, 252 f.; founders of, 533 note
Reliquia insignis, 533 and note
Remedium sempiternum, 785 and note
Remissio, 410 and note
Remission of sin, 176-81
Remission of temporal punishment, 181-84: for the dead, 208; merits of Christ and, 181
Repentance, as act of sacrifice, 23
Repetition of Masses, 179: for the dead, 208; for the remission of punishment, 182; for the same intention, 150 f.
Requiem Masses
Agnus Dei, 752 f.
blessing of water omitted in, 560 f.
chants in the plural, 708 note
color of vestments used, 346 and note
Communion distributed at, 759 note
the dismissal, 800 f. and notes
Gradual of, 490 f.
Introit of, 429 f.
last blessing omitted in, 560 f., 805
last kissing of the altar, 805
obligation of, 159 f. and note
Offertory for, 541 f. and note
omissions in, 560
prayer for peace omitted in, 758 f. note
psalm 42 and *Gloria Patri* omitted, 401
reading of the Gospel in, 522 note
restricted, 159 f. and note
Sequence for, 507 f.: author of, 503 note
Tract for, 495 f.
value and efficacy of, 158-60

Requiescant in pace, 799 and note, 801 and notes
Responsorium, 489 note
Resurrection of Christ
  commemorated in the *Unde et memores*, 685 f.
  in the Easter Sequence, 503
  joy over, 500
  part in redemption, 65 note
  renewed in the Mass, 586 f.
  on Sunday, 529
  symbolized by the mingling of the elements, 744-46
Rite of administering Communion, 779 f. and note
Rites of the Mass (*see also* Liturgy)
  Ambrosian, 373 note; *see also* Ambrosian rite
  Carmelite, 375 note
  Carthusian, 375 note
  common characteristics of, 370, 371 note
  development of, 370-76
  different divisions, 371 f. and note
  Dominican, 375 note
  Eastern liturgies, 372: recitation of the canon in, 622 note; use of incense in, 418 note, 419 and note; *see also* Greek liturgy
  Gallican, 372 f. note
  Mozarabic, 372 f. note; *see also* Mozarabic rite
  Roman; *see* Roman rite
  Western liturgies, 372 f. and note
Robert of France (king), 503 note
Rogation days, 356, 427
Roman rite, 370-83
  beauty of, 375-77, 379: Wiseman on, 375 f.
  brevity of, 372
  ceremonies of, 378-81
  compared with the Ambrosian, 373 note
  development of, 370 f., 373-76
  divisions of the Mass, 383
  esteem for, 381
  incense used in, 418 note, 419 and note, 422-24
  observance of, 381
  St. Innocent I, on origin of, 373
  St. Peter as founder of, 373 f.
  simplicity of, 372
  source of devotion, 377-81
  symbolical ceremonies, 378, 380 f. and note

Roman rite (*continued*)
  unleavened bread used in, 545 f. and note
  Wiseman on perfection of, 375 f.
Rosa aurea, 291 f. and note
Rose vestments, 345 note
Rumanian language, used in the Mass, 359 note
Russians, use of Greek, 364 note
Ruthenian language, used in the Mass, 359 note
Ruysbroek, on praise of God, 166

Sabbatum in albis, 501 note
Sacerdos, 34 note
Sacramenta (mysteria), 786 note
Sacramentals, 422 and note, 807: means of salvation, 228-30; *see also* Blessing, Consecration (a sacramental)
Sacramentaries, 374 and note
Sacraments, the: efficacy of, 227; the Eucharist and, 226-31; means of grace, 70, 226-29; symbolized by blood and water, 228, 549
Sacrarium, 586 note
Sacred Heart, symbolized by the chalice, 304
Sacrifice
  of Abel, 26, 691, 693 f.
  of Abraham, 691, 693-95: depicted in the catacombs, 118-20; figure of the Eucharist, 118-20
  act of religion, 3 and note, 13, 15
  acts of charity as, 22, 253 note
  acts of virtue as, 21-25, 253 note
  adoration and, 18 f.
  of adoration: Mass as, 165-68, 173, 195 f., 644 f.; in the Old Law, 26 f. and note
  altar and, 20, 82: the Fathers on, 105; in heaven, 700
  atonement and, 18 f., 58
  of atonement: Mass as, 146, 149 f., 173-86, 195 f.; in the Old Law, 27 and note, 174
  authoritative institution of, 19 f.
  bloody, 26, 28, 81, 83
  chief act of religion, 658
  Christian life a, 234-37, 241 f., 244-58
  Christ's life a, 24, 40 f.
  definition of, 15
  dispositions necessary for, 27
  divine institution of, 19 f.
  excellence of, 20, 82

Sacrifice (*continued*)
  explanation of, 15-20
  expressed in religious life, 24, 252-55
  exterior, 129: of Christ, 131 f.
  in a figurative sense, 21-25
  four ends of, 18 f.
  of holocaust, 26 f. and note
  human nature and, 80 f.
  of incense, 419, 420 note
  interior, 129: of Christ, 131 f.; symbolized by incense, 420 f.
  internal dispositions for, 17
  in the life of the saints, 250-55
  manner of offering, 16 f.
  martyrdom and, 24, 253 note
  of Melchisedech, 85 f., 105: St. Augustine on, 113; St. Leo on, 696; in the *Supra quae*, 691, 693-96
  mortification as, 22 f.
  necessity of, 21 and note, 80 f.
  pagan, 101 f.
  of peace offering, 27 and note
  perpetual: necessity of, 80-85; in Christianity, 80-85, 103, 121
  petition and, 18 f.
  of petition: Mass as, 146, 149, 183 f., 188-96; in the Old Law, 27 and note
  place of; *see* Altar
  of praise: the Mass as, 145 f., 149, 165-68, 173, 195 f.; in the Old Law, 26 f. and note
  prayer and, 13, 23
  priesthood and, 20, 34, 82: the Fathers on, 105
  proper to God alone, 21
  of propitiation: Mass as, 146, 149 f., 173-86, 195 f.; in the Old Law, 27 and note, 174
  repentance as act of, 23
  requirements for, 129: the Fathers on, 110
  scriptural use of the word, 22 note
  seal of the Old and New Covenants, 99 f.
  spiritual, 253 note
  suffering as act of, 23 f.
  thanksgiving and, 18 f.
  of thanksgiving: Mass as, 146, 149, 168, 170-73, 195 f.; in the Old Law, 27 and note
  unbloody: in the New Law, 83, 89; prophesied by Malachias, 88 f. and note
  universality of, 81: in the New Law, 87-90, 93, 121

Sacrifice in the New Law, 80-85
  altar and, 82
  announced by the prophets, 85-94
  food oblation, 89 f.
  perpetual, 80-85, 103, 121
  priesthood and, 82: the Fathers on, 105
  unbloody, 83, 89
  universality of, 87-90, 93, 121
Sacrifice in the Old Law, 26-30, 81, 83, 88
  bloody and unbloody, 81, 83
  efficacy of, 28-30
  ends of, 146
  figure of Christ's sacrifice, 132, 694-96: St. Leo on, 114 f.
  fulfilled in the Mass, 146
  insufficiency of, 29 f.
  propitiatory character of, 28 f.
  significance of, 27 ff., 42 f., 81
Sacrifice of Christ
  act of adoration, 58
  atonement for sin, 57 ff.
  effects of, 55-64
  efficacy of, 30, 43, 45
  desired in the Old Law, 30
  foundation of Christianity, 82
  fruits of, 55-64
  fulfillment of the Old Law, 79, 81
  in heaven, 76 f. and note, 700 f.
  infinite merit of, 67 f.
  love for, 143 f.
  meritorious character of, 57, 60 f.
  object of, 45, 48 f.
  our restoration to grace, 57, 60 f.
  prefigured by paschal lamb, 100 f.
  prefigured in the Old Law, 27 ff., 42 f., 81, 132, 694-96: St. Leo on, 114 f.
  prophecies concerning, 43
  propitiatory character of, 30 ff., 44 f., 58, 67
  purpose of, 30 f.
  renewed in the Mass, 83, 131-44, 215-17, 226, 677: as sacrifice of atonement, 177, 186; as sacrifice of praise, 165 f.; *see also* Relation of Mass to Calvary
  source of all grace, 70 f., 82
  source of all salvation, 82
  superadundance of, 30, 33, 52 f., 67
  support of New Testament, 82
  a true sacrifice, 40-53
  uniqueness of, 70 note
  veneration for, 50, 52, 54
  vicarious, 30 ff., 44 f.
  voluntary, 47 f.

Sacrifice of the cross, the
  effects of, 55-64
  foundation of Christianity, 82
  fruits of, 55-64: bestowed in the Mass, 216
  fulfillment of Old Testament sacrifices, 79, 81
  infinite value of, 147
  the Last Supper and, 94-98, 102-4
  love for, 143 f.
  not undervalued by Mass, 142 f., 173
  object of, 140
  perpetual sacrifice and, 82
  prefigured in Old Law, 694 f.
  priest of, 46 f., 49, 55
  propitiatory character of, 32, 34
  remission of temporal punishment, 181
  renewed in the Mass, 83, 131-44, 215-17, 226, 677: as sacrifice of atonement, 177, 186; as sacrifice of praise, 165 f.; *see also* Relation
  source of: all merit, 173 f.; Christ's merits, 148; grace, 226; the treasures of the Mass, 140 f., 226
  transient act, 80
  a true sacrifice, 40-53
  veneration for, 50, 52, 54
  victim of, 45 f., 49, 55
Sacrificial banquet, 128 f., 688, 727: of the heathens, 101 f.; indicated by the Fraction, 741; participation in the sacrifice, 780; St. Gregory of Nyssa on, 129
Sacrificial character of the Eucharist
  the Consecration, 127-32, 135-40, 675-77, 682 f.
  de fide, 129
  essence of, 122-32
  necessity of sacrifice, 82-84
  painless sacrifice, 140
  proved from ancient liturgies, 115-17
  proved from the catacombs, 117-20
  proved from the Fathers, 104-15
  proved from the New Testament, 94-104
  proved from the Old Testament, 85-94
  symbolized by the Fraction, 739-41
  unbloody, 139 f. and note
Sacrificium, 16 f. and notes
Sacrilege, 766
Sacristan, 303 note
Sadness, indicated by violet, 355-57
Saints, the
  Collects on feasts of, 476
  communion of, 657
  communion with, 416 f., 649 f., 716 f.

Saints (*continued*)
  death of, 521
  devotion to, 212
  the Eucharist and, 210-14, 252 f., 289
  fruits of Christ's sacrifice, 68
  God praised by, 164, 166, 443
  gratitude of, 172
  happiness of, 713
  honored by incense, 578
  honored by the Mass, 222
  images of, 289 f. and notes: incensing of, 422, 424, 577 f. and note; Laurent on, 265
  imitation of, 212, 476
  intercession of, 212-14, 278: invoked in the *Communicantes*, 650-55; invoked in the Confiteor, 404 f.; invoked by incensing relics, 424; obtained through the Mass, 588 f.; St. Bonaventure on, 404
  invocation of, 416: in the *Communicantes*, 650-55; in the *Suscipe, Sancta Trinitas*, 588 f.
  life of sacrifice, 250-55
  Mass offered in honor of, 587-89 and note
  mentioned in the *Nobis quoque*, 714-16 and notes, 718-20 note
  merits of, 416
  names mentioned in the Orations, 468 note
  number of, 659
  order of, 407 note
  prayers in honor of, 212-14 and notes
  relics of; *see* Relics
  sacrifice offered in heaven, 700 f.
  singing of alleluja, 498 f.
  splendor surrounding, 347
  symbolized by the altar, 456
  symbolized by the altar cloths, 285
  thanksgiving and, 603 f.
  titular, 289 note
  united with Christ, 210
  united with the angels, 614 f. note
  unknown, 252 f.
  veneration of, 212-14, 424
Salus, 646
Salutare (in the Preface), 604
Salvation
  Church as means of, 215
  church decoration and, 264 f.
  effected in the Mass, 645 f.
  of the individual, 68-71
  in the Old Testament, 26, 29
  purpose of the Mass, 559
  way of, 69 f.

INDEX

Sancta sacrificia illibata, 634 and note
Sanctum sacrificium, 695 note
Sanctus, 608-15
  angels and men united in, 614 f. and note, 617
  bell at, 310 and note
  Gloria Patri and, 400
  grandeur of, 614 f.
  in the Mozarabic rite, 609 note, 611 note
  praise expressed in, 612 f., 615
  recitation of, 614
  Scriptural text, 609-13
  singing of, 614 note
Sanctus candle, 618
Satan: dominion of, 61; vanquished by Christ, 61 f.
Satisfactio, 182
Satisfactio pro poena, 59 note
Satisfaction (*see also* Atonement)
  merit and, 60 note
  merited on Calvary, 148
  necessity of personal, 70
  for sin, 57 ff.
  for temporal punishment, 182
Satispassio, 59 note, 182
Schism and national language, 360 and note, 369
Schismatics, Mass offered for, 206
Scripture: author of, 480, 484; excellence of, 480 f., 486 f.; used in the Mass, 479-87; used in the Sanctus, 609-13
Secrecy, discipline of, 105, 816
Secret cards, 288 and note, 290 note
Secreta, 592-95
  in the Ambrosian rite, 592 note
  the *Amen,* 594 f.
  Berthold on, 592 notes
  Collect and, 593
  conclusion of, 594
  contents of, 593
  examples of, 594
  only Offertory prayers, 538
  Post communion and, 792
  recitation of, 592 f.
Secretus (the Canon), 623 note
Self-denial; *see* Mortification
Self-immolation, the, 567-69
Self-sacrifice; *see* Mortification
Sensuality, diminished by the Eucharist, 768 f.
Sepulcher of Christ: symbolized by the altar, 272, 278; symbolized by chalice and paten, 304, 308
Sepulcher of the altar, 273 and note: violation of, 276 note

Sequence, 502-9
  authors of, 503 and note
  for Corpus Christi, 505 f.: author of, 503 note, 505
  development of, 502
  for Easter, 503 f.: author of, 503 note
  excellence of, 503
  Guéranger on, 503
  number of, 502 f.
  for Pentecost, 504 f.: author of, 503 note
  for Requiem Mass, 507 f.: author of, 503 note
  Stabat mater, 506 and note, 508: author of, 503 note
  Wiseman on, 503
Sequentia, 502
Seraphim, 606 note, 607 f., 614: the Consecration and the, 677; "Hymn of," 609 and note
Serenus, 693 note
Sergius I, St. (pope): and the Agnus Dei, 748
Sericus, 309
Server at Mass, 392 note
Servi, 684 and note
Service of God, *Imitation of Christ* on, 337
Severus (emperor), 716 note
Sfondrati (cardinal), 720 note
Ships, blessing of, 229
Side of Christ, piercing of, 549 f. and note
Sign of the cross
  at the blessing of incense, 575 f.
  with the chalice, 563, 777
  by Christ, 670 note: at the Ascension, 808
  at Communion, 777
  before the Confiteor, 402
  before the Consecration, 689
  at the Consecration, 670, 674
  after the Consecration, 688 f. and notes, 725: Bossuet on, 690 note
  at the Creed, 455 note, 528
  efficacy of, 394 f., 517, 689
  at the Embolism, 736 and note
  at the end of the Canon, 725 f.
  at the Epiklesis, 570, 572
  at the final blessing, 805 f.
  at the foot of the altar, 392, 395
  at the Fraction, 738, 744 f. and note
  at the Gloria, 449 f., 455
  at the Gospel, 516 f. and notes
  on the Gospel book, 516 and note
  history of, 392 f. note, 393

Sign of the cross (*continued*)
  with the host, 725 f. and note
  at the Introit, 430
  kinds of, 392 notes
  kissing of the altar and, 630 f.
  making of, 392-94
  meaning of, 393-95
  before the mingling, 758 note
  number during the Canon, 631 note
  at the offering of the host, 554
  at the *Quam oblationem*, 664 f.
  at the receiving of the host, 773
  St. Francis de Sales on, 394
  at the Sanctus, 455 note, 614
  during the *Supplices te*, 703
  symbolism of, 690 and note
  at the *Te igitur*, 630 f.
  Tertullian on, 393
  at the *Unde et memores*, 689 f. and note
  use of, 689
  over the water, 560
Silence: during the Canon, 618, 622-25; at the Consecration, 666; at the Nativity, 625
Silk, origin of the word, 209
Silver: cruets of, 310; sacred vessels of, 301 note, 302
Silvester I (pope), 271
Sin
  acknowledgment of, 408 f.
  forgiveness of, 409-12, 415 f.: effected by the Eucharist, 176-81, 763
  grace withheld on account of, 178-81
  guilt and punishment, 57 ff.
  kinds of, 409
  Mass and the remission of, 176-81, 763
  nature of, 57
Sin offering, 27 and note
Sinfulness: expressed by striking of the breast, 750; of mankind, 184 ff.
Sinners: disposition required for grace, 180; grace withheld from, 178-81; Mass offered for, 205; participation in the Mass, 199
Sirmond, use of leavened bread, 545 note
Sixtus I, St. (pope), 609, 653 note
Sixtus II, St. (pope), 653 note, 654 note
Slander, St. Chrysostom on, 809 note
Slavs, conversion of, 359 note
Solemn Mass: incensing of the altar; *see* Incensing; kiss of peace restricted to, 758; light at, 300 note; without ordained subdeacon, 483 note
Solomon, hands extended, 471

Solus, 448 note
Sorrow
  Benedicamus Domino and spirit of, 800 and note
  expressed in the Gradual chants, 491 f., 509
  expressed in the Tract, 492-94, 497
  and joy, in Christian life, 256 ff.
  relieved by song, 508
  signified by striking of the breast, 408, 712, 750
  symbolized by the maniple, 331 f.
  symbolized by violet, 355-57
Sorrowful mysteries: red vestments and, 351 f.; renewed in the Mass, 586 f.
Sorrows, Man of, 31, 51
Sorrows of Christ, 38, 50 ff.
South, symbol of life, 518
Sovereignty of God, 5 f., 9, 13 f.: expressed by sacrifice, 15, 17
Speech: control of, 322; purity of, 512 f., 580, 787
Spoon for the wine, 310 and note
Spring, symbol of hope, 353
Stabat mater, 506 and note, 508: author of, 503 note
Stars and flowers, 291
Statio, 425-27 and notes
Station, the, 425-27: *Oratio ad Collectam*, 453
Statues; *see* Images
Stephen, St. (martyr), 714 and notes
Stipends for Mass, 154, 204: origin of, 540 note
Stola, 333
Stole, 333-39: historical development, 333 f. and notes; kissing of, 320 note; symbolism of, 319, 335-38; wearing of, 333 f. and notes, 336
Stone: material for the altar, 272 f. and note, 279; symbol of Christ, 279 f.
Stowe Missal, 443 f. note
Streets, blessing of, 229
Striking of the breast: at the Agnus Dei, 750; at the Confiteor, 408 f.; at the *Nobis quoque*, 712; symbolism of, 408 f.
Subdeacon
  cleric acting as, 483 note
  duties of, 320
  handling of the chalice, 303 note
  holding of the paten, 559 note
  humeral veil and, 309 note
  Levate, 462 note
  reader of the Epistle, 483 and note
  stole not worn by, 334 note

INDEX 865

Subdiaconate, 234
Submission of man, 4, 9 f.: church decoration and, 263; expressed by sacrifice, 15, 17
Sudarium, 307, 330 note
Suffering: as act of sacrifice, 23 f., 253 note; love and, 351 f.; of souls in purgatory, 709 and note; symbolized by the maniple, 332; way of sanctification, 63 f.
Sufferings of Christ, 31 f., 38, 50 ff., 59: model for us, 63 f.; offered in the Mass, 165 f.; part in redemption, 65
Sundays, Creed recited on, 529
Supplex, 632 note
Supplication; *see* Petition
Supplices te rogamus, 682, 696-703: angels implored, 696-99, 701 f.; Bossuet on, 697 note; ceremonies during, 702 f. and note; mystery of, 701
Supra quae, 681 f., 691-96
Sursum corda, 599-601
Suscipe, sancta Trinitas, 586-89
Suscipe, sancte Pater, 555-59
Suscipiat, the, 591 f. and note
Suso, Blessed Henry
  on the angels, 350
  the Blessed Virgin, 349
  on flowers, 293
  insufficiency of human praise, 164, 166
  May pole, 64 f.
  mother of, 240
  praise due to God, 164, 166 f.
  on suffering, 64
  sufferings of Christ, 66
  veneration for the Cross, 54, 64-66
Suspension *a divinis*, 112
Symbol; *see* Creed
Symbolism
  of the alb, 318, 324-26
  of the altar, 278-81
  of the amice, 318, 320-23
  in Catholic worship, 316 f.
  of ceremonies of the Mass, 380 f. and note
  of the chalice, 304, 308
  of the chasuble, 319
  of the cincture, 318, 326-28
  of the corporal, 306-8
  of flowers, 291 ff.
  of gold, 304 note
  of incense, 420 f., 576 f., 580: at the Gospel, 520 f.
  of light, 296-300, 519 f.
  of linen, 307, 324 f.
  of liturgical objects, 268 f.

Symbolism (*continued*)
  of liturgical worship, 268 f.
  of the maniple, 318 f., 330 note, 331 f.
  of the pall, 306-8
  of the paschal candle, 297
  of the paten, 304, 308
  of the sign of the cross, 393-95
  of the stole, 319, 335-38
  of the vestments, 316-19
Symbols (creeds), 525 and note
Symbols of the Eucharist, 118-20
Symbolum, 525 note
Symbolum apostolorum, 525
Symbolum patrum, 525
Symmachus, St. (pope): recitation of the Gloria, 438 note
Synagogue, St. Michael defender of, 406
Synaxis, 453 note
Syriac language, 359 note, 364 note
Syro-Chaldaic, 359 note, 364 note
Syro-Maronite rite, unleavened bread used in, 545 note

T at the beginning of the Canon, 627 and notes
Tabernacle: beauty of, 265; images on, 289 note; use of flowers and, 290 note
Te Deum, 437 note
  Gloria and, 437 f. notes, 439, 799 note
  Gloria Patri and, 400
  Hanc igitur and, 659
  hymn of petition, 794 f.
  St. Elizabeth and singing of, 605
  song of thanksgiving, 438 note, 602, 794 f.
Te igitur, 625-41
  addressed to the Father, 631 f.
  blessing of the elements, 633 f.
  ceremonies at, 629 f. and notes
  guidance implored in, 638
  hierarchy prayed for, 638-40
  humility in, 632
  peace implored in, 636
  protection implored in, 637
  unity implored in, 637
Teacher, Christ as, 216 f., 479 f., 484; at the Gospel, 519
Telesphorus, St. (pope): recitation of the Gloria, 438 note
Temporal welfare, 658 f.
Tenebrae: candles used during, 294 note; darkness of, 297
Tertullian: angel at Mass, 698; the Pater noster, 731; posture at prayer, 462 note, 470; sign of the cross, 393; the station, 427 and note

"Testament," 99 f. and note
Thanksgiving
  as act of religion, 10
  blessing and, 671
  in the Collects, 464 f.
  after Communion, 789, 793 f., 796
  at the Consecration of the host, 670 f.
  at the dismissal, 800
  due to God, 169 f.
  an end of sacrifice, 18 f.
  after the Epistle, 486 f.
  equity and, 604
  Eucharist as source of, 173
  expressed by the Gloria, 438 note, 441, 443-45
  expressed in the prayers at Mass, 171
  expressed in the Preface, 596, 602-5, 615
  extent of, 605
  Imitation of Christ on, 604 f.
  infinite, 168, 170-73, 220 f.
  justice and, 604
  at the Last Gospel, 811
  at the Last Supper, 553 f. note, 596, 670, 674
  after Mass, 811 f. note: necessity of, 812 f. and note
  Mass as sacrifice of, 146, 149, 168-73, 195 f.: in honor of the saints, 211
  necessity of, 10, 168 f., 172, 221
  offered in heaven, 700 f.
  Old Testament sacrifice of, 27 and note
  petition and, 794 f.
  Postcommunion as prayer of, 793-95
  after receiving the host, 775 f.
  the saints and, 603 f.
  symbolized by the kiss, 757 note
  Te Deum a song of, 438 note, 602, 794 f.
  virtue of, 168
Theca, 308 note
Theodulus, St., 715 note
Theological virtues, 3 note: as acts glorifying God, 7 f.; in Christian life, 8
Theresa, St.: on interior peace, 755
Thomas Aquinas, St.
  author of the *Lauda Sion*, 503 note, 505
  author of the Office of Corpus Christi, 505
  Collect on feast of, 476
  essence of the Eucharistic sacrifice, 134 note
  Laurent on, 505
  praying toward the east, 472
  sacrifice of the cross and the Mass, 134 note

Thomas of Celano, author of the *Dies irae*, 503 note
Thomasius, Blessed J. M.: meaning of ceremonies, 378 note
"Three young men" in the furnace, 568
Thrones (angelic choir), 606 note, 607 note
Thus, 420 note
Tiburtius, St., 720 note
Time: for granting petitions, 190; spent in purgatory, 208
Tintinnabulum, 310 note
Titulus altaris, 275 note
Titulus ecclesiae, 532 and note
Tobias, vision of Jerusalem, 498
Toledan liturgy; *see* Mozarabic rite
Tones of voice, 623 note, 712
Tongue, control of; *see* Speech
Tono recto, 482 note
Tools, blessing of, 229
Touching of liturgical objects, 268
Towel for the hands, 310 note
Tract, 493-97: Gradual and, 492 f., 494 note, 496; during Lent, 494 f.; manner of singing, 493 and note; of Requiem Masses, 495 f.
Tractus, 493 and note
Tradition, sacrificial character of the Eucharist, 104-21
Trajan (emperor), 653 note, 715 note
Transfiguration of Christ, 347
Translation: of the Collects, 474; of the Mass prayers, 363 f., 366
Transubstantiation, 130-32, 672 f., 675-77, 722 f.: petition for, 657, 661, 663 f.
"Tree of knowledge," 616 note
"Tree of life," 145
Trent, Council of
  assistance at Mass, 381 f.
  the Canon, 620
  celebration of Mass, 381 f.
  ceremonies at Mass, 378
  explanation of the Mass, 361
  frequent Communion, 780
  institution of the Eucharist, 94 f.
  instructional character of Mass, 361, 365
  the Last Supper, 94 f.
  propitiatory character of the Mass, 174
  remission of venial sins, 180
  sacrifice of the cross and of the Mass, 134
  sacrificial character of the Mass, 122
  use of incense, 420
  wearing of vestments, 313

INDEX

Trinity, the
  circumincession, 725
  feast of, 485: Creed on, 529 f.; Preface for, 616 and note
  glorified at the end of the Canon, 725 f.
  Mass offered to, 587, 725 f.: in the *Placeat*, 803
  praised by the Sanctus, 610
  prayers addressed to, 466
  symbolized by the sign of the cross, 394, 664 f.
  symbolized by the three particles, 742
  work of redemption by, 763 and note
Trisagion, 609 and notes; *see also* Sanctus
Triumph of the Church, 247 f.
Tropes, 438 note
Truth: Christ as teacher of, 479 f.; the Eucharist and, 480; symbolized by light, 297 f.
Tu solus, 448 and note

Unde et memores, 681-90: gift offered at, 688 and note; mysteries of Christ, 685-87 and note; signs of the cross at, 688-90 and notes
Understanding, required for participation, 365 f.
Uniformity of worship, 367 ff.
Union with Christ, 764: after Communion, 786; through the Eucharist, 562 and note, 769; St. Cyril on, 562 note; symbolized by water and wine, 550 f., 560-62, 565
Unity
  of the Eucharistic sacrifice, 742
  implored in the *Te igitur*, 637 f.
  manifested in invocation of the saints, 404
  peace and, 756
  promoted by use of Latin, 367 ff.
  symbolized by the Eucharist, 748
Universality of the Mass, 87-90, 93, 121, 367 f.
Unworthiness: before Communion, 779; confession of, 764 f.; spirit of, 693
Urban I, St. (pope): sacred vessels of silver, 301 note
Urban II (pope): number of Prefaces, 597 and note
Urban IV (pope): feast of Corpus Christi, 505; a memorial sacrifice, 687
Urban VIII (pope), 374 f.
Use of light, 293 ff. and notes: in the catacombs, 295

Vaison, Council of, 609 note
Valerian (emperor), 653 note
Valerian, St.: and St. Cecilia, 720 note
Valor of the Mass, 145 note
Value of the Mass, 124, 146-62
  Christ as chief offerer, 147-55
  High Mass, 157
  holiness of Christ, 147 f., 155
  holiness of the Church, 156 f.
  infinite, 147-50, 155, 161
  as offered by the Church, 156-60
  as offered by the priest, 160 f.
  Requiem Mass, 158-60
  Solemn Mass, 158
  votive Mass, 158-60
Veil for the chalice, 309 and notes
Veil of the Temple, 79 f.
Velum, 309 note
Veni Creator Spiritus, 505 note
Veni Sancte Spiritus, 504 f.: author of, 503 note
Venial sin: moral sin and, 181; remission of, 176, 180 f.
Vernacular in the liturgy, 360
Vesperal, 284 note
Vespers: after Mass, 795 note; *Oratio super populum* and, 795 note; Pater noster at, 733 note
Vessels, sacred
  beauty of, 223: Laurent on, 265
  blessing of, 229, 267 f., 302 f.
  handling of, 303 and note
  material used in, 301 note, 302 and note
  poverty and, 266
  symbolism of, 268 f.
Vestments
  beauty of, 223, 315: in Holy Scripture, 312
  black: symbolism of, 357 f.; use of, 346 notes, 355 note, 357 f.
  blessing of, 229, 267 f., 315 f. and note: loss of, 316 note
  blue, 346 and note
  form of, 314
  gold cloth, 315, 346
  green, 353-55: symbolism of, 353 note, 354 f.; use of, 346 note, 354
  historical development of, 313 f. and note
  Imitation of Christ on, 343 f.
  kissing of, 320 and note
  lace on, 323 f. note
  Laurent on, 265
  material for, 314 f.
  poverty and, 266

Vestments (*continued*)
  reason for wearing, 312 f., 343
  red, 350-53: symbolism of, 351-53; use of, 346 note, 351-53
  rose-colored, 345 note
  symbolism of, 268 f., 316-19, 343
  value of, 315
  violet: symbolism of, 355-57; use of, 346 and notes, 355 note, 356
  white: symbolism of, 347-50; use of, 345, 346 note, 348-50, 358 note
  worn-out, 316
  yellow, 346
Viaticum, 780 note
Victim of the Mass, 122 f., 132, 138, 142, 155
  in ancient liturgies, 116
  infinite value of, 147 f., 688
  as sacrifice of petition, 190
  as sacrifice of praise, 165
  as sacrifice of thanksgiving, 171
  St. Ambrose on, 113
Victim of the sacrifice of the cross, 45 f., 49, 55
Victimae paschali, 503 f.: author of, 503 note
Vigil of Pentecost: *Flectamus genua*, 462; Mass without Introit, 429 and note
Vigils, 356
Violet vestments: symbolism of, 355-57; use of, 346 and notes, 355 note, 356
Virginity
  martyrdom and, 352, 353 note
  of virgins, 251 f.
  St. Agnes on, 251
  St. Ambrose on, 254 note, 280 note
  St. Cecilia on, 251
  symbolized by the bee, 295
Virgins
  Creed omitted on feasts of, 531
  Eucharist as support of, 254 f.
  martyrs and, 352, 353 note
  purity of, 251 f.
  self-sacrifice of, 251, 254 f.
  spiritual altars, 280
  Virgin of, 651
  white vestments on feasts of, 350
Virtue, acts of, 21-25, 253 note
Virtues
  of Christ, 37 and note
  fostered by the Eucharist, 223-25, 237 f., 767
  moral: sanctifying grace and the, 3; theological virtues and the, 8

Virtues (*continued*)
  symbolized by flowers, 292
  symbolized by incense, 521 and note
  symbolized by light, 297
  theological, 3 note: as acts glorifying God, 7 f.; in Christian life, 8
Virtues (angelic choir), 606 note, 607 f. and note
Viscera, 786 note
Vision of God, 713
Vivificas, 723 and note
Vocation to the priesthood, 35
Voice: protected by the amice, 321 f.; tones of, 623 note, 712
Votive Masses: Creed recited in, 533; *de Passione Domini*, 613; greater impetratory power of, 158-60; obligation of, 159; restricted, 158-60 and note
Votum, 647 and note
Vow, liturgical meaning of, 647 and note
Vultus, 693 note

Washing of liturgical objects, 268
Washing of the hands, 581-85: Apostolic Constitutions on, 582; on Epistle side, 586 note; prayers at, 583-85; St. Cyril on, 582
Water: at the ablution, 781 note; blessing of, 229 f., 560; at the Offertory, 548-51
Water mixed with wine, 548-51, 560: amount of, 548 and note; before Mass, 553 note; prayer at, 561 note; symbolism of, 549-51, 560-62, 565, 692
Wax: kinds of, 294 note; symbolism of, 294 f.; use of, 293 f. and notes
Weapons, blessing of, 229
Weather, prayers for good, 194
Wenceslaus, St.: preparation of bread and wine, 552 note
Western liturgies, 372 f. and note
Wheat: Laurent on, 746; product of man's labor, 543 f.; symbol of the faithful, 141
White and red, 350
White vestments: burial of children in, 358 note; symbolism of, 347-50; use of, 345, 346 note, 348-50
Widows, spiritual altars, 280 note
Will of Christ, in application of graces, 151
Will of God and release from purgatory, 208
Winding sheet of Christ, 306, 308

INDEX 869

Wine (*see also* Bread and wine)
  blessing of: at the Consecration, 674; at the Last Supper, 674
  consecration of, 673-77: ceremonies during, 674, 676
  containers for, 309 note
  Laurent on, 746 f.
  matter of the Eucharist, 545, 547-51
  offering of; *see* Offering
  preparation of, 552
  water mingled with; *see* Water
Wipo of Burgundy, 503 note
Wisdom, Books of, 482 note
Wiseman
  beauty of liturgical worship, 375 f.
  the Collects, 474 f.
  the Gloria, 436, 451
  the Introit, 432
  the Kyrie and Gloria, 436
  perfection of Mass prayers, 375 f.
  the Preface, 618
  the Sequences, 503
  songs of sorrow, 508
Wolter, on praying with arms extended, 471
Works, necessity of good, 69 f.
Works of mercy
  the Church and, 242-45, 265
  decline of, 245
  Eberhard on, 242 f.
  the Eucharist and, 245, 254 f.
  Hettinger on, 254 f.
  religious and, 254 f.

Worship: dogma and, 368 and note; exterior, 11 ff.; interior and exterior, 379 f., 382; St. Augustine on, 380; social, 12 f.
Wounds of Christ: retained in heaven, 74 f.; symbolized by five signs of the cross, 665, 690 and note
Wrath of God, 184 ff., 194, 566
Wretchedness of man, 184 ff., 194

Year, ecclesiastical
  chants at Mass and, 490
  Collects and, 463 f., 475-78
  dressing of the altar and, 283
  the Eucharist and, 219, 222
  Gradual and, 490
  means of instruction, 464
  means of sanctification, 463 f.
  mysteries of Christ and, 219
  Prefaces of, 615 f.
  rank of feasts in, 473 f.
  selection of Epistle and Gospel, 481 and note, 517 and note
  selection of Mass chants, 431 f.
Yellow vestments forbidden, 346
Yoke of the Lord: symbolized by the chasuble, 341 note, 342; symbolized by the stole, 335 f.

Zeal, effect of love, 341
Zona, 326 note